taste of home

THE taste of home BAKING BOOK

TIMELESS RECIPES FROM TRUSTED HOME COOKS

taste of home
BOOKS

REIMAN MEDIA GROUP, INC. · GREENDALE, WISCONSIN

taste of home · Reader's Digest

A TASTE OF HOME/READER'S DIGEST BOOK

© 2010 Reiman Media Group, Inc.
  5400 S. 60th St., Greendale WI 53129
  All rights reserved.

Taste of Home and Reader's Digest are registered trademarks of The Reader's Digest Association, Inc.

Editor in Chief: Catherine Cassidy
Vice President, Executive Editor/Books: Heidi Reuter Lloyd
Creative Director: Ardyth Cope
U.S. Chief Marketing Officer: Lisa Karpinski
Food Director: Diane Werner RD
Senior Editor/Books: Mark Hagen
Editor: Janet Briggs
Associate Project Editor: Julie Schnittka

Art Director: Edwin Robles, Jr.
Content Production Supervisor: Julie Wagner
Design Layout Artists: Catherine Fletcher, Kathy Crawford
Proofreader: Linne Bruskewitz
Project Proofreader: Jean Duerst
Recipe Asset System Manager: Coleen Martin
Premedia Supervisor: Scott Berger
Recipe Testing & Editing: Taste of Home Test Kitchen
Food Photography: Taste of Home Photo Studio
Administrative Assistant: Barb Czysz

The Reader's Digest Association, Inc.
President and Chief Executive Officer: Mary G. Berner
President, U.S. Affinities: Suzanne M. Grimes
SVP, Global Chief Marketing Officer: Amy J. Radin
President/Publisher Trade Publishing: Harold Clarke
Associate Publisher: Rosanne McManus
Vice President, Sales and Marketing: Stacey Ashton

Cover Photographers: Rob Hagen, James Wieland

"Timeless Recipes from Trusted Home Cooks" is a registered trademark of Reiman Media Group, Inc.

For other *Taste of Home* books and products,
visit us at **tasteofhome.com.**

For more Reader's Digest products and information,
visit **rd.com** (in the United States)
or see **rd.ca** (in Canada).

International Standard Book Number (10): 0-89821-815-2
International Standard Book Number (13): 978-0-89821-815-2
Library of Congress Control Number: 2007921835

PRINTED IN CHINA
1 3 5 7 9 10 8 6 4 2

Pictured on front cover:
1 Maple Butter Twists (p. 407)
2 Rich Chocolate Brownies (p. 96)
3 Pecan Squares (p. 94)
4 Raspberry Chocolate Cake (p. 120)
5 Apple Cranberry Tart (p. 230)
6 Italian Horn Cookies (p. 451)
7 Chocolate Thumbprints (p. 57)
8 Zucchini Chip Bread (p. 290)

CONTENTS

OUR BEST BAKING SECRETS REVEALED!

Taste of Home, America's No. 1 food magazine, presents its biggest-ever collection of baking recipes! These 725+ recipes from great home bakers have been tasted and reviewed by the professional home economists of the Taste of Home Test Kitchen, so you can trust they'll turn out every time!

Whether you're a beginner just learning the time-honored tips and tricks of home baking or an experienced family baker searching for new taste sensations, you'll discover a bounty of delicious options in *The Taste of Home Baking Book*. Here's what you'll find inside:

• **725+ recipes for irresistible baked goods**—from cookies, bars, brownies, cakes, cheesecakes, pies, bread puddings and meringues…to yeast breads, quick breads, coffee cakes, muffins, biscuits and more! These recipes are made with easy-to-find ingredients already stocked in your pantry or refrigerator.

• **Over 675 color photos** illustrate mixing and baking methods and then reveal their delectable final results! See what an egg white beaten to a stiff peak looks like…the perfect spritz cookie…goof-proof frosting techniques …even how to make phyllo triangles.

• **Step-by-step baking directions** written in a clear and concise style take the guesswork out of baking. These easy-to-understand, quick-read directions will have a novice baking like a pro in no time!

• **Prep and bake times** with every recipe give a clear idea of how long each recipe will take so you can plan your kitchen time.

• **150+ proven tips from test kitchen experts** are generously sprinkled throughout the book. With simple solutions for common baking dilemmas and pointers for high altitude adjustments, your breads, cakes, cookies and pies will turn out picture-perfect.

• **Baking Basics,** an in-depth, quick reference section, features general measuring and mixing techniques, handy charts, tips about the tools and bakeware in a well-supplied kitchen and an expansive glossary of common baking ingredients and terms.

• **Comprehensive indexes,** including alphabetical listings in each chapter, subject index and a special index for all the reference materials, give you instant access to everything inside this definitive baking guide.

Best of all, with this book you get the everyday, home-style goodness for which *Taste of Home* is trusted and loved. Whether you're a new friend or a longtime fan, you'll be sure to find a delectable fresh-from-the-oven treat for every occasion in *The Taste of Home Baking Book*.

Taste of Home.com

5

Baking Basics

secrets for *successful baking*

- Read the entire recipe before you begin. Make sure you understand the cooking techniques.
- Check to see that you have all the ingredients for the recipe.
- Prepare the ingredients before you start mixing. Let the butter soften, toast the coconut, chop the nuts, etc.
- Measure the ingredients correctly, using proper techniques and measuring utensils.
- Prepare the recipe according to directions. It's best to use the baking pan or dish called for in the recipe.
- Preheat the oven before baking.
- Use a kitchen timer to accurately time the recipe. If you use a pan size other than the one called for in the recipe, you may need to adjust the baking time.
- Use an oven thermometer to verify the accuracy of your oven. To check the accuracy of your oven, preheat it to the desired temperature. Place an oven thermometer on the center rack. Close the oven door and leave the oven on at the set temperature. Keep the thermometer in the oven for 15 minutes, then check. If the thermometer does not agree with the set oven temperature, the oven temperature is inaccurate. Adjust the oven temperature accordingly.
- Cool baked goods on a wire rack to allow air to circulate around the food.

Measuring Tools

To ensure good and consistent baking results, every cook needs to know how to accurately and correctly measure ingredients. Not all measuring cups are the same and not all ingredients are measured in the same manner.

- A liquid measuring cup is either clear glass or transparent plastic with a handle and a pour spout. They are available in 1-cup, 2-cup, 4-cup and 8-cup sizes. Liquid measures are used for milk, honey, molasses, corn syrup, water and oil.

- A dry measuring cup is made from metal or plastic and has a handle. The food to be measured should be even with the rim of the cup. Dry measuring cups usually come in a set with 1/4-cup, 1/3-cup, 1/2-cup and 1-cup sizes. Some sets may have additional sizes such as 1/8 cup or 2/3 cup. Dry measures are used for flour and sugar. They also are used to measure shortening, sour cream, yogurt and applesauce. While these ingredients are not "dry," they can mound when measured. The dry measure allows you to level the ingredient at the top of the cup for an accurate measurement.

- Standard measuring spoons are used to measure both liquid and dry ingredients. Sets include a 1/4 teaspoon, 1/2 teaspoon, 1 teaspoon and 1 tablespoon. Some sets are available with a 1/8 teaspoon.

proper
measuring *techniques*

MEASURING LIQUIDS

Place liquid measuring cup on a level surface. For a traditional liquid measuring cup, view the amount at eye level to be sure of an accurate measure. Do not lift cup to check the level. Some newer liquid measuring cups are designed so that they can be accurately read from above.

For sticky liquids such as molasses, corn syrup or honey, spray the measuring cup with nonstick cooking spray before adding the liquid. This will make it easier to pour out the liquid and clean the cup.

MEASURING DRY INGREDIENTS

For dry ingredients such as flour, sugar or cornmeal, spoon ingredients into a dry measuring cup over a canister or waxed paper. Fill cup to overflowing, then level by sweeping a metal spatula or flat side of a knife across the top.

MEASURING BULK DRY INGREDIENTS

Spoon bulky dry ingredients such as cranberries, raisins, chocolate chips or oats into the measuring cup. If necessary, level the top with a spatula or flat side of knife.

MEASURING BROWN SUGAR

Since brown sugar has a unique moist texture, it needs to be packed into a dry measuring cup. Firmly press brown sugar into the cup with your fingers or the back of a spoon. Level with the rim of the cup. Brown sugar should hold the shape of the cup when it is turned out.

MEASURING SOUR CREAM AND YOGURT

Spoon sour cream and yogurt into a dry measuring cup, then level top by sweeping a metal spatula or flat side of a knife across the top of the cup.

MEASURING SHORTENING

Press shortening into a dry measuring cup with a spatula to make sure it is solidly packed without air pockets. With a metal spatula or flat side of a knife, level with the rim. Some shortenings come in sticks and may be measured like butter (see below).

MEASURING BUTTER

The wrappers for sticks of butter come with markings for tablespoons, 1/4 cup, 1/3 cup and 1/2 cup. Use a knife to cut off the desired amount.

USING MEASURING SPOONS

For dry ingredients such as flour, sugar or spices, heap the ingredient into the spoon over a canister or waxed paper. With a metal spatula or the flat side of a knife, level with the rim of the spoon.

For shortening or butter, spread into spoon and level off. For liquids, pour into measuring spoon over a bowl or custard cup. Never measure over the batter, because some may spill and you may end up with too much in the batter.

Bakeware
Stocking Your Kitchen with Bakeware

A well-stocked kitchen should have the following items for baking:

1) 9-in. x 1-1/2-in. round baking pan (two to three)

2) 13-in. x 9-in. x 2-in. baking pan and/or dish (3 qt.)

3) 10-in. fluted tube pan

4) 15-in. x 10-in. x 1-in. baking pan (jelly-roll pan)

5) Baking sheets (without sides) in assorted sizes

6) 9-in. springform pan

7) 9-in. pie plate

8) 12-cup muffin pan (standard size)

9) 6-oz. custard cups (set of six)

10) 9-in. x 5-in. x 3-in. loaf pan (two) and 8-in. x 4-in. x 2-in. loaf pan (two)

11) 9-in. x 9-in. x 2-in. and 8-in. x 8-in. x 2-in. square baking dishes and/or pans

12) 10-in. tube pan

These other items are also convenient to have on hand:

• 11-in. x 7-in. x 2-in. baking pan and/or dish (2 qt.)

• 9-in. deep-dish pie plate

• 9-in. fluted tart pan with removable bottom

• 10-in. springform pan

• 5-3/4-in. x 3-in. x 2-in. loaf pan (three to four)

• Miniature muffin pans

• 10-oz. custard cups (set of six)

• 8-in. fluted tube pan

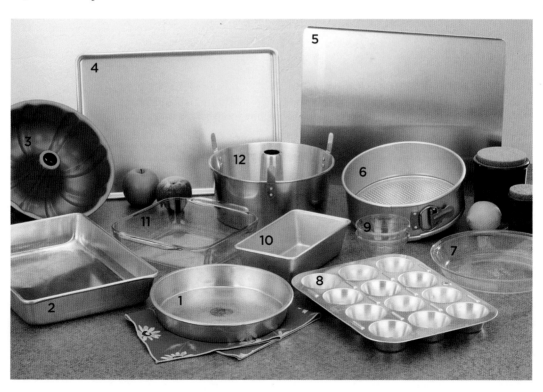

Choosing Bakeware

The recipes in this book call for standard-size baking pans and baking dishes. For best results, use the pan size called for in the recipe. However, there are some practical substitutions (see chart below).

Baking pans are made of metal. Aluminum pans with dull finishes give the best overall baking results. Pans with dark finishes often cook and brown foods more quickly. If you use pans with dark finishes, you may need to adjust the baking time and cover tops of baked goods with foil to prevent overbrowning. Insulated pans generally take longer to bake and brown foods.

Baking dishes are made of ovenproof glass or ceramic. If you substitute a glass baking dish in a recipe calling for a metal baking pan, reduce the oven temperature by 25° to avoid overbaking and overbrowning.

To measure your bakeware's diameter, length or width, use a ruler and measure from one inside top edge to the opposite inside top edge. To measure the height, place a ruler on the outside of the dish and measure from the bottom to a top edge. For volume, fill the pan or dish full to the rim with water.

Bakeware Substitution

If you don't have the right pan for a recipe, here are a few substitutions. Remember that using smaller pans will require less baking time, and a larger pan may require more baking time.

IF YOU DON'T HAVE THIS PAN(S):	USE THIS PAN(S) INSTEAD:
One 9-in. x 5-in. x 3-in. loaf pan	Three 5-3/4-in. x 3-in. x 2-in. loaf pans
One 8-in. x 4-in. x 2-in. loaf pan	Two 5-3/4-in. x 3-in. x 2-in. loaf pans
One 9-in. round baking pan	One 8-in. square baking dish
Two 9-in. round baking pans	One 13-in. x 9-in. x 2-in. baking pan
One 10-in. fluted tube pan	One 10-in. tube pan or two 9-in. x 5-in. x 3-in. loaf pans
One 13-in. x 9-in. x 2-in. baking pan	Two 9-in. round baking pans or two 8-in. square baking dishes

Mixing Tools & Appliances

When baking, it's handy to have a variety of tools and appliances to make the job easier. Here are a few essentials for a well-stocked kitchen:

1) Mixing bowls
2) Food processor
3) Mixer (stand)
4) Blender
5) Mixer (portable)
6) Measuring cups (dry and liquid)
7) Sieve
8) Juicer
9) Timers
10) Rolling pin
11) Wire rack
12) Pastry brushes
13) Spatulas (rubber or plastic)
14) Dough cutter/scraper
15) Metal spatula
16) Wire whisk
17) Measuring spoons
18) Grater
19) Wooden spoons
20) Pastry blender
21) Pastry bag and tips

Common Baking Ingredients

Chocolate

Chocolate is one of the most popular flavorings in baked goods. Chocolate comes from cocoa beans, which are processed to produce cocoa powder, cocoa butter and chocolate liquor (the liquid created when the meat of the cocoa bean "nibs" are crushed). The various forms and flavors of chocolate products are a combination of these and other ingredients. For best results, we recommend using the type of chocolate listed in the recipe.

Baking cocoa is the powdery residue that remains after the cocoa butter is removed from the chocolate liquor. This form of chocolate contains the least amount of fat. Dutch-processed cocoa has been treated during processing with an alkalizing agent, which produces a smoother flavor and darker color than untreated baking cocoa.

Candy coating or almond bark is not considered true chocolate because it uses other vegetable fats instead of cocoa butter. Candy coatings come in a variety of flavors. They are mainly used as a coating on cookies, fruits or nuts or in candy making. Candy coatings are rarely used as a baking ingredient.

Chocolate chips are available in standard, miniature and larger "chunk" sizes. Chocolate chips come in a variety of flavors: semisweet, milk and vanilla or white. Specialty flavors such as raspberry or mint are sometimes available.

Chocolate syrup is a liquid made from cocoa, corn syrup and flavorings.

German sweet chocolate comes in a bar and is a sweeter chocolate than semisweet.

Milk chocolate contains cocoa butter, sugar, vanilla, chocolate liquor and 12% milk solids. It's available in chips and candy bars.

Semisweet and bittersweet chocolate are sometimes used interchangeably. However, bittersweet chocolate is less sweet than semisweet chocolate. Semisweet chocolate is made with chocolate liquor, additional cocoa butter, sugar and vanilla. It is available in packages of 1-ounce squares, chips and candy bars.

Unsweetened chocolate may also be referred to as baking chocolate. It is solidified chocolate liquor and does not contain sugar. It is available in packages of 1-ounce squares.

White chocolate is not a true chocolate because it does not contain chocolate liquor. White chocolate is made with cocoa butter, sugar, milk solids and vanilla. It is available in packages of 1-ounce squares and chips.

Storing Chocolate

Store chocolate tightly wrapped in a cool dry place. If stored improperly, the appearance of the chocolate will change. When chocolate is stored at too warm a temperature, a fat bloom occurs, causing grayish-white streaks or blotches in the chocolate. When chocolate is stored in a damp place, a sugar bloom occurs, giving a rough feel to the chocolate. You can still melt chocolate with blooms and incorporate it into batter or dough for baked goods.

Melting Chocolate

Break or chop large pieces of chocolate so it will melt more evenly. Melt chocolate in a dry heavy saucepan over low heat and stir until smooth. Even small amounts of water will cause the chocolate to seize (become thick and lumpy), making it unusable. If the chocolate needs to set up after melting (such as when it's used for dipping or garnishes), add 1/4 to 1/2 teaspoon of shortening for every 6 ounces of chocolate.

To melt chocolate in the microwave, place chocolate in a microwave-safe bowl. Melt semisweet chocolate at 50% power, and milk chocolate and vanilla or white chocolate at 30% power. Stir frequently until the chocolate is melted; do not overheat.

Dairy Products

Dairy products add moisture to bake goods. They also impart flavor and tenderness and aid in browning. Unless otherwise stated, the recipes in this book were tested with whole milk. You may substitute reduced-fat or fat-free milk for the whole milk, but the texture and richness of the final product may be affected.

Buttermilk is made by adding a bacteria to fat-free or reduced-fat milk. The result is a tangy flavor and a slightly thicker consistency. Buttermilk was originally the low-fat liquid that remained when cream was churned into butter.

Evaporated milk is whole milk with 60% of the water removed and contains about 7.9% milk fat. An unopened can of evaporated milk is shelf stable. Do not use evaporated milk as a substitute for sweetened condensed milk. Reduced-fat and fat-free evaporated milk are also available.

Fat-free milk, also called skim or nonfat milk, contains no more than 1/2% milk fat.

Half-and-half cream is a blend of whole milk and cream that contains from 10-1/2% to 18% milk fat.

Heavy whipping cream contains at least 36% milk fat. When whipped, it should double in volume and hold stiff peaks.

Nonfat dry milk powder is fat-free milk with all the moisture removed. It is reconstituted with water.

Reduced-fat milk has 2% milk fat.

Sour cream is half-and-half cream that has been soured by using a lactic acid-producing bacteria or acidifiers. It has a tangy flavor and a thick texture.

Sweetened condensed milk is made from whole milk with about 50% of the water removed and has added sugar. It is a thick, sweet product. An unopened can of sweetened condensed milk is shelf stable. Do not use sweetened condensed milk as a substitute for evaporated milk. Reduced-fat and fat-free sweetened condensed milk are also available.

Whole milk, referred to as milk in this cookbook, has about 3-1/2% milk fat.

Yogurt is made from whole, reduced-fat or fat-free milk. The milk is fermented with lactic acid-producing bacteria. It has a tangy flavor and a thick texture. Yogurt may have added sweeteners, flavorings and fruit.

Eggs

Eggs perform many functions in baking. They add color, flavor, texture (give a tender crumb), structure and help leaven. Egg yolks add fat and act as an emulsifier, which helps blend the shortening or oil into the liquid ingredients. Egg whites are used for their drying properties, especially for meringues.

Purchase eggs with unbroken shells from a refrigerated case. Refrigerate them as soon as possible after purchase. Store eggs in their carton on an inside refrigerator shelf, not in a compartment on the door. The carton cushions the eggs and helps prevent moisture loss and odor adsorption. Use eggs by the expiration date printed on the carton.

Never use a recipe where the eggs will not be completely cooked. Eggs are thoroughly cooked when they reach a temperature of 160°. For food safety reasons, do not leave eggs at room temperature for over 2 hours. Discard any eggs that have cracked or broken shells.

Egg substitutes are available in cartons in the refrigerated and frozen section of grocery stores. Egg substitutes use egg whites and contain no cholesterol and little or no fat. One-fourth cup of egg substitute is equal to one egg. Do not use egg substitute for items such as cream puffs, popovers and sponge cakes. Baking with egg substitutes may affect the quality of your baked item. Generally, it is best to use egg substitutes for only a portion of the eggs called for in a recipe.

Egg Size Equivalents

The recipes in this cookbook were tested with large eggs. The following are some guidelines for substituting other size eggs for large eggs.

1 large egg	= 1 jumbo;	1 extra-large;	1 medium	
2 large eggs	= 2 jumbo;	2 extra-large;	2 medium;	3 small
3 large eggs	= 2 jumbo;	3 extra-large;	3 medium;	4 small
4 large eggs	= 3 jumbo;	4 extra-large;	5 medium;	5 small
5 large eggs	= 4 jumbo;	4 extra-large;	6 medium;	7 small
6 large eggs	= 5 jumbo;	5 extra-large;	7 medium;	8 small

separating *eggs*

Place an egg separator over a custard cup; crack egg into the separator. As each egg is separated, place yolk in another bowl and empty egg whites into a mixing bowl. It is easier to separate eggs when they are cold.

beating *eggs*

LIGHTLY BEATEN

To beat the egg with a fork until the yolk and white are combined.

LEMON-COLORED

To beat eggs with an electric mixer on high speed for about 5 minutes. The volume of the beaten eggs will increase, the texture will go from liquid to thick and foamy, and the color will be a light yellow.

THICK AND PALE YELLOW

To beat eggs and sugar with an electric mixer on high speed for about 7-8 minutes or until mixture has thickened and turned a very pale yellow. Mixture will fall in ribbons from a spoon.

SOFT PEAKS

To beat egg whites with an electric mixer on medium speed until they are thick and white. To test for soft peaks, lift the beaters from the whites—the egg white peaks should curl down.

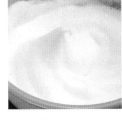

For best results, make sure the bowl and beaters are free from oil and the egg whites contain no specks of yolk. Both will prevent the whites from reaching full volume.

STIFF PEAKS

To continue beating the egg whites after they have reached the soft-peak stage with an electric mixer on high speed until the volume increases more and they are thicker. To test for stiff peaks, lift the beaters from the whites—the egg white peaks should stand straight up and if you tilt the bowl, the whites should not slide around.

Fats

Fats in baked goods can perform many functions—they tenderize, add moisture, carry flavors and give a richness to the flavors. Fats act as a leavener when creamed, because the creaming process incorporates air into the batter or dough. They also help keep baked goods fresh.

Butter adds flavor and may add color. In some recipes (such as shortbread) butter is the main or only flavoring component, and the use of butter is essential to that recipe. Recipes for this cookbook were tested with butter, not margarine.

creaming *butter*

When creaming butter, it should be softened (a table knife will be able to glide through the butter). When butter is cut into a mixture, it generally should be cold from the refrigerator.

Margarine is made from a variety of vegetable oils, usually soybean and corn oils. Not all margarines are alike. They vary in oil content and form. For baking, use stick margarine with an 80% fat content. Margarine with lower fat content, usually labeled as margarine spread or whipped margarine, has more water and air in it and will adversely affect the quality of your baked goods.

Shortening is a solid fat (it holds its shape at room temperature) that is made from 100% vegetable oils. Shortening is not as temperature-sensitive as butter and margarine, so shortening makes cookies spread less during baking and makes pastries flakier. Regular vegetable shortening adds no flavor to baked goods. Butter-flavored shortening adds flavor and some color.

Oil is most frequently used in cakes to add tenderness and moistness. Because oil cannot be creamed like butter, margarine and shortening, it does not help in leavening. Oil cannot be used interchangeably with solid shortening.

Flours

Flours are made from the finely ground meal of edible grains. Wheat flour, the most commonly used flour, contains gluten—an elastic protein that traps the gases produced by leaveners. The trapped gases push against the protein, causing the product to rise. During baking, the protein is set by the heat and gives the baked good its structure. The terms soft and hard wheat refer to the amount of protein (gluten) in the flour—soft has less and hard has more. The amount of gluten will affect the texture of the baked product.

Wheat flour will bleach naturally when exposed to air over many weeks. In commercially bleached flour, this whitening process is accelerated with a small amount of bleaching agents. Unbleached flour does not use bleaching agents and may give baked goods an off-white color.

All-purpose flour is a blend of hard (high-gluten) wheat and soft (low-gluten) wheat flours. It is a general-purpose flour, which means it is suitable for all types of baking.

Bread flour is made from hard (high-gluten) wheat and is specifically formulated for yeast breads.

Cake flour is made from soft (low-gluten) wheat and has a fine texture. It gives a tender delicate crumb to cakes.

Rye flour contains less gluten than wheat flours like all-purpose flour and should be used in combination with wheat flour. Rye flour produces breads with a darker color, denser texture and more distinctive flavor. Medium rye flour is available in most grocery stores, but light and dark rye flours are also sold in specialty markets.

Self-rising flour is all-purpose flour to which salt and baking powder have been added. Self-rising flour is used as a shortcut in some biscuit and cake recipes.

Whole wheat flour, also called graham flour, is a wheat flour that is processed from the entire wheat kernel, which contains the bran and the germ. Whole wheat flour has more fiber, nutrition and fat than all-purpose flour. Because of the fat from the bran and germ, whole wheat flour has a shorter shelf life than white flours. Store whole wheat flour in the refrigerator for up to 6 months.

Leaveners

Leaveners cause baked goods to rise and have a light texture. Baking powder, baking soda, yeast and eggs are leavening agents.

Creaming fat also helps leaven baked goods by incorporating air into the batter. The air expands during baking, causing the product to rise. Liquids such as water create steam during baking, which can also cause baked products to rise.

Baking powder is available in single-acting and double-acting varieties. Double-acting baking powder is the most readily available type and is the type used in this cookbook. Double-acting baking powder produces carbon dioxide gas in two stages: when it is mixed with liquid and when it is heated. Single-acting baking powder creates carbon dioxide gas only when it is mixed with liquid. Baking powder can lose its ability to leaven. Discard any baking powder that is past the expiration date on the can.

Baking soda is an alkaline substance used in batters that have acidic ingredients such as buttermilk, molasses and sour cream. When the baking soda is mixed with the acidic ingredient, there is an immediate release of carbon dioxide gas. Batters and doughs that only use baking soda as a leavening agent should be baked immediately. Otherwise, the baked product might not rise as high and the texture won't be as light.

Yeast is a microorganism that becomes activated when combined with warm water and sugar. It consumes the sugars in sweeteners and flours and produces carbon dioxide gas that helps give bread its light airy texture. There are several different types of yeast and each is handled differently. Check the expiration date on the package before using and discard yeast if it is past the date.

- *Active dry yeast* is available in 1/4-ounce foil packages or 4-ounce jars. With the Traditional Mixing Method on page 337, the active yeast is dissolved in liquid that has been warmed to 110° to 115°. If the liquid temperature is too low, the yeast will not be activated. If the liquid temperature is too high, the yeast will be killed, preventing the bread from rising.

- With the Rapid Mixing Method on page 351, the active dry yeast is added directly to the flour and other dry ingredients. Then warm liquid (120° to 130°) is added.

- *Quick-rise yeast* is available in 1/4-ounce foil packages or 4-ounce jars. Quick-rise yeast is finely granulated and should only be combined with the other ingredients using the Rapid Mixing Method on page 351. Quick-rise yeast will raise bread dough in about a third to half the traditional time.

- *Bread machine yeast* is available in 4-ounce jars. This is an instant yeast with finer granules. The smaller granules allow the yeast to mix into the dough more evenly.

- *Fresh or cake yeast* is most commonly available in 2-ounce cakes, which is equivalent to three 1/4-ounce packages of active dry yeast. A third of the fresh yeast cake (about .6 ounce) is equal to one packet of active dry yeast. Older bread recipes often call for a "cake of yeast."

- *Cake yeast* is a fresh product found in your grocer's dairy case. It should be used within 10 days of purchase. To use, crumble the yeast into dry ingredients or soften in tepid water (70° to 80°).

Eggs are whipped to incorporate air to create a foam. The incorporated air expands when heated, causing the baked product to rise. Foam cakes such as angel foods and chiffon use egg whites as a leavening agent.

Salt

Salt helps round out flavors. In bread making, salt also controls the growth of the yeast. Too much salt in the bread dough will inhibit the growth of the yeast, resulting in a dense loaf.

Confectioners' sugar, also known as powdered sugar, is granulated sugar that has been ground into a fine powder and mixed with a little cornstarch to prevent clumping. It is mainly used for frostings and glazes. For smooth frostings without any lumps, sift confectioners' sugar after measuring.

Granulated sugar, also know as sugar or white sugar, is made from refined sugarcane or beets. In this cookbook, it's simply referred to as sugar.

Corn syrup is made from corn. It helps keep baked goods moist. It is available in light and dark. Dark corn syrup has caramel color and flavor added to it, so it will cause baked goods to be darker in color.

Honey adds a distinct flavor and sweetness to baked items and also keeps them moist. Honey's flavor is affected by the type of flowers from which the bees collect nectar. Honey caramelizes at a lower temperature than sugar and may cause baked good to brown more quickly. It's available in liquid and whipped form. The recipes in this cookbook were tested with liquid honey.

Molasses is the by-product of refining sugarcane. It adds sweetness, a distinct flavor and color to baked goods. Molasses is available in light, dark and black strap. As you would expect, the light has the mildest flavor and the lightest color and black strap has the strongest flavor and darkest color.

Sugars and Other Sweeteners

Sugars and other sweeteners perform many functions in baked goods. They tenderize, add sweetness and flavor, promote browning and enhance the keeping quality. Sugar is used in meringues for stability. Sweeteners are used in small amounts to feed the yeast when making bread.

Brown sugar is a combination of granulated sugar and molasses. Available in light and dark, brown sugars can be used interchangeably. Dark brown sugar has more molasses and therefore, a more distinctive molasses flavor than light brown sugar. Dark brown sugar will also cause the color of the baked good to be slightly darker.

Common Baking Terms

Bake—To cook in an oven surrounded by dry heat. When baking, it's important to preheat the oven before placing the food inside.

Batter—A mixture made of flour and a liquid such as milk. It may also include ingredients such as sugar, butter, shortening or oil, eggs, leaveners and flavorings. The consistency of batters range from thin to thick. Thin batters are pourable such as pancakes or cakes. Thick batters can be dropped from a spoon such as quick breads or muffins.

Beat—To rapidly mix with a spoon, fork, wire whisk or electric mixer.

Blend—To combine several ingredients with a spoon, electric mixer, blender or food processor.

Boil—To heat liquids until bubbles form that cannot be stirred down. In the case of water, the temperature will reach 212° at sea level.

Caramelize—To heat sugar in a skillet or saucepan over low heat until melted and golden brown in color.

Chill—To cool foods to below room temperature (40° or less) by placing in the refrigerator, freezer or an ice bath.

Chop—To cut foods into 1/4-inch to 1/2-inch pieces.

Coats Spoon—To leave a thin even smooth film on the back of a metal spoon. This is a doneness test for stirred custards.

Combine—To place several ingredients in a single bowl or container and thoroughly mix.

Cool—To bring foods to room temperature (about 70°).

Core—To remove the seed area of an apple or pear using a coring tool or a small knife.

Cream—To beat softened butter, margarine or shortening alone or with sugar using a spoon or mixer until light and fluffy.

Crimp—To seal the edge of a double-crust pie by pinching or pressing the bottom and top pastry together with your fingers, fork or other utensil.

Cube—To cut foods into 1/2-inch to 1-inch square pieces.

Cut In—To break down and distribute cold butter, margarine or shortening into a flour mixture using a pastry blender or two knives.

Dash—A measurement less than 1/8 teaspoon that is used for herbs, spices or hot pepper sauce. This is not an accurate measurement.

Dice—To cut foods into 1/8-inch to 1/4-inch cubes.

Dissolve—To stir a solid food with a liquid until none of the solid remains, such as yeast with warm water or gelatin in boiling water.

Dot—To break up small pieces of butter and distribute over the top of pie filling or dough.

Dough— A thick mixture made of flour and a liquid that is not pourable. It may also include ingredients such as sugar, butter, shortening or oil, eggs, leaveners and flavorings. It is stiff enough to be worked with by hand, for example, kneading bread dough.

Drizzle—To slowly spoon or pour a thin stream of icing, melted butter or other liquid.

Dust—To lightly sprinkle confectioners' sugar, baking cocoa or flour.

Egg Wash—A mixture of beaten egg, egg yolk or egg white and water that is brushed over breads, rolls, pastries or pie crusts before baking. Egg washes give the final baked product a shiny brown finish.

Extracts—The distilled essential oils from plant materials, which are then dissolved in alcohol. Common examples are vanilla and almond.

Flavorings—Chemical compounds that replicate the flavor of a particular food or plant. Flavorings do not originate from the plant material. Common examples are maple, banana and coconut.

Flute—To make a V shape or scalloped edge on pie crust with your thumb and fingers.

Fold—A method of mixing to combine light or delicate ingredients such as whipped cream or egg whites with other ingredients without beating. A rubber spatula is used to gently cut down through the ingredients, move across the bottom of the bowl and bring up part of the mixture.

Food Coloring—Used to tint foods and is available in liquid, gel or paste.

Frost—To cover a cake, cupcake or cookie with a spreadable frosting.

Glaze—To coat the exterior of sweet or savory foods with a thin glossy mixture.

Grate—To rub ingredients such as citrus peel, spices and chocolate over a grater to produce very fine particles.

Grease—To rub the inside of a baking dish or pan with shortening, butter or oil or to coat with nonstick cooking spray.

Grease and Flour—To rub a thin layer of shortening, butter or oil over the inside of a baking pan or dish and then dust with flour. The excess flour is shaken out of the pan. Cakes baked in round baking pans or fluted tube pans generally require that the pan be greased and floured.

Grind—To transform a solid piece of food into smaller pieces using a food processor, blender or a mortar and pestle.

Ice—To spread a thin icing over cakes or cookies.

Jelly Roll—A dessert made by spreading a filling of jelly, cream or whipped cream over a sponge cake baked in a 15-inch x 10-inch x 1-inch pan and rolling into a log. Jelly-roll style is used when any food is filled and rolled into a log shape.

Knead—To work dough by using a pressing and folding action to make it smooth and elastic.

Line—To cover a baking sheet with a piece of parchment paper, waxed paper or foil to prevent sticking.

Marble—To swirl light and dark batters for a cake, bar, pie or cheesecake. The batters should not be combined into one color; there should still be two distinctive batters after marbling.

Mince—To cut foods into very fine pieces no larger than 1/8 inch.

Mix—To stir or beat two or more ingredients together with a spoon or a fork until well combined.

Moisten—To add enough liquid to dry ingredients while stirring gently to make a wet but not runny mixture. Often used in the preparation of muffins.

Peel—To remove the skin from fruits and vegetables. Also, the outer portion of a citrus fruit is known as peel. To remove the peel, use small sharp knife, grater, vegetable peeler or zester.

Pinch—A small amount (less than 1/8 teaspoon) of a seasoning or spice that is easily held between the thumb and index finger. This is not an accurate measurement.

Pipe—To force a soft mixture such as whipped cream, frosting or meringue through a pastry bag or tip for a fancy shape.

Plump—To soak dried fruit such as raisins and cherries in liquid until softened.

Press—Often called a cookie press. Used to form cookie dough into decorative shapes.

Prick—To pierce food or pastry with the tines of a fork to prevent them from bursting or rising during baking.

Proof—To check the quality of yeast before using in bread making. To proof yeast, dissolve yeast and a little sugar in warm water (110° to 115°) and let stand for 5 minutes. If the yeast is alive, there will be a thick foam on the surface. To proof also refers to letting yeast dough rise after it's been shaped and before baking.

Punch Down—To use a fist to deflate risen yeast dough after the first rising.

Puree—To mash solid foods into a smooth mixture using a food processor, food mill, blender or sieve.

Refrigerate—To place in the refrigerator to chill.

Rounded Teaspoon or Tablespoon—To mound dough slightly in the measuring spoon.

Score—To make thin slashes on the surface of breads to decorate and allow steam to escape during baking.

Seize—To become thick and lumpy. Seizing refers to when a small amount of liquid comes in contact with melted chocolate.

Separate—To remove the egg white from the egg yolk.

Sift—To pass dry ingredients such as flour or confectioners' sugar through a fine-mesh strainer to remove lumps, add air and combine several dry ingredients.

Soften—To bring butter, margarine or cream cheese to a soft consistency by letting it stand at room temperature for a short time.

Soft Peaks—The stage when beating egg whites or heavy whipping cream when the beater is lifted from the mixture and points of the peaks curl over.

Stiff Peaks—The stage when beating egg whites or heavy whipping cream when the beater is lifted from the mixture and points of the peaks stand straight up.

Stir—To blend a combination of ingredients by hand using a spoon in a circular motion.

Strain—To separate solids from liquid by pouring through a sieve or colander.

Toss—To quickly and gently mix ingredients with a spoon or fork. Often done with flour and candied fruit in baked goods.

Whip—To beat rapidly by hand or with an electric mixer to add air and increase volume.

Whisk—A multi-looped wire mixing utensil with a handle used to whip sauces, eggs, cream, etc. to a smooth, airy consistency. To whisk means to whip ingredients together.

Zest—See Peel.

weight and measure *equivalents*

TEASPOON AND TABLESPOON MEASURES

Dash or pinch	=	less than 1/8 teaspoon
1-1/2 teaspoons	=	1/2 tablespoon
3 teaspoons	=	1 tablespoon; 1/2 fluid ounce
4-1/2 teaspoons	=	1-1/2 tablespoons
2 tablespoons	=	1/8 cup; 1 fluid ounce
4 tablespoons	=	1/4 cup; 2 fluid ounces
5-1/3 tablespoons	=	1/3 cup; 5 tablespoons plus 1 teaspoon
8 tablespoons	=	1/2 cup; 4 fluid ounces
10-2/3 tablespoons	=	2/3 cup; 10 tablespoons plus 2 teaspoons
12 tablespoons	=	3/4 cup; 6 fluid ounces
16 tablespoons	=	1 cup; 8 fluid ounces; 1/2 pint

CUP MEASURES

1/8 cup	=	2 tablespoons; 1 fluid ounce
1/4 cup	=	4 tablespoons; 2 fluid ounces
1/3 cup	=	5-1/3 tablespoons
1/2 cup	=	8 tablespoons; 4 fluid ounces
2/3 cup	=	10-2/3 tablespoons
3/4 cup	=	12 tablespoons; 6 fluid ounces
7/8 cup	=	3/4 cup plus 2 tablespoons
1 cup	=	16 tablespoons; 8 fluid ounces; 1/2 pint
2 cups	=	1 pint; 16 fluid ounces
4 cups	=	2 pints; 1 quart; 32 fluid ounces

PINTS, QUARTS, GALLONS AND POUNDS

1/2 pint	=	1 cup; 8 fluid ounces
1 pint	=	2 cups; 16 fluid ounces
1 quart	=	4 cups; 32 fluid ounces
4 quarts	=	16 cups; 1 gallon
16 ounces	=	1 pound

COOKIES

Cookies

The Basics of Cookies

Cookies are grouped into five categories according to how they're shaped: drop, refrigerator, shaped, cutout and bars. (Bars and brownies appear in the next chapter.)

• The consistency of drop cookie dough allows it to simply be dropped from a spoon onto a baking sheet, making it the easiest kind of cookie to bake.

• For refrigerator cookies (also known as icebox cookies), the dough is shaped into logs, wrapped in plastic, then refrigerated until firm enough to slice and bake.

• Shaped cookies are formed by hand into various shapes (such as balls, logs and crescents) or are pressed through a cookie press (such as spritz).

• Cutout cookies have a firmer dough. To make it easier to handle, the dough may need to be chilled before being rolled out. Then the dough is cut into shapes with a cookie cutter or knife.

secrets for *successful cookies*

• Use butter, stick margarine (with at least 80% oil) or shortening. Whipped, tub, soft, liquid or reduced-fat products contain air and water and will produce flat, tough, underbrowned cookies.

• Measure ingredients accurately, using the measuring tools and techniques on pages 7 and 8.

• Avoid overmixing the dough. If it's handled too much, the cookies will be tough.

• Use heavy-gauge dull aluminum baking sheets with one or two low sides. When a recipe calls for greased baking sheets, use shortening or nonstick cooking spray. Dark finishes may cause the cookies to become overly browned.

• Preheat the oven for 10 to 15 minutes.

• For even baking, make cookies the same size and thickness.

• Unless the recipe states otherwise, place cookie dough 2 to 3 in. apart on a cool baking sheet.

• Leave at least 2 in. around the baking sheet and the oven walls for good heat circulation. For best results, bake only one sheet of cookies at a time. If you need to bake two sheets at once, switch the position of the baking sheets halfway through the baking time.

• Check the cookies when the minimum baking time has been reached, baking longer if needed. Follow doneness tests given in individual recipes.

• Unless otherwise directed, let cookies cool for 1 minute on the baking sheet before removing to a wire rack. Cool completely before storing.

• Let baking sheets cool before placing the next batch of cookie dough on them. Otherwise, the heat from the baking sheet will soften the dough and cause it to spread.

Drop Cookies

CHOCOLATE CHIP COOKIES

Chocolate Chip Cookies

PREP: 10 min. **BAKE:** 10 min. per batch
YIELD: about 11 dozen

Cindy Utter, Jacksonville, Illinois

Chocolate chip cookies are a mainstay in every cookie jar. They have mass appeal, making them perfect for gifts, bake sales or everyday snacking.

1	cup butter, softened
1	cup shortening
2	cups packed light brown sugar
1	cup sugar
4	eggs
2	teaspoons vanilla extract
4-1/2	cups all-purpose flour
2	teaspoons baking soda
2	teaspoons salt
2	cups (12 ounces) semisweet chocolate chips
1	cup chopped pecans

1 In a large mixing bowl, cream the butter, shortening and sugars until light and fluffy. Beat in eggs and vanilla. Combine the flour, baking soda and salt; add to creamed mixture and mix well. Stir in chocolate chips and nuts (dough will be slightly sticky).

2 Drop by tablespoonfuls 2 in. apart onto greased baking sheets. Bake at 350° for 10-12 minutes or until lightly browned. Remove to wire racks to cool.

Whoopie Pies

PREP: 15 min. **BAKE:** 5 min. per batch + cooling
YIELD: about 3 dozen

Ruth Ann Stelfox, Raymond, Alberta

This confection features an irresistible cream filling, which is sandwiched between two chocolate cupcake-like cookies. Enlist the kids to help assemble and eat these old-fashioned favorites.

1	cup butter, softened
1-1/2	cups sugar
2	eggs
2	teaspoons vanilla extract
4	cups all-purpose flour
3/4	cup baking cocoa
2	teaspoons baking soda
1/2	teaspoon salt
1	cup water
1	cup buttermilk

FILLING:

2	cups marshmallow creme
2	cups confectioners' sugar
1/2	cup butter, softened
2	teaspoons vanilla extract

1 In a large mixing bowl, cream butter and sugar until light and fluffy. Add the eggs and vanilla; mix well. Combine the flour, cocoa, baking soda and salt; add to creamed mixture alternately with water and buttermilk, beating well after each addition.

2 Drop by teaspoonfuls 2 in. apart onto greased baking sheets. Bake at 375° for 5-7 minutes or until set. Remove to wire racks to cool completely.

3 In a small mixing bowl, beat filling ingredients until fluffy. Spread filling on the bottom of half of the cookies; top with remaining cookies.

tips for making *drop cookies*

- If your mixer begins to strain because the cookie dough is too thick, use a wooden spoon to stir in the last of the flour or ingredients such as nuts, chips or dried fruit.

- For even baking, it's important that you make cookies the same size. Use a teaspoon or tablespoon from your flatware set (see Shaping Drop Cookies on page 25) or a small ice cream scoop (see Using an Ice Cream Scoop to Make Drop Cookies on page 29).

- Drop cookies generally melt and spread during baking. But sometimes a recipe may instruct you to flatten the cookies with the bottom of a glass dipped in sugar or with a fork making a crisscross pattern.

Double Chocolate Crisps

PREP: 15 min. **BAKE:** 10 min. per batch **YIELD:** 4 dozen

Marilyn Spangler, Oak Creek, Wisconsin

Chock-full of chocolate, these crispy cookies have a tantalizing aroma while baking. They'll surely satisfy a sweet tooth.

- 1 cup butter, softened
- 2 cups sugar
- 2 eggs
- 4 squares (1 ounce *each*) unsweetened chocolate, melted and cooled
- 2 teaspoons vanilla extract
- 2-1/4 cups all-purpose flour
- 1 teaspoon baking soda
- 1 teaspoon salt
- 1/4 teaspoon ground cinnamon
- 1 cup (6 ounces) semisweet chocolate chips
- 1 cup chopped pecans

1 In a large mixing bowl, cream butter and sugar until light and fluffy. Add eggs, one at time, beating well after each addition. Beat in chocolate and vanilla. Combine the flour, baking soda, salt and cinnamon; gradually add to the creamed mixture. Stir in chocolate chips and pecans.

2 Drop by tablespoonfuls 2 in. apart onto ungreased baking sheets. Bake at 375° for 10-12 minutes or until tops are cracked. Remove to wire racks to cool.

DOUBLE CHOCOLATE CRISPS

shaping *drop cookies*

Fill a teaspoon or tablespoon with dough. Use another spoon or small rubber spatula to push the mound of dough off the spoon onto a cool baking sheet. Place dough 2 to 3 in. apart or as recipe directs.

Toffee Chip Thins

PREP: 10 min. **BAKE:** 10 min. per batch + cooling
YIELD: about 4-1/2 dozen

Lynae Lang, Wolf Point, Montana

Every bite of these crisp cookies is bursting with the flavors of toffee, chocolate and coconut. Graham cracker crumbs add to their deliciously different flavor.

- 1/2 cup butter, softened
- 1 can (14 ounces) sweetened condensed milk
- 2 cups graham cracker crumbs (about 32 squares)
- 3/4 cup all-purpose flour
- 2 teaspoons baking powder
- 2 cups (12 ounces) semisweet chocolate chips
- 1 cup English toffee bits *or* almond brickle chips
- 1-1/2 cups flaked coconut, optional

1 In a large mixing bowl, combine the butter and milk. Combine the graham cracker crumbs, flour and baking powder; gradually add to the butter mixture. Stir in chocolate chips, toffee bits and coconut if desired.

2 Drop by rounded tablespoonfuls 2 in. apart onto greased baking sheets. Bake at 375° for 10-12 minutes or until edges are lightly browned. Cool for 2 minutes before removing to wire racks to cool completely.

Frosted Pineapple Cookies

PREP: 15 min. **BAKE:** 20 min. per batch + cooling
YIELD: 3 dozen

Mary DeVoe, Bradenton, Florida

Never thought of using pineapple to make cookies? Then give this recipe a try! Sweet and moist with real tropical flavor, these cookies will be a hit whenever you serve them.

1	can (8 ounces) crushed pineapple
1/2	cup shortening
1	cup packed brown sugar
1	egg
1	teaspoon vanilla extract
2	cups all-purpose flour
1-1/2	teaspoons baking powder
1/4	teaspoon baking soda
1/4	teaspoon salt
1-1/2	cups confectioners' sugar

1 Drain pineapple, reserving 3 tablespoons juice. Set pineapple aside; set reserved juice aside for frosting. In a mixing bowl, cream shortening and brown sugar until light and fluffy. Beat in egg. Add pineapple and vanilla; mix well. Combine the flour, baking powder, baking soda and salt; gradually add to the creamed mixture.

2 Drop by tablespoonfuls 2 in. apart onto greased baking sheets. Bake at 325° for 17-20 minutes or until golden. Remove to wire racks to cool.

3 For frosting, in a bowl, combine confectioners' sugar with enough of the reserved pineapple juice to achieve spreading consistency. Frost cooled cookies.

German Chocolate Cookies

PREP: 5 min. **BAKE:** 10 min. per batch
YIELD: about 3-1/2 dozen

Leslie Henke, Louisville, Colorado

A handy boxed cake mix hurries along the preparation of chewy cookies studded with chips and raisins. Even with only six ingredients, they have wonderful bakery-shop flavor.

1	package (18-1/4 ounces) German chocolate cake mix
2	eggs
1/2	cup butter, melted
1/2	cup quick-cooking oats
1	cup (6 ounces) semisweet chocolate chips
1/2	cup raisins

1 In a large mixing bowl, combine the dry cake mix, eggs, butter and oats; mix well. Stir in the chocolate chips and raisins.

2 Drop by rounded tablespoonfuls 3 in. apart onto ungreased baking sheets. Bake at 350° for 9-11 minutes or until set. Cool for 5 minutes before removing to wire racks.

CHOCOLATE MARSHMALLOW COOKIES

1 In a large mixing bowl, cream butter and sugar until light and fluffy. Beat in the egg, milk and vanilla. Combine the flour, cocoa, baking soda and salt; beat into creamed mixture.

2 Drop by rounded teaspoonfuls 2 in. apart onto ungreased baking sheets. Bake at 350° for 8 minutes. Meanwhile, cut marshmallows in half. Press a marshmallow half cut side down onto each cookie. Bake 2 minutes longer. Remove to wire racks to cool.

3 For icing, combine the butter, cocoa and milk in a saucepan. Bring to a boil; boil for 1 minute, stirring constantly. Cool slightly; transfer to a small mixing bowl. Add confectioners' sugar and vanilla; beat well. Spread over the cooled cookies. Top each with a pecan half.

packing & shipping *cookies*

Here are some pointers to ensure that cookies arrive at their destination as delicious and attractive as when you baked them.

- First, select cookies that are sturdy and will travel well, such as bars and brownies, drop, icebox and sandwich cookies. Cutouts and other thin cookies might break or crumble during shipping. Cookies requiring refrigeration are a poor choice for shipping because they'll spoil.

- Bake and completely cool cookies just before packing and shipping so they arrive as fresh as possible.

- Wrap them in bundles of two (for drop cookies, place their bottoms together) with plastic wrap. Wrap bars individually. Pack crisp and soft cookies in separate tins and pack strong-flavored cookies, such as gingersnaps, separate from mild-flavored cookies.

- Line a tin or box with crumpled waxed paper to cushion the cookies. Snugly pack the cookies to within 1 inch of the top. Use crumpled waxed paper or bubble wrap to fill in any gaps between cookies and side of container and to cover tops of cookies. Close box or tin.

- Wrap the cookie container in a slightly larger cardboard box and cushion with bubble wrap, crumpled paper or shipping peanuts. Seal box and label it as "Fragile and Perishable."

Chocolate Marshmallow Cookies

PREP: 25 min. + cooling **BAKE:** 10 min. per batch + cooling **YIELD:** about 3 dozen

June Formanek, Belle Plaine, Iowa

These double-chocolaty delights have a surprise inside. Atop the chocolate cookie base, marshmallow peeks out under chocolate icing. Kids love them!

1/2	cup butter, softened
1	cup sugar
1	egg
1/4	cup milk
1	teaspoon vanilla extract
1-3/4	cups all-purpose flour
1/3	cup baking cocoa
1/2	teaspoon baking soda
1/2	teaspoon salt
16	to 18 large marshmallows

ICING:

6	tablespoons butter
2	tablespoons baking cocoa
1/4	cup milk
1-3/4	cups confectioners' sugar
1/2	teaspoon vanilla extract

Pecan halves

APRICOT COCONUT COOKIES

Oatmeal Sandwich Cremes

PREP: 20 min. **BAKE:** 15 min. per batch + cooling
YIELD: 3 dozen

Lesley Mansfield, Monroe, North Carolina

Sandwich cookies can be a little time-consuming but are well worth it. To save some time, bake the cookies, cool and freeze. When ready to serve, thaw the cookies, make the filling and assemble the sandwiches.

3/4	cup shortening
1	cup sugar
1	cup packed brown sugar
1	egg
1/4	cup water
1	teaspoon vanilla extract
1-1/2	cups self-rising flour
1	teaspoon baking soda
1	teaspoon ground cinnamon
3	cups quick-cooking oats
3/4	cup raisins

FILLING:

1/2	cup butter, softened
1/2	cup shortening
3-3/4	cups confectioners' sugar
2	tablespoons milk
1	teaspoon vanilla extract

Dash salt

1 In a large mixing bowl, cream shortening and sugars until light and fluffy. Beat in the egg, water and vanilla. Combine the flour, baking soda and cinnamon; gradually add to the creamed mixture. Stir in oats and raisins.

2 Drop by tablespoonfuls 2 in. apart onto ungreased baking sheets. Flatten with a greased glass. Bake at 325° for 13-14 minutes or until lightly browned. Remove to wire racks to cool.

3 Combine filling ingredients in a large mixing bowl; beat until smooth. Spread on the bottom of half of the cooled cookies; top with the remaining cookies.

Editor's Note: As a substitute for the self-rising flour, place 2-1/4 teaspoons baking powder and 3/4 teaspoon salt in a 1-cup measuring cup; add all-purpose flour to measure 1 cup. Add an additional 1/2 cup all-purpose flour.

Apricot Coconut Cookies

PREP: 15 min. **BAKE:** 10 min. per batch + cooling
YIELD: about 3 dozen

Sara Kennedy, Manassas, Virginia

These fancy, chewy cookies are made without eggs. They make a delicious treat, especially for people allergic to eggs.

1-1/4	cups all-purpose flour
1/4	cup sugar
1-1/2	teaspoons baking powder
1/2	cup cold butter
1	package (3 ounces) cream cheese
1/2	cup shredded coconut
1/2	cup apricot preserves

GLAZE:

1/2	cup confectioners' sugar
2	tablespoons apricot preserves
1-1/2	teaspoons butter, softened
1-1/2	teaspoons milk

1 In a large bowl, combine the flour, sugar and baking powder. Cut in butter and cream cheese until mixture resembles coarse crumbs. Add coconut and preserves; mix well.

2 Drop by rounded teaspoonfuls 2 in. apart onto greased baking sheet. Bake at 350° for 10-12 minutes or until golden brown. Remove to wire racks to cool completely.

3 In a small bowl, combine all the glaze ingredients. Spoon over cookies.

using an
ice cream scoop
to make *drop cookies*

An ice cream scoop is the perfect utensil for making uniformly sized drop cookies.

(A 1 tablespoon-size ice cream scoop will result in a standard-size 2-in. cookie.) Just scoop the dough, even off the top with a flat-edge metal spatula and release onto a baking sheet.

Iced Orange Cookies

PREP: 15 min. **BAKE:** 10 min. per batch + cooling
YIELD: about 5-1/2 dozen

Lori DiPietro, New Port Richey, Florida

Orange juice in both the dough and icing lends to the tropical flavor of these bite-size cookies.

- 1/2 **cup shortening**
- 1 **cup sugar**
- 2 **eggs**
- 1/2 **cup orange juice**
- 1 **tablespoon grated orange peel**
- 2-1/2 **cups all-purpose flour**
- 1-1/2 **teaspoons baking powder**
- 1/2 **teaspoon salt**

ICING:
- 2 **cups confectioners' sugar**
- 1/4 **cup orange juice**
- 2 **tablespoons butter, melted**

1 In a large mixing bowl, cream shortening and sugar until light and fluffy. Add eggs, one at a time, beating well after each addition. Beat in orange juice and peel. Combine the flour, baking powder and salt; gradually add to the creamed mixture.

2 Drop by rounded teaspoonfuls 2 in. apart onto ungreased baking sheets. Bake at 350° for 10-12 minutes or until edges begin to brown. Remove to wire racks to cool. In a small bowl, combine icing ingredients until smooth; drizzle over cooled cookies.

Sour Cream Drops

PREP: 20 min. + chilling **BAKE:** 10 min. per batch + cooling **YIELD:** about 2-1/2 dozen

Tracy Betzler, Reston, Virginia

This unique frosting combines melted butter and confectioners' sugar for a rich flavor.

- 1/4 **cup shortening**
- 3/4 **cup sugar**
- 1 **egg**
- 1/2 **cup sour cream**
- 1/2 **teaspoon vanilla extract**
- 1-1/3 **cups all-purpose flour**
- 1/4 **teaspoon baking powder**
- 1/4 **teaspoon baking soda**
- 1/4 **teaspoon salt**

FROSTING:
- 2 **tablespoons butter**
- 1/2 **cup confectioners' sugar**
- 1/4 **teaspoon vanilla extract**
- 3 **to 4 teaspoons hot water**

1 In a large mixing bowl, cream shortening and sugar until light and fluffy. Beat in the egg, sour cream and vanilla. Combine the flour, baking powder, baking soda and salt; add to the creamed mixture. Cover and refrigerate for at least 1 hour.

2 Drop by tablespoonfuls 2 in. apart onto greased baking sheets. Bake at 425° for 7-8 minutes or until lightly browned. Remove to wire racks to cool.

3 For frosting, melt butter in a saucepan until golden brown; stir in the confectioners' sugar, vanilla and enough water to achieve a spreading consistency. Frost cooled cookies.

SOUR CREAM DROPS

Nutty Sugar Crisps

PREP: 15 min. **BAKE:** 10 min. per batch
YIELD: 8-1/2 dozen

Eleanore Kovach, Lakeview, Oregon

These slightly crisp drop cookies are especially appealing to folks who don't want to hassle with cutout sugar cookies.

1	cup butter, softened
1/2	cup vegetable oil
1	cup sugar
1	cup confectioners' sugar
2	eggs
1	teaspoon vanilla extract
4-1/2	cups all-purpose flour
1	teaspoon baking soda
1	teaspoon cream of tartar
1	cup chopped walnuts

1 In a large mixing bowl, beat the butter, oil and sugars until smooth. Add eggs, one at a time, beating well after each addition. Beat in vanilla. Combine the flour, baking soda and cream of tartar; gradually add to the creamed mixture. Stir in walnuts.

2 Drop by teaspoonfuls 2 in. apart onto ungreased baking sheets. Flatten slightly with a glass dipped in sugar. Bake at 375° for 10-12 minutes or until the edges are golden brown. Remove to wire racks to cool.

CHEWY PECAN COOKIES

chocolate and raspberries. Combine the flour, baking soda and salt; gradually add to the creamed mixture. Stir in vanilla chips.

2 Drop by teaspoonfuls 2 in. apart onto ungreased baking sheets. Bake at 375° for 10-12 minutes or until edges begin to brown. Remove to wire racks to cool.

Chocolate Raspberry Cookies

PREP: 15 min. **BAKE:** 10 min. per batch **YIELD:** 6 dozen

Sherri Crotwell, Shasta Lake, California

Raspberries and chocolate give each bite of these luscious cookies an elegant feel. Serve them for special occasions or "just because!"

1	cup butter, softened
3/4	cup sugar
3/4	cup packed brown sugar
2	eggs
3/4	cup semisweet chocolate chips, melted and cooled
1/2	cup fresh raspberries, pureed
3	cups all-purpose flour
3/4	teaspoon baking soda
3/4	teaspoon salt
1	cup vanilla *or* white chips

1 In a large mixing bowl, cream butter and sugars until light and fluffy. Add eggs, one at a time, beating well after each addition. Beat in melted

Chewy Pecan Cookies

PREP: 25 min. **BAKE:** 10 min. per batch
YIELD: 5-6 dozen

Janice Jackson, Haleyville, Alabama

The pecans add a real Southern touch to these deliciously spiced oatmeal cookies.

1	cup butter, softened
1	cup sugar
3/4	cup packed brown sugar
3	eggs
1/4	cup milk
1	teaspoon vanilla extract
2-1/2	cups all-purpose flour
1	tablespoon ground cinnamon
1	teaspoon baking soda
1	teaspoon salt
1	teaspoon pumpkin pie *or* apple pie spice
2	cups quick-cooking oats
2	cups raisins
1-1/2	cups chopped pecans

1 In a large mixing bowl, cream butter and sugars until light and fluffy. Beat in the eggs, milk and vanilla. Combine the flour, cinnamon, baking soda, salt and pie spice; add to creamed mixture and mix well. Stir in the oats, raisins and nuts; mix well.

2 Drop by tablespoonfuls 2 in. apart onto greased baking sheets. Bake at 350° for 10-12 minutes or until light golden brown. Remove to wire racks to cool.

German Chocolate Toffee Cookies

PREP: 20 min. **BAKE:** 15 min. per batch **YIELD:** 13 dozen

Joyce Robb, Dillon, Montana

German sweet chocolate gives these crisp cookies a unique taste twist. So don't be surprised if the big batch disappears quickly!

1	cup butter, softened
1	cup shortening
2-1/2	cups sugar
1/2	cup packed brown sugar
1	package (4 ounces) German sweet chocolate, melted and cooled
4	eggs
2	teaspoons water
2	teaspoons vanilla extract
6-1/2	cups all-purpose flour
2	teaspoons baking soda
1-1/2	teaspoons salt
1-1/2	cups English toffee bits *or* almond brickle chips
1-1/2	cups chopped walnuts

1 In a large mixing bowl, cream the butter, shortening and sugars until light and fluffy. Beat in chocolate. Add eggs, one at a time, beating well after each addition. Beat in water and vanilla. Combine the flour, baking soda and salt; gradually add to the creamed mixture. Stir in toffee bits and walnuts.

2 Drop by tablespoonfuls 2 in. apart onto greased baking sheets. Bake at 350° for 12-15 minutes or until golden brown. Remove to wire racks to cool.

the history of *cookies*

Cookies started out as little cakes used to test the oven temperature before the larger cake was baked. In fact, the word cookie is derived from the Dutch word "koekje," meaning little cake.

GERMAN CHOCOLATE TOFFEE COOKIES

Chewy Macaroons

PREP: 15 min. **BAKE:** 25 min. **YIELD:** about 2 dozen

Herbert Borland, Des Moines, Washington

A perfectly prepared macaroon will be lightly crisp on the outside and chewy on the inside. Macaroons are primarily made with coconut, but some varieties feature nuts.

>   2   egg whites
>   1/2   teaspoon vanilla extract
> Pinch salt
>   6   tablespoons sugar
>   1   cup flaked coconut

1 In a small mixing bowl, beat egg whites, vanilla and salt on medium speed until soft peaks form. Gradually add sugar, one tablespoon at a time, beating on high until stiff peaks form. Fold in the coconut.

2 Drop by tablespoonfuls 2 in. apart onto well-greased baking sheets. Bake at 300° for 25 minutes or until lightly browned. Immediately remove to wire racks to cool.

Pumpkin Raisin Cookies

PREP: 15 min. **BAKE:** 15 min. per batch + cooling
YIELD: about 3 dozen

Carol Preston, Bloomington, Indiana

Fall is the perfect time to turn on the oven and bake up a batch of nicely spiced pumpkin cookies.

CHEWY MACAROONS

>   1/2   cup shortening
>   1   cup sugar
>   1   cup canned pumpkin
>   1   teaspoon vanilla extract
>   2   cups all-purpose flour
>   1   teaspoon baking powder
>   1   teaspoon baking soda
>   1   teaspoon ground cinnamon
> Dash salt
>   1   cup raisins
> FROSTING:
>   2   tablespoons butter
> 1-1/2   cups confectioners' sugar
>   2   tablespoons milk
>   1   teaspoon vanilla extract

1 In a large mixing bowl, cream shortening and sugar until light and fluffy. Add pumpkin and vanilla. Combine the flour, baking powder, baking soda, cinnamon and salt; add to the creamed mixture and mix well. Fold in raisins.

2 Drop by teaspoonfuls 2 in. apart onto greased baking sheets. Bake at 350° for 12-14 minutes or until lightly browned. Remove to wire racks to cool.

3 For frosting, melt butter in a small saucepan. Stir in the sugar, milk and vanilla until smooth. Frost cooled cookies.

Banana Spice Cookies

PREP: 15 min. + chilling **BAKE:** 10 min. per batch
YIELD: 3 dozen

Peggy Burdick, Burlington, Michigan

This is a great way to use up overripe bananas. They make these soft cookies quite tasty.

>   1/2   cup shortening
>   1   cup packed brown sugar
>   2   eggs
>   1   cup mashed ripe bananas (2 to 3 medium)
>   2   cups all-purpose flour
>   2   teaspoons baking powder
>   1/2   teaspoon ground cinnamon
>   1/4   teaspoon baking soda
>   1/4   teaspoon salt
>   1/4   teaspoon ground cloves
>   1/2   cup chopped walnuts
>   1/2   cup raisins

1 In a large mixing bowl, cream shortening and brown sugar until light and fluffy. Add eggs and bananas; mix well. Combine the flour, baking

LACE COOKIES

powder, cinnamon, baking soda, salt and cloves; add to creamed mixture and mix well. Stir in nuts and raisins. Cover and refrigerate until dough is easier to handle (dough will be very soft).

2 Drop by rounded teaspoonfuls 2 in. apart onto greased baking sheets. Bake at 350° for 8-10 minutes or until lightly browned. Remove to wire racks to cool.

Lace Cookies

PREP: 20 min. **BAKE:** 10 min. per batch + cooling
YIELD: about 4-1/2 dozen

Bonnie Thompson, Cave City, Kentucky

Light and crispy, these cookies melt in your mouth, while the plump pecan perched on top provides a little crunch. They're delicate when they come out of the oven, so keep them on the foil until completely cool, then carefully remove them from the foil.

1	cup chopped pecans
1	cup sugar
1/4	cup all-purpose flour
1/4	teaspoon baking powder
1/8	teaspoon salt
1	egg
1/2	cup butter, melted
1	teaspoon vanilla extract

Pecan halves

1 In a food processor, combine chopped pecans and sugar; cover and process until nuts are ground. Transfer to a small mixing bowl; add the flour, baking powder and salt. In a bowl, beat egg; add butter and vanilla. Stir into pecan mixture.

2 Drop by teaspoonfuls about 3 in. apart onto lightly greased foil-lined baking sheets. Place a pecan half in the center of each cookie. Bake at 325° for 8-10 minutes or until golden brown and lacy. Allow cookies to cool completely before carefully removing from foil.

removing cookies from a *baking sheet*

If cookies seem to crumble when you remove them from the baking sheet, let them cool for 1 to 2 minutes first.

But be aware that if cookies cool too long, they become hard and can break when removed. If this happens, return the baking sheet to the oven to warm the cookies slightly so they'll release more easily.

GOLDEN RAISIN OATMEAL COOKIES

Golden Raisin Oatmeal Cookies

PREP: 15 min. **BAKE:** 15 min. per batch
YIELD: 4 dozen

Marion Lowery, Medford, Oregon

Here's a slightly different twist on a traditional favorite. These crisp, chewy oatmeal cookies feature golden raisins and have a mild orange tang.

- 3/4 **cup butter, softened**
- 1 **cup packed brown sugar**
- 1/2 **cup sugar**
- 1 **egg**
- 2 **tablespoons water**
- 1 **teaspoon vanilla extract**
- 3 **cups quick-cooking oats**
- 2/3 **cup all-purpose flour**
- 2 **tablespoons grated orange peel**
- 1 **teaspoon ground cinnamon**
- 1/2 **teaspoon baking soda**
- 2/3 **cup golden raisins**

1 In a large mixing bowl, cream butter and sugars until light and fluffy. Beat in the egg, water and vanilla. Combine the oats, flour, orange peel, cinnamon and baking soda; gradually add to the creamed mixture. Stir in the raisins (dough will be stiff).

2 Drop by level tablespoonfuls 2 in. apart onto ungreased baking sheets. Bake at 350° for 12-15 minutes or until the edges are lightly browned. Remove to wire racks to cool.

Brown Sugar Crinkles

PREP: 20 min. **BAKE:** 10 min. per batch
YIELD: about 13 dozen

Donna Frame
Montgomery Village, Maryland

The addition of brown sugar makes these deliciously different from traditional sugar cookies. They're attractive and simple to make.

- 1 **cup butter, softened**
- 1 **cup shortening**
- 3 **cups sugar**
- 1-1/2 **cups packed brown sugar**
- 6 **eggs**
- 1 **tablespoon vanilla extract**
- 6 **cups all-purpose flour**
- 1 **tablespoon baking soda**
- 1-1/2 **teaspoons salt**

1 In a large mixing bowl, cream butter, shortening and sugars until light and fluffy. Add eggs, one at a time, beating well after each addition. Beat in vanilla. Combine the flour, baking soda and salt; gradually add to the creamed mixture (the dough will be soft).

2 Drop by rounded teaspoonfuls 2 in. apart onto ungreased baking sheets. Flatten with a glass dipped in sugar. Bake at 350° for 10-12 minutes or until lightly browned. Cool for 2 minutes before removing to wire racks.

Soft Lemonade Cookies

PREP: 10 min. **BAKE:** 10 min. per batch **YIELD:** 6 dozen

Margo Neuhauser, Bakersfield, California

These lovely lemon cookies are so moist, you won't be able to stop eating them! Frozen lemonade concentrate is the surprise ingredient.

- 1 **cup butter, softened**
- 1 **cup sugar**
- 2 **eggs**
- 3 **cups all-purpose flour**
- 1 **teaspoon baking soda**
- 1 **can (6 ounces) frozen lemonade concentrate, thawed, *divided***

Additional sugar

1 In a large mixing bowl, cream butter and sugar until light and fluffy. Add eggs, one at a time, beating well after each addition. Combine flour and baking soda; add to the creamed mixture alternately with 1/3 cup of lemonade concentrate, beating well after each addition.

2 Drop by rounded teaspoonfuls 2 in. apart onto ungreased baking sheets. Bake at 400° for 8-10 minutes. Remove to wire racks. Brush warm cookies with remaining lemonade concentrate; sprinkle with sugar. Cool.

Super Chunky Cookies

PREP: 15 min. **BAKE:** 10 min. per batch
YIELD: about 8-1/2 dozen

Rebecca Jendry, Spring Branch, Texas

Chocolate lovers will go crazy over these cookies—they have four kinds of chocolate! One of these will keep you going until mealtime.

- 1/2 **cup butter, softened**
- 1/2 **cup butter-flavored shortening**
- 1 **cup packed brown sugar**
- 3/4 **cup sugar**
- 2 **eggs**
- 2 **teaspoons vanilla extract**
- 2-1/2 **cups all-purpose flour**
- 1 **teaspoon baking soda**
- 1/8 **teaspoon salt**
- 1 **cup miniature semisweet chocolate chips**
- 1 **cup milk chocolate chips**
- 1 **cup vanilla *or* white chips**
- 4 **squares (1 ounces *each*) bittersweet chocolate, coarsely chopped**

SUPER CHUNKY COOKIES

- 3/4 **cup English toffee bits *or* almond brickle chips**
- 1/2 **cup chopped pecans**

1 In a large mixing bowl, cream the butter, shortening and sugars until light and fluffy. Add eggs, one at a time, beating well after each addition. Beat in vanilla. Combine the flour, baking soda and salt; gradually add to the creamed mixture. Stir in the remaining ingredients.

2 Drop by tablespoonfuls 3 in. apart on ungreased baking sheets. Bake at 350° for 10-12 minutes or until lightly browned. Cool for 2-3 minutes before removing to wire racks to cool completely.

Cherry Almond Chews

PREP: 15 min. **BAKE:** 15 min. per batch
YIELD: about 7 dozen

Alma Chaney, Trenton, Ohio

Topped with bright red cherries, coconut cookies are terrific for the holidays. During that busy time of year, you'll appreciate the fact that these freeze well, so you can make them ahead.

- 1 **cup shortening**
- 1 **cup sugar**
- 1 **cup packed brown sugar**
- 2 **eggs**
- 3/4 **teaspoon almond extract**
- 2-1/2 **cups all-purpose flour**
- 1 **teaspoon baking soda**
- 1 **teaspoon salt**
- 2-1/2 **cups flaked coconut**
- 3/4 **cup chopped almonds *or* pecans, optional**
- 1 **jar (16 ounces) maraschino cherries, drained and halved**

1 In a large mixing bowl, cream shortening and sugars until light and fluffy. Add eggs, one at a time, beating well after each addition. Beat in extract. Combine the flour, baking soda and salt; gradually add to the creamed mixture. Stir in coconut and nuts if desired.

2 Drop by rounded teaspoonfuls 2 in. apart onto lightly greased baking sheets. Place a cherry half in the center of each. Bake at 350° for 12-14 minutes or until lightly browned. Remove to wire racks to cool.

Banana Oatmeal Cookies

PREP: 15 min. **BAKE:** 10 min. per batch
YIELD: about 4 dozen

Yvonne Miller, Chenango Forks, New York

Bananas and chocolate chips give ordinary oatmeal cookies a flavorful twist. Keep some ripe bananas in the freezer to make these treats on a moment's notice.

   1   **cup butter-flavored shortening**
   1   **cup sugar**
   2   **eggs**
   1   **teaspoon vanilla extract**
   2   **cups all-purpose flour**
   1   **teaspoon baking soda**
   1   **teaspoon ground cinnamon**
   1   **teaspoon ground cloves**
   3   **medium bananas, mashed**
   2   **cups quick-cooking oats**
   1   **cup (6 ounces) semisweet chocolate chips**

1 In a large mixing bowl, cream shortening and sugar until light and fluffy. Beat in eggs and vanilla. Combine flour, baking soda, cinnamon and cloves; add to creamed mixture and mix well. Stir in the bananas, oats and chocolate chips.

2 Drop by rounded teaspoonfuls 2 in. apart onto greased baking sheets. Bake at 375° for 10-12 minutes. Immediately remove to wire racks to cool.

Frosted Chocolate Delights

PREP: 20 min. **BAKE:** 15 min. per batch + cooling
YIELD: 5-1/2 dozen

Patricia Ramczyk, Appleton, Wisconsin

These simple chocolate drop cookies are crowned with a creamy vanilla frosting.

   1/2   **cup shortening**
     1   **cup packed brown sugar**
     1   **egg**
   1/2   **cup milk**
     1   **teaspoon vanilla extract**
     2   **squares (1 ounce *each*) unsweetened chocolate, melted and cooled**
 1-3/4   **cups all-purpose flour**
     1   **teaspoon baking powder**
   1/2   **teaspoon salt**
   1/4   **teaspoon baking soda**
   1/2   **cup chopped walnuts**
FROSTING:
     9   **tablespoons butter, softened**
 4-1/2   **cups confectioners' sugar**
 1-1/2   **teaspoons vanilla extract**
     6   **to 8 tablespoons milk**

1 In a large mixing bowl, cream shortening and brown sugar until light and fluffy. Beat in the egg, milk and vanilla. Beat in chocolate until blended. Combine the flour, baking powder, salt and baking soda; gradually add to the creamed mixture. Stir in walnuts.

2 Drop by tablespoonfuls 2 in. apart onto ungreased baking sheets. Bake at 350° for 11-13 minutes or until firm. Remove to wire racks to cool completely.

3 For frosting, in a mixing bowl, cream butter and sugar until light and fluffy. Beat in vanilla and enough milk to achieve spreading consistency. Frost cooled cookies.

Pineapple Chocolate Chip Cookies

PREP: 10 min. **BAKE:** 10 min. per batch
YIELD: about 4-1/2 dozen

Karen Bontrager, Macon, Mississippi

These cookies are always popular at bake sales. You can use 1 cup of coconut instead of the chopped walnuts.

> 1 cup shortening
> 1 cup sugar
> 1 cup packed brown sugar
> 2 eggs
> 2 cans (8 ounces *each*) crushed pineapple, drained
> 2 teaspoons vanilla extract
> 4 cups all-purpose flour
> 2 teaspoons baking soda
> 2 teaspoons baking powder
> 1/2 teaspoon salt
> 1 cup (6 ounces) semisweet chocolate chips
> 1 cup chopped walnuts, optional

1 In a mixing bowl, cream shortening and sugars until light and fluffy. Add eggs, one at a time, beating well after each addition. Beat in pineapple and vanilla. Combine the flour, baking soda, baking powder and salt; gradually add to creamed mixture. Stir in chocolate chips and walnuts if desired.

2 Drop by rounded tablespoonfuls 2 in. apart onto greased baking sheets. Press down lightly. Bake at 375° for 10-12 minutes or until lightly browned. Remove to wire racks to cool.

Cream Cheese Macadamia Cookies

PREP: 15 min. + chilling **BAKE:** 10 min. per batch
YIELD: about 3-1/2 dozen

Lillie Grove, Beaver, Oklahoma

A soft cake-like texture and subtle orange flavor make these tender drop cookies a tasty treat.

> 1/2 cup butter, softened
> 1 package (8 ounces) cream cheese, softened
> 3/4 cup packed brown sugar
> 4 teaspoons grated orange peel
> 2 teaspoons vanilla extract
> 1-1/2 cups all-purpose flour
> 2 teaspoons baking powder
> 3/4 cup coarsely chopped salted macadamia nuts *or* almonds

1 In a large mixing bowl, cream the butter, cream cheese, brown sugar, orange peel and vanilla until light and fluffy. Combine flour and baking powder. Gradually add to the creamed mixture; mix well. Fold in nuts. Cover and refrigerate for 1 hour or until firm.

2 Drop by rounded teaspoonfuls 2 in. apart onto ungreased baking sheets; flatten slightly with a greased glass. Bake at 400° for 9-11 minutes or until lightly browned. Remove to wire racks to cool.

Editor's Note: If using unsalted macadamia nuts, add 1/4 teaspoon salt to the dough.

PINEAPPLE CHOCOLATE CHIP COOKIES

Refrigerator Cookies

refrigerator *cookie facts*

- To make refrigerator cookie dough easier to slice, use nuts and fruits that are finely chopped. If the nuts and fruit are too large, the cookie dough may break apart when sliced.

- Wrap dough tightly to prevent it from drying out in the refrigerator. Refrigerate dough until firm.

- Generally, the dough can be refrigerated up to 1 week or frozen up to 6 months.

- To keep a nice round shape for refrigerated cookie dough, place each roll inside a tall glass and place the glass on its side in the refrigerator. The rounded glass will prevent the bottom of the roll from flattening out. A cardboard tube from a roll of paper towels or wrapping paper will also work.

- Use a thin sharp knife to slice through the dough. Cut one roll at a time, keeping additional rolls refrigerated until ready to use. After each slice, rotate the roll to avoid having one side that's flat.

Cream Cheese-Filled Cookies

PREP: 20 min. + cooling **BAKE:** 10 min. per batch + cooling **YIELD:** about 2-1/2 dozen

Ruth Glick, New Holland, Pennsylvania

With a cream cheese filling and chocolate topping, these rich cookies are more fancy than others. Their eye-catching appeal makes them perfect for special occasions.

- 1/3   cup butter, softened
- 1/3   cup shortening
- 3/4   cup sugar
- 1   egg
- 1   teaspoon vanilla extract
- 1-3/4   cups all-purpose flour
- 1   teaspoon baking powder
- 1/2   teaspoon salt

FILLING:
- 2   packages (3 ounces *each*) cream cheese, softened
- 1-1/2   cups confectioners' sugar
- 2   tablespoons all-purpose flour
- 1   teaspoon vanilla extract
- 1   drop yellow food coloring, optional

TOPPING:
- 3/4   cup semisweet chocolate chips
- 3   tablespoons butter

1 In a large mixing bowl, cream the butter, shortening and sugar until light and fluffy. Beat in egg and vanilla. Combine the flour, baking powder and salt; gradually add to the creamed mixture. Shape into two 12-in. rolls; wrap each in plastic wrap. Refrigerate for 4 hours or overnight.

2 Unwrap dough; cut into 1-in. slices. Place 1 in. apart on greased baking sheets. Bake at 375° for 10-12 minutes or until lightly browned. Immediately make an indentation in the center of each cookie using the end of a wooden spoon handle. Remove to wire racks to cool completely.

3 In a mixing bowl, combine the filling ingredients; mix well. Place 2 teaspoonfuls in the center of each cookie. Let stand until set. Melt chocolate chips and butter; stir until smooth. Drizzle over cooled cookies. Store in the refrigerator.

Neapolitan Cookies

PREP: 20 min. + chilling **BAKE:** 10 min. per batch
YIELD: 12 dozen

Jan Mallo, White Pigeon, Michigan

These eye-catching cookies may look complicated, but they're actually easy to prepare.

- 1   cup butter, softened
- 1-1/2   cups sugar
- 1   egg
- 1   teaspoon vanilla extract
- 2-1/2   cups all-purpose flour
- 1-1/2   teaspoons baking powder
- 1/2   teaspoon salt
- 1/2   teaspoon almond extract
- 6   drops red liquid food coloring
- 1/2   cup chopped walnuts
- 1   square (1 ounce) unsweetened baking chocolate, melted and cooled

NEAPOLITAN COOKIES

1 Line a 9-in. x 5-in. x 3-in. loaf pan with waxed paper; set aside. In a large mixing bowl, cream butter and sugar until light and fluffy. Beat in egg and vanilla. Combine the flour, baking powder and salt; gradually add to the creamed mixture. Divide the dough into thirds. Add almond extract and food coloring to one portion; spread evenly into prepared pan. Add nuts to second portion; spread evenly over first layer. Add melted chocolate to third portion; spread over second layer. Cover with waxed paper; refrigerate overnight.

2 Unwrap dough; cut loaf in half lengthwise. Cut each portion into 1/8-in. slices. Place 1 in. apart on ungreased baking sheets. Bake at 350° for 10-12 minutes or until edges are firm. Remove to wire racks to cool.

CUTE KITTY COOKIES

Cute Kitty Cookies

PREP: 25 min. + chilling **BAKE:** 10 min. per batch
YIELD: 3 dozen

Kay Curtis, Guthrie, Oklahoma

Here's a fun dessert idea to serve children. Half of the dough is chocolate, which frames the playful cat faces.

- 1/2   **cup butter, softened**
- 1/4   **cup shortening**
-   1   **cup sugar**
-   2   **eggs**
-   1   **teaspoon vanilla extract**
- 2-1/4   **cups all-purpose flour**
- 3/4   **teaspoon baking powder**
- 1/2   **teaspoon salt**
-   1   **cup quick-cooking oats**
-   2   **squares (1 ounce *each*) unsweetened chocolate, melted and cooled**
- **Semisweet chocolate chips**
- **Red-hot candies**
- **Black shoestring licorice, cut into 1-1/2-inch pieces**

1 In a large mixing bowl, cream the butter, shortening and sugar until light and fluffy. Add eggs, one at a time, beating well after each addition. Beat in vanilla. Combine the flour, baking powder and salt; gradually add to the creamed mixture. Stir in oats. Divide dough in half. Add melted chocolate to one portion.

2 Shape the plain dough into an 8-in. roll. Roll chocolate dough between waxed paper into an 8-in. square. Place plain dough roll at one end of square; roll up. Seal seam. Wrap in plastic wrap; refrigerate for 3 hours or overnight.

3 Unwrap dough; cut into 1/4-in. slices. Place 2 in. apart on ungreased baking sheets. To form ears, pinch two triangles on the top of each cookie. Bake at 350° for 8-10 minutes or until lightly browned. Immediately place two chocolate chips for eyes, a red-hot for the nose and six pieces of licorice on each for whiskers. Remove to wire racks to cool.

making cute *kitty cookies*

Cute Kitty Cookies have a solid center of vanilla dough encased in a chocolate dough. To make these two-toned cookies, shape the vanilla dough into an 8-in. roll. Roll out the chocolate dough into an 8-in. square between two sheets of waxed paper. Remove the top sheet of waxed paper and place the vanilla roll at one edge of the square. Trim if necessary. Roll up jelly-roll style, peeling waxed paper away while rolling. Seal seam. Wrap the roll in plastic wrap and refrigerate.

Black Walnut Cookies

PREP: 20 min. + chilling **BAKE:** 10 min. per batch
YIELD: 10 dozen

Mrs. Doug Black, Conover, North Carolina

Like most nuts, walnuts can be stored in a cool dark place for several months. An open bag of shelled chopped nuts can become rancid quickly and should be used within a week. For long-term storage, refrigerate them for up to 6 months or freeze for up to 1 year.

- 1 **cup butter, softened**
- 2 **cups packed brown sugar**
- 2 **eggs**
- 1 **teaspoon vanilla extract**
- 3-1/2 **cups all-purpose flour**
- 1 **teaspoon baking soda**
- 1/4 **teaspoon salt**
- 2 **cups chopped black walnuts *or* walnuts, *divided***

1 In a large mixing bowl, cream the butter and brown sugar until light and fluffy. Beat in the eggs and vanilla. Combine the flour, baking soda and salt; gradually add to the creamed mixture. Stir in 1-1/4 cups of walnuts. Finely chop the remaining nuts. Shape dough into two 15-in. rolls. Roll in chopped nuts, pressing gently. Wrap each in plastic wrap. Refrigerate for 2 hours or until firm.

2 Unwrap dough; cut into 1/4-in. slices. Place 2 in. apart on greased baking sheets. Bake at 350° for 8-11 minutes. Remove to wire racks to cool.

BLACK WALNUT COOKIES

Rainbow Butter Cookies

PREP: 30 min. + chilling **BAKE:** 10 min. per batch
YIELD: about 4 dozen

Lanette Tate, Sandy, Utah

Use this recipe year-round simply by changing the color scheme of the dough to reflect the season or holiday.

- 1/2 **cup plus 2 tablespoons butter, softened**
- 1/2 **cup packed brown sugar**
- 1/4 **cup sugar**
- 1 **egg**
- 1 **teaspoon vanilla extract**
- 2 **cups all-purpose flour**
- 1/2 **teaspoon baking powder**
- 1/2 **teaspoon salt**
- 1/8 **teaspoon baking soda**
- **Green, red and yellow food coloring**
- **Milk**

1 In a large mixing bowl, cream butter and sugars until light and fluffy. Beat in egg and vanilla. Combine the flour, baking powder, salt and baking soda; gradually add to creamed mixture. Divide dough into three portions; tint each a different color. Roll each portion of dough on waxed paper into a 9-in. x 5-in. rectangle. Freeze for 10 minutes.

2 Cut each rectangle in half lengthwise. Lightly brush top of one rectangle with milk. Top with another colored dough. Remove waxed paper; brush top with milk. Repeat with remaining

coating
the edge
of *refrigerated cookies*

To give a little twist to refrigerated cookies, coat the edge in nuts, colored sugar, jimmies, nonpareils, coconut or cinnamon-sugar. Spread the coating lengthwise down a piece of waxed paper. Place the roll of dough on top of the coating and roll gently, pressing coating onto dough with your hands.

dough, alternating colors, to make six layers. Press together lightly; cut in half lengthwise. Wrap each with plastic wrap. Refrigerate several hours or overnight.

3 Unwrap dough; cut into 1/8-in. slices. Place 2 in. apart on ungreased baking sheets. Bake at 350° for 8-10 minutes. Cool for 1-2 minutes before removing from pans to wire racks to cool completely.

Chewy Date Pinwheels

PREP: 25 min. + chilling **BAKE:** 15 min. per batch
YIELD: about 4 dozen

Naomi Cross, Goshen, Indiana

For a lovely look on your holiday cookie tray, make a batch of these pretty pinwheel cookies. The date and pecan filling gives them an old-fashioned flavor.

FILLING:
- 1-1/2 cups chopped dates
- 1 cup sugar
- 1 cup water
- 1/2 cup chopped pecans

DOUGH:
- 1 cup butter, softened
- 2 cups packed brown sugar
- 1/2 cup sugar
- 3 eggs
- 4-1/2 cups all-purpose flour
- 1 teaspoon baking soda
- 1 teaspoon salt
- 1 teaspoon ground cinnamon

CHEWY DATE PINWHEELS

1 In a large saucepan, combine the dates, sugar and water. Cook and stir over medium heat for 8 minutes or until thick. Add nuts; cool. In a large mixing bowl, cream butter and sugars until light and fluffy. Add eggs, one at a time, beating well after each addition. Combine the flour, baking soda, salt and cinnamon; gradually add to creamed mixture. Divide dough in half.

2 On a floured surface, roll out one portion of dough into a 1/4-in.-thick rectangle. Spread with half of the filling. Roll up jelly-roll style, starting with a long side. Repeat with remaining dough and filling. Wrap each roll in plastic wrap; refrigerate overnight.

3 Unwrap dough; cut into 1/2-in. slices. Place 2 in. apart on greased baking sheets. Bake at 375° for 12-14 minutes. Remove to wire racks to cool.

Chocolate Almond Cookies

PREP: 15 min. + chilling **BAKE:** 10 min. + cooling
YIELD: 2 dozen

Kathryn Werner, Peterborough, Ontario

These sandwich cookies are not only jam-filled but also dipped in chocolate for a doubly delicious treat. Raspberry jam and chocolate pair well together, but feel free to use whatever flavor jam you prefer.

- 1/2 cup butter, softened
- 6 tablespoons sugar
- 1-1/2 teaspoons vanilla extract
- 1 cup all-purpose flour
- 1 cup finely chopped blanched almonds
- 1/4 to 1/2 cup raspberry jam *or* jam of your choice
- 3 squares (1 ounce *each*) semisweet chocolate

1 In a large mixing bowl, cream the butter, sugar and vanilla until light and fluffy. Combine flour and almonds; gradually add to the creamed mixture. Shape into a 12-in. roll; wrap in plastic wrap. Refrigerate for 4 hours or until firm.

2 Unwrap dough; cut into 1/4-in. slices. Place 2 in. apart on ungreased baking sheets. Bake at 350° for 8-10 minutes or until lightly browned. Remove to wire racks to cool.

3 Spread 1 teaspoon jam on the bottom of half of the cookies; top with remaining cookies. Melt chocolate. Dip cookies halfway into chocolate; shake off excess. Place on waxed paper until chocolate is set.

HAZELNUT SHORTBREAD

2 Unwrap dough; cut into 1/4-in. slices. Place 2 in. apart on ungreased baking sheets. Bake at 325° for 14-16 minutes or until edges begin to brown. Remove to wire racks to cool completely. Melt chocolate chips; drizzle over cookies. Let stand until chocolate is set.

Orange Pecan Cookies

PREP: 15 min. + chilling **BAKE:** 10 min. per batch
YIELD: 6 dozen

Eleanor Henry, Derry, New Hampshire

This cookie is pure heaven with a subtle orange flavor and just a sprinkling of chopped pecans throughout.

    1   cup butter, softened
  1/2   cup sugar
  1/2   cup packed brown sugar
    1   egg
    2   tablespoons orange juice
    1   tablespoon grated orange peel
2-1/2   cups all-purpose flour
  1/2   teaspoon baking soda
  1/2   teaspoon salt
  1/2   cup chopped pecans

1 In a large mixing bowl, cream butter and sugars until light and fluffy. Beat in the egg, orange juice and peel. Combine the flour, baking soda and salt; gradually add to creamed mixture and mix well. Stir in pecans. Shape into two 11-1/2-in. rolls; wrap each in plastic wrap. Refrigerate for 4 hours or overnight.

2 Unwrap dough; cut into 1/4-in. slices. Place 2 in. apart on lightly greased baking sheets. Bake at 400° for 7-8 minutes or until golden brown. Remove to wire racks to cool.

Hazelnut Shortbread

PREP: 15 min. + chilling **BAKE:** 15 min. per batch + cooling **YIELD:** about 6 dozen

Karen Morrell, Canby, Oregon

Traditional shortbread only contains flour, sugar and butter, resulting in a rich crumbly cookie. This version gets added flavor from chopped hazelnuts, some maple syrup and a touch of chocolate.

    1   cup butter, softened
  1/2   cup sugar
    2   tablespoons maple syrup *or* honey
    2   teaspoons vanilla extract
    2   cups all-purpose flour
1-1/4   cups finely chopped hazelnuts
  1/2   cup semisweet chocolate chips

1 In a large mixing bowl, cream butter and sugar until light and fluffy. Add syrup and vanilla. Add flour; mix just until combined. Fold in the nuts. Shape into two 1-1/2-in. rolls; wrap each in plastic wrap. Refrigerate for 2 hours or until firm.

removing skins *from* hazelnuts

To easily remove skins from shelled hazelnuts—and, in the process, to enrich their flavor by toasting—try this trick:

Spread the nuts in a single layer in a baking pan. Bake at 350° for 10 to 15 minutes or until the nuts are toasted and the skins begin to flake. Transfer nuts to a clean kitchen towel; rub against the towel to remove skins.

Simple Sugar Cookies

PREP: 15 min. + chilling **BAKE:** 10 min. per batch
YIELD: 3-1/2 dozen

Maxine Guin, Barnhart, Missouri

Confectioners' sugar takes the place of granulated sugar in this sweet standby. They're a nice alternative to traditional cutout sugar cookies.

    1   cup butter, softened
1-1/4   cups confectioners' sugar
    1   egg
    1   teaspoon vanilla extract
    2   cups all-purpose flour

1 teaspoon baking soda
1 teaspoon cream of tartar
1/8 teaspoon salt

1 In a large mixing bowl, cream butter and confectioners' sugar until light and fluffy. Beat in egg and vanilla. Combine the flour, baking soda, cream of tartar and salt; gradually add to the creamed mixture. Shape into two 5-in. rolls; wrap each in plastic wrap. Refrigerate for 1 hour or until firm.

2 Unwrap dough; cut into 1/4-in. slices. Place 2 in. apart on ungreased baking sheets. Bake at 350° for 8-10 minutes. Remove to wire racks to cool.

Butterscotch Bonanza Cookies

PREP: 25 min. + chilling **BAKE:** 10 min. per batch
YIELD: 12 dozen

Dorothy Hankey, Waukesha, Wisconsin

These cookies store well for about 2 weeks in an airtight container. So when you have some time to spare, make a batch and enjoy them for days to come.

  1 **cup butter, softened**
  3 **cups packed brown sugar**
  4 **eggs,** *separated*
5-1/2 **cups all-purpose flour**
  1 **teaspoon baking soda**
  1 **teaspoon cream of tartar**
  1 **cup chopped almonds**

1 In a large mixing bowl, cream butter and brown sugar until light and fluffy. Add egg yolks, one at a time, beating well after each addition. Combine the flour, baking soda and cream of tartar; gradually add to the creamed mixture. Stir in almonds.

2 In small mixing bowl, beat egg whites on high speed until stiff peaks form; fold into dough. Shape into four 9-in. rolls; wrap each in plastic wrap. Refrigerate overnight.

3 Unwrap dough; cut into 1/8- to 1/4-in. slices. Place 1 in. apart on greased baking sheets. Bake at 350° for 10-12 minutes or until edges are golden brown. Remove to wire racks to cool.

Snickers Cookies

PREP: 10 min. **BAKE:** 10 min. **YIELD:** 2 to 2-1/2 dozen

Kari Pease, Conconully, Washington

A sweet surprise is inside these two-ingredient cookies. It's a great way to dress up refrigerated cookie dough.

  1 **tube (18 ounces) refrigerated chocolate chip cookie dough**
24 **to 30 miniature Snickers candy bars**

1 Cut dough into 1/4-in.-thick slices. Place a candy bar on each slice and wrap dough around it.

2 Place 2 in. apart on ungreased baking sheets. Bake at 350° for 8-10 minutes or until lightly browned. Remove to wire racks to cool.

Editor's Note: Two cups of any chocolate chip cookie dough can be substituted for the refrigerated dough. Use 1 tablespoon of dough for each cookie.

SNICKERS COOKIES

DOUBLE PEANUT BUTTER COOKIES

Chocolate Monster Cookies

PREP: 20 min. + chilling **BAKE:** 15 min. per batch
YIELD: 7-1/2 dozen

Helen Hilbert, Liverpool, New York

Young children may like to help stir in all the added ingredients. Use an extra-large bowl to prevent spillage.

 2 **cups butter, softened**
 2 **cups sugar**
 2 **cups packed brown sugar**
 4 **eggs**
 2 **teaspoons vanilla extract**
 4 **cups all-purpose flour**
 3 **teaspoons baking powder**
 2 **teaspoons baking soda**
 1 **teaspoon salt**
 2 **cups cornflakes**
 2 **cups rolled oats**
 1 **package (8 ounces) flaked coconut**
 1 **package (12 ounces) semisweet chocolate chips**
 1 **cup chopped walnuts**

1 In a large mixing bowl, cream butter and sugars until light and fluffy. Beat in eggs and vanilla. Combine the flour, baking powder, baking soda and salt; gradually add to creamed mixture and mix well. Stir in the cornflakes, oats and coconut. (It may be necessary to transfer to a larger bowl to stir in the cornflakes, oats and coconut.) Stir in chocolate chips and nuts.

2 Divide dough into six sections. Shape each into a 7-in. x 1-1/2-in. roll. Wrap each in plastic wrap. Refrigerate several hours or overnight.

3 Unwrap dough; cut into 1/2-in. slices. Place 3 in. apart on ungreased baking sheets. Bake at 350° for 13-15 minutes or until edges are browned. Remove to wire racks to cool.

Double Peanut Butter Cookies

PREP: 15 min. + chilling **BAKE:** 15 min. + cooling
YIELD: 20 cookies

Jeannette Mack, Rushville, New York

The extra taste of peanut butter in the middle of the cookie is a delicious surprise the first time you bite into one. It's a nice soft cookie and fun to make with little helpers.

1-1/2 **cups all-purpose flour**
 1/2 **cup sugar**
 1/2 **teaspoon baking soda**
 1/4 **teaspoon salt**
 1/2 **cup shortening**
 1/2 **cup creamy peanut butter**
 1/4 **cup light corn syrup**
 1 **tablespoon milk**
Additional peanut butter

1 In a large bowl, combine the flour, sugar, baking soda and salt. Cut in shortening and peanut butter until mixture resembles coarse crumbs. Stir in the corn syrup and milk; mix well. Shape into a 10-in. roll; wrap in plastic wrap. Refrigerate for 3 hours or overnight.

2 Unwrap dough; cut into 1/4-in. slices. Place half of the slices 2 in. apart on ungreased baking sheets. Top each with 1/2 teaspoon of peanut butter. Top with remaining slices; seal edges with a fork. Bake at 350° for 12-14 minutes or until lightly browned. Cool for 2 minutes before removing to wire racks to cool completely.

Lemon Refrigerator Cookies

PREP: 10 min. + chilling **BAKE:** 25 min. per batch
YIELD: about 8 dozen

Dessa Black, Dallas, Texas

This old-fashioned, lemon-flavored cookie is thin, crisp and delicious.

 1/2 **cup butter, softened**
 1/2 **cup sugar**
 1/2 **cup packed brown sugar**
 1 **egg**
 1 **teaspoon lemon extract**

1 teaspoon vanilla extract
1-3/4 cups all-purpose flour
1/2 teaspoon baking soda
1/4 teaspoon salt
1/2 cup finely chopped pecans

1 In a large mixing bowl, cream butter and sugars until light and fluffy. Beat in the egg and extracts. Combine the flour, baking soda and salt; gradually add to the creamed mixture. Stir in pecans. Shape into two 9-in. rolls; wrap each in plastic wrap. Refrigerate for 2 hours or until firm.

2 Unwrap dough; cut into 1/8-in. slices. Place 1 in. apart on ungreased baking sheets. Bake at 250° for 21-22 minutes or until edges are golden brown. Remove to wire racks to cool.

Editor's Note: The oven temperature is correct as printed.

Shaped Cookies

tips for making *shaped cookies*

- Refrigerate the dough until it is chilled for easier handling. If there is a high butter content in the dough, the heat from your hands can soften the butter in the dough, making it harder to shape.
- Dust hands lightly with flour to prevent dough from sticking while shaping it.

Split-Second Cookies

PREP: 20 min. **BAKE:** 15 min. per batch
YIELD: about 5 dozen

Mrs. Richard Foust
Stoneboro, Pennsylvania

These easy-to-bake cookies feature flavorful raspberry jam. Their rectangular shape makes them a nice addition to the traditional round varieties found on most cookie trays.

3/4 cup butter, softened
2/3 cup sugar
1 egg
1 teaspoon vanilla extract
2 cups all-purpose flour
1/2 teaspoon baking powder
1/2 teaspoon salt
1/3 cup raspberry jam

1 In a large mixing bowl, cream butter and sugar until light and fluffy. Beat in egg and vanilla. Combine the flour, baking powder and salt; gradually add to creamed mixture and mix well.

2 Divide dough into four equal portions; shape each into a 12-in. x 3/4-in. roll. Place 4 in. apart on two greased baking sheets. Make a 1/2-in. depression down center of logs; fill with jam. Bake at 350° for 15-20 minutes or until lightly browned. Cool for 2 minutes; cut diagonally into 3/4-in. slices. Remove to wire racks to cool.

SPLIT-SECOND COOKIES

Strawberry Cream Cookies

PREP: 25 min. + chilling **BAKE:** 10 min. per batch
YIELD: 5 dozen

Glenna Aberle, Sabetha, Kansas

Vary the look of these delicate cream cheese cookies with just one change by using a different jam flavor.

1 cup butter, softened
1 cup sugar
1 package (3 ounces) cream cheese, softened
1 egg yolk
1 tablespoon vanilla extract
2-1/2 cups all-purpose flour
Seedless strawberry jam

1 In a large mixing bowl, cream the butter, sugar and cream cheese until light and fluffy. Beat in egg yolk and vanilla. Add flour and blend. Cover and refrigerate for 1 hour or until dough is easy to handle.

2 Shape dough into 1-in. balls. Place 2 in. apart on ungreased baking sheets. Using a wooden spoon handle, press a hole in center of each cookie; fill with 1/4 teaspoon jam. Bake at 350° for 10-12 minutes or until set. Remove to wire racks to cool.

Cinnamon Crackle Cookies

PREP: 15 min. **BAKE:** 10 min. per batch
YIELD: about 6 dozen

Vicki Lair, Apple Valley, Minnesota

A blend of cinnamon, nutmeg and orange and lemon peel gives these sugar cookies excellent flavor. Keep a batch in the freezer for a speedy snack.

1/2 cup butter, softened
1/2 cup shortening
1 cup sugar
1/2 cup packed brown sugar
1 egg
1 teaspoon vanilla extract
1/2 teaspoon almond extract

shaping
cookie dough
into balls

Roll the dough between your palms until it forms a ball. A 1-in. ball requires about 2 teaspoons of dough. If the dough is sticky, you can refrigerate it until it is easy to handle, lightly flour your hands or spray your hands with nonstick cooking spray.

2-1/2 **cups all-purpose flour**
   3 **teaspoons ground cinnamon**
   2 **teaspoons baking soda**
   2 **teaspoons cream of tartar**
   2 **teaspoons ground nutmeg**
   2 **teaspoons grated orange peel**
   1 **teaspoon grated lemon peel**
1/2 **teaspoon salt**
Additional sugar

1 In a large mixing bowl, cream the butter, shortening and sugars until light and fluffy. Beat in egg and extracts. Combine flour, cinnamon, baking soda, cream of tartar, nutmeg, orange and lemon peel and salt; gradually add to the creamed mixture.

2 Shape into 1-in. balls; roll in sugar. Place 2 in. apart on ungreased baking sheets. Bake at 350° for 10-15 minutes or until lightly browned. Remove to wire racks to cool.

Chocolate Meringue Stars

PREP: 25 min. **BAKE:** 30 min. per batch + cooling
YIELD: about 4 dozen

Edna Lee, Greeley, Colorado

These light, delicate cookies are perfect for merry munching. Their big chocolate flavor makes it difficult to keep the kids away from them long enough to get any on the cookie tray.

   3 **egg whites**
3/4 **teaspoon vanilla extract**
3/4 **cup sugar**
1/4 **cup baking cocoa**
GLAZE:
   3 **squares (1 ounce *each*) semisweet chocolate**
   1 **tablespoon shortening**

CHOCOLATE MERINGUE STARS

1 In a large mixing bowl, beat egg whites and vanilla on medium speed until soft peaks form. Gradually add sugar, about 2 tablespoons at a time, beating on high until stiff peaks form. Gently fold in cocoa.

2 Insert a #8b large open star tip into a pastry or plastic bag; fill half full with meringue. Pipe stars, about 1-1/4-in. diameter, or drop by rounded teaspoonfuls onto ungreased parchment paper-lined baking sheets. Bake at 300° for 30-35 minutes or until lightly browned. Remove from paper; cool on wire racks.

3 In a heavy saucepan or microwave, melt chocolate and shortening; stir until smooth. Dip the cookies halfway into glaze; place on waxed paper until set.

piping *meringue cookies*

- Insert a decorating tip that has a large opening into a pastry bag or heavy-duty resealable plastic bag. (If using a plastic bag, first cut a small hole in the corner of the bag.)

- Fill the bag about half full with meringue. Smooth the meringue down toward the decorating tip to remove any air bubbles that could cause breaks in the design when piping. Twist the top of the bag shut.

- Line a baking sheet with parchment paper. Hold the pastry bag straight up and position the tip about 1/8 to 1/4 in. above the baking sheet. Hold the tip with one hand and squeeze the pastry bag with other. Stop squeezing before you lift up the decorating tip.

CHOCOLATE-TIPPED BUTTER COOKIES

Chocolate-Tipped Butter Cookies

PREP: 25 min. + chilling **BAKE:** 15 min. per batch
YIELD: about 5 dozen

Thara Baker-Alley, Columbia, Missouri

After dipping these cookies in melted chocolate and coating with chopped nuts, let them stand at room temperature until set before you stack them on a platter.

  1 **cup plus 3 tablespoons butter, softened, *divided***
1/2 **cup confectioners' sugar**
  2 **cups all-purpose flour**
  1 **teaspoon vanilla extract**
  1 **cup (6 ounces) semisweet chocolate chips**
1/2 **cup finely chopped pecans *or* walnuts**

1 In a large mixing bowl, cream 1 cup butter and confectioners' sugar until light and fluffy. Add flour and vanilla; mix well. Cover and refrigerate for 1 hour.

2 Shape 1/4 cupfuls of dough into 1/2-in.-thick logs. Cut logs into 2-1/2-in. pieces; place 1 in. apart on ungreased baking sheets. Bake at 350° for 12-14 minutes or until lightly browned. Remove to wire racks to cool.

3 In a heavy saucepan or microwave, melt chocolate and remaining butter; stir until smooth. Dip one end of each cookie into chocolate, then dip into nuts. Place on waxed paper until chocolate is set.

shaping
chocolate-tipped
butter cookies

Shape 1/4 cupfuls of dough into logs that are 1/2 in. thick. Cut the logs into 2-1/2-in. pieces, using a ruler as your guide.

Snickerdoodles

PREP/TOTAL TIME: 25 min. **YIELD:** 2-1/2 dozen

Taste of Home Test Kitchen

The history of this whimsically named treat is widely disputed, but the popularity of this classic cinnamon-sugar-coated cookie is undeniable!

1/2 **cup butter, softened**
  1 **cup plus 2 tablespoons sugar, *divided***
  1 **egg**
1/2 **teaspoon vanilla extract**
1-1/2 **cups all-purpose flour**
1/4 **teaspoon baking soda**
1/4 **teaspoon cream of tartar**
  1 **teaspoon ground cinnamon**

1 In a large mixing bowl, cream butter and 1 cup sugar until light and fluffy. Beat in egg and vanilla. Combine the flour, baking soda and cream of tartar; gradually add to the creamed mixture. In a small bowl, combine cinnamon and remaining sugar.

2 Shape dough into 1-in. balls; roll in cinnamon-sugar. Place 2 in. apart on ungreased baking sheets. Bake at 375° for 10-12 minutes or until lightly browned. Remove to wire racks to cool.

Butter Pecan Cookies

PREP: 25 min. + chilling **BAKE:** 10 min. per batch
YIELD: about 4 dozen

Martha Thefield, Cedartown, Georgia

These cookies are country fair blue-ribbons winners. You'll agree these mouth-watering morsels are real winners, too!

1-3/4	**cups chopped pecans**
1	**tablespoon plus 1 cup butter, softened, *divided***
1	**cup packed brown sugar**
1	**egg, *separated***
1	**teaspoon vanilla extract**
2	**cups self-rising flour**
1	**cup pecan halves**

1 Place chopped pecans and 1 tablespoon butter in a baking pan. Bake at 325° for 5-7 minutes or until toasted and browned, stirring frequently. Set aside to cool.

2 In a mixing bowl, cream brown sugar and remaining butter until light and fluffy. Beat in egg yolk and vanilla. Gradually add flour. Cover and refrigerate for 1 hour or until easy to handle.

3 Shape dough into 1-in. balls, then roll in toasted pecans, pressing nuts into dough. Place 2 in. apart on ungreased baking sheets. Beat egg white until foamy. Dip pecan halves in egg white, then gently press one into each ball. Bake at 375° for 10-12 minutes or until golden brown. Cool for 2 minutes before removing to wire racks.

Editor's Note: As a substitute for self-rising flour, place 3 teaspoons baking powder and 1 teaspoon salt in a measuring cup. Add all-purpose flour to measure 1 cup. Then add an additional cup of all-purpose flour.

dipping cookies in *chocolate*

- Melt the chocolate chips, baking chocolate or candy coating according to recipe directions. If necessary, transfer chocolate to a narrow container.

- Dip cookie partway into chocolate and scrape bottom of the cookie across the edge of the container to remove excess chocolate. Place on a baking sheet lined with waxed paper and allow to set at room temperature.

- Toward the end of the process, when the chocolate is running low, it might be necessary to spoon the chocolate over the cookies.

- If chocolate cools too much to coat the cookies properly, rewarm before finishing dipping.

BUTTER PECAN COOKIES

Cookie Jar Gingersnaps

PREP: 20 min. **BAKE:** 15 min. per batch
YIELD: 3-4 dozen

Deb Handy, Pomona, Kansas

Each time you take a bite of these crisp, chewy gingersnaps, you'll be reminded of your grandma's cozy kitchen.

- 3/4 cup shortening
- 1 cup sugar
- 1 egg
- 1/4 cup molasses
- 2 cups all-purpose flour
- 2 teaspoons baking soda
- 1-1/2 teaspoons ground ginger
- 1 teaspoon ground cinnamon
- 1/2 teaspoon salt

Additional sugar

1 In a large mixing bowl, cream the shortening and sugar until light and fluffy. Beat in egg and molasses. Combine the flour, baking soda, ginger, cinnamon and salt; gradually add to creamed mixture and mix well.

2 Shape teaspoonfuls of dough into balls. Dip one side into sugar; place sugar side up 2 in. apart on greased baking sheets. Bake at 350° for 12-15 minutes or until lightly browned and crinkly. Remove to wire racks to cool.

PEANUT BUTTER SANDWICH COOKIES

shaping
peanut butter *cookies*

Peanut butter cookie dough is generally a stiff dough and needs to be flattened before baking. Using a floured fork, press the balls of dough until 3/8 in. thick. Press again in the opposite direction to make a crisscross pattern.

Peanut Butter Sandwich Cookies

PREP: 20 min. **BAKE:** 10 min. per batch + cooling
YIELD: about 4 dozen

Debbie Kokes, Tabor, South Dakota

A creamy filling gives traditional peanut butter cookies a new twist.

- 1 cup butter-flavored shortening
- 1 cup creamy peanut butter
- 1 cup sugar
- 1 cup packed brown sugar
- 3 eggs
- 1 teaspoon vanilla extract
- 3 cups all-purpose flour
- 2 teaspoons baking soda
- 1/4 teaspoon salt

FILLING:
- 1/2 cup creamy peanut butter
- 3 cups confectioners' sugar
- 1 teaspoon vanilla extract
- 5 to 6 tablespoons milk

making
crescent shape
cookies

Shape rounded teaspoonfuls of dough into 2-1/2-in. logs, then bend slightly to form the crescent shape.

1 In a large mixing bowl, cream the shortening, peanut butter and sugars until light and fluffy. Add eggs, one at a time, beating well after each addition. Beat in vanilla. Combine the flour, baking soda and salt; gradually add to the creamed mixture.

2 Shape into 1-in. balls. Place 2 in. apart on ungreased baking sheets. Flatten to 3/8-in. thickness with a fork. Bake at 375° for 7-8 minutes or until golden. Remove to wire racks to cool completely.

3 In a mixing bowl, combine filling ingredients; beat until smooth. Spread on the bottom of half of the cookies; top with remaining cookies.

Pecan Crescent Cookies

PREP: 20 min. **BAKE:** 20 min. per batch + cooling
YIELD: 6 dozen

Grace Yaskovic, Branchville, New Jersey

Dust these rich buttery cookies with confectioners' sugar just before serving; otherwise, the sugar will be absorbed into the cookie.

    1 **cup butter, softened**
  1/2 **cup sugar**
    1 **teaspoon vanilla extract**
    2 **cups all-purpose flour**
    1 **cup finely chopped pecans**
Confectioners' sugar

1 In a large mixing bowl, cream the butter, sugar and vanilla until light and fluffy. Gradually add flour. Stir in pecans.

PECAN CRESCENT COOKIES

2 Shape rounded teaspoonfuls of dough into 2-1/2-in. logs and shape into crescents. Place 1 in. apart on ungreased baking sheets. Bake at 325° for 20-22 minutes or until set and bottoms are lightly browned. Let stand for 2-3 minutes before removing to wire racks to cool completely. Dust with confectioners' sugar before serving.

Lemon Crisp Cookies

PREP: 10 min. **BAKE:** 10 min. per batch
YIELD: about 4 dozen

Julia Livingston, Frostproof, Florida

The sunny yellow color and big lemon flavor of these quick-to-fix cookies are sure to bring smiles.

    1 **package (18-1/4 ounces) lemon cake mix**
    1 **cup crisp rice cereal**
  1/2 **cup butter, melted**
    1 **egg, beaten**
    1 **teaspoon grated lemon peel**

1 In a large bowl, combine all ingredients until well mixed (dough will be crumbly). Shape into 1-in. balls. Place 2 in. apart on ungreased baking sheets.

2 Bake at 350° for 10-12 minutes or until set. Cool for 1 minute before removing from wire racks to cool completely.

LEMON CRISP COOKIES

CHERRY CRUNCH COOKIES

Cherry Crunch Cookies

PREP: 20 min. + chilling BAKE: 15 min. per batch
YIELD: 5-1/2 dozen

Lora Reynolds, Grants Pass, Oregon

These crispy cookies provide a nice change of pace from the traditional chocolate chip, sugar and peanut butter cookies. The cornflakes give them a tasty coating.

3/4	cup butter, softened
1	cup sugar
2	eggs
2	tablespoons milk
1	teaspoon vanilla extract
2-1/4	cups all-purpose flour
1	teaspoon baking powder
1/2	teaspoon salt
1/2	teaspoon baking soda
1	cup chopped pecans
1	cup chopped dates
1/3	cup chopped maraschino cherries
1-3/4	cups finely crushed cornflakes
30	to 34 maraschino cherries, halved

1 In a mixing bowl, cream butter and sugar until light and fluffy. Add eggs, one at a time, beating well after each addition. Add milk and vanilla; mix well. Combine the flour, baking powder, salt and baking soda; add to creamed mixture. Stir in the pecans, dates and chopped cherries. Cover and refrigerate for 30 minutes.

2 Shape dough into 1-in. balls; roll in cornflakes. Place 2 in. apart on ungreased baking sheets; press a cherry half into center of each. Bake at 350° for 14-15 minutes or until golden brown. Remove to wire racks to cool.

Almond Biscotti

PREP: 15 min. BAKE: 35 min. + cooling
YIELD: 3-1/2 dozen

Mrs. H. Michaelsen, St. Charles, Illinois

In Italian, biscotti means twice-baked. The dough is first formed into a rectangle and baked. Then it's cut into slices, which are baked again. A crisp texture makes them great dunking cookies.

1/2	cup butter, softened
1-1/4	cups sugar, *divided*
3	eggs
1	teaspoon anise *or* vanilla extract
2	cups all-purpose flour
2	teaspoons baking powder
Dash salt	
1/2	cup chopped almonds
2	teaspoons milk

1 In a large mixing bowl, cream butter and 1 cup sugar until light and fluffy. Add eggs, one at a time, beating well after each addition. Stir in extract. Combine the flour, baking powder and salt; add to creamed mixture and mix well. Stir in almonds.

2 Line a baking sheet with parchment paper and grease the paper. Divide dough in half; spread each portion into a 12-in. x 3-in. rectangle on prepared pan. Brush with milk and sprinkle with remaining sugar. Bake at 375° for 15-20 minutes or until golden brown and firm to the touch.

3 Remove from oven and reduce heat to 300°. Lift rectangles with paper onto a wire rack; cool for 15 minutes. Place on a cutting board; cut with a serrated knife at a 45° angle into 1/2-in.-thick slices. Place slices cut side down on ungreased baking sheets. Bake for 10 minutes on each side. Turn oven off; leave cookies in oven with door ajar to cool.

ALMOND BISCOTTI

Brownie Alpine Biscotti

PREP: 25 min. **BAKE:** 40 min. + cooling
YIELD: 2-1/2 dozen

Jeanie Williams, Minnetonka, Minnesota

Brownie mix makes these biscotti cookies easy to stir up, and a white chocolate and almond topping adds a special touch.

1	package fudge brownie mix (13-inch x 9-inch size)
3/4	cup ground almonds
1/2	cup all-purpose flour
3/4	teaspoon baking powder
1	egg
3	egg whites
1	teaspoon almond extract
1/4	cup sliced almonds, optional
3	squares (1 ounce *each*) white baking chocolate, melted, optional

1 In a large bowl, combine dry brownie mix, ground almonds, flour and baking powder; mix well. In a small bowl, whisk egg, egg whites and extract. Add to brownie mixture; stir until combined. Divide dough into thirds.

2 On a greased baking sheet and using greased hands, shape each portion of dough into a 7-in. x 3-1/2-in. rectangle. Bake at 350° for 24 minutes.

cutting *biscotti*

After the rectangular biscotti dough is baked, it needs to be cut into slices, which will be baked longer.

With a serrated knife, cut the cookie diagonally into 1/2- or 3/4-in.-thick slices. Place the sliced cookies cut side down on a baking sheet and bake as directed.

Remove from the oven; cool on baking sheet for 5 minutes. Transfer to a cutting board; cut with a serrated knife at a 45° angle into 3/4-in.-thick slices. Place cut side down on greased baking sheets. Bake for 6-7 minutes on each side or until firm. Remove to wire racks to cool.

3 If desired, sprinkle with sliced almonds and drizzle with white chocolate. Let stand until chocolate is set.

BROWNIE ALPINE BISCOTTI

Coconut Washboards

PREP: 25 min. + chilling BAKE: 10 min. per batch
YIELD: about 9 dozen

Tommie Sue Shaw, McAlester, Oklahoma

This simple yet satisfying coconut cookie recipe has been around for generations. Pressing a fork into the top gives the look of an old-fashioned washboard.

1/2	cup butter, softened
1/2	cup shortening
2	cups packed brown sugar
2	eggs
1/4	cup water
1	teaspoon vanilla extract
4	cups all-purpose flour
1-1/2	teaspoons baking powder
1/2	teaspoon baking soda
1/4	teaspoon salt
1	cup flaked coconut

1 In a large mixing bowl, cream the butter, shortening and brown sugar until light and fluffy. Beat in eggs. Gradually add water and vanilla. Combine the flour, baking powder, baking soda and salt; add to the creamed mixture and mix well. Fold in coconut. Cover and refrigerate for 2-4 hours.

2 Shape into 1-in. balls. Place 2 in. apart on greased baking sheets; flatten with fingers into 2-1/2-in. x 1-in. rectangular shapes. Press lengthwise with a floured fork. Bake at 400° for 8-10 minutes or until lightly browned. Cool for 2 minutes before removing to a wire rack to cool completely.

COCONUT WASHBOARDS

forming *coconut washboard cookies*

With your hands, shape 1-in. balls of dough into 2-1/2-in. x 1-in. rectangles. Using a floured fork, press the tines lengthwise across the dough, giving it a washboard look.

Brown Sugar Cookies

PREP: 30 min. + chilling BAKE: 10 min. per batch + cooling YIELD: 5-1/2 dozen

Leonora Cloon, Ironwood, Michigan

Dark brown sugar and ground pecans give these cookies added richness. They're sure to solicit recipe requests!

1	cup butter, softened
3/4	cup sugar, *divided*
1/2	cup packed dark brown sugar
1	egg
1	teaspoon vanilla extract
2	cups all-purpose flour
1/2	cup finely ground pecans
1	teaspoon salt
1/2	teaspoon baking soda

ICING:

1	cup packed dark brown sugar
1/2	cup half-and-half cream
1	cup confectioners' sugar

1 In a large mixing bowl, cream the butter, 1/2 cup sugar and brown sugar until light and fluffy. Beat in egg and vanilla. Combine the flour, pecans, salt and baking soda; gradually add to creamed mixture and mix well. Cover and refrigerate for 20 minutes or until easy to handle.

2 Shape into 1-in. balls; roll in remaining sugar. Place 2 in. apart on ungreased baking sheets. Flatten with a glass dipped in sugar. Bake at 350° for 10-12 minutes or until edges are lightly browned. Remove to wire racks to cool completely.

3 For icing, combine brown sugar and cream in a saucepan. Bring to a boil; boil and stir for 4 minutes. Remove from the heat. Sift the confectioners' sugar into the hot mixture; stir until combined. Drizzle over cookies.

Chinese Almond Cookies

PREP: 20 min. **BAKE:** 15 min. per batch
YIELD: about 5 dozen

Jane Garing, Talladega, Alabama

These tender butter cookies make a nice addition to a holiday cookie tray. They keep when stored in an airtight container.

    1 cup butter, softened
    1 cup sugar
    1 egg
    1 teaspoon almond extract
    3 cups all-purpose flour
    1 teaspoon baking soda
  1/2 teaspoon salt
  1/4 cup sliced almonds
    1 egg white
  1/2 teaspoon water

1 In a large mixing bowl, cream butter and sugar until light and fluffy. Beat in egg and extract. Combine the flour, baking soda and salt; gradually add to creamed mixture.

2 Shape dough into 1-in. balls. Place 2 in. apart on ungreased baking sheets. Flatten with a fork. Sprinkle with almonds.

3 In a small bowl, beat egg white and water. Brush over cookies. Bake at 325° for 14-16 minutes or until edges and bottoms are lightly browned. Cool for 2 minutes before removing from pans to wire racks.

Apricot Pecan Tassies

PREP: 30 min. **BAKE:** 25 min. **YIELD:** 2 dozen

Paula Magnus, Republic, Washington

The apricot filling makes these adorable little tarts extra special. You could also try dried cranberries or cherries in the filling.

  1/2 cup plus 1 tablespoon butter, softened, *divided*
    6 tablespoons cream cheese, softened
    1 cup all-purpose flour
  3/4 cup packed brown sugar
    1 egg, lightly beaten
  1/2 teaspoon vanilla extract
  1/4 teaspoon salt
  2/3 cup diced dried apricots
  1/3 cup chopped pecans

1 In a large mixing bowl, cream 1/2 cup butter and cream cheese until light and fluffy. Gradually add flour, beating until mixture forms a ball. Cover and refrigerate for 15 minutes.

2 Meanwhile, in a bowl, combine the brown sugar, egg, vanilla, salt and remaining butter. Stir in apricots and pecans; set aside.

3 Shape dough into 1-in. balls. Press onto the bottom and up the sides of greased miniature muffin cups. Spoon 1 teaspoon apricot mixture into each cup. Bake at 325° for 25 minutes or until golden brown. Cool in pans on wire racks.

storing *cookies*

- Allow cookies to cool completely before storing.
- Store soft cookies and crisp cookies in separate airtight containers. If stored together, the moisture from the soft cookies will soften the crisp cookies, making them lose their crunch.
- Flavors can also blend during storage, so don't store strong-flavored cookies with delicate-flavored ones.
- Layer cookies in a container, separating each layer with waxed paper.
- Allow icing on cookies to completely dry before storing.
- Unfrosted cookies can be stored in a cool dry place in airtight containers for about 3 days. Cookies topped with a cream cheese frosting should be stored in the refrigerator.
- For longer storage, wrap unfrosted cookies in plastic wrap, stack in an airtight container, seal and freeze for up to 3 months. Thaw wrapped cookies at room temperature before frosting and serving.
- If your crisp cookies became soft during storage, crisp them up by heating in a 300° oven for 5 minutes.

Chocolate Truffle Cookies

PREP: 15 min. + chilling **BAKE:** 10 min. per batch
YIELD: about 5-1/2 dozen

Sharon Miller, Thousand Oaks, California

Chocolate lovers will gobble up these sweet treats featuring baking cocoa, chocolate chips and chocolate sprinkles. Pair them with a mug of coffee or cup of milk for a snack.

1-1/4	cups butter, softened
2-1/4	cups confectioners' sugar
1/3	cup baking cocoa
1/4	cup sour cream
1	tablespoon vanilla extract
2-1/4	cups all-purpose flour
2	cups (12 ounces) semisweet chocolate chips
1/4	cup chocolate sprinkles

1 In a large mixing bowl, cream the butter, confectioners' sugar and cocoa until light and fluffy. Beat in sour cream and vanilla. Add flour; mix well. Stir in chocolate chips. Cover and refrigerate for 1 hour.

2 Shape into 1-in. balls; dip one side in chocolate sprinkles. Place sprinkled side up 2 in. apart on ungreased baking sheets. Bake at 325° for 10-12 minutes or until set. Cool for 5 minutes before removing to wire racks.

Chocolate Pretzel Cookies

PREP: 30 min. + chilling **BAKE:** 5 min. per batch + cooling **YIELD:** 4 dozen

Priscilla Anderson, Salt Lake City, Utah

These pretzel-shaped buttery cookies are covered in a rich mocha glaze and drizzled with white chocolate. Your family will go wild over their chocolaty crunch.

1/2	cup butter, softened
2/3	cup sugar
1	egg
2	squares (1 ounce *each*) unsweetened chocolate, melted and cooled
2	teaspoons vanilla extract
1-3/4	cups all-purpose flour
1/2	teaspoon salt

MOCHA GLAZE:

1	cup (6 ounces) semisweet chocolate chips
1	teaspoon shortening
1	teaspoon light corn syrup
1	cup confectioners' sugar
4	to 5 tablespoons strong brewed coffee
2	squares (1 ounce *each*) white baking chocolate

1 In a large mixing bowl, cream butter and sugar until light and fluffy. Add the egg, chocolate and vanilla; mix well. Combine flour and salt; gradually add to creamed mixture and mix well. Cover and refrigerate for 1 hour or until firm.

2 Divide dough into fourths; shape each portion into a 6-in. roll. Cut each roll into 1/2-in. slices; roll each into a 9-in. rope. Place ropes on greased baking sheets; form into pretzel shapes and space 2 in. apart. Bake at 400° for 5-7 minutes or until firm. Cool for 1 minute before removing to wire racks to cool completely.

CHOCOLATE TRUFFLE COOKIES

CHOCOLATE PRETZEL COOKIES

3 For glaze, melt the chocolate chips and shortening with corn syrup in a heavy saucepan or microwave; stir until smooth. Stir in confectioners' sugar and enough coffee to make a smooth glaze. Dip pretzels in glaze; place on waxed paper until set. Melt white chocolate; drizzle over pretzels. Let stand until completely set. Store in an airtight container.

Chocolate Thumbprints

PREP: 25 min. + chilling **BAKE:** 10 min. + cooling
YIELD: about 2 dozen

Laura Bryant German
West Warren, Massachusetts

Stunning shaped cookies like this are a real standout on any cookie tray. A chocolate cookie base is a nice change of pace from the traditional vanilla-based cookie.

- 1/2 cup butter, softened
- 2/3 cup sugar
- 1 egg, *separated*
- 2 tablespoons milk
- 1 teaspoon vanilla extract
- 1 cup all-purpose flour
- 1/3 cup baking cocoa
- 1/4 teaspoon salt
- 1 cup finely chopped walnuts

FILLING:
- 1/2 cup confectioners' sugar
- 1 tablespoon butter, softened
- 2 teaspoons milk
- 1/4 teaspoon vanilla extract
- 26 milk chocolate kisses

1 In a large mixing bowl, cream butter and sugar until light and fluffy. Beat in the egg yolk, milk and vanilla. Combine the flour, cocoa and salt; gradually add to creamed mixture and mix well. Cover and refrigerate for 1 hour or until easy to handle.

2 In a small bowl, whisk egg white until foamy. Shape dough into 1-in. balls; dip in egg white, then roll in nuts. Place 2-in. apart on greased baking sheets. Using a wooden spoon handle, make an indentation in the center of each cookie. Bake at 350° for 10-12 minutes or until center is set.

3 For filling, combine the confectioners' sugar, butter, milk and vanilla in a small bowl; stir until smooth. Spoon 1/4 teaspoon into each warm cookie; gently press a chocolate kiss in the center. Carefully remove from pans to wire racks to cool.

CHOCOLATE THUMBPRINTS

CHOCOLATE-DIPPED SPRITZ

Chocolate-Dipped Spritz

PREP: 25 min. **BAKE:** 10 min. per batch + cooling
YIELD: about 6 dozen

Nancy Ross, Alvordton, Ohio

Give traditional spritz cookies a tasty twist by dipping them in chocolate. Tuck some in a coffee mug, add a ribbon and use it as a holiday gift for a neighbor, teacher or friend.

1	cup butter, softened
3/4	cup sugar
1	egg
1	teaspoon vanilla extract
2-1/4	cups all-purpose flour
1/2	teaspoon salt
1/4	teaspoon baking powder
11	ounces dark, white *or* milk chocolate candy coating

Finely chopped walnuts *or* colored sprinkles,
   optional

1 In a large mixing bowl, cream butter and sugar until light and fluffy. Beat in egg and vanilla. Combine the flour, salt and baking powder; gradually add to the creamed mixture.

2 Using a cookie press fitted with the disk of your choice, press dough 1 in. apart onto ungreased baking sheets. Bake at 375° for 7-9 minutes or until set (do not brown). Remove to wire racks to cool completely.

3 In a heavy saucepan or microwave, melt candy coating; stir until smooth. Dip each cookie halfway into coating. If desired, sprinkle walnuts or sprinkles over chocolate. Place on waxed paper until set.

perfectly shaped *spritz*

If you are making spritz cookies for the first time, it may take a little practice with the cookie press to make perfectly shaped cookies.

JUST RIGHT

When just the right amount of dough is pressed out, the baked cookie will have a uniform design and crisp indentations.

TOO SMALL

When too little dough is pressed out, the design will not meet at all the indentations. The cookie will be too small and break easily.

TOO BIG

When too much dough is pressed out, the design will lose its form.

Swedish Spritz

PREP: 15 min. **BAKE:** 10 min. per batch + cooling
YIELD: 4-5 dozen

Irmgard Sinn, Sherwood Park, Alberta

A touch of almond extract gives these spritz wonderful flavor. For Christmas, you could tint half of the dough with red food coloring and the other half with green.

1	cup butter, softened
2/3	cup sugar
1	egg
1/2	teaspoon almond extract
1/2	teaspoon vanilla extract
2-1/4	cups all-purpose flour
1	teaspoon baking powder

Prepared frosting

1 In a large mixing bowl, cream butter and sugar until light and fluffy. Beat in egg and extracts. Combine the flour and baking powder; gradually add to the creamed mixture.

2 Using a cookie press fitted with the disk of your choice, press dough 1 in. apart onto ungreased baking sheets. Bake at 400° for 7-9 minutes or until edges are firm and lightly browned. Remove to wire racks to cool. Frost as desired.

Cinnamon Almond Strips

PREP: 15 min. **BAKE:** 10 min. per batch
YIELD: about 10 dozen

Fred Grover, Lake Havasu City, Arizona

These rich, buttery cookies are proof that sometimes the most simple ingredients can result in delicious foods.

1-1/2 **cups butter, softened**
   1 **cup sugar**
   3 **eggs,** *separated*
   3 **cups all-purpose flour**
TOPPING:
1-1/2 **cups sugar**
   1 **cup finely chopped almonds**
1-1/2 **teaspoons ground cinnamon**

1 In a large mixing bowl, cream butter and sugar until light and fluffy. Beat in egg yolks. Gradually add flour; mix well.

2 Using a cookie press fitted with a bar disk, press dough 1 in. apart into long strips onto ungreased baking sheets. In a small mixing bowl, beat egg whites until stiff peaks form; brush over dough. Combine topping ingredients; sprinkle over strips. Cut each strip into 2-in. pieces (there is no need to separate the pieces).

3 Bake at 350° for 8-10 minutes or until edges are firm (do not brown). Cut into pieces again if necessary. Remove to wire racks to cool.

Shortbread Sandwich Cookies

PREP: 20 min. **BAKE:** 10 min. per batch + cooling
YIELD: about 4 dozen

Bertha Seyer, Oak Ridge, Missouri

A creamy coffee-flavored filling is layered between strips of buttery shortbread sandwich, which is then dipped in chocolate. What an impressive cookie to serve to guests!

   1 **cup butter, softened**
1/2 **cup confectioners' sugar**
1/2 **teaspoon vanilla extract**
   2 **cups all-purpose flour**
1/4 **teaspoon baking powder**

FILLING:
1/4 **cup butter, softened**
1-1/3 **cups confectioners' sugar**
   2 **teaspoons instant coffee granules**
   2 **teaspoons hot water**
TOPPING:
1-1/3 **cups semisweet chocolate chips**
   1 **tablespoon shortening**
Nonpareils

1 Place ungreased baking sheets in the refrigerator. In a large mixing bowl, cream butter and sugar until light and fluffy. Beat in vanilla. Combine flour and baking powder; add to creamed mixture and mix well.

2 Using a cookie press fitted with a ribbon disk; press dough into 2-in.-long ribbons on chilled baking sheets. Bake at 375° for 6-8 minutes or until lightly browned around edges. Cool for 1 minute before removing from pan to wire racks to cool completely.

3 For filling, in a small mixing bowl, cream butter and sugar until light and fluffy. Dissolve coffee in hot water; add to creamed mixture and mix until smooth. Spread 1/2 teaspoon filling on the bottom of one cookie; top with another cookie to form a sandwich. Repeat.

4 In a heavy saucepan or microwave, melt chocolate chips with shortening; stir until smooth. Dip one end of each cookie into chocolate, then in nonpareils. Place on waxed paper-lined baking sheets until set.

success with *spritz cookies*

- Be sure your butter or cream cheese is softened before beginning.
- Always press cookies onto a cool baking sheet.
- Hold the cookie press so that it is upright and touching the baking sheet. Force the dough through the press until you see it at the end of the rim of the cookie press. Lift the press straight up when the shape is formed.
- If the dough is too soft and not making a sharp design, refrigerate briefly. If the dough is too stiff and won't move through the press, let the dough stand at room temperature briefly until it is the right consistency.

Cutout Cookies

Lemon Sugar Cookies

PREP: 30 min. + chilling **BAKE:** 10 min. per batch
YIELD: about 13 dozen

Vivian Hines, New Philadelphia, Ohio

These light cookies are crisp on the outside and soft inside. Each bite has an appealing hint of lemon.

- 2 **cups butter, softened**
- 4 **cups confectioners' sugar**
- 4 **eggs**
- 3 **tablespoons lemon juice**
- 3 **tablespoons half-and-half cream**
- 2 **teaspoons grated lemon peel**
- 6-1/2 **cups all-purpose flour**
- 1 **teaspoon baking soda**
- 1/4 **teaspoon salt**
- **Sugar**

1 In a large mixing bowl, cream butter and confectioners' sugar until light and fluffy. Add the eggs, one at a time, beating well after each addition. Beat in the lemon juice, cream and lemon peel. Combine the flour, baking soda and salt; gradually add to the creamed mixture. Cover and refrigerate for 2 hours or until easy to handle.

2 On a lightly floured surface, roll out dough to 1/8-in. thickness. Cut with floured 2-1/2-in. cookie cutters. Place 1 in. apart on ungreased baking sheets. Sprinkle with sugar. Bake at 350° for 8-10 minutes or until lightly browned. Remove to wire racks to cool.

Crispy Almond Strips

PREP: 25 min. + freezing **BAKE:** 15 min. per batch
YIELD: 6 dozen

Darlene Brenden, Salem, Oregon

Remember sprinkling cinnamon and sugar on pieces of pastry dough and popping them in the oven along with the pie? That's what these crisp strips are like.

- 1 **cup cold butter**
- 2 **cups all-purpose flour**
- 1/2 **cup sour cream**
- 2/3 **cup sugar, *divided***
- 1 **cup ground almonds**
- 1 **teaspoon ground cinnamon**

1 In a large bowl, cut butter in flour until mixture resembles coarse crumbs. With a fork, stir in sour cream until blended. Divide dough in half; shape each half into a ball and flatten. Wrap tightly and freeze for 20 minutes.

2 Sprinkle 1/3 cup sugar on a lightly floured surface; roll each portion of dough into a 12-in. square. Combine the almonds, cinnamon and remaining sugar; sprinkle over dough. Using a rolling pin, press nut mixture into dough. Cut into 1-in. strips; cut each strip widthwise into thirds.

3 Place 1 in. apart on greased baking sheets. Bake at 400° for 12-14 minutes or until golden brown. Remove to wire racks to cool.

CRISPY ALMOND STRIPS

tips for *cutout cookies*

- Use a light touch when handling the dough; overhandling will cause the cookies to be tough.

- For easier handling, refrigerate the dough before rolling. This is especially true if the dough was made with butter rather than shortening.

- Lightly dust the rolling pin and work surface with flour to prevent sticking. Working too much extra flour into the dough will result in tough cookies.

- Roll out a portion of the dough at a time and keep the remaining dough in the refrigerator. Roll out from the center to the edge, keeping a uniform thickness and checking the thickness with a ruler. If the thickness of the dough is uneven, the cookies will bake unevenly. Thinner cookies will be crisp and may burn, while thicker cookies will be chewy.

- To prevent the dough from sticking to the cookie cutter, dip the cutter in flour or spray it with nonstick cooking spray.

- After the dough is rolled out, position the shapes from the cookie cutters close together to avoid having too many scraps. Save all the scraps and reroll them just once to prevent tough cookies.

- To keep the cutouts intact before and after baking, transfer them to and from the baking sheet with a large metal spatula or pancake turner that supports the entire cutout.

Maple Leaf Cookies

PREP: 30 min. **BAKE:** 10 min. per batch + cooling
YIELD: about 6 dozen

Lynda Harnish, Pembroke, Ontario

The shape of these cutout cookies hints at the maple syrup in the frosting. If you don't have a leaf cookie cutter, use whatever shape you have on hand.

- 1 cup butter, softened
- 1 cup sugar
- 2 eggs
- 1 teaspoon vanilla extract
- 3 cups all-purpose flour
- 2 teaspoons cream of tartar
- 1 teaspoon baking soda
- Dash salt
- FROSTING:
- 4 cups confectioners' sugar
- 2 tablespoons butter, softened
- 1 teaspoon vanilla extract
- 1/2 teaspoon salt
- 3/4 cup maple syrup
- Red paste *or* liquid food coloring

1 In a large mixing bowl, cream butter and sugar until light and fluffy. Beat in eggs and vanilla. Combine the flour, cream of tartar, baking soda and salt; add to creamed mixture and mix well. Cover and refrigerate for at least 1 hour or until easy to handle.

2 On a floured surface, roll out dough to 1/8-in. thickness. Cut with a floured 2-3/4-in. maple leaf-shape cookie cutter. Place 1 in. apart on the ungreased baking sheets. Bake at 350° for 8-10 minutes or until edges are lightly browned (do not overbake). Remove to wire racks to cool.

3 For frosting, beat the confectioners' sugar, butter, vanilla and salt in a mixing bowl. Add syrup; beat until smooth. If leaf veins are desired, set aside 1/2 cup; add food coloring to remaining frosting. Spread red frosting on cookies. Cut a small hole in the corner of a pastry or plastic bag; insert a #3 round tip into bag. Fill bag with reserved frosting; pipe veins on leaves.

Chewy Tangerine Cookies

PREP: 20 min. + chilling **BAKE:** 10 min. per batch
YIELD: about 3 dozen

Janyce Barstad, Anchorange, Alaska

This Scandinavian cookie has a blend of spices and a hint of tangerine. They are great served with a mug of hot coffee for a delicious snack.

- 1/2 cup butter, softened
- 1/2 cup sugar
- 1/2 cup dark corn syrup
- 1 egg
- 1 tablespoon grated tangerine *or* orange peel
- 2-1/4 cups all-purpose flour
- 1/2 teaspoon baking soda
- 1/2 teaspoon ground cloves
- 1/2 teaspoon ground nutmeg
- 1/4 teaspoon salt

1 In a large mixing bowl, cream butter and sugar until light and fluffy. In a small saucepan, bring corn syrup to a boil; gradually add to the creamed mixture. Beat in egg and tangerine peel. Combine the flour, baking soda, cloves, nutmeg and salt; gradually add to the creamed mixture. Cover and refrigerate for 2 hours or until easy to handle.

2 On a lightly floured surface, roll out dough to 1/4-in. thickness. Cut with floured 2-1/2-in. cookie cutters. Place 1 in. apart on greased baking sheets. Bake at 375° for 8-10 minutes or until edges are firm. Remove to wire racks to cool.

GINGERBREAD CUTOUTS

1. For easier handling, chill dough for 1 to 2 hours before rolling out. Lightly flour the surface and rolling pin. Roll out dough as evenly as possible to the recommended thickness.

2. Dip the cutter in flour, then press into the dough. With a large metal spatula or pancake turner, move cookies to baking sheet.

3. Bake according to recipe directions. Remove cookies from the baking sheet to a wire rack, being careful to support the entire cookie. Cool completely before frosting and/or storing.

Gingerbread Cutouts

PREP: 25 min. + chilling **BAKE:** 10 min. per batch
YIELD: about 6 dozen

LaJunta Malone, Camden, Alabama

For the young and young at heart, Christmas isn't complete without Gingerbread Cutouts adorning a holiday table. You can make them like a pro with this recipe.

> 1 **cup butter, softened**
> 1 **cup sugar**
> 1/2 **cup dark corn syrup**
> 1 **teaspoon** *each* **ground cinnamon, nutmeg, cloves and ginger**
> 2 **eggs, beaten**
> 1 **teaspoon white vinegar**
> 5 **cups all-purpose flour**
> 1 **teaspoon baking soda**
> **Red-hot candies**

1 In a large saucepan, combine the butter, sugar, corn syrup and spices; bring to a boil, stirring constantly. Remove from the heat and cool to lukewarm. Stir in eggs and vinegar. Combine the flour and baking soda; stir into sugar mixture to form a soft dough. Cover and refrigerate for several hours or until easy to handle.

2 On a lightly floured surface, roll dough to 1/4-in. thickness. Cut with a floured 2-1/2-in. gingerbread man cookie cutter. Place 2 in. apart on greased baking sheets. Use red-hots for eyes and buttons. Bake at 350° for 8-10 minutes. Remove to wire racks to cool.

Cream Cheese Dainties

PREP: 20 min. + chilling **BAKE:** 15 min. per batch
YIELD: 4 dozen

Melissa Boder, Salem, Virginia

Cream cheese makes these tender, tasty treats just melt in your mouth.

> 1 **cup butter, softened**
> 1 **package (8 ounces) cream cheese, softened**
> 2-1/2 **cups all-purpose flour**
> 1/2 **cup 100% apricot spreadable fruit** *or* **seedless raspberry preserves**

1 In a large mixing bowl, cream the butter and cream cheese until light and fluffy. Gradually add flour to the creamed mixture. Divide dough into four portions; cover and refrigerate until easy to handle.

2 On a floured surface, roll one portion of dough at a time into a 10-in. x 7-1/2-in. rectangle. Trim edges if necessary. Cut into 2-1/2-in. squares.

3 Place 1/4 teaspoon spreadable fruit or preserves near each end of two diagonal corners. Moisten the remaining two corners with water; fold over and press lightly.

4 Place on ungreased baking sheets. Bake at 350° for 12-15 minutes or until corners are lightly browned. Cool 2-3 minutes before removing to wire racks to cool.

Poinsettia Cookies

PREP: 20 min. + chilling BAKE: 10 min. per batch
YIELD: about 4 dozen

Helen Burch, Jamestown, New York

These sugar-sprinkled treats are as pretty to see as they are to eat! They look nice on a cookie tray.

1	**cup butter, softened**
1	**cup confectioners' sugar**
1	**egg**
1-1/2	**teaspoons almond extract**
1	**teaspoon vanilla extract**
2-1/2	**cups all-purpose flour**
1	**teaspoon salt**

Red decorator's sugar
Red and green candied cherries, quartered

1 In a large mixing bowl, cream butter and sugar until light and fluffy. Add egg and extracts; mix well. Combine flour and salt; gradually add to creamed mixture. Divide dough in half; wrap in plastic wrap. Chill overnight or until firm.

POINSETTIA COOKIES

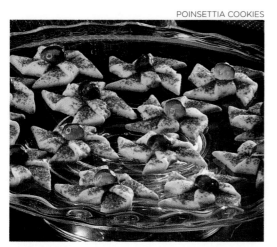

2 On a lightly floured surface, roll out one portion of dough to a 12-in. x 10-in. rectangle about 1/8 in. thick. Cut into 2-in. squares. In each square, make 1-in. slits in each corner. Bring every other corner up into center to form a pinwheel; press lightly. Sprinkle cookies with red sugar and press a candied cherry piece into the center of each.

3 Place 1 in. apart on ungreased baking sheets. Bake at 350° for 8-10 minutes. Cool 1-2 minutes before removing to a wire rack.

Cashew Sandwich Cookies

PREP: 30 min. + chilling BAKE: 15 min. per batch
YIELD: 4 dozen

Melissa Boder, Salem, Virginia

Filled with chocolate and cashews, the cookies have melt-in-your-mouth appeal.

1	**cup butter, softened**
3/4	**cup sugar**
2	**eggs yolks**
1/2	**cup sour cream**
1	**teaspoon vanilla extract**
1	**teaspoon lemon juice**
3	**cups all-purpose flour**

FILLING:

2	**cups (12 ounces) semisweet chocolate chips**
1/2	**cup butter**
1	**can (10 ounces) salted cashews, finely chopped**

Confectioners' sugar, optional

1 In a large mixing bowl, cream butter and sugar until light and fluffy. Beat in the egg yolks, sour cream, vanilla and lemon juice. Add flour; mix well. Cover and refrigerate for at least 2 hours or until easy to handle.

2 On a floured surface, roll out dough to 1/8-in. thickness. Cut with a floured 2-in.-round cookie cutter. Place 1 in. apart on ungreased baking sheets. Bake at 350° for 11-13 minutes or until edges are lightly browned. Remove to wire racks to cool.

3 For filling, melt chocolate chips and butter in a small heavy saucepan or microwave; stir until smooth. Stir in cashews. Spread on the bottom of half of the cookies; top each with another cookie. Dust tops with confectioners' sugar if desired.

Apricot-Filled Cookies

PREP: 45 min. + chilling **BAKE:** 10 min. per batch
YIELD: about 1-1/2 dozen

Bonnie Waliezer, Brush Prairie, Washington

Canned apricots are a versatile ingredient all year long. One delicious way to take advantage of their goodness is in these sandwich cookies.

    1/2 cup shortening
      1 cup sugar
      2 eggs
      1 teaspoon vanilla extract
  2-1/2 cups all-purpose flour
    1/2 teaspoon salt
    1/4 teaspoon baking soda
FILLING:
      2 cups canned apricots, mashed
    2/3 cup sugar
    2/3 cup water
    1/2 cup finely chopped almonds
      1 teaspoon lemon juice

1 In a large mixing bowl, cream shortening and sugar until light and fluffy. Beat in eggs and vanilla. Combine the flour, salt and baking soda; gradually add to the creamed mixture. Cover and refrigerate for 1 hour. Meanwhile, in a large saucepan, combine filling ingredients. Cook and stir until thickened, about 15 minutes. Cool completely.

2 Divide the dough in half. On a lightly floured surface, roll out each portion to 1/8-in. thickness. Cut half of the dough with a floured 2-1/2-in. round cookie cutter. Cut the other half with a floured 2-1/2-in. doughnut cutter. Place 1 in. apart on ungreased baking sheets.

APRICOT-FILLED COOKIES

3 Bake at 375° for 8-10 minutes or until edges are very lightly browned. Remove to wire racks to cool. To assemble, spread bottom of solid cookies with filling; top with cutout cookies.

Almond Raspberry Stars

PREP: 35 min. + chilling **BAKE:** 10 min. per batch + cooling **YIELD:** about 3 dozen

Darlene Weaver, Lebanon, Pennsylvania

Guests will think you bought these impressive-looking cookies at a gourmet bakery. They may take some time to prepare, but the oohs and aahs you'll hear make it well worth it!

    3/4 cup butter, softened
    1/2 cup confectioners' sugar
      1 teaspoon vanilla extract
    1/2 teaspoon almond extract
  1-3/4 cups plus 2 tablespoons all-purpose flour
      2 tablespoons finely chopped almonds
      1 tablespoon sugar
    1/2 teaspoon ground cinnamon
      1 egg white, lightly beaten
    1/3 cup raspberry jam

1 In a large mixing bowl, cream the butter and confectioners' sugar until light and fluffy. Beat in

making sandwich cookies

Spread filling over the bottoms of half of the cookies. Place another cookie over the filling, bottom side down.

extracts. Stir in flour. Shape into a ball; cover and refrigerate for 15 minutes.

2 On a lightly floured surface, roll out dough to 1/4-in. thickness. Cut into about 72 stars, half 2-1/2 in. and half 1-1/2 in. Combine the almonds, sugar and cinnamon. Brush small stars with egg white and immediately sprinkle with almond mixture. Leave large stars plain.

3 Place 1 in. apart on ungreased baking sheets. Bake small stars at 350° for 10 minutes and large stars for 12 minutes or until the tips just begin to brown. Remove to wire racks to cool.

4 To assemble, spread enough jam over large stars to cover the centers. Top with small stars; press lightly (jam should show around edge of small stars). Let jam set before storing.

Chocolate Orange Cookies

PREP: 30 min. + chilling **BAKE:** 15 min. per batch
YIELD: about 3 dozen

Ruth Rumple, Rockford, Ohio

Cutout cookies are a time-honored holiday tradition for most every family. This version combines the fabulous flavors of orange and chocolate.

   1 **cup butter, softened**
3/4 **cup sugar, *divided***
   1 **egg**
   1 **teaspoon vanilla extract**
2-1/2 **cups all-purpose flour**

CHOCOLATE ORANGE COOKIES

1/2 **teaspoon salt**
1/4 **cup finely grated orange peel**
   1 **cup (6 ounces) semisweet chocolate chips**

1 In a large mixing bowl, cream butter and 1/2 cup sugar until light and fluffy. Beat in egg and vanilla. Gradually add flour and salt; mix well. Cover and refrigerate for 15 minutes.

2 On a floured surface, roll out dough to 1/4-in. thickness. Cut with a floured 2-in. cookie cutter or shape into 2-in. x 1-in. rectangles. Place 2 in. apart on ungreased baking sheets. Combine orange peel and remaining sugar; sprinkle over cookies.

3 Bake at 350° for 14-16 minutes or until the edges just begin to brown. Remove to wire racks to cool. Melt chocolate chips; decorate cookies.

Grandma's Oatmeal Cookies

PREP: 35 min. **BAKE:** 15 min. per batch
YIELD: 12 dozen

Mary Ann Konechne, Kimball, South Dakota

For a festive touch to these cookies use colored sugar. Match the color of the sugar to the occasion.

   2 **cups sugar**
1-1/2 **cups shortening**
   4 **eggs**
   4 **teaspoons water**
   4 **cups all-purpose flour**
   2 **teaspoons baking soda**
   2 **teaspoons ground cinnamon**
1/2 **teaspoon salt**
   4 **cups quick-cooking oats**
   2 **cups chopped raisins**
   1 **cup chopped walnuts**
Additional granulated sugar *or* colored sugar

1 In a large mixing bowl, cream sugar and shortening until light and fluffy. Add eggs, one at a time, beating well after each addition. Beat in water. Combine the flour, baking soda, cinnamon and salt; add to creamed mixture and mix well. Stir in the oats, raisins and walnuts.

2 On a surface sprinkled with additional sugar or colored sugar, roll out dough to 1/4-in. thickness. Cut out with desired cookie cutters. Place 2 in. apart on greased baking sheets. Bake at 350° for 12-15 minutes or until set. Remove to wire racks to cool.

Feathered Friend Cookies

PREP: 1 hour + chilling   **BAKE:** 10 min. per batch
YIELD: 3-1/2 dozen

Taste of Home Test Kitchen

Let your imagination soar as an egg yolk glaze transforms plain sugar cookies into fanciful winged wonders. Use paste food coloring instead of liquid for more intense color.

- 1/2   **cup butter, softened**
- 1/4   **cup shortening**
- 1   **cup sugar**
- 2   **eggs**
- 2   **tablespoons sour cream**
- 1   **teaspoon vanilla extract**
- 1/4   **teaspoon almond extract**
- 2-3/4   **cups all-purpose flour**
- 1-1/2   **teaspoons baking powder**
- 1   **teaspoon salt**

GLAZE:
- 4   **to 6 egg yolks**
- 1   **to 1-1/2 teaspoons water**

Paste *or* gel food coloring

1 In a large mixing bowl, cream the butter, shortening and sugar until light and fluffy. Beat in the eggs, sour cream and extracts. Combine the flour, baking powder and salt; add to the creamed mixture and mix well. Cover and refrigerate for about 1 hour or until easy to handle.

2 On a floured surface, roll out dough to 1/4-in. thickness. Cut with a floured 4-in. bird-shaped cookie cutter. Place 1 in. apart on ungreased baking sheets.

3 For each color of glaze, beat 1 egg yolk and 1/4 teaspoon water in a custard cup; tint with food coloring. Decorate cookies as desired. Bake at 375° for 7-9 minutes or until edges are lightly browned. Cool for 1-2 minutes before removing to wire racks to cool.

FEATHERED FRIEND COOKIES

painting with *egg yolks*

In a small bowl combine egg yolk, water and food coloring. With a small new paintbrush, decorate the unbaked cookies, then bake as directed. If the glaze thickens, stir in a few drops of water.

Pineapple Star Cookies

PREP: 25 min. + chilling   **BAKE:** 10 min. per batch
YIELD: 5 dozen

Sarah Lukaszewicz, Batavia, New York

When you see the pretty shape of these treats and savor the pineapple filling and sweet frosting, you'll know they're worth the effort. Use a fluted pastry wheel for a more interesting effect.

- 1   **cup butter, softened**
- 1   **package (8 ounces) cream cheese, softened**
- 2   **cups all-purpose flour**

FILLING:
- 3/4   **cup sugar**
- 4-1/2   **teaspoons all-purpose flour**
- 1   **can (8 ounces) crushed pineapple, drained**

FROSTING:
- 1   **cup confectioners' sugar**
- 2   **tablespoons butter, melted**
- 2   **tablespoons milk**
- 1/2   **teaspoon vanilla extract**
- 1/2   **cup chopped walnuts**

1 In a large mixing bowl, cream the butter and cream cheese until light and fluffy. Add flour and mix well. Cover and refrigerate for 2 hours or until easy to handle. Meanwhile, in a saucepan, combine sugar and flour; add pineapple and stir until blended. Cook over low heat until mixture comes to a boil and is thickened, stirring frequently. Cover and refrigerate.

2 Divide dough in half. On a lightly floured surface, roll out each portion to 1/8-in. thickness. Cut into 3-in. squares. Place 1 in. apart on ungreased baking sheets. To form star, make a 1-1/4-in. cut from each corner toward center (do not cut

through center). Place 1/4 teaspoon of pineapple filling in the center of each. Fold every other point toward the center, overlapping pieces; press lightly to seal. Bake at 375° for 8-10 minutes or until set. Remove to wire racks to cool.

3 For frosting, combine the confectioners' sugar, butter, milk and vanilla in a bowl until smooth. Drizzle over cookies; sprinkle with walnuts.

Sweetheart Coconut Cookies

PREP: 30 min. **BAKE:** 10 min. per batch
YIELD: about 3-1/2 dozen

Jo Ellen Helmlinger, Columbus, Ohio

Ruby-red jam and colored sugar add a festive look to these crisp sandwich cookies that are perfect for Valentine's Day.

> 1 **cup flaked coconut**
> 1 **cup sugar**
> 3/4 **cup cold butter**
> 2-1/4 **cups all-purpose flour**
> 2 **eggs, lightly beaten**
> 1/2 **teaspoon vanilla extract**
> **GLAZE:**
> 3/4 **cup confectioners' sugar**
> 1 **tablespoon water**
> 1/2 **teaspoon vanilla extract**
> **Red colored sugar, optional**
> 1/2 **cup seedless raspberry jam**

1 Place coconut and sugar in a food processor; cover and process until coconut is coarsely chopped. In a large bowl, cut butter into flour until crumbly. Stir in coconut mixture. Stir in eggs and vanilla.

2 On a lightly floured surface, roll out dough to 1/8-in. thickness. Cut with a 2-1/2-in. heart-shaped cookie cutter dipped in flour. Using a 1-in. heart-shaped cookie cutter, cut out the center of half of the cookies. Reroll small cutouts if desired. Place solid and cutout cookies 1 in. apart on greased baking sheets. Bake at 375° for 7-9 minutes or until edges are lightly browned. Remove to wire racks.

3 In a small bowl, combine the confectioners' sugar, water and vanilla; brush over warm cookies with cutout centers. Immediately sprinkle with colored sugar if desired. Spread 1/2 teaspoon of jam over the bottom of each solid cookie; place cookies with cutout centers over jam.

Chocolate Mint Wafers

PREP: 30 min. + chilling **BAKE:** 5 min. per batch + cooling **YIELD:** about 7-1/2 dozen

Annette Esau, Durham, Ontario

We guarantee a batch of these chocolaty treats with cool mint filling won't last long around your house. They're so pretty piled high on a glass plate.

- 2/3 cup butter, softened
- 1/2 cup sugar
- 1/2 cup packed brown sugar
- 1/4 cup milk
-   1 egg
-   2 cups all-purpose flour
- 3/4 cup baking cocoa
-   1 teaspoon baking powder
- 1/2 teaspoon baking soda
- 1/4 teaspoon salt

FILLING:
- 2-3/4 cups confectioners' sugar
-   1/4 cup half-and-half cream
-   1/4 teaspoon peppermint extract
-   1/4 teaspoon salt

Green food coloring

CHOCOLATE MINT WAFERS

1 In a large mixing bowl, cream butter and sugars until light and fluffy. Add milk and egg; mix well. Combine the flour, cocoa, baking powder, baking soda and salt; gradually add to creamed mixture and mix well. Cover and refrigerate for 2 hours or until firm.

2 On a floured surface, roll out dough to 1/8-in. thickness. Cut with a floured 1-1/2-in. cookie cutter. Place 1 in. apart on greased baking sheets. Bake at 375° for 5-6 minutes or until edges are lightly browned. Remove to wire racks to cool.

3 Combine filling ingredients; spread on the bottom of half of the cookies; top with remaining cookies.

Tea Cakes with Butter Frosting

PREP: 25 min. + chilling **BAKE:** 10 min. per batch + cooling **YIELD:** about 5-1/2 dozen

Sandy Glenn, Booneville, Mississippi

You'll treasure this simple tender cookie. Tint the frosting with food coloring for a festive look throughout the year.

-   1 cup butter, softened
-   2 cups sugar
-   3 eggs
-   1 teaspoon vanilla extract
-   5 cups all-purpose flour
-   2 teaspoons baking powder
-   1 teaspoon baking soda
- 1/4 teaspoon salt
-   1 cup buttermilk

FROSTING:
- 1/2 cup butter, softened
-   4 cups confectioners' sugar
-   1 teaspoon vanilla extract
-   3 to 5 tablespoons milk

Food coloring, optional

1 In a large mixing bowl, cream butter and sugar until light and fluffy. Add eggs, one at a time, beating well after each addition. Beat in vanilla. Combine the flour, baking powder, baking soda and salt; add to the creamed mixture alternately with buttermilk, beating well after each addition. Cover and refrigerate for 1 hour or until easy to handle.

2 On a lightly floured surface, roll out dough to 1/4-in. thickness. Cut with floured 2-1/2-in. cookie cutters. Using a floured spatula, place 1 in. apart on greased baking sheets. Bake at 350° for 8-10 minutes or until lightly browned. Remove to wire racks to cool.

RAISIN-FILLED COOKIES

3 In a large mixing bowl, cream the butter, sugar, vanilla and enough milk to achieve spreading consistency. Add food coloring if desired. Frost the cooled cookies.

Raisin-Filled Cookies

PREP: 30 min. + chilling **BAKE:** 10 min. per batch
YIELD: about 3-1/2 dozen

Barbara Noel, Junction City, Kansas

A sweet raisin filling is hidden in these delicious, old-fashioned cookies.

- 1 **cup butter, softened**
- 1 **cup packed brown sugar**
- 1 **cup sugar**
- 3 **eggs**
- 2 **tablespoons vanilla extract**
- 5 **cups all-purpose flour**
- 1 **teaspoon baking powder**
- 1 **teaspoon baking soda**
- 1/2 **teaspoon salt**
- 1/4 **teaspoon ground nutmeg**
- 3 **tablespoons buttermilk**

FILLING:
- 1 **tablespoon cornstarch**
- 3 **tablespoons all-purpose flour**
- 1 **cup packed brown sugar**
- 2 **cups boiling water**
- 1-1/2 **cups seedless raisins**

1 In a large mixing bowl, cream butter and sugars until light and fluffy. Add eggs, one at a time, beating well after each addition. Beat in vanilla. Combine the flour, baking powder, baking soda, salt and nutmeg; add to creamed mixture alternately with buttermilk, beating well after each addition. Cover and chill until easy to handle.

2 For filling, in a saucepan, combine the cornstarch, flour and brown sugar. Stir in water until smooth. Add raisins. Bring to a boil over medium heat; cook and stir and cook for 3 minutes or until thickened. Cool.

3 On a floured surface, roll out dough into 1/8-in. thickness. Cut with floured 3-in.-round cookie cutters. Spoon 2 teaspoons filling on top of half the circles and top each with another circle. Pinch edges together and cut slit in top.

4 Place 2 in. apart on ungreased baking sheets. Bake at 350° for 10-13 minutes or until lightly browned. Remove to wire racks to cool.

POLKA-DOT COOKIES

Polka-Dot Cookies

PREP: 30 min. + chilling **BAKE:** 10 min. per batch
YIELD: 4 dozen

Mary Ann Rafalski
North Huntingdon, Pennsylvania

While living in Florida, I found this cookie recipe in a book on cooking with oranges. It's fun to use for bake sales or a child's party.

    1/2 cup butter, softened
    1/2 cup sugar
      1 egg
      2 tablespoons orange juice concentrate
      1 tablespoon grated orange peel
      2 cups all-purpose flour
  1-1/4 teaspoons baking powder
    1/4 teaspoon salt
CHOCOLATE FROSTING:
    1/4 cup semisweet chocolate chips, melted
  1-1/2 teaspoons butter, melted
      1 tablespoon milk
    1/2 cup confectioners' sugar

1 In a large mixing bowl, cream butter and sugar until light and fluffy. Add egg, concentrate and orange peel. Combine the flour, baking powder and salt; gradually add to creamed mixture. Cover and refrigerate for 2 hours.

2 Divide dough in half. On a lightly floured surface, roll out each portion to 1/8-in. thickness. Cut with a floured 2-in. round cookie cutter. Place 2 in. apart on greased baking sheets. Bake at 350° for 6-7 minutes or until edges begin to brown. Remove to wire racks to cool.

3 Combine all the frosting ingredients. Place in a heavy-duty resealable plastic bag; cut a small hole in corner of bag. Pipe polka dots on cookies.

Shortbread Cutouts

PREP: 25 min. + chilling **BAKE:** 15 min. per batch
YIELD: 3 dozen

Carole Vogel, Allison Park, Pennsylvania

Almonds give these cookies a special flavor. Use your favorite cookie cutters to make different shapes, then let the kids have a hand in adding the finishing touches.

      1 cup all-purpose flour
    1/2 cup blanched almonds
    1/4 cup sugar
    1/4 teaspoon salt
    1/2 cup cold butter
      1 egg yolk
      2 teaspoons cold water
    1/4 teaspoon almond extract

1 In a food processor, combine the flour, almonds, sugar and salt; cover and process until almonds are finely ground. Cut butter into cubes; add to processor. Pulse on and off until mixture resembles coarse crumbs.

2 Combine the yolk, water and almond extract. While processing, gradually add yolk mixture; process until dough forms a ball. Wrap in plastic wrap and refrigerate for at least 30 minutes.

3 On a lightly floured surface, roll out half of the dough to 1/4-in. thickness. Cut into desired shapes with floured cookie cutters. Place 1 in. apart on ungreased baking sheets. Repeat with remaining dough.

4 Bake at 325° for 12-14 minutes or until edges are lightly browned. Cool for 1 minute before removing from pans to wire racks to cool.

Welsh Tea Cakes

PREP: 15 min. **BAKE:** 15 min. per batch + cooling **YIELD:** 3 dozen

Wendy Lehman, Huron, Ohio

These old-fashioned cookies are crisp on the outside and slightly chewy in the center, which is full of currants. The dough is not overly sweet, so sprinkling the tops with sugar enhances the flavor and gives them a nice look.

2-1/2 cups all-purpose flour
1 cup cold butter
3/4 cup sugar
1/4 cup quick-cooking oats
1/2 teaspoon ground nutmeg
2 eggs
1/4 cup milk
1 cup dried currants
Additional sugar, optional

1 Place flour in a bowl; cut in butter until mixture resembles coarse crumbs. Add the sugar, oats, and nutmeg. Stir in the eggs and milk. Add currants.

2 On a heavily floured surface, roll out dough to 1/4-in. thickness. Cut with a floured 2-1/2-in.-round cookie cutter. Place 2 in. apart on greased baking sheets. Sprinkle with additional sugar if desired. Bake at 350° for 12-16 minutes or until lightly browned. Remove to wire racks to cool.

GLAZED ANISE COOKIES

Glazed Anise Cookies

PREP: 30 min. + chilling **BAKE:** 10 min.
per batch + cooling **YIELD:** about 6 dozen

Armetta Keeney, Carlisle, Iowa

At Christmastime hang these cookies on your tree instead of gingerbread cookies.

2/3 cup butter, softened
1 cup sugar
2 eggs
1 tablespoon aniseed
2 teaspoons anise extract
2-1/2 cups all-purpose flour
1 teaspoon baking powder
1/2 teaspoon salt
GLAZE:
2 cups sugar
1 cup hot water
1/8 teaspoon cream of tartar
1 teaspoon anise extract
Paste food coloring, optional
2-1/2 to 3 cups confectioners' sugar

1 In a large mixing bowl, cream butter and sugar until light and fluffy. Add eggs, one at a time, beating well after each addition. Beat in aniseed and extract. Combine the flour, baking powder and salt; gradually add to the creamed mixture. Cover and refrigerate for 1 hour or until easy to handle.

2 On a lightly floured surface, roll out to 1/4-in. thickness. Cut with floured 2-1/2-in. cookie cutters. Place 1 in. apart on ungreased baking sheets. Bake 375° for 10-12 minutes or until lightly browned. Remove to wire racks to cool.

3 In a large heavy saucepan, combine the sugar, water and cream of tartar; bring to a boil over low heat. Cook and stir until a candy thermometer reads 226° (thread stage). Cool to 110° (do not stir). Stir in the extract, food coloring if desired and enough confectioners' sugar to achieve spreading consistency. Spread over cookies.

Editor's Note: We recommend that you test your candy thermometer before each use by bringing water to a boil; the thermometer should read 212°. Adjust your recipe temperature up or down based on your test.

Peanut Butter Bears

PREP: 30 min. + chilling **BAKE:** 10 min. per batch
YIELD: about 3 dozen

Rose Reiser, Greenfield, Illinois

These cute, peanut butter bears are as fun to eat as they are to make.

- 1   **cup butter, softened**
- 1   **cup creamy peanut butter**
- 1   **cup packed brown sugar**
- 2/3   **cup light corn syrup**
- 2   **eggs**
- 4   **cups all-purpose flour**
- 3   **teaspoons baking powder**
- 1/4   **teaspoon salt**

Decorating gel *or* frosting, colors of your choice

1 In a large mixing bowl, cream the butter, peanut butter and brown sugar until light and fluffy. Beat in the corn syrup and eggs. Combine the flour, baking powder and salt; gradually add to the creamed mixture. Cover and refrigerate for 2 hours or until easy to handle.

2 On a lightly floured surface, roll out dough to 1/8-in. thickness. Cut with a floured 4-in. bear-shaped cookie cutter. Place 2 in. apart on ungreased baking sheets. Roll leftover dough into small balls; press gently into each cookie, forming the bear's muzzle, nose and eyes.

3 Bake at 350° for 10-12 minutes or until set. Remove to wire racks to cool. Using gel or frosting, decorate each bear's face, paws and ears and form a bow tie.

Editor's Note: Reduced-fat or generic brands of peanut butter are not recommended for this recipe.

PEANUT BUTTER BEARS

---

problem-solving **pointers** *for Cookies*

COOKIES ARE SPREADING TOO MUCH

- Place the dough on a cool baking sheet.
- Chill the dough before baking.
- Next time, replace part of the butter in the recipe with shortening. If using margarine, check the label and make sure it contains 80% vegetable oil.

COOKIES ARE NOT SPREADING ENOUGH

- Add 1 to 2 tablespoons of liquid, such as milk or water, to the remaining dough.
- Let the dough stand at room temperature before baking.
- Next time use butter, not margarine or shortening.

COOKIES ARE TOUGH

- Too much flour was worked into the dough. Add 1 or 2 tablespoons of shortening, butter or sugar to the remaining dough.
- The dough was overhandled or overmixed. Next time, use a lighter touch when mixing.

COOKIES ARE TOO BROWN

- Oven temperature is too high. Check with an oven thermometer.
- Use heavy-gauge dull aluminum baking sheets. Dark baking sheets will cause the cookies to become overly browned.

COOKIES ARE TOO PALE

- Oven temperature is too low. Check with an oven thermometer.
- Use heavy-gauged dull aluminum baking sheets. Insulated baking sheets cause cookies to be pale in color.
- Next time use butter, not margarine or shortening. Or substitute 1 to 2 tablespoons corn syrup for the sugar.

Bars
& Brownies

The Basics of Bars & Brownies

Bars and brownies are easy to make but difficult to define since they can be made in endless variations. They can be crisp with a rich buttery shortbread crust, cake-like or fudgy. They can have layers, fruit, jam or a cooked filling and be topped with frosting, glaze or icing. Or, they can be deliciously humble like a chocolate chip cookie bar.

- Bar cookies may be made with a pourable batter, spreadable dough or a crumbly crust that needs to be patted into the pan. The one thing they all have in common is that they are baked in a pan, rather than on a baking sheet. After cooling, they are cut into bars, squares, fingers, triangles or diamonds.

- Brownies are generally chocolate, flour, sugar and eggs with or without nuts. They may be cake-like, fudgy, chewy, dense or moist. They may also be frosted or plain. Brownies are usually baked in a square or rectangular pan. Those with a butterscotch or vanilla flavor are called blondies. Most people have a preference as to the type of brownie they think is the best.

secrets for *successful* *bars & brownies*

- Use butter, stick margarine (with at least 80% oil) or shortening. Whipped, tub, soft, liquid or reduced-fat products contain air and water and will produce flat, tough bars or brownies.

- Measure ingredients accurately, using the measuring tools and techniques suggested on pages 7 and 8.

- Avoid overmixing the batter. If it's handled too much, the gluten in the flour will be developed and the bars or brownies will be tough.

- Use dull aluminum baking pans or glass dishes. Dark-colored pans may cause overbrowning.

- Grease the pan with shortening or coat with nonstick cooking spray.

- To easily remove bars and brownies from a pan, line the bottom of the pan with foil, then grease. Add the batter and bake as directed. (See Lining a Baking Pan with Foil on page 79.)

- Preheat oven for 10 to 15 minutes before baking.

- It's important to evenly spread batter in the pan. If one corner is thinner than another, it will bake faster and be overbaked when the rest of the pan is done.

- Center the pan in the middle of the oven.

- Use a kitchen timer. Check bars when the minimum baking time has been reached, baking longer if needed. Follow doneness tests given in individual recipes.

- Generally, bars and brownies should cool completely on a wire rack before being cut. However, crisp bars should be cut while still slightly warm.

Marbled Chocolate Cheesecake Bars

PREP: 20 min. **BAKE:** 20 min. + cooling
YIELD: about 6 dozen

Elaine Hanson, Waite Park, Minnesota

Gently swirl the cheesecake layer into the batter–otherwise, you'll lose the pretty swirl effect.

3/4	cup water
1/2	cup butter
1-1/2	squares (1-1/2 ounces) unsweetened chocolate
2	cups all-purpose flour
1-1/2	cups packed brown sugar
1	teaspoon baking soda
1/2	teaspoon salt
2	eggs
1/2	cup sour cream

CREAM CHEESE MIXTURE:

1	package (8 ounces) cream cheese, softened
1/3	cup sugar
1	egg, beaten
1	tablespoon vanilla extract
1	cup (6 ounces) semisweet chocolate chips

marbling *batters*

To give batters a marbled look, spoon one batter in a random pattern over the other batter. Cut through the batter with a knife. Be careful not to overdo it, or the two batters will blend together and you'll lose the effect.

1 In a small saucepan, combine the water, butter and chocolate; cook and stir over low heat until smooth. Cool.

2 In a large mixing bowl, combine the flour, brown sugar, baking soda and salt. Add eggs and sour cream; beat on low just until combined. Stir in chocolate mixture until smooth.

3 In another bowl, beat the cream cheese, sugar, egg and vanilla; set aside. Spread chocolate batter into a greased 15-in. x 10-in. x 1-in. baking pan. Drop cream cheese mixture by tablespoonfuls over batter; cut through the batter with a knife to swirl. Sprinkle with chocolate chips.

4 Bake at 375° for 20-25 minutes or until a toothpick inserted near the center comes out clean. Cool on a wire rack. Cut into bars.

MARBLED CHOCOLATE CHEESECAKE BARS

Chocolate Oat Squares

PREP: 20 min. **BAKE:** 25 min. **YIELD:** 4 dozen

Jennifer Eilts, Central City, Nebraska

When you bring these chewy treats to a group meal, guests will be tempted to start at the dessert table. Chock-full of chocolate and walnuts, they'll satisfy any sweet tooth.

1	cup plus 2 tablespoons butter, softened, *divided*
2	cups packed brown sugar
2	eggs
4	teaspoons vanilla extract, *divided*
3	cups quick-cooking oats
2-1/2	cups all-purpose flour
1-1/2	teaspoons salt, *divided*
1	teaspoon baking soda
1	can (14 ounces) sweetened condensed milk

CHOCOLATE OAT SQUARES

2 **cups (12 ounces) semisweet chocolate
chips**
1 **cup chopped walnuts**

1 In a large mixing bowl, cream 1 cup butter and brown sugar until light and fluffy. Beat in eggs and 2 teaspoons vanilla. Combine the oats, flour, 1 teaspoon salt and baking soda; stir into creamed mixture. Press two-thirds of oat mixture into a greased 15-in. x 10-in. x 1-in. baking pan.

2 In a saucepan, combine the milk, chocolate chips and remaining butter and salt. Cook and stir over low heat until chocolate is melted. Remove from the heat; stir in walnuts and remaining vanilla. Spread over crust. Sprinkle with remaining oat mixture.

3 Bake at 350° for 25 minutes or until golden brown. Cool on a wire rack. Cut into squares.

Chocolate Cherry Bars

PREP: 15 min. + chilling **BAKE:** 35 min. + cooling
YIELD: 3 dozen

Tina Dierking, Skohegan, Maine

These tempting bars are simple to make with cherry pie filling, crunchy almonds and chocolate chips. The taste is reminiscent of chocolate-covered cherries.

1-3/4 **cups all-purpose flour**
1 **cup sugar**
1/4 **cup baking cocoa**
1 **cup cold butter**
1 **egg, lightly beaten**
1 **teaspoon almond extract**
1 **can (21 ounces) cherry pie filling**
2 **cups (12 ounces) semisweet chocolate
chips**
1 **cup chopped almonds**

1 In a bowl, combine the flour, sugar and cocoa. Cut in butter until the mixture is crumbly. Add egg and almond extract until blended. Set aside 1 cup for topping. Press remaining crumb mixture into a greased 13-in. x 9-in. x 2-in. baking pan. Carefully top with pie filling. Combine chocolate chips, almonds and reserved crumb mixture; sprinkle over pie filling.

2 Bake at 350° for 35-40 minutes or until a toothpick inserted near the center comes out clean. Cool on a wire rack. Refrigerate for at least 2 hours before cutting into bars.

CHOCOLATE CHERRY BARS

Celestial Bars

PREP: 35 min. **BAKE:** 20 min. + cooling **YIELD:** 4 dozen

Maribeth Gregg, Cable, Ohio

With their marbled base, fluffy icing and pretty chocolate glaze, these nutty bars will be the stars of bake sales, cookie gift packs and parties.

- 1/2 **cup butter, softened**
- 2 **cups packed brown sugar**
- 3 **eggs**
- 1 **teaspoon vanilla extract**
- 1/2 **teaspoon almond extract**
- 2 **cups all-purpose flour**
- 1/2 **teaspoon salt**
- 1-1/2 **cups chopped pecans**
- 2 **squares (1 ounce *each*) unsweetened chocolate, melted and cooled**

ICING:
- 1/2 **cup butter, softened**
- 3 **cups confectioners' sugar**
- 3 **to 4 tablespoons milk**
- 1 **teaspoon vanilla extract**

GLAZE:
- 1/2 **cup semisweet chocolate chips**
- 2 **teaspoons shortening**

1 In a large mixing bowl, cream butter and brown sugar until light and fluffy. Add eggs, one at a time, beating well after each addition. Add extracts; beat well. Combine flour and salt; add to creamed mixture. Stir in pecans (batter will be thick). Divide batter in half; stir chocolate into one portion. Alternately spoon plain and chocolate batters into a greased 13-in. x 9-in. x 2-in. baking pan. Swirl with a knife.

2 Bake at 350° for 16-20 minutes or until a toothpick inserted near the center comes out clean. Cool completely on a wire rack.

3 For icing, in a large mixing bowl, cream butter and confectioners' sugar. Add milk and vanilla; beat until smooth. Spread over bars.

4 For glaze, melt chocolate chips and shortening in a heavy saucepan or microwave; stir until smooth. Drizzle over bars. Let stand until chocolate is completely set before cutting.

drizzling chocolate *over bars*

Melt chocolate according to recipe directions. Transfer to a resealable plastic bag and cut a small hole in one corner. While moving the bag back and forth over the bars, gently squeeze out the melted chocolate.

You can also put the melted chocolate in a small bowl and use a spoon or fork to drizzle it.

Fun Marshmallow Bars

PREP: 10 min. BAKE: 25 min. + cooling
YIELD: 3-1/2 dozen

Debbie Brunssen, Randolph, Nebraska

*These colorful, kid-tested treats will go fast at bake sales.
Cake mix really cuts your prep time.*

- 1   **package (18-1/4 ounces) devil's food cake mix**
- 1/4   **cup butter, melted**
- 1/4   **cup water**
- 1   **egg**
- 3   **cups miniature marshmallows**
- 1   **cup milk chocolate M&M's**
- 1/2   **cup chopped peanuts**

1 In a large mixing bowl, combine the dry cake mix, butter, water and egg; mix well. Press into a greased 13-in. x 9-in. x 2-in. baking pan. Bake at 375° for 20-22 minutes or until a toothpick inserted near the center comes out clean.

2 Sprinkle with marshmallows, M&M's and peanuts. Bake 2-3 minutes longer or until the marshmallows begin to melt. Cool on a wire rack. Cut into bars.

FUN MARSHMALLOW BARS

lining a
baking pan *with foil*

To easily remove bars and brownies from the pan, first line it with foil. Cut a piece of foil that is larger than the pan. Turn the pan upside down and mold the foil around the bottom and sides of the pan. Remove the foil, turn the pan right side up and place the formed foil in the pan, allowing the foil to extend beyond the edges of the pan.

   Grease the foil, add the batter and bake as directed. After bars or brownies are completely cooled, lift the foil out of the pan.

Peppermint Crumb Squares

PREP: 15 min. BAKE: 30 min. + cooling YIELD: 4 dozen

Martha Kerr, Abilene, Texas

To crush the peppermint candy for this recipe, place the candy in a resealable plastic bag and seal. With the flat side of a meat mallet, pound the candy until crushed.

- 3/4   **cup butter, softened**
- 1/2   **cup packed brown sugar**
- 2   **cups all-purpose flour**
- 1   **can (14 ounces) sweetened condensed milk**
- 1   **package (10 to 12 ounces) vanilla *or* white chips**
- 2/3   **cup crushed peppermint candy**

1 In a large mixing bowl, cream butter and brown sugar until light and fluffy. Add flour; beat until crumbly. Press 2 cups into a greased 13-in. x 9-in. x 2-in. baking pan; set remaining crumb mixture aside. Bake the crust at 350° for 8-10 minutes.

2 In a heavy saucepan or microwave, heat milk and vanilla chips until the chips are melted; stir until smooth. Pour over hot crust and spread evenly. Combine the candy and reserved crumb mixture; sprinkle over the top.

3 Bake 18-22 minutes longer or until lightly browned. Cool on a wire rack. Cut into squares.

Polka-Dot Cookie Bars

PREP: 15 min. **BAKE:** 20 min. + cooling
YIELD: 4 dozen

Elizabeth Poire, Kailua-Kona, Hawaii

When you're serving a group, these lightly sweet bars are a lot easier to make than fussing with individual cookies. For the true chocolate lover, substitute semisweet chips for the vanilla chips.

- 1 **cup butter, softened**
- 3/4 **cup sugar**
- 3/4 **cup packed brown sugar**
- 2 **eggs**
- 1/2 **teaspoon almond extract**
- 2-1/4 **cups all-purpose flour**
- 1/3 **cup baking cocoa**
- 1 **teaspoon baking soda**
- 1/2 **teaspoon salt**
- 1 **package (10 to 12 ounces) vanilla *or* white chips**

1 In a large mixing bowl, cream butter and sugars until light and fluffy. Add eggs, one at a time, beating well after each addition. Beat in extract. Combine the flour, cocoa, baking soda and salt; gradually add to the creamed mixture. Set aside 1/4 cup vanilla chips; stir remaining chips into batter. Spread into a greased 15-in. x 10-in. x 1-in. baking pan. Sprinkle with the reserved chips.

2 Bake at 375° for 18-23 minutes or until a toothpick inserted near the center comes out clean. Cool on a wire rack. Cut into bars.

Chocolate Raspberry Bars

PREP: 20 min. + chilling **BAKE:** 15 min. + cooling
YIELD: 3 dozen

Kathy Smedstad, Silverton, Oregon

Chocolate and raspberry jam go together so well in these rich, sweet bars. Their make-ahead convenience is perfect for hectic days.

- 1 **cup all-purpose flour**
- 1/4 **cup confectioners' sugar**
- 1/2 **cup cold butter**
- **FILLING:**
- 1/2 **cup seedless raspberry jam**
- 4 **ounces cream cheese, softened**
- 2 **tablespoons milk**
- 1 **cup vanilla *or* white chips, melted**
- **GLAZE:**
- 3/4 **cup semisweet chocolate chips**
- 2 **tablespoons shortening**

1 In a bowl, combine flour and confectioners' sugar; cut in butter until mixture is crumbly. Press into an ungreased 9-in. square baking pan. Bake at 375° for 15-18 minutes or until browned.

2 Spread jam over warm crust. In a small mixing bowl, beat cream cheese and milk until smooth. Add vanilla chips; beat until smooth. Spread carefully over jam layer. Cool completely. Refrigerate for 1 hour or until set.

3 For glaze, melt chocolate chips and shortening in a heavy saucepan or microwave; stir until smooth. Spread over filling. Refrigerate for 10 minutes. Cut into bars; chill 1 hour longer. Store in the refrigerator.

POLKA-DOT COOKIE BARS

CHOCOLATE RASPBERRY BARS

Chocolate Oatmeal Bars

PREP: 10 min. **BAKE:** 15 min. + cooling
YIELD: about 1-1/2 dozen

Donna Gonda, North Canton, Ohio

A sprinkle of chocolate chips over the just-from-the-oven bars softens the chips. Then you can spread them over the bars for a super easy topping.

- 1/2 **cup butter, softened**
- 1/2 **cup packed brown sugar**
- 1 **egg**
- 1 **teaspoon vanilla extract**
- 1/2 **cup all-purpose flour**
- 1/2 **cup quick-cooking oats**
- 1 **cup (6 ounces) semisweet chocolate chips**
- 1/2 **cup chopped pecans**

1 In a large mixing bowl, cream butter and sugar until light and fluffy. Beat in egg and vanilla. Add the flour and oats; mix well. Pour into a lightly greased 11-in. x 7-in. x 2-in. baking pan.

2 Bake at 375° for 15-20 minutes or until lightly browned. Cool on a wire rack for 3-5 minutes. Sprinkle with chips; when melted, spread chocolate over bars. Top with nuts. Cool completely. Cut into bars.

Double Chip Meringue Bars

PREP: 20 min. **BAKE:** 25 min. + cooling **YIELD:** 4 dozen

Dawn Onuffer, Freeport, Florida

The meringue topping and blend of chocolate and peanut butter chips make these bars extra special. Keep a pan in your refrigerator for late-night snacking.

- 1 **cup butter, melted**
- 1/2 **cup sugar**
- 1/2 **cup packed brown sugar**
- 2 **egg yolks**
- 1 **teaspoon water**
- 1 **teaspoon vanilla extract**
- 2 **cups all-purpose flour**
- 1 **teaspoon baking powder**
- 1/4 **teaspoon baking soda**
- 1/4 **teaspoon salt**
- 1 **cup semisweet chocolate chips**
- 1 **cup peanut butter chips**

TOPPING:
- 2 **egg whites**
- 1 **cup packed brown sugar**

1 In a large mixing bowl, cream butter and sugars until light and fluffy. Beat in the egg yolks, water and vanilla; mix well. Combine the flour, baking powder, baking soda and salt; gradually add to creamed mixture.

2 Spread into a greased 13-in. x 9-in. x 2-in. baking pan. Sprinkle with chips and pat lightly. For topping, in a small mixing bowl, beat egg whites on medium speed until soft peaks form. Gradually beat in brown sugar, 2 tablespoons at a time, on high until stiff peaks form. Spread evenly over chips.

3 Bake at 350° for 25-30 minutes or until golden brown. Cool on a wire rack. Cut into bars. Store in the refrigerator.

CHOCOLATE OATMEAL BARS

Triple-Layer Cookie Bars

PREP: 15 min. **BAKE:** 30 min. **YIELD:** 2-3 dozen

Diane Bradley, Sparta, Michigan

With chocolate, coconut and peanut butter, these bars are the perfect treat when you crave something sweet.

1-1/4 cups all-purpose flour
  2/3 cup sugar
  1/3 cup baking cocoa
  1/4 cup packed brown sugar
    1 teaspoon baking powder
  1/4 teaspoon salt
  1/2 cup cold butter
    2 eggs
TOPPING:
    1 package (7 ounces) flaked coconut
    1 can (14 ounces) sweetened condensed milk
    2 cups (12 ounces) semisweet chocolate chips
  1/2 cup creamy peanut butter

1 In a large mixing bowl, combine the first six ingredients. Cut in butter until mixture is crumbly. Add eggs; mix well. Spread into a greased 13-in. x 9-in. x 2-in. baking pan.

2 Bake at 350° for 8 minutes. Sprinkle coconut over crust; drizzle with milk. Bake 20-25 minutes longer or until lightly browned. In a heavy saucepan or microwave, melt chocolate chips and peanut butter; stir until smooth. Spread over top. Cool on a wire rack. Cut into bars.

Chocolate Chip Cookie Bars

PREP: 20 min. **BAKE:** 15 min. **YIELD:** 8 dozen

Barbara Witte, Irving, Texas

When you have a craving for chocolate chip cookies but don't have time to spend in the kitchen, reach for this bar recipe. The big batch is great for potlucks.

    2 cups butter, softened
1-1/2 cups sugar
1-1/2 cups packed brown sugar
    4 eggs
    2 teaspoons vanilla extract
    1 teaspoon water
4-1/2 cups all-purpose flour
    2 teaspoons baking soda
1-1/2 teaspoons salt
    3 cups (18 ounces) semisweet chocolate chips
    1 cup chopped walnuts

TRIPLE-LAYER COOKIE BARS

1 In a large mixing bowl, cream butter and sugars until light and fluffy. Beat in the eggs, vanilla and water. Combine the flour, baking soda and salt; gradually add to creamed mixture and mix well. Fold in chocolate chips and nuts.

2 Press into three greased 15-in. x 10-in. x 1-in. baking pans. Bake at 375° for 15-18 minutes or until golden brown. Cool on wire racks. Cut into bars.

Toffee Squares

PREP: 15 min. **BAKE:** 20 min. + cooling
YIELD: 4-1/2 dozen

Judy Scholovich, Waukesha, Wisconsin

These candy-like bars are very rich, so cut them into smaller bars. Using German sweet chocolate gives them a delightfully different taste.

  1 cup butter, softened
  1 cup packed brown sugar
  1 egg yolk
  1 teaspoon vanilla extract
  2 cups all-purpose flour
1/4 teaspoon salt
  2 packages (4 ounces *each*) German sweet chocolate
1/2 cup chopped nuts

1 In a large mixing bowl, cream butter and brown sugar until light and fluffy. Add the egg yolk, vanilla, flour and salt; mix well. Spread into a greased 13-in. x 9-in. x 2-in. baking pan.

patting
a crust
into a *pan*

Transfer the dough or crumb mixture to a greased pan and spread evenly. Press into the pan, using your fingers. Make sure to go into the corners and along the sides.

2 Bake at 350° for 20-25 minutes or until golden brown. In a heavy saucepan or microwave, melt chocolate; stir until smooth. Spread over hot bars. Immediately sprinkle with nuts. Cool on a wire rack. Cut into 1-1/4-in. squares.

Butterscotch Bars

PREP: 20 min. **BAKE:** 40 min. + cooling
YIELD: about 1-1/2 dozen

Romagene Deuel, Clarkston, Michigan

A cream cheese filling sets these apart from other butterscotch bars. They'd be a cool summer treat served from the refrigerator.

    1   cup butter-flavored shortening
    1   cup sugar
    1   cup packed brown sugar
    2   eggs
    1   teaspoon vanilla extract
    2   cups all-purpose flour
    1   cup old-fashioned oats
  1/2   teaspoon baking soda
    1   package (10 ounces) butterscotch chips
    1   cup chopped pecans
FILLING:
    1   package (3 ounces) cream cheese, softened
    2   tablespoons butter, softened
  1/4   cup sugar
    1   egg
    1   tablespoon all-purpose flour

1 In a large mixing bowl, cream the shortening and sugars until light and fluffy. Add eggs, one at a time, beating well after each addition. Beat in vanilla. Combine the flour, oats and baking soda;

gradually add to the creamed mixture. Stir in chips and pecans. Reserve 2 cups. Spread remaining dough into a greased 13-in. x 9-in. x 2-in. baking pan.

2 In a small mixing bowl, combine filling ingredients; beat until smooth. Spread evenly over crust. Crumble reserved dough over filling.

3 Bake at 375° for 40-42 minutes or until golden brown. Cool on a wire rack. Cut into bars. Store in the refrigerator.

Scotch Shortbread

PREP: 15 min. **BAKE:** 25 min. **YIELD:** 4 dozen

Marlene Hellickson, Big Bear City, California

This simple three-ingredient recipe makes wonderfully rich, buttery bars. Serve with fresh berries of the season for a delicious dessert.

    4   cups all-purpose flour
    1   cup sugar
    1   pound cold butter

1 In a large mixing bowl, combine flour and sugar. Cut in butter until mixture resembles fine crumbs. Knead dough until smooth, about 6-10 minutes. Pat into an ungreased 15-in. x 10-in. x 1-in. baking pan. Pierce with a fork.

2 Bake at 325° for 25-30 minutes or until lightly browned. Cut into squares while warm. Cool on a wire rack.

Editor's Note: This recipe makes a dense, crisp bar, so it does not call for baking powder or soda.

SCOTCH SHORTBREAD

Lemon Bars

PREP: 10 min. **BAKE:** 45 min. + cooling
YIELD: 9 bars

Etta Soucy, Mesa, Arizona

Basic lemon bars have been popular for years. The wonderful tangy flavor is a nice change from chocolate-laden desserts.

> 1 cup all-purpose flour
> 1/2 cup butter, softened
> 1/4 cup confectioners' sugar
> FILLING:
> 2 eggs
> 1 cup sugar
> 2 tablespoons all-purpose flour
> 1/2 teaspoon baking powder
> 2 tablespoons lemon juice
> 1 teaspoon grated lemon peel
> Additional confectioners' sugar

1 In a bowl, combine the flour, butter and confectioners' sugar. Pat into an ungreased 8-in. square baking dish. Bake at 350° for 20 minutes.

2 For filling, in a small mixing bowl, beat eggs. Add the sugar, flour, baking powder, lemon juice and peel; beat until frothy. Pour over the crust. Bake 25 minutes longer or until light golden brown. Cool on a wire rack. Dust with confectioners' sugar. Cut into bars.

LEMON BARS

Rich 'n' Buttery Bars

PREP: 20 min. **BAKE:** 35 min. + cooling **YIELD:** 4 dozen

Ann Horst, Boonsboro, Maryland

You'll keep a cake mix on hand just to make these rich bars. They're fancy enough to serve company, yet easy enough to stir up for a bake sale.

> 1/2 cup cold butter
> 1 package (18-1/4 ounces) yellow cake mix
> 1 egg, beaten
> FILLING:
> 1 package (8 ounces) cream cheese, softened
> 2 cups confectioners' sugar
> 2 eggs
> 1 teaspoon vanilla extract
> Additional confectioners' sugar

1 In a bowl, cut butter into cake mix until crumbly. Add egg and mix well. Press into a greased 13-in. x 9-in. x 2-in. baking pan. For filling, in a small mixing bowl, beat cream cheese and sugar. Add eggs and vanilla; beat until smooth. Spread evenly over crust.

2 Bake at 325° for 35-40 minutes or until the center is just set. Dust with confectioners' sugar while warm. Cool to room temperature before cutting. Store in the refrigerator.

Frosted Cinnamon Zucchini Bars

PREP: 20 min. **BAKE:** 25 min. + cooling
YIELD: about 5 dozen

Bonita Holzbacher, Batesville, Indiana

When your garden is at its peak, you can never have enough recipes calling for zucchini! These cake-like bars with a cinnamon-flavored frosting are unbelievably good.

> 3/4 cup butter, softened
> 1/2 cup sugar
> 1/2 cup packed brown sugar
> 2 eggs
> 1 teaspoon vanilla extract
> 1-3/4 cups all-purpose flour
> 1-1/2 teaspoons baking powder
> 2 cups shredded zucchini
> 1 cup flaked coconut
> 3/4 cup chopped walnuts
> FROSTING:
> 2 cups confectioners' sugar
> 1 teaspoon ground cinnamon

BEST DATE BARS

Best Date Bars

PREP: 25 min. **BAKE:** 35 min. **YIELD:** 4 dozen

Dorothy DeLeske, Scottsdale, Arizona

These date treats are very easy to bake, and one pan will yield 48 good-size bars to share at a church bazaar or any group function.

2-1/2 **cups pitted dates, cut up**
  1/4 **cup sugar**
1-1/2 **cups water**
  1/3 **cup coarsely chopped walnuts, optional**
1-1/4 **cups all-purpose flour**
    1 **teaspoon salt**
  1/2 **teaspoon baking soda**
1-1/2 **cups quick-cooking oats**
    1 **cup packed brown sugar**
  1/2 **cup cold butter**
    1 **tablespoon water**

1 In a saucepan, combine the dates, sugar and water. Cook, stirring frequently, until very thick. Stir in walnuts if desired; cool.

2 Sift the flour, salt and baking soda together in a large bowl; add oats and brown sugar. Cut in butter until mixture is crumbly. Sprinkle water over mixture; stir lightly. Pat half into a greased 13-in. x 9-in. x 2-in. baking pan. Spread with date mixture; cover with remaining oat mixture and pat lightly.

3 Bake at 350° for 35-40 minutes or until lightly browned. Cool on a wire rack. Cut into bars.

  2 **tablespoons butter, melted**
  1 **teaspoon vanilla extract**
  2 **to 3 tablespoons milk**

1 In a large mixing bowl, cream butter and sugars until light and fluffy. Add eggs, one at a time, beating well after each addition. Beat in vanilla. Combine flour and baking powder; gradually add to the creamed mixture. Stir in zucchini, coconut and nuts. Spread into a greased 15-in. x 10-in. x 1-in. baking pan.

2 Bake at 350° for 25-30 minutes or until a toothpick inserted near the center comes out clean. Cool on a wire rack. For frosting, combine confectioners' sugar and cinnamon in a bowl. Stir in the butter, vanilla and enough milk to achieve spreading consistency. Frost bars before cutting.

tips for
cutting *bars & brownies*

- With a knife, use a gentle sawing motion. Remove the corner piece first. Then the rest will be easier to remove.
- For perfectly sized bars, lay a clean ruler on top of the bars and make cut marks with the point of a knife. Use the edge of the ruler as a cutting guide.
- For basic bars and brownies (those without soft fillings or toppings), line the pan with foil before baking. (See page 79.) When cool, lift the foil from the pan. Trim the edges of the bars or brownies, then cut into bars, squares or diamonds. The scraps can be crumbled and used as a topping for ice cream or pudding.
- An 8-in. square pan will yield 16 (2-in.) squares or 64 (1-in.) squares. A 9-in. square pan will yield 54 (1-1/2-in. x 1-in.) bars or 81 (1-in.) squares. A 13-in. x 9-in. x 2-in. pan will yield 78 (1-1/2-in. x 1-in.) bars.

Cool Lime Triangles

PREP: 15 min. **BAKE:** 35 min. + cooling **YIELD:** 4 dozen

TerryAnn Moore, Oaklyn, New Jersey

Folks will enjoy this variation on the popular lemon bars. Lime juice adds fresh flavor while nuts add some crunch. They're especially refreshing during the summer months.

      2 cups all-purpose flour
    1/2 cup confectioners' sugar
    1/2 cup ground almonds
      1 cup butter, melted
FILLING:
      4 eggs
      2 cups sugar
    1/3 cup lime juice
    1/4 cup all-purpose flour
      1 teaspoon baking powder
    1/2 teaspoon grated lime peel
      1 to 2 drops green food coloring, optional
    1/2 cup sliced almonds
Confectioners' sugar

1 In a large mixing bowl, combine the first four ingredients. Press into a greased 13-in. x 9-in. x 2-in. baking pan. Bake at 350° for 13-15 minutes or just until edges are lightly browned.

2 For filling, in a large mixing bowl, combine eggs, sugar, lime juice, flour, baking powder, lime peel and food coloring if desired; beat until frothy. Pour over hot crust. Sprinkle with almonds.

3 Bake 20-25 minutes longer or until light golden brown. Cool on a wire rack. Dust with confectioners' sugar. Cut into triangles.

cutting bars into *triangles*

Triangle-shaped bars give a festive look to a cookie platter. Simply cut the bars into squares, then cut each square in half diagonally.

SHORTBREAD LEMON BARS

Shortbread Lemon Bars

PREP: 25 min. **BAKE:** 40 min. + chilling **YIELD:** 3 dozen

Margaret Peterson, Forest City, Iowa

A yummy shortbread crust puts a special spin on these lemon bars. You don't need to be afraid to make this dessert for guests—it's bound to be a hit!

  1-1/2 cups all-purpose flour
    1/2 cup confectioners' sugar
      1 teaspoon grated lemon peel
      1 teaspoon grated orange peel
    3/4 cup cold butter
FILLING:
      4 eggs
      2 cups sugar
    1/3 cup lemon juice
    1/4 cup all-purpose flour
      2 teaspoons grated lemon peel
      2 teaspoons grated orange peel
      1 teaspoon baking powder
TOPPING:
      2 cups (16 ounces) sour cream
    1/3 cup sugar
    1/2 teaspoon vanilla extract

1 In a food processor, combine the flour, confectioners' sugar, lemon peel and orange peel. Cut in butter until the mixture is crumbly; process until mixture forms a ball. Pat into a greased 13-in. x 9-in. x 2-in. baking pan. Bake at 350° for 12-14 minutes or until set and edges are lightly browned.

2 In a large mixing bowl, combine the filling ingredients; mix well. Pour over hot crust. Bake for 14-16 minutes or until set and lightly browned.

3 In a bowl, combine the topping ingredients. Spread over filling. Bake 7-9 minutes longer or until topping is set. Cool on a wire rack. Refrigerate overnight. Cut into bars just before serving. Store in the refrigerator.

Chewy Cinnamon Bars

PREP: 15 min. **BAKE:** 35 min. **YIELD:** 3 dozen.

Donna Halbert, Potosi, Missouri

The cinnamon flavor really comes through in these sweet, nutty bars.

 1/2 cup butter, softened
 1 cup sugar
 1 egg
 1/2 cup all-purpose flour
 1-1/4 teaspoons ground cinnamon
 1/4 teaspoon salt
 1 cup finely chopped pecans
Confectioners' sugar

1 In a large mixing bowl, cream butter and sugar until light and fluffy. Add egg; beat well. Combine the flour, cinnamon and salt; add to creamed mixture and beat until smooth. Stir in pecans. Spread into a greased 8-in. square baking pan.

2 Bake at 350° for 35-40 minutes or until a toothpick inserted near the center comes out clean. Cut into small bars while warm; roll in confectioners' sugar.

Easy Company Bars

PREP: 20 min. **BAKE:** 25 min. + cooling
YIELD: 1-1/2 dozen

Ruby Lee Hughes, Lynchburg, Virginia

Keep ingredients on hand for this fast-to-fix dessert, so you can easily make a treat for unexpected company.

 2 tablespoons butter, melted
 2 eggs
 1 cup packed brown sugar
 1 teaspoon vanilla extract
 1/3 cup all-purpose flour
 1/8 teaspoon baking soda
 1 cup finely chopped nuts
Confectioners' sugar

1 Coat the bottom of an 8-in. square baking dish with melted butter. In a large mixing bowl, beat eggs. Gradually beat in brown sugar and vanilla just until combined. Combine flour and baking soda; stir into the egg mixture. Fold in nuts. Pour batter evenly over butter; do not stir.

2 Bake at 350° for 25 minutes or until a toothpick inserted near the center comes out clean. Cool slightly on a wire rack. Dust with confectioners' sugar; cut into bars. Cool completely.

Peanut Butter Bars

PREP: 15 min. **BAKE:** 20 min. + cooling
YIELD: 3-4 dozen

Patricia Staudt, Marble Rock, Iowa

These bars can be dressed up for festive occasions by substituting colored icing for the peanut butter frosting. Drizzle them with pastel colors for Easter; red, white and blue for the Fourth of July; and orange and chocolate for Halloween.

 1/2 cup butter, softened
 1/2 cup sugar
 1/2 cup packed brown sugar
 1/2 cup creamy peanut butter
 1 egg
 1 teaspoon vanilla extract
 1 cup all-purpose flour
 1/2 cup quick-cooking oats
 1 teaspoon baking soda
 1/4 teaspoon salt
 1 cup (6 ounces) semisweet chocolate chips
ICING:
 1/2 cup confectioners' sugar
 2 tablespoons creamy peanut butter
 2 tablespoons milk

1 In a large mixing bowl, cream the butter, sugars and peanut butter until light and fluffy. Beat in egg and vanilla. Combine the flour, oats, baking soda and salt; stir into the creamed mixture. Spread into a greased 13-in. x 9-in. x 2-in. baking pan. Sprinkle with chocolate chips.

2 Bake at 350° for 20-25 minutes or until lightly browned. Cool on a wire rack for 10 minutes. Combine icing ingredients; drizzle over the top. Cool completely. Cut into bars.

Chewy Peanut Butter Bars

PREP: 15 min. **BAKE:** 30 min. **YIELD:** 3 dozen

Mrs. Sanford Wickham, Holbrook, Nebraska

This mouth-watering dessert is very rich and filling, so a small piece usually satisfies even a real sweet tooth.

    1 cup all-purpose flour
  1/3 cup sugar
  1/2 cup cold butter
FILLING:
    2 eggs
  1/2 cup sugar
  1/2 cup corn syrup
  1/4 cup crunchy peanut butter
  1/4 teaspoon salt
  1/2 cup flaked coconut
  1/2 cup semisweet chocolate chips

1 In a bowl, combine flour and sugar; cut in the butter until mixture is crumbly. Press into a greased 13-in. x 9-in. x 2-in. baking pan. Bake at 350° for 14-16 minutes or until lightly browned.

2 For filling, in a large mixing bowl, beat the eggs, sugar, corn syrup, peanut butter and salt until smooth. Fold in coconut and chocolate chips. Pour over crust. Bake 15-20 minutes longer or until golden. Cool on a wire rack. Cut into bars.

Soft Spice Bars

PREP: 10 min. **BAKE:** 10 min. + cooling
YIELD: 2-1/2 dozen

Sharon Nichols, Brookings, South Dakota

These bars have the old-fashioned taste of gingersnaps, but they're chewy and very easy to make.

  3/4 cup butter, melted
    1 cup plus 2 tablespoons sugar, *divided*
  1/4 cup molasses
    1 egg
    2 cups all-purpose flour
    2 teaspoons baking soda
    1 teaspoon ground cinnamon
  1/2 teaspoon salt
  1/2 teaspoon ground ginger
  1/2 teaspoon ground cloves

1 In a large mixing bowl, combine butter, 1 cup of sugar and molasses. Beat in egg until smooth. Combine the flour, baking soda, cinnamon, salt, ginger and cloves; stir into the molasses mixture.

2 Spread into a greased 15-in. x 10-in. x 1-in. baking pan. Sprinkle with remaining sugar. Bake at 375° for 10-12 minutes or until lightly browned (do not overbake). Cool on a wire rack. Cut into bars.

Oatmeal Apricot Squares

PREP: 10 Min. **BAKE:** 40 min. + cooling
YIELD: 16 bars

Veronica Roza, Bayport, New York

Easy to prepare and designed to make a small amount, these fruity oatmeal squares are a marvelous blend of flavors. They can be served warm from the oven or as a treat later.

    1 cup all-purpose flour
    1 cup quick-cooking oats
  1/2 cup packed brown sugar
  1/4 teaspoon salt
  1/4 teaspoon baking soda
  1/2 cup cold butter
  3/4 cup apricot preserves

1 In a large bowl, combine the flour, oats, sugar, salt and baking soda. Cut in butter until the mixture resembles coarse crumbs.

2 Press half of the mixture into a greased 8-in. square baking pan. Spread with preserves. Sprinkle with remaining oat mixture; gently press down.

3 Bake at 350° for 38-42 minutes or until golden brown. Cool on a wire rack. Cut into squares.

CHEWY PEANUT BUTTER BARS

Lattice Fruit Bars

PREP: 20 min. + chilling **BAKE:** 30 min. + cooling
YIELD: about 3-1/2 dozen

Betty Keisling, Knoxville, Tennessee

A pretty lattice top makes these an eye-catching addition to any table. You'll like the fact that one batch goes a long way.

3	cups all-purpose flour
1	cup sugar
1	teaspoon baking powder
1/2	teaspoon salt
1	cup cold butter
2	eggs
2	teaspoons vanilla extract
3/4	cup apricot preserves
3/4	cup raspberry preserves

1 In a bowl, combine the flour, sugar, baking powder and salt; cut in butter until the mixture is crumbly. Combine eggs and vanilla; stir into crumb mixture until blended. Cover and refrigerate a fourth of the dough for at least 45 minutes.

2 Press remaining dough into an ungreased 15-in. x 10-in. x 1-in. baking pan. Spread 1/4 cup apricot preserves in a 1-3/4-in. strip over one long side of crust. Spread 1/4 cup of raspberry preserves in a 1-3/4-in. strip adjoining the apricot strip. Repeat twice.

3 Roll out chilled dough to 1/8-in. thickness. Cut into 1/2-in. strips; place over filling to make a lattice top. Bake at 325° for 30-35 minutes or until lightly browned. Cool. Cut into bars.

Fruitcake Bars

PREP: 15 min. **BAKE:** 45 min. + cooling **YIELD:** 8 dozen

Terry Mercede, Danbury, Connecticut

These bars are easy to make, and they're colorful, too—chock-full of candied pineapple and red and green cherries.

3/4	cup butter, softened
1-3/4	cups packed brown sugar
3	eggs
1	tablespoon vanilla extract
1-1/2	cups all-purpose flour
3	cups coarsely chopped walnuts
1-1/2	cups coarsely chopped candied pineapple
1-3/4	cups red and green candied cherries, halved
2	cups pitted dates, halved

1 In a large mixing bowl, cream the butter and brown sugar until light and fluffy. Add eggs, one at time, beating well after each addition. Stir in vanilla. Add flour and walnuts; mix well. Spread evenly into a greased and floured 15-in. x 10-in. x 1-in. baking pan. Sprinkle with pineapple, cherries and dates; press lightly into dough.

2 Bake at 325° for 45-50 minutes or until lightly browned. Cool on a wire rack. Cut into bars.

Apple-Berry Streusel Bars

PREP: 10 min. **BAKE:** 45 min. **YIELD:** 4 dozen

Jane Acree, Holcomb, Illinois

The flavor combination of apples and raspberries is fabulous in these easy-to-make bars.

- 2-1/2 cups plus 2 tablespoons all-purpose flour, *divided*
- 2 cups old-fashioned oats
- 1-1/4 cups sugar
- 2 teaspoons baking powder
- 1 teaspoon ground cinnamon
- 1 cup butter, melted
- 3 cups thinly sliced peeled tart apples
- 1 jar (12 ounces) raspberry preserves
- 1/2 cup finely chopped walnuts

1 In a large mixing bowl, combine 2-1/2 cups flour, oats, sugar, baking powder and cinnamon. Beat in butter just until moistened. Set aside 2 cups for topping. Pat remaining oat mixture into a greased 13-in. x 9-in. x 2-in. baking pan. Bake at 375° for 15 minutes.

2 Meanwhile, toss apples with remaining flour. Stir in the preserves; spread over hot crust to within 1/2 in. of edges. Combine nuts and reserved oat mixture; sprinkle over fruit mixture. Bake 30-35 minutes longer or until lightly browned. Cool completely on a wire rack. Cut into bars.

Cranberry Bars

PREP: 30 min. **BAKE:** 30 min. + cooling
YIELD: about 2-1/2 dozen

Betty Noga, Milwaukie, Oregon

Keep some cranberries in the freezer all year so you can make these bars whenever you get a craving for their tart flavor.

FILLING:
- 3/4 cup sugar
- 1/2 cup water
- 2 cups fresh *or* frozen cranberries
- 1/4 cup orange juice
- 1 tablespoon grated orange peel
- 1 tablespoon butter
- 1/2 teaspoon ground cinnamon
- 1/4 teaspoon salt
- 1 cup chopped walnuts

CRUST:
- 2 cups all-purpose flour
- 1/4 teaspoon salt
- 1-1/4 cups cold butter
- 1 cup sugar
- 3 cups quick-cooking oats

1 In a saucepan, bring sugar and water to a boil. Add cranberries and cook until they pop, about 4-6 minutes. Add the orange juice, orange peel, butter, cinnamon and salt. Cook 5 minutes longer or until mixture thickens. Remove from the heat; stir in walnuts and set aside.

APPLE-BERRY STREUSEL BARS

2 For crust, combine the flour and salt in a bowl; cut in butter until mixture is crumbly. Add sugar and oats; mix well. Spoon half into an ungreased 13-in. x 9-in. x 2-in. baking pan; pat firmly into pan. Spread filling evenly over crust. Top with remaining crumb mixture; pat lightly.

3 Bake at 400° for 30-35 minutes. Cool on a wire rack. Cut into bars.

Strawberry Jam Bars

PREP: 15 min. **BAKE:** 25 min. + cooling **YIELD:** 16 bars

Patricia Olson, Barstow, California

A golden crust nicely seasoned with nutmeg, allspice and honey complements these sweet bars. You can replace the strawberry jam with any flavor you prefer.

1/2	cup butter, softened
3/4	cup sugar
1	egg
1	tablespoon honey
1-1/4	cups all-purpose flour
1/4	teaspoon baking powder
1/8	teaspoon ground allspice
1/8	teaspoon ground nutmeg
2/3	cup strawberry jam
1/2	cup chopped walnuts

1 In a large mixing bowl, cream butter and sugar until light and fluffy. Beat in egg and honey. Combine the flour, baking powder, allspice and nutmeg; gradually add to the creamed mixture.

2 Divide the dough in half; spread one portion into a lightly greased 9-in. square baking pan. Spread with jam. Drop remaining dough by teaspoonfuls over jam. Sprinkle with walnuts.

3 Bake at 350° for 25-30 minutes or until top is golden brown. Cool on a wire rack. Cut into bars.

storing *bars & brownies*

- Cover a pan of uncut brownies and bars with foil—or put the pan in a large resealable plastic bag. (If made with perishable ingredients, like cream cheese, they should be covered and refrigerated.) Once the bars are cut, store them in an airtight container.

- Most bars and brownies freeze well for up to 3 months. To freeze a pan of uncut bars, place in an airtight container or resealable plastic bag. Or wrap individual bars in plastic wrap and stack in an airtight container. Thaw at room temperature before serving.

CHOCOLATE-DRIZZLED CHERRY BARS

Chocolate-Drizzled Cherry Bars

PREP: 15 min. **BAKE:** 35 min. + cooling **YIELD:** 3 dozen

Janice Heikkila, Deer Creek, Minnesota

These special bars are fabulous for Christmas parties and other festive gatherings. Have copies of the recipe available to hand out—as you'll be asked for the recipe.

2	cups all-purpose flour
2	cups quick-cooking oats
1-1/2	cups sugar
1-1/4	cups butter, softened
1	can (21 ounces) cherry pie filling
1	teaspoon almond extract
1/4	cup semisweet chocolate chips
3/4	teaspoon shortening

1 In a mixing bowl, combine flour, oats, sugar and butter until crumbly; set aside 1-1/2 cups. Press remaining crumb mixture into an ungreased 13-in. x 9-in. x 2-in. baking dish. Bake at 350° for 15-18 minutes or until edges begin to brown.

2 In a bowl, combine pie filling and extract; carefully spread over crust. Sprinkle with reserved crumb mixture.

3 Bake 20-25 minutes longer or until edges and topping are lightly browned. In a microwave or heavy saucepan, melt chocolate chips and shortening; stir until smooth. Drizzle over warm bars. Cool completely on a wire rack.

TRIPLE-NUT DIAMONDS

Pecan Lemon Bars

PREP: 15 min. **BAKE:** 30 min. **YIELD:** 2 to 2-1/2 dozen

June Trom, Blooming Prairie, Minnesota

Refrigerated cookie dough makes it easy to whip up these luscious lemon squares.

- 1 tube (18 ounces) refrigerated sugar cookie dough
- 1 cup chopped pecans, *divided*
- 1/3 cup corn syrup
- 1/4 cup lemon juice
- 1 egg, beaten
- 1 tablespoon butter, melted
- 1 tablespoon grated lemon peel
- 1/2 cup sugar
- 5 teaspoons all-purpose flour

Confectioners' sugar

1 Cut dough into 1/2-in. slices; press into an ungreased 13-in. x 9-in. x 2-in. baking pan. Sprinkle with 1/2 cup pecans; press firmly into crust. Bake at 375° for 10-12 minutes or until light golden brown. Reduce heat to 350°.

2 In a small bowl, combine the corn syrup, lemon juice, egg, butter and lemon peel. Combine the sugar, flour and remaining pecans; stir into lemon mixture until blended. Pour over crust.

3 Bake for 18-20 minutes or until golden brown. Cool on a wire rack. Dust with confectioners' sugar. Cut into bars.

Triple-Nut Diamonds

PREP: 10 min. **BAKE:** 30 min. + chilling **YIELD:** 4 dozen

Darlene King, Estevan, Saskatchewan

Every delectable bite of these rich nutty bars is like a slice of pecan pie. One pan makes a nice sized batch.

- 1 cup all-purpose flour
- 1/2 cup sugar
- 1/2 cup cold butter, *divided*
- 1/2 cup packed brown sugar
- 2 tablespoons honey
- 1/4 cup heavy whipping cream
- 2/3 cup *each* chopped pecans, walnuts and almonds

1 Line a greased 9-in. square baking pan with foil; grease the foil and set aside. In a bowl, combine the flour and sugar. Cut in 1/4 cup butter until mixture resembles coarse crumbs. Press into prepared pan. Bake at 350° for 10 minutes.

2 In a saucepan, heat the brown sugar, honey and remaining butter until bubbly. Boil for 1 minute. Remove from the heat; stir in cream and nuts. Pour over crust. Bake 16-20 minutes longer or until surface is bubbly. Cool on a wire rack.

3 Refrigerate for 30 minutes. Using foil, lift bars out of the pan; cut into diamonds.

cutting bars into *diamond shapes*

With a large knife, make a diagonal cut from one corner of the pan to the opposite corner. Make diagonal cuts at 1-1/2-in. intervals parallel to the first cut.

Make a lengthwise cut through the middle of the pan. Make lengthwise cuts at 1-1/2-in. intervals parallel to the first lengthwise cut, forming diamonds.

Caramel Peanut Bars

PREP: 25 min. **BAKE:** 15 min. + cooling **YIELD:** 3 dozen

Ardyce Piehl, Wisconsin Dells, Wisconsin

With chocolate, peanuts and caramel between golden oat and crumb layers, these bars are very popular. They taste like candy bars but with homemade goodness.

1-1/2	cups quick-cooking oats
1-1/2	cups all-purpose flour
1-1/4	cups packed brown sugar
3/4	teaspoon baking soda
1/4	teaspoon salt
3/4	cup butter, melted
1	package (14 ounces) caramels
1/2	cup heavy whipping cream
1-1/2	cups semisweet chocolate chips
3/4	cup chopped peanuts

1 In a bowl, combine the first five ingredients; stir in the butter. Set aside 1 cup for topping. Press the remaining oat mixture into a greased 13-in. x 9-in. x 2-in. baking pan. Bake at 350° for 10 minutes or until lightly browned.

2 In a heavy saucepan or microwave, melt caramels with cream, stirring often. Sprinkle chocolate chips and peanuts over the crust; top with the caramel mixture. Sprinkle with reserved oat mixture. Bake 15-20 minutes longer or until topping is golden brown. Cool completely on a wire rack. Cut into bars.

Diamond Bars

PREP/TOTAL TIME: 30 min. **YIELD:** 5 dozen

Lois Lipker, Ormond Beach, Florida

You'll need just seven basic ingredients to stir up a batch of these delicious bars. Cutting them into diamonds makes for an interesting presentation.

1	cup butter, softened
1	cup packed brown sugar
2	egg yolks
2	cups all-purpose flour
2	cups (12 ounces) semisweet chocolate chips
1	cup chopped walnuts
1	cup flaked coconut

1 In a large mixing bowl, cream the butter and brown sugar until light and fluffy. Beat in egg yolks. Add flour and mix well. Spread into a greased 15-in. x 10-in. x 1-in. baking pan. Bake at 325° for 20-25 minutes or until golden brown.

2 Sprinkle with chocolate chips. Bake 1 minute longer or until chips are melted. Spread chocolate over crust. Sprinkle with walnuts and coconut. Cool on a wire rack. Cut into diamond shapes.

JEWEL NUT BARS

Jewel Nut Bars

PREP: 10 min. **BAKE:** 35 min. + cooling **YIELD:** 3 dozen

Joyce Fitt, Listowel, Ontario

With the eye-catching appeal of candied cherries and the crunchy goodness of mixed nuts,these colorful bars are certain to become a holiday favorite year after year.

- 1-1/4 cups all-purpose flour
-   2/3 cup packed brown sugar, *divided*
-   3/4 cup cold butter
-     1 egg
-   1/2 teaspoon salt
- 1-1/2 cups salted mixed nuts
- 1-1/2 cups halved green and red candied cherries
-     1 cup (6 ounces) semisweet chocolate chips

1 In a bowl, combine flour and 1/3 cup brown sugar; cut in butter until the mixture resembles coarse crumbs. Press into a lightly greased 13-in. x 9-in. x 2-in. baking pan. Bake at 350° for 15 minutes.

2 In a large mixing bowl, beat the egg. Add salt and remaining brown sugar. Stir in the nuts, cherries and chocolate chips. Spoon evenly over crust. Bake 20-25 minutes longer or until set. Cool on a wire rack. Cut into bars.

Pecan Squares

PREP: 10 min. **BAKE:** 45 min. + cooling **YIELD:** 4 dozen

Sylvia Ford, Kennett, Missouri

These bars are good for snacking when you're on the road or for taking to gatherings. They're different from ordinary dessert bars. If you love pecan pie, you'll find them irresistible!

-     2 cups all-purpose flour
-   1/3 cup sugar
-   1/4 teaspoon salt
-   3/4 cup cold butter

FILLING:

-     4 eggs, lightly beaten
- 1-1/2 cups corn syrup
- 1-1/2 cups sugar
-     3 tablespoons butter, melted
- 1-1/2 teaspoons vanilla extract
- 2-1/2 cups chopped pecans

1 In a large bowl, combine the flour, sugar and salt. Cut into butter until the mixture resembles coarse crumbs. Press firmly and evenly into a greased 15-in. x 10-in. x 1-in. baking pan. Bake at 350° for 20 minutes.

2 For filling, combine the eggs, corn syrup, sugar, butter and vanilla in a bowl. Stir in pecans. Spread evenly over hot crust. Bake 25-30 minutes longer or until set. Cool on a wire rack. Cut into squares.

PECAN SQUARES

Brownie Bonanza

Best Cake Brownies

PREP: 20 min. BAKE: 20 min. + cooling
YIELD: about 3 dozen

Jean Kennedy, Springfield, Oregon

Chocolate lovers will be delighted to know this recipe calls for a whole can of chocolate syrup! Plus, the smooth chocolate glaze features creamy marshmallows.

1/2	cup butter, softened
1	cup sugar
4	eggs
1	can (16 ounces) chocolate syrup
1	teaspoon vanilla extract
1	cup all-purpose flour
1/2	teaspoon salt

GLAZE:

1	cup sugar
1/3	cup butter
1/3	cup milk
2/3	cup semisweet chocolate chips
2/3	cup miniature marshmallows

1 In a large mixing bowl, cream butter and sugar until light and fluffy. Add the eggs, one at a time, beating well after each addition. Beat in chocolate syrup and vanilla. Add the flour and salt until blended.

2 Pour into a greased 15-in. x 10-in. x 1-in. baking pan. Bake at 350° for 20-25 minutes or until a toothpick inserted near the center comes out clean (top of brownies will still appear wet). Cool on a wire rack for 15-20 minutes.

3 For glaze, combine sugar, butter and milk in a saucepan. Bring to a boil; boil until the sugar is dissolved. Remove from the heat; stir in chocolate chips and marshmallows until melted. Pour over the brownies and spread evenly. Refrigerate for 5 minutes before cutting.

Black Forest Brownies

PREP: 20 min. BAKE: 30 min. + cooling YIELD: 3 dozen

Toni Reeves, Medicine Hat, Alberta

This chocolate and cherry treat tastes just like a traditional Black Forest Cake but with less work.

1-1/3	cups all-purpose flour
1	teaspoon baking powder
1/2	teaspoon salt

BEST CAKE BROWNIES

1	cup butter
1	cup baking cocoa
4	eggs
2	cups sugar
1-1/2	teaspoons vanilla extract
1	teaspoon almond extract
1	cup chopped maraschino cherries
1/2	cup chopped nuts

ICING:

1/4	cup butter, softened
1	teaspoon vanilla extract
2	cups confectioners' sugar
6	tablespoons baking cocoa
1/4	cup milk
1/4	cup chopped nuts

1 Combine the flour, baking powder and salt; set aside. In a saucepan, melt butter. Remove from the heat and stir in cocoa until smooth. Blend in the eggs, sugar and extracts. Stir in the flour mixture, cherries and nuts. Pour into a greased 13-in. x 9-in. x 2-in. baking pan. Bake at 350° for 30-35 minutes or until a toothpick inserted near the center comes out clean.

2 For icing, in a bowl, blend the butter, vanilla, confectioners' sugar, cocoa and milk until smooth; spread over hot brownies. Sprinkle with nuts. Cool on a wire rack. Cut into bars.

CHOCOLATE-DIPPED BROWNIES

Chocolate-Dipped Brownies

PREP: 30 min. + freezing **BAKE:** 35 min. + cooling
YIELD: 3 dozen

Jackie Archer, Clinton, Iowa

Dipping brownies in melted chocolate just might make these the world's most chocolaty brownies! It's best to store them in a single layer.

- 3/4 cup sugar
- 1/3 cup butter
- 2 tablespoons water
- 4 cups (24 ounces) semisweet chocolate chips, *divided*

dipping bars *in chocolate*

Melt the chocolate chips, baking chocolate or candy coating according to recipe directions. If necessary, transfer chocolate to a narrow container.

   To cover an entire bar in chocolate, use two forks to dip the bar into the chocolate and lift up. Gently shake the bar to remove excess chocolate. Place on a waxed paper-lined baking sheet to set at room temperature.

   If the chocolate cools too much to coat the bars properly, rewarm and continue dipping.

- 1 teaspoon vanilla extract
- 2 eggs
- 3/4 cup all-purpose flour
- 1/2 teaspoon salt
- 1/4 teaspoon baking soda
- 2 tablespoons shortening
- 1/2 cup chopped pecans, toasted

1 In a saucepan, bring the sugar, butter and water to a boil over medium heat; remove from the heat. Stir in 1 cup chocolate chips and vanilla; stir until smooth. Cool for 5 minutes. Add eggs, one at a time, beating well after each addition. Combine the flour, salt and baking soda; stir into the chocolate mixture. Stir in 1 cup chips.

2 Pour into a greased 9-in. square baking pan. Bake at 325° for 35 minutes or until set. Cool completely on a wire rack. Place in the freezer for 30-40 minutes (do not freeze completely). Cut into bars.

3 In a heavy saucepan or microwave, melt remaining chips with shortening; stir until smooth. Using a small fork, dip brownies in chocolate to completely coat; shake off excess. Place on waxed paper; immediately sprinkle with pecans. Let stand until set. Store in an airtight container in a cool dry place.

Rich Chocolate Brownies

PREP: 15 min. **BAKE:** 25 min. + cooling
YIELD: 12 servings

Karen Trapp
North Weymouth, Massachusetts

This rich cocoa-based brownie is fabulous. They'll go quickly as you serve them.

- 1 cup sugar
- 2 eggs
- 1/2 teaspoon vanilla extract
- 1/2 cup butter, melted
- 1/2 cup all-purpose flour
- 1/3 cup baking cocoa
- 1/4 teaspoon baking powder
- 1/4 teaspoon salt

FROSTING:
- 3 tablespoons baking cocoa
- 3 tablespoons butter, melted
- 1 teaspoon instant coffee granules
- 1-1/2 cups confectioners' sugar
- 2 to 3 tablespoons warm water

RICH CHOCOLATE BROWNIES

1 In a large mixing bowl, beat the sugar, eggs and vanilla. Add butter; mix well. Combine the flour, cocoa, baking powder and salt; add to batter and mix well.

2 Pour into a greased 8-in. square baking pan. Bake at 350° for 25-30 minutes or until a toothpick inserted near the center comes out clean. Cool on a wire rack.

3 For frosting, combine the cocoa, butter and coffee. Gradually stir in confectioners' sugar and enough water to achieve a spreading consistency. Frost brownies.

Fudgy Nut Brownies

PREP: 30 min. **BAKE:** 25 min. + cooling
YIELD: about 2-1/2 dozen

Ruth Sparer Stern, Shadow Hills, California

A brownie like this never goes out of style. A semisweet chocolate frosting and white chocolate drizzle make every bite irresistible.

2-1/2 **cups semisweet chocolate chips**
   1 **cup butter**
   1 **cup sugar**
1/4 **teaspoon salt**
   4 **eggs**
   2 **teaspoons vanilla extract**
3/4 **cup all-purpose flour**
   1 **cup coarsely chopped hazelnuts** *or* **almonds, toasted**

TOPPING:
12 **squares (1 ounce** *each***) semisweet chocolate**
   1 **tablespoon shortening**
   3 **squares (1 ounce** *each***) white baking chocolate**

1 In a heavy saucepan or microwave, melt chocolate chips and butter; stir until smooth. Add sugar and salt; stir until dissolved. Cool for 10 minutes. Stir in the eggs, vanilla, flour and nuts.

2 Spread into a greased 15-in. x 10-in. x 1-in. baking pan. Bake at 350° for 25-30 minutes or until a toothpick inserted near the center comes out with moist crumbs (do not overbake). Cool completely on a wire rack.

3 For topping, melt semisweet chocolate and shortening in a heavy saucepan or microwave; stir until smooth. Spread over brownies. Melt white chocolate; cool slightly. Pour into a small heavy-duty resealable plastic bag; cut a small hole in corner of bag. Pipe thin lines 1 in. apart widthwise. Beginning about 1 in. from a long side, gently pull a toothpick lengthwise through the lines to the opposite side. Wipe toothpick clean. Pull toothpick through lines in opposite direction. Repeat over entire top at 1-in. intervals. Cut into bars.

FUDGY NUT BROWNIES

Fudge Brownies

PREP: 15 min. + cooling **BAKE:** 45 min. + cooling
YIELD: 16 servings

Hazel Fritchie, Palestine, Illinois

These brownies are so fudgy, they don't need icing.

- 1 **cup butter**
- 6 **squares (1 ounce *each*) unsweetened chocolate**
- 4 **eggs**
- 2 **cups sugar**
- 1 **teaspoon vanilla extract**
- 1/2 **teaspoon salt**
- 1 **cup all-purpose flour**
- 2 **cups chopped walnuts**

Confectioners' sugar, optional

1 In a small saucepan, melt butter and chocolate over low heat; cool for 10 minutes. In a large mixing bowl, beat the eggs, sugar, vanilla and salt. Stir in the chocolate mixture. Add flour and nuts; mix well.

2 Pour into a greased 11-in. x 7-in. x 2-in. baking dish. Bake at 325° for 45-50 minutes or until a toothpick inserted near the center comes out with moist crumbs. Cool on a wire rack. Dust with confectioners' sugar if desired. Cut into bars.

FUDGE BROWNIES

Frosted Cake Brownies

PREP: 15 min. **BAKE:** 30 min. + cooling
YIELD: 2-1/2 dozen

Mary Fox, Forest City, Iowa

A boxed mix is the base for these moist brownies with a from-scratch taste. It uses about half of a can of prepared frosting. Save the rest, because you'll make them again.

- 1 **package fudge brownie mix (13-inch x 9-inch pan size)**
- 1 **cup (8 ounces) sour cream**
- 1 **cup milk chocolate chips**
- 1/2 **cup chopped walnuts**
- 1 **cup milk chocolate frosting**

1 Prepare brownie mix according to package directions. Fold in sour cream, chocolate chips and walnuts into batter. Pour into a greased 13-in. x 9-in. x 2-in. baking pan.

2 Bake at 350° for 30-35 minutes or until a toothpick inserted near the center comes out clean. Cool completely on a wire rack. Frost. Cut into bars.

Cookies 'n' Cream Brownies

PREP: 15 min. **BAKE:** 25 min. + cooling **YIELD:** 2 dozen

Darlene Brenden, Salem, Oregon

You won't want to frost these brownies, since the marbled top is too pretty to cover up. Besides, the tasty cream cheese layer makes them taste like they're already frosted. The crushed cookies add extra chocolate flavor.

- 1 **package (8 ounces) cream cheese, softened**
- 1/4 **cup sugar**
- 1 **egg**
- 1/2 **teaspoon vanilla extract**

BROWNIE LAYER:

- 1/2 **cup butter, melted**
- 1/2 **cup sugar**
- 1/2 **cup packed brown sugar**
- 1/2 **cup baking cocoa**
- 2 **eggs**
- 1/2 **cup all-purpose flour**
- 1 **teaspoon baking powder**
- 1 **teaspoon vanilla extract**
- 12 **cream-filled chocolate sandwich cookies, crushed**

1 In a small mixing bowl, beat the cream cheese, sugar, egg and vanilla until smooth; set aside. For brownie layer, combine the butter, sugars and

COOKIES 'N' CREAM BROWNIES

cocoa in a large mixing bowl; blend well. Add eggs, one at a time, beating well after each addition. Combine flour and baking powder; stir into the cocoa mixture. Stir in vanilla and cookie crumbs.

2 Pour into a greased 11-in. x 7-in. x 2-in. baking pan. Spoon cream cheese mixture over batter; cut through batter with a knife to swirl. Bake at 350° for 25-30 minutes or until a toothpick inserted near the center comes out with moist crumbs. Cool completely on a wire rack. Cut into bars. Store in the refrigerator.

Chocolate Cream Cheese Brownies

PREP: 20 min. **BAKE:** 35 min. + cooling
YIELD: about 2 dozen

Lisa Godfrey, Temple, Georgia

This is a good brownie to take to gatherings because it won't crumble in your hand. It's easy to achieve the attractive marbled effect.

- 1 package (4 ounces) German sweet chocolate, broken into squares
- 3 tablespoons butter
- 2 eggs
- 3/4 cup sugar
- 1/2 cup all-purpose flour
- 1/2 teaspoon baking powder
- 1/4 teaspoon salt
- 1 teaspoon vanilla extract
- 1/4 teaspoon almond extract
- 1/2 cup chopped nuts

FILLING:
- 2 tablespoons butter, softened
- 1 package (3 ounces) cream cheese, softened
- 1/4 cup sugar
- 1 egg
- 1 tablespoon all-purpose flour
- 1/2 teaspoon vanilla extract

1 In a saucepan or microwave, melt chocolate and butter; stir until smooth. Cool. In a large mixing bowl, beat the eggs. Gradually add sugar, beating until thick and pale yellow. Combine the flour, baking powder and salt; add to egg mixture. Stir in melted chocolate, extracts and nuts. Pour half of the batter into a greased 8-in. square baking dish; set aside.

2 For filling, in a small mixing bowl, beat butter and cream cheese until light and fluffy. Gradually add sugar, beating until fluffy. Blend in the egg, flour and vanilla; mix well. Pour over batter in pan. Spoon remaining batter over filling. With a knife, cut through batter to create a marbled effect.

3 Bake at 325° for 35-40 minutes or until a toothpick inserted near the center comes out clean. Cool on a wire rack. Cut into bars. Store in the refrigerator.

CHOCOLATE CREAM CHEESE BROWNIES

DOUBLE BROWNIES

Double Brownies

PREP: 30 min. **BAKE:** 35 min. + cooling **YIELD:** 2 dozen

Rosanne Stevenson, Melfort, Saskatchewan

A caramel icing tops this sensational blond and chocolate brownie treat.

BOTTOM LAYER:
- 1/2 cup butter, softened
- 1-1/4 cups packed brown sugar
- 2 eggs
- 2 teaspoons vanilla extract
- 1-1/2 cups all-purpose flour
- 1/4 teaspoon salt
- 1/2 cup chopped walnuts

MIDDLE LAYER:
- 1/2 cup butter, softened
- 1 cup sugar
- 2 eggs
- 3/4 cup all-purpose flour
- 1/4 cup baking cocoa
- 1/8 teaspoon salt
- 1/2 cup chopped walnuts

CARAMEL ICING:
- 6 tablespoons butter
- 3/4 cup packed brown sugar
- 4 to 6 tablespoons milk
- 2-1/2 cups confectioners' sugar

1 In a large mixing bowl, cream the butter and brown sugar until light and fluffy. Beat in eggs and vanilla. Combine flour and salt. Stir into creamed mixture. Stir in nuts. Spread into a greased 13-in. x 9-in. x 2-in. baking pan; set aside.

2 For middle layer, cream butter and sugar until light and fluffy. Beat in eggs. Combine the flour, cocoa and salt. Stir into creamed mixture. Add nuts. Spread over the bottom layer. Bake at 350° for 35-40 minutes or until a toothpick inserted near the center comes out clean. Cool completely on wire rack.

3 For icing, melt butter in a saucepan over medium heat. Stir in brown sugar and milk; bring to a boil. Remove from the heat. Cool just until warm; beat in confectioners' sugar until the icing achieves spreading consistency. Spread over brownies. Let stand until set. Cut into bars.

Fudge-Topped Brownies

PREP: 25 min. + freezing **BAKE:** 25 min. + cooling
YIELD: about 10 dozen

Judy Olson, Whitecourt, Alberta

Why have only brownies or fudge when you can combine them? These exquisite brownies are the ultimate dessert.

- 1 cup butter
- 4 squares (1 ounce *each*) unsweetened chocolate
- 2 cups sugar
- 2 teaspoons vanilla extract
- 4 eggs, beaten
- 1-1/2 cups all-purpose flour
- 1 teaspoon baking powder
- 1/2 teaspoon salt
- 1 cup chopped walnuts

FUDGE-TOPPED BROWNIES

TOPPING:

- 4-1/2 **cups sugar**
- 1 **can (12 ounces) evaporated milk**
- 1/2 **cup butter**
- 1 **package (12 ounces) semisweet chocolate chips**
- 1 **package (11-1/2 ounces) milk chocolate chips**
- 1 **jar (7 ounces) marshmallow creme**
- 2 **teaspoons vanilla extract**
- 2 **cups coarsely chopped walnuts**

1 In a heavy saucepan or microwave, melt butter and chocolate; stir until smooth. Remove from the heat; blend in sugar and vanilla. Add eggs; mix well. Combine the flour, baking powder and salt; add to chocolate mixture. Stir in walnuts. Pour into a greased 13-in. x 9-in. x 2-in. baking pan. Bake at 350° for 25-30 minutes or until top springs back when lightly touched.

2 For topping, combine the sugar, milk and butter in a large heavy saucepan; bring to a boil over medium heat. Reduce heat; simmer, uncovered, for 5 minutes, stirring constantly. Remove from the heat. Stir in the chocolate chips, marshmallow creme and vanilla until smooth. Add nuts. Spread over warm brownies. Freeze for 3 hours or until firm. Cut into 1-in. squares. Store in refrigerator.

Fudge Ripple Brownies

PREP: 35 min. **BAKE:** 25 min. + cooling **YIELD:** 4 dozen

Bobi Raab, St. Paul, Minnesota

A yummy, browned butter frosting tops this rich brownie. Chocolate topping drizzled over them adds to the appeal.

- 1 **cup butter, softened**
- 2 **cups sugar**
- 4 **eggs**
- 2 **squares (1 ounce *each*) unsweetened chocolate, melted and cooled**
- 2 **teaspoons vanilla extract**
- 1-1/2 **cups all-purpose flour**
- 1 **teaspoon baking powder**
- 1 **teaspoon salt**
- 1 **cup chopped walnuts**

FROSTING:
- 1/3 **cup butter**
- 3 **cups confectioners' sugar**
- 1-1/2 **teaspoons vanilla extract**
- 4 **to 5 tablespoons heavy whipping cream**

FUDGE RIPPLE BROWNIES

TOPPING:
- 1 **square (1 ounce) unsweetened chocolate**
- 1 **tablespoon butter**
- 1 **tablespoon confectioners' sugar**

1 In a large mixing bowl, cream butter and sugar until light and fluffy. Add eggs, one at a time, beating well after each addition. Add chocolate and vanilla; mix well. Combine the flour, baking powder and salt; add to creamed mixture and mix well. Stir in nuts.

2 Spread into a greased 15-in. x 10-in. x 1-in. baking pan. Bake at 350° for 25-30 minutes or until a toothpick inserted near the center comes out clean. Cool on a wire rack.

3 For frosting, cook and stir butter in a saucepan over medium heat for 6-7 minutes or until golden brown. Pour into a large mixing bowl; add the confectioners' sugar, vanilla and enough cream to achieve spreading consistency. Frost cooled brownies.

4 For topping, melt chocolate and butter in a heavy saucepan or microwave; stir until smooth. Add confectioners' sugar; stir until smooth. Drizzle over frosting. Cut into bars.

Almond Coconut Brownies

PREP: 25 min. + chilling **BAKE:** 30 min. + cooling
YIELD: 4 dozen

Wendy Wilkins, Prattville, Alabama

You'll make your taste buds happy with the first bite of these sensational brownies. It's a triple delight with a delicious brownie base, coconut filling and smooth chocolate topping.

1-1/2 **cups butter**
   4 **squares (1 ounce *each*) unsweetened chocolate**
2-1/4 **cups sugar**
   3 **eggs, beaten**
   1 **cup all-purpose flour**
 3/4 **cup chopped slivered almonds**
   1 **teaspoon vanilla extract**
FILLING:
   1 **cup sugar**
   1 **cup milk**
 24 **large marshmallows**
   1 **package (14 ounces) flaked coconut**
TOPPING:
   1 **cup (6 ounces) semisweet chocolate chips**
 3/4 **cup sugar**
 1/4 **cup butter**
 1/4 **cup milk**
 1/4 **cup chopped slivered almonds, toasted**

1 In a saucepan, over low heat, melt butter and chocolate; cool slightly. Add sugar. Stir in the eggs, flour, almonds and vanilla. Transfer to a greased 13-in. x 9-in. x 2-in. baking pan. Bake at 350° for 30 minutes or until a toothpick inserted in the center comes out clean. Cool on a wire rack.

2 In a large saucepan, combine filling ingredients; bring to a boil. Pour over cooled brownies.

3 In another saucepan, combine chocolate chips, sugar, butter and milk; bring to a boil. Spoon over the filling. Sprinkle with almonds. Refrigerate for 2 hours or until set. Store in the refrigerator.

Double Frosted Brownies

PREP: 15 min. + chilling **BAKE:** 25 min. + cooling
YIELD: 3 dozen

Jean Kolessar, Orland Park, Illinois

For a quick dessert or bake sale contribution, this recipe is ideal. A packaged brownie mix is dressed up with two kinds of frosting, creating a two-toned treat with a luscious look and sweet taste.

   1 **package fudge brownie mix (13-inch x 9-inch pan size)**
 1/2 **cup butter, softened**
1-1/2 **cups confectioners' sugar**
   2 **tablespoons instant vanilla pudding mix**
   2 **to 3 tablespoons milk**
   1 **can (16 ounces) chocolate fudge frosting**

1 Prepare brownie mix according to package directions. Spread the batter into a greased 13-in. x 9-in. x 2-in. baking pan. Bake at 350° for 25-30 minutes or until a toothpick inserted 2 in. from side of pan comes out clean. Cool completely on a wire rack.

2 In a large mixing bowl, beat the butter, sugar and pudding mix until blended. Add enough milk to achieve spreading consistency. Frost brownies. Cover and chill for 30 minutes. Spread with fudge frosting. Cut into bars. Store in the refrigerator.

ALMOND COCONUT BROWNIES

DOUBLE FROSTED BROWNIES

Mocha Truffle Brownies

PREP: 30 min. + cooling **BAKE:** 30 min. + chilling
YIELD: about 6-1/2 dozen

Margaret Roberts, Kuna, Idaho

Even folks who don't care for coffee can't resist these mocha morsels. For a little more visual appeal, use vanilla or white chips instead of chocolate chips for the glaze.

1-1/4 **cups semisweet chocolate chips**
  1/2 **cup butter**
    1 **teaspoon instant coffee granules**
    2 **tablespoons hot water**
    2 **eggs**
  3/4 **cup packed brown sugar**
  3/4 **cup all-purpose flour**
  1/2 **teaspoon baking powder**

FILLING:
    1 **tablespoon instant coffee granules**
    1 **tablespoon hot water**
    1 **package (8 ounces) cream cheese, softened**
  1/3 **cup confectioners' sugar**
    1 **cup (6 ounces) semisweet chocolate chips, melted**

GLAZE:
  1/4 **cup semisweet chocolate chips**
    1 **teaspoon shortening**

1 In a heavy saucepan or microwave, melt chocolate chips and butter; stir until smooth. Cool for 5 minutes. Dissolve coffee granules in hot water; set aside. In a large mixing bowl, beat eggs and brown sugar on medium speed for 1 minute. Stir in chocolate mixture and coffee. Combine flour and baking powder; gradually add to chocolate mixture.

2 Transfer to a greased 9-in. square baking pan. Bake at 350° for 30-35 minutes or until a toothpick inserted near the center comes out with moist crumbs. Cool completely on a wire rack.

3 For filling, dissolve coffee granules in water; set aside. In a mixing bowl, beat cream cheese until smooth. Beat in the confectioners' sugar, melted chocolate and coffee. Spread over brownies.

4 For glaze, melt the chocolate chips and shortening in a heavy saucepan or microwave; stir until smooth. Drizzle over filling. Chill for at least 2 hours before cutting. Store in the refrigerator.

MOCHA TRUFFLE BROWNIES

MACAROON BROWNIES

Macaroon Brownies

PREP: 25 min. **BAKE:** 40 min. + cooling **YIELD:** 4 dozen

Christine Foust, Stoneboro, Pennsylvania

These three-layer brownies make for a pretty presentation on any dessert table.

> 1   cup butter, softened
> 2   cups sugar
> 4   eggs
> 1   teaspoon vanilla extract
> 2   cups all-purpose flour
> 1/2   cup baking cocoa
> 1/2   teaspoon cream of tartar
> 1/2   cup chopped walnuts

MACAROON FILLING:

> 1   package (14 ounces) flaked coconut
> 1   can (14 ounces) sweetened condensed milk
> 2   teaspoons vanilla extract

FROSTING:

> 3/4   cup sugar
> 1/4   cup milk
> 2   tablespoons butter
> 1   cup miniature marshmallows
> 1   cup (6 ounces) semisweet chocolate chips
> 1   teaspoon vanilla extract

1 In a large mixing bowl, cream butter and sugar until light and fluffy. Add eggs and vanilla; mix well. Combine the flour, cocoa and cream of tartar; gradually add to creamed mixture. Stir in nuts. Spread half into a greased 13-in. x 9-in. x 2-in. baking pan.

2 For filling, combine the coconut, condensed milk and vanilla; carefully spread over batter in pan. Top with the remaining batter. Bake at 350° for 40-45 minutes or until a toothpick inserted near the center comes out clean. Cool on a wire rack.

3 For frosting, combine the sugar, milk and butter in a saucepan; cook and stir until sugar is dissolved. Add the marshmallows and chocolate chips; cook and stir until melted. Remove from the heat; stir in vanilla. Cool until frosting reaches spreading consistency, about 25 minutes. Spread over the cooled brownies. Cut into bars.

Peppermint Patty Brownies

PREP: 20 min. **BAKE:** 35 min. + cooling
YIELD: 2 to 2-1/2 dozen

Clara Bakke, Coon Rapids, Minnesota

A layer of chocolate-covered mint patties provides a rich, refreshing surprise.

> 1-1/2   cups butter, softened
> 3   cups sugar
> 5   eggs
> 1   tablespoon vanilla extract
> 2   cups all-purpose flour
> 1   cup baking cocoa
> 1   teaspoon baking powder
> 1   teaspoon salt
> 1   package (13 ounces) chocolate-covered peppermint patties

PEPPERMINT PATTY BROWNIES

GERMAN CHOCOLATE BROWNIES

1 In a large mixing bowl, cream butter and sugar until light and fluffy. Add eggs, one at a time, beating well after each addition. Beat in vanilla. Combine the flour, cocoa, baking powder and salt; add to creamed mixture and mix well.

2 Spread about two-thirds of the batter into a greased 13-in. x 9-in. x 2-in. baking pan. Arrange peppermint patties over top. Carefully spread remaining batter over patties. Bake at 350° for 35-40 minutes or until edges begin to pull away from sides of pan and a toothpick inserted near the center comes out clean (top will appear uneven). Cool completely on a wire rack. Cut into bars.

German Chocolate Brownies

PREP: 20 min. **BAKE:** 25 min. **YIELD:** 16 brownies

Karen Grimes, Stephens City, Virginia

These saucepan brownies capture the rich flavor of a favorite cake with a few easy steps. Broiling the sweet coconut topping makes them gooey and good!

1/2	cup butter
1	package (4 ounces) **German sweet chocolate**, broken into squares
1/2	cup sugar
1	teaspoon vanilla extract
2	eggs, beaten
1	cup all-purpose flour
1/2	teaspoon baking powder
1/4	teaspoon salt

TOPPING:

2	tablespoons butter, melted
1/2	cup packed brown sugar
1	cup flaked coconut
1/2	cup chopped pecans
2	tablespoons corn syrup
2	tablespoons milk

1 In a heavy saucepan or microwave, melt butter and chocolate; stir until smooth. Remove from the heat; cool slightly. Stir in sugar and vanilla. Add eggs; mix well. Combine the flour, baking powder and salt; add to chocolate mixture. Pour into a greased 9-in. square baking pan. Bake at 350° for 18-22 minutes or until a toothpick inserted near the center comes out clean.

2 For topping, combine butter and brown sugar in a bowl. Add the coconut, pecans, corn syrup and milk; mix well. Drop by teaspoonfuls onto warm brownies; spread evenly. Broil several inches from the heat for 2-4 minutes or until top is browned and bubbly. Cool on a wire rack. Cut into bars.

Cashew Blondies

PREP: 15 min. **BAKE:** 25 min. + cooling **YIELD:** 2 dozen

Kathey Skarie, Vergas, Minnesota

These easy-to-make, white chocolate brownies are a hit at potlucks and other gatherings.

2	eggs
2/3	cup sugar
1	teaspoon vanilla extract
8	squares (1 ounce *each*) white baking chocolate, melted and cooled
1/3	cup butter, melted
1-1/2	cups all-purpose flour
1-1/2	teaspoons baking powder
1/4	teaspoon salt
1/2	**to 1 cup chopped salted cashews** *or* pecans

1 In a large mixing bowl, beat the eggs, sugar and vanilla on medium speed for 1 minute. Beat in chocolate and butter. Combine the flour, baking powder and salt; gradually add to chocolate mixture. Stir in cashews. Spread into a greased 9-in. square baking pan.

2 Bake at 350° for 25-30 minutes or until a toothpick inserted near the center comes out clean. Cool on a wire rack. Cut into bars.

Chunky Blond Brownies

PREP: 15 min. **BAKE:** 25 min. + cooling **YIELD:** 2 dozen

Rosemary Dreiske, Keldron, South Dakota

Every bite of these chewy blond brownies is packed with chunks of white and semisweet chocolate and macadamia nuts. It's a potluck offering that stands out.

- 1/2 cup butter, softened
- 3/4 cup sugar
- 3/4 cup packed brown sugar
- 2 eggs
- 2 teaspoons vanilla extract
- 1-1/2 cups all-purpose flour
- 1 teaspoon baking powder
- 1/2 teaspoon salt
- 1 cup vanilla *or* white chips
- 1 cup semisweet chocolate chunks
- 1 jar (3-1/2 ounces) macadamia nuts *or* 3/4 cup blanched almonds, chopped, *divided*

1 In a large mixing bowl, cream butter and sugars until light and fluffy. Add eggs and vanilla; mix well. Combine the flour, baking powder and salt; add to creamed mixture and mix well. Stir in the vanilla chips, chocolate chunks and 1/2 cup nuts.

2 Spoon into a greased 13-in. x 9-in. x 2-in. baking pan; spread to evenly cover bottom of pan. Sprinkle with the remaining nuts. Bake at 350° for 25-30 minutes or until top begins to crack and is golden brown. Cool on a wire rack. Cut into bars.

CHUNKY BLOND BROWNIES

COCONUT PECAN BLONDIES

Coconut Pecan Blondies

PREP: 10 min. **BAKE:** 30 min. + cooling
YIELD: 16 brownies

Anna Tokash Henry, Keller, Texas

Here's a classic white chocolate brownie that's perfect when feeding a smaller group.

- 1 egg
- 3/4 cup plus 2 tablespoons packed brown sugar
- 1/2 cup butter, melted and cooled
- 1-1/2 teaspoons vanilla extract
- 3/4 cup plus 2 tablespoons all-purpose flour
- 1/2 teaspoon baking soda
- 1/8 teaspoon salt
- 3/4 cup coarsely chopped pecans, toasted
- 2/3 cup flaked coconut
- 4 squares (1 ounce *each*) white baking chocolate, coarsely chopped

1 In a large mixing bowl, beat egg and brown sugar for 3 minutes. Add butter and vanilla; mix well. Combine the flour, baking soda and salt; gradually add to the brown sugar mixture, beating just until blended. Stir in the pecans, coconut and white chocolate.

2 Spread into a greased 8-in. square baking dish. Bake at 325° for 30-40 minutes or until a toothpick inserted near the center comes out with moist crumbs (do not overbake). Cool on a wire rack. Cut into bars.

Butterscotch Brownies

PREP: 15 min. **BAKE:** 20 min. **YIELD:** about 2 dozen

Lois Culberson, Pana, Illinois

Brownies get an extra-special, rich flavor from butterscotch chips and marshmallows in this recipe.

- 3/4 **cup butter**
- 1 **cup butterscotch chips**
- 1-1/2 **cups all-purpose flour**
- 2/3 **cup packed brown sugar**
- 2 **teaspoons baking powder**
- 1/4 **teaspoon salt**
- 2 **eggs**
- 2 **teaspoons vanilla extract**
- 2 **cups miniature marshmallows**
- 2 **cups semisweet chocolate chips**
- 1/2 **cup chopped walnuts**

1 In a saucepan, melt butter and butterscotch chips; stir until smooth. Cool. In a large mixing bowl, combine the flour, brown sugar, baking powder and salt. Add the eggs, vanilla and butterscotch mixture; mix well (batter will be thick). Fold in the marshmallows, chocolate chips and walnuts.

2 Spread into a well-greased 15-in. x 10-in. x 1-in. baking pan. Bake at 350° for 20-25 minutes or until a toothpick inserted near the center comes out clean. Cool on a wire rack. Cut into bars.

Maple Butterscotch Brownies

PREP: 15 min. **BAKE:** 30 min. + cooling
YIELD: 16 brownies

Grace Vanhold, Rochester, New York

Here's a great treat when cooking for a smaller group. But with these brownies' terrific maple flavor, don't be surprised if you're asked to make more!

- 1-1/4 **cups packed brown sugar**
- 1/2 **cup butter, melted**
- 1-1/2 **teaspoons maple flavoring**
- 2 **eggs**
- 1-1/2 **cups all-purpose flour**
- 1 **teaspoon baking powder**
- 1 **cup chopped walnuts**
- **Confectioners' sugar, optional**

1 In a bowl, combine the brown sugar, butter and maple flavoring. Add the eggs, one at a time, beating well after each addition. Combine flour and baking powder; add to egg mixture. Stir in the nuts.

2 Pour into a greased 9-in. square baking pan. Bake at 350° for 27-32 minutes or until a toothpick inserted near the center comes out clean. Cool on a wire rack. Dust with confectioners' sugar if desired. Cut into bars.

Oatmeal Brownies

PREP: 15 min. **BAKE:** 25 min. + cooling **YIELD:** 5 dozen

Jennifer Trenhaile, Emerson, Nebraska

Top these M&M-studded fudgy brownies with ice cream for a fabulous dessert.

- 1-1/2 **cups quick-cooking oats**
- 1 **cup M&M miniature baking bits**
- 1/2 **cup all-purpose flour**
- 1/2 **cup packed brown sugar**
- 1/2 **cup chopped walnuts**
- 1/2 **teaspoon baking soda**
- 1/2 **cup butter, melted**
- 1 **package fudge brownie mix (13-inch x 9-inch pan size)**

1 In a bowl, combine the oats, baking bits, flour, sugar, walnuts, baking soda and butter. Set aside 1 cup for topping. Pat the remaining mixture into a greased 15-in. x 10-in. x 1-in. baking pan. Prepare brownie batter according to package directions. Spread over the crust. Sprinkle with the reserved oat mixture.

2 Bake at 350° for 25-30 minutes or until a toothpick inserted near the center comes out clean. Cool on a wire rack. Cut into bars.

OATMEAL BROWNIES

Peanut Butter Swirl Brownies

PREP: 15 min. **BAKE:** 25 min. + cooling **YIELD:** 3 dozen

Linda Craig
Hay River, Northwest Territories

A delicious duo of peanut better and chocolate makes this tempting treat extra special. The marbled look prompts curious tasters—the flavor brings them back for seconds.

- 1/2 cup butter, softened
- 2/3 cup sugar
- 1/2 cup packed brown sugar
- 2 eggs
- 2 tablespoons milk
- 3/4 cup all-purpose flour
- 1/2 teaspoon baking powder
- 1/4 teaspoon salt
- 1/4 cup creamy peanut butter
- 1/3 cup peanut butter chips
- 1/3 cup baking cocoa
- 1/2 cup semisweet chocolate chips

1 In a large mixing bowl, cream butter and sugars until light and fluffy. Add eggs and milk; mix well. Combine the flour, baking powder and salt; add to creamed mixture and mix well.

2 Divide batter in half. To one portion, add peanut butter and peanut butter chips; mix well. To the other portion, add the cocoa and chocolate chips; mix well.

3 In a greased 9-in. square baking pan, spoon chocolate batter in eight mounds in a checker-board pattern. Spoon seven mounds of peanut butter batter between the chocolate batter. Cut through batters with a knife to swirl.

4 Bake at 350° for 25-30 minutes or until a tooth-pick inserted near the center comes out clean. Cool on a wire rack. Cut into bars.

PEANUT BUTTER SWIRL BROWNIES

problem-solving pointers
for Bars & Brownies

BAKED UNEVENLY

- The batter wasn't spread evenly in the pan.
- The oven rack wasn't level.

ARE OVERBAKED

- A pan larger than called for in the recipe was used, causing the batter to be thin and dry.
- Oven temperature is too high. Check with an oven thermometer.
- Next time, check the bars 5 minutes sooner than the baking time given in the recipe.

ARE GUMMY

- A pan smaller than called for in the recipe was used.

ARE TOUGH

- Stir in dry ingredients with a wooden spoon and don't overmix, which can develop the gluten in the flour and cause the bars to be tough.

HAVE A SOGGY CRUST

- The crust was not baked long enough before placing the filling on top.

HAVE A CRUMBLY CRUST

- Next time, cut in a little more butter so that the crust will stick together.

CRUMBLE WHEN THEY ARE CUT

- Cool the bars completely before cutting.
- Use a sawing motion when cutting.
- Warm the blade of knife in hot water, dry, then cut. Clean and rewarm the knife after each cut.

Cakes

secrets for
successful butter cakes

- Use butter, stick margarine (with at least 80% oil) or shortening. The fat should be softened (at room temperature), meaning it is pliable when touched. Whipped, tub, soft, liquid or reduced-fat products should not be used.

- Measure ingredients accurately, using the measuring tools and techniques suggested on pages 7 and 8.

- Arrange the oven racks so that the cake will bake in the center of the oven.

- Preheat oven for 10 to 15 minutes before baking.

- Most butter cake recipes call for creaming the butter and sugar. Beat the softened butter or shortening and sugar with an electric mixer or wooden spoon to a light and fluffy consistency, about 5 minutes.

- For better volume, allow eggs to stand at room temperature for 30 minutes before using. Or, place eggs in their shell in a bowl of warm water while assembling the remaining ingredients.

- Mix dry ingredients together to evenly distribute the leavener throughout the flour. This will ensure that it's evenly incorporated into the batter.

- Stop the mixer occasionally—or between additions of ingredients—and scrape the batter down sides of bowl with a rubber or plastic spatula.

- It's best to use the pan size recommended in the recipe. For substitutions, check the Bakeware Substitution Chart on page 10. Baking times may need to be adjusted.

- For a tender golden crust, use aluminum pans with a dull rather than shiny or dark finish. If using glass baking dishes, reduce the oven temperature 25°.

- Grease and flour baking pans for butter cakes that will be removed from the pans. Cakes that will be served from the pans should be greased but not floured. Some cake recipes call for the pan to be lined with waxed paper for easier removal of the cake from the pan. (See Lining a Baking Pan with Waxed Paper on page 117.)

- Fill pans half to three-fourths full. A thin batter will rise more than a heavy batter, so allow more room for thin batters to rise.

- Pour thinner batters into pans, then tap pans on the countertop to remove air bubbles. Spoon firmer batters into pans, then spread gently to even out the batter.

- Leave at least 1 in. of space between pans and between pans and sides of oven for good heat circulation. If using two oven racks, stagger pans in the oven so that they are not directly over one another. Switch pan positions and rotate pans from front to back halfway through baking.

- Use a kitchen timer. Check for doneness at the minimum recommended baking time, then check every 2 minutes after that. Butter cakes are done when a toothpick inserted near the center of the cake comes out clean. (See Testing Butter Cakes for Doneness on page 118.)

- Cool cakes for 10 minutes in the pan, unless recipe directs otherwise. Loosen the cake by running a knife around the edge of the pan. Turn out onto a wire rack, place another rack over the cake and flip right side up. Cool completely before filling or frosting unless directed otherwise by recipe.

- If a cake sticks to the pan and will not come out when inverted, return to a heated oven for 1 minute, then try again to turn it out.

- Use a serrated knife or use a sawing motion when cutting. Warm the blade of knife in hot water, then dry and make a cut. Clean and rewarm knife before each cut.

the basics of *cakes*

Cakes add a festive air to any meal and usually make an appearance at special-occasion dinners. Cakes can be rich and moist, dense, buttery or airy and are divided into two basic categories:

- Butter cakes get their name because the batter is made from creaming fat—such as butter or shortening—with sugar. The creaming traps air in the batter; this trapped air expands during baking and gives the cake its height. Butter cakes have a fine moist texture and a tender crumb.

- Foam cakes contain a high proportion of eggs or egg whites to flour. Beaten eggs give foam cakes their light, fluffy texture.

- There are three kinds of foam cakes: angel food, sponge and chiffon. Angel food is made with whipped egg whites but without fat and has a delicate crumb. Sponge cake also is made without fat but contains both egg whites and yolks (the fat in the cake comes only from egg yolks). Sponge cakes have a richer texture than angel food. Chiffon cake, which has the richest texture of the three types, is made with fat and both egg whites and yolks.

Butter Cakes

White Layer Cake

PREP: 15 min. **BAKE:** 30 min. + cooling
YIELD: 10-12 servings

Taste of Home Test Kitchen

Every recipe file should contain a standard delicious cake like this. Topped with your favorite flavor of frosting, it's great for any occasion.

 1/2   cup butter, softened
1-1/2   cups sugar
    4   egg whites
    2   teaspoons vanilla extract
    2   cups all-purpose flour
    1   teaspoon baking powder
 1/2   teaspoon baking soda
 1/4   teaspoon salt
1-1/3   cups buttermilk
2-1/2   cups frosting of your choice

1 In a large mixing bowl, cream butter and sugar until light and fluffy. Add egg whites, one at a time, beating well after each addition. Beat in vanilla. Combine the flour, baking powder, baking soda and salt; add to creamed mixture alternately with buttermilk, beating well after each addition.

2 Spread evenly into two greased and floured 9-in. round baking pans. Bake at 350° for 30-35 minutes or until a toothpick inserted near the center comes out clean. Cool for 10 minutes before removing from pans to wire racks to cool completely. Spread frosting between layers and over the top and sides of cake.

Yellow Layer Cake

PREP: 10 min. **BAKE:** 25 min. + cooling
YIELD: 10-12 servings

Taste of Home Test Kitchen

Instead of turning to a boxed cake mix, why not try your hand at this easy recipe for a basic yellow cake? You just can't beat the homemade goodness!

 2/3   cup butter, softened
1-3/4   cups sugar
    2   eggs
1-1/2   teaspoons vanilla extract
2-1/2   cups all-purpose flour
2-1/2   teaspoons baking powder
 1/2   teaspoon salt
1-1/4   cups milk
2-1/2   cups frosting of your choice

1 In a large mixing bowl, cream butter and sugar until light and fluffy. Add eggs, one at a time, beating well after each addition. Stir in vanilla. Combine the flour, baking powder and salt; add to the creamed mixture alternately with milk, beating well after each addition.

2 Pour into two greased and floured 9-in. round baking pans. Bake at 350° for 25-30 minutes or until a toothpick inserted near the center comes out clean. Cool for 10 minutes before removing from pans to wire racks to cool completely. Spread frosting between layers and over the top and sides of cake.

Butter Pecan Cake

PREP: 40 min. **BAKE:** 25 min. + cooling
YIELD: 12-16 servings

Becky Miller, Tallahassee, Florida

Pecans and butter give this cake the same irresistible flavor as the popular ice cream.

2-2/3   **cups chopped pecans**
1-1/4   **cups butter, softened, *divided***
   2   **cups sugar**
   4   **eggs**
   2   **teaspoons vanilla extract**
   3   **cups all-purpose flour**
   2   **teaspoons baking powder**
1/2   **teaspoon salt**
   1   **cup milk**
FROSTING:
   1   **cup butter, softened**
   8   **to 8-1/2 cups confectioners' sugar**
   1   **can (5 ounces) evaporated milk**
   2   **teaspoons vanilla extract**

1 Place pecans and 1/4 cup of butter in a baking pan. Bake at 350° for 20-25 minutes or until toasted, stirring frequently; set aside. In a large mixing bowl, cream sugar and remaining butter until light and fluffy. Add eggs, one at a time, beating well after each addition. Stir in vanilla. Combine the flour, baking powder and salt; add to the creamed mixture alternately with milk, beating well after each addition. Stir in 1-1/3 cups of toasted pecans.

2 Pour into three greased and floured 9-in. round baking pans. Bake at 350° for 25-30 minutes or until a toothpick inserted near the center comes out clean. Cool for 10 minutes before removing from pans to wire racks to cool completely.

3 For frosting, cream butter and confectioners' sugar in a large mixing bowl until light and fluffy. Add milk and vanilla; beat until smooth. Stir in remaining toasted pecans. Spread frosting between layers and over top and sides of cake.

Spice Cake

PREP: 25 min. **BAKE:** 25 min. + cooling
YIELD: 12 servings

Linda Peffer, Denison, Iowa

If you don't have time to make Fluffy White Frosting, this cake would also be quite tasty with the Cream Cheese Frosting on page 165.

1/2   **cup butter, softened**
   2   **cups packed dark brown sugar**
   2   **eggs**
   2   **cups all-purpose flour**
   2   **teaspoons ground cinnamon**
1/2   **teaspoon baking soda**
1/2   **teaspoon ground cloves**
1/2   **teaspoon ground nutmeg**
   1   **cup buttermilk**
Fluffy White Frosting (page 165)

1 In a large mixing bowl, cream butter and sugar until light and fluffy. Add eggs, one at a time, beating well after each addition. Combine the flour, cinnamon, baking soda, cloves and nutmeg; add to creamed mixture alternately with buttermilk, beating well after each addition.

2 Pour into two greased 9-in. round baking pans. Bake at 350° for 25-30 minutes or until a toothpick inserted near the center comes out clean. Cool for 10 minutes before removing from pans to wire racks to cool completely.

3 Spread frosting between layers and over the top and sides of cake. Do not seal cake tightly when storing.

preparing a *cake pan*

1. Grease the sides and bottom of the pan by spreading shortening with a paper towel over the interior of the pan.

2. Sprinkle 1 to 2 tablespoons of flour into the greased pan; tilt the pan to coat bottom and sides. Turn pan over and tap to remove excess flour.

Sunny Coconut Cake

PREP: 20 min. **BAKE:** 30 min. + cooling
YIELD: 12-14 servings

Annette Buckner, Charlotte, North Carolina

For a refreshing finale to any dinner, present this appealing cake. Orange gelatin in the batter and mandarin oranges on top give it beautiful color.

- 2 cups (16 ounces) sour cream
- 2 cups sugar
- 1/4 cup orange juice
- 1 package (14 ounces) flaked coconut
- 1 package (18-1/4 ounces) yellow cake mix
- 1 package (3 ounces) orange gelatin
- 1 cup water
- 1/3 cup vegetable oil
- 2 eggs
- 1 cup heavy whipping cream
- 1 can (11 ounces) mandarin oranges, well drained

1 In a small mixing bowl, combine the sour cream, sugar and orange juice. Beat in coconut. Cover and refrigerate. In a large mixing bowl, combine the dry cake mix, gelatin powder, water, oil and eggs; mix well.

2 Pour into two greased and floured 9-in. round baking pans. Bake at 350° for 30-35 minutes or until a toothpick inserted near the center comes out clean. Cool for 10 minutes before removing from pans to wire racks to cool completely.

3 Split each cake into two horizontal layers. Set aside 1 cup of the coconut filling; spread remaining filling between cake layers. Refrigerate. In a chilled large mixing bowl, beat cream until stiff peaks form; fold into reserved filling. Frost the top and sides of cake. Garnish with oranges. Store in the refrigerator.

Pineapple Layer Cake

PREP: 45 min. + cooling **BAKE:** 30 min. + cooling
YIELD: 12 servings

Debbie Norling, Harris, Minnesota

A sunny yellow filling and topping plus the fluffy white frosting complements this tender yellow cake.

- 1/2 cup shortening
- 1-2/3 cups sugar
- 3 egg yolks
- 1 egg
- 1/2 teaspoon vanilla extract
- 2-1/2 cups cake flour
- 1 teaspoon salt
- 1/2 teaspoon baking powder
- 1/2 teaspoon baking soda
- 1-1/4 cups buttermilk

FILLING:

- 1/2 cup sugar
- 3 tablespoons cornstarch
- 1/2 teaspoon salt
- 1 can (8 ounces) crushed pineapple
- 1 tablespoon butter
- 1 teaspoon lemon juice

Fluffy White Frosting (page 165)

1 In a mixing bowl, cream shortening and sugar until light and fluffy. Add egg yolks and egg, one at a time, beating well after each. Add vanilla. Combine the flour, salt, baking powder and baking soda; add to the creamed mixture alternately with buttermilk, beating well after each addition.

2 Pour into two greased and floured 9-in. round baking pans. Bake at 350° for 30-35 minutes or until a toothpick inserted near the center comes out clean. Cool for 10 minutes before removing from pans to wire racks.

3 In a saucepan, combine the sugar, cornstarch and salt. Drain the pineapple, reserving juice. Add pineapple to pan. Add water to juice to measure 3/4 cup; pour into pan and mix well. Bring to a boil over medium heat; cook and stir for 2 minutes or until thickened. Remove from the heat. Add butter and lemon juice. Cool completely without stirring.

PINEAPPLE LAYER CAKE

4 Set aside a third of the filling. Spread remaining filling between cake layers. Spread reserved filling in a 4-in. circle in the center of top layer. Frost the sides of cake and around the filling on top with Fluffy White Frosting.

Buttermilk Banana Cake

PREP: 35 min. **BAKE:** 25 min. + cooling
YIELD: 12-16 servings

Arlene Grenz, Linton, North Dakota

A rich, light frosting tastefully tops off this banana cake. The pecan filling nicely complements the banana flavor.

3/4	cup butter, softened
1	cup sugar
1/2	cup packed brown sugar
2	eggs
1	cup mashed ripe bananas (about 2 medium)
1	teaspoon vanilla extract
2	cups cake flour
1	teaspoon baking powder
1	teaspoon baking soda
1/2	teaspoon salt
1/2	cup buttermilk

FILLING:

1/2	cup sugar
2	tablespoons all-purpose flour
1/4	teaspoon salt
1/2	cup half-and-half cream
2	tablespoons butter
1	teaspoon vanilla extract
1/2	cup chopped pecans

FROSTING:

2	cups heavy whipping cream
1/4	cup confectioners' sugar

1 In a large mixing bowl, cream butter and sugars until light and fluffy. Add eggs; beat for 2 minutes. Add bananas and vanilla; beat for 2 minutes. Combine the flour, baking powder, baking soda and salt; add to creamed mixture alternately with buttermilk, beating well after each addition.

2 Pour into two greased and floured 9-in. round baking pans. Bake at 375° for 25-30 minutes or until a toothpick inserted near the center comes out clean. Cool for 10 minutes before removing from pans to wire racks to cool completely.

3 For filling, combine the sugar, flour and salt in a saucepan. Stir in half-and-half cream until smooth; add butter. Bring to a boil; cook and stir for 2 minutes. Remove from the heat; stir in vanilla and pecans. Cool. Spread between cake layers.

4 For frosting, beat heavy whipping cream in a chilled large mixing bowl until soft peaks form. Gradually add confectioners' sugar, a tablespoon at a time, beating until stiff peaks form. Spread over top and sides of cake. Store in the refrigerator.

Strawberry Cake

PREP: 25 min. **BAKE:** 25 min. + cooling
YIELD: 12-16 servings

Pam Anderson, Billings, Montana

When you cut into this cake, people will be delighted to see the pretty pink tint. To hint at the flavor before cutting, garnish the top with whole strawberries.

1	package (18-1/4 ounces) white cake mix
1	package (3 ounces) strawberry gelatin
1	cup water
1/2	cup vegetable oil
4	egg whites
1/2	cup mashed unsweetened strawberries
3-1/2	cups whipped cream *or* frosting of your choice

1 In a large mixing bowl, combine the dry cake mix, gelatin powder, water and oil. Beat on low speed for 1 minute or until moistened; beat on medium for 4 minutes. In a small mixing bowl and with clean beaters, beat egg whites on high speed until stiff peaks form. Fold egg whites and mashed strawberries into cake batter.

2 Pour into three greased and floured 9-in. round baking pans. Bake at 350° for 20-25 minutes or until a toothpick inserted near the center comes out clean. Cool for 10 minutes before removing from pans to wire racks to cool completely. Frost with whipped cream or frosting. If frosted with whipped cream, store in the refrigerator.

ORANGE BONBON CAKE

Orange Bonbon Cake

PREP: 1 hour **BAKE:** 25 min. + cooling
YIELD: 12-16 servings

Ann Loveland, Dothan, Alabama

You'll get real orange flavor in every bite of this cake. Orange juice is used in the cake's layers, filling and frosting!

7	egg whites
3/4	cup butter, softened
2	cups sugar
1/3	cup sour cream
1-1/4	teaspoons vanilla extract
2-2/3	cups all-purpose flour
2-1/2	teaspoons baking powder
1/2	teaspoon salt
1/4	teaspoon baking soda
2/3	cup orange juice

FILLING:

3/4	cup sugar
2	tablespoons all-purpose flour
1/2	cup orange juice
1/2	cup butter, melted
5	egg yolks, beaten
1/2	cup chopped pecans
1/2	cup flaked coconut

FROSTING:

1/4	cup all-purpose flour
1	cup orange juice
1/2	cup butter, softened
1/2	cup shortening
1	cup sugar
1	teaspoon vanilla extract
1/2	teaspoon salt

Candied fruit, optional

1 Let egg whites stand at room temperature for 30 minutes. In a large mixing bowl, cream butter and sugar until light and fluffy. Beat in the sour cream and vanilla. Combine the flour, baking powder, salt and baking soda; add to creamed mixture alternately with orange juice. In another large mixing bowl and with clean beaters, beat egg whites until stiff peaks form; fold into batter.

2 Pour into two greased and floured 9-in. round baking pans. Bake at 350° for 35-40 minutes or until a toothpick inserted near the center comes out clean. Cool for 10 minutes before removing from pans to wire racks to cool completely.

3 For filling, combine sugar and flour in a saucepan. Gradually stir in orange juice and butter until smooth. Cook and stir over medium-high heat until thickened and bubbly. Reduce heat; cook and stir 2 minutes longer. Remove from the heat. Stir a small amount of hot filling into egg yolks; return all to pan, stirring constantly. Bring to a gentle boil; cook and stir 2 minutes longer. Remove from the heat; stir in the pecans and coconut. Cool to room temperature without stirring.

4 For the frosting, combine flour and orange juice in a saucepan until smooth. Bring to a boil over medium heat; cook and stir for 2 minutes or until thickened. Cool to room temperature. In another large mixing bowl, cream the butter, shortening and sugar until light and fluffy. Beat in vanilla and salt. Add cooled orange juice mixture; beat for 5 minutes or until fluffy.

5 Split each cake into two horizontal layers; place one on a serving plate. Spread with a third of the filling. Repeat layers twice. Top with remaining cake layer. Frost top and sides of cake. Garnish with candied fruit if desired.

Cookies-and-Cream Cake

PREP: 25 min. **BAKE:** 30 min. + cooling
YIELD: 12 servings

Pat Habiger, Spearville, Kansas

This moist, fun-to-eat cake will remind you of the classic chocolate sandwich cookies.

1	package (18-1/4 ounces) white cake mix
1-1/4	cups water
1/3	cup vegetable oil
3	egg whites
1	cup coarsely crushed cream-filled chocolate sandwich cookies (about 8)

FROSTING:
- 4 to 4-1/2 cups confectioners' sugar
- 1/2 cup shortening
- 1/4 cup milk
- 1 teaspoon vanilla extract

Additional cream-filled chocolate sandwich cookies, halved *and/or* crushed, optional

1 In a large mixing bowl, combine the dry cake mix, water, oil and egg whites. Beat on low speed until moistened; beat on high for 2 minutes. Gently fold in crushed cookies.

2 Pour into two greased and floured 9-in. round baking pans. Bake at 350° for 30-35 minutes or until a toothpick inserted near the center comes out clean. Cool for 10 minutes before removing from pans to wire racks to cool completely.

3 For frosting, beat the sugar, shortening, milk and vanilla in another large mixing bowl until smooth. Spread frosting between layers and over top and sides of cake. If desired, decorate the top with cookie halves and the sides with crushed cookies.

Coconut Layer Cake

PREP: 30 min. **BAKE:** 40 min. + cooling
YIELD: 12-16 servings

Marilyn Dick, Centralia, Missouri

You can make this delectable coconut cake without the pecans if you prefer.

- 5 eggs, *separated*
- 1/2 cup butter, softened
- 1/2 cup shortening

COCONUT LAYER CAKE

To easily remove cakes from the pan, consider lining the pan with waxed paper. Place pan on a piece of waxed paper. Trace the shape of the pan onto the waxed paper, then cut out. Grease the pan; place the waxed paper in the pan and grease it. Remove the paper as soon as the baked cake is inverted onto a wire rack to cool.

- 2 cups sugar
- 1 teaspoon vanilla extract
- 2 cups all-purpose flour
- 1/2 teaspoon baking soda
- 1 cup buttermilk
- 2 cups flaked coconut
- 1/2 cup chopped pecans

FROSTING:
- 1 package (8 ounces) cream cheese, softened
- 4 cups (1 pound) confectioners' sugar
- 1/4 cup butter, softened
- 1 teaspoon vanilla extract
- 1/4 cup flaked coconut, toasted

Pecan halves

1 Let eggs stand at room temperature for 30 minutes. In a large mixing bowl, cream the butter, shortening and sugar until light and fluffy. Add egg yolks and beat well. Stir in vanilla. Combine flour and baking soda; add to creamed mixture alternately with buttermilk, beating well after each addition. Stir in coconut and pecans. In a small mixing bowl and with clean beaters, beat egg whites until stiff peaks form; gently fold into batter.

2 Pour into two greased and floured 9-in. round baking pans. Bake at 325° for 40-45 minutes or until a toothpick inserted near the center comes out clean. Cool for 10 minutes before removing from pans to wire racks to cool completely.

3 For frosting, beat the cream cheese, sugar, butter and vanilla in a large mixing bowl until smooth and creamy. Spread between layers and over top and sides of cake. Sprinkle with coconut; garnish with pecans. Store in the refrigerator.

Peanut Butter Lover's Cake

PREP: 20 min. + cooling **BAKE:** 25 min. + cooling
YIELD: 12-14 servings

Teresa Mozingo, Camden, South Carolina

The combination of chocolate and peanut butter gives this cake the flavor of a popular candy bar. Folks will be impressed when you serve this cake.

- 3 **eggs**
- 1-2/3 **cups sugar,** *divided*
- 1-1/2 **cups milk,** *divided*
- 3 **squares (1 ounce** *each***) unsweetened chocolate, finely chopped**
- 1/2 **cup shortening**
- 1 **teaspoon vanilla extract**
- 2 **cups cake flour**
- 1 **teaspoon baking soda**
- 1/2 **teaspoon salt**

PEANUT BUTTER FROSTING:

- 2 **packages (8 ounces** *each***) cream cheese, softened**
- 1 **can (14 ounces) sweetened condensed milk**
- 1-1/2 **cups peanut butter**
- 1/4 **cup salted peanuts, chopped**
- 3 **milk chocolate candy bars (1.55 ounces** *each***), broken into squares**

1 In a saucepan, whisk one egg until blended. Stir in 2/3 cup sugar, 1/2 cup milk and chocolate. Cook and stir over medium heat until chocolate is melted and mixture just comes to a boil. Remove from the heat; cool to room temperature.

2 In a large mixing bowl, cream shortening and remaining sugar until light and fluffy. Add remaining eggs, one at a time, beating well after each addition. Beat in vanilla. Combine the flour, baking soda and salt; add to creamed mixture alternately with remaining milk, beating well after each addition. Add chocolate mixture; mix well.

3 Pour into three greased and floured 9-in. round baking pans. Bake at 325° for 25-30 minutes or until a toothpick inserted near the center comes out clean. Cool for 10 minutes before removing from pans to wire racks to cool completely.

4 For frosting, beat cream cheese in a large mixing bowl until light and fluffy. Gradually add milk and peanut butter, beating well after each addition. Spread between layers and over top and sides of cake. Sprinkle with peanuts. Garnish with candy bars. Store in the refrigerator.

testing
butter cakes
for doneness

Insert a toothpick in several spots near the center of the cake. If the toothpick comes out clean, the cake is done.

If the toothpick comes out with crumbs, the cake needs to bake longer.

PEANUT BUTTER LOVER'S CAKE

VICTORIAN STRAWBERRY CHOCOLATE CAKE

Victorian Strawberry Chocolate Cake

PREP: 35 min. **BAKE:** 30 min. + cooling
YIELD: 10-12 servings

Amy Parker, Ponca City, Oklahoma

With its alternating light and dark layers, rich chocolate frosting and fresh strawberry garnishes, this heart-shaped cake will be a hit for any occasion.

- 2 cups boiling water
- 1 cup baking cocoa
- 1 cup butter, softened
- 2-1/2 cups sugar
- 4 eggs
- 1-1/2 teaspoons vanilla extract
- 2-3/4 cups all-purpose flour
- 2 teaspoons baking powder
- 2 teaspoons baking soda
- 1 quart fresh strawberries
- 1 cup (6 ounces) semisweet chocolate chips, melted

FROSTING:
- 2/3 cup shortening
- 1 package (32 ounces) confectioners' sugar
- 1/2 cup water

ICING:
- 1-1/2 cups semisweet chocolate chips
- 1/3 cup heavy whipping cream

Chocolate shavings and additional confectioners' sugar, optional

1 In a small bowl, stir water into cocoa until blended; set aside. In a large mixing bowl, cream butter and sugar until light and fluffy. Add eggs, one at a time, beating well after each addition. Beat in vanilla. Combine the flour, baking powder and baking soda; add to the creamed mixture alternately with cocoa mixture, beating well after each addition.

2 Pour into two greased and floured 9-in. heart-shaped pans. Bake at 350° for 35-40 minutes or until a toothpick inserted near the center comes out clean. Cool for 10 minutes before removing from pans to wire racks to cool completely.

3 Slice 10 strawberries; set aside. Dip remaining whole strawberries into melted chocolate, about three-fourths to top. Place on a waxed paper-lined baking sheet; refrigerate until set.

4 For frosting, cream shortening and confectioners' sugar in a large mixing bowl until light and fluffy; gradually add water, beating until smooth. Spread between layers and over top and sides of cake. Set aside to dry, about 30 minutes.

5 For icing, heat chocolate chips and cream in a saucepan over medium heat until chocolate is melted, stirring occasionally. Spread over frosted cake until smooth. Refrigerate until set. Before serving, arrange two rows of sliced strawberries on top of cake in a heart shape. Fill center with chocolate shavings and dust with confectioners' sugar if desired. Place dipped strawberries around base. Store in the refrigerator.

Editor's Note: Cake may also be baked in two greased and floured 9-in. square pans.

leveling *cake layers*

Stacking layers for a layered cake is easier when the layers are level. When the cake is cool, use a long serrated knife to slice the high spot from the bottom layer of a two-layer cake or the bottom and middle layers of a three-layer cake. You can trim off the crown of the top layer or leave it for a domed effect.

Raspberry Chocolate Cake

PREP: 45 min. + standing **BAKE:** 35 min. + cooling
YIELD: 12-16 servings

Marlene Sanders, Paradise, Texas

With this elegant chocolate creation, you'll get a triple treat—raspberry flavor on the cake and in the filling and frosting.

3	cups sugar
2-3/4	cups all-purpose flour
1	cup baking cocoa
2	teaspoons baking soda
1-1/2	teaspoons salt
3/4	teaspoon baking powder
1-1/4	cups buttermilk
3/4	cup vegetable oil
3	teaspoons vanilla extract
3	eggs
1-1/2	cups strong brewed coffee, room temperature

FILLING:

3	tablespoons all-purpose flour
6	tablespoons milk
6	tablespoons shortening
3	tablespoons butter, softened
3	cups confectioners' sugar
2	tablespoons raspberry liqueur
1/4	teaspoon salt
2	drops red food coloring, optional
4	tablespoons raspberry jam, melted

FROSTING:

1	package (8 ounces) cold cream cheese
1/3	cup butter, softened
1/2	cup baking cocoa
1	tablespoon raspberry liqueur
4	cups confectioners' sugar

Raspberries and chocolate curls, optional

1 Line three greased 9-in. round baking pans with waxed paper and grease paper; set aside. In a large mixing bowl, combine the first six ingredients.

Combine the buttermilk, oil and vanilla; add to the dry ingredients. Add eggs, one at a time, beating well after each addition; beat for 2 minutes. Gradually add coffee (batter will be thin).

2 Pour batter into prepared pans. Bake at 350° for 35-40 minutes or until a toothpick inserted near the center comes out clean. Cool for 10 minutes before removing from pans to wire racks to cool completely; discard waxed paper.

3 For filling, in a saucepan, whisk together flour and milk until smooth. Cook over medium heat for 1 minute or until thickened, stirring constantly. Remove from the heat and let stand until cool. In a large mixing bowl, cream shortening and butter. Gradually add confectioners' sugar; mix well. Gradually add cooled milk mixture; beat for 4 minutes or until light and fluffy. Beat in liqueur, salt and food coloring if desired.

4 Level tops of cakes if necessary. Place one layer on a serving plate; spread with about 2 tablespoons jam. Place remaining layers on waxed paper; spread one of the remaining layers with remaining jam. Let stand for 30 minutes. Spread 1/2 cup filling over layer on the plate to within 1/4 in. of edges. Top with jam-covered cake, then spread with remaining filling. Top with the remaining cake layer.

5 In a large mixing bowl, beat cream cheese and butter until smooth. Add cocoa and liqueur; mix well. Gradually beat in confectioners' sugar until light and fluffy. Frost top and sides of cake; top with raspberries and chocolate curls if desired. Store in the refrigerator.

HEAVENLY WHITE CHOCOLATE CAKE

Heavenly White Chocolate Cake

PREP: 20 min. **BAKE:** 25 min. + cooling
YIELD: 14-16 servings

Norma Van Devander, Calais, Maine

Looking for a change from heavy, chocolate desserts? Try this luscious white chocolate cake! It's wonderfully moist and slices well.

- 1 **cup butter, softened**
- 2 **cups sugar**
- 4 **squares (1 ounce *each*) white baking chocolate, melted and cooled**
- 4 **eggs**
- 1-1/2 **teaspoons clear vanilla extract**
- 3 **cups all-purpose flour**
- 1 **teaspoon baking soda**
- 1 **cup buttermilk**
- 1/2 **cup water**
- 1/2 **cup chopped pecans, toasted**

FROSTING:
- 2 **packages (one 8 ounces, one 3 ounces) cream cheese, softened**
- 1/3 **cup butter, softened**
- 4 **squares (1 ounce *each*) white baking chocolate, melted and cooled**
- 1-1/2 **teaspoons clear vanilla extract**
- 6-1/2 **cups confectioners' sugar**

White chocolate curls

1 Line three greased 9-in. round baking pans with waxed paper and grease the paper; set aside. In a large mixing bowl, cream butter and sugar until light and fluffy. Add chocolate; mix well. Add eggs, one at a time, beating well after each. Beat in vanilla. Combine flour and baking soda; add to creamed mixture alternately with buttermilk and water, beating well after each addition. Fold in pecans. Pour batter into prepared pans.

2 Bake at 350° for 23-27 minutes or until a toothpick inserted near the center comes out clean. Cool for 10 minutes before removing from pans to wire racks; discard waxed paper.

3 For frosting, in a large mixing bowl, beat cream cheese and butter until smooth. Add chocolate and vanilla; mix well. Gradually add confectioners' sugar, beating until light and fluffy. Spread frosting between layers and over top and sides of cake. Garnish with chocolate curls. Store in the refrigerator.

TRIPLE-LAYER BROWNIE CAKE

3 For frosting, melt semisweet chocolate in a heavy saucepan over medium heat. Gradually stir in cream until well blended. Heat to a gentle boil; boil and stir for 1 minute. Transfer to a large mixing bowl. Refrigerate for 2-3 hours or until mixture reaches a pudding-like consistency, stirring occasionally. Beat until soft peaks form. Immediately spread between layers and over top and sides of cake. Sprinkle with grated chocolate. Store in the refrigerator.

Triple-Layer Brownie Cake

PREP: 30 min. + chilling **BAKE:** 25 min. + cooling
YIELD: 16-20 servings

Barbara Dean, Littleton, Colorado

A little of this rich brownie cake goes a long way, so you'll have plenty to share with grateful family members and friends. It's a sure way to satisfy chocolate lovers.

1-1/2	cups butter
6	squares (1 ounce *each*) unsweetened chocolate
3	cups sugar
5	eggs
1-1/2	teaspoons vanilla extract
1-1/2	cups all-purpose flour
3/4	teaspoon salt

FROSTING:

2	packages (8 ounces *each*) semisweet baking chocolate
3	cups heavy whipping cream
2	milk chocolate candy bars (1.55 ounces *each*), grated

1 In a heavy saucepan or microwave, melt butter and chocolate; stir until smooth. Stir in sugar. Transfer to a large mixing bowl. Add eggs, one at a time, beating well after each addition. Stir in vanilla. Combine flour and salt; stir into chocolate mixture.

2 Pour into three greased and floured 9-in. round baking pans. Bake at 350° for 23-25 minutes or until a toothpick inserted near the center comes out clean. Cool for 10 minutes before removing from pans to wire racks to cool completely.

Zucchini Fudge Cake

PREP: 20 min. **BAKE:** 25 min. + cooling
YIELD: 10-12 servings

Robert Keith, Rochester, Minnesota

Zucchini makes each bite of this fudgy cake moist and delicious. Chocolate provides the perfect disguise!

1	cup butter, softened
2-1/2	cups sugar
4	eggs
2	teaspoons vanilla extract
3	cups all-purpose flour
1/2	cup baking cocoa
2	teaspoons baking powder
1	teaspoon baking soda
3/4	teaspoon salt
1	cup buttermilk
3	cups shredded zucchini
3-1/2	cups prepared chocolate frosting

1 In a large mixing bowl, cream butter and sugar until light and fluffy. Add the eggs, one at a time, beating well after each addition. Beat in vanilla. Combine the flour, cocoa, baking powder, baking soda and salt; add to the creamed mixture alternately with buttermilk, beating well after each addition. Stir in zucchini.

2 Pour into three greased and floured 9-in. round baking pans. Bake at 350° for 25-30 minutes or until a toothpick inserted near the center comes out clean. Cool for 10 minutes before removing from pans to wire racks to cool completely. Spread frosting between layers and over the top and sides of cake.

Mocha Layer Cake

PREP: 30 min. **BAKE:** 25 min. + cooling
YIELD: 12-14 servings

Mark Brown, Birmingham, Alabama

This rich cake is tall and delicious with a special flavored frosting. It makes a dramatic presentation.

- 5 **eggs,** *separated*
- 1 **cup shortening**
- 2-1/2 **cups sugar**
- 5 **tablespoons strong brewed coffee**
- 2 **teaspoons vanilla extract**
- 3 **cups cake flour**
- 4 **teaspoons baking cocoa**
- 1 **teaspoon baking soda**
- 1/2 **teaspoon salt**
- 1 **cup buttermilk**

FROSTING:
- 5-1/2 **to 6 cups confectioners' sugar**
- 1 **tablespoon baking cocoa**
- 1-1/2 **cups butter, softened**
- 3 **tablespoons plus 1-1/2 teaspoons strong brewed coffee**
- 1-1/2 **teaspoons vanilla extract**

1 Let eggs stand at room temperature for 30 minutes. In a large mixing bowl, cream shortening and sugar until light and fluffy. Add egg yolks, one at a time, beating well after each addition. Beat in coffee and vanilla. Combine the flour, cocoa, baking soda and salt; add to the creamed mixture alternately with buttermilk. In another mixing bowl and with clean beaters, beat egg whites on high speed until stiff peaks form; fold into batter.

2 Pour into three greased and floured 9-in. round baking pans. Bake at 350° for 25-30 minutes or until a toothpick inserted near the center comes out clean. Cool for 10 minutes before removing from pans to wire racks to cool completely.

3 For frosting, combine confectioners' sugar and cocoa. In another large mixing bowl, cream butter and sugar mixture. Beat in coffee and vanilla. Spread between layers and over top and sides of cake.

---

problem-solving pointers
for Butter Cakes

CAKE HAS A SUNKEN CENTER

- Oven temperature was too low. Check temperature with an oven thermometer.
- Cake was underbaked, resulting in a sticky layer in the center of the cake under the top crust.
- Too much sugar was used, resulting in a thick, firm and overly brown crust.
- Too much liquid was used, resulting in a sticky layer above the bottom crust.
- Too much leavener was used, resulting in a chemical or bitter taste.

CAKE HAS A PEAKED OR CRACKED CENTER

- Oven temperature was too high.
- Batter was overbeaten after the flour was added, causing the gluten in the flour to be developed.
- A hard wheat (high-gluten) flour was used. Next time, try a soft wheat flour like cake flour.

CAKE IS HEAVY

- The fat and sugar were not creamed long enough.
- Either too much sugar, flour or fat was used or not enough leavener was used.

CAKE HAS TUNNELS

- Oven temperature was too high.
- Batter was overbeaten after the flour was added, causing the gluten in the flour to be developed.

CAKE IS DRY

- Oven temperature was too high.
- Too small a baking pan was used. The pan should be filled from half to three-fourths full.

CAKE OVERFLOWED PAN

- The cake was overbaked.
- Too small a baking pan was used. The pan should be filled from half to three-fourths full.

CAKE HAS A DARK CRUST

- The baking pan was a dark color. For best results, use aluminum pans with a dull finish.
- Too much sugar was used, resulting in a thick, firm and overly brown crust.

Lemon Meringue Cake

PREP: 30 min. **BAKE:** 40 min. + cooling
YIELD: 6-8 servings

Debra Blair, Glenwood, Minnesota

When you can't decide whether to make a cake or pie, reach for this unique recipe and make both in one!

- 1/4 **cup butter, softened**
- 1/2 **cup sugar**
- 1 **egg**
- 2 **egg yolks**
- 1/2 **teaspoon vanilla extract**
- 1 **cup all-purpose flour**
- 1 **teaspoon baking powder**
- 1/3 **cup milk**

FILLING:
- 3/4 **cup sugar**
- 1/3 **cup all-purpose flour**
- 1 **cup water**
- 2 **egg yolks, lightly beaten**
- 1/4 **cup lemon juice**
- 1 **tablespoon butter**
- 1/2 **teaspoon grated lemon peel**

MERINGUE:
- 4 **egg whites**
- 1/2 **teaspoon cream of tartar**
- 1/2 **cup sugar**

1 In a large mixing bowl, cream butter and sugar until light and fluffy. Add the egg and yolks; mix well. Beat in vanilla. Combine the flour and baking powder; add to the creamed mixture alternately with milk, beating well after each addition.

2 Pour into a greased and floured 9-in. round baking pan. Bake at 350° for 25-30 minutes or until a toothpick inserted near the center comes out clean. Cool for 10 minutes before removing to a wire rack to cool completely.

LEMON MERINGUE CAKE

3 For filling, combine sugar and flour in a heavy saucepan. Stir in water until smooth. Cook and stir over medium-high heat until thickened and bubbly. Reduce heat; cook and stir 2 minutes longer. Remove from the heat. Stir a small amount of hot filling into egg yolks; return all to the pan, stirring constantly. Bring to a gentle boil; cook and stir 2 minutes longer. Remove from the heat. Gently stir in lemon juice, butter and lemon peel. Cool to room temperature without stirring. Place cake on a baking sheet; spoon filling on top of cake to within 1/2 in. of edge.

4 For meringue, let egg whites stand at room temperature for 30 minutes. In a small mixing bowl and with clean beaters, beat egg whites and cream of tartar on medium speed until soft peaks form. Gradually add sugar, 1 tablespoon at a time, beating on high until stiff peaks form. Carefully spread over filling, sealing to edges of cake. Bake at 350° for 12-15 minutes or until lightly browned.

Pistachio Coconut Cake

PREP: 15 min. **BAKE:** 40 min. + cooling
YIELD: 12-15 servings

Arlene Bontager, Haven, Kansas

White cake mix is dressed up with pudding mix and coconut, then is topped off with a pistachio-flavored icing.

- 1 **package (18-1/4 ounces) white cake mix**
- 3/4 **cup vegetable oil**
- 3 **eggs**
- 1 **cup lemon-lime *or* club soda**
- 1 **package (3/4 ounce) instant pistachio pudding mix**
- 1 **cup chopped pecans**
- 1/2 **cup flaked coconut**

ICING:
- 1-1/2 **cups milk**
- 2 **envelopes whipped topping mix**
- 1 **package (3/4 ounce) instant pistachio pudding mix**
- 3/4 **cup chopped pecans**
- 1/2 **cup flaked coconut**

1 In a mixing bowl, combine dry cake mix, oil, eggs, soda and dry pudding mix; mix well. Stir in pecans and coconut. Pour into a greased 13-in. x 9-in. x 2-in. baking pan. Bake at 350° for 40-45 minutes or until a toothpick inserted comes out clean. Cool completely on a wire rack.

2 For icing, combine the milk, topping mix and dry pudding mix in mixing bowl; beat until thickened, about 4 minutes. Spread over cake. Sprinkle with pecans and coconut. Store in the refrigerator.

WHITE TEXAS SHEET CAKE

White Texas Sheet Cake

PREP: 15 min. **BAKE:** 20 min. + cooling
YIELD: 16-20 servings

Joanie Ward, Brownsburg, Indiana

Try to make this cake a day ahead because it will get better the longer it sits.

1	cup butter
1	cup water
2	cups all-purpose flour
2	cups sugar
2	eggs, beaten
1/2	cup sour cream
1	teaspoon salt
1	teaspoon baking powder
1	teaspoon almond extract
1/4	teaspoon baking soda

FROSTING:

1/2	cup butter
1/4	cup milk
4-1/2	cups confectioners' sugar
1/2	teaspoon almond extract
1	cup chopped walnuts

1 In a large saucepan, bring butter and water just to a boil. Immediately remove from the heat; stir in the flour, sugar, eggs, sour cream, salt, baking powder, almond extract and baking soda until smooth.

2 Pour into a greased 15-in. x 10-in. x 1-in. baking pan. Bake at 375° for 20-22 minutes or until a toothpick inserted near the center comes out clean and cake is golden brown. Cool for 20 minutes.

3 For frosting, in a large saucepan, combine butter and milk. Bring to a boil. Remove from the heat; stir in sugar and extract. Stir in walnuts; spread over warm cake.

Hawaiian Cake

PREP: 25 min. **BAKE:** 20 min. + cooling
YIELD: 16-20 servings

Estella Traeger, Milwaukee, Wisconsin

Pineapple, coconut and a delightful blend of instant pudding, cream cheese and whipped topping dress up a yellow cake mix. This is a favorite dessert that suits any occasion.

1	package (18-1/4 ounces) yellow cake mix
2	cups cold milk
2	packages (3.4 ounces *each*) instant vanilla pudding mix
1	package (8 ounces) cream cheese, softened
1	carton (8 ounces) frozen whipped topping, thawed
1	can (20 ounces) crushed pineapple, drained
1/2	cup chopped maraschino cherries, drained
1/2	cup flaked coconut
1/2	cup chopped walnuts

1 Prepare cake batter according to package directions. Pour into a greased 15-in. x 10-in. x 1-in. baking pan. Bake at 350° for 20-25 minutes or until a toothpick inserted near the center comes out clean. Cool on a wire rack.

2 In a large mixing bowl, combine milk and pudding mixes; beat in cream cheese until smooth. Fold in whipped topping. Spread over cooled cake. Top with pineapple, cherries, coconut and walnuts. Store in the refrigerator.

MOIST CHOCOLATE CAKE

Chocolate Chip Cake

PREP: 15 min. **BAKE:** 45 min. **YIELD:** 9 servings

Sue Reichenbach, Langhorne, Pennsylvania

A delightful chocolate and cinnamon filling is sandwiched between tender white cake layers. It's the perfect size for a smaller group.

1/2	cup butter, softened
1-1/2	cups sugar, *divided*
2	eggs
1	teaspoon vanilla extract
2	cups all-purpose flour
1	teaspoon baking powder
1/2	teaspoon baking soda
1	cup (8 ounces) sour cream
3/4	cup semisweet chocolate chips
1	teaspoon ground cinnamon

1 In a large mixing bowl, cream butter and 1 cup sugar until light and fluffy. Add eggs, one at a time, beating well after each addition. Beat in vanilla. Combine the flour, baking powder and baking soda; add to the creamed mixture alternately with sour cream, beating well after each addition.

2 Spread half of the batter into a greased 9-in. square baking pan. Sprinkle with chocolate chips. Combine cinnamon and remaining sugar; sprinkle over chips. Spread with remaining batter. Bake at 350° for 40-45 minutes or until a toothpick inserted near the center comes out clean. Cool on a wire rack.

Moist Chocolate Cake

PREP: 10 min. **BAKE:** 30 min. + cooling
YIELD: 9 servings

Beulah Sak, Fairport, New York

This cake is so moist it doesn't need frosting. Simply sprinkle confectioners' sugar over the top.

1-1/2	cups all-purpose flour
1	cup sugar
3	tablespoons baking cocoa
1	teaspoon baking soda
1/2	teaspoon salt
6	tablespoons vegetable oil
1	tablespoon white vinegar
1	teaspoon vanilla extract
1	cup cold water

Confectioners' sugar

1 In a large mixing bowl, combine the flour, sugar, cocoa, baking soda and salt. Using a spoon, make three wells in the dry ingredients. Pour oil into one, vinegar into another and vanilla into the third. Slowly pour water over all. Beat on low speed until thoroughly combined (batter will be thin).

2 Pour into a greased 8-in. square baking dish. Bake at 350° for 30-35 minutes or until a toothpick inserted near the center comes out clean. Cool on a wire rack. Dust with confectioners' sugar.

dusting cakes with
confectioners' sugar

Place confectioners' sugar in a small metal sieve or sifter; shake or sift over the top of the baked and cooled cake. To make a pattern, lay a doily over the cake; sift an even layer of sugar over all. Lift the doily straight up, leaving the pattern on the cake.

Chocolate Almond Sheet Cake

PREP: 20 min. **BAKE:** 20 min. + cooling
YIELD: 16-20 servings

Mary Ann Kosmas, Minneapolis, Minnesota

This tender almond cake is perfect to make for potlucks or other occasions where you need to serve a crowd.

  3/4 cup butter
    1 cup water
  1/4 cup baking cocoa
2-1/2 cups all-purpose flour
    2 cups sugar
    1 teaspoon baking soda
  1/2 teaspoon salt
    2 eggs
  1/2 cup buttermilk
    1 teaspoon vanilla extract
    1 teaspoon almond extract
FROSTING:
  1/2 cup butter
  1/4 cup milk
    3 cups confectioners' sugar
  1/4 cup baking cocoa
    1 teaspoon vanilla extract

1 In a saucepan, bring the butter, water and cocoa to boil over medium heat. Remove from the heat and cool to room temperature.

2 In a large mixing bowl, combine the flour, sugar, baking soda and salt. Beat in cocoa mixture. Add the eggs, buttermilk and extracts; mix well.

3 Pour into a greased 15-in. x 10-in. x 1-in. baking pan. Bake at 375° for 20-22 minutes or until a toothpick inserted near the center comes out clean. Cool for 10 minutes on a wire rack.

4 For frosting, place butter and milk in a saucepan. Cook and stir over medium heat until butter is melted. Remove from the heat; add remaining ingredients and beat well. Carefully spread over warm cake. Cool completely.

CHOCOLATE ALMOND SHEET CAKE

German Chocolate Cake

PREP: 25 min. **BAKE:** 50 min. + cooling
YIELD: 12-15 servings

Lisa Andis, Morristown, Indiana

German chocolate is similar to milk chocolate and sweeter than regular baking chocolate.

    4 eggs, *separated*
    1 package (4 ounces) German sweet
       chocolate
  1/2 cup water
    1 cup butter, softened
    2 cups sugar
    1 teaspoon vanilla extract
2-1/2 cups cake flour
    1 teaspoon baking soda
  1/2 teaspoon salt
    1 cup buttermilk
COCONUT-PECAN FROSTING:
    1 cup evaporated milk
    1 cup sugar
    3 egg yolks, lightly beaten
  1/2 cup butter
1-1/3 cups flaked coconut
    1 cup chopped pecans
    1 teaspoon vanilla extract

1 Let eggs stand at room temperature for 30 minutes. Line a greased 13-in. x 9-in. x 2-in. baking pan with waxed paper. Grease and flour the paper; set aside.

2 In a saucepan, melt chocolate in water over low heat; cool. In a large mixing bowl, cream butter and sugar until light and fluffy. Add egg yolks, one at a time, beating well after each addition. Add chocolate mixture and vanilla; mix well. Combine the flour, baking soda and salt; add to creamed mixture alternately with buttermilk, beating well after each addition. In a small mixing bowl and with clean beaters, beat egg whites until stiff peaks form; fold into batter.

3 Spread batter evenly into prepared pan. Bake at 350° for 50-55 minutes or until a toothpick inserted near the center comes out clean. Cool for 10 minutes before inverting onto a wire rack to cool completely. Remove waxed paper.

4 For frosting, combine the milk, sugar, egg yolks and butter in a large saucepan; cook and stir over medium heat until thickened. Remove from the heat; stir in coconut, pecans and vanilla. Beat until frosting is cool and achieves spreading consistency. Place cake on a serving platter; spread frosting over top and sides.

Chocolate Marshmallow Cake

PREP: 30 min. **BAKE:** 20 min. **YIELD:** 12-16 servings

Teresa Ingebrand, Perham, Minnesota

This awesome dessert consists of a tender chocolate cake, fluffy marshmallow layer and fudgy topping. It's very difficult to stop at one piece.

- 1/2 **cup butter**
- 2 **squares (1 ounce *each*) unsweetened chocolate**
- 1 **cup all-purpose flour**
- 1/2 **teaspoon baking powder**
- 1/4 **teaspoon baking soda**
- 1/4 **teaspoon salt**
- 2 **eggs**
- 1 **cup sugar**
- 1/2 **cup unsweetened applesauce**
- 1 **teaspoon vanilla extract**
- 1 **package (10-1/2 ounces) miniature marshmallows, *divided***

GLAZE:
- 1/2 **cup sugar**
- 2 **tablespoons milk**
- 2 **tablespoons butter**
- 1/4 **cup semisweet chocolate chips**

1 In a heavy saucepan or microwave, melt butter and chocolate; stir until smooth. Cool for 10 minutes. Combine the flour, baking powder, baking soda and salt; set aside. In a mixing bowl, beat the eggs, sugar, applesauce and vanilla. Stir in the chocolate mixture. Add the dry ingredients; mix well.

CHOCOLATE MARSHMALLOW CAKE

2 Pour into a greased 13-in. x 9-in. x 2-in. baking pan. Bake at 350° for 20-30 minutes or until a toothpick inserted near the center comes out clean. Set aside 1/2 cup marshmallows for glaze. Sprinkle remaining marshmallows over cake. Bake 2 minutes longer or until marshmallows are softened.

3 In a saucepan, combine the sugar, milk and butter. Bring to a boil; boil for 1-1/2 minutes. Remove from the heat; stir in chocolate chips and reserved marshmallows until melted. Quickly drizzle over the cake (glaze will harden as it cools).

Lemon Cherry Cake

PREP: 20 min. **BAKE:** 30 min. + cooling
YIELD: 12-15 servings

Janice Greenhalgh, Florence, Kentucky

The combination of sweet cherries and lemon peel gives the cake a distinctive flavor, and no one can resist the yummy cream cheese topping.

- 1-1/2 **cups coarsely chopped fresh *or* frozen pitted sweet cherries**
- 3/4 **cup butter, softened**
- 1-3/4 **cups sugar**
- 3 **eggs**
- 2 **teaspoons grated lemon peel**
- 1-1/2 **teaspoons vanilla extract**
- 2-1/2 **cups all-purpose flour**
- 2-1/2 **teaspoons baking powder**
- 1/2 **teaspoon salt**
- 1-1/4 **cups milk**

TOPPING:
- 1 **package (8 ounces) cream cheese, softened**
- 2 **tablespoons lemon juice**
- 2 **teaspoons grated lemon peel**
- 3-1/2 **to 4 cups confectioners' sugar**

1 Pat cherries dry with paper towels; set aside. In a large mixing bowl, cream butter and sugar until light and fluffy. Add eggs, one at a time, beating well after each addition. Beat in lemon peel and vanilla. Combine the flour, baking powder and salt; add to creamed mixture alternately with milk, beating well after each addition.

2 Pour into a greased 13-in. x 9-in. x 2-in. baking pan. Sprinkle with cherries. Bake at 375° for 30-35 minutes or until a toothpick inserted near the center comes out clean. Cool on a wire rack.

CARROT CAKE

CREAM CHEESE FROSTING:
- 2 packages (3 ounces *each*) cream cheese, softened
- 3 cups confectioners' sugar
- 6 tablespoons butter, softened
- 1 teaspoon vanilla extract
- 1/2 cup chopped nuts

1 In a large mixing bowl, combine the flour, sugar, cinnamon, baking soda and salt. Add the eggs, oil, carrots and vanilla; beat until combined. Stir in the pineapple, coconut and nuts.

2 Pour into a greased 13-in. x 9-in. x 2-in. baking pan. Bake at 350° for 50-60 minutes or until a toothpick inserted near the center comes out clean. Cool on a wire rack.

3 For frosting, beat cream cheese in a small mixing bowl until fluffy. Add the confectioners' sugar, butter and vanilla; beat until smooth. Frost cake. Sprinkle with nuts. Store in the refrigerator.

Butterscotch Snack Cake

PREP: 10 min. **BAKE:** 35 min. **YIELD:** 12-16 servings

Joanie Ward, Brownsburg, Indiana

Handy pantry ingredients, including cake and pudding mixes, are the key to this moist, golden cake.

- 1 package (3-1/2 ounces) cook-and-serve butterscotch pudding mix
- 2 cups milk
- 1 package (18-1/4 ounces) yellow cake mix
- 1 package (11 ounces) butterscotch chips
- 1/2 cup chopped pecans *or* walnuts

1 In a large saucepan, combine the pudding mix and milk. Bring to a boil over medium heat, stirring constantly. Remove from the heat; stir in the dry cake mix.

2 Pour into a greased 13-in. x 9-in. x 2-in. baking pan. Sprinkle with butterscotch chips and nuts. Bake at 350° for 35-40 minutes or until a toothpick inserted near the center comes out clean. Cool on a wire rack.

3 For topping, in mixing bowl, beat cream cheese, lemon juice and peel until smooth. Beat in enough confectioners' sugar until mixture achieves desired consistency. Cut cake; top each piece with a dollop of topping.

Carrot Cake

PREP: 20 min. **BAKE:** 50 min. + cooling
YIELD: 12-16 servings

Debbie Jones, California, Maryland

You'll love the texture this pretty, moist cake gets from pineapple, coconut and, of course, carrots. The traditional cream cheese frosting adds just the right amount of sweetness.

- 2 cups all-purpose flour
- 2 cups sugar
- 2 teaspoons ground cinnamon
- 1 teaspoon baking soda
- 1/2 teaspoon salt
- 3 eggs
- 1-1/2 cups vegetable oil
- 2 cups finely grated carrots
- 1 teaspoon vanilla extract
- 1 cup well-drained crushed pineapple
- 1 cup flaked coconut
- 1/2 cup chopped nuts

Plantation Gingerbread

PREP: 20 min. **BAKE:** 30 min. + cooling
YIELD: 12-16 servings

Wanda Burchell, Lynnville, Tennessee

When you make this dessert the wonderful aroma of gingerbread will fill the house. A dollop of sweetened whipped cream crowns each piece.

  1   **cup butter, softened**
  1   **cup sugar**
  3   **eggs**
  1   **cup molasses**
  3/4   **cup hot water**
2-1/2   **cups all-purpose flour**
1-1/2   **teaspoons ground ginger**
  1   **teaspoon baking soda**
  1   **teaspoon ground cinnamon**
1/2   **teaspoon salt**
1/2   **teaspoon ground nutmeg**
  1   **cup heavy whipping cream**
  1   **to 2 tablespoons confectioners' sugar**
Additional nutmeg, optional

1 In a large mixing bowl, cream butter and sugar until light and fluffy. Add eggs; beat on low speed for 2 minutes. Gradually add the molasses and hot water. Combine the flour, ginger, baking soda, cinnamon, salt and nutmeg; gradually add to creamed mixture. Beat on low for 1 minute.

2 Pour into a greased 13-in. x 9-in. x 2-in. baking pan. Bake at 350° for 30-35 minutes or until a toothpick inserted near the center comes out clean. Cool on a wire rack.

3 In a chilled small mixing bowl, beat cream until it begins to thicken. Add confectioners' sugar; beat until soft peaks form. Serve with the gingerbread. Sprinkle with nutmeg if desired.

PLANTATION GINGERBREAD

Plum Upside-Down Cake

PREP: 15 min. **BAKE:** 40 min. **YIELD:** 8-10 servings

Bobbie Talbott, Veneta, Oregon

The delicate flavor of plums is a pleasing change of pace in this upside-down cake.

1/3   **cup butter**
1/2   **cup packed brown sugar**
  2   **pounds fresh plums, pitted and halved**
  2   **eggs**
2/3   **cup sugar**
  1   **cup all-purpose flour**
  1   **teaspoon baking powder**
1/4   **teaspoon salt**
1/3   **cup hot water**
1/2   **teaspoon lemon extract**
Whipped cream, optional

1 Melt butter in a 10-in. cast-iron or ovenproof skillet. Sprinkle brown sugar over butter. Arrange plum halves cut side down in a single layer over sugar; set aside.

2 In a large mixing bowl, beat eggs until thick and lemon-colored; gradually beat in sugar. Combine the flour, baking powder and salt; add to egg mixture and mix well. Blend water and lemon extract; beat into batter. Pour over plums.

3 Bake at 350° for 40-45 minutes or until a toothpick inserted near the center comes out clean. Immediately invert onto a serving plate. Serve warm with whipped cream if desired.

Spiced Pineapple Upside-Down Cake

PREP: 15 min. **BAKE:** 40 min. **YIELD:** 12 servings

Jennifer Sergesketter, Newburgh, Indiana

This tried-and-true cake can be prepared either in an ovenproof skillet or in a 13-inch x 19-inch baking pan.

1-1/3   cups butter, softened, *divided*
   1   cup packed brown sugar
   1   can (20 ounces) pineapple slices, drained
  10   to 12 maraschino cherries
 1/2   cup chopped pecans
1-1/2   cups sugar
   2   eggs
   1   teaspoon vanilla extract
   2   cups all-purpose flour
   2   teaspoons baking powder
 1/2   teaspoon baking soda
 1/2   teaspoon salt
 1/2   teaspoon ground cinnamon
 1/2   teaspoon ground nutmeg
   1   cup buttermilk

1 In a saucepan, melt 2/3 cup butter; stir in brown sugar. Spread on the bottom of an ungreased heavy 12-in. ovenproof skillet or a 13-in. x 9-in. x 2-in. baking pan. Arrange pineapple in a single layer over sugar mixture; place a cherry in the center of each slice. Sprinkle with pecans; set aside.

2 In a large mixing bowl, cream the sugar and remaining butter until light and fluffy. Beat in eggs and vanilla. Combine the flour, baking powder, baking soda, salt, cinnamon and nutmeg; add to creamed mixture alternately with buttermilk, beating well after each addition. Carefully pour over the pineapple.

3 Bake at 350° for 40 minutes for skillet (50-60 minutes for baking pan) or until a toothpick inserted near the center comes out clean. Immediately invert onto a serving platter. Serve warm.

GRANDMA'S BLACKBERRY CAKE

Grandma's Blackberry Cake

PREP: 15 min. **BAKE:** 45 min. + cooling
YIELD: 9 servings

Diana Martin, Moundsville, West Virginia

A lightly seasoned spice cake lets the wonderful flavor of blackberries shine through.

- 1 cup fresh blackberries
- 2 cups all-purpose flour, *divided*
- 1/2 cup butter, softened
- 1 cup sugar
- 2 eggs
- 1 teaspoon baking soda
- 1 teaspoon ground cinnamon
- 1 teaspoon ground nutmeg
- 1/2 teaspoon salt
- 1/4 teaspoon ground cloves
- 1/4 teaspoon ground allspice
- 3/4 cup buttermilk

Whipped cream, optional

1 Toss blackberries with 2 tablespoons of flour; set aside. In a large mixing bowl, cream butter and sugar until light and fluffy. Add eggs; beat well. Combine the baking soda, cinnamon, nutmeg, salt, cloves, allspice and remaining flour; add to creamed mixture alternately with buttermilk, beating well after each addition. Fold in blackberries.

2 Pour into a greased 9-in. square baking pan. Bake at 350° for 45-50 minutes or until a toothpick inserted near the center comes out clean. Cool on a wire rack. Serve cake with whipped cream if desired.

Pumpkin Cake with Caramel Sauce

PREP: 20 min. **BAKE:** 40 min. + cooling
YIELD: 12-16 servings

Roberta Peck, Fort Hill, Pennsylvania

This variation of a spice cake has pumpkin and is served with a delicious caramel sauce.

- 2 cups all-purpose flour
- 2 cups sugar
- 2 teaspoons ground cinnamon
- 1-1/2 teaspoons baking soda
- 1 teaspoon ground nutmeg
- 1/2 teaspoon salt
- 4 eggs
- 1 can (15 ounces) solid-pack pumpkin
- 1 cup vegetable oil

CARAMEL SAUCE:
- 1-1/2 cups packed brown sugar
- 3 tablespoons all-purpose flour

Dash salt
- 1-1/4 cups water
- 2 tablespoons butter
- 1/2 teaspoon vanilla extract

1 In a mixing bowl, combine the flour, sugar, cinnamon, baking soda, nutmeg and salt. In another bowl, beat the eggs, pumpkin and oil until smooth; add to the dry ingredients. Mix until well blended, about 1 minute.

2 Pour into a greased 13-in. x 9-in. x 2-in. baking pan. Bake at 350° for 40-45 minutes or until a toothpick inserted near the center comes out clean. Cool on a wire rack.

3 For sauce, combine the brown sugar, flour and salt in a saucepan. Stir in water and butter. Bring to a boil over medium heat; boil and stir for 3 minutes. Remove from the heat; stir in vanilla. Cut cake into squares and serve with warm sauce.

PUMPKIN CAKE WITH CARAMEL SAUCE

APPLE CAKE

Boston Cream Cake

PREP: 20 min. + chilling **BAKE:** 25 min. + cooling
YIELD: 6-8 servings

Michelle Mirich, Youngstown, Ohio

Boston Cream Pie (which is truly more like a cake) is believed to have originated at Boston's Parker House restaurant in 1856. A boxed cake mix makes this version easy to prepare.

- 1 package (9 ounces) yellow cake mix
- 1/2 teaspoon lemon extract
- 2 cups cold milk
- 1 package (3.4 ounces) instant vanilla pudding mix
- 1 square (1 ounce) semisweet chocolate
- 1 tablespoon butter
- 1/2 cup confectioners' sugar
- 2 to 3 teaspoons hot water

1 Prepare cake batter according to package directions, adding lemon extract. Pour into a greased and floured 9-in. round baking pan. Bake at 350° for 25 minutes or until a toothpick inserted near the center comes out clean. Cool for 10 minutes before removing from pan to a wire rack to cool completely.

2 In a bowl, whisk milk and pudding mix for 2 minutes; refrigerate. In a heavy saucepan or microwave, melt chocolate and butter; stir until smooth. Stir in confectioners' sugar until crumbly. Stir in hot water, 1 teaspoon at a time, until smooth. Split cake into two horizontal layers. Spread pudding on bottom layer. Place second layer over pudding. Pour chocolate glaze over top, letting it drizzle down the sides. Store in the refrigerator.

Apple Cake

PREP: 15 min. **BAKE:** 35 min. **YIELD:** 9 servings

Iona Redemer, Calumet, Oklahoma

Every bite of this perfectly sized cake is packed with tender and juicy apples. Served warm or cold, with or without cream or ice cream, it's a treat every time.

- 3 tablespoons butter, softened
- 1 cup sugar
- 1 egg
- 1 teaspoon vanilla extract
- 1 cup all-purpose flour
- 1 teaspoon baking soda
- 1/2 teaspoon salt
- 1/2 teaspoon ground cinnamon
- 1/2 teaspoon ground nutmeg
- 3 cups diced peeled apples
- 1/4 cup chopped nuts

Whipped cream *or* ice cream, optional

1 In a large mixing bowl, cream butter and sugar until light and fluffy. Beat in egg and vanilla. Combine the flour, baking soda, salt, cinnamon and nutmeg; add to creamed mixture (batter will be thick). Stir in apples and nuts.

2 Spread into a greased 8-in. square baking dish. Bake at 350° for 35-45 minutes or until a toothpick inserted near the center comes out with just a few crumbs. Serve warm or cold with whipped cream or ice cream if desired.

Fancy Cream Cupcakes

PREP: 25 min. **BAKE:** 20 min. + cooling
YIELD: 22 cupcakes

Merrilee Chambers
Haines Junction, Yukon Territory

These cute, filled cupcakes are creamy and not too sweet. They look fancy but are actually quick to fix.

- 1/2 cup shortening
- 1-1/2 cups sugar
- 4 egg whites
- 1 teaspoon vanilla extract
- 2 cups all-purpose flour
- 3-1/2 teaspoons baking powder
- 1 teaspoon salt
- 1 cup milk

FILLING:
- 1 cup heavy whipping cream
- 2 tablespoons confectioners' sugar
- 4 to 5 drops red food coloring, optional
- 1/4 teaspoon almond extract

1 In a large mixing bowl, cream shortening and sugar until light and fluffy. Add egg whites, one at a time, beating well after each addition. Beat in vanilla. Combine flour, baking powder and salt; add to creamed mixture alternately with milk, beating well after each addition.

2 Fill paper- or foil-lined muffin cups two-thirds full. Bake at 350° for 20-25 minutes or until a toothpick comes out clean. Cool for 10 minutes before removing from pans to wire racks to cool completely.

3 For filling, beat cream in a chilled small mixing bowl until it begins to thicken. Gradually beat in confectioners' sugar and food coloring if desired until stiff peaks form. Beat in almond extract. Cut a 1-in. cone shape from the center of each cupcake; set cone aside. Fill indentation with filling. Cut each cone in half from top to bottom; place

FANCY CREAM CUPCAKES

two halves on filling for butterfly wings. If desired, pipe a thin strip of filling between wings for butterfly body.

Orange Applesauce Cupcakes

PREP: 20 min. **BAKE:** 20 min. + cooling
YIELD: 1 dozen

Janis Plourde, Smooth Rock Falls, Ontario

Kids of all ages will rave about these fruity cupcakes. For a tasty variation, substitute crushed pineapple for the applesauce.

- 6 tablespoons butter, softened
- 1 cup packed brown sugar
- 1 egg
- 1/2 cup unsweetened applesauce
- 1 teaspoon vanilla extract
- 1 teaspoon grated orange peel
- 1 cup all-purpose flour
- 1 teaspoon baking powder
- 1/2 teaspoon salt
- 1/4 teaspoon baking soda
- 1/2 cup chopped pecans

FROSTING:
- 1/4 cup butter, softened
- 2 cups confectioners' sugar
- 1-1/2 teaspoons grated orange peel
- 2 to 4 teaspoons orange juice

cupcake *capers*

- Batter for a two-layer 9-in. cake can be used to make 2 to 2-1/2 dozen cupcakes. Fill greased or paper-lined muffin cups two-thirds full. Bake at 350° for 20 to 30 minutes or until a toothpick comes out clean. Cool cupcakes for 10 minutes before removing from pans to wire racks to cool completely. Frost as desired.

- To make cupcakes of the same size, use a solid plastic ice cream scoop to measure out the batter and fill the muffin cups.

1 In a mixing bowl, cream the butter and brown sugar until light and fluffy. Add egg; beat well. Beat in the applesauce, vanilla and orange peel. Combine the flour, baking powder, salt and baking soda; add to creamed mixture. Stir in pecans.

2 Fill paper-lined muffin cups half full. Bake at 350° for 20-25 minutes or until a toothpick comes out clean. Cool for 10 minutes before removing from pan to a wire rack to cool completely.

3 For frosting, in a small mixing bowl, best butter and confectioners' sugar. Add orange peel and enough orange juice to achieve spreading consistency. Frost cupcakes.

Lemon Cream Cupcakes

PREP: 20 min. **BAKE:** 25 min. + cooling
YIELD: about 2-1/2 dozen

Ruth Ann Stelfox, Raymond, Alberta

Delicate cupcakes like these are sure to disappear at your next potluck or bake sale.

- 1 cup butter, softened
- 2 cups sugar
- 3 eggs
- 2 teaspoons grated lemon peel
- 1 teaspoon vanilla extract
- 3-1/2 cups all-purpose flour
- 1 teaspoon baking soda
- 1/2 teaspoon baking powder
- 1/2 teaspoon salt
- 2 cups (16 ounces) sour cream

FROSTING:

- 3 tablespoons butter, softened
- 2-1/4 cups confectioners' sugar
- 2 tablespoons lemon juice
- 3/4 teaspoon vanilla extract
- 1/4 teaspoon grated lemon peel
- 1 to 2 tablespoons milk

1 In a large mixing bowl, cream butter and sugar until light and fluffy. Add eggs, one at a time, beating well after each addition. Beat in lemon peel and vanilla. Combine the flour, baking soda, baking powder and salt; add to creamed mixture alternately with sour cream, beating well after each addition (batter will be thick).

2 Fill greased or paper-lined muffin cups with 1/4 cup of batter. Bake at 350° for 25-30 minutes or until a toothpick comes out clean. Cool for 10 minutes before removing from pans to wire racks to cool completely.

3 For the frosting, cream butter and confectioners' sugar in a small mixing bowl until light and fluffy. Add the lemon juice, vanilla, lemon peel and milk; beat until smooth. Frost cupcakes.

LEMON CREAM CUPCAKES

Peanut Butter Cup Cupcakes

PREP: 15 min. **BAKE:** 25 min. + cooling
YIELD: 16 cupcakes

Heidi Harrington, Steuben, Maine

The mini peanut butter cups eliminate the need to frost these yummy cupcakes.

1/3	cup shortening
1/3	cup peanut butter
1-1/4	cups packed brown sugar
2	eggs
1	teaspoon vanilla extract
1-3/4	cups all-purpose flour
1-3/4	teaspoons baking powder
1	teaspoon salt
1	cup milk
16	miniature peanut butter cups

1 In a mixing bowl, cream the shortening, peanut butter and brown sugar until light and fluffy. Beat in eggs, one at a time, beating well after each addition. Add vanilla. Combine the flour, baking powder and salt; add to creamed mixture alternately with milk, beating well after each addition.

2 Fill paper-lined muffin cups with 1/4 cup of batter. Press a peanut butter cup into the center of each until top edge is even with batter. Bake at 350° for 22-24 minutes or until a toothpick inserted on an angle toward the center of the cupcakes comes out clean. Cool for 10 minutes before removing from pans to wire racks to cool completely.

Editor's Note: Reduced-fat or generic brands of peanut butter are not recommended for this recipe.

PEANUT BUTTER CUP CUPCAKES

ZUCCHINI CHIP CUPCAKES

Zucchini Chip Cupcakes

PREP: 15 min. **BAKE:** 20 min. + cooling
YIELD: about 2 dozen

Debra Forshee, Stockton, Kansas

These moist, nut-topped cupcakes don't even need frosting, and they're a great way to use up zucchini.

1/2	cup butter, softened
1/2	cup vegetable oil
1-3/4	cups sugar
2	eggs
1/2	cup milk
1	teaspoon vanilla extract
2-1/2	cups all-purpose flour
1/4	cup baking cocoa
1	teaspoon baking soda
1/2	teaspoon salt
1/2	teaspoon ground cinnamon
2	cups shredded zucchini
1/4	cup miniature semisweet chocolate chips
1/4	cup chopped pecans

1 In a large mixing bowl, beat the butter, oil and sugar. Add the eggs, milk and vanilla; mix well. Combine the flour, cocoa, baking soda, salt and cinnamon; add to the creamed mixture. Fold in zucchini and chocolate chips.

2 Fill greased or paper-lined muffin cups two-thirds full. Top with pecans. Bake at 375° for 20-25 minutes or until top springs back when lightly touched. Cool for 10 minutes before removing from pans to wire racks to cool completely.

Creamy Chocolate Cupcakes

PREP: 15 min. **BAKE:** 25 min. + cooling
YIELD: 1-1/2 dozen

Mrs. Walter Jacobson, Ashland, Ohio

The surprise inside these rich chocolate cupcakes is the smooth cream cheese filling.

- 1-1/2   cups all-purpose flour
- 1   cup sugar
- 1/4   cup baking cocoa
- 1   teaspoon baking soda
- 1/2   teaspoon salt
- 2   eggs
- 3/4   cup water
- 1/3   cup vegetable oil
- 1   tablespoon white vinegar
- 1   teaspoon vanilla extract

FILLING:
- 1   package (8 ounces) cream cheese, softened
- 1/3   cup sugar
- 1   egg, lightly beaten
- 1/8   teaspoon salt
- 1   cup (6 ounces) semisweet chocolate chips
- 1   cup chopped walnuts

1 In a large mixing bowl, combine the flour, sugar, cocoa, baking soda and salt. In a bowl, whisk the eggs, water, oil, vinegar and vanilla. Add to dry ingredients; mix well.

2 Pour into 18 greased or paper-lined muffin cups. For filling, beat cream cheese and sugar in another large mixing bowl until blended. Add egg and salt; mix well. Fold in the chocolate chips. Drop by tablespoonfuls into the center of each cupcake. Sprinkle with nuts.

3 Bake at 350° for 25-30 minutes or until a toothpick inserted in the cake and not the filling comes out clean. Cool for 10 minutes before removing from pans to wire racks to cool completely. Store in the refrigerator.

Mocha Cupcakes

PREP: 15 min. + chilling **BAKE:** 20 min. + cooling
YIELD: about 1-1/2 dozen

Lorna Smith
New Hazelton, British Columbia

Instant coffee granules add the right amount of mocha flavor to the chocolate frosting.

CREAMY CHOCOLATE CUPCAKES

- 1   cup boiling water
- 1   cup mayonnaise
- 1   teaspoon vanilla extract
- 2   cups all-purpose flour
- 1   cup sugar
- 1/2   cup baking cocoa
- 2   teaspoons baking soda

MOCHA FROSTING:
- 3/4   cup confectioners' sugar
- 1/4   cup baking cocoa
- 1/2   to 1 teaspoon instant coffee granules

Pinch salt
- 1-1/2   cups heavy whipping cream

1 In a large mixing bowl, combine the water, mayonnaise and vanilla. Combine the flour, sugar, cocoa and baking soda; add to the mayonnaise mixture and beat until well mixed.

2 Fill greased or paper-lined muffin cups two-thirds full. Bake at 350° for 20-25 minutes or until a toothpick comes out clean. Cool for 10 minutes before removing from pans to wire racks to cool completely.

3 For frosting, combine the confectioners' sugar, cocoa, coffee granules and salt in a large mixing bowl. Stir in cream. Place mixer beaters in bowl; cover and chill for 30 minutes. Beat frosting until stiff peaks form. Frost the cupcakes.

Editor's Note: Reduced-fat or fat-free mayonnaise may not be substituted for regular mayonnaise in this recipe.

Adams County Apple Bundt

PREP: 15 min. **BAKE:** 1-1/2 hours + cooling
YIELD: 12-16 servings

Gretchen Berendt
Carroll Valley, Pennsylvania

Cinnamon-sugar coated apples are tucked inside this tempting tube cake.

3	cups all-purpose flour
3	teaspoons baking powder
2	cups plus 5 tablespoons sugar, *divided*
1	cup vegetable oil
4	eggs
1/3	cup orange juice
1/2	teaspoon salt
2-1/2	teaspoons vanilla extract
4	medium tart apples, peeled and thinly sliced
2	teaspoons ground cinnamon

Confectioners' sugar, optional

1 In a large mixing bowl, combine the flour, baking powder, 2 cups sugar, oil, eggs, orange juice, salt and vanilla. Beat until thoroughly combined. In another bowl, toss apples with cinnamon and remaining sugar. Spread a third of the batter into a greased and floured 10-in. tube pan. Cover with half of the apples. Repeat layers. Spoon remaining batter over top.

2 Bake at 350° for 1-1/2 hours or until a toothpick inserted near the center comes out clean. Cool for 20 minutes before removing from pan to a wire rack to cool completely. Just before serving, dust with confectioners' sugar if desired.

Packable Chocolate Chip Cake

PREP: 10 min. **BAKE:** 45 min. + cooling
YIELD: 12-16 servings

Barbara Hofstede, Waukesha, Wisconsin

Since this recipe doesn't call for frosting, it travels well to potlucks and in brown-bag lunches. Sour cream in the batter makes the cake deliciously moist.

1	package (18-1/4 ounces) yellow cake mix
1	cup (8 ounces) sour cream
1/2	cup vegetable oil
1/4	cup water
4	eggs
1	to 1-1/2 cups semisweet chocolate chips

Confectioners' sugar

1 In a large mixing bowl, combine the dry cake mix, sour cream, oil, water and eggs. Beat on medium speed for 2 minutes. Fold in the chocolate chips.

2 Pour into a greased and floured 10-in. fluted tube pan. Bake at 350° for 45-50 minutes or until a toothpick inserted near the center comes out clean. Cool for 20 minutes before removing from pan to a wire rack to cool completely. Just before serving, dust with confectioners' sugar.

Pecan Pound Cake

PREP: 20 min. **BAKE:** 1 hour + cooling
YIELD: 12-16 servings

Fleta West, Hayes, Virginia

This cake always turns out great. It's wonderful with a steaming cup of coffee on a chilly winter day.

1-1/2	cups butter, softened
3-3/4	cups confectioners' sugar
6	eggs
1	tablespoon vanilla extract
2-1/2	cups all-purpose flour
1/2	teaspoon salt
1	cup flaked coconut
2/3	cup chopped pecans, toasted

1 In a large mixing bowl, cream butter and confectioners' sugar until light and fluffy. Add eggs, one at a time, beating well after each addition. Add vanilla. Combine flour and salt; add to creamed mixture just until combined. Stir in coconut and pecans.

2 Pour into a greased and floured 10-in. tube pan; spread evenly. Bake at 325° for 60-65 minutes or until a toothpick inserted near the center comes out clean. Cool for 10 minutes before removing from pan to a wire rack to cool completely.

Great-Grandma's Lemon Cake

PREP: 20 min. **BAKE:** 65 min. + cooling
YIELD: 2 cakes (24 servings)

Glenda Stokes, Florence, South Carolina

This old-fashioned cake has great lemon flavor, which it gets from both the lemon juice and peel.

> 5 **eggs,** *separated*
> 1 **cup butter, softened**
> 3 **cups sugar**
> 1 **tablespoon finely shredded lemon peel**
> 3 **tablespoons lemon juice**
> 4 **cups all-purpose flour**
> 1/2 **teaspoon baking soda**
> 1 **cup milk**
>
> **Confectioners' sugar**

1 Let eggs stand at room temperature for 30 minutes. In a large mixing bowl, cream butter and sugar until light and fluffy. In a small mixing bowl, beat egg yolks until thick and lemon-colored. Add to creamed mixture and beat well.

GREAT-GRANDMA'S LEMON CAKE

Stir in lemon peel and juice. Combine flour and baking soda; add alternately with milk. In another mixing bowl, beat egg whites on high speed until stiff peaks form; fold into batter.

2 Pour into two well-greased 9-in. x 5-in. x 3-in. loaf pans. Bake at 325° for 65-70 minutes or until a toothpick inserted near the center comes out clean. Cool for 10 minutes before removing from pans to wire racks to cool completely. Dust tops with confectioners' sugar.

Fresh Pear Cake

PREP: 15 min. **BAKE:** 1 hour + cooling
YIELD: 14-16 servings

Mrs. Frances Lanier, Metter, Georgia

Suitable for dessert, breakfast or a coffee break, this moist cake serves a lot, but the leftovers keep well.

> 3 **eggs**
> 2 **cups sugar**
> 1-1/2 **cups vegetable oil**
> 3 **cups all-purpose flour**
> 2 **teaspoons ground cinnamon**
> 1 **teaspoon salt**
> 1 **teaspoon baking soda**
> 1-1/2 **cups finely chopped peeled pears (about 2 medium)**
> 1 **teaspoon vanilla extract**
> 1-1/4 **cups confectioners' sugar**
> 2 **tablespoons milk**

1 In a large mixing bowl, beat eggs on medium speed. Gradually add sugar and oil; beat thoroughly. Combine the flour, cinnamon, salt and baking soda; add to egg mixture and mix well. Stir in pears and vanilla, (the batter will be stiff).

2 Spoon into a greased and floured 10-in. tube pan. Bake at 350° for 60-65 minutes or until a toothpick inserted near the center comes out clean. Cool for10 minutes before inverting onto a serving plate.

3 In a small bowl, combine confectioners' sugar and milk until smooth. Drizzle over warm cake. Cool completely.

Pastel Pound Cake

PREP: 10 min. **BAKE:** 55 min. + cooling
YIELD: 12-16 servings

Jean Karolewicz, Elmwood Park, Illinois

Mini tinted marshmallows create a marbled look in this bundt-shaped pound cake. It's special enough to offer at a festive gathering or to slice up for a weekday snack.

- 1 **cup butter, softened**
- 2 **cups sugar**
- 4 **eggs**
- 1 **teaspoon almond extract**
- 1 **teaspoon vanilla extract**
- 3 **cups all-purpose flour**
- 3/4 **teaspoon salt**
- 1/2 **teaspoon baking powder**
- 1/2 **teaspoon baking soda**
- 1 **cup buttermilk**
- 1 **cup pastel miniature marshmallows**

Confectioners' sugar

1 In a large mixing bowl, cream butter and sugar until light and fluffy. Add eggs, one at a time, beating well after each addition. Add extracts. Combine the flour, salt, baking powder and baking soda; add to creamed mixture alternately with buttermilk, beating well after each addition.

2 Pour half of the batter into a greased and floured 10-in. fluted tube pan. Sprinkle with marshmallows. Top with remaining batter. Bake at 350° for 55-60 minutes or until a toothpick inserted near the center comes out clean.

3 Cool for 10 minutes before removing from pan to a wire rack to cool completely. Dust with confectioners' sugar.

PASTEL POUND CAKE

MINCEMEAT APPLE CAKE

Mincemeat Apple Cake

PREP: 20 min. **BAKE:** 35 min. + cooling
YIELD: 10 servings

Priscilla Gilbert
Indian Harbour Beach, Florida

For a holiday touch, glaze the cake top and decorate with red and green candied cherries.

- 2 **cups all-purpose flour**
- 1/2 **cup packed brown sugar**
- 1 **teaspoon baking powder**
- 1/2 **teaspoon baking soda**
- 1/2 **teaspoon ground cinnamon**
- 1/4 **teaspoon ground cloves**
- 2 **eggs, beaten**
- 1 **cup prepared mincemeat**
- 1/3 **cup applesauce**
- 1/3 **cup apple juice**
- 3 **tablespoons butter, melted**

LEMON SAUCE:
- 1/2 **cup sugar**
- 4-1/2 **teaspoons cornstarch**
- 1 **cup water**
- 2 **tablespoons butter**
- 1-1/2 **teaspoons grated lemon peel**
- 1 **teaspoon lemon juice**

1 In a large bowl, combine the flour, brown sugar, baking powder, baking soda, cinnamon and cloves. In another bowl, combine the eggs, mincemeat, applesauce, juice and butter; stir into dry ingredients just until moistened.

2 Pour into a greased 9-in. fluted tube pan. Bake at 350° for 35-40 minutes or until a toothpick inserted near the center comes out clean. Cool for 10 minutes before removing from pan to a wire rack to cool completely.

3 For sauce, combine sugar and cornstarch in a saucepan. Stir in water until smooth. Bring to a boil; cook and stir for 2 minutes or until thickened. Remove from the heat; stir in butter until melted. Add lemon peel and juice. Serve warm with the cake.

Pumpkin Spice Cake

PREP: 15 min. **BAKE:** 45 min. + cooling
YIELD: 12-16 servings

Kathy Rhoads, Circleville, Ohio

Canned pumpkin and pudding mix dress up a boxed spice cake and make every bite moist and mouth-watering! This cake is a delicious alternative to pumpkin pie.

  1 **package (18-1/4 ounces) spice cake mix**
  3 **eggs**
  1 **cup canned pumpkin**
1/2 **cup water**
1/2 **cup vegetable oil**
  1 **package (3.4 ounces) instant vanilla pudding mix**
  1 **teaspoon ground cinnamon**
1/2 **cup chopped pecans**
Cream Cheese Frosting (page 165) *or* whipped cream

1 In a large mixing bowl, combine the dry cake mix, eggs, pumpkin, water, oil, pudding mix and cinnamon. Beat on medium speed for 5 minutes. Stir in pecans.

2 Pour into a greased and floured 10-in. fluted tube pan. Bake at 350° for 45-55 minutes or until a toothpick inserted near the center comes out clean. Cool for 10 minutes before removing from pan to a wire rack to cool completely. Frost cake or serve with whipped cream. Store in the refrigerator.

Glazed Lemon Bundt Cake

PREP: 15 min. **BAKE:** 1 hour + cooling
YIELD: 12-16 servings

John Thompson, Vandalia, Illinois

A sunny lemon-flavored cake brightens up any day. Lemon peel provides a nice zing, and a light glaze gives the golden cake a delicate crust.

  1 **cup butter, softened**
  2 **cups sugar**
  4 **eggs**
1-1/2 **teaspoons lemon extract**
1-1/2 **teaspoons vanilla extract**
  3 **cups all-purpose flour**
  2 **teaspoons baking powder**
1/2 **teaspoon salt**
  1 **cup milk**
  1 **tablespoon grated lemon peel**
GLAZE:
1/4 **cup lemon juice**
  1 **tablespoon water**
1/2 **teaspoon lemon extract**
3/4 **cup sugar**

1 In a large mixing bowl, cream butter and sugar until light and fluffy. Add the eggs, one at a time, beating well after each addition. Beat in extracts. Combine the flour, baking powder and salt; add to the creamed mixture alternately with milk, beating well after each addition. Stir in lemon peel.

2 Pour into a greased and floured 10-in. fluted tube pan. Bake at 350° for 60-70 minutes or until a toothpick inserted near the center comes out clean. Cool for 10 minutes before removing from pan to a wire rack. Cool 10 minutes longer.

3 Place waxed paper under rack. Combine glaze ingredients; drizzle over the warm cake. Cool completely before serving.

GLAZED LEMON BUNDT CAKE

Blueberry Sour Cream Pound Cake

PREP: 20 min. **BAKE:** 1 hour + cooling
YIELD: 12-16 servings

Juanita Miller, Arnett, Oklahoma

Original recipes for pound cake called for a pound each of butter, sugar, eggs and flour! Through the years, recipes have been adjusted to be a little lighter yet still have outstanding results.

- 6 **eggs,** *separated*
- 1 **cup butter, softened**
- 3 **cups sugar**
- 1 **teaspoon almond extract**
- 1 **teaspoon vanilla extract**
- 1 **teaspoon butter flavoring**
- 3 **cups all-purpose flour**
- 1/4 **teaspoon baking soda**
- 1 **cup (8 ounces) sour cream**
- 1-1/2 **cups fresh** *or* **frozen blueberries**

1 Let eggs stand at room temperature for 30 minutes. In a large mixing bowl, cream butter and sugar until light and fluffy. Add egg yolks, one at a time, beating well after each addition. Add the extracts and butter flavoring. Combine flour and baking soda; add to creamed mixture alternately with sour cream, beating well after each addition. In another mixing bowl and with clean beaters, beat egg whites on high speed until stiff peaks form. Fold into batter. Fold in blueberries.

2 Spoon into a greased and floured 10-in. tube pan. Bake at 350° for 60-70 minutes or until a toothpick inserted near the center comes out clean. Cool for 10 minutes before removing from pan to a wire rack to cool completely.

Editor's Note: If using frozen blueberries, do not thaw before adding to batter.

Bananas 'n' Cream Bundt Cake

PREP: 20 min. **BAKE:** 50 min. + cooling
YIELD: 12-16 servings

Oma Rollison, El Cajon, California

This absolutely scrumptious cake needs no icing…just a dusting of confectioners' sugar. Ripe bananas will provide the most intense flavor.

- 1/3 **cup shortening**
- 1-1/4 **cups sugar**
- 2 **eggs**
- 1 **teaspoon vanilla extract**

BANANAS 'N' CREAM BUNDT CAKE

- 1-1/4 **cups mashed ripe bananas (2 to 3 medium)**
- 2 **cups all-purpose flour**
- 1-1/4 **teaspoons baking powder**
- 1 **teaspoon baking soda**
- 1/2 **teaspoon salt**
- 1 **cup (8 ounces) sour cream**
- 3/4 **cup chopped walnuts**

Confectioners' sugar

1 In a large mixing bowl, cream the shortening and sugar until light and fluffy. Add the eggs, one at a time, beating well after each addition. Beat in vanilla. Add bananas and mix well. Combine the flour, baking powder, baking soda and salt; add to the creamed mixture alternately with sour cream, stirring just until combined. Stir in walnuts.

2 Pour into a greased and floured 10-in. fluted tube pan. Bake at 350° for 50-55 minutes or until a toothpick inserted near the center comes out clean. Cool for 10 minutes before removing from pan to a wire rack to cool completely. Dust with confectioners' sugar.

Chocolate Almond Bundt

PREP: 20 min. **BAKE:** 50 min. + cooling
YIELD: 12-16 servings

Sherri Gentry, Dallas, Oregon

Folks will be pleasantly surprised to see a rich chocolate cake beneath the fluffy white frosting. Sliced toasted almonds on top add a little crunch.

       3/4 **cup butter, softened**
    1-2/3 **cups sugar**
         2 **eggs**
       3/4 **cup sour cream**
         1 **teaspoon vanilla extract**
         1 **teaspoon almond extract**
         2 **cups all-purpose flour**
       2/3 **cup baking cocoa**
         2 **teaspoons baking soda**
       1/2 **teaspoon salt**
         1 **cup buttermilk**
FROSTING:
         5 **tablespoons butter, softened**
    2-1/2 **cups confectioners' sugar**
         1 **teaspoon vanilla extract**
       1/2 **teaspoon almond extract**
         3 **to 4 tablespoons milk**
Sliced almonds, toasted

1 In a large mixing bowl, cream butter and sugar until light and fluffy. Add eggs, one at a time, beating well after each addition. Add sour cream and extracts; mix well. Combine the flour, cocoa, baking soda and salt; add to the creamed mixture alternately with buttermilk, beating well after each addition.

CHOCOLATE ALMOND BUNDT

2 Pour into a greased and floured 10-in. fluted tube pan. Bake at 350° for 50-55 minutes or until a toothpick inserted near the center comes out clean. Cool for 10 minutes before removing from pan to a wire rack to cool completely.

3 For frosting, beat butter, sugar and extracts in a small mixing bowl until smooth. Add enough milk until frosting achieves desired spreading consistency. Spread over cake. Decorate with almonds.

Cherry Chocolate Marble Cake

PREP: 20 min. **BAKE:** 1-1/4 hours + cooling
YIELD: 12-16 servings

Sandra Campbell, Chase Mills, New York

Cherries and chocolate are natural partners that make desserts such as this simply scrumptious! The marbled effect is achieved by layering the two different batters.

         1 **cup butter, softened**
         2 **cups sugar**
         3 **eggs**
         6 **tablespoons maraschino cherry juice**
         6 **tablespoons water**
         1 **teaspoon almond extract**
    3-3/4 **cups all-purpose flour**
    2-1/4 **teaspoons baking soda**
       3/4 **teaspoon salt**
    1-1/2 **cups (12 ounces) sour cream**
       3/4 **cup chopped maraschino cherries, drained**
       3/4 **cup chopped walnuts, toasted**
         3 **squares (1 ounce *each*) unsweetened chocolate, melted**
Confectioners' sugar, optional

1 In a large mixing bowl, cream butter and sugar until light and fluffy. Add the eggs, one at a time, beating well after each addition. Add the cherry juice, water and extract; mix well. Combine the flour, baking soda and salt; add to creamed mixture alternately with sour cream, beating well after each addition.

2 Divide batter in half. To one portion, add cherries and walnuts; mix well. To the second portion, add chocolate; mix well. Spoon half of the cherry mixture into a greased and floured 10-in. fluted tube pan. Cover with half of the chocolate mixture. Repeat layers.

3 Bake at 350° for 1 hour and 15 minutes or until a toothpick inserted near the center comes out clean. Cool for 15 minutes before removing from pan to a wire rack to cool completely. Dust with confectioners' sugar if desired.

MILK CHOCOLATE BUNDT CAKE

1 milk chocolate candy bar (7 ounces), broken into pieces
1/2 cup chocolate syrup
1 cup butter, softened
1-1/2 cups sugar
4 eggs
1 teaspoon vanilla extract
2-3/4 cups all-purpose flour
3/4 teaspoon baking powder
1/2 teaspoon baking soda
1/2 teaspoon salt
1 cup buttermilk
Confectioners' sugar, optional

1 In a heavy saucepan or in a microwave, melt the candy bar with chocolate syrup; stir until smooth. Set aside to cool. In a large mixing bowl, cream butter and sugar until light and fluffy. Add eggs, one at a time, beating well after each addition. Stir in chocolate mixture and vanilla. Combine the flour, baking powder, baking soda and salt; add to creamed mixture alternately with buttermilk.

2 Pour into a greased and floured 10-in. fluted tube pan. Bake at 350° for 50-60 minutes or until a toothpick inserted near the center comes out clean. Cool for 15 minutes before removing from pan to a wire rack to cool completely. Dust with confectioners' sugar if desired.

Milk Chocolate Bundt Cake

PREP: 10 min. + cooling **BAKE:** 50 min. + cooling
YIELD: 12-14 servings

Sharan Williams, Spanish Fork, Utah

Try this recipe for a moist, mild chocolate cake that cuts cleanly and doesn't need frosting. This scrumptious snack cake travels very well, so it's a snap to share anywhere.

baking cakes at *high altitudes*

High altitude (over 3,000 feet) has less air pressure and drier air. These conditions affect baked goods. The lower air pressure allows the gases created by the leavening agents to expand more quickly and causes liquids to evaporate and boil at lower temperatures. The drier air also dries out the flour.

For cakes, this means that there might be excessive rising from the gases produced by the leavening. This could cause the texture to be coarse or the cake to fall before the structure is set by baking. Faster evaporation of the liquid, due to lower boiling point, would reduce the amount of liquid and increase the concentration of sugar. This higher sugar concentration may also weaken the structure of the cake.

Some measures to take for butter cakes are to increase the oven temperature 15° to 25°, which allows cakes to set faster and prevent falling. Fill baking pans half full not two-thirds full, since cakes rise higher. Reduce the leavener and the sugar and increase the liquid. Here are some general guidelines for adjusting ingredients for butter cakes.

ADJUSTMENT	3,000 FEET	5,000 FEET	7,000 FEET
For each teaspoon of baking powder, reduce by:	1/8 teaspoon	1/8-1/4 teaspoon	1/4 teaspoon
For each cup of sugar, reduce by:	0-1 tablespoon	0-2 tablespoons	1-3 tablespoons
For each cup of liquid, increase by:	1-2 tablespoons	2-4 tablespoons	3-4 tablespoons

For foam cakes, only beat the egg whites until soft peaks form (see page 14). To strengthen the structure of the cake, decrease the amount of sugar by a tablespoon or two and increase the amount of flour or egg component of the cake a little. Increasing the oven temperature by 15° to 25° will also help set the cake structure sooner.

Banana Pecan Torte

PREP: 15 min. **BAKE:** 30 min. + cooling
YIELD: 12-16 servings

Linda Fryar, Stanton, Texas

The pecans in this banana torte give it a delicious twist.

- 1 **cup butter, softened**
- 2-1/2 **cups sugar**
- 4 **eggs**
- 2 **cups mashed ripe bananas (about 3 to 4 medium)**
- 2 **teaspoons vanilla extract**
- 3-1/2 **cups all-purpose flour**
- 2 **teaspoons baking soda**
- 3/4 **teaspoon salt**
- 1/2 **cup buttermilk**
- 1 **cup chopped pecans, toasted**

FROSTING:
- 1 **package (8 ounces) cream cheese, softened**
- 1/2 **cup butter, softened**
- 3-1/2 **cups confectioners' sugar**
- 1 **teaspoon vanilla extract**

Toasted chopped pecans

1 In a mixing bowl, cream butter and sugar until light and fluffy. Add the eggs, one at a time, beating well after each addition. Beat in bananas and vanilla. Combine the flour, baking soda and salt; add to creamed mixture alternately with buttermilk. Stir in pecans.

2 Pour into three greased and floured 9-in. round baking pans. Bake at 350° for 30-35 minutes or until a toothpick inserted near the center comes out clean. Cool for 10 minutes before removing from pans to wire racks to cool completely.

BANANA PECAN TORTE

3 For the frosting, beat the cream cheese, butter and sugar in a small mixing bowl. Add vanilla. Spread between layers and over top of cake. Sprinkle with pecans. Store in the refrigerator.

Apricot Hazelnut Torte

PREP: 20 min. **BAKE:** 20 min. + cooling
YIELD: 12-14 servings

Enid Stoehr, Emsdale, Ontario

You'll elicit oohs and aahs from guests when you present this pretty torte.

- 4 **eggs,** *separated*
- 1 **cup ground hazelnuts**
- 3/4 **cup all-purpose flour**
- 2 **teaspoons baking powder**
- 1/2 **teaspoon salt**
- 2 **tablespoons water**
- 1 **teaspoon vanilla extract**
- 1 **cup sugar,** *divided*
- 2 **cups heavy whipping cream**
- 1/4 **cup confectioners' sugar**
- 2/3 **cup pureed canned apricots**
- 1/2 **cup apricot jam, warmed**

Whipped cream, sliced apricots and whole *or* **chopped hazelnuts, optional**

1 Let eggs stand at room temperature for 30 minutes. Line two greased 9-in. round baking pans with waxed paper; grease the paper and set aside. In a bowl, combine the hazelnuts, flour, baking powder and salt; set aside. In a large mixing bowl, beat the egg yolks, water and vanilla until lemon-colored. Gradually add 3/4 cup sugar; set aside. In a small mixing bowl and with clean beaters, beat egg whites on medium speed until soft peaks form. Gradually add remaining sugar, 1 tablespoon at a time, beating on high until stiff peaks form. Fold a fourth of the dry ingredients into egg yolk mixture. Repeat three times. Fold in egg white mixture.

2 Spread batter evenly into prepared pans. Bake at 350° for 20-25 minutes or until cake springs back when lightly touched. Cool for 10 minutes before removing from pans to wire racks to cool completely.

3 In a chilled large mixing bowl, beat cream until it begins to thicken. Add confectioners' sugar; beat until stiff peaks form. Fold in apricots. Split each cake into two horizontal layers. Spread filling between layers and over sides of torte. Spread jam over the top. Garnish with whipped cream, apricots and hazelnuts if desired. Store in the refrigerator.

California Cranberry Torte

PREP: 30 min. + chilling **BAKE:** 1 hour + cooling
YIELD: 12-16 servings

Pat Parsons, Bakersfield, California

Three meringue layers serve as the "cake" in this pretty dessert. A cool cranberry filling is just right for the holidays.

      6   **egg whites**
Pinch salt
  1/4   **teaspoon cream of tartar**
1-1/2   **cups sugar**
      1   **teaspoon vanilla extract**
      1   **can (16 ounces) jellied cranberry sauce**
      2   **tablespoons raspberry gelatin powder**
1-1/2   **cups heavy whipping cream**
      2   **tablespoons confectioners' sugar**
Fresh cranberries, raspberries and mint

1 Let egg whites stand at room temperature for 30 minutes. Line baking sheets with parchment paper. Draw three 8-in. circles on the paper; set aside.

2 In a large mixing bowl, beat the egg whites, salt and cream of tartar on medium speed until soft peaks form. Gradually add sugar, 2 tablespoons at a time, beating on high for 5 minutes or until stiff peaks form. Add vanilla.

3 Insert a 1/2-in. round pastry tip, #A1, in a pastry bag or heavy-duty plastic bag. Fill bag with meringue. Starting in the center of each circle on prepared sheets, pipe meringue in a spiral pattern until circle is completely filled. Bake at 250° for 1 hour. Turn oven off and let meringue dry in oven for 1 hour with door closed.

4 Meanwhile, in a saucepan, melt cranberry sauce over medium heat. Add gelatin powder; stir until dissolved. Cool. In a chilled large mixing bowl, beat cream and confectioners' sugar; fold 1 cup into cranberry mixture.

5 To assemble, place 1 tablespoon of whipped cream in the center of serving plate to hold meringue in place. Top with a meringue shell; spread a third of the cranberry mixture on top. Repeat with remaining meringues and cranberry mixture. Frost sides with reserved whipped cream. If desired, a pastry bag can be used to decorate edges of torte. Refrigerate for 6 hours or overnight. Garnish with berries and mint just before serving. Refrigerate leftovers.

HUNGARIAN WALNUT TORTE

Hungarian Walnut Torte

PREP: 35 min. + chilling **BAKE:** 20 min. + cooling
YIELD: 12 servings

Jeannette Jeremias, Kitchener, Ontario

This special cake has a creamy, not-too-sweet filling. It's impressive to serve to guests.

- 6 **eggs,** *separated*
- 1 **cup sugar**
- 1 **teaspoon vanilla extract**
- 1 **cup cake flour**
- 1 **teaspoon baking powder**
- 5 **tablespoons water**
- 1/2 **cup ground walnuts**

FILLING:

- 1-1/4 **cups milk**
- 1 **package (3.4 ounces) cook-and-serve chocolate pudding mix**
- 1/2 **cup butter, softened**
- 1/2 **cup shortening**
- 1 **cup confectioners' sugar**
- 1 **teaspoon vanilla extract**

White and dark chocolate curls, optional

1 Let eggs stand at room temperature for 30 minutes. In a large mixing bowl, beat egg yolks and sugar for 10 minutes or until light lemon-colored. Beat in vanilla. Combine cake flour and baking powder; add to egg mixture alternately with water, beating well after each addition. Fold in walnuts. In another mixing bowl and with clean beaters, beat the egg whites on high until stiff peaks form. Fold a fourth of the egg whites into batter; fold in remaining whites.

2 Pour into two greased and floured 9-in. round baking pans. Bake at 350° for 20-25 minutes or until a toothpick inserted near the center comes out clean. Cool for 10 minutes before removing from pans to wire racks to cool completely.

3 In a small saucepan, whisk the milk and pudding mix. Bring to a boil, stirring constantly. Remove from the heat. Pour into a bowl; press a piece of plastic wrap over pudding. Refrigerate for 30 minutes.

4 In a mixing bowl, cream the butter, shortening and confectioners' sugar until light and fluffy. Beat in vanilla and cooled pudding. Split each cake into two layers. Place one bottom layer on a serving plate; spread with about 3/4 cup filling. Repeat layers. Garnish with chocolate curls if desired.

Pretty Pineapple Torte

PREP: 30 min. **BAKE:** 30 min. + cooling
YIELD: 10-12 servings

Iola Egle, McCook, Nebraska

Pineapple stars in both the cake and filling in this tall, beautiful dessert.

- 3   **eggs,** *separated*
- 1/2   **cup butter, softened**
- 1   **cup sugar,** *divided*
- 1   **can (20 ounces) crushed pineapple**
- 1   **teaspoon vanilla extract**
- 2-1/2   **cups cake flour**
- 2   **teaspoons baking powder**
- 1/2   **teaspoon baking soda**
- 1/2   **teaspoon salt**

FILLING:
- 1-1/2   **cups heavy whipping cream**
- 1/4   **cup confectioners' sugar**
- 1/2   **teaspoon almond extract**
- 2   **tablespoons slivered almonds, toasted**

1 Let eggs stand at room temperature for 30 minutes. In a large mixing bowl, cream butter and 3/4 cup sugar until light and fluffy. Beat in egg yolks. Drain pineapple, reserving 2/3 cup juice. In a bowl, combine the juice, 3/4 cup pineapple and vanilla (set remaining pineapple aside for the filling). Combine the flour, baking powder, baking soda and salt; add to the creamed mixture alternately with pineapple mixture, beating well after each addition.

2 In a small mixing bowl and with clean beaters, beat egg whites on medium speed until soft peaks form. Gradually add remaining sugar, 1 tablespoon at a time, beating on high until stiff peaks form. Fold a fourth of the egg whites into batter; fold in remaining whites.

PRETTY PINEAPPLE TORTE

3 Spoon into two greased and floured 9-in. round baking pans. Bake at 350° for 28-32 minutes or until cake springs back when lightly touched. Cool for 10 minutes before removing from pans to wire racks to cool completely.

4 For filling, beat the cream, confectioners' sugar and extract in a chilled large mixing bowl until stiff peaks form. Fold in reserved pineapple. Split each cake into two horizontal layers. Spread about 3/4 cup filling between each layer; spread remaining filling over top. Sprinkle with almonds. Store in the refrigerator.

Grandma Zauner's Dobosh Torte

PREP: 30 min. **BAKE:** 15 min. + cooling
YIELD: 16 servings

Kathy Wells, Brodhead, Wisconsin

This rich, special torte makes an ideal holiday dessert.

- 6   **eggs,** *separated*
- 1   **cup sugar,** *divided*
- 2   **teaspoons vanilla extract**

Pinch salt
- 1   **cup cake flour**

FROSTING:
- 1   **cup butter, softened**
- 2   **cups confectioners' sugar**
- 4   **squares (1 ounce** *each***) semisweet chocolate, melted and cooled**
- 3   **tablespoons milk**
- 1   **teaspoon vanilla extract**
- 1   **cup heavy whipping cream**

1 Let eggs stand at room temperature for 30 minutes. Line two greased 9-in. round baking pans with waxed paper and grease and flour the paper; set aside. In a mixing bowl, beat egg yolks for 2 minutes. Add 3/4 cup sugar; beat for 3 minutes until mixture is thick, pale yellow and falls in a ribbon from beaters. Beat in vanilla.

2 In another large mixing bowl and with clean beaters, beat egg whites and salt on medium speed until soft peaks form. Gradually beat in remaining sugar, 1 tablespoon at a time, on high until stiff peaks form. Fold flour into egg yolk a third at a time. Stir in a third of the whites. Fold in remaining whites. Spread into prepared pans.

3 Bake at 350° for 15-18 minutes or until cake springs back when lightly touched. Cool for 10 minutes before removing from pans to wire racks to cool completely.

BLACK FOREST TORTE

4 In another mixing bowl, beat the first five frosting ingredients until smooth. In a chilled small mixing bowl, beat cream until stiff peaks form; fold into chocolate mixture.

5 To assemble, split each cake into two horizontal layers. Spread 1 cup frosting on one layer. Repeat using all layers. Frost top and sides of cake with remaining frosting. Sprinkle with grated chocolate if desired. Store in the refrigerator.

Black Forest Torte

PREP: 35 min. **BAKE:** 25 min. + cooling
YIELD: 12-16 servings

Glatis McNiel, Constantine, Michigan

Looking for a surefire way to impress guests? This torte features a moist chocolate cake and both a chocolate filling and a smooth cream filling.

- 2/3 cup butter
- 4 squares (1 ounce *each*) unsweetened chocolate
- 1-1/3 cups all-purpose flour
- 1-3/4 cups sugar
- 1 teaspoon baking soda
- 1/4 teaspoon baking powder
- 1-1/4 cups water
- 1 teaspoon vanilla extract
- 3 eggs

CHOCOLATE FILLING:
- 2 bars (4 ounces *each*) German sweet chocolate, *divided*
- 3/4 cup butter
- 1/2 cup chopped pecans

CREAM FILLING:
- 2 cups heavy whipping cream
- 1 tablespoon confectioners' sugar
- 1 teaspoon vanilla extract

1 Line two greased 9-in. round baking pans with waxed paper; set aside. In a heavy saucepan or microwave, melt butter and chocolate; stir until smooth and cool. In a large mixing bowl, combine the flour, sugar, baking soda and baking powder. Add the chocolate mixture, water and vanilla. Beat on low speed for 1 minute; beat on medium for 2 minutes. Add eggs, one at a time, beating well after each addition.

2 Pour into the prepared pans. Bake at 350° for 25-30 minutes or until a toothpick inserted near the center comes out clean. Cool for 10 minutes before removing from pans to wire racks to cool completely.

3 For chocolate filling, melt 1-1/2 bars of German chocolate in a heavy saucepan or microwave; stir until smooth. Stir in butter and nuts. Watching closely, cool filling just until it reaches spreading consistency. For cream filling, beat cream in a chilled large mixing bowl until it begins to thicken. Add confectioners' sugar and vanilla; beat until stiff peaks form.

4 Split each cake into two horizontal layers. Place one layer on a serving plate; cover with half of the chocolate filling. Top with a second cake layer; spread with half of the cream filling. Repeat layers. Grate remaining German chocolate; sprinkle on the top. Store in the refrigerator.

splitting
cakes into *layers*

Using a ruler, mark the center of the side of the cake with a toothpick. Continue inserting toothpicks around the cake. Using the toothpicks as a guide, cut the cake horizontally in half with a long serrated knife. Carefully remove the top half. Frost or fill

the bottom half as recipe instructs and replace the top cut side down.

Foam Cakes

Lemon Angel Food Supreme

PREP: 20 min. + standing **BAKE:** 30 min. + cooling
YIELD: 12-16 servings

Linda Blaska, Dunwoody, Georgia

This delicate cake topped with a tart, creamy lemon sauce is perfect for folks who want a little lighter dessert.

1-1/2   cups egg whites (about 12)
   1   cup cake flour
1-1/2   cups plus 2 tablespoons sugar, *divided*
1-1/2   teaspoons cream of tartar
1-1/2   teaspoons vanilla extract
 1/2   teaspoon lemon extract
 1/4   teaspoon salt
LEMON SAUCE:
   3   eggs
   1   cup sugar
 1/2   cup lemon juice
 1/4   cup butter, melted
   1   tablespoon grated lemon peel
 1/2   cup heavy whipping cream, whipped
Yellow food coloring, optional

1 Let egg whites stand at room temperature for 30 minutes. Sift cake flour and 3/4 cup plus 2 tablespoons sugar together twice; set aside. In a large mixing bowl, beat egg whites, cream of tartar, extracts and salt on medium speed until soft peaks form. Gradually add remaining sugar, 2 tablespoons at a time, beating on high until stiff peaks form. Gradually fold in flour mixture, about a fourth at a time.

LEMON ANGEL FOOD SUPREME

2 Gently spoon into an ungreased 10-in. tube pan. Cut through the batter with a knife to remove air pockets. Bake on the lowest rack at 375° for 30-35 minutes or until top springs back when lightly touched and cracks feel dry. Immediately invert baking pan; cool completely. Run a knife around sides and center tube of pan. Invert cake onto a serving plate.

3 For sauce, beat eggs and sugar in a heavy saucepan over low heat. Stir in the lemon juice, butter and lemon peel. Cook until the mixture thickens and reaches 160°, about 15 minutes; chill. Fold in whipped cream and food coloring if desired. Serve with cake. Store sauce in the refrigerator.

Homemade Angel Food Cake

PREP: 30 min. **BAKE:** 50 min. + cooling
YIELD: 12-16 servings

Joan Schroeder, Pinedale, Wyoming

Nothing can compare to the heavenly taste of homemade angel food cake. You can skip the frosting and serve slices with fresh fruit and sweetened whipped cream.

1-1/2   cups egg whites (about 12)
   1   cup cake flour
   1   cup confectioners' sugar
   1   teaspoon cream of tartar
   1   teaspoon vanilla extract
Pinch salt
1-1/4   cups sugar

FROSTING:

   1 **plain milk chocolate candy bar (7 ounces)**
   2 **cups heavy whipping cream**
   3 **tablespoons confectioners' sugar**
   1 **teaspoon vanilla extract**

Chocolate shavings, optional

1 Let egg whites stand at room temperature for 30 minutes. Sift flour and confectioners' sugar together twice; set aside. In a large mixing bowl, beat the egg whites, cream of tartar, vanilla and salt on medium speed until soft peaks form. Gradually add sugar, about 2 tablespoons at a time, beating on high until stiff glossy peaks form and sugar is dissolved. Gradually fold in flour mixture, about 1/2 cup at a time.

2 Gently spoon into an ungreased 10-in. tube pan. Cut through the batter with a knife to remove air pockets. Bake on the lowest rack at 325° for 50-60 minutes or until top springs back when lightly touched and cracks feel dry. Immediately invert baking pan; cool completely.

3 For frosting, melt the candy bar in a heavy saucepan or microwave; stir until smooth. Cool for 5 minutes. In a chilled large mixing bowl, beat cream until it begins to thicken. Add confectioners' sugar; beat until stiff peaks form. Stir in vanilla. Fold in melted chocolate.

4 Run a knife around sides and center tube of pan. Invert cake onto a serving plate; frost top and sides. Garnish with chocolate shavings if desired. Store in the refrigerator.

secrets for
successful foam cakes

- Measure ingredients accurately, using the measuring tools and techniques suggested on pages 7 and 8.
- When baking foam cakes in tube pans, set the oven rack in the lowest position.
- Preheat oven for 10 to 15 minutes before baking.
- Separate eggs when they are cold. (See Separating Eggs on page 14.)
- To ensure egg whites reach their maximum volume, they should stand at room temperature no more than 30 minutes before beating. Also, make sure there are no specks of egg yolk in the white.
- Before beating egg whites, make sure your mixing bowl and beaters are clean by washing them thoroughly in hot soapy water and drying with a clean kitchen towel. Use metal or glass mixing bowls. Plastic bowls, even freshly washed and dried ones, may have an oily film on them.
- Beat whole eggs or egg yolks until they are thick and lemon-colored.
- Gently fold in the ingredients. Using a rubber spatula, gently cut down through the ingredients/batter, move across the bottom of the bowl and bring up part of the mixture. (See Folding in Ingredients on page 163.)
- Use only the pan size recommended in the recipe.
- For a tender golden crust, use aluminum pans with a dull rather than a shiny or dark finish.

- Do not grease or flour tube pans when baking foam cakes. To rise properly, the batter needs to cling to the sides of the pan.
- To avoid large air pockets in a baked cake, cut through the batter with a knife to break air bubbles.
- Use a kitchen timer. Foam cakes are done when the top springs back when touched and the cracks at the top of the cake look and feel dry. (See Testing Foam Cakes for Doneness on page 150.)
- It's important to cool foam cakes upside down in the pan, otherwise they will collapse and flatten. If using a tube pan with legs, invert the pan onto its legs. If using a tube pan without legs, invert the pan and place the neck over a funnel or narrow bottle. (See Cooling a Foam Cake on page 153.)
- Cool cakes completely in the pan before removing. To loosen from the pan, run a thin metal spatula around the edge of the pan and around the center tube using a sawing motion. Gently press the metal spatula between the pan and the cake to loosen more. If the cake pan has a removable bottom, lift out the cake and run a knife along the bottom of the cake. If the pan is one piece, invert the pan onto a plate; tap the side of the pan with the flat side of a knife and lift the pan away from the cake.
- Cool the cake completely before filling or frosting.
- Cut foam cakes with a serrated knife or electric knife with a sawing motion.

CHOCOLATE ANGEL FOOD CAKE

3 Run a knife around the sides and center tube of pan. Invert cake onto a serving plate. Frost if desired. If frosted, store in the refrigerator.

Rainbow Angel Food Cake

PREP: 20 min. **BAKE:** 30 min. + cooling
YIELD: 12-16 servings

Pat Habiger, Spearville, Kansas

Bring the colors of spring flowers to your table with this attractive angel food cake. On the Fourth of July, keep a third of the batter plain, then tint one third red and another third blue.

1-1/2	cups egg whites (about 12)
1	cup cake flour
1-1/2	cups sugar, *divided*
1-1/2	teaspoons cream of tartar
1-1/2	teaspoons vanilla extract
1/2	teaspoon almond extract
1/4	teaspoon salt

Red, yellow and green food coloring
| 1-1/2 | cups confectioners' sugar |
| 2 | to 3 tablespoons milk |

1 Let egg whites stand at room temperature for 30 minutes. Sift flour and 3/4 cup sugar together twice; set aside. In a large mixing bowl, beat the egg whites, cream of tartar, extracts and salt on medium speed until soft peaks form. Gradually add remaining sugar, 2 tablespoons at a time, beating on high until stiff glossy peaks form and sugar is dissolved. Gradually fold in the flour mixture, a fourth at a time.

Chocolate Angel Food Cake

PREP: 25 min. **BAKE:** 45 min. + cooling
YIELD: 12-16 servings

Mary Ann Iverson, Woodville, Wisconsin

To achieve the look of the frosting in the photo above, refer to the cake comb technique in Simple Frosting Finishes on page 169.

1-1/2	cups egg whites (about 12)
3/4	cup cake flour
1-1/2	cups plus 2 tablespoons sugar, *divided*
1/4	cup baking cocoa
1-1/2	teaspoons cream of tartar
1-1/2	teaspoons vanilla extract
1/4	teaspoon salt

Rich 'n' Fluffy Chocolate Frosting (page 168), optional

1 Let egg whites stand at room temperature for 30 minutes. Sift flour, 3/4 cup plus 2 tablespoons sugar and cocoa together twice; set aside. In a large mixing bowl, beat the egg whites, cream of tartar, vanilla and salt on medium speed until soft peaks form. Gradually add remaining sugar, about 2 tablespoons at a time, beating on high until stiff glossy peaks form and sugar is dissolved. Gradually fold in the flour mixture, about 1/2 cup at a time.

2 Gently spoon into an ungreased 10-in. tube pan. Cut through the batter with a knife to remove air pockets. Bake on the lowest rack at 350° for 45-50 minutes or until the top springs back when lightly touched and cracks feel dry. Immediately invert baking pan; cool completely.

RAINBOW ANGEL FOOD CAKE

2 Divide batter into three bowls. To the first bowl, add 1 drop red and 1 drop yellow food coloring. To the second bowl, add 2 drops yellow food coloring. To the third bowl, add 2 drops green food coloring. Fold food coloring into each batter.

3 Spoon orange batter into an ungreased 10-in. tube pan; carefully spread to cover bottom. Spoon yellow batter over orange layer (do not mix). Spoon green batter over yellow layer. Bake on the lowest rack at 375° for 30-35 minutes or until top springs back when lightly touched and cracks feel dry. Immediately invert baking pan; cool completely. Run a knife around sides and center tube of pan. Invert cake onto a serving plate. Combine confectioners' sugar and milk until smooth; drizzle over cake.

Lemon Daffodil Cake

PREP: 30 min. **BAKE:** 50 min. + cooling
YIELD: 12 servings

Eunice Richardson, Shullsburg, Wisconsin

You're sure to impress dinner guests when you present this eye-catching sponge cake. A light lemon filling and frosting make it a perfect springtime dessert.

1-1/4   cups egg whites (about 10)
   1   teaspoon cream of tartar
 1/2   teaspoon salt
1-1/3   cups sugar
   1   cup all-purpose flour
 1/2   teaspoon vanilla extract
   4   egg yolks
 1/4   teaspoon almond extract
LEMON FILLING:
   1   tablespoon unflavored gelatin
 3/4   cup cold water, *divided*
   1   cup sugar
   3   tablespoons cornstarch
   4   egg yolks, beaten
 1/3   cup butter
   2   tablespoons grated lemon peel
 1/2   cup lemon juice
   1   cup heavy whipping cream, **whipped**

1 Let egg whites stand at room temperature for 30 minutes. In a large mixing bowl, beat the egg whites, cream of tartar and salt on medium speed until soft peaks form. Gradually add sugar, 2 tablespoons at a time, beating on high until stiff glossy peaks form and sugar is dissolved. Fold in flour, 1/4 cup at a time. Divide mixture in half. Fold vanilla into one portion; set aside. In another large mixing bowl, beat egg yolks on high speed

cooling a *foam cake*

If your tube pan has legs, invert the pan onto its legs until the cake is completely cool.

If your tube pan does not have legs, place pan over a funnel or the neck of a narrow bottle until cake is completely cool.

until thick and lemon-colored. Stir in almond extract. Fold in unflavored egg white batter.

2 Alternately spoon batters into an ungreased 10-in. tube pan. Gently cut through batter with a knife to swirl. Bake on the lowest rack at 325° for 50-60 minutes or until top springs back when lightly touched. Immediately invert pan; cool completely.

3 For filling, soften gelatin in 1/4 cup cold water; let stand for 1 minute. In a heavy saucepan, combine the sugar, cornstarch and remaining water until smooth. Bring to a boil over medium heat; cook and stir 2 minutes longer. Remove from the heat. Gradually stir 1/2 cup hot filling into egg yolks; return all to the pan, stirring constantly. Bring to a gentle boil, stirring constantly. Cook and stir 2 minutes longer. Remove from the heat; stir in butter and lemon peel. Gently stir in lemon juice and softened gelatin until gelatin is dissolved.

4 Cool to room temperature without stirring. Fold in whipped cream. Refrigerate until mixture achieves spreading consistency, about 40-50 minutes.

5 Run a knife around sides and center tube of pan. Remove cake; split into two horizontal layers. Spread filling between layers and over top of cake. Store in the refrigerator.

Classic Sponge Torte

PREP: 45 min. + standing **BAKE:** 15 min. + cooling
YIELD: 12 servings

Kathy Wells, Brodhead, Wisconsin

Sponge cakes call for both egg whites and egg yolks, giving them a richer texture than angel food cakes.

- 6 **eggs,** *separated*
- 1 **cup sugar,** *divided*
- 2 **teaspoons vanilla extract**

Pinch salt

- 1 **cup cake flour**

FROSTING:

- 1 **cup butter, softened**
- 2 **cups confectioners' sugar**
- 4 **squares (1 ounce** *each***) semisweet chocolate, melted**
- 3 **tablespoons milk**
- 1 **teaspoon vanilla extract**
- 1 **cup heavy whipping cream**

Grated chocolate, optional

1 Let eggs stand at room temperature for 30 minutes. Line two greased 9-in. round baking pans with waxed paper; grease and flour the waxed paper. Set aside. In a large mixing bowl, beat egg yolks for 2 minutes. Add 3/4 cup sugar; beat for 3 minutes or until mixture is thick and lemon-colored and falls in a ribbon from beaters. Beat in vanilla.

2 In another large mixing bowl and with clean beaters, beat egg whites and salt on medium speed until soft peaks form. Gradually add remaining sugar, 1 tablespoon at a time, beating on high until stiff peaks form. Fold flour into egg yolk a third at a time. Stir in a third of the whites. Fold in remaining whites.

3 Spread batter into prepared pans. Bake at 350° for 15-18 minutes or until top springs back when lightly touched. Cool for 10 minutes before removing from pans to wire racks to cool completely.

4 For frosting, in a large mixing bowl, beat the butter, confectioners' sugar, chocolate, milk and vanilla until smooth. In a chilled small mixing bowl, beat cream until stiff peaks form; fold into chocolate mixture.

5 To assemble, split each cake into two horizontal layers. Spread frosting between layers and over top and sides of cake. Sprinkle with grated chocolate if desired. Store in the refrigerator.

making a *sponge cake*

1. Beat egg yolks in a mixing bowl until they begin to thicken. Gradually add 3/4 cup sugar, beating until the mixture is lemon-colored (shown at right). Blend in flavorings. Sift together flour and salt; beat into egg yolk mixture.

2. In another mixing bowl, beat egg whites on medium speed until soft peaks form. Gradually add sugar, beating on high until stiff peaks form.

3. Spoon a fourth of the egg white mixture into the yolk mixture; carefully fold in with a rubber spatula. Fold in the remaining egg white mixture just until combined. Don't overmix. Proceed with the recipe as directed.

Confetti Cream Cake

PREP: 40 min. **BAKE:** 25 min. + cooling
YIELD: 10-12 servings

Jennie Moshier, Fresno, California

Luscious layers of cake and creamy filling form this attractive dessert. If you're short on time, ready the filling ingredients a day ahead. Then assemble and frost right before serving.

- 5 **eggs**
- 1 **teaspoon vanilla extract**
- 1 **cup sugar**
- 1 **cup all-purpose flour**

1/2 teaspoon baking powder
1/2 teaspoon salt
FILLING:
  1 package (8 ounces) cream cheese, softened
  1 cup sugar, *divided*
  1 teaspoon vanilla extract
1/4 teaspoon ground cinnamon
  1 cup (8 ounces) sour cream
1/2 cup finely chopped walnuts
1/2 cup flaked coconut, optional
1/3 cup chopped maraschino cherries
  2 milk chocolate candy bars (1.55 ounces *each*), shaved *or* finely chopped
1-1/2 cups heavy whipping cream

1 In a large mixing bowl, beat eggs and vanilla on high speed until foamy. Add sugar; beat until thick and lemon-colored. Combine the flour, baking powder and salt; fold into egg mixture, a third at a time.

2 Pour into two greased and floured 9-in. round baking pans. Bake at 350° for 25-30 minutes or until top springs back when lightly touched. Cool for 5 minutes before removing from pans to wire racks to cool completely.

3 In a large mixing bowl, beat the cream cheese, 2/3 cup sugar, vanilla and cinnamon until smooth. Stir in the sour cream, walnuts, coconut if desired and cherries. Fold in chocolate. In a chilled large mixing bowl, beat cream until it begins to thicken. Add remaining sugar; beat until soft peaks form. Fold half of the whipped cream into the cream cheese mixture. Set remaining whipped cream aside.

4 Split each cake into two horizontal layers; spread a fourth of the cream cheese mixture on one layer. Repeat. Frost sides with reserved whipped cream. Store in the refrigerator.

Flourless Chocolate Cake

PREP: 20 min. + standing **BAKE:** 40 min. + cooling
YIELD: 16 servings

Taste of Home Test Kitchen

One bite of fudgy Flourless Chocolate Cake and you'll see why it's pure pleasure for confirmed chocoholics! A small slice of this rich, dense dessert goes a long way.

  4 eggs, *separated*
10 tablespoons butter
1/2 cup sugar, *divided*

  6 squares (1 ounce *each*) semisweet chocolate, chopped
  3 squares (1 ounce *each*) unsweetened chocolate, chopped
  2 teaspoons vanilla extract
1/4 cup finely ground pecans, toasted
Chocolate Ganache (page 167), optional
Sliced strawberries and fresh mint, optional

1 Let eggs stand at room temperature for 30 minutes. In a heavy saucepan, melt butter, 1/4 cup sugar and chocolate over low heat, stirring constantly. Cool until mixture is lukewarm. In a large mixing bowl, beat egg yolks until thick and lemon-colored, about 3 minutes. Beat in vanilla. Gradually beat in pecans and chocolate mixture.

2 In a small mixing bowl and with clean beaters, beat egg whites on medium speed until soft peaks form. Gradually add remaining sugar, 1 tablespoon at a time, beating on high speed until stiff peaks form. Stir a small amount of whites into chocolate mixture. Fold in remaining whites.

3 Pour into a greased 9-in. springform pan. Place on a baking sheet. Bake at 350° for 40-50 minutes or until a toothpick inserted near the center comes out with a few moist crumbs. Cool on a wire rack for 20 minutes. Carefully run a knife around edge of pan to loosen; remove sides of pan and cool completely. Frost with Chocolate Ganache if desired. Garnish with strawberries and mint if desired.

FLOURLESS CHOCOLATE CAKE

PECAN CAKE ROLL

Pecan Cake Roll

PREP: 20 min. + chilling **BAKE:** 10 min. + cooling
YIELD: 10-12 servings

Shirley Awald, Walkerton, Indiana

Cake rolls are easy to make and bake in minutes, but the results really look like you fussed.

- 4 **eggs,** *separated*
- 1 **cup confectioners' sugar**
- 2 **cups ground pecans**
- 1 **cup heavy whipping cream**
- 3 **tablespoons sugar**
- 2 **teaspoons baking cocoa**
- 1/2 **teaspoon vanilla extract**

Chocolate shavings and additional confectioners' sugar, optional

1 Let eggs stand at room temperature for 30 minutes. Line a greased 15-in. x 10-in. x 1-in. baking pan with waxed paper; grease and flour paper and set aside.

2 In a large mixing bowl, beat egg yolks and confectioners' sugar until thick and lemon-colored, about 5 minutes. In another mixing bowl and with clean beaters, beat whites until soft peaks form; fold into yolk mixture. Fold in pecans until well blended (batter will be thin).

3 Spread batter into prepared pan. Bake at 375° for 10-15 minutes or until cake springs back when lightly touched. Cool in pan for 5 minutes. Turn the cake onto a kitchen towel dusted with confectioners' sugar. Gently peel off waxed paper.

Roll up cake in towel jelly-roll style, starting with short end. Cool completely on wire rack.

4 Meanwhile, beat the cream until it begins to thicken. Add the sugar, cocoa and vanilla; beat until soft peaks form.

5 Unroll cake; spread filling over cake to within 1/2 in. of edges. Roll up again. Cover and refrigerate for 1 hour before serving. If desired, garnish with chocolate shavings and confectioners' sugar. Refrigerate leftovers.

Editor's Note: This recipe does not use flour.

making a *cake roll*

1. Cool cake in the pan for 5 minutes. Turn out onto a kitchen towel dusted with confectioners' sugar; gently peel off waxed paper. Roll up cake in the towel jelly-roll style, starting with a short side. Cool completely on a wire rack.

2. Unroll cake and spread filling evenly over cake to within 1/2 in. of edges.

3. Starting with a short side, roll up the cake loosely, pulling away the towel. Place seam side down on a serving platter.

Gingerbread Cake Roll

PREP: 25 min. **BAKE:** 10 min. + cooling
YIELD: 10 servings

Bernadette Colvin, Houston, Texas

Instead of making ordinary gingerbread, turn it into this awesome cake roll. The creamy spiced filling is a delightful complement to the moist cake.

- 3 **eggs,** *separated*
- 1/2 **cup molasses**
- 1 **tablespoon butter, melted**
- 1/4 **cup sugar**
- 1 **cup all-purpose flour**
- 1/4 **teaspoon baking soda**
- 1/2 **teaspoon** *each* **ground cinnamon, ginger and cloves**
- 1/8 **teaspoon salt**
- 1 **to 2 tablespoons confectioners' sugar**

SPICED CREAM FILLING:
- 1-1/2 **cups heavy whipping cream**
- 1/3 **cup confectioners' sugar**
- 1 **teaspoon ground cinnamon**
- 1 **teaspoon vanilla extract**
- 1/4 **teaspoon ground cloves**

Additional ground cinnamon, optional

1 Let eggs stand at room temperature for 30 minutes. Line a greased 15-in. x 10-in. x 1-in. baking pan with waxed paper; grease and flour the paper. Set aside. In a large mixing bowl, beat egg yolks on high speed until thickened, about 3 minutes. Beat in molasses and butter. In a small mixing bowl and with clean beaters, beat egg whites on medium speed until foamy. Gradually add sugar, 1 tablespoon at a time, beating on high until soft peaks form. Fold into yolk mixture. Combine the flour, baking soda, spices and salt; gently fold into egg mixture until combined.

2 Spread batter into prepared pan. Bake at 375° for 9-12 minutes or until top springs back when lightly touched. Cool in pan for 5 minutes. Turn the cake onto a kitchen towel dusted with confectioners' sugar. Gently peel off waxed paper. Roll up cake in the towel jelly-roll style, starting with a short side. Cool completely on a wire rack.

3 In a chilled large mixing bowl, combine the first five filling ingredients; beat until soft peaks form. Unroll cake; spread half of the filling evenly over cake to within 1/2 in. of edges. Roll up again. Spread remaining filling over cake. Sprinkle with cinnamon if desired. Store in the refrigerator.

Rainbow Sherbet Cake Roll

PREP: 20 min. + freezing **BAKE:** 20 min. + cooling
YIELD: 2 cake rolls (10 servings each)

Karen Edland, McHenry, North Dakota

A cake roll doesn't have to be complicated, especially when you start out with an angel food cake mix. For added convenience, this sherbet-filled dessert can be kept in the freezer for weeks.

- 1 **package (16 ounces) one-step angel food cake mix**
- 1 **to 2 tablespoons confectioners' sugar**
- 1/2 **gallon berry rainbow sherbet**

1 Coat two 15-in. x 10-in. x 1-in. baking pans with nonstick cooking spray; line pans with waxed paper and spray the paper. Prepare cake mix according to package directions; spread batter into prepared pans. Bake at 375° for 18-22 minutes or until the top springs back when lightly touched. Cool in pans for 5 minutes.

2 Turn each cake onto a kitchen towel dusted with confectioners' sugar. Gently peel off waxed paper. Roll up cakes in the towels jelly-roll style, starting with a short side. Cool completely on a wire rack.

3 Unroll cakes; spread each with 4 cups sherbet to within 1/2 in. of edges. Roll up again. Place seam side down on plastic wrap. Wrap securely; freeze until firm, about 6 hours. Remove from the freezer 15 minutes before serving. Cut into 1-in. slices. Freeze leftovers.

GINGERBREAD CAKE ROLL

Genoise with Fruit 'n' Cream Filling

PREP: 35 min. **BAKE:** 25 min. + cooling
YIELD: 10-12 servings

Taste of Home Test Kitchen

Sweet syrup soaks into the tender layers of this classic French sponge cake. Complete the presentation with sweetened cream and assorted fresh berries.

- 6 eggs, lightly beaten
- 1 cup sugar
- 1 teaspoon grated lemon peel
- 1 teaspoon lemon extract
- 1 cup all-purpose flour
- 1/2 cup butter, melted and cooled

SUGAR SYRUP:

- 3 tablespoons boiling water
- 2 tablespoons sugar
- 1/4 cup cold water
- 1-1/2 teaspoons lemon extract

FILLING:

- 1 cup heavy whipping cream
- 1/2 cup confectioners' sugar
- 1 teaspoon vanilla extract, optional
- 3 cups mixed fresh berries

1 Line two greased 9-in. round baking pans with waxed paper and grease the paper; set aside. In a large heatproof mixing bowl, combine eggs and sugar; place over a large saucepan filled with 1-2 in. of simmering water. Heat over low heat, stirring occasionally, until mixture reaches 110°, about 8-10 minutes.

2 Remove from the heat; add lemon peel and extract. Beat on high speed until mixture is lemon-colored and more than doubles in volume. Fold in flour, 1/4 cup at a time. Gently fold in butter. Spread into prepared pans.

3 Bake at 350° for 25-30 minutes or until a toothpick inserted near the center comes out clean. Cool for 10 minutes before removing from pans to wire racks to cool completely.

4 In a bowl, combine boiling water and sugar; stir until sugar is dissolved. Stir in cold water and extract. Using a fork, evenly poke 1/2-in.-deep holes in each cake. Spoon sugar syrup over cake surface. In a small mixing bowl, beat cream until it begins to thicken. Add sugar and vanilla if desired; beat until soft peaks form.

5 Place one cake on a serving platter; spread with half of the whipped cream and top with half of the berries. Repeat layers. Store in the refrigerator.

Banana Chiffon Cake

PREP: 20 min. **BAKE:** 1 hour + cooling
YIELD: 12-16 servings

Nancy Horsburgh, Everett, Ontario

Stock up on overripe bananas when they're on sale. Freeze them whole and unpeeled in a large resealable plastic bag. Take out what you need from the freezer, then thaw and peel before mashing.

        5 **eggs,** *separated*
   2-1/4 **cups cake flour**
   1-1/2 **cups sugar**
        1 **tablespoon baking powder**
        1 **teaspoon salt**
      1/3 **cup vegetable oil**
      1/3 **cup water**
        1 **teaspoon vanilla extract**
        1 **cup mashed ripe bananas (about 2 medium)**
Chocolate frosting *or* **frosting of your choice**

1 Let eggs stand at room temperature for 30 minutes. In a large mixing bowl, combine the flour, sugar, baking powder and salt. In a bowl, whisk the egg yolks, oil, water and vanilla; add to dry ingredients along with bananas. Beat until well blended. In another large mixing bowl and with clean beaters, beat egg whites on high speed until stiff peaks form. Fold into yolk mixture.

2 Gently spoon batter into an ungreased 10-in. tube pan. Cut through batter with a knife to remove air pockets. Bake on lowest rack at 325° for 60-65 minutes or until top springs back when lightly touched. Immediately invert baking pan; cool completely. Run a knife around sides and center tube of pan. Invert cake onto serving plate; frost top and sides.

Orange Chiffon Cake

PREP: 15 min. + standing **BAKE:** 45 min. + cooling
YIELD: 12-16 servings

Marjorie Ebert, South Dayton, New York

The delicate orange flavor of this simply delicious cake is perfect for rounding out a rich meal. The orange glaze would also be a nice way to top off slices of your favorite angel food cake.

        6 **eggs,** *separated*
        2 **cups all-purpose flour**
   1-1/2 **cups sugar**
        1 **teaspoon salt**
      1/2 **teaspoon baking soda**
      3/4 **cup fresh orange juice**
      1/2 **cup vegetable oil**
        2 **tablespoons grated orange peel**
      1/2 **teaspoon cream of tartar**
ORANGE GLAZE:
      1/2 **cup butter**
        2 **cups confectioners' sugar**
        2 **to 4 tablespoons fresh orange juice**
      1/2 **teaspoon grated orange peel**

1 Let eggs stand at room temperature for 30 minutes. In a large mixing bowl, combine the flour, sugar, salt, and baking soda. In a bowl, whisk the egg yolks, orange juice, oil and orange peel; add to dry ingredients. Beat until well blended.

2 In another large mixing bowl and with clean beaters, beat egg whites and cream of tartar on high speed until stiff peaks form. Fold into orange mixture.

3 Gently spoon batter into an ungreased 10-in. tube pan. Cut through the batter with a knife to remove air pockets. Bake on the lowest rack at 350° for 45-50 minutes or until top springs back when lightly touched. Immediately invert pan; cool completely. Run a knife around sides and center tube of pan. Invert cake onto a serving plate.

4 For glaze, melt the butter in a saucepan; add remaining glaze ingredients. Stir until smooth. Pour over the top of the cake, allowing it to drizzle down sides.

problem-solving pointers *for Foam Cakes*

CAKE IS HEAVY AND DENSE

- Oven temperature was too low. Check temperature with an oven thermometer.
- Didn't use large eggs.
- Ingredients were folded in too vigorously.
- Eggs were underbeaten.
- There was egg yolk in the egg whites before beating.
- Egg whites were beaten in a bowl with a greasy film.

CAKE TOP HAS SUNK

- Oven temperature was too high. Check temperature with an oven thermometer.
- Cake was underbaked.

Marble Chiffon Cake

PREP: 15 min. + standing **BAKE:** 1 hour + cooling
YIELD: 16 servings

LuAnn Heikkila, Floodwood, Minnesota

This confection's a real winner—in taste and in looks!

- 7 **eggs**, *separated*
- 2 **squares (1 ounce *each*) unsweetened chocolate**
- 1-3/4 **cups sugar**, *divided*
- 1/4 **cup hot water**
- 2 **cups all-purpose flour**
- 2 **teaspoons baking powder**
- 1 **teaspoon salt**
- 1/4 **teaspoon baking soda**
- 3/4 **cup water**
- 1/2 **cup vegetable oil**
- 2 **teaspoons vanilla extract**
- 1/2 **teaspoon cream of tartar**

FROSTING:

- 4 **squares (1 ounce *each*) semisweet chocolate**
- 1 **tablespoon butter**
- 7 **tablespoons heavy whipping cream**
- 1 **teaspoon vanilla extract**
- 1-1/2 **cups confectioners' sugar**

1 Let eggs stand at room temperature for 30 minutes. In a small saucepan or microwave, melt unsweetened chocolate; stir until smooth. Add 1/4 cup sugar and hot water; mix well and set aside.

2 In a large mixing bowl, combine the flour, baking powder, salt, baking soda and remaining sugar. Whisk together the egg yolks, water, oil and vanilla; add to flour mixture and beat until moistened. Beat for 3 minutes on medium speed; set aside.

3 In another large mixing bowl and with clean beaters, beat egg whites and cream of tartar on high speed until stiff peaks form. Stir a fourth of egg whites into the batter, then fold in remaining whites. Divide batter in half; gradually fold chocolate mixture into one portion.

4 Alternately spoon the plain and chocolate batters into an ungreased 10-in. tube pan. Swirl with a knife. Bake on the lowest rack at 325° for 60-65 minutes or until top springs back when lightly touched. Immediately invert the cake; cool completely. Run a knife around sides and center tube of pan; remove cake to serving plate.

5 For frosting, melt semisweet chocolate and butter in a small saucepan or microwave; stir until smooth. Remove from the heat; stir in cream and vanilla. Whisk in confectioners' sugar until smooth. Immediately spoon over cake.

MARBLE CHIFFON CAKE

Chiffon Nut Cake

PREP: 15 min. **BAKE:** 1 hour + cooling
YIELD: 12-16 servings

Anna Knauser, Robesonia, Pennsylvania

Chopped hickory nuts add rich taste and a subtle crunch to every slice. If you can't find hickory nuts, you can use pecans instead.

- 7 **eggs**, *separated*
- 2 **cups all-purpose flour, sifted**
- 1-1/2 **cups sugar**
- 1 **teaspoon baking powder**
- 1 **teaspoon salt**
- 1/2 **cup vegetable oil**
- 3/4 **cup water**
- 1 **teaspoon vanilla extract**
- 1/2 **teaspoon cream of tartar**
- 1 **cup chopped hickory nuts *or* pecans**

CREAMY VANILLA FROSTING:

- 4 **cups confectioners' sugar**
- 1/2 **cup butter, softened**
- 1-1/2 **teaspoons vanilla extract**
- 4 **to 6 tablespoons milk**

Chopped hickory nuts *or* pecan halves

CHIFFON NUT CAKE

Poppy Seed Chiffon Cake

PREP: 25 min. **BAKE:** 55 min. + cooling
YIELD: 12-16 servings

Irene Hirsch, Tustin, California

There's just something about the combination of poppy seeds and lemon that people can't resist. With a flavorful frosting, this cake melts in your mouth.

7	egg whites
2-1/2	cups all-purpose flour
1	cup sugar
1	tablespoon baking powder
1/2	teaspoon salt
5	egg yolks
3/4	cup water
1/2	cup vegetable oil
1	teaspoon lemon extract
1	teaspoon grated lemon peel
1	can (12-1/2 ounces) poppy seed filling
1/2	teaspoon cream of tartar

LEMON BUTTER FROSTING:

6	tablespoons butter, softened
4	cups confectioners' sugar
3	to 5 tablespoons milk
1	tablespoon lemon juice
1	teaspoon lemon extract

1 Let egg whites stand at room temperature for 30 minutes. In a large mixing bowl, combine the flour, sugar, baking powder and salt. In a bowl, whisk the egg yolks, water, oil, lemon extract, lemon peel and poppy seed filling. Add to dry ingredients; beat until well blended. In another mixing bowl and with clean beaters, beat egg whites and cream of tartar on high speed until stiff peaks form. Fold into egg yolk mixture.

2 Gently spoon batter into an ungreased 10-in. tube pan. Cut through the batter with a knife to remove air pockets. Bake on the lowest rack at 350° for 55-60 minutes or until top springs back when lightly touched. Immediately invert pan; cool completely. Run a knife around edge and center tube of pan. Invert cake onto a serving plate.

3 For frosting, beat butter and confectioners' sugar in a large mixing bowl. Add the milk, lemon juice and extract; beat until smooth. Frost cake.

1 Let eggs stand at room temperature for 30 minutes. In a large mixing bowl, combine the flour, sugar, baking powder and salt. Add the oil, egg yolks, water and vanilla; beat until smooth. In another mixing bowl and with clean beaters, beat egg whites and cream of tartar on high speed until stiff peaks form. Gradually fold into egg yolk mixture. Fold in nuts.

2 Gently spoon batter into an ungreased 10-in. tube pan. Cut through the batter with a knife to remove air pockets. Bake on the lowest rack at 325° for 60-65 minutes or until top springs back when lightly touched and cracks feel dry. Immediately invert pan; cool completely. Run a knife around the sides and center tube of pan. Invert cake onto a serving plate.

3 For frosting, in a bowl, combine the confectioners' sugar, butter, vanilla and enough milk to achieve desired consistency. Frost top and sides of cake; garnish with nut halves.

Tunnel of Berries Cake

PREP: 30 min. **BAKE:** 1 hour + cooling
YIELD: 12-16 servings

Shirley Noe, Lebanon Junction, Kentucky

A tunnel of strawberries is tucked inside this frosted cake.

TUNNEL OF BERRIES CAKE

6	eggs, *separated*
2-1/4	cups cake flour
2	cups sugar, *divided*
1	tablespoon baking powder
1	teaspoon ground cinnamon
3/4	teaspoon salt
3/4	cup water
1/2	cup vegetable oil
1-1/2	teaspoons vanilla extract, *divided*
1/4	teaspoon cream of tartar
4	cups fresh whole strawberries, *divided*
2-1/2	cups heavy whipping cream

1 Let eggs stand at room temperature for 30 minutes. In a large mixing bowl, combine flour, 1 cup sugar, baking powder, cinnamon and salt. In a bowl, whisk the egg yolks, water, oil and 1 teaspoon vanilla; add to dry ingredients. Beat until well blended. In another large mixing bowl and with clean beaters, beat egg whites and cream of tartar on medium speed until soft peaks form. Fold into yolk mixture.

2 Gently spoon batter into an ungreased 10-in. tube pan. Cut through the batter with a knife to remove air pockets. Bake on the lowest rack at 325° for 60-70 minutes or until top springs back when lightly touched. Immediately invert pan; cool completely. Run a knife around sides and center tube of pan. Invert cake onto a serving plate.

3 Slice off the top 1 in. of the cake; set aside. With a knife, cut a tunnel about 1-1/2 in. deep in bottom of cake, leaving a 3/4-in. shell. Remove cake from tunnel and save for another use. Chop half of the strawberries; set aside. In a chilled large mixing bowl, beat cream until it begins to thicken. Gradually add the remaining sugar and vanilla, beating until stiff peaks form. Combine 1-1/2 cups cream mixture and chopped berries.

4 Fill the tunnel with strawberry mixture. Replace cake top. Frost cake with the remaining cream mixture. Refrigerate. Just before serving, cut the remaining strawberries in half for garnish. Refrigerate leftovers.

filling and frosting a *tube cake*

1. Cut a 1-in. slice off the top of the cake; carefully set aside. Using a very sharp knife, carve a 1-1/2-in. deep tunnel in the cake, leaving a 3/4-in. wall on all sides. Carefully remove cake and save for another use.

2. Spoon filling into the tunnel.

3. Carefully replace cake top. Frost top and sides of cake. Chill for 2 to 8 hours before serving.

Chocolate Chiffon Cake

PREP: 25 min. + cooling **BAKE:** 1 hour + cooling
YIELD: 12-16 servings

Erma Fox, Memphis, Missouri

If you want to offer family and friends a dessert that really stands out from the rest, this is the cake to make. Beautiful high layers of rich sponge cake are drizzled with a succulent chocolate glaze.

7	eggs, *separated*
1/2	cup baking cocoa
3/4	cup boiling water
1-3/4	cups cake flour
1-3/4	cups sugar
1/2	teaspoon baking soda
1	teaspoon salt
1/2	cup vegetable oil
2	teaspoons vanilla extract
1/4	teaspoon cream of tartar

ICING:

1/3	cup butter
2	cups confectioners' sugar
2	squares (1 ounce *each*) unsweetened chocolate, melted and cooled
1-1/2	teaspoons vanilla extract
3	to 4 tablespoons hot water

Chopped nuts, optional

1 Let eggs stand at room temperature for 30 minutes. In a bowl, combine the cocoa and water until smooth; cool for 20 minutes. In a large mixing bowl, combine the flour, sugar, baking soda and salt. In a bowl, whisk the egg yolks,

CHOCOLATE CHIFFON CAKE

folding in *ingredients*

To fold a lighter mixture into a heavier one, use a rubber spatula to gently cut down through the middle of the ingredients. Move the spatula across the bottom of the bowl and bring up part of the heavier mixture. Repeat this circular motion just until mixture is combined.

oil and vanilla; add to dry ingredients along with the cocoa mixture. Beat until well blended. In another large mixing bowl and with clean beaters, beat egg whites and cream of tartar on high speed until stiff peaks form. Gradually fold into egg yolk mixture.

2 Gently spoon batter into an ungreased 10-in. tube pan. Cut through the batter with a knife to remove air pockets. Bake on lowest rack at 325° for 60-65 minutes or until top springs back when lightly touched. Immediately invert pan; cool completely. Run a knife around sides and center tube of pan. Invert cake onto a serving plate.

3 For icing, melt butter in a saucepan. Remove from the heat; stir in the confectioners' sugar, chocolate, vanilla and water. Drizzle over cake. Sprinkle with nuts if desired.

Flavorful Frostings

secrets for *successful frosting*

- Always sift confectioners' sugar before using it for frosting. If there are any lumps in the sugar, there will be lumps in the frosting, which will clog decorating tips.
- Frosting needs to be just the right consistency for spreading and decorating. If it's too thin, add a little confectioners' sugar. If it's too thick, add a little milk.
- Tint white frosting with liquid, gel or paste food coloring. Liquid will give a pastel color; gel and paste give a deeper color. Add a little at a time, stir in and check the color. You can always add more, but it's hard to lighten the color. The color generally darkens as the frosting dries.

Easy Vanilla Buttercream Frosting

PREP/TOTAL TIME: 10 min. **YIELD:** about 3 cups

Diana Wilson, Denver, Colorado

This basic buttery frosting has unmatchable homemade taste. With a few simple variations, you can come up with different colors and flavors.

- 1/2 cup butter, softened
- 4-1/2 cups confectioners' sugar
- 1-1/2 teaspoons vanilla extract
- 5 to 6 tablespoons milk

In a large mixing bowl, cream butter until light and fluffy. Beat in confectioners' sugar and vanilla. Add enough milk to achieve desired consistency.

Easy Chocolate Buttercream Frosting: Prepare as directed above, except use 4 cups confectioners' sugar, 1/2 cup baking cocoa and 6-7 tablespoons milk.

Easy Peanut Butter Frosting: Prepare as directed above, except use 1/2 cup peanut butter instead of the butter and use 6-8 tablespoons milk.

Easy Lemon Buttercream Frosting: Prepare as directed above, except use 5-6 tablespoons lemon juice instead of the milk and add 1 teaspoon grated lemon peel.

Easy Orange Buttercream Frosting: Prepare as directed above, except use 5-6 tablespoons orange juice instead of the milk and add 1 teaspoon grated orange peel.

Easy Almond Buttercream Frosting: Prepare as directed at left, except use 1/2 to 3/4 teaspoon almond extract instead of the vanilla.

Easy Peppermint Buttercream Frosting: Prepare as directed at left, except use 1/2 to 3/4 teaspoon peppermint extract instead of the vanilla.

Favorite White Frosting

PREP: 20 min. + chilling **YIELD:** about 3-1/3 cups

Martha Mills, Walterboro, South Carolina

A light texture and buttery flavor makes this an ideal frosting for so many cakes. It allows the fabulous taste of the cake to shine.

- 2 tablespoons cornstarch
- 1 cup cold water
- 1 cup butter, softened
- 1 cup sugar
- 1/2 teaspoon almond extract

1 In a saucepan, combine cornstarch and water until smooth. Bring to a boil over medium heat; cook and stir for 2 minutes or until thickened. Refrigerate for 1 hour.

2 In a large mixing bowl, cream butter and sugar until light and fluffy. Beat in almond extract. Add cornstarch mixture and beat until sugar is dissolved and frosting is fluffy, about 4 minutes. Store in the refrigerator.

Soft Lemon Frosting

PREP/TOTAL TIME: 5 min. **YIELD:** about 4 cups

Madge Robertson, Murfreesboro, Arkansas

The lemonade concentrate gives this frosting a fresh citrus flavor. It makes a pretty topping for white cake or cupcakes, especially when garnished with grated lemon peel. Plus, it's a snap to stir up in a jiffy.

- 1 can (14 ounces) sweetened condensed milk
- 3/4 cup lemonade concentrate
- 1 carton (8 ounces) frozen whipped topping, thawed

In a bowl, combine milk and lemonade concentrate. Fold in whipped topping. Store in the refrigerator.

Classic Vanilla Buttercream Frosting

PREP/TOTAL TIME: 30 min.   **YIELD:** 3 cups

Taste of Home Test Kitchen

This rich, classic frosting has just the right amount of sweetness. It complements any flavor of cake.

- 1 cup sugar
- 1/3 cup water
- 6 egg yolks, lightly beaten
- 1-1/2 teaspoons vanilla extract
- 1-1/2 cups butter, softened
- 6 tablespoons confectioners' sugar

1 In a heavy saucepan, bring sugar and water to a boil; cook over medium-high heat until sugar is dissolved. Remove from the heat. Add a small amount of hot mixture to egg yolks; return all to the pan, stirring constantly. Cook 2 minutes longer or until mixture thickens, stirring constantly. Remove from the heat; stir in vanilla. Cool to room temperature.

2 In a mixing bowl, with the whisk attachment, cream butter until fluffy, about 5 minutes. Gradually beat in cooked sugar mixture. Beat in confectioners' sugar until fluffy, about 5 minutes. If necessary, refrigerate until frosting reaches spreading consistency. Store in the refrigerator.

Classic Chocolate Buttercream Frosting: Prepare buttercream frosting as directed above and set aside. In a saucepan or microwave, melt 1 cup semisweet chocolate chips with 3 tablespoons water; stir until smooth. Remove from the heat; cool to room temperature. Stir into buttercream frosting.

Cream Cheese Frosting

PREP/TOTAL TIME: 10 min.   **YIELD:** about 3 cups

Sharon Lugdon, Costigan, Maine

Cream cheese plus a hint of vanilla makes this smooth versatile frosting perfect for carrot cake and pumpkin bars.

- 2 packages (3 ounces *each*) cream cheese, softened
- 1/2 cup butter, softened
- 2 teaspoons vanilla extract
- 1/4 teaspoon salt
- 5 to 6 cups confectioners' sugar

In a large mixing bowl, beat cream cheese, butter, vanilla and salt until smooth. Gradually beat in confectioners' sugar. Store in the refrigerator.

FLUFFY WHITE FROSTING

Fluffy White Frosting

PREP/TOTAL TIME: 15 min.   **YIELD:** about 5 cups

Georgie Bohmann, West Allis, Wisconsin

For a heavenly light and fluffy frosting, you can't top this variation of the classic 7-minute frosting.

- 1-1/2 cups sugar
- 2 egg whites
- 1/3 cup water
- 1/4 teaspoon cream of tartar
- 1 teaspoon vanilla extract

In a large heavy saucepan over low heat or double boiler over simmering water, combine the sugar, egg whites, water and cream of tartar. With a portable mixer, beat mixture on low speed for 1 minute. Continue beating on low speed over low heat until frosting reaches 160°, about 8-10 minutes. Pour into a large mixing bowl; add vanilla. Beat on high speed until stiff peaks form, about 7 minutes. Store in refrigerator.

Editor's Note: A stand mixer is recommended for beating the frosting after it reaches 160°.

filling & frosting a *layer cake*

1. After the cake layers have completely cooled to room temperature, use a soft pastry brush to carefully remove any loose crumbs on the top and sides of each layer. Trim off any crisp edges with a knife or kitchen scissors.

2. To keep crumbs from loosening from the cake and mixing into the frosting, first spread a very thin layer of frosting over the top and sides. If the frosting is very thick, it may need to be thinned with a teaspoon or two of milk or cream.

3. To keep the serving plate clean, line it with 3-in. strips of waxed paper. Center the first cake layer over the strips. To use frosting as the cake filling, dollop about 1/2 cup frosting over the top of the cake and spread to the edges. Repeat with the second layer, if frosting a three-layer cake.

4. If your cake filling is different from the frosting, it might spill out the edges and discolor the frosting. To prevent this, pipe or spread a 1/2-in. strip of icing around the top edge of each layer before spreading the filling in the center. This keeps the filling inside.

5. Top with the last layer. Frost the sides of the cake, building up the top edge of the cake slightly. Make large swirling strokes in a vertical pattern.

6. Spread remaining frosting over the top of the cake, smoothing right to the edges of the cake. Swirl top to match sides. Garnish or decorate if desired. Carefully remove waxed paper by pulling one piece at a time out from under the cake.

Caramel Frosting

PREP: 20 min. + cooling **YIELD:** about 2-1/4 cups

Virginia Breitmeyer, Craftsbury, Vermont

I love this creamy caramel frosting, which is an ideal complement to spice cupcakes. The recipe originated with my grandmother.

- 1 cup packed brown sugar
- 1/2 cup butter
- 1/4 cup milk
- 1 teaspoon vanilla extract
- 2-1/2 to 3 cups confectioners' sugar

In a heavy saucepan, combine the brown sugar, butter and milk; bring to a boil over medium heat. Cook and stir for 2 minutes. Remove from the heat; stir in vanilla. Cool to lukewarm. Gradually beat in confectioners' sugar until the frosting achieves spreading consistency.

frosting amounts for *cakes*

For cooked fluffy frostings, double the amounts needed.
Plan on an extra 1/2 to 1 cup frosting to use for decorating.

PAN SIZE AND SHAPE	BETWEEN EACH LAYER	SIDES	TOP	TOTAL
8- or 9-in. round, two layers	1/2 cup	1-1/4 cups	3/4 cup	2-1/2 cups
8- or 9-in. square, one layer	—	1 cup	3/4 cup	1-3/4 cups
8- or 9-in. square, two layers	3/4 cup	1-1/2 cups	3/4 cup	3 cups
13- x 9-in. rectangle	—	1 cup	1-1/4 cups	2-1/4 cups
10-in. tube pan (angel food) or 10-in. fluted tube pan (bundt)	—	1-1/2 cups	3/4 cup	2-1/4 cups
24 cupcakes	—	—	2-1/4 cups	2-1/4 cups

Chocolate Ganache

PREP: 5 min. **COOK:** 15 min. + chilling
YIELD: 1-1/4 cups

Taste of Home Test Kitchen

This smooth satin chocolate frosting will bring a touch of elegance to even the most basic cake.

- 1 **cup (6 ounces) semisweet chocolate chips**
- 2/3 **cup heavy whipping cream**

1 In a heavy saucepan, melt chocolate chips with cream over low heat. Remove from the heat. Refrigerate, stirring occasionally.

2 For a pourable ganache, cool until mixture reaches 85°-90° and is slightly thickened, about 40 minutes. Pour over cake, allowing some to flow down the edges to completely coat. Spread ganache with a spatula if necessary to evenly coat, working quickly before it thickens. Chill until set.

3 For a spreadable ganache, chill until mixture reaches a spreading consistency. Spread over cake. Chill until set. Store in the refrigerator.

Sweetened Whipping Cream

PREP/TOTAL TIME: 10 min. **YIELD:** 2 cups

Taste of Home Test Kitchen

Sometimes a dollop of sweetened whipped cream is all you need to top your favorite cake or other dessert. To make ahead, slightly underwhip the cream, then cover and refrigerate for several hours. Beat briefly just before using.

- 1 **cup heavy whipping cream**
- 3 **tablespoons confectioners' sugar**
- 1/2 **teaspoon vanilla extract**

In a chilled small mixing bowl and with chilled beaters, beat cream until it begins to thicken. Add confectioners' sugar and vanilla; beat until soft peaks form. Store in the refrigerator.

Bakery Frosting

PREP/TOTAL TIME: 10 min. **YIELD:** 8 cups

Barbara Jones, Pana, Illinois

This recipe makes it easy to capture the fabulous flavor of cakes from the best bakeries. A big batch of this sweet frosting keeps for 3 months in the refrigerator.

- 2 **cups shortening**
- 1/2 **cup nondairy creamer**
- 1 **teaspoon almond extract**
- 1 **package (32 ounces) confectioners' sugar**
- 1/2 **to 3/4 cup water**

Food coloring, optional

In a large mixing bowl, beat the shortening, creamer and extract. Gradually beat in confectioners' sugar. Add enough water until frosting reaches desired consistency. If desired, add food coloring. Store in the refrigerator for up to 3 months. Bring to room temperature before spreading.

CHOCOLATE MOUSSE FROSTING

Chocolate Peanut Butter Frosting

PREP/TOTAL TIME: 10 min. **YIELD:** 1-2/3 cups

Ruthe Stevenson, Minneapolis, Minnesota

Chocolate and peanut butter are such an enjoyable combination. This delicious frosting makes a satisfying topping to moist chocolate cupcakes.

1/3	cup creamy peanut butter
1/3	cup butter, softened
1-1/2	teaspoons vanilla extract
2-1/2	cups confectioners' sugar
1/3	cup baking cocoa
1/4	teaspoon salt
4	to 5 tablespoons milk

In a mixing bowl, cream the peanut butter and butter until light and fluffy. Mix in vanilla. Stir in confectioners' sugar, cocoa and salt. Add enough milk to achieve spreading consistency.

Chocolate Mousse Frosting

PREP/TOTAL TIME: 10 min. **YIELD:** 3-1/2 cups

Kim Marie Van Rheenen, Mendota, Illinois

This smooth, fluffy frosting is a real treat for cake lovers.

1	cup cold milk
1	package (3.9 ounces) instant chocolate fudge pudding mix
1	carton (8 ounces) frozen whipped topping, thawed

In a large mixing bowl, whisk milk and pudding mix for 2 minutes. Fold in whipped topping. Store in the refrigerator.

Rich 'n' Fluffy Chocolate Frosting

PREP/TOTAL TIME: 15 min. **YIELD:** 2-1/2 cups

Jeanette Mack, Rushville, New York

Whisking up a batch of smooth-as-silk fudgy chocolate icing is a snap using this short recipe and your favorite flavor of baking chips.

1	cup heavy whipping cream
1	cup semisweet chocolate, milk chocolate *or* vanilla *or* white chips
3-3/4	to 4-1/4 cups confectioners' sugar

In a saucepan, bring cream to a simmer, about 180°; remove from the heat. Stir in chips until melted. Place pan in a bowl of ice water; stir constantly until cooled. Gradually whisk in confectioners' sugar until smooth and thick. Store in the refrigerator.

Browned Butter Frosting

PREP/TOTAL TIME: 20 min. **YIELD:** 2-1/2 cups

Taste of Home Test Kitchen

This old-fashioned frosting is great on an apple cake, or spice cake or cupcakes.

3/4	cup butter, cubed
6	cups confectioners' sugar
3	to 5 tablespoons milk
1-1/2	teaspoons vanilla extract

1 In a small saucepan, cook butter over low heat until lightly browned. Remove from the heat; cool slightly.

2 In a mixing bowl, beat sugar, butter, 3 tablespoons milk and vanilla until blended. Beat in enough remaining milk to achieve spreading consistency.

leftover *frosting*

If you have a little frosting leftover after decorating a cake, you can use it to make the following sweet treats.

- Spread some frosting over a graham cracker or the flat side of cookie, such as a vanilla wafer or gingersnap. Top with another cracker or cookie.
- Spread frosting on top of an ice cream bar, then top with another bar and cut widthwise in half. Cover with whipped topping and freeze. When ready to serve, drizzle each serving with ice cream topping and sprinkle with chopped nuts if desired.

simple frosting *finishes*

To give cakes a little pizzazz without a lot of fuss, try these easy decorating techniques. For the best results, use a fluffy creamy frosting, such as Easy Vanilla Buttercream Frosting (page 164) or Bakery Frosting (page 167).

SCALLOPS

Smooth frosting over top of cake. Turn a teaspoon tip side down and press the tip in rows across the top of the cake, making scallop marks in frosting.

WAVES

Run the tines of a table fork through the frosting in a wavy motion. You can also use a cake comb.

PEAKS

Smooth frosting over top and sides of cake. With an icing spatula or small flat metal spatula, press a flat side of the spatula tip in frosting and pull straight up, forming a peak. Repeat over top and sides of cake.

CAKE COMB

Smooth frosting over top and sides of cake. It is easier if you can place the cake on a turntable. Hold a cake comb at a 45° angle to the side of the cake and rotate the turntable until entire side of the cake is scored. If a turntable is not available, just sweep the comb around the side of the cake.

For the top of the cake, sweep the comb over the top in a circular pattern.

SWIRLS

Smooth frosting over top and sides of cake. With the tip of an icing spatula or small flat metal spatula, make a swirling or waving movement over top and sides of cake.

For more texture, use the back of a tablespoon or teaspoon to make a small twisting motion in one direction. Then move the spoon over a little and make another twist in the opposite direction. Repeat until entire cake is covered.

fancy *frosting & patterns*

Decorate cakes like a pro with decorating tips and pastry or resealable plastic bags. Cut a small hole in the corner of the bag and insert a decorating tip. Reinforce the seal between the bag and tip with tape or use a plastic coupler. The coupler lets you easily change decorating tips. For very simple decorations, you can just snip the corner off of a heavy-duty resealable plastic bag.

To fill a pastry or resealable plastic bag with frosting, insert a decorating tip if desired and place bag in a measuring cup. Roll down top edge to make a cuff. Fill about half full with frosting. Roll up cuff. Smooth filling down toward tip to remove air bubbles, which will cause breaks in the design when piping. Twist top of bag shut.

WRITING, PRINTING, VINES

Use a small round tip and hold the bag at a 45° angle. Touch the surface lightly with the tip and squeeze frosting out evenly as you go. Release pressure and touch the cake surface to stop each line, letter or vine.

DROP FLOWERS OR STARS

Use a flower or star tip and hold the bag at a 90° angle. Position tip just above the surface, and holding tip in place, squeeze bag as flower or star is formed. Stop pressure and pull tip up. Increase or decrease pressure to slightly change the size.

SHELL BORDER

Use a star tip and hold the bag at a 45° angle. Squeeze bag and slightly lift tip as frosting builds and fans out. Relax pressure as you lower tip to make the tail. Stop pressure completely and pull tip away. Work from left to right, resting the head of one shell on the tail of the previous shell.

LEAVES

Use a leaf tip and hold the bag at a 45° angle. Touch the surface lightly with the tip, and holding tip in place, squeeze bag to let frosting fan out to create wide base of leaf. Relax and stop pressure as you pull tip away from leaf and draw it up to a point.

BASKET WEAVE PATTERN

With serrated side of a basket weave tip facing up, pipe a vertical line of frosting. Squeeze out a short horizontal bar over the top of the vertical line. Add additional bars, each about a tip width apart, to cover line.

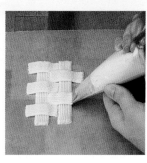

Make another vertical line of frosting to the right of first one, a tip width apart, overlapping ends of horizontal bars. Repeat the procedure of covering lines with bars by gently tucking tip under the line first to create a basket weave effect.

Cheesecakes

Whether served as an appetizer or a dessert, cheesecakes are a real crowd-pleaser. Their eye-catching look will give folks the impression that you spent hours in the kitchen! While cheesecakes do require advance planning to allow for chilling, they are actually easy to make.

secrets for successful cheesecakes

- Measure ingredients accurately, using the measuring tools and techniques suggested on pages 7 and 8.
- Before preheating the oven, arrange the oven racks so that the cheesecake will bake in the center of the oven.
- Preheat the oven for 10 to 15 minutes.
- Grease the bottom and sides of the springform pan to help prevent the filling from cracking when the cheesecake cools. It will naturally pull away from the sides.
- For best results, we recommend using regular cream cheese and sour cream, unless a recipe specifically calls for reduced-fat or fat-free products.
- To avoid lumps, always soften cream cheese at room temperature for about 30 minutes before mixing. If the cream cheese is not softened before mixing, the cream cheese won't be smoothed after blending.
- Make sure the batter is completely smooth and free of lumps before adding eggs. Add the eggs all at once and beat on low speed just until blended. Avoid overbeating at this step. If too much air is beaten into the mixture, the cheesecake will puff during baking, then collapse and split when cooled.
- Stop the mixer occasionally and scrape the batter down from the sides of the bowl.
- For best results, the springform pan should not be warped and should seal tightly. If in doubt about the tightness of the seal, tightly wrap heavy-duty foil around the outside of the pan to prevent butter in the crust from leaking out. Place on a baking sheet.

- Open the oven door as little as possible while baking the cheesecake, especially during the first 30 minutes. Drafts can cause a cheesecake to crack.
- Use a kitchen timer. Check for doneness at the minimum recommended baking time. A cheesecake is done when the edges are slightly puffed and when the center (about 1 in. in diameter) jiggles slightly when the side of the pan is tapped with a spoon. The retained heat will continue to cook the center while the cheesecake is cooling. A cheesecake cooked in a water bath will be just set across the top. The top will look dull, not shiny. Don't use a knife to test for doneness...doing so will cause the top to crack.
- Cool the cheesecake for 10 minutes on a wire rack, then run a knife around the inside edge to loosen from the springform pan. Don't remove the sides of the pan yet.
- Allowing cheesecake to set will make it easier to cut. Cool the cheesecake on a wire rack in a draft-free location for 1 hour. Refrigerate, uncovered, for at least 3 to 4 hours. When the cheesecake is cold, cover it with a piece of foil or plastic wrap across the top of the pan and refrigerate for at least 6 hours or overnight.
- When ready to serve, loosen the latch of the springform and carefully lift the rim of the pan straight up. Slice the cheesecake while it's cold. For maximum flavor, let slices stand at room temperature 15 to 30 minutes before serving.
- Use a straight-edge knife to cut a cheesecake. Warm the blade in hot water, dry and slice. Clean and rewarm the knife after each cut.

Classic Cheesecakes

Luscious Almond Cheesecake

PREP: 15 min. **BAKE:** 1 hour + chilling
YIELD: 14-16 servings

Brenda Clifford, Overland Park, Kansas

Almonds and almond extract give a traditional sour cream-topped cheesecake a tasty twist.

- 1-1/4 cups crushed vanilla wafers (about 28 wafers)
- 3/4 cup finely chopped almonds
- 1/4 cup sugar
- 1/3 cup butter, melted

FILLING:

- 4 packages (8 ounces *each*) cream cheese, softened
- 1-1/4 cups sugar
- 4 eggs, lightly beaten
- 1-1/2 teaspoons almond extract
- 1 teaspoon vanilla extract

TOPPING:

- 2 cups (16 ounces) sour cream
- 1/4 cup sugar
- 1 teaspoon vanilla extract
- 2 tablespoons sliced almonds, toasted

1 In a bowl, combine the wafer crumbs, almonds and sugar; stir in butter. Press onto the bottom of a greased 10-in. springform pan; set aside.

LUSCIOUS ALMOND CHEESECAKE

topping a cheesecake with *sour cream*

Sour cream toppings are frequently spread over cheesecakes a few minutes before the end of baking. Remove the cheesecake from oven and let stand for 5 to 15 minutes. Spoon sour cream topping around the edge of the cheesecake, then carefully spread toward the center.

2 In a large mixing bowl, beat cream cheese and sugar until smooth. Add eggs; beat on low speed just until combined. Stir in extracts. Pour into crust. Place pan on a baking sheet.

3 Bake at 350° for 50-55 minutes or until center is almost set. Remove from the oven; let stand for 5 minutes (leave oven on). Combine the sour cream, sugar and vanilla. Spoon around edge of cheesecake; carefully spread over filling. Bake 5 minutes longer. Cool pan on a wire rack for 10 minutes. Carefully run a knife around edge of pan to loosen; cool 1 hour longer. Refrigerate overnight.

4 Just before serving, sprinkle with almonds and remove sides of pan. Refrigerate leftovers.

Honey Pecan Cheesecake

PREP: 20 min. + chilling **BAKE:** 40 min. + chilling
YIELD: 12 servings

Tish Frish, Hampden, Maine

Bits of chopped pecans accent the crust, filling and topping of this maple-flavored cheesecake.

- 1 cup crushed vanilla wafers (about 22 wafers)
- 1/4 cup ground pecans
- 2 tablespoons sugar
- 5 tablespoons butter, melted

FILLING:

- 3 packages (8 ounces *each*) cream cheese, softened
- 3/4 cup packed dark brown sugar
- 3 eggs, lightly beaten
- 2 tablespoons all-purpose flour
- 1 tablespoon maple flavoring
- 1 teaspoon vanilla extract
- 1/2 cup chopped pecans

TOPPING:

- 1/4 cup honey
- 1 tablespoon butter
- 1 tablespoon water
- 1/2 cup chopped pecans

1 In a small bowl, combine the wafer crumbs, pecans and sugar; stir in butter. Press onto the bottom of a greased 9-in. springform pan. Refrigerate.

2 In a large mixing bowl, beat cream cheese and sugar until smooth. Add eggs; beat on low just until combined. Add the flour, maple flavoring and vanilla; beat until blended. Stir in pecans. Pour into crust. Place pan on a double-thickness of heavy-duty foil (about 16 in. x 16 in.). Securely wrap foil around pan.

3 Place in a large baking pan. Fill larger pan with hot water to a depth of 1 in. Bake at 350° for 40-45 minutes or until center is just set. Cool on a wire rack for 10 minutes. Remove foil. Carefully run a knife around edge of pan to loosen; cool for 1 hour longer. Refrigerate overnight.

4 For topping, combine the honey, butter and water in a small saucepan; cook and stir over medium heat for 2 minutes. Add nuts; cook 2 minutes longer (mixture will be thin). Spoon over cheesecake. Carefully remove sides of pan before serving. Refrigerate leftovers.

Chocolate Swirl Cheesecake

PREP: 25 min. **BAKE:** 1-1/4 hours + chilling
YIELD: 12-14 servings

Aida Babbel, Coquitlam, British Columbia

The wonderful flavors of orange and chocolate combine in this smooth, creamy cheesecake. The swirl makes it look extra special.

- 1/3 cup graham cracker crumbs (about 6 squares)
- 4 packages (8 ounces *each*) cream cheese, softened
- 1-1/3 cups sugar

- 4 eggs, lightly beaten
- 2 tablespoons orange juice
- 2 teaspoons grated orange peel
- 2 squares (1 ounce *each*) semisweet chocolate, melted and cooled

Whipped cream, optional

1 Sprinkle cracker crumbs over bottom and sides of a lightly greased 9-in. springform pan; set aside. In a large mixing bowl, beat cream cheese until smooth. Add sugar; beat for 1 minute. Add eggs; beat on low speed just until combined. Add orange juice and peel; beat on medium for 2-3 minutes. Set aside 3/4 cup; pour remaining filling into pan. Combine chocolate and reserved filling. Drop by spoonfuls over filling in pan and swirl with a knife. Place pan on a double thickness of heavy-duty foil (about 16 in. x 16 in.). Securely wrap foil around pan.

2 Place pan in a large baking pan. Fill larger pan with hot water to a depth of 1 in. (Refer to Preparing a Water Bath for Cheesecakes on page 181.) Bake at 350° for 75-80 minutes or until center is just set. Remove springform pan from water bath. Cool on a wire rack for 10 minutes. Carefully run a knife around edge of pan to loosen; cool 1 hour longer. Remove foil. Refrigerate 3-4 hours or overnight.

3 Remove sides of pan. Serve with whipped cream if desired. Refrigerate leftovers.

swirling filling into a *cheesecake*

Spoon small amounts of the filling to be swirled in a random pattern onto cheesecake batter. Cut through cheesecake batter with a knife to swirl in the filling. Be careful not to draw the blade through the filling too often, or the filling will blend into the rest of the batter and you'll lose the pretty pattern.

Strawberry Cheesecake

PREP: 30 min. **BAKE:** 50 min. + chilling
YIELD: 14-16 servings

L.C. Herschap, Luling, Texas

Juicy whole strawberries top off this impressive dessert.

- 3/4 **cup ground pecans**
- 3/4 **cup graham cracker crumbs (about 12 squares)**
- 3 **tablespoons butter, melted**

FILLING:
- 4 **packages (8 ounces *each*) cream cheese, softened**
- 1-1/4 **cups sugar**
- 1 **tablespoon lemon juice**
- 2 **teaspoons vanilla extract**
- 4 **eggs, lightly beaten**

TOPPING:
- 2 **cups (16 ounces) sour cream**
- 1/4 **cup sugar**
- 1 **teaspoon vanilla extract**

STRAWBERRY GLAZE:
- 2 **tablespoons cornstarch**
- 1/4 **cup water**
- 1 **jar (12 ounces) strawberry jelly**
- 3 **tablespoons orange juice**

Red food coloring, optional
- 1 **quart whole fresh strawberries**

1 In a bowl, combine the pecans and cracker crumbs; stir in butter. Press onto the bottom of a greased 10-in. springform pan; set aside.

2 In a large mixing bowl, beat the cream cheese until smooth. Add the sugar, lemon juice and vanilla; beat well. Add eggs; beat on low speed just until combined. Spoon over crust. Place pan on a baking sheet.

3 Bake at 350° for 45-50 minutes or until center is almost set. Remove from the oven; let stand for 15 minutes (leave oven on). For topping, combine all the ingredients; spoon around edge of cheesecake. Carefully spread over filling. Bake 5 minutes longer. Cool pan on a wire rack for 10 minutes. Carefully run a knife around the edge of pan to loosen; cool 1 hour longer. Refrigerate overnight.

4 Several hours before serving, prepare glaze. In a saucepan, combine cornstarch and water until smooth; add jelly. Bring to a boil over medium-high heat; cook and stir for 1-2 minutes or until jelly is melted and glaze is thickened. Remove from the heat; stir in orange juice and food coloring if desired. Cool to room temperature.

STRAWBERRY CHEESECAKE

5 Just before serving, remove sides of pan. Arrange strawberries on top of cheesecake with pointed ends up. Spoon glaze over berries, allowing some to drip down sides of cake. Refrigerate leftovers.

Tiny Cherry Cheesecakes

PREP: 25 min. **BAKE:** 15 min. + cooling
YIELD: 2 dozen

Janice Hertlein, Esterhazy, Saskatchewan

Individual cheesecakes are a nice alternative to a large cheesecake because they take less time to bake. Plus, they're a pretty addition to any dessert tray.

- 1 **cup all-purpose flour**
- 1/3 **cup sugar**
- 1/4 **cup baking cocoa**
- 1/2 **cup cold butter**
- 2 **tablespoons cold water**

FILLING:
- 2 **packages (3 ounces *each*) cream cheese, softened**
- 1/4 **cup sugar**
- 2 **tablespoons milk**
- 1 **teaspoon vanilla extract**

1   **egg, lightly beaten**
1   **can (21 ounces) cherry *or* strawberry pie filling**

1 In a small bowl, combine the flour, sugar and cocoa; cut in butter until mixture is crumbly. Gradually add water, tossing with a fork until dough forms a ball. Shape into 24 balls. Place in greased miniature muffin cups; press dough onto the bottom and up the sides of each cup.

2 In a large mixing bowl, beat cream cheese and sugar until smooth. Beat in milk and vanilla. Add egg; beat on low speed just until combined. Spoon about 1 tablespoonful into each cup.

3 Bake at 325° for 15-18 minutes or until set. Cool on a wire rack for 30 minutes. Carefully remove from pans to cool completely. Top with pie filling. Store in the refrigerator.

Golden Lemon-Glazed Cheesecake

PREP: 20 min. + cooling **BAKE:** 40 min. + chilling
YIELD: 12-14 servings

Betty Jacques, Hemet, California

A light lemon glaze adds the perfect finishing touch to a rich and creamy cheesecake.

2-1/2   **cups graham cracker crumbs (about 40 squares)**
1/4   **cup sugar**
2/3   **cup butter, melted**
FILLING:
3   **packages (8 ounces *each*) cream cheese, softened**
1-1/4   **cups sugar**
3   **eggs, lightly beaten**
3   **tablespoons lemon juice**
1   **tablespoon grated lemon peel**
1   **teaspoon vanilla extract**
GLAZE:
1   **small lemon, thinly sliced, *divided***
3   **cups water, *divided***
1   **cup sugar**
3   **tablespoons cornstarch**
1/3   **cup lemon juice**

1 In a bowl, combine cracker crumbs and sugar; stir in butter. Press onto the bottom and 2-in. up the sides of a greased 9-in. springform pan. Place pan on a baking sheet. Bake at 350° for 10 minutes or until set. Place pan on a wire rack. (leave oven on).

2 In a large mixing bowl, beat the cream cheese and sugar until smooth. Add eggs; beat on low speed just until combined. Stir in the lemon juice, lemon peel and vanilla just until blended. Pour into the crust. Return pan to baking sheet. Bake for 40-45 minutes or until center is almost set. Cool pan on a wire rack for 10 minutes. Carefully run a knife around edge of pan to loosen; cool 1 hour longer. Refrigerate overnight.

3 Set aside 1 lemon slice; coarsely chop remaining lemon slices. In a saucepan, bring the chopped lemon and 2 cups water to a boil. Reduce heat; simmer for 15 minutes. Drain and discard the liquid. In another saucepan, combine sugar and cornstarch; stir in remaining water until smooth. Add lemon juice and lemon pulp. Bring to a boil; cook and stir for 3 minutes or until thickened. Chill until cooled, stirring occasionally.

4 Remove sides of pan. Pour the lemon glaze over the cheesecake; garnish with the reserved lemon slice. Refrigerate leftovers.

making *a cheesecake crumb crust*

1. Place cookies or crackers in a heavy-duty resealable plastic bag. Seal bag, pushing out as much air as possible. Press a rolling pin over the bag, crushing the cookies or crackers into fine crumbs. Or, process (cookies and crackers) in a food processor.

2. Use a flat-bottomed measuring cup or glass to firmly press the prepared crumb mixture onto the bottom (and up the sides if recipe directs) of a springform pan.

Citrus Cheesecake

PREP: 30 min. + chilling **BAKE:** 65 min. + chilling
YIELD: 12-14 servings

Marcy Cella, L'Anse, Michigan

Here's the perfect cheesecake for spring. The rich, cookie-like crust and creamy filling make the zesty, citrus taste a wonderful surprise.

- 1/2 **cup butter, softened**
- 1/3 **cup sugar**
- 1 **egg yolk**
- 1/2 **teaspoon vanilla extract**
- 1-1/4 **cups all-purpose flour**
- 1 **teaspoon grated lemon peel**

FILLING:

- 5 **packages (8 ounces *each*) cream cheese, softened**
- 1-3/4 **cups sugar**
- 3 **tablespoons all-purpose flour**
- 1-1/2 **teaspoons grated lemon peel**
- 1-1/2 **teaspoons grated orange peel**
- 1/4 **teaspoon vanilla extract**
- 5 **eggs, lightly beaten**
- 2 **egg yolks, lightly beaten**
- 1/4 **cup heavy whipping cream**

TOPPING:

- 1-1/2 **cups (about 12 ounces) sour cream**
- 3 **tablespoons sugar**
- 1 **teaspoon vanilla extract**

1 In a large mixing bowl, cream butter and sugar until light and fluffy. Beat in egg yolk and vanilla. Combine flour and lemon peel; gradually add to creamed mixture. Mix until dough forms a ball and pulls away from the sides of the bowl. Divide dough in half; cover and refrigerate for 1 hour or until easy to handle.

2 Remove sides of a 9-in. springform pan. Grease bottom. Between waxed paper, roll one half dough to fit bottom of pan. Peel off top paper; invert dough onto bottom of pan. Remove paper; trim dough to fit pan. Place on a baking sheet. Bake at 400° for 6-8 minutes or until light browned. Cool completely on a wire rack.

3 Attach sides of the pan and grease sides. Pat remaining dough 1-1/2 in. up sides of pan, pressing dough to bottom crust to seal.

4 For filling, in another large mixing bowl, beat the cream cheese, sugar, flour, peels and vanilla until smooth. Add eggs and yolks; beat on low just until combined. Stir in cream just until combined. Pour into crust. Return pan to baking sheet.

5 Bake at 400° for 10 minutes. Reduce heat to 325°; bake 55-65 minutes or until center is almost set. Cool on a wire rack for 10 minutes. Carefully run a knife around edge of pan to loosen; cool 1 hour longer. Combine topping ingredients; spread over cheesecake. Refrigerate overnight. Remove sides of pan. Refrigerate leftovers.

Royal Raspberry Cheesecake

PREP: 20 min. **BAKE:** 35 min. + chilling
YIELD: 12-14 servings

Lori Monthorpe, Ile Bizard, Quebec

Every bite of this creamy cheesecake is bursting with a succulent raspberry topping. Instead of the usual cracker crust, it features a rich pastry crust.

- 3/4 **cup all-purpose flour**
- 3 **tablespoons sugar**
- 1/2 **teaspoon finely grated lemon peel**
- 6 **tablespoons butter, softened**
- 1 **egg yolk, lightly beaten**
- 1/4 **teaspoon vanilla extract**

FILLING:
- 3 **packages (8 ounces *each*) cream cheese, softened**
- 1/2 **teaspoon finely grated lemon peel**
- 1/4 **teaspoon vanilla extract**
- 1 **cup sugar**
- 2 **tablespoons all-purpose flour**
- 1/4 **teaspoon salt**
- 2 **eggs, lightly beaten**
- 1 **egg yolk, lightly beaten**
- 1/4 **cup milk**

RASPBERRY SAUCE:
- 1 **tablespoon cornstarch**
- 1 **package (10 ounces) frozen sweetened raspberries, thawed and crushed**
- 1/2 **cup currant jelly**
- 3 **cups whole raspberries**

1 In a bowl, combine the flour, sugar and lemon peel. Cut in butter until crumbly. Stir in egg yolk and vanilla. Pat half of dough onto bottom of a greased 9-in. springform pan with sides removed. Bake at 400° for 7 minutes or until golden. Cool completely on a wire rack. Attach sides of pan

ROYAL RASPBERRY CHEESECAKE

making a pastry crust for *cheesecakes*

1. Prepare crust according to recipe directions. Remove the bottom from a springform pan. Pat about half of the dough onto the bottom of a springform pan. Or, if recipe directs, roll out half of dough, then place on bottom of pan and trim to fit. Bake as directed.

2. Cool completely. Attach sides of pan and grease sides. Pat remaining dough 1-1/2-in. up the sides of the pan and press onto the bottom crust along the sides of the pan.

and grease sides. Pat remaining dough 1-1/2 in. up the sides and press onto bottom crust along the sides of pan. Set aside.

2 For filling, in a large mixing bowl, beat the cream cheese, lemon peel and vanilla until smooth. Combine the sugar, flour and salt; add to cream cheese mixture, beating until smooth. Add eggs and yolk; beat on low speed just until combined. Stir in milk. Pour into crust. Place pan on a baking sheet.

3 Bake at 375° for 35-40 minutes or until center is almost set. Cool pan on a wire rack for 10 minutes. Carefully run a knife around edge of pan to loosen; cool 1 hour. Chill overnight.

4 For sauce, combine the cornstarch and crushed raspberries in a saucepan until blended. Stir in jelly. Bring to a boil over medium heat; cook and stir for 1 minute or until thickened. Remove from the heat; strain to remove berry seeds. Discard seeds. Cool sauce; refrigerate until serving.

5 Just before serving, remove sides of pan. Cut cheesecake into slices; garnish with sauce and fresh berries. Refrigerate leftovers.

Caramel Fudge Cheesecake

PREP: 30 min. + cooling **BAKE:** 35 min. + chilling
YIELD: 12-14 servings

Brenda Ruse, Truro, Nova Scotia

It's hard to resist this chocolaty cheesecake with its fudgy crust, crunchy pecans and gooey layer of caramel.

- 1 **package fudge brownie mix (8-inch square pan size)**
- 1 **package (14 ounces) caramels**
- 1/4 **cup evaporated milk**
- 1-1/4 **cups coarsely chopped pecans**
- 2 **packages (8 ounces *each*) cream cheese, softened**
- 1/2 **cup sugar**
- 2 **eggs, lightly beaten**
- 2 **squares (1 ounce *each*) semisweet chocolate, melted and cooled**
- 2 **squares (1 ounce *each*) unsweetened chocolate, melted and cooled**

1 Prepare brownie batter according to package directions. Spread into a greased 9-in. springform pan. Place pan on a baking sheet. Bake at 350° for 20 minutes. Place pan on a wire rack for 10 minutes (leave oven on).

2 Meanwhile, in a microwave-safe bowl, melt the caramels with milk. Pour over brownie crust; sprinkle with pecans. In a large mixing bowl, beat cream cheese and sugar. Add eggs; beat on low speed just until combined. Stir in melted chocolate. Pour over pecans. Return pan to baking sheet.

3 Bake for 35-40 minutes or until center is almost set. Cool pan on a wire rack for 10 minutes. Run a knife around edge of pan to loosen; cool 1 hour longer. Refrigerate overnight. Remove sides of pan. Refrigerate leftovers.

CARAMEL FUDGE CHEESECAKE

Old-World Ricotta Cheesecake

PREP: 20 min. **BAKE:** 1 hour + chilling
YIELD: 12-14 servings

Mary Beth Jung
Hendersonville, North Carolina

Zwieback crumbs give the crust a subtle cinnamon flavor, and the dense texture of the ricotta cheese is reminiscent of old-fashioned cheesecakes.

- 1-2/3 **cups zwieback crumbs**
- 3 **tablespoons sugar**
- 1/2 **teaspoon ground cinnamon**
- 1/3 **cup butter, softened**

FILLING:

- 2 **cartons (15 ounces *each*) ricotta cheese**
- 1/2 **cup sugar**
- 1/2 **cup half-and-half cream**
- 2 **tablespoons all-purpose flour**
- 1 **tablespoon lemon juice**
- 1 **teaspoon finely grated lemon peel**
- 1/4 **teaspoon salt**
- 2 **eggs, lightly beaten**

TOPPING:

- 1 **cup (8 ounces) sour cream**
- 2 **tablespoons sugar**
- 1 **teaspoon vanilla extract**

1 In a bowl, combine the zwieback crumbs, sugar and cinnamon; mix in butter until mixture is crumbly. Press onto the bottom and 1-1/2 in. up the sides of a greased 9-in. springform pan. Refrigerate until chilled.

2 For filling, beat the ricotta cheese, sugar, cream, flour, lemon juice, lemon peel and salt in a large mixing bowl. Blend until smooth. Add eggs; beat on low speed just until combined. Pour into crust. Place pan on a baking sheet.

3 Bake at 350° for 50-55 minutes or until center is almost set. Remove from the oven; let stand for 15 minutes (leave oven on). Combine topping ingredients; spoon around edge of cheesecake. Carefully spread over filling. Bake 10 minutes longer. Cool pan on a wire rack for 10 minutes. Carefully run a knife around edge of pan to loosen; cool 1 hour longer. Refrigerate for 3 hours or overnight. Remove sides of pan. Refrigerate leftovers.

1. Using a double thickness of heavy-duty foil, make a 16-in. square. Center springform pan on foil, then tightly mold foil around pan.

2. Place springform pan in a larger pan, such as a large shallow baking dish or roasting pan. Set dish on rack in oven. Using a kettle or large measuring cup, carefully pour hot water into larger pan to a depth of 1 in.

Chocolate-Covered White Cheesecake

PREP: 30 min. + cooling **BAKE:** 65 min. + chilling
YIELD: 12-14 servings

Carol Staniger, Springdale, Arkansas

The inside scoop on this tasty treat is the white chocolate center. A drizzle of melted vanilla chips over the chocolate glaze makes for a pretty presentation.

1-1/2 cups chocolate wafer crumbs (about
    27 wafers)
  3 tablespoons butter, melted
FILLING:
  3 packages (8 ounces *each*) cream cheese,
    softened
1/2 cup sugar
1/4 cup heavy whipping cream
  1 teaspoon vanilla extract
  3 eggs, lightly beaten
1-1/2 cups vanilla *or* white chips, melted and
    cooled

GLAZE:
  2 cups (12 ounces) semisweet chocolate
    chips
  1 cup heavy whipping cream
  2 tablespoons butter
  2 tablespoons sugar
  1 cup vanilla *or* white chips
Striped chocolate kisses, optional
Raspberries, optional

1 In a small bowl, combine wafer crumbs and butter; press onto the bottom of a greased 9-in. springform pan. Place pan on a baking sheet. Bake at 350° for 10 minutes. Place pan on a wire rack (leave oven on).

2 In a large mixing bowl, beat the cream cheese, sugar, cream and vanilla until well blended. Add eggs; beat on low speed just until combined. Stir in melted vanilla chips. Pour into crust. Place pan on a double thickness of heavy-duty foil (about 16 in. x 16 in.). Securely wrap foil around pan.

3 Place springform pan in a larger baking pan. Fill larger pan with hot water to a depth of 1 in. Bake for 65-70 minutes until center is just set. Remove springform pan from water bath. Cool on a wire rack for 10 minutes. Carefully run a knife around edge of pan to loosen; cool 1 hour longer. Refrigerate for 4 hours or overnight.

4 For glaze, place chocolate chips in a bowl; set aside. In a heavy saucepan, bring the cream, butter and sugar to a boil over medium-high heat, stirring constantly. Pour over chocolate chips. Cool for 3 minutes; stir until smooth and cooled. Remove sides of pan. Spread glaze over top and sides of cheesecake. Refrigerate for 2 hours. Melt remaining vanilla chips; drizzle over cheesecake. Garnish with kisses and raspberries if desired. Refrigerate leftovers.

Chocolate Chip Cookie Dough Cheesecake

PREP: 25 min. **BAKE:** 45 min. + chilling
YIELD: 12-14 servings

Julie Craig, Jackson, Wisconsin

This recipe captures the flavor of a popular ice cream.

1-3/4   cups crushed chocolate chip cookies *or* chocolate wafer crumbs
1/4   cup sugar
1/3   cup butter, melted

FILLING:

3   packages (8 ounces *each*) cream cheese, softened
1   cup sugar
3   eggs, lightly beaten
1   cup (8 ounces) sour cream
1/2   teaspoon vanilla extract

COOKIE DOUGH:

1/4   cup butter, softened
1/4   cup sugar
1/4   cup packed brown sugar
1   tablespoon water
1   teaspoon vanilla extract
1/2   cup all-purpose flour
1-1/2   cups miniature semisweet chocolate chips, *divided*

1 In a small bowl, combine cookie crumbs and sugar; stir in butter. Press onto the bottom and 1 in. up the sides of a greased 9-in. springform pan; set aside.

2 In a large mixing bowl, beat the cream cheese and sugar until smooth. Add eggs; beat on low just until combined. Add sour cream and vanilla; beat just until blended. Pour over crust; set aside. In another large mixing bowl, cream butter and sugars until light and fluffy. Add water and vanilla. Gradually add the flour. Stir in 1 cup chocolate chips. Drop dough by teaspoonfuls over filling, gently pushing dough below surface (dough should be completely covered by filling). Place pan on a baking sheet.

3 Bake at 350° for 45-55 minutes or until center is almost set. Cool pan on a wire rack for 10 minutes. Carefully run a knife around edge of pan to loosen; cool 1 hour longer. Refrigerate overnight. Remove sides of pan. Sprinkle with remaining chips. Refrigerate leftovers.

Brownie Cheesecake

PREP: 20 min. **BAKE:** 50 min. + chilling
YIELD: 10-12 servings

Dorothy Olivares, El Paso, Texas

Crumbled brownies are stirred into the batter before baking, which gives this chocolate cheesecake a delectable taste.

1-1/2   cups crushed vanilla wafers (about 45 cookies)
6   tablespoons confectioners' sugar
6   tablespoons baking cocoa
6   tablespoons butter, melted

FILLING:

3   packages (8 ounces *each*) cream cheese, softened
1/4   cup butter, melted
1   can (14 ounces) sweetened condensed milk
3   teaspoons vanilla extract
1/2   cup baking cocoa
4   eggs, lightly beaten
1-1/2   cups crumbled brownies

Whipped topping and pecan halves, optional

1 In a small bowl, combine the wafer crumbs, confectioners' sugar and cocoa; stir in the butter. Press onto the bottom of a greased 9-in. springform pan; set aside.

2 In a large mixing bowl, beat the cream cheese and butter until smooth. Add the milk and vanilla; mix well. Add the cocoa; mix well. Add eggs; beat on low just until combined. Fold in brownies. Spoon into crust. Place pan on a baking sheet.

CHOCOLATE CHIP COOKIE DOUGH CHEESECAKE

CHOCOLATE CARAMEL CHEESECAKE

3 Bake at 350° for 50-55 minutes or until center is almost set. Cool on a wire rack for 10 minutes. Carefully run a knife around the edge of pan to loosen. Cool 1 hour longer. Refrigerate overnight.

4 Remove sides of pan. Garnish with whipped topping and pecans if desired. Refrigerate leftovers.

Chocolate Caramel Cheesecake

PREP: 35 min. + cooling **BAKE:** 55 min. + chilling
YIELD: 14-16 servings

Jo Groth, Plainfield, Iowa

Guests love this rich, delicious make-ahead dessert. It turns out perfect every time and is impressive on the table.

- 2 **cups crushed vanilla wafers (about 44 cookies)**
- 1/2 **cup butter, melted**
- 1 **package (14 ounces) caramels**
- 1 **can (5 ounces) evaporated milk**
- 2 **cups chopped pecans, toasted, *divided***
- 4 **packages (8 ounces *each*) cream cheese, softened**
- 1 **cup sugar**
- 2 **teaspoons vanilla extract**
- 4 **eggs, lightly beaten**
- 1 **cup (6 ounces) semisweet chocolate chips, melted and slightly cooled**

Whipped cream, optional

1 In a bowl, combine wafer crumbs and butter; blend well. Press into the bottom and 2 in. up the sides of a greased 10-in. springform pan. Place pan on a baking sheet. Bake at 350° for 8-10 minutes or until set. Cool on a wire rack.

2 In a saucepan or microwave melt caramels with milk; stir until smooth. Cool for 5 minutes. Pour into crust; top with 1-1/2 cups of pecans.

3 In a large mixing bowl, beat cream cheese until smooth. Add sugar and vanilla; mix well. Add eggs; beat on low just until combined. Add chocolate; mix just until blended. Carefully spread over pecans. Return to baking sheet.

4 Bake at 350° for 55-65 minutes or until center is almost set. Cool on a wire rack for 10 minutes. Carefully run a knife around the edge of pan to loosen; cool 1 hour longer. Refrigerate overnight.

5 Remove sides of pan. Garnish with remaining pecans and whipped cream if desired. Refrigerate leftovers.

CHOCOLATE MALT CHEESECAKE

Stir in the melted chocolate and vanilla just until blended. Pour into the crust. Place pan on a baking sheet.

3 Bake at 325° for 60-65 minutes or until center is almost set. Cool on a wire rack for 10 minutes. Carefully run a knife around the edge of the pan to loosen; cool 1 hour longer. Refrigerate overnight.

4 Remove the sides of the pan. Garnish with confectioners' sugar and chocolate curls if desired. Refrigerate leftovers.

Chocolate Truffle Cheesecake

PREP: 30 min. **BAKE:** 45 min. + chilling
YIELD: 12-14 servings

Mary Jones, Cumberland, Maine

If you delight in the taste of chocolate, this is the cheesecake for you! Every creamy bite melts in your mouth. It looks elegant yet is so easy to prepare.

1-1/2 cups chocolate wafer crumbs (about 27 wafers)
   2 tablespoons sugar
1/4 cup butter, melted
FILLING:
1/4 cup semisweet chocolate chips
1/4 cup heavy whipping cream
   3 packages (8 ounces *each*) cream cheese, softened
   1 cup sugar
1/3 cup baking cocoa
   3 eggs, lightly beaten
   1 teaspoon vanilla extract

Chocolate Malt Cheesecake

PREP: 25 min. **BAKE:** 1 hour + chilling
YIELD: 12-14 servings

Anita Moffett, Rewey, Wisconsin

For a change of pace, substitute pretzel crumbs for the graham cracker crumbs. They make a surprisingly good crust!

   1 cup graham cracker crumbs (about 16 squares)
1/4 cup sugar
1/3 cup butter, melted
FILLING:
   3 packages (8 ounces *each*) cream cheese, softened
   1 can (14 ounces) sweetened condensed milk
3/4 cup chocolate malt powder
   4 eggs, lightly beaten
   1 cup semisweet chocolate chips, melted and cooled
   1 teaspoon vanilla extract
Confectioners' sugar and chocolate curls, optional

1 In a bowl, combine cracker crumbs and sugar; stir in butter. Press onto the bottom of a greased 9-in. springform pan; set aside.

2 In a large mixing bowl, beat the cream cheese and milk until smooth. Add the malt powder; beat well. Add eggs; beat on low just until combined.

CHOCOLATE TRUFFLE CHEESECAKE

TOPPING:

1-1/2 **cups semisweet chocolate chips**
1/4 **cup heavy whipping cream**
1 **teaspoon vanilla extract**
Whipped cream and miniature chocolate kisses, optional

1 In a small bowl, combine wafer crumbs and sugar; stir in butter. Press onto the bottom and 1-1/2 in. up the sides of a greased 9-in. springform pan. Place pan on a baking sheet. Bake at 350° for 10 minutes. Place pan on a wire rack. Reduce heat to 325°.

2 For filling, melt chocolate chips in a small heavy saucepan or microwave; stir until smooth. Remove from the heat; add cream and mix well. Set aside. In a large mixing bowl, beat cream cheese and sugar until smooth. Add cocoa and beat well. Add eggs; beat on low just until combined. Stir in vanilla and reserved chocolate mixture just until blended. Pour over crust. Return pan to baking sheet.

3 Bake for 45-50 minutes or until center is almost set. For topping, melt chocolate chips in a heavy saucepan or microwave; stir until smooth. Stir in cream and vanilla; mix well. Spread over filling. Cool pan on a wire rack for 10 minutes. Carefully run a knife around edge of pan to loosen; cool 1 hour longer. Refrigerate overnight.

4 Remove sides of pan. Just before serving, garnish with whipped cream and miniature chocolate kisses if desired. Refrigerate leftovers.

Bittersweet Chocolate Cheesecake

PREP: 20 min. + chilling **BAKE:** 1 hour + cooling
YIELD: 16 servings

Amelia Gregory, Omemee, Ontario

Very chocolaty describes this recipe—from the rich wafer crust and bittersweet filling to the satiny glaze.

1 **cup chocolate wafer crumbs**
1/2 **cup finely chopped toasted hazelnuts**
1/3 **cup butter, melted**
3 **packages (8 ounces *each*) cream cheese, softened**
1 **cup sugar**
12 **squares (1 ounce *each*) bittersweet baking chocolate, melted and cooled**
3 **eggs, lightly beaten**
1 **cup (8 ounces) sour cream**
1-1/2 **teaspoons vanilla extract**

BITTERSWEET CHOCOLATE CHEESECAKE

1/2 **teaspoon almond extract**
Dash salt
GLAZE:
4 **squares (1 ounce *each*) bittersweet baking chocolate**
1/4 **cup heavy whipping cream**
1 **teaspoon vanilla extract**
Whipped cream and toasted chopped hazelnuts, optional

1 In a small bowl, combine the crumbs and hazelnuts; stir in butter. Press onto the bottom of a greased 9-in. springform pan.

2 In a large mixing bowl, beat cream cheese and sugar until smooth. Add chocolate. Add eggs; beat on low just until combined. Add sour cream, extracts and salt; beat just until blended. Pour over crust. Place pan on a baking sheet.

3 Bake at 350° for 60-65 minutes or until the center is almost set. Cool on a wire rack for 10 minutes. Carefully run a knife around edge of pan to loosen; cool 1 hour longer. Refrigerate for 3 hours.

4 For glaze, in a heavy saucepan or microwave, melt chocolate with cream, stirring until smooth. Remove from the heat. Stir in vanilla. Remove sides of pan. Spread glaze over top. Refrigerate overnight. Garnish with whipped cream and hazelnuts if desired.

Editor's Note: Semisweet baking chocolate may be substituted for the bittersweet chocolate.

Mocha Cheesecake

PREP: 35 min. + cooling **BAKE:** 20 min. + chilling
YIELD: 8-10 servings

Jane Manges, Cameron Park, California

"Simple to make" describes this cheesecake. It will be well received by family and friends alike.

1-1/4   cups confectioners' sugar
   1   cup all-purpose flour
 1/2   cup baking cocoa
 1/4   teaspoon baking soda
Dash salt
 1/2   cup butter, melted
FILLING:
   1   package (8 ounces) cream cheese, softened
   1   can (14 ounces) sweetened condensed milk
   2   eggs, lightly beaten
   1   tablespoon hot water
   2   to 3 teaspoons instant coffee granules
Whipped topping, baking cocoa, fresh raspberries and mint, optional

1 In a bowl, combine the first five ingredients; stir in butter. Press onto the bottom and 1 in. up the sides of a greased 9-in. springform pan. Place pan on a baking sheet. Bake at 350° for 12-15 minutes or until the edges are browned. Cool on a wire rack.

2 In a large mixing bowl, beat cream cheese and milk until smooth. Add eggs, beating on low, just until combined. In a small bowl, combine water and coffee granules; let stand for 1 minute. Add to the creamed mixture; beat just until mixed. Pour into crust. Return pan to baking sheet.

3 Bake at 350° for 20-25 minutes or until center is almost set. Cool on a wire rack for 10 minutes. Carefully run a knife around edge of pan to loosen; cool 1 hour longer. Refrigerate overnight.

4 Remove sides of pan. Let stand at room temperature for 30 minutes before cutting. If desired, pipe whipping topping around edges and dust with cocoa; garnish with berries and mint. Refrigerate leftovers.

Neapolitan Cheesecake

PREP: 35 min. **BAKE:** 70 min. + chilling
YIELD: 12-14 servings

Sherri Regalbuto, Carp, Ontario

This rich, creamy cheesecake has two chocolate layers—semisweet and white—and a strawberry layer.

- 1 **cup chocolate wafer crumbs (18 wafers)**
- 3 **tablespoons butter, melted**

FILLING:
- 3 **packages (8 ounces *each*) cream cheese, softened**
- 3/4 **cup sugar**
- 1/4 **cup heavy whipping cream**
- 3 **eggs, lightly beaten**
- 1 **teaspoon vanilla extract**
- 2 **squares (1 ounce *each*) semisweet chocolate, melted and cooled**
- 2 **squares (1 ounce *each*) white baking chocolate, melted and cooled**
- 1/3 **cup mashed frozen sweetened sliced strawberries, well-drained**

Red liquid food coloring, optional

TOPPING:
- 3 **squares (1 ounce *each*) semisweet chocolate**
- 2 **tablespoons butter**
- 2 **teaspoons shortening, *divided***
- 1 **square (1 ounce) white baking chocolate**

1 In a small bowl, combine wafer crumbs and butter. Press onto the bottom of an ungreased 9-in. springform pan. Place pan on a baking sheet. Bake at 350° for 10 minutes. Cool on a wire rack. Reduce heat to 325°.

NEAPOLITAN CHEESECAKE

loosening *cheesecakes* from sides of pan

- To prevent cracks during cooling, it's important to loosen the cheesecake from the sides of the pan after baking.

- First cool the cheesecake on a wire rack for 10 minutes. Then carefully run a table knife or small metal spatula between the cheesecake and the inside of the pan. Cool 1 hour longer. Refrigerate overnight before removing the sides of the pan.

2 In a large mixing bowl, beat cream cheese until smooth. Gradually beat in sugar and cream. Add eggs and vanilla; beat on low just until combined. Divide batter into thirds. Add melted semisweet chocolate to a third. Spread over crust. Add melted white chocolate to another third. Spread over semisweet layer. Stir strawberries and a few drops of food coloring if desired into remaining portion. Spread over white chocolate layer. Place pan on a double-thickness of heavy-duty foil (about 16 in. x 16 in.). Securely wrap foil around pan.

3 Place springform pan in a large baking pan. Fill larger pan with hot water to a depth of 1 in. Bake at 325° for 70-75 minutes or until center is just set. Remove springform pan from water bath. Cool on a wire rack for 10 minutes. Remove foil. Carefully run a knife around the edge of pan to loosen; cool for 1 hour longer. Remove foil. Refrigerate overnight.

4 For topping, melt semisweet chocolate, butter and 1 teaspoon shortening in a heavy saucepan or microwave; stir until smooth. Cool 5 minutes. Remove sides of springform pan. Pour melted chocolate mixture over cheesecake. Melt white chocolate and remaining shortening. Drizzle over cheesecake. Refrigerate until chocolate is firm. Refrigerate leftovers.

S'More Cheesecake

PREP: 20 min. **BAKE:** 45 min. + chilling
YIELD: 12 servings

Robin Andrews, Cary, North Carolina

This luscious dessert is just as wonderfully tasty as the campfire snack that inspired it. It's a great way to savor a summer classic anytime of year.

- 2-1/4 **cups graham cracker crumbs (about 36 squares)**
- 1/3 **cup sugar**
- 1/2 **cup butter, melted**

FILLING:
- 2 **packages (8 ounces *each*) cream cheese, softened**
- 1 **can (14 ounces) sweetened condensed milk**
- 2 **teaspoons vanilla extract**
- 3 **eggs, lightly beaten**
- 1 **cup (6 ounces) miniature semisweet chocolate chips**
- 1 **cup miniature marshmallows**

TOPPING:
- 1 **cup miniature marshmallows**
- 1/2 **cup semisweet chocolate chips**
- 1 **tablespoon shortening**

1 In a small bowl, combine cracker crumbs and sugar; stir in butter. Press onto the bottom and 1-3/4 in. up the sides of a greased 10-in. springform pan; set aside.

2 In a large mixing bowl, beat the cream cheese, milk and vanilla until smooth. Add eggs; beat on low just until combined. Stir in chocolate chips

S'MORE CHEESECAKE

and marshmallows. Pour over crust. Place on a baking sheet.

3 Bake at 325° for 40-45 minutes or until center is almost set. Sprinkle with marshmallows. Bake 4-6 minutes longer or until marshmallows are puffed.

4 Meanwhile, melt chocolate chips and shortening in a heavy saucepan or microwave; stir until smooth. Drizzle over marshmallows.

5 Cool on a wire rack for 10 minutes. Carefully run a knife around edge of pan to loosen; cool 1 hour longer. Refrigerate overnight. Remove sides of pan. Refrigerate leftovers.

Pumpkin Mousse Cheesecake

PREP: 30 min. + cooling **BAKE:** 45 min. + chilling
YIELD: 12-14 servings

Dawn Oswald, Kailua, Hawaii

A scrumptious pumpkin filling makes this cheesecake different from most, and the glaze adds a nice touch.

- 1 **cup graham cracker crumbs (about 16 squares)**
- 3 **tablespoons sugar**
- 1/4 **cup butter, melted**

FILLING:
- 3 **packages (8 ounces *each*) cream cheese, softened**
- 1 **cup sugar**
- 1 **cup canned pumpkin**
- 3 **tablespoons all-purpose flour**
- 1 **teaspoon ground cinnamon**
- 1/4 **teaspoon ground nutmeg**
- 4 **eggs, lightly beaten**

GLAZE:
- 1/2 **cup vanilla *or* white chips**
- 1 **tablespoon shortening**

1 In a small bowl, combine cracker crumbs and sugar; stir in butter. Press into a greased 9-in. springform pan. Place pan on a baking sheet. Bake at 325° for 10 minutes. Cool on a wire rack.

2 Meanwhile, in a large mixing bowl, beat cream cheese and sugar until smooth. Add the pumpkin, flour, cinnamon and nutmeg. Add eggs; beat on low just until combined. Pour into crust. Return to baking sheet.

3 Bake at 325° for 45-50 minutes or until center is almost set. Cool on a wire rack for 10 minutes. Carefully run a knife around edge of pan to loosen; cool 1 hour longer. Refrigerate overnight.

COOL LIME CHEESECAKE

Cool Lime Cheesecake

PREP: 20 min. + cooling **BAKE:** 50 min. + chilling
YIELD: 14-16 servings

Karen Donhauser, Frazer, Pennsylvania

The mixture of tart lime and sweet creamy cheesecake is absolutely scrumptious. At any get-together, it's a show-stopping dessert that's always enjoyed.

> 2-1/4 **cups graham cracker crumbs (about 36 squares)**
> 1/3 **cup sugar**
> 1/2 **cup butter, melted**
> **FILLING:**
> 20 **ounces cream cheese, softened**
> 3/4 **cup sugar**
> 1 **cup (8 ounces) sour cream**
> 3 **tablespoons all-purpose flour**
> 3 **eggs, lightly beaten**
> 2/3 **cup lime juice**
> 1 **teaspoon vanilla extract**
> 1 **drop green food coloring, optional**
> **Whipped cream and lime slices**

1 In a bowl, combine cookie crumbs and sugar; stir in butter. Press onto the bottom and 1 in. up the sides of a greased 10-in. springform pan. Place pan on a baking sheet. Bake at 375° for 8 minutes. Place pan on a wire rack. Reduce heat to 325°.

2 In a large mixing bowl, beat cream cheese and sugar until smooth. Add sour cream and flour; beat well. Add eggs; beat on low speed just until combined. Stir in the lime juice, vanilla and food coloring if desired just until mixed. Pour into crust. Return pan to baking sheet.

3 Bake for 50-55 minutes or until center is almost set. Cool pan on a wire rack for 10 minutes. Carefully run a knife around edge of pan to loosen; cool 1 hour longer. Refrigerate overnight. Remove sides of pan. Garnish with whipped cream and lime. Refrigerate leftovers.

4 Remove sides of pan. For glaze, melt chips and shortening in a small heavy saucepan or micro-wave; stir until smooth. Drizzle over cheesecake. Refrigerate until firm, about 30 minutes. Refrigerate leftovers.

Mini Apricot Cheesecakes

PREP: 10 min. **BAKE:** 20 min. + cooling
YIELD: 2 dozen

Carol Twardzik, Spy Hill, Saskatchewan

Vanilla wafers are used to create the no-fuss crusts for these darling bite-size treats. For a different look and taste, vary the kind of preserves on top.

> 24 **vanilla wafers**
> 2 **packages (8 ounces *each*) cream cheese, softened**
> 3/4 **cup sugar**
> 2 **eggs, lightly beaten**
> 1 **tablespoon lemon juice**
> 1 **teaspoon vanilla extract**
> 1 **cup apricot preserves**

1 Place wafers flat side down in paper- or foil-lined muffin cups; set aside. In a large mixing bowl, beat cream cheese and sugar until smooth. Add the eggs, lemon juice and vanilla; beat well. Fill muffin cups three-fourths full.

2 Bake at 375° for 17-20 minutes or until top is set. Cool on a wire rack for 20 minutes. Carefully remove from pans to cool completely. Top each cheesecake with 2 teaspoons preserves. Store in the refrigerator.

storing *cheesecakes*

Cover and refrigerate cheesecake for up to 3 days. To freeze, place entire cheesecake or individual slices on a baking sheet and freeze until firm. Wrap in heavy-duty plastic wrap and place in a freezer bag. Freeze for up to 2 months. Thaw in the refrigerator.

CRANBERRY CHEESECAKE

Cranberry Cheesecake

PREP: 30 min. + cooling **BAKE:** 60 min. + chilling
YIELD: 12 servings

Nancy Zimmerman
Cape May Court House, New Jersey

This lovely cheesecake, which uses cranberries and eggnog, is a perfect Christmas dessert.

   1   **cup sugar**
   2   **tablespoons cornstarch**
   1   **cup cranberry juice**
 1-1/2 **cups fresh *or* frozen cranberries**
CRUST:
   1   **cup graham cracker crumbs (about 16 squares)**
   3   **tablespoons sugar**
   3   **tablespoons butter, melted**
FILLING:
   4   **packages (8 ounces *each*) cream cheese, softened**
   1   **cup sugar**
   3   **tablespoons all-purpose flour**
   4   **eggs, lightly beaten**
   1   **cup eggnog**
   1   **tablespoon vanilla extract**

1 In a large saucepan, combine sugar and cornstarch. Stir in cranberry juice until smooth. Add cranberries. Bring to a boil over medium heat; cook and stir for 2 minutes or until thickened. Remove from the heat; set aside.

2 In a small bowl, combine cracker crumbs and sugar; stir in butter. Press onto the bottom of a greased 9-in. springform pan. Place pan on a baking sheet. Bake at 325° for 10 minutes. Cool on a wire rack.

3 In a large mixing bowl, beat cream cheese and sugar until smooth. Add flour and beat well. Add eggs, beat on low just until combined. Add eggnog and vanilla; beat just until blended. Pour two-thirds of the filling over crust. Top with half of the cranberry mixture (cover and refrigerate remaining cranberry mixture). Carefully spoon remaining filling on top. Return pan to baking sheet.

4 Bake at 325° for 60-70 minutes or until center is almost set. Cool on a wire rack for 10 minutes. Carefully run a knife around edge of pan to loosen; cool 1 hour longer.

5 Refrigerate overnight. Remove sides of pan. Spoon remaining cranberry mixture over cheesecake. Refrigerate leftovers.

Editor's Note: This recipe was tested with commercially prepared eggnog.

Apple Strudel Cheesecake

PREP: 30 min. + chilling **BAKE:** 60 min. + chilling
YIELD: 12-14 servings

Janice White, Encampment, Wyoming

The apples lighten up this cheesecake without sacrificing any taste. It makes a great dessert or snack.

   1   **cup all-purpose flour**
 1/3   **cup sugar**
 1/3   **cup cold butter**
   1   **egg yolk**
 1/4   **teaspoon vanilla extract**
FILLING:
   4   **cups sliced peeled tart apples**
   2   **packages (8 ounces *each*) cream cheese, softened**
 3/4   **cup sugar, *divided***
   1   **teaspoon vanilla extract**
   2   **eggs, lightly beaten**
   1   **teaspoon ground cinnamon**
 1/4   **cup chopped walnuts**

1 In a bowl, combine flour and sugar; cut in butter until crumbly. In a small bowl, combine egg yolk and vanilla; stir into flour mixture. Press onto the bottom of an ungreased 9-in. springform pan. Place pan on a baking sheet. Bake at 400° for 10-12 minutes or until set. Cool on a wire rack. Reduce heat to 350°.

2 Place apples in an ungreased 13-in. x 9-in. x 2-in. baking dish. Cover and bake at 350° for 20 minutes or until tender; drain and cool.

3 Meanwhile, in a large bowl, beat the cream cheese, 1/2 cup sugar and vanilla until smooth. Add eggs; beat on low just until combined. Pour over crust. Toss baked apples with cinnamon and remaining sugar. Arrange apples over cream cheese layer; drizzle with any remaining cinnamon mixture. Sprinkle with nuts. Return pan to baking sheet.

4 Bake at 350° for 40-45 minutes or until center is almost set. Cool on a wire rack for 10 minutes. Carefully run a knife around the edge of pan to loosen; cool 1 hour longer. Refrigerate for 4 hours or overnight. Remove sides of pan. Use a sharp knife to cut. Refrigerate leftovers.

APPLE-OF-YOUR-EYE CHEESECAKE

Apple-of-Your-Eye Cheesecake

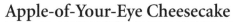

PREP: 30 min. **BAKE:** 55 min. + chilling
YIELD: 12-14 servings

Debbie Wilson, Sellersburg, Indiana

With apples, caramel and pecans, this exquisite cheesecake will win you many compliments.

1 cup graham cracker crumbs (about 16 squares)
3 tablespoons sugar
2 tablespoons finely chopped pecans
1/2 teaspoon ground cinnamon
1/4 cup butter, melted

APPLE STRUDEL CHEESECAKE

FILLING:
3 packages (8 ounces *each*) cream cheese, softened
3/4 cup sugar
3 eggs, lightly beaten
3/4 teaspoon vanilla extract

TOPPING:
2-1/2 cups chopped peeled apples
1 tablespoon lemon juice
1/4 cup sugar
1/2 teaspoon ground cinnamon
6 tablespoons caramel ice cream topping, *divided*

Sweetened whipped cream
2 tablespoons chopped pecans

1 In a bowl, combine the cracker crumbs, sugar, pecans and cinnamon; stir in butter. Press onto the bottom of a lightly greased 9-in. springform pan. Place pan on a baking sheet. Bake at 350° for 10 minutes. Place pan on a wire rack (leave oven on).

2 In a large mixing bowl, beat cream cheese and sugar until smooth. Add eggs; beat on low speed just until combined. Stir in vanilla. Pour over crust. Toss apples with lemon juice, sugar and cinnamon; spoon over filling. Return pan to baking sheet.

3 Bake at 350° for 55-60 minutes or until center is almost set. Cool on a wire rack for 10 minutes. Run a knife around edge of pan to loosen. Drizzle with 4 tablespoons caramel topping. Cool 1 hour longer. Refrigerate overnight.

4 Remove sides of pan. Garnish with whipped cream. Drizzle with remaining caramel topping; sprinkle with pecans. Refrigerate leftovers.

Apricot Swirl Cheesecake

PREP: 30 min. **BAKE:** 50 min. + chilling
YIELD: 12 servings

Ardyth Voss, Rosholt, South Dakota

Apricots make this cheesecake different. You'll get a taste of fruit in every bite.

- 1/2 cup finely ground almonds
- 1 cup dried apricots
- 1 cup water
- 1 tablespoon grated lemon peel
- 3 packages (8 ounces *each*) cream cheese, softened
- 1 cup sugar
- 2 tablespoons all-purpose flour
- 4 eggs, lightly beaten
- 1/2 cup heavy whipping cream
- 1 cup apricot preserves

Whipped cream and toasted sliced almonds

1 Grease the bottom and sides of a 10-in. spring-form pan; sprinkle with ground almonds and set aside.

2 In a saucepan, cook apricots and water for 15 minutes over medium heat or until the water is nearly absorbed and apricots are tender, stirring occasionally. Stir in lemon peel; cool slightly. Transfer to a blender; cover and process until smooth and set aside.

3 In a mixing bowl, beat cream cheese and sugar until smooth. Add flour; mix well. Add eggs; beat on low just until combined. Beat in cream just until blended. Stir 1 cup into pureed apricots; set aside. Pour remaining mixture into prepared pan. Drop apricot mixture by 1/2 teaspoonfuls over filling. Cut through filling with a knife to swirl apricot mixture. Place pan on a baking sheet.

4 Bake at 350° for 50-55 minutes or until center is almost set. Cool on a wire rack for 10 minutes. Carefully run a knife around edge of pan to loosen. Cool 1 hour longer.

5 In a small saucepan, heat preserves. Press through a strainer (discard pulp). Spread over cheesecake. Refrigerate overnight. Remove sides of pan. Garnish with whipped cream and sliced almonds. Refrigerate leftovers.

Macaroon Cheesecake

PREP: 20 min. **BAKE:** 55 min. + chilling
YIELD: 12-14 servings

Tracy Powers, Cedar Springs, Michigan

Coconut is featured in both the crust and topping of this irresistible cheesecake.

- 1 cup flaked coconut, toasted
- 1/2 cup ground pecans
- 2 tablespoons butter, melted

FILLING:

- 3 packages (8 ounces *each*) cream cheese, softened
- 1/2 cup sugar
- 3 eggs, lightly beaten
- 1/2 teaspoon vanilla extract
- 1/4 teaspoon almond extract

TOPPING:

- 1 egg white
- 1/2 teaspoon vanilla extract
- 1/3 cup sugar
- 2/3 cup flaked coconut, toasted

1 In a small bowl, combine the coconut and pecans; stir in butter. Press onto the bottom of a greased 9-in. springform pan; set aside.

2 In a large mixing bowl, beat cream cheese and sugar until smooth. Add eggs; beat on low just until combined. Beat in extracts just until blended. Pour over crust. Place pan on a baking sheet.

3 Bake at 350° for 35 minutes. In a small mixing bowl, beat egg white and vanilla until soft peaks form. Gradually beat in sugar, 1 tablespoon at a time, on high until stiff peaks form. Fold in coconut. Carefully spread over top of cheesecake. Bake 20-25 minutes longer or until center is almost set. Cool on a wire rack for 10 minutes. Carefully run a knife around edge of pan to loosen; cool 1 hour longer. Refrigerate overnight. Remove sides of pan. Refrigerate leftovers.

Peanut Butter Cheesecake

PREP: 20 min. + cooling **BAKE:** 55 min. + chilling
YIELD: 12-14 servings

Lois Brooks, Newark, Delaware

This cheesecake with its pretzel crust creates delicious pairings of sweet and salty—creamy and crunchy, plus peanut butter and chocolate.

1-1/2   **cups crushed pretzels**
1/3   **cup butter, melted**
FILLING:
5   **packages (8 ounces *each*) cream cheese, softened**
1-1/2   **cups sugar**
3/4   **cup creamy peanut butter**
2   **teaspoons vanilla extract**
3   **eggs, lightly beaten**
1   **cup peanut butter chips**
1   **cup (6 ounces) semisweet chocolate chips**
TOPPING:
1   **cup (8 ounces) sour cream**
3   **tablespoons creamy peanut butter**
1/2   **cup sugar**
1/2   **cup finely chopped unsalted peanuts**

1 In a small bowl, combine pretzels and butter. Press onto the bottom and 1 in. up the sides of a greased 10-in. springform pan. Place pan on a baking sheet. Bake at 350° for 5 minutes. Cool on a wire rack.

2 In a large mixing bowl, beat cream cheese and sugar until smooth. Add peanut butter and vanilla; mix well. Add eggs; beat on low just until combined. Stir in chips. Pour over the crust. Return pan to baking sheet.

3 Bake at 350° for 50-55 minutes or until center is almost set. Remove from the oven; let stand for 15 minutes (leave oven on).

4 For topping, in a small mixing bowl, combine the sour cream, peanut butter and sugar; spread over filling. Sprinkle with nuts. Bake 5 minutes longer.

5 Cool on a wire rack for 10 minutes. Carefully run a knife around the edge of the pan to loosen; cool 1 hour longer. Refrigerate overnight. Remove sides of pan. Refrigerate leftovers.

PEANUT BUTTER CHEESECAKE

Savory Cheesecakes

Creamy Crab Cheesecake

PREP: 25 min. + cooling **BAKE:** 35 min. + chilling
YIELD: 20-24 appetizer servings

Cathy Sarrels, Tucson, Arizona

A savory appetizer cheesecake such as this one, dotted with tender crabmeat, is sure to grab the attention and tempt the taste buds of guests.

- 1 **cup crushed butter-flavored crackers (about 25 crackers)**
- 3 **tablespoons butter, melted**
- 2 **packages (8 ounces *each*) cream cheese, softened**
- 3/4 **cup sour cream, *divided***
- 3 **eggs, lightly beaten**
- 2 **teaspoons grated onion**
- 1 **teaspoon lemon juice**
- 1/4 **teaspoon seafood seasoning**
- 2 **drops hot pepper sauce**
- 1/8 **teaspoon pepper**
- 1 **cup crabmeat, drained, flaked and cartilage removed**

Additional seafood seasoning, optional

1 In a small bowl, combine the cracker crumbs and butter. Press onto the bottom of a greased 9-in. springform pan. Place pan on a baking sheet. Bake at 350° for 10 minutes. Place pan on a wire rack. Reduce heat to 325°.

2 In a large mixing bowl, beat cream cheese and 1/4 cup sour cream until smooth. Add eggs; beat on low speed just until combined. Add the onion, lemon juice, seafood seasoning, hot pepper sauce and pepper; beat just until blended. Fold in crab. Pour over crust. Return pan to baking sheet.

3 Bake for 35-40 minutes or until center is almost set. Cool pan on a wire rack for 10 minutes. Carefully run a knife around edge of pan to loosen; cool 1 hour longer. Carefully spread remaining sour cream over top. Refrigerate overnight.

4 Remove sides of pan. Let cheesecake stand at room temperature for 30 minutes before serving. Sprinkle with additional seafood seasoning if desired. Refrigerate leftovers.

Savory Appetizer Cheesecake

PREP: 20 min. **BAKE:** 35 min.
YIELD: 16-20 appetizer servings

Joy Burke, Punxsutawney, Pennsylvania

Unlike most other appetizer cheesecakes, this version is best served warm from the oven.

- 6 **bacon strips, diced**
- 1 **large onion, chopped**
- 1 **garlic clove, minced**
- 1 **carton (15 ounces) ricotta cheese**
- 1/2 **cup half-and-half cream**
- 2 **tablespoons all-purpose flour**
- 1/2 **teaspoon salt**
- 1/8 **to 1/4 teaspoon cayenne pepper**
- 2 **eggs, lightly beaten**
- 1/2 **cup sliced green onions**

Assorted crackers and fresh fruit

1 In a skillet, cook bacon over medium heat until crisp. Using a slotted spoon, remove to paper towels to drain. In the drippings, saute onion and garlic until tender; remove with a slotted spoon.

2 In a large mixing bowl, beat the ricotta cheese, cream, flour, salt and cayenne until smooth. Add eggs; beat on low speed just until combined. Set aside 3 tablespoons bacon for garnish. Stir green onions, sauteed onion and remaining bacon into egg mixture. Pour into a greased 8-in. springform pan. Place pan on a baking sheet.

3 Bake at 350° for 35-40 minutes or until center is almost set. Cool pan on a wire rack for 10 minutes. Carefully run a knife around the edge of pan to loosen. Remove sides of pan. Sprinkle with reserved bacon. Serve warm with crackers and fruit. Refrigerate leftovers.

CREAMY CRAB CHEESECAKE

LAYERED VEGETABLE CHEESECAKE

Layered Vegetable Cheesecake

PREP: 35 min. + cooling **BAKE:** 35 min. + chilling
YIELD: 20 appetizer servings

Donna Cline, Pensacola, Florida

Everyone who tastes this cheesy concoction, topped with a dilly of a cucumber sauce, will relish its richness and come back for more.

1-1/3 cups dry bread crumbs
1/3 cup butter, melted
FILLING:
    2 packages (8 ounces *each*) cream cheese, softened
    2 eggs, lightly beaten
    1 cup (8 ounces) sour cream
    1/3 cup all-purpose flour
    1/4 cup finely chopped onion
    1/4 teaspoon salt
    1/4 teaspoon white pepper
    3/4 cup shredded carrots
    3/4 cup diced green pepper
    3/4 cup diced sweet red pepper
CUCUMBER DILL SAUCE:
    1 cup (8 ounces) plain yogurt
    1/3 cup mayonnaise
    1/2 cup finely chopped unpeeled cucumber
    1/4 teaspoon salt
    1/4 teaspoon dill weed

1 Combine bread crumbs and butter; press onto the bottom and 1 in. up the sides of a greased 9-in. springform pan. Set aside.

2 In a large mixing bowl, beat cream cheese until smooth. Add eggs; beat on low speed just until combined. Add the sour cream, flour, onion, salt and pepper; beat just until combined. Pour 1 cup into crust; sprinkle with carrots. Continue layering 1 cup cream cheese mixture, green pepper, 1 cup cream cheese mixture, red pepper, then remaining cream cheese mixture. Place pan on a baking sheet.

3 Bake at 325° for 35-40 minutes or until center is almost set. Cool pan on a wire rack for 10 minutes. Carefully run a knife around edge of pan to loosen; cool 1 hour longer. Refrigerate overnight. In a small bowl, combine sauce ingredients; refrigerate.

4 Remove sides of pan. Serve chilled or warm with cucumber dill sauce.

5 To serve warm, remove from the refrigerator 1 hour before serving. Let cheesecake come to room temperature for 30 minutes, then reheat at 300° for 20-25 minutes or until warm. Refrigerate leftovers.

problem-solving pointers *for Cheesecakes*

THE CHEESECAKE HAS LUMPS

- The cream cheese was not softened before mixing and/or was not thoroughly blended before adding the eggs.

THE CHEESECAKE HAS A CRACKED TOP

- The batter was overbeaten.
- The oven temperature was too high. Check temperature with an oven thermometer.
- The cheesecake was overbaked.
- Doneness was checked with a knife or toothpick.
- The cheesecake was cooled in a drafty area or the oven door was opened during baking.
- Next time, try baking the cheesecake in a water bath. (See page 181.)

THE TOP CRACKED WHEN THE SIDES OF THE PAN WERE REMOVED

- You didn't loosen the cheesecake from the sides of the pan with a knife while it was cooling.

Cheese Pies & Bars

Raspberry Swirl Cheesecake Pie

PREP: 20 min. **BAKE:** 25 min. + chilling
YIELD: 8 servings

Sandra McKenzie, Braham, Minnesota

Raspberry jam gives this attractive dessert its marbled effect. While the cheesecake refrigerates overnight, its flavors blend beautifully.

Pastry for single-crust pie (9 inches)
- 2   packages (8 ounces *each*) cream cheese, softened
- 1/2   cup sugar
- 1/2   teaspoon vanilla extract
- 2   eggs, lightly beaten
- 3   tablespoons raspberry jam

Whipped topping, optional

1 Line unpricked pastry shell with a double thickness of heavy-duty foil. Bake at 450° for 5 minutes; remove foil. Bake 5 minutes longer. Place on a wire rack. Reduce heat to 350°.

2 In a large mixing bowl, beat the cream cheese, sugar and vanilla until smooth. Add eggs; beat on low speed just until combined. Pour into pastry shell. Stir jam; drizzle over the filling. Cut through filling with a knife to swirl the jam.

CHOCOLATE CHEESE PIE

3 Bake for 25-30 minutes or until center is almost set. Cool on a wire rack for 1 hour. Refrigerate overnight. Let stand at room temperature for 30 minutes before slicing. If desired, pipe whipped topping around pie. Refrigerate leftovers.

Chocolate Cheese Pie

PREP: 35 min. + chilling **BAKE:** 40 min. + chilling
YIELD: 2 pies (8 servings each)

Lorra Rhyner, Poynette, Wisconsin

A chocolate chain of hearts on top of this cheesecake makes it a lovely dessert on Valentine's Day.

- 3   cups graham cracker crumbs (about 48 squares)
- 1/2   cup sugar
- 2/3   cup butter, melted

FILLING:
- 3   packages (8 ounces *each*) cream cheese, softened
- 1   cup sugar
- 5   eggs, lightly beaten
- 1   tablespoon vanilla extract
- 1   package (4 ounces) German sweet chocolate, melted and cooled

RASPBERRY SWIRL CHEESECAKE PIE

1. In a bowl, combine cracker crumbs and sugar; stir in butter. Press onto the bottom and up the sides of two ungreased 9-in. pie plates. Refrigerate while preparing filling.

2. In a large mixing bowl, beat cream cheese until fluffy. Gradually add sugar, beating until smooth. Add eggs; beat on low speed just until combined. Beat in vanilla. Remove 1-1/2 cups to a small bowl; fold in melted chocolate. Divide remaining filling mixture between crusts.

3. To make the chain of hearts on each pie, drop teaspoonfuls of chocolate filling equally spaced around outside edges and four drops in center. Starting in the center of one outer drop, run a knife through the center of each to connect, forming a circle of hearts. Repeat with center drops.

4. Bake at 350° for 40-45 minutes or until center is almost set. Cool on wire racks for 1 hour. Refrigerate for at least 6 hours or overnight. Refrigerate leftovers.

Blueberry Swirl Cheesecake

PREP: 15 min. **BAKE:** 35 min. + chilling
YIELD: 8 servings

Suzanne McKinley, Lyons, Georgia

Convenient canned blueberry pie filling and a prepared graham cracker crust make this dessert extra easy.

- 2 packages (8 ounces *each*) cream cheese, softened
- 1/2 cup sugar
- 1/4 teaspoon vanilla extract
- 2 eggs, lightly beaten
- 1 graham cracker crust (9 inches)
- 1 can (21 ounces) blueberry pie filling, *divided*

BLUEBERRY SWIRL CHEESECAKE

1. In a large mixing bowl, beat the cream cheese, sugar and vanilla until smooth. Add eggs; beat on low speed just until combined. Pour into crust. Drop 1/2 cup of pie filling by heaping teaspoonfuls onto the cream cheese mixture; cut through with a knife to swirl the pie filling.

2. Bake at 350° for 35-40 minutes or until center is almost set. Cool on a wire rack for 1 hour. Refrigerate for 2 hours. Top with remaining pie filling. Refrigerate leftovers.

Lemon Cheesecake Pie

PREP: 20 min. + chilling **BAKE:** 25 min. + chilling
YIELD: 8 servings

Hope Huggins, Santa Cruz, California

Lemon peel lightly flavors this smaller-serving version of a traditional cheesecake.

- 1-1/4 cups graham cracker crumbs (about 20 squares)
- 1/3 cup butter, melted

FILLING:
- 2 packages (8 ounces *each*) cream cheese, softened
- 1/2 cup sugar
- 2 eggs, lightly beaten
- 1 teaspoon vanilla extract
- 1/2 teaspoon finely grated lemon peel

TOPPING:
- 1 cup (8 ounces) sour cream
- 2 tablespoons sugar
- 1/2 teaspoon vanilla extract

Fresh mint and lemon peel strips, optional

1. In a bowl, combine cracker crumbs and butter; press onto the bottom and up the sides of an ungreased 9-in. pie plate. Cover and refrigerate for 30 minutes.

2. In a large mixing bowl, beat the cream cheese and sugar until smooth. Add eggs; beat on low speed just until combined. Stir in vanilla and lemon peel just until blended. Pour into prepared crust.

3. Bake at 325° for 20-25 minutes or until center is almost set. Remove from the oven; let stand for 5 minutes (leave oven on). Combine the sour cream, sugar and vanilla; spread carefully over pie. Bake 5 minutes longer. Cool on a wire rack for 1 hour. Refrigerate overnight. Garnish with mint and lemon peel if desired. Refrigerate leftovers.

Pineapple Cheesecake Squares

PREP: 20 min. + cooling **BAKE:** 1 hour + cooling
YIELD: 9 servings

Elisabeth Garrison, Elmer, New Jersey

For a fun, tropical twist, prepare these cheese bars starring crushed pineapple. Because they're not too sweet, it's hard to eat just one!

1/2	cup all-purpose flour
3	tablespoons sugar
1/4	teaspoon salt
1/4	cup cold butter

FILLING:

1	can (8 ounces) crushed pineapple
1	package (8 ounces) cream cheese, softened
3	tablespoons sugar
1	tablespoon all-purpose flour
1	egg, lightly beaten
1	cup milk
1	teaspoon vanilla extract

Ground cinnamon

1 In a bowl, combine the flour, sugar and salt; cut in butter until mixture is crumbly. Press onto the bottom of an ungreased 8-in. square baking dish. Bake at 325° for 12 minutes. Cool on a wire rack.

2 For filling, drain pineapple, reserving the juice; set pineapple and juice aside. In a large mixing bowl, beat the cream cheese, sugar and flour until smooth. Add egg; beat on low speed just until combined. Add pineapple juice. Gradually add milk and vanilla. Sprinkle pineapple over the crust. Slowly pour filling over pineapple. Sprinkle with cinnamon.

3 Bake at 325° for 1 hour or until a knife inserted near the center comes out clean. Cool on a wire rack for 1 hour. Store in the refrigerator.

Brown Sugar Cheese Pie

PREP: 30 min. **BAKE:** 30 min. + chilling
YIELD: 8 servings

Francis & Sybyl Pressly
Valle Crucis, North Carolina

This easy-to-prepare cheese pie is full of old-fashioned flavor from the brown sugar and buttermilk.

1-1/2	cups graham cracker crumbs (about 24 squares)
1/4	cup sugar
1/2	cup butter, melted

FILLING:

1	package (8 ounces) cream cheese, softened
1/2	cup firmly packed brown sugar
2	eggs, lightly beaten
1/4	cup buttermilk
1	teaspoon vanilla extract
1/3	cup slivered almonds, toasted

1 In a small bowl, combine the crumbs and sugar; stir in the butter. Press onto bottom and sides of 9-in. pie plate. Bake at 350° for 5 minutes or until set. Cool on a wire rack.

2 For filling, in a large mixing bowl, beat cream cheese and brown sugar until smooth. Add the eggs, buttermilk and vanilla; beat just until combined. Pour into crust; sprinkle with almonds.

3 Bake at 350° for 25-30 minutes until center is almost set. Cool on a wire rack. Refrigerate for at least 3 hours. Refrigerate leftovers.

Lemon Ricotta Cheesecake Squares

PREP: 15 min. **BAKE:** 1 hour + chilling
YIELD: 16-20 servings

Mrs. Glenn Holcomb
Torrington, Connecticut

The ricotta cheese layer sinks down in the cheesecake, creating a luscious, dense cake that's just bursting with lemon flavor.

   3   **eggs, lightly beaten**
   2   **cartons (15 ounces *each*) ricotta cheese**
3/4   **cup sugar**
   2   **teaspoons grated lemon peel**
CAKE:
   1   **package (18-1/4 ounces) lemon cake mix**
   1   **cup water**
1/3   **cup vegetable oil**
1/4   **cup lemon juice**
   3   **eggs**
   2   **teaspoons confectioners' sugar**

1 In a large bowl, combine the eggs, ricotta cheese,

LEMON RICOTTA CHEESECAKE SQUARES

sugar and lemon peel; set aside. In a large mixing bowl, combine the dry cake mix, water, oil, lemon juice and eggs; beat on low speed for 30 seconds. Beat on medium for 2 minutes. Pour into a greased 13-in. x 9-in. x 2-in. baking pan. Carefully spoon ricotta mixture on top of cake batter.

2 Bake at 350° for 60-65 minutes or until lightly browned. Cool on a wire rack for 1 hour. Refrigerate overnight. Dust with confectioners' sugar; cut into squares. Refrigerate leftovers.

Cinnamon Cherry Cheesecake Squares

PREP: 20 min. **BAKE:** 30 min. + chilling
YIELD: 12-15 servings

Vera Kramer, Jenera, Ohio

Cinnamon graham crackers are used in this recipe and give each bite a deliciously different taste.

1-3/4   **cups crushed cinnamon graham crackers (about 28 crackers)**
 1/4   **cup sugar**
 1/2   **cup butter, melted**
FILLING:
   2   **packages (8 ounces *each*) cream cheese, softened**
 1/2   **cup sugar**
   3   **eggs, lightly beaten**
   1   **teaspoon vanilla extract**
TOPPING:
   2   **cups (16 ounces) sour cream**
 1/4   **cup sugar**
   1   **teaspoon vanilla**
   1   **can (16 ounces) cherry pie filling**

1 In a bowl, combine graham crackers and sugar; stir in butter. Press onto the bottom of a greased 11-in. x 7-in. x 2-in. baking dish. Set aside.

2 For filling, beat cream cheese and sugar in a large mixing bowl until smooth. Add eggs; beat on low speed until just combined. Add vanilla. Pour into the crust.

3 Bake at 350° for 25 minutes. Remove from the oven; let stand for 5 minutes (leave oven on). For topping, combine the sour cream, sugar and vanilla; carefully spread over pie. Bake 5 minutes longer. Cool on a wire rack for 1 hour. Refrigerate for 4 hours or overnight. Cut into squares; top each with a spoonful of cherry pie filling. Refrigerate leftovers.

Nutty Cheesecake Squares

PREP: 20 min. **BAKE:** 20 min. + cooling
YIELD: 16-20 servings

Ruth Simon, Buffalo, New York

Easy to make, but special enough for company describes these bars. They also travel well to potlucks and picnics.

- 2 **cups all-purpose flour**
- 1 **cup finely chopped walnuts**
- 2/3 **cup packed brown sugar**
- 1/2 **teaspoon salt**
- 2/3 **cup cold butter**

FILLING:
- 2 **packages (8 ounces *each*) cream cheese, softened**
- 1/2 **cup sugar**
- 2 **eggs, lightly beaten**
- 1/4 **cup milk**
- 1 **teaspoon vanilla extract**

1 In a bowl, combine the flour, walnuts, brown sugar and salt; cut in butter until the mixture resembles coarse crumbs. Set half aside; press remaining crumb mixture onto the bottom of a greased 13-in. x 9-in. x 2-in. baking pan. Bake at 350° for 10-15 minutes or until lightly browned.

2 In a large mixing bowl, beat filling ingredients until smooth; pour over crust. Sprinkle with reserved crumb mixture. Bake for 20-25 minutes or until a knife inserted near the center comes out clean. Cool on a wire rack for 1 hour. Store in the refrigerator.

RHUBARB CHEESECAKE DESSERT

Rhubarb Cheesecake Dessert

PREP: 30 min. + cooling **BAKE:** 20 min. + chilling
YIELD: 12-15 servings

Joyce Krumwiede, Mankato, Minnesota

These pretty rhubarb-topped squares will signal the arrival of spring!

- 1 **cup all-purpose flour**
- 1/2 **cup packed brown sugar**
- 1/4 **teaspoon salt**
- 1/4 **cup cold butter**
- 1/2 **cup chopped walnuts**
- 1 **teaspoon vanilla extract**

FILLING:
- 2 **packages (8 ounces *each*) cream cheese, softened**
- 3/4 **cup sugar**
- 3 **eggs, lightly beaten**
- 1 **teaspoon vanilla extract**

TOPPING:
- 1 **cup sugar**
- 1 **tablespoon cornstarch**
- 1/4 **teaspoon ground cinnamon**
- 1/4 **cup water**
- 3 **cups chopped fresh *or* frozen rhubarb**

1 In a bowl, combine the flour, brown sugar and salt; cut in butter until mixture resembles coarse crumbs. Stir in walnuts and vanilla. Set half aside; press remaining crumb mixture onto the bottom of a greased 13-in. x 9-in. x 2-in. baking dish. Bake at 375° for 10 minutes. Cool slightly.

2 In a large mixing bowl, beat cream cheese and sugar until smooth. Add eggs; beat on low speed just until combined. Add vanilla. Pour over crust. Bake at 375° for 20-25 minutes or until center is almost set and edges are light brown. Cool on a wire rack for 1 hour.

3 In a large saucepan, combine the sugar, cornstarch and cinnamon. Gradually stir in water until smooth. Add rhubarb. Bring to a boil over medium heat; cook and stir until for 5 minutes or until thickened. Cool. Pour over filling. Refrigerate at least 1 hour. Refrigerate leftovers.

Editor's Note: If using frozen rhubarb, measure rhubarb while still frozen, then thaw completely. Drain in a colander, but do not press liquid out.

PIES & TARTS

Pies & Tarts

The Basics of Pies & Tarts

Pies and their fancier cousin, tarts, make a delightfully delicious treat or ending to a meal. The pies and tarts featured in this chapter have sweetened centers from a selection of fruit fillings to smooth custards and creamy puddings.

Pies and tarts can use similar fillings, and they both have a crust. The main difference is that tarts are more shallow than pies. Tarts are typically about 1 inch high and can be full size, individual-serving size or even bite size. Pies are typically 9 inches, but can also have a single or double crust, a pastry or crumb crust, and some even have a meringue crust.

Pies and tarts offer so much variety in flavors and textures that there is sure to be a special favorite to suit everyone's taste buds.

secrets for *successful pie pastry*

- Classic pie pastry recipes are prepared with solid shortening. Lard or butter-flavored shortening can be substitutes for plain shortening if desired.

- Measure ingredients accurately, using the measuring tools and techniques suggested on pages 7 and 8.

- Use all-purpose or pastry flour for pie crusts. Bread or cake flour will not give the desired texture to the crust.

- Combine flour and salt thoroughly before adding the shortening and water.

- Be sure to use ice-cold water. Before you measure out the flour and shortening, place about 1/2 cup water in a glass measuring cup and some ice cubes. This way, the water will be icy cold when you are ready to measure it out.

- The key to producing a flaky crust is to avoid overmixing when adding the water to the flour and shortening mixture. Overmixing will cause the gluten in the flour to develop and the pastry to be tough.

- Chill pie pastry dough for 30 minutes before rolling to make it easier to handle.

- Pie pastry can be made 1 or 2 days before using. Shape it into a flat disk and wrap the dough in plastic wrap. Store it in the refrigerator until ready to use.

- A floured surface is essential to prevent sticking when rolling out pastry. A pastry cloth and rolling pin cover are good investments—they will keep the pastry from sticking and minimize the amount of flour used. The less flour you add while rolling, the flakier and lighter the pastry will be.

- Pie pastry can also be rolled out between two sheets of waxed paper. When the pastry dough is rolled out, just peel off the top sheet, invert it into the pie plate and peel off the remaining waxed paper.

- Gently ease the pie pastry into the pie plate. Stretching it will cause it to shrink during baking.

- Choose dull-finish aluminum or glass pie plates for crisp golden crusts. Shiny pans can produce soggy crusts.

- Because of the high fat content in a pastry, do not grease the pie plate unless the recipe directs.

- Never prick the bottom of a pastry crust when the filling and crust are to be baked together.

- Arrange the oven racks so that the pie will bake in the center of the oven.

- Preheat the oven for 10-15 minutes before baking.

- If the edge of the crust is browning too quickly during baking, shield the edge with a ring of foil. (See Protecting Pastry Edges from Overbrowning, page 215.)

- Cool pies on a wire rack.

Pie Pastries

Classic Pie Pastry

PREP: 15 min + chilling **YIELD:** pastry for single- or double-crust pie (9 or 10 inches)

Taste of Home Test Kitchen

Just four ingredients are all you need to create a fabulous flaky pie crust. The double-crust recipe should be used when making a lattice-topped pie.

INGREDIENTS FOR SINGLE-CRUST PIE:
- 1-1/4 cups all-purpose flour
- 1/2 teaspoon salt
- 1/3 cup shortening
- 4 to 5 tablespoons cold water

INGREDIENTS FOR DOUBLE-CRUST PIE:
- 2 cups all-purpose flour
- 3/4 teaspoon salt
- 2/3 cup shortening
- 6 to 7 tablespoons cold water

In a small bowl, combine the flour and salt; cut in shortening until mixture resembles course crumbs. Gradually add the water, tossing with a fork until a ball forms. Cover and refrigerate for 30 minutes or until easy to handle.

Pastry for a single-crust (9-in. to 10-in.) pie: Roll out pastry to fit a 9-in. or 10-in. pie plate. Transfer pastry to pie plate. Trim pastry to 1/2 in. beyond edge of plate; flute edges. Fill or bake shell according to recipe directions.

Pastry for a double-crust (9-in. to 10-in.) pie: Divide dough in half so that one ball is slightly larger than the other. Roll out larger ball to fit a 9-in. or 10-in. pie plate. Transfer pastry to pie plate. Trim pastry even with edge of plate. Add filling. Roll out remaining pastry to fit top of pie; place over filling. Trim, seal and flute edges. Cut slits in top. Bake according to recipe directions.

Never-Fail Pie Crust

PREP: 15 min. + chilling **YIELD:** pastry for single- or double-crust pie (9 or 10 inches)

Ruth Gritter, Grand Rapids, Michigan

Even novice bakers who normally shy away from homemade pie pastry can't go wrong with this recipe. It's so easy to roll out and produces a tender, flaky crust.

INGREDIENTS FOR SINGLE-CRUST PIE:
- 1 cup all-purpose flour
- 1/4 teaspoon salt

prebaking
a pastry shell

1. After placing pastry in the pie plate and fluting edges, line unpricked shell with a double thickness of heavy-duty foil. If desired, fill with dried beans, uncooked rice or pie weights. The weight will keep the crust from puffing up, shrinking and slipping down the pie plate during baking.

2. Bake at 450° for 8 minutes. With oven mitts, carefully remove the foil and beans, rice or weights. Bake 5-6 minutes longer or until light golden brown. Cool on a wire rack. Let beans or rice cool, then store. They may be reused for pie weights, but cannot be cooked and used in recipes.

- 1/3 cup shortening
- 1-1/2 teaspoons white vinegar
- 2 to 3 tablespoons milk

INGREDIENTS FOR DOUBLE-CRUST PIE:
- 2 cups all-purpose flour
- 1/2 teaspoon salt
- 2/3 cup shortening
- 1 tablespoon white vinegar
- 5 to 6 tablespoons milk

In a small bowl, combine the flour and salt; cut in shortening until mixture resembles course crumbs. Sprinkle with vinegar. Gradually add the milk, tossing with a fork until a ball forms. Cover and refrigerate for 30 minutes or until easy to handle.

Pastry for a single-crust (9-in. to 10-in.) pie: Roll out pastry to fit a 9-in. or 10-in. pie plate. Transfer pastry to pie plate. Trim pastry to 1/2 in. beyond edge of plate; flute edges. Fill or bake shell according to recipe directions.

Pastry for a double-crust (9-in. to 10-in.) pie: Divide pastry in half so that one ball is slightly larger than the other. Roll out larger ball to fit a 9-in. or 10-in. pie plate. Transfer pastry to pie plate. Trim pastry even with edge of plate. Add filling. Roll out remaining pastry to fit top of pie; place over filling. Trim, seal and flute edges. Cut slits in top. Bake according to recipe directions.

Basic Pastry Mix

PREP/TOTAL TIME: 15 min. **YIELD:** 8 cups

Kathleen Koziolek, Hartland, Minnesota

You can turn out a finished pie crust in a matter of minutes using this Basic Pastry Mix. With several flavors of crust to choose from, you're sure to find one that's a hit at your house!

- 6 cups all-purpose flour
- 2 teaspoons salt
- 2-1/3 cups shortening

In a large mixing bowl, combine flour and salt. Cut in half of the shortening until the mixture resembles coarse crumbs. Cut in remaining shortening. Place in an airtight container and store in the refrigerator for up to 6 weeks.

Pastry for a single-crust (9-in. to 10-in.) pie:
1 Place 1-1/4 to 1-3/4 cups Basic Pastry Mix in a large bowl. Gradually add 2 to 4 tablespoons cold water, tossing with a fork until dough forms a ball. Cover and refrigerate for 30 minutes if desired.

2 Roll out pastry to fit a 9-in. to 10-in. pie plate. Transfer pastry to pie plate. Trim pastry to 1/2 in. beyond edge of pie plate; flute edges. Fill or bake shell according to recipe directions. Or bake without filling at 400° for 10 minutes or until the pastry is light golden brown.

Pastry for a double-crust (9-in. to 10-in.) pie:
1 Place 2 to 2-3/4 cups Basic Pastry Mix in a large bowl. Gradually add 4 to 6 tablespoons cold water, tossing with a fork until dough forms a ball. Cover and refrigerate for 30 minutes if desired.

2 Divide dough in half so that one ball is slightly larger than the other. Roll out larger ball to fit a 9-in. to 10-in. pie plate. Trim pastry even with

edge. Fill crust with desired filling. Roll out remaining pastry to fit top of pie. Place over filling. Trim, seal and flute edges. Cut slits in top. Bake according to recipe directions.

Spicy Pastry: Prepare as directed for a single-crust pie, except add 1 teaspoon pumpkin pie spice to the Basic Pastry Mix. Add 1 tablespoon light molasses and 1 to 3 tablespoons cold water until dough forms a ball.

Chocolate Pastry: Prepare as directed for a single-crust pie, except add 2 tablespoons instant chocolate drink mix to the Basic Pastry Mix. Add 2 to 3 tablespoons cold water until dough forms a ball.

Egg Yolk Pastry

PREP: 20 min. + chilling **YIELD:** pastry for 2 single-crust or double-crust pies (9 inches)

Dolores Skrout, Summerhill, Pennsylvania

Egg yolk lends an attractive golden color to this pie pastry.

- 2-1/2 cups all-purpose flour
- 2 teaspoons sugar
- 1/4 teaspoon baking powder
- 1/4 teaspoon salt
- 3/4 cup shortening
- 1 egg yolk, lightly beaten
- 5 to 6 tablespoons cold water

In a small bowl, combine the flour, sugar, baking powder and salt; cut in shortening until mixture resembles coarse crumbs. Combine the egg yolk and water; gradually add to flour mixture, tossing with a fork until a ball forms. Cover and refrigerate for 30 minutes or until easy to handle.

Pastry for a single-crust (9-in. to 10-in.) pie: Divide pastry in half. Roll out each portion to fit a 9-in. pie plate. Transfer pastry to pie plate. Trim pastry to 1/2 in. beyond edge of plate; flute edges. Fill or bake shell according to recipe directions.

Pastry for a double-crust (9-in. to 10-in.) pie: Divide pastry in half so that one ball is slightly larger than the other. Roll out larger ball to fit a 9-in. pie plate. Transfer pastry to pie plate. Trim pastry even with edge of plate. Add filling. Roll out remaining pastry to fit top of pie; place over filling. Trim, seal and flute edges. Cut slits in top. Bake according to recipe directions.

making and
shaping *single- and double-crust pie pastry*

1. Combine flour and salt in a bowl. With a pastry blender or two knives, cut in shortening until the mixture resembles coarse crumbs (the size of small peas).

2. Sprinkle 1 tablespoon of cold water at a time over the mixture and toss gently with a fork. Repeat until the dry ingredients are moist and mixture forms a ball. Use only as much water as necessary to moisten the flour.

3. Shape into a ball. (For a double-crust pie, divide pastry in half so that one ball is slightly larger than the other.) On a floured surface or floured pastry cloth, flatten the ball (the larger one, if making a double-crust pie) into a circle, pressing together any cracks or breaks.

4. Roll with a floured rolling pin from the center of the pastry to the edges, forming a circle 2 in. larger than the pie plate. The pastry should be about 1/8 in. thick.

5. To move pastry to the pie plate, roll up onto the rolling pin. Position over the edge of pie plate and unroll. Let the pastry ease into the plate. Do not stretch the pastry to fit. For a single-crust pie, trim pastry with a scissors to 1/2 in. beyond plate edge; turn under and flute as in step 8. For a double-crust pie, trim pastry even with the edge of plate. For a lattice-crust pie, trim pastry to 1 in. beyond plate edge. Either bake the shell or fill according to recipe directions.

6. For a double-crust pie, roll out second ball into a 12-in. circle about 1/8 in. thick. Roll up pastry onto the rolling pin; position over filling. With a knife, cut several slits in top to allow steam to escape while baking.

7. With scissors, trim top pastry to 1 in. beyond plate edge. Fold top pastry over bottom pastry.

8. To flute the edge as shown at right, position your thumb on the inside of the crust. Place the thumb and index finger of your other hand on the outside edge and pinch pastry around the thumb to form a V shape and seal dough together. Continue around the edge.

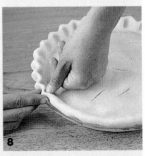

Pat-in-the-Pan Pie Crust

PREP: 10 min. **BAKE:** 10 min. + cooling
YIELD: 1 pie crust (9 inches)

Mrs. Anton Sohrwiede, McGraw, New York

This pie crust requires no rolling pin—it's just simply patted into the pan.

1 cup all-purpose flour
1/3 cup sugar
1 teaspoon baking powder
1/4 teaspoon salt
2 tablespoons cold butter
1 egg, beaten
2 tablespoons milk

1 In a bowl, combine the flour, sugar, baking powder and salt; cut in butter until mixture resembles coarse crumbs. Combine egg and milk; stir into flour mixture (dough will be sticky). Press into the bottom and up the sides of a greased 9-in. pie plate. Bake at 375° for 8-10 minutes or until set. Cool on a wire rack.

2 Fill as desired. If baking the filling, shield edges with foil to prevent overbrowning.

decorative *pie crust edges*

RUFFLE EDGE

Use for a single- or double-crust pie. Trim pastry 1/2 in. beyond edge of pie plate (1 in. for a double-crust pie). Turn the overhanging pastry under to form the rolled edge.

Position your thumb and index finger about 1 in. apart on the edge of the crust, pointing out. Position the index finger on your other hand between the two fingers and gently push the pastry toward the center in an upward direction. Continue around the edge.

ROPE EDGE

Use for a single- or double-crust pie. Trim pastry 1/2 in. beyond edge of pie plate (1 in. for a double-crust pie). Turn the overhanging pastry under to form the rolled edge.

Make a fist with one hand and press your thumb at an angle into the pastry. Pinch some of the pastry between your thumb and index finger. Repeat at about 1/2-in. intervals around the crust. For a looser-looking rope, position your thumb at a wider angle and repeat at 1-in. intervals.

CUT SCALLOPED EDGE

Use for a single-crust pie. Line a 9-in. pie plate with the bottom pastry and trim pastry even with edge of pie plate. Hold a teaspoon or tablespoon upside down and roll the tip of

the spoon around the edge of the pastry, cutting it. Remove and discard the cut pieces to create a scalloped look.

BRAIDED EDGE

Use for a single-crust pie. Make enough pastry for a double crust. Line a 9-in. pie plate with the bottom pastry and trim pastry even with edge of pie plate.

Roll remaining pastry into a 10-in. x 8-in. rectangle. With a sharp knife, cut twelve 1/4-in.-wide strips; gently braid three strips. Brush edge of crust with water; place braid on edge and press lightly to secure. Repeat with remaining strips, attaching additional braids until entire edge is covered. Cover with foil to protect edges from overbrowning.

LEAF TRIM

Use for a single-crust pie. Make enough pastry for a double crust. Line a 9-in. pie plate with the bottom pastry and trim pastry even with edge of pie plate. Roll out remaining pastry to 1/8-in. thickness.

Cut out leaf shapes, using 1-in. to 1-1/2-in. cookie cutters. With a sharp knife, score pastry to create leaf veins. Brush bottom of each leaf with water. Place one or two layers of leaves around the edge of crust; press lightly to secure. Cover with foil to protect edges from overbrowning. ·

You can also use this technique with other cookie cutter designs such as stars, hearts and apples. Vary them to suit the occasion or season you are celebrating.

Fruit Pies

Dutch Apple Pie

PREP: 10 min. **BAKE:** 65 min. + cooling
YIELD: 6-8 servings

Eugenia McQueen, Tampa, Florida

Sour cream adds extra richness to this classic pie's unbeatable crust. A not-too-sweet streusel topping provides the finishing touch.

    3/4 cup sugar
      2 tablespoons all-purpose flour
Pinch salt
      1 egg, beaten
    1/2 teaspoon vanilla extract
      1 cup (8 ounces) sour cream
      2 cups chopped peeled tart apples
         (about 3 medium)
      1 unbaked pastry shell (9 inches)
STREUSEL TOPPING:
    1/3 cup all-purpose flour
    1/3 cup packed brown sugar
      2 tablespoons cold butter

1 In a large mixing bowl, combine the sugar, flour and salt. Stir in the egg, vanilla and sour cream until smooth. Add apples; mix well. Pour into pastry shell. Bake at 375° for 15 minutes. Reduce heat to 325°; bake for 30 minutes.

DUTCH APPLE PIE

2 For topping, combine flour and sugar in a small bowl. Cut in butter until mixture is crumbly. Sprinkle over pie; bake 20 minutes longer or until filling is bubbly and topping is browned. Cool on a wire rack. Serve warm or chilled. Store in the refrigerator.

Apple Custard Pie

PREP: 15 min. **BAKE:** 45 min. + chilling
YIELD: 6-8 servings

Carol Adams, Medina, Texas

There's no need to pull out your rolling pin to make this sweet treat. It has an easy press-in crust under a mouth-watering apple and custard filling.

  1-1/2 cups all-purpose flour
    1/2 teaspoon salt
    1/2 cup cold butter
      3 cups sliced peeled tart apples
         (about 4 medium)
    1/3 cup sugar
      1 teaspoon ground cinnamon
CUSTARD:
      1 cup evaporated milk
      1 egg
    1/2 cup sugar

1 In a small bowl, combine flour and salt; cut in butter until mixture resembles course crumbs. Press onto the bottom and up the sides of a 9-in. pie plate. Arrange apples over the crust. Combine sugar and cinnamon; sprinkle over apples. Bake at 375° for 20 minutes.

2 For custard, whisk the milk, egg and sugar in another small bowl until smooth; pour over apples. Bake 25-30 minutes longer or until a knife inserted near the center comes out clean. Cool on a wire rack for 1 hour. Refrigerate for at least 3 hours before serving. Refrigerate leftovers.

Apple Praline Pie

PREP: 20 min. **BAKE:** 55 min. + cooling
YIELD: 6-8 servings

Bev Higley, Londonderry, Ohio

After this double-crust pie is baked, it's covered with a deliciously rich brown sugar, butter and pecan topping. Then the pie is returned to the oven so the topping can bubble and bake onto the crust.

      7 cups thinly sliced peeled tart apples
         (about 8 medium)

1 cup sugar
6 tablespoons all-purpose flour
1 teaspoon ground cinnamon
1 teaspoon ground nutmeg
Pastry for double-crust pie (9 inches)
3 tablespoons apple cider *or* apple juice
2 tablespoons butter, melted
PRALINE TOPPING:
2 tablespoons butter
1/4 cup packed brown sugar
2 tablespoons apple cider *or* apple juice
1 tablespoon half-and-half cream
1/2 cup chopped pecans

1 In a large bowl, combine the apples, sugar, flour, cinnamon and nutmeg; toss gently to coat. Line a 9-in. pie plate with bottom pastry; trim even with edge of plate. Brush well with apple cider. Add apple mixture; pour any remaining cider over top. Drizzle with butter. Roll out remaining pastry to fit top of pie; place over filling. Trim, seal and flute edges. Cut slits in top. Bake at 350° for 50 minutes.

2 For topping, melt butter in a small saucepan. Add the brown sugar, cider and cream. Bring to a full rolling boil over low heat, stirring occasionally. Remove from the heat. Stir in pecans.

3 Remove pie from the oven (leave oven on) and place on a baking sheet. Slowly pour topping over pie. Bake 5-10 minutes longer or until topping bubbles. Cool on a wire rack for at least 1 hour before serving.

Golden Apple Pie

PREP: 30 min. + cooling **BAKE:** 40 min. + cooling
YIELD: 6-8 servings

Theresa Brazil, Petaluma, California

A classic double-crust apple pie like this never goes out of fashion. Serve slices alone or a la mode.

6 cups sliced peeled Golden Delicious apples (about 7 medium)
3/4 cup plus 2 tablespoons apple juice, *divided*
3/4 cup sugar
1 teaspoon ground cinnamon
1/2 teaspoon apple pie spice
2 tablespoons cornstarch
1/4 teaspoon vanilla extract

GOLDEN APPLE PIE

CRUST:
2-1/2 cups all-purpose flour
1 teaspoon salt
1 cup cold butter
6 to 8 tablespoons cold water

1 In a large saucepan, combine the apples, 3/4 cup apple juice, sugar, cinnamon and apple pie spice; bring to a boil over medium heat, stirring occasionally. Combine cornstarch and remaining apple juice until smooth; stir into apple mixture. Bring to a boil; cook and stir for 1 minute or until thickened. Remove from the heat. Stir in vanilla. Cool to room temperature, stirring occasionally.

2 For crust, combine flour and salt in a bowl; cut in butter until mixture resembles coarse crumbs. Gradually add water, tossing with a fork until mixture forms a ball. Divide in half, making one half slightly larger. On a lightly floured surface, roll out larger portion.

3 Line a 9-in. pie plate with bottom pastry; trim even with edge of plate. Add filling. Roll out remaining pastry to fit top of pie; place over filling. Trim, seal and flute edges. Cut slits in top.

4 Bake at 400° for 40-45 minutes or until crust is golden brown and apples are tender. Cool on a wire rack.

Four-Fruit Pie

PREP: 15 min. + standing **BAKE:** 50 min.
YIELD: 6-8 servings

Joan Rose, Langley, British Columbia

Buy the rhubarb, blueberries and raspberries when they are in season and freeze. That way you can make this fruit-filled pie any time of the year.

- 1 cup sliced rhubarb (1-inch pieces)
- 1 cup chopped peeled apple
- 1 cup blueberries
- 1 cup raspberries
- 1 teaspoon lemon juice
- 3/4 cup sugar
- 1/4 cup all-purpose flour

Pastry for double-crust pie (9 inches)
- 2 tablespoons butter

Additional sugar, optional

1 In a large bowl, gently toss the rhubarb, apple, berries and lemon juice. Combine sugar and flour; stir into the fruit and let stand for 30 minutes.

2 Line a pie plate with bottom crust. Add filling; dot with butter. Roll out remaining pastry to fit top of pie. Place over filling. Trim, seal and flute edges. Cut slits in top. Bake at 400° for 50-60 minutes or until crust is golden brown. Sprinkle with sugar if desired. Cool on a wire rack. Store in the refrigerator.

Fresh Apricot Pie

PREP: 15 min. **BAKE:** 45 min. + cooling
YIELD: 6-8 servings

Ruth Peterson, Jenison, Michigan

Apricot pie is a nice change of pace from the more traditional apple or cherry pies.

- 4 cups sliced fresh apricots (about 1-3/4 pounds)
- 1 tablespoon lemon juice
- 1 cup sugar
- 1/3 cup all-purpose flour

Pinch ground nutmeg
Pastry for double-crust pie (9 inches)
Milk
Additional sugar

1 In a large bowl, sprinkle apricots with lemon juice. Combine the sugar, flour and nutmeg. Add to apricots; toss gently to coat.

2 Line a 9-in. pie plate with bottom pastry; trim to 1 in. beyond edge of pie plate. Add filling. Roll out remaining pastry; make a lattice crust. Trim, seal and flute edges. Brush with milk and sprinkle with additional sugar. Cover the edges loosely with foil.

3 Bake at 375° for 45-55 minutes or until crust is golden brown and filling is bubbly. Cool on a wire rack.

FOUR-FRUIT PIE

Blueberry Pie

PREP: 30 min. **BAKE:** 50 min. + cooling
YIELD: 6-8 servings

Richard Case, Johnstown, Pennsylvania

This pie has a wonderful fresh blueberry flavor and a bit of tang from the lemon peel.

- 4 cups blueberries
- 1 tablespoon lemon juice
- 1/2 teaspoon grated lemon peel
- 1-1/4 to 1-1/2 cups sugar
- 1/4 cup quick-cooking tapioca
- 1 tablespoon cornstarch
- 1/2 teaspoon ground cinnamon

Pastry for a double-crust pie (9 inches)
- 1 tablespoon butter

1 In a large bowl, combine the blueberries, lemon juice and lemon peel. Combine the sugar, tapioca, cornstarch and cinnamon. Add to berries; toss gently to coat. Let stand for 15 minutes.

2 Line a 9-in. pie plate with bottom pastry; trim pastry even with edge. Add filling; dot with butter. Roll out remaining pastry to fit top of pie. Place over filling. Trim, seal and flute edges. Cut slits in top. Cover edges loosely with foil.

3 Bake at 350° for 30 minutes. Remove foil; bake 20-30 minutes longer or until crust is golden brown and filling is bubbly. Cool on a wire rack.

Fresh Strawberry Pie

PREP: 25 min. + chilling **BAKE:** 15 min. + cooling
YIELD: 6-8 servings

Florence Robinson, Lenox, Iowa

A pretty pie like this will elicit many compliments when you present it to family and friends. Serve with whipped cream or ice cream.

> 3/4 **cup all-purpose flour**
> 1/2 **cup quick-cooking oats**
> 1/2 **cup chopped pecans**
> 2 **tablespoons sugar**
> 1/8 **teaspoon salt**
> 1/2 **cup butter, melted**
>
> **FILLING:**
> 3/4 **cup sugar**
> 2 **tablespoons cornstarch**
> 1 **cup water**
> 2 **tablespoons light corn syrup**
> 2 **tablespoons strawberry gelatin powder**
> 1 **quart fresh strawberries**

1 In a large bowl, combine the flour, oats, pecans, sugar and salt; stir in the butter until blended. Press onto the bottom and up the sides of a 9-in. pie plate. Bake at 400° for 12-15 minutes or until lightly browned. Cool on a wire rack.

2 For filling, combine sugar and cornstarch in a saucepan. Gradually stir in water and corn syrup until smooth. Bring to a boil over medium heat; cook and stir for 2 minutes or until thickened. Remove from the heat; stir in gelatin until dissolved. Cool to room temperature.

3 Arrange berries in the crust. Carefully pour gelatin mixture over berries. Refrigerate for 2 hours or until set. Refrigerate leftovers.

FRESH STRAWBERRY PIE

thickeners
for *fruit pies*

- Thickeners help prevent fruit pies from being too runny. All-purpose flour, cornstarch and quick-cooking tapioca are the thickeners commonly used in fruit pies. Flour gives the filling an opaque appearance, cornstarch gives a clear appearance and tapioca gives a clear to almost gel-like appearance.

- One thickener can be substituted for another; however, the thickening power of each is different and you may need to make adjustments. Equal amounts of quick-cooking tapioca and cornstarch can be substituted for each other. When replacing flour in a recipe, use half the amount of cornstarch or use 2 teaspoons of quick-cooking tapioca for every 1 tablespoon of flour.

- When using tapioca, mix it with the filling ingredients and allow the mixture to stand for 15 minutes before proceeding with the recipe.

BLACKBERRY APPLE PIE

creating a
lattice-topped *pie*

- Make pastry for a double-crust pie.
- Line a 9-in. pie plate with the bottom pastry and trim to 1 in. beyond edge of plate.

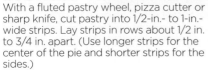

- Roll out remaining pastry to a 12-in. circle. With a fluted pastry wheel, pizza cutter or sharp knife, cut pastry into 1/2-in.- to 1-in.-wide strips. Lay strips in rows about 1/2 in. to 3/4 in. apart. (Use longer strips for the center of the pie and shorter strips for the sides.)
- Fold every other strip halfway back. Starting at the center, add strips at right angles, lifting every other strip as the cross strips are put down. Continue to add strips, lifting and weaving until lattice top is completed.
- Trim strips even with pastry edge. Fold bottom pastry up and over ends of strips and seal. Flute edges.

Blackberry Apple Pie

PREP: 20 min. **BAKE:** 50 min. + cooling
YIELD: 6-8 servings

Fran Stanfield, Wilmington, Ohio

You'll need about 2 cups fresh blackberries for this tasty pie.

Pastry for double-crust pie (9 inches)
- 5 cups thinly sliced peeled tart apples (about 5 medium)
- 1 pint blackberries
- 1 tablespoon lemon juice
- 3/4 cup sugar
- 2 tablespoons cornstarch
- 2 tablespoons butter
- 1 egg
- 1 tablespoon water *or* milk

Additional sugar

1 Line a 9-in. pie plate with bottom pastry; trim to 1 in. beyond edge of plate. Top with a thin layer of apples. In a large bowl, combine blackberries and remaining apples; sprinkle with lemon juice. Combine sugar and cornstarch. Add to fruit mixture; toss gently to coat. Spoon into pie shell; dot with butter.

2 Roll out remaining pastry; make a lattice crust. Trim, seal and flute edges. Beat egg with water or milk; brush over lattice top and pie edges.

3 Bake at 375° for 50 minutes or until filling is bubbly and apples are tender. Cool on a wire rack. Sprinkle with additional sugar. Serve warm or at room temperature.

Cherry Pie

PREP: 20 min. **BAKE:** 55 min. + cooling
YIELD: 6-8 servings

Frances Poste, Wall, South Dakota

A traditionally delicious treat—this pretty cherry pie is always a favorite.

PASTRY:
- 1-1/2 cups all-purpose flour
- 1/2 teaspoon salt
- 1/2 cup shortening
- 1/4 cup ice water

FILLING:
- 2 cans (16 ounces *each*) tart cherries
- 1 cup sugar
- 3 tablespoons quick-cooking tapioca
- 1/4 teaspoon almond extract
- 1/4 teaspoon salt

Red food coloring, optional
- 1 tablespoon butter

1 In a bowl, combine flour and salt; cut in shortening until crumbly. Gradually add water tossing with a fork until dough forms a ball.

2 Divide dough in half. Roll one portion to fit a 9-in. pie plate.

3 Drain cherries, reserving 1/4 cup juice. In a large bowl, combine the cherries, juice, sugar, tapioca, extract, salt and food coloring if desired; let stand for 15 minutes. Pour into the crust. Dot with butter. Top with a lattice crust. Bake at 375° for 55-60 minutes. Cool on a wire rack.

Three-Berry Pie with Crumb Topping

PREP: 15 min. **BAKE:** 45 min. **YIELD:** 6-8 servings

Jan Meinke, Parma, Ohio

This pie has broad appeal since it uses different types of berries that will suit most people.

1-1/2 **cups fresh *or* frozen blueberries**
1-1/2 **cups fresh *or* frozen blackberries**
1-1/2 **cups fresh *or* frozen elderberries *or* raspberries**
   1 **tablespoon lemon juice**
   1 **cup sugar**
   4 **tablespoons quick-cooking tapioca**
   1 **unbaked pastry shell (9 inches)**
TOPPING:
  3/4 **cup all-purpose flour**
  1/2 **cup sugar**
  1/3 **cup cold butter**

1 In a large bowl, sprinkle berries with lemon juice. Combine sugar and tapioca. Add to berries; toss gently to coat. Let stand for 15 minutes. Spoon into pastry shell.

2 For topping, combine flour and sugar in a bowl. Cut in butter until crumbly. Sprinkle over filling. Bake at 400° for 45 minutes or until filling is bubbly and topping is browned. Cool on a wire rack.

Peach-Pear Pie

PREP: 15 min. **BAKE:** 1 hour + cooling
YIELD: 6-8 servings

Jayne Littlefield, Ft. Morgan, Colorado

With both peaches and pears, this special pie is twice as pleasing. A nutty streusel topping gives it a little crunch.

2-1/2 **cups sliced peeled fresh peaches (about 3 medium)**
2-1/2 **cups sliced peeled fresh pears (about 3 medium)**

   1 **tablespoon lemon juice**
  1/3 **cup packed brown sugar**
  1/4 **cup sugar**
   3 **tablespoons cornstarch**
  1/2 **teaspoon ground cinnamon**
  1/4 **teaspoon ground allspice**
   1 **unbaked pastry shell (9 inches)**
WALNUT STREUSEL:
  1/2 **cup all-purpose flour**
  1/4 **cup sugar**
   3 **tablespoons brown sugar**
  1/4 **teaspoon ground cinnamon**
  1/4 **teaspoon ground nutmeg**
  1/4 **cup cold butter**
  1/3 **cup chopped walnuts**

1 In a large bowl, sprinkle the peaches and pears with lemon juice. Combine sugars, cornstarch, cinnamon and allspice. Add to fruit; toss gently to coat. Pour into pastry shell.

2 For streusel, combine the flour, sugars, cinnamon and nutmeg in a small bowl; cut in butter until mixture is crumbly. Stir in walnuts. Sprinkle over filling. Cover edges loosely with foil. Bake at 375° for 1 hour or until bubbly. Cool on a wire rack.

PEACH-PEAR PIE

GOLDEN PEACH PIE

edges. Brush pastry and cutouts with milk; place cutouts on top of pie. Cover the edges loosely with foil.

3 Bake at 400° for 40 minutes. Remove the foil; bake 10-15 minutes longer or until the crust is golden brown and filling is bubbly. Cool on a wire rack.

Ginger Pear Pie

PREP: 20 min. **BAKE:** 20 min. + cooling
YIELD: 6 servings

Delilah Stauffer
Mt. Pleasant Mills, Pennsylvania

Ginger and lemon make this pear pie exceptional.

> 3 **tablespoons cornstarch**
> 1/4 **teaspoon ground ginger**
> 1/2 **cup water**
> 1/2 **cup dark corn syrup**
> 1 **teaspoon lemon juice**
> 1/8 **teaspoon grated lemon peel**
> 4 **large pears, peeled and thinly sliced**
> 1 **tablespoon butter**
> 1 **unbaked pastry shell (9 inches)**

TOPPING:
> 1/2 **cup all-purpose flour**

Golden Peach Pie

PREP: 15 min. **BAKE:** 50 min. + cooling
YIELD: 6-8 servings

Shirley Olson, Polson, Montana

Here's an easy way to peel a peach: With a slotted spoon, dip the peach into boiling water for 20 to 30 seconds. Remove and immediately place in a bowl of ice water. Peel off the skin with a paring knife.

Pastry for double-crust pie (9 inches)
> 5 **cups sliced peeled fresh peaches**
>   **(about 7 medium)**
> 2 **teaspoons lemon juice**
> 1/2 **teaspoon grated orange peel**
> 1/8 **teaspoon almond extract**
> 1 **cup sugar**
> 1/4 **cup cornstarch**
> 1/4 **teaspoon ground nutmeg**
> 1/8 **teaspoon salt**
> 2 **tablespoons butter**

Milk

1 Line a 9-in. pie plate with bottom pastry; trim even with edge of plate. Set aside. In a large bowl, combine the peaches, lemon juice, orange peel and extract. Combine the sugar, cornstarch, nutmeg and salt. Add to peach mixture; toss gently to coat. Pour into crust; dot with butter.

2 Roll out remaining pastry to fit top of pie; make decorative cutouts in pastry. Set cutouts aside. Place top crust over filling. Trim, seal and flute

making pastry cutouts *for a pie*

• Pastry cutouts can be used for a single- or double-crust pie. To make cutouts, roll out dough to 1/8-in. thickness. Cut out with 1-in. to 1-1/2-in. cookie cutters of desired shape. With a sharp knife, score designs (if desired) on cutouts.

• For a single-crust pie, bake cutouts on an ungreased baking sheet at 400° for 6-8 minutes or until golden brown. Remove to a wire rack to cool. Arrange over cooled filling on baked pie.

• For a double-crust pie, brush bottom of each unbaked cutout with water or milk and arrange over top crust of an unbaked pie. Press lightly to secure. Bake pie according to recipe.

1/4 cup packed brown sugar
1/8 teaspoon ground ginger
1/4 cup cold butter
1/4 cup chopped pecans

1 In a large saucepan, combine the cornstarch and ginger. Stir in the water, corn syrup, lemon juice and peel until smooth. Gently stir in pears. Bring to a boil over medium heat; cook and stir for 1 minute or until thickened. Remove from the heat; add butter. Pour into pastry shell.

2 For topping, combine the flour, brown sugar and ginger in a small bowl; cut in butter until crumbly. Stir in pecans. Sprinkle over pears. Bake at 425° for 20-25 minutes or until filling is bubbly and topping is browned. Cool on a wire rack.

Purple Plum Pie

PREP: 20 min. **BAKE:** 50 min. + cooling
YIELD: 6-8 servings

Michelle Beran, Claflin, Kansas

This pie is a terrific way to enjoy the bounty of summer plums. Use ripe, but firm plums that are free of blemishes like cracks, soft spots and brown discoloration.

4 cups sliced fresh plums (about 1-1/2 pounds)
1 tablespoon lemon juice
1/2 cup sugar
1/4 cup all-purpose flour
1/4 teaspoon salt
1/4 teaspoon ground cinnamon
1 unbaked deep-dish pastry shell (9 inches)

TOPPING:
1/2 cup sugar
1/2 cup all-purpose flour
1/4 teaspoon ground cinnamon
1/4 teaspoon ground nutmeg
3 tablespoons cold butter

1 In a large bowl, sprinkle the plums with lemon juice. Combine the sugar, flour, salt and cinnamon. Add to plums; toss gently to coat. Pour into the pastry shell.

2 For topping, combine the sugar, flour, cinnamon and nutmeg in a small bowl; cut in butter until mixture is crumbly. Sprinkle over filling. Bake at 375° for 50-60 minutes or until filling is bubbly. Cover edges of crust with foil during the last 20 minutes to prevent overbrowning. Cool on a wire rack.

protecting pastry edges from *overbrowning*

- The edges of a pie pastry often brown before the rest of the pie is thoroughly baked. To protect the edges, fold a 12-in. piece of foil in quarters. Place the folded corner toward you. Measure 3-3/4 in. up each adjacent side and cut out an arc joining the two sides. Discard the center.

- Unfold the remaining foil and place it over the unbaked pie. Trim corners if necessary. Gently crimp foil around edge of crust to secure. Bake the pie for 20 to 30 minutes before removing the foil. Or add during the final 10 to 20 minutes of baking.

PURPLE PLUM PIE

CHEDDAR PEAR PIE

Old-Fashioned Raisin Pie

PREP: 20 min. **BAKE:** 40 min. + cooling
YIELD: 8 servings

Pat Sisk, South Elgin, Illinois

The wonderful flavor of this old-fashioned pie will take you back in taste and time to Grandma's kitchen.

      3/4 **cup sugar**
        2 **tablespoons cornstarch**
      1/4 **teaspoon salt**
        1 **cup water**
      1/2 **cup dark corn syrup**
    1-1/2 **cups raisins**
        1 **tablespoon lemon juice**
        2 **teaspoons butter**
Pastry for double-crust pie (9 inches)

1 In a saucepan, combine the sugar, cornstarch and salt. Stir in the water and corn syrup until blended. Add raisins. Bring to a boil over medium heat; cook and stir for 2 minutes or until thickened. Remove from the heat; stir in lemon juice and butter (filling will be thin).

2 Line a 9-in. pie plate with bottom pastry; trim even with edge of plate. Add filling. Roll out remaining pastry to fit top of pie; place over filling. Trim, seal and flute edges. Cut slits in top.

3 Bake at 425° for 10 minutes. Reduce heat to 375°; bake 30 minutes longer or until crust is golden brown. Cool on a wire rack.

Cheddar Pear Pie

PREP: 10 min. **BAKE:** 25 min. + cooling
YIELD: 6-8 servings

Cynthia LaBree, Elmer, New Jersey

With the sprinkling of cheddar on top, some people may think this is an apple pie. They will be delightfully surprised when they discover the subtle sweetness of the pears.

        4 **large ripe pears, peeled and thinly sliced**
      1/3 **cup sugar**
        1 **tablespoon cornstarch**
      1/8 **teaspoon salt**
        1 **unbaked pastry shell (9 inches)**
TOPPING:
      1/2 **cup shredded cheddar cheese**
      1/2 **cup all-purpose flour**
      1/4 **cup sugar**
      1/4 **teaspoon salt**
      1/4 **cup butter, melted**

1 In a large bowl, combine the pears, sugar, cornstarch and salt; toss gently to coat. Pour into pastry shell.

2 For topping, combine the cheese, flour, sugar and salt; stir in butter until crumbly. Sprinkle over filling. Bake at 425° for 25-35 minutes or until crust is golden and cheese is melted. Cool on a wire rack for 15-20 minutes. Serve warm. Store in the refrigerator.

Rhubarb Berry Pie

PREP: 10 min. + standing **BAKE:** 45 min. + cooling
YIELD: 8 servings

Mrs. Bill Lawson, Tacoma, Washington

The pairing of rhubarb and berries in this pie is enhanced with a touch of almond and nutmeg.

        3 **cups diced fresh *or* frozen rhubarb, thawed and drained**
        1 **cup fresh raspberries *or* strawberries**
      1/2 **teaspoon lemon juice**
      1/8 **teaspoon almond extract**
    1-1/3 **cups sugar**
        3 **tablespoons quick-cooking tapioca**
        1 **tablespoon all-purpose flour**
      1/8 **teaspoon salt**
      1/8 **teaspoon ground nutmeg**
Pastry for double-crust pie (9 inches)
        1 **tablespoon butter**

1 In a large bowl, combine the rhubarb, berries,

lemon juice and extract. Add the sugar, tapioca, flour, salt and nutmeg. Add to the fruit mixture; toss gently to coat. Let stand for 15 minutes.

2 Line a 9-in. pie plate with bottom crust. Add filling. Dot with butter. Roll out remaining pastry to fit top of pie. Place over filling. Trim, seal and flute edges. Cut slits in top. Bake at 425° for 15 minutes. Reduce heat to 350°; bake 30-35 minutes longer or until crust is golden brown and filling is bubbly. Cool on a wire rack.

Editor's Note: If using frozen rhubarb, measure rhubarb while still frozen, then thaw completely. Drain in a colander, but do not press liquid out.

Green Tomato Pie

PREP: 15 min. **BAKE:** 1 hour + cooling
YIELD: 6-8 servings

Violet Thompson, Port Ludlow, Washington

This pie is a delicious way to use up your green tomatoes at the end of the summer.

1-1/2	cups sugar
5	tablespoons all-purpose flour
1	teaspoon ground cinnamon

Pinch salt

3	cups thinly sliced green tomatoes (about 4 to 5 medium)
1	tablespoon cider vinegar

Pastry for double-crust pie (9 inches)

1	tablespoon butter

1 In a bowl, combine the sugar, flour, cinnamon and salt. Add tomatoes and vinegar; toss to coat.

GREEN TOMATO PIE

2 Line a pie plate with bottom crust. Add filling; dot with butter. Roll out remaining pastry; make a lattice crust. Trim, seal and flute edges. Bake at 350° for 1 hour or until tomatoes are tender. Cool on a wire rack to room temperature. Store in the refrigerator.

Walnut Mincemeat Pie

PREP: 15 min. **BAKE:** 50 min. + cooling
YIELD: 8 servings

Laverne Kamp, Kutztown, Pennsylvania

As a cold and tasty finishing touch, try a scoop of ice cream on top of this pie.

2	eggs
1	cup sugar
2	tablespoons all-purpose flour
1/8	teaspoon salt
2	cups prepared mincemeat
1/2	cup chopped walnuts
1/4	cup butter, melted
1	unbaked pastry shell (9 inches)

1 In a large mixing bowl, lightly beat eggs. Combine the sugar, flour and salt; gradually add to eggs. Stir in the mincemeat, walnuts and butter; pour into pie shell.

2 Bake at 400° for 15 minutes. Reduce heat to 325°; bake 35-40 minutes longer or until a knife inserted near the center comes out clean. Cool completely. Store in the refrigerator.

finishing touches
for *pie crusts*

To top off double-crust pies before baking, use a pastry brush to lightly and evenly apply one of the following washes to the top crust, avoiding the edges:

- For a shine and light browning, brush with an egg white that was lightly beaten with 1 teaspoon of water.

- For a glossy golden appearance, brush with an egg yolk that was beaten with 1 teaspoon of water.

- For a slight shine, brush with half-and-half cream or heavy whipping cream.

- For a crisp brown crust, brush with water.

- For a little sparkle, sprinkle with sugar or decorator sugar after brushing with one of the washes.

- To give a little more shine to a baked double-crust pie, warm 1 tablespoon of light corn syrup. Gently brush over the baked warm crust.

Meringue, Cream & Custard Pies

Meringue Berry Pie

PREP: 25 min. **BAKE:** 1 hour + cooling
YIELD: 6-8 servings

Page Alexander, Baldwin City, Kansas

A hot day calls for a cool dessert like this tempting pie. Fresh berries and a sweet raspberry sauce over ice cream in a meringue crust make each slice absolutely irresistible.

- 1/2 cup sugar, *divided*
- 1/4 cup slivered almonds, toasted and ground
- 2 tablespoons cornstarch
- 2 egg whites
- 1/8 teaspoon cream of tartar

SAUCE AND TOPPING:
- 1/2 cup sugar
- 1 tablespoon cornstarch
- 1/3 cup water
- 1 pint fresh raspberries
- 1 quart vanilla ice cream
- 2 cups fresh mixed berries

1 In a small bowl, combine 1/4 cup sugar, almonds and cornstarch. In a small mixing bowl, beat egg whites and cream of tartar on medium speed until soft peaks form. Gradually beat in remaining sugar, 1 tablespoon at a time, on high until stiff glossy peaks form and sugar is dissolved. Fold in almond mixture. Spread evenly over the bottom and up the sides of a greased 9-in. pie plate.

2 Bake at 275° for 1 to 1-1/2 hours or until light golden brown. Turn off oven and do not open door; let crust dry for 1 hour. Cool on a wire rack.

3 For sauce, combine sugar and cornstarch in a saucepan. Gradually stir in water until smooth; add raspberries. Bring to a boil over medium heat; cook and stir for 1 minute or until thickened. Set aside to cool.

4 To serve, scoop ice cream into crust; top with mixed berries and sauce. Serve immediately. Freeze leftovers.

MERINGUE BERRY PIE

Strawberry Meringue Pie

PREP: 20 min. **BAKE:** 45 min. + cooling
YIELD: 6-8 servings

Kathleen Mercier, Orrington, Maine

This recipe is simple, so don't be put off by the detailed directions. The meringue crust filled with chocolate and berries makes an impressive dessert to dress up any meal.

- 3 egg whites
- 1/3 cup finely crushed saltines (about 12 crackers), *divided*
- 1 teaspoon vanilla extract
- 1/4 teaspoon cream of tartar
- 1/8 teaspoon salt
- 1 cup sugar
- 1/2 cup chopped pecans, toasted
- 1 package (4 ounces) German sweet chocolate
- 2 tablespoons butter
- 4 cups fresh strawberries, halved
- 1 cup heavy whipping cream
- 2 tablespoons confectioners' sugar

1 Let egg whites stand at room temperature for 30 minutes. Sprinkle 2 tablespoons of cracker crumbs into a greased 9-in. pie plate; set aside. In a large mixing bowl, beat the egg whites, vanilla, cream of tartar and salt on medium speed until soft peaks form. Gradually add the sugar, 2 tablespoons at a time, beating on high until stiff glossy peaks form and sugar is dissolved. Fold in pecans and remaining cracker crumbs.

STRAWBERRY MERINGUE PIE

2 Spread evenly onto the bottom and up the sides of prepared pan. Bake at 300° for 45 minutes. Turn off oven and do not open door; let crust cool in oven overnight.

3 In a small heavy saucepan or microwave, melt chocolate and butter; stir until smooth. Drizzle over crust. Let stand for 15 minutes or until set. Top with strawberries. In a chilled small mixing bowl, beat cream until it begins to thicken. Add confectioners' sugar; beat until soft peaks form. Spoon over berries. Refrigerate leftovers.

Grandma's Lemon Meringue Pie

PREP: 30 min. **BAKE:** 25 min. + chilling
YIELD: 6-8 servings

Gwen Johnson, Medford, Oregon

For a refreshing change from heavier desserts, nothing can compare to lemon meringue pie. Meringues take some time to prepare, but it's a surefire way to impress dinner guests.

- 1-1/4   cups sugar
-     6   tablespoons cornstarch
-     2   cups water
-     3   egg yolks, beaten
-     3   tablespoons butter, cubed
-   1/3   cup lemon juice
-     2   teaspoons white vinegar
- 1-1/2   teaspoons lemon extract
-     1   pastry shell (9 inches), baked

MERINGUE:
- 1/2   cup plus 2 tablespoons water
-   1   tablespoon cornstarch
-   3   egg whites
-   1   teaspoon vanilla extract

Pinch salt
-   6   tablespoons sugar

1 In a large saucepan, combine sugar and cornstarch. Stir in water until smooth. Cook and stir over medium-high heat until thickened and bubbly. Reduce heat to low; cook and stir 2 minutes longer. Remove from the heat. Stir 1 cup of hot filling into egg yolks; return all to the pan, stirring constantly. Bring to a gentle boil; cook and stir for 2 minutes. Remove from the heat. Stir in butter. Gently stir in lemon juice, vinegar and extract. Pour hot filling into pastry shell.

2 For meringue, combine water and cornstarch in a saucepan until smooth. Cook and stir until thickened and clear, about 2 minutes. Meanwhile, beat the egg whites, vanilla and salt in a large mixing bowl on medium speed until soft peaks form. Gradually beat in sugar, 1 tablespoon at a time, on high until stiff glossy peaks form and sugar is dissolved. Gradually add cornstarch mixture, beating well on high. Immediately spread over hot filling, sealing edges to crust.

3 Bake at 350° for 12-15 minutes or until meringue is golden brown. Cool on a wire rack for 1 hour. Refrigerate for at least 3 hours before serving. Refrigerate leftovers.

GRANDMA'S LEMON MERINGUE PIE

ORANGE MERINGUE PIE

Orange Meringue Pie

PREP: 30 min. + chilling **BAKE:** 20 min. + chilling
YIELD: 6-8 servings

June Nehmer, Las Vegas, Nevada

*Most folks are accustomed to lemon meringue pie. So
surprise them with this taste twist. It's colorful, refreshing
and looks so pretty on the plate.*

1-1/2 **cups graham cracker crumbs (about**
 24 squares)
 1/4 **cup sugar**
 1/3 **cup butter, melted**
FILLING:
 1 **cup sugar**
 1/4 **cup cornstarch**
 1/4 **teaspoon salt**
 1 **cup orange juice**
 1/2 **cup water**
 3 **egg yolks, beaten**
 2 **tablespoons lime juice**
 4 **teaspoons grated orange peel**
 1 **tablespoon butter**
MERINGUE:
 3 **egg whites**
 1/8 **teaspoon cream of tartar**
 6 **tablespoons sugar**

1 In a small bowl, combine cracker crumbs and
sugar; stir in butter. Press onto the bottom and
up the sides of a 9-in. pie plate. Bake at 375° for
8-10 minutes or until lightly browned. Cool on a
wire rack.

2 For filling, combine the sugar, cornstarch and salt
in a small saucepan. Stir in orange juice and water
until smooth. Cook and stir over medium heat
until thickened and bubbly. Reduce heat; cook
and stir 2 minutes longer. Remove from the heat.
Stir 1 cup hot filling into egg yolks; return all to
the pan, stirring constantly. Bring to a gentle boil;
cook and stir 2 minutes longer. Remove from the
heat; stir in the lime juice, orange peel and butter.
Pour hot filling into pie crust.

3 For meringue, beat egg whites and cream of
tartar in a small mixing bowl on medium speed
until soft peaks form. Gradually beat in sugar,
1 tablespoon at a time, on high until stiff glossy
peaks form and sugar is dissolved. Spread evenly
over hot filling, sealing edges to crust.

4 Bake at 350° for 12-15 minutes or until meringue
is golden brown. Cool on a wire rack for 1 hour.
Refrigerate for at least 3 hours before serving.
Refrigerate leftovers.

Coconut Cream Meringue Pie

PREP: 30 min. + chilling **BAKE:** 25 min. + cooling
YIELD: 6-8 servings

Joyce Reece, Mena, Arkansas

Coconut not only appears in this pie's filling but on top of the meringue as well.

- 1 **unbaked pastry shell (9 inches)**
- 6 **tablespoons sugar**
- 5 **tablespoons all-purpose flour**
- 1/4 **teaspoon salt**
- 2 **cups milk**
- 3 **egg yolks, beaten**
- 2 **teaspoons vanilla extract**
- 1 **cup flaked coconut**

MERINGUE:
- 3 **egg whites**
- 1/4 **teaspoon cream of tartar**
- 6 **tablespoons sugar**
- 1/2 **cup flaked coconut**

1 Line unpricked pastry shell with a double thickness of heavy-duty foil. Bake at 450° for 8 minutes. Remove foil; bake 5 minutes longer. Cool on a wire rack.

2 In a saucepan, combine the sugar, flour and salt. Stir in milk until smooth. Cook and stir over medium-high heat until thickened and bubbly. Reduce heat; cook and stir 2 minutes longer. Remove from the heat. Stir a small amount of hot filling into egg yolks; return all to the pan, stirring constantly. Bring to a gentle boil; cook and stir 2 minutes longer. Remove from the heat. Gently stir in vanilla and coconut. Pour into crust.

3 For meringue, beat egg whites and cream of tartar in a small mixing bowl on medium speed until soft peaks form. Gradually beat in sugar, 1 tablespoon at a time, on high until stiff glossy peaks form and sugar is dissolved. Spread evenly over hot filling, sealing edges to crust. Sprinkle with coconut.

4 Bake at 350° for 12-15 minutes or until meringue is golden brown. Cool on a wire rack for 1 hour. Refrigerate for 3 hours before serving. Refrigerate leftovers.

tips for *making meringue*

- Since humidity is the most critical factor in making a successful meringue, choose a dry day. Meringues can absorb moisture on a humid day and become limp or sticky.

- Separate the eggs while they are still cold from the refrigerator, then allow the egg whites to stand at room temperature for 30 minutes before beating.

- For the greatest volume, place whites in a small clean metal or glass mixing bowl. Even a drop of fat from the egg yolk or a film sometimes found on plastic bowls will prevent egg whites from foaming. For this reason, be sure to use clean beaters.

- After stiff peaks form, check that the sugar is dissolved. It should feel silky smooth when rubbed between your thumb and index finger.

- Spread the meringue over hot filling to minimize "weeping" (the watery layer between the meringue and filling). Use a metal spatula for spreading the meringue. Seal it to the edges of the pastry to prevent shrinkage while baking.

- Cool the pie away from drafts on a wire rack at room temperature for 1 hour. Refrigerate for at least 3 hours before cutting and serving. Store leftovers in the refrigerator.

COCONUT CREAM MERINGUE PIE

Chocolate Angel Pie

PREP: 15 min. + standing **BAKE:** 50 min. + chilling
YIELD: 6-8 servings

Miriam Seitz, Ottawa, Ohio

Chocolate lovers will really go for this pie. The filling is not too rich, making it a delicious complement to the sweet meringue shell.

- 2 egg whites
- 1/8 teaspoon cream of tartar
- 1/2 cup sugar

FILLING:
- 1 cup (6 ounces) semisweet chocolate chips
- 3 tablespoons strong-brewed coffee
- 1 teaspoon vanilla extract
- 1-1/2 cups heavy whipping cream

Chopped nuts, optional

1 Place egg whites in a small mixing bowl and let stand at room temperature for 30 minutes. Add cream of tartar to egg whites and beat on medium speed until soft peaks form. Gradually beat in sugar, 1 tablespoon at a time, on high until soft glossy peaks form and sugar is dissolved. Spread evenly into a well-greased 9-in. pie pan. Bake at 275° for 50 minutes. Cool on a wire rack.

2 For filling, melt chocolate in a small heavy saucepan or microwave; stir until smooth. Stir in coffee and vanilla. Cool to room temperature.

3 In a chilled small mixing bowl, beat cream until soft peaks form. Fold into chocolate mixture. Pour into the meringue shell. Sprinkle with nuts

CHOCOLATE ANGEL PIE

if desired. Refrigerate for several hours before serving. Refrigerate leftovers.

Chocolate Chip Pecan Pie

PREP: 15 min. **BAKE:** 50 min. + cooling
YIELD: 10-12 servings

Maggie Garrett, Kosciusko, Mississippi

Chocolate chips give ordinary pecan pie a tasty twist. Top with a scoop of vanilla ice cream for added indulgence.

- 4 eggs
- 1 cup sugar
- 1 cup light corn syrup
- 1 teaspoon vanilla extract
- 1/2 cup butter, melted
- 1 cup chopped pecans
- 1/2 cup semisweet chocolate chips
- 1 unbaked pastry shell (10 inches)

1 In a large mixing bowl, beat the eggs, sugar, corn syrup and vanilla. Add butter and mix well. Stir in pecans and chocolate chips. Pour into pie shell.

2 Bake at 350° for 50-55 minutes or until set. Cool on a wire rack.

Chocolate Almond Silk Pie

PREP: 20 min. **COOK:** 30 min. + cooling
YIELD: 8-10 servings

Diane Larson, Roland, Iowa

Looking for a special dessert for the chocolate lovers in your family? Try this pie! With a rich, velvet-like texture, even a small slice will satisfy.

- 2/3 cup all-purpose flour
- 1/4 cup butter, softened
- 3 tablespoons finely chopped almonds, toasted
- 2 tablespoons confectioners' sugar
- 1/8 teaspoon vanilla extract

FILLING:
- 3/4 cup sugar
- 3 eggs
- 3 squares (1 ounce *each*) unsweetened chocolate, coarsely chopped
- 1/8 teaspoon almond extract
- 1/2 cup butter, softened

Sweetened whipped cream and toasted sliced almonds, optional

CHOCOLATE ALMOND SILK PIE

1 In a small mixing bowl, combine the first five ingredients. Beat on low speed until well combined, about 2-3 minutes. Press onto the bottom and up the sides of a greased 9-in. pie plate. Bake at 400° for 8-10 minutes or until golden. Cool on a wire rack.

2 For filling, combine sugar and eggs in a small saucepan until well blended. Cook over low heat, stirring constantly, until mixture coats the back of a metal spoon and reaches 160°. Remove from the heat. Stir in chocolate and almond extract until smooth. Cool to lukewarm (90°), stirring occasionally.

3 In a large mixing bowl, cream butter until light and fluffy. Add cooled egg mixture; beat on high speed for 5 minutes. Pour into cooled pie shell. Refrigerate for at least 6 hours before serving. Garnish with whipped cream and almonds if desired. Refrigerate leftovers.

homemade
crumb crusts

In a mixing bowl, combine the crumbs and sugar; add the melted butter and blend well. Press the mixture onto the bottom and up the sides of an ungreased 9-in. pie plate. Refrigerate for 30 minutes before filling, or bake at 375° for 8-10 minutes or until crust is lightly browned. Cool completely on a wire rack before filling.

For desserts made in a 9-in. springform pan (such as cheesecakes), you may need to add an additional 1/4 to 1/2 cup crumbs and 1 tablespoon butter.

TYPE OF CRUST	AMOUNT OF CRUMBS	SUGAR	BUTTER, MELTED
Graham Cracker	1-1/2 cups (24 squares)	1/4 cup	1/3 cup
Chocolate Wafer	1-1/4 cups (20 wafers)	1/4 cup	1/4 cup
Vanilla Wafer	1-1/2 cups (30 wafers)	none	1/4 cup
Cream-Filled Chocolate	1-1/2 cups (15 cookies)	none	1/4 cup
Gingersnap	1-1/2 cups (24 cookies)	none	1/4 cup
Macaroon	1-1/2 cups	none	1/4 cup
Pretzel (use a greased pie plate)	1-1/4 cups	1/4 cup	1/2 cup

Southern Sweet Potato Pie

PREP: 15 min. **BAKE:** 55 min. + chilling
YIELD: 6-8 servings

Bonnie Holcomb, Fulton, Mississippi

Sweet potatoe pie is a Southern classic that is reminiscent of pumpkin pie.

- 3 **tablespoons all-purpose flour**
- 1-2/3 **cups sugar**
- 1 **cup mashed sweet potatoes**
- 2 **eggs**
- 1/4 **cup light corn syrup**
- 1/4 **teaspoon ground nutmeg**

Pinch salt

- 1/2 **cup butter, softened**
- 3/4 **cup evaporated milk**
- 1 **unbaked pastry shell (9 inches)**

1 In a large mixing bowl, combine flour and sugar. Add the sweet potatoes, eggs, corn syrup, nutmeg, salt, butter and evaporated milk; beat well. Pour into pastry shell.

2 Bake at 350° for 55-60 minutes. Cool on a wire rack for 1 hour. Refrigerate for at least 3 hours before serving. Refrigerate leftovers.

Creamy Maple Pie

PREP: 30 min. + chilling **BAKE:** 15 min. + cooling
YIELD: 8 servings

Emma Magielda, Amsterdam, New York

Every bite of this cool and creamy pie is bursting with rich maple flavor. It slices well for a pretty presentation.

Pastry for single-crust pie (9 inches)
- 1/4 **cup cornstarch**
- 1/4 **teaspoon salt**
- 1-3/4 **cups milk**
- 3/4 **cup plus 1 tablespoon maple syrup, *divided***
- 2 **egg yolks, lightly beaten**
- 2 **tablespoons butter, cubed**
- 1 **cup heavy whipping cream**

Toasted sliced almonds

1 Line a 9-in. pie plate with pastry; trim to 1/2 in. beyond edge of plate. Flute edges. Line unpricked pastry shell with a double thickness of heavy-duty foil. Bake at 450° for 8 minutes. Remove foil; bake 5 minutes longer. Cool on a wire rack.

2 For filling, combine cornstarch and salt in a large saucepan. Stir in 1/2 cup milk until smooth. Gradually stir in remaining milk and 3/4 cup maple syrup. Cook and stir over medium heat until thickened and bubbly. Reduce heat; cook and stir 2 minutes longer. Remove from the heat. Stir a small amount of hot filling into egg yolks; return all to the pan, stirring constantly. Bring to a gentle boil; cook and stir 2 minutes longer. Remove from the heat. Gently stir in butter. Cool to room temperature without stirring.

3 In a chilled small mixing bowl, beat cream on high speed until stiff peaks form. Fold 1 cup cream into cooled filling; spoon into crust. Fold remaining syrup into remaining cream; frost top of pie. Refrigerate overnight. Garnish with toasted almonds. Refrigerate leftovers.

Peanut Butter Pie

PREP: 20 min. + cooling **YIELD:** 8-10 servings

Doris Doherty, Albany, Oregon

Who can resist a tempting chocolate crumb crust and a creamy filling with big peanut butter taste? Be prepared to take an empty plate home when you serve this pie at your next potluck.

- 1-1/4 **cups chocolate wafer crumbs (20 wafers)**
- 1/4 **cup sugar**
- 1/4 **cup butter, melted**

FILLING:
- 1 **package (8 ounces) cream cheese, softened**
- 1 **cup creamy peanut butter**
- 1 **cup sugar**

1   tablespoon butter, softened
1   teaspoon vanilla extract
1   cup heavy whipping cream, whipped
Grated chocolate *or* chocolate wafer crumbs, optional

1 In a small bowl, combine cookie crumbs and sugar; stir in butter. Press onto the bottom and up the sides of a 9-in. pie plate. Bake at 375° for 10 minutes. Cool on a wire rack.

2 For filling, beat the cream cheese, peanut butter, sugar, butter and vanilla in a large mixing bowl until smooth. Fold in whipped cream. Gently spoon into crust. Garnish with chocolate or cookie crumbs if desired. Store in the refrigerator.

Coconut Banana Cream Pie

PREP: 30 min. + chilling   **YIELD:** 6-8 servings

Tammy Olson, Bruce, South Dakota

This pie features the perfect pairing of bananas and coconut, giving it a slightly tropical taste.

3   **cups flaked coconut**
7   **tablespoons butter**
3/4   **cup sugar**
1/4   **cup all-purpose flour**
3   **tablespoons cornstarch**
1/4   **teaspoon salt**

PEANUT BUTTER PIE

COCONUT BANANA CREAM PIE

3   **cups half-and-half cream**
4   **egg yolks, lightly beaten**
2   **teaspoons vanilla extract**
2   **large firm bananas, sliced**
Whipped cream and sliced bananas, optional

1 In a large skillet, saute coconut in butter until golden. Reserve 2 tablespoons for garnish. Press remaining toasted coconut onto the bottom and up the sides of a greased 9-in. pie plate. Bake at 350° for 7 minutes. Cool on a wire rack.

2 For filling, combine the sugar, flour, cornstarch and salt in a large saucepan. Stir in cream until smooth. Cook and stir over medium-high heat until thickened and bubbly. Reduce heat; cook and stir 2 minutes longer. Remove from the heat. Stir a small amount of hot filling into egg yolks; return all to the pan, stirring constantly. Bring to a gentle boil; cook and stir 2 minutes longer. Remove from the heat. Gently stir in vanilla. Cool to room temperature without stirring.

3 Place bananas in the crust. Cover with cream mixture. Refrigerate until set, about 2 hours. Sprinkle with reserved toasted coconut. If desired, garnish with whipped cream and bananas. Refrigerate leftovers.

CREAMY BANANA PECAN PIE

bananas. Top with remaining whipped topping. Garnish with pecans if desired. Refrigerate for at least 3 hours before serving. Refrigerate leftovers.

Cream Cheese Lime Pie

PREP: 15 min. **COOK:** 20 min. + chilling
YIELD: 6-8 servings

Taste of Home Test Kitchen

The shortbread cookie crust and lime filling are delicious changes from the typical lemon pie. You can substitute graham cracker crumbs for the cookie crumbs.

1-1/2 **cups shortbread cookie crumbs**
   3 **tablespoons butter, melted**
LIME FILLING:
   1 **cup sugar**
1/4 **cup cornstarch**
   3 **tablespoons all-purpose flour**
1/4 **teaspoon salt**
   2 **cups water**
   3 **egg yolks, beaten**
   1 **tablespoon butter**
   1 **teaspoon grated lime peel**
Green liquid food coloring, optional
1/4 **cup lime juice**
CREAM CHEESE FILLING:
   1 **package (8 ounces) cream cheese, softened**
1/2 **cup confectioners' sugar**
   2 **teaspoons lime juice**
   1 **cup whipped topping**

1 Combine cookie crumbs and butter; press onto the bottom and up the sides of an ungreased 9-in. pie plate. Bake at 375° for 8-10 minutes or until crust just begins to brown. Cool completely on a wire rack.

2 For lime filling, combine the sugar, cornstarch, flour and salt in a saucepan. Stir in water until smooth. Cook and stir over medium-high heat until thickened and bubbly. Reduce heat; cook and stir 2 minutes longer. Remove from the heat. Stir a small amount of hot filling into egg yolks; return all to the pan, stirring constantly. Bring to a gentle boil; cook and stir 2 minutes longer. Remove from the heat. Stir in butter, lime peel and food coloring if desired. Gently stir in lime juice. Cool to room temperature without stirring.

3 For cream cheese filling, beat cream cheese, confectioners' sugar and lime juice in a small mixing bowl until smooth. Fold in whipped

Creamy Banana Pecan Pie

PREP: 20 min. **BAKE:** 25 min. + cooling
YIELD: 6-8 servings

Isabel Fowler, Anchorage, Alaska

You'll get many compliments when you serve this layered banana beauty. It's a snap to prepare because the filling starts with instant pudding mix.

   1 **cup all-purpose flour**
   1 **cup finely chopped pecans**
1/2 **cup butter, softened**
   1 **package (8 ounces) cream cheese, softened**
   1 **cup confectioners' sugar**
   1 **carton (8 ounces) frozen whipped topping, thawed, *divided***
   3 **large firm bananas, sliced**
1-1/3 **cups cold milk**
   1 **package (3.4 ounces) instant vanilla pudding mix**
Additional chopped pecans, optional

1 In a small bowl, combine the flour, pecans and butter. Press onto the bottom and up the sides of a greased 9-in. pie plate. Bake at 350° for 25 minutes. Cool completely on a wire rack.

2 In a small mixing bowl, beat cream cheese and confectioners' sugar. Fold in 1 cup whipped topping. Spread over crust. Arrange bananas on top. In another bowl, whisk milk and pudding mix for 2 minutes. Immediately pour over

topping. Spread evenly in crust; top with lime filling. Refrigerate for 3 hours or until firm. Refrigerate leftovers.

Butterscotch Pie

PREP: 30 min. **BAKE:** 15 min. + chilling
YIELD: 6-8 servings

Cary Letsche, Brandenton, Florida

This creamy pudding-like pie filling is crowned with golden peaks of meringue.

6	tablespoons butter
6	tablespoons all-purpose flour
1-1/2	cups packed brown sugar
2	cups milk
1/4	teaspoon salt
3	eggs yolks, beaten
1	teaspoon vanilla extract
1	pastry shell (9 inches), baked

MERINGUE:

3	egg whites
1/4	teaspoon cream of tartar
1/2	cup sugar

1 In a saucepan, melt the butter. Remove from the heat; add flour and stir until smooth. Stir in brown sugar. Return to heat; stir in milk and salt until blended. Cook and stir over medium-high heat until thickened and bubbly. Reduce heat; cook and stir 2 minutes longer. Remove from the heat. Stir about 1 cup hot filling into the egg yolks; return all to pan, stirring constantly. Bring to a gentle boil; cook and stir for 2 minutes longer. Remove from the heat. Gently stir in vanilla. Pour into pastry shell.

2 For meringue, beat egg whites and cream of tartar in a small bowl on medium speed until soft peaks form. Gradually beat in sugar, about 1 tablespoon at a time, on high until stiff glossy peaks form and sugar is dissolved. Spread evenly over hot filling, sealing edges to crust.

3 Bake at 350° for 12-15 minutes or until meringue is golden brown. Cool on a wire rack for 1 hour. Refrigerate for at least 3 hours before serving. Refrigerate leftovers.

Praline Pumpkin Pie

PREP: 20 min. **BAKE:** 45 min. + cooling
YIELD: 10 servings

Sandra Haase, Baltimore, Maryland

This makes a sweet ending to winter meals. The sweet pecans are a delightful contrast to the pumpkin filling.

1/3	cup finely chopped pecans
1/3	cup packed brown sugar
3	tablespoons butter, softened
1	unbaked pastry shell (10 inches)

FILLING:

3	eggs, lightly beaten
1/2	cup sugar
1/2	cup packed brown sugar
2	tablespoons all-purpose flour
3/4	teaspoon ground cinnamon
1/2	teaspoon salt
1/2	teaspoon ground ginger
1/4	teaspoon ground cloves
1	can (15 ounces) solid-packed pumpkin
1-1/2	cups half-and-half cream

Additional chopped pecans, optional

1 In a small bowl, combine the pecans, sugar and butter; press into the bottom of pie shell. Prick sides of pastry with a fork. Bake at 450° for 10 minutes. Cool on a wire rack for 5 minutes. Reduce heat to 350°.

2 For filling, combine the eggs, sugars, flour and spices in a large bowl; stir in pumpkin. Gradually add cream. Pour into pastry shell. If desired, sprinkle chopped pecans on top. Bake at 350° for 45-50 minutes or until a knife inserted near the center comes out clean. Cool on a wire rack for 1 hour. Refrigerate for at least 3 hours before serving. Refrigerate leftovers.

PRALINE PUMPKIN PIE

Lemon Supreme Pie

PREP: 25 min. + chilling **BAKE:** 15 min. + chilling
YIELD: 6-8 servings

Jana Beckman, Wamego, Kansas

The combination of the cream cheese topping and tart lemon filling is wonderful.

    1 unbaked deep-dish pastry shell
       (9 inches)
LEMON FILLING:
1-1/4 cups sugar, *divided*
    6 tablespoons cornstarch
  1/2 teaspoon salt
1-1/4 cups water
    2 tablespoons butter
    2 teaspoons grated lemon peel
    4 to 5 drops yellow food coloring,
       optional
  1/2 cup fresh lemon juice
CREAM CHEESE FILLING:
    2 packages (one 8 ounces, one 3 ounces)
       cream cheese, softened
  3/4 cup confectioners' sugar
1-1/2 cups whipped topping
    1 tablespoon lemon juice

1 Line unpricked pastry shell with a double thickness of heavy-duty foil. Bake at 450° for 8 minutes. Remove foil; bake 5 minutes longer. Cool on a wire rack.

2 For lemon filling, combine 3/4 cup sugar, cornstarch and salt. Stir in water until smooth. Bring to a boil over medium-high heat. Reduce heat; add the remaining sugar. Cook and stir for 2 minutes or until thickened and bubbly. Remove

from the heat; stir in the butter, lemon peel and food coloring if desired. Gently stir in lemon juice. Cool to room temperature, about 1 hour.

3 For cream cheese filling, beat the cream cheese and sugar in a large mixing bowl until smooth. Fold in whipped topping and lemon juice. Refrigerate 1/2 cup for garnish. Spread remaining cream cheese mixture into pastry shell; top with lemon filling. Refrigerate overnight.

4 Place reserved cream cheese mixture in a pastry bag with a #21 star tip; pipe stars onto pie. Store in the refrigerator.

Fudgy Pecan Pie

PREP: 30 min. + chilling **BAKE:** 40 min. + chilling
YIELD: 6-8 servings

Ellen Arndt, Cologne, Minnesota

This pie looks too good to eat. It has two layers of chocolate filling, which are topped with sweetened whipped cream.

    1 unbaked pastry shell (9 inches)
    1 package (4 ounces) German sweet
       chocolate
  1/4 cup butter
    1 can (14 ounces) sweetened condensed
       milk
  1/2 cup water
    2 eggs, beaten
    1 teaspoon vanilla extract
  1/4 teaspoon salt
  1/2 cup chopped pecans
FILLING:
    1 cup cold milk
    1 package (3.9 ounces) instant chocolate
       pudding mix
    1 cup whipped topping

TOPPING:

- 1 **cup heavy whipping cream**
- 1 **tablespoon confectioners' sugar**
- 1 **teaspoon vanilla extract**

1 Line unpricked pastry shell with a double thickness of heavy-duty foil. Bake at 450° for 5 minutes. Remove foil and set shell aside. Reduce heat to 375°.

2 In a saucepan, melt chocolate and butter. Remove from heat; stir in milk and water. Add a small amount of hot chocolate mixture to eggs; return all to pan, stirring constantly. Stir in vanilla and salt. Pour into shell; sprinkle with nuts. Cover edges with foil. Bake for 35 minutes or until a knife inserted near the center comes out clean. Remove to a wire rack to cool completely.

3 In a mixing bowl, whisk milk and pudding mix for 2 minutes. Fold in whipped topping. Spread over nut layer; cover and refrigerate.

4 In a chilled mixing bowl, beat cream until soft peaks form. Add sugar and vanilla; beat until stiff peaks form. Spread over the pudding layer. Refrigerate until set, about 4 hours.

Old-Fashioned Custard Pie

PREP: 20 min. **BAKE:** 20 min. + cooling
YIELD: 6-8 servings

Maxine Linkenauger, Montverde, Florida

If you wish to make a braided crust, prepare a double-crust pastry. Otherwise, you'll just need need a single-crust pastry.

Pastry for single- *or* **double-crust pie (9 inches)**
- 4 **eggs**
- 2-1/2 **cups milk**
- 1/2 **cup sugar**
- 1 **teaspoon ground nutmeg**
- 1 **teaspoon vanilla extract**
- 1 **teaspoon almond extract**
- 1/2 **teaspoon salt**

1 Line a 9-in. pie plate with bottom pastry; trim to 1/2 in. beyond edge of plate; flute edges or prepare a braided edge (see page 207). Bake at 400° for 10 minutes.

2 In a mixing bowl, beat eggs. Beat in remaining ingredients. Pour into crust. Cover edges loosely with foil. Bake for 20-25 minutes or until a knife inserted near the center comes out clean. Cool on a wire rack for 1 hour. Chill for at least 3 hours before serving. Refrigerate leftovers.

problem-solving pointers *for Pies*

CRUST IS NOT FLAKY

- The shortening was cut in too much. Cut in shortening so it resembles coarse crumbs, not any smaller.

CRUST IS TOUGH AND/OR HAS SHRUNK

- The pastry was overhandled.
- Too much water was used. Stir in only enough water to moisten the flour so a ball forms.

CRUST IS SOGGY

- Next time, bake the crust longer or at a higher temperature.
- Before adding the filling, brush the crust with a beaten egg white, then bake.
- Add the filling to the crust right before baking.

CRUST IS BURNT IN SPOTS

- Make sure the crust is rolled out evenly.
- Your oven may bake unevenly. Next time, rotate the pie during baking.

PIE BUBBLES OVER

- Too much filling was used. Reduce the amount of filling or use a deep-dish pie plate.

THERE'S A WATERY LAYER BETWEEN THE MERINGUE AND FILLING

- Keep the filling warm while making the meringue. Then spread the meringue over hot filling.

MERINGUE SHRUNK DURING BAKING

- Be sure to seal the meringue to the edge of the pastry before baking.

BEADS FORMED ON THE TOP OF THE MERINGUE AND/OR THE MERINGUE IS STICKY

- Meringue was baked at too high a temperature or was underbaked.
- For best results, meringue should not be made on a humid or rainy day.

BUBBLES FORMED IN A CUSTARD-TYPE PIE

- Beat the filling only until combined.

Tasty Tarts

RUSTIC APPLE RASPBERRY TART

Rustic Apple Raspberry Tart

PREP: 25 min. + chilling **BAKE:** 35 min. + cooling
YIELD: 6 servings

Taste of Home Test Kitchen

This free-form tart requires no pie plate. Just roll out the dough and place on a pizza pan or baking sheet. Place the filling in center of dough and fold up the edge of the pastry to hold in the fruit and juices.

1-1/3 cups all-purpose flour
1/4 cup sugar
1/8 teaspoon salt
6 tablespoons cold butter
1 egg yolk
3 tablespoons cold water
FILLING:
2-1/2 cups thinly sliced peeled tart apples
(about 2 medium)
1 cup fresh *or* frozen raspberries
1/4 cup sugar
1 tablespoon cornstarch
3/4 teaspoon ground cinnamon
1 tablespoon milk
Coarse decorating sugar

1 In a small bowl, combine the flour, sugar and salt; cut in butter until mixture is crumbly. Gradually add egg yolk and water, tossing with a fork until a ball forms. Shape into a disk; wrap in plastic wrap and refrigerate for at least 1 hour.

2 On a lightly floured surface, roll out pastry into a 14-in. circle. Transfer to a parchment paper-lined 14-in. pizza pan.

3 For filling, combine apples and raspberries in a large bowl. Combine the sugar, cornstarch and cinnamon. Add to the fruit; toss gently to coat. Spoon over pastry to within 2 in. of edges. Fold up edges of pastry over filling, leaving center uncovered. Brush folded pastry with milk; sprinkle with coarse sugar. Bake at 375° for 35-40 minutes or until crust is golden and filling is bubbly. Using parchment paper, slide tart onto a wire rack to cool.

Apple Cranberry Tart

PREP: 15 min. **BAKE:** 35 min. **YIELD:** 12-16 servings

Suzanne Strocsher, Bothell, Washington
You'll love the tangy sweetness of this quick but elegant-looking dessert.

Pastry for double-crust pie (9 inches)
2 cups fresh *or* frozen cranberries,
coarsely chopped
2 medium tart apples, peeled and coarsely
chopped
1-1/4 cups packed brown sugar
2 tablespoons all-purpose flour
1/2 teaspoon ground cinnamon
1 to 2 tablespoons butter

1 On a lightly floured surface, roll out half of the pastry into a 13-in. circle. Press onto the bottom and up the sides of an ungreased 11-in. fluted tart pan with removable bottom, or press onto the bottom and 1 in. up the sides of a 10-in. spring-form pan.

2 In a large bowl, combine the cranberries, apples, brown sugar, flour and cinnamon; pour into crust. Dot with butter. Roll out remaining pastry and cut with a 1-in. apple cookie cutter. Cut leaf shapes from remaining pastry. Place cutouts over filling.

APPLE CRANBERRY TART

3 Place pan on a baking sheet. Bake at 425° for 35-40 minutes or until filling is bubbly and crust is golden. Cool on a wire rack. Serve warm.

White Chocolate Fruit Tart

PREP: 30 min. + chilling **BAKE:** 25 min. + cooling
YIELD: 12-16 servings

Claire Darby, New Castle, Delaware

It takes a little time to make, but this tart is marvelous, especially in summer when fresh fruit is in abundance.

3/4　cup butter, softened
1/2　cup confectioners' sugar
1-1/2　cups all-purpose flour
FILLING:
　1　package (10 to 12 ounces) vanilla *or* white chips, melted and cooled
1/4　cup heavy whipping cream
　1　package (8 ounces) cream cheese, softened

preventing
soggy *tart crusts*

Brush tart crusts with melted jelly before layering with fruit. That will help seal the crust and keep the fruit juices from absorbing into the crust.

　1　can (20 ounces) pineapple chunks
　1　pint fresh strawberries, sliced
　1　can (11 ounces) mandarin oranges, drained
　2　kiwifruit, peeled and sliced
GLAZE:
　3　tablespoons sugar
　2　teaspoons cornstarch
1/2　teaspoon lemon juice

1 In a small mixing bowl, cream butter and confectioners' sugar until light and fluffy. Gradually add flour; mix well. Press into an ungreased 11-in. tart pan with removable bottom or 12-in. pizza pan with sides. Place pan on a baking sheet. Bake at 300° for 25-30 minutes or until lightly browned. Cool on a wire rack.

2 For filling, beat melted chips and cream in a small mixing bowl. Add the cream cheese; beat until smooth. Spread over crust. Refrigerate for 30 minutes. Drain the pineapple, reserving 1/2 cup juice; set juice aside. Arrange pineapple, strawberries, oranges and kiwi over filling.

3 For glaze, combine sugar and cornstarch in a small saucepan. Stir in lemon juice and reserved pineapple juice until smooth. Bring to a boil over medium heat; cook and stir for 2 minutes or until thickened. Cool; brush over fruit. Refrigerate for 1 hour before serving. Refrigerate leftovers.

Peaches 'n' Cream Tart

PREP: 20 min. + chilling **BAKE:** 25 min. + cooling
YIELD: 6-8 servings

Mary Ann Kosmas, Minneapolis, Minnesota

You'll find that this luscious dessert is as easy as it is elegant. You can bake the crust ahead, then whip together the filling later.

1	cup finely chopped pecans
2/3	cup all-purpose flour
1/2	cup butter, melted
1/2	cup heavy whipping cream
1	package (8 ounces) cream cheese, softened
1/3	cup sugar
1	teaspoon vanilla extract
1/2	teaspoon almond extract
1	teaspoon grated orange peel
1	can (16 ounces) sliced peaches, well drained
1/2	cup fresh raspberries
1/4	cup apricot preserves
2	tablespoons honey

1 In a small bowl, combine the pecans, flour and butter; press onto the bottom and up the sides of an ungreased 9-in. tart pan with removable bottom. Place pan on a baking sheet. Bake at 350° for 25-30 minutes or until golden brown. Cool completely on a wire rack.

2 In a chilled small mixing bowl, beat cream until soft peaks form; set aside. In another small mixing bowl, beat the cream cheese and sugar until fluffy. Add extracts and orange peel; mix well. Beat in the whipped cream on low speed. Spoon into crust. Refrigerate for 2-4 hours.

3 Just before serving, arrange peaches and raspberries over filling. In a small saucepan or microwave, melt preserves and honey; mix well. Carefully spoon or brush over fruit. Cut into wedges to serve. Refrigerate leftovers.

Nectarine Blueberry Tart

PREP: 40 min. **BAKE:** 20 min. + chilling
YIELD: 10-12 servings

Taste of Home Test Kitchen

If nectarines are not available, you may use peeled peaches for an equally delicious dessert.

1/2	cup butter, softened
1/3	cup sugar
1	cup all-purpose flour
Pinch salt	
PASTRY CREAM:	
1/2	cup sugar
2	tablespoons plus 2 teaspoons cornstarch
Pinch salt	
1-1/2	cups milk
2	egg yolks
1	teaspoon vanilla extract
1-1/2	cups sliced fresh nectarines
1/2	cup fresh blueberries

1 In a small mixing bowl, cream the butter and sugar until light and fluffy. Add the flour and salt; mix until a ball forms. Cover and refrigerate for 1 hour. Press pastry onto the bottom and up the sides of a greased 9-in. tart pan with removable bottom. Place pan on a baking sheet. Bake at 350° for 18-20 minutes or until golden brown. Cool on a wire rack.

2 For pastry cream, combine the sugar, cornstarch and salt in a saucepan. Stir in milk until smooth. Cook and stir over medium heat until thickened and bubbly. Reduce heat; cook and stir 2 minutes longer. Remove from the heat. Beat a small amount of hot filling into egg yolks; return all to the pan, stirring constantly. Bring to a gentle boil; cook and stir 2 minutes longer. Remove from the heat. Gently stir in vanilla. Pour into another small bowl; cover with plastic wrap and refrigerate, without stirring, until chilled.

3 Just before serving, pour pastry cream into tart shell. Arrange nectarines and blueberries on top. Refrigerate leftovers.

Heavenly Blueberry Tart

PREP: 20 min. **BAKE:** 55 min. + cooling
YIELD: 6-8 servings

Lyin Schramm, Berwick, Maine

Mmm—this tart is bursting with the fresh flavor of blueberries! The berries are not only baked with the crust, but additional fresh berries are scattered across the top.

- 1 **cup all-purpose flour**
- 2 **tablespoons sugar**
- 1/8 **teaspoon salt**
- 1/2 **cup cold butter**
- 1 **tablespoon white vinegar**

FILLING:
- 2 **pints fresh blueberries,** *divided*
- 2/3 **cup sugar**
- 2 **tablespoons all-purpose flour**
- 1/2 **teaspoon ground cinnamon**
- 1/8 **teaspoon ground nutmeg**

1 In a small bowl, combine the flour, sugar and salt; cut in butter until crumbly. Add vinegar, tossing with a fork to moisten. Press onto bottom and up the sides of a lightly greased 9-in. tart pan with removable bottom.

2 For filling, place 1 pint of blueberries over crust. Combine the sugar, flour, cinnamon and nutmeg; sprinkle over blueberries. Place tart pan on a baking sheet.

3 Bake at 400° for 55-60 minutes or until crust is browned and filling is bubbly. Remove from the oven; arrange and press remaining berries in a single layer over top. Cool on a wire rack. Store in the refrigerator.

CRUMB-TOPPED APPLE RASPBERRY TARTS

Crumb-Topped Apple Raspberry Tarts

PREP: 20 min. + standing **BAKE:** 35 min.
YIELD: 2 servings

Margie Portenier, Orleans, Nebraska

These are the perfect size for dessert. If you want more than two tarts, just double the recipe.

- 1 **cup fresh** *or* **frozen unsweetened raspberries**
- 3/4 **cup halved thinly sliced peeled tart apple**
- 1/4 **cup sugar**
- 1 **tablespoon quick-cooking tapioca**

Dash to 1/8 teaspoon ground cinnamon
Dash ground nutmeg
- 1 **sheet refrigerated pie pastry**
- 2 **teaspoons butter, melted**

TOPPING:
- 1 **tablespoon all-purpose flour**
- 1-1/2 **teaspoons brown sugar**
- 1 **teaspoon cold butter**

1 In a bowl, combine the raspberries and apple. In a small bowl, combine the sugar, tapioca, cinnamon and nutmeg. Sprinkle over apple mixture; gently toss to coat evenly. Let stand for 15 minutes.

2 Divide pie pastry in half and roll each half into a 7-in. circle. Transfer pastry to two ungreased 4-in. fluted tart pans with removal bottoms. Trim pastry even with edge. Spoon raspberry mixture into pastry shells. Drizzle with melted butter.

3 For topping, in a bowl, combine flour and brown sugar. Cut in butter until crumbly. Sprinkle over raspberry mixture. Bake at 375° for 35-40 minutes or until bubbly. Serve warm or chilled.

HEAVENLY BLUEBERRY TART

Raspberry Curd Tartlets

PREP: 45 min. + chilling **BAKE:** 30 min. + cooling
YIELD: about 2 dozen

Taste of Home Test Kitchen

If you're pressed for time, use purchased lemon curd in place of the homemade raspberry curd and garnish with fresh raspberries.

> 1 cup butter, softened
> 1/2 cup confectioners' sugar
> 1 teaspoon vanilla extract
> 2 cups all-purpose flour
> Pinch salt
> 1/2 cup finely chopped almonds
> **RASPBERRY CURD:**
> 1 package (10 ounces) frozen unsweetened raspberries, thawed
> 3 tablespoons lemon juice
> 1/2 cup butter
> 3 tablespoons sugar
> 4 eggs
> Red liquid food coloring, optional
> Whipped cream, fresh raspberries and mint

1 In a large mixing bowl, cream butter and confectioners' sugar until light and fluffy. Add the vanilla. Combine flour and salt; add to creamed mixture and beat until smooth. Stir in almonds. Press into 2-1/2-in. tartlet pans; trim edges. Place pans on a baking sheet. Bake at 375° for 20-25 minutes or until golden brown. Cool on a wire rack. Remove from pans.

2 For raspberry curd, combine raspberries and lemon juice in a blender or food processor; cover and process until pureed. Press through a strainer to remove seeds.

3 In a saucepan, melt butter over medium heat. Reduce heat to low; add the raspberry puree, sugar and eggs. Cook and stir for 10-15 minutes or until mixture is smooth and thickened and reaches 160°. Remove from the heat. Add food coloring if desired. Press plastic wrap on surface of curd. Refrigerate for several hours or overnight.

4 Spoon about 3 tablespoons of curd into each tart shell; top with whipped cream, raspberries and mint. Refrigerate leftovers.

Walnut Tart

PREP: 30 min. **BAKE:** 22 min. + cooling
YIELD: 10-12 servings

Rovena Wallace, Trafford, Pennsylvania

Don't have a tart pan? No problem! This dessert can be prepared in an 11-in. x 7-in. x 2-in. baking pan instead.

> 1/3 cup butter, softened
> 1/4 cup sugar

RASPBERRY CURD TARTLETS

1 egg yolk
1 cup all-purpose flour
FILLING:
2 cups coarsely chopped walnuts
2/3 cup packed brown sugar
1/4 cup butter
1/4 cup dark corn syrup
1/2 cup heavy whipping cream, *divided*

1 In a small mixing bowl, cream butter and sugar until light and fluffy. Add egg yolk; mix well. Add the flour just until blended (mixture will be crumbly). Press onto the bottom and up the sides of an ungreased 9-in. tart pan with removable bottom. Place pan on a baking sheet. Bake at 375° for 12-14 minutes. Cool on a wire rack.

2 Sprinkle nuts over crust. In a small heavy saucepan, combine the brown sugar, butter, corn syrup and 2 tablespoons cream. Bring to a boil over medium heat; cook and stir 1 minute longer. Pour over walnuts.

3 Return pan to baking sheet. Bake at 375° for 10-12 minutes or until bubbly. Cool on a wire rack.

4 In a chilled small mixing bowl, beat remaining cream until stiff peaks form. Serve tart at room temperature with whipped cream.

PECAN TARTLETS

Pecan Tartlets

PREP: 20 min. + chilling BAKE: 25 min. + cooling
YIELD: about 20

Jean Rhodes, Tignall, Georgia

The flaky crust combined with a rich center makes these little tarts a satisfying snack. They look so appealing on a pretty platter and make a great finger-food dessert when you're entertaining. They also freeze well.

1 package (3 ounces) cream cheese, softened
1/2 cup butter, softened
1 cup all-purpose flour
1/4 teaspoon salt
FILLING:
1 egg
3/4 cup packed dark brown sugar
1 tablespoon butter, melted
1 teaspoon vanilla extract
2/3 cup chopped pecans
Maraschino cherry halves, optional

1 In a small mixing bowl, beat cream cheese and butter until fluffy; blend in flour and salt. Refrigerate for 1 hour. Shape into 1-in. balls; press onto the bottom and up the sides of greased miniature muffin cups.

2 For filling, in a small mixing bowl, beat the egg. Add the brown sugar, butter and vanilla; mix well. Stir in pecans. Spoon into tart shells. Bake at 325° for 25-30 minutes. Cool for 15 minutes before carefully removing from pans. Decorate with maraschino cherries if desired.

Tiny Shortbread Tarts

PREP: 20 min. BAKE: 20 min. per batch + cooling
YIELD: about 3 dozen

Kim Marie Van Rheenen, Mendota, Illinois

To save time when making these bite-size treats, bake the crusts the day before, cool and store in an airtight container. Top with your favorite filling just before serving.

1 cup butter, softened
1/2 cup confectioners' sugar
2 cups all-purpose flour
1 can (21 ounces) raspberry, cherry *or* strawberry pie filling

1 In a large mixing bowl, cream butter and confectioners' sugar until light and fluffy. Add flour; mix well. Shape into 1-in. balls; press onto the bottom and up the sides of greased miniature muffin cups.

2 Bake at 300° for 17-22 minutes. Cool for 15 minutes before carefully removing from pans to wire racks. Spoon 1 teaspoon of pie filling into each tart.

Rustic Fruit Tart

PREP: 20 min. + standing **BAKE:** 25 min.
YIELD: 2 servings

Naomi Olson, Hamilton, Michigan

This rustic fruit tart is ideal for two. You can also substitute apples, peaches or blueberries for the rhubarb.

   1   cup all-purpose flour
 1/2   teaspoon salt
 1/4   cup vegetable oil
   2   tablespoons milk
   1   cup diced fresh *or* frozen rhubarb, thawed
   1   cup fresh *or* frozen raspberries, thawed
 1/2   cup sugar
   2   tablespoons quick-cooking tapioca
GLAZE:
   6   tablespoons confectioners' sugar
   1   teaspoon water
 1/8   teaspoon almond extract

1 In a bowl, combine flour and salt. Add oil and milk, tossing with a fork until mixture forms a ball. Shape dough into a disk; wrap in plastic wrap. Refrigerate for at least 1 hour.

2 In another bowl, combine the rhubarb, raspberries, sugar and tapioca; let stand for 15 minutes. Unwrap the dough and place on a parchment-lined baking sheet. Cover with waxed paper and roll the dough into an 11-in. circle. Discard waxed paper.

3 Spoon fruit mixture into the center of dough to within 2 in. of the edges. Fold edges of dough over fruit, leaving center uncovered. Bake at 400° for 25-30 minutes or until crust is golden brown

and filling is bubbly. Remove to a wire rack. Combine the glaze ingredients until smooth. Drizzle over warm tart.

Citrus Cream Tartlets

PREP: 20 min. **BAKE:** 15 min. + chilling
YIELD: 2 servings

Brian Barger, Chevy Chase, Maryland

This rich, creamy dessert can be made ahead of time.

 1/2   cup chopped macadamia nuts, toasted
   3   tablespoons sugar
   2   tablespoons all-purpose flour
   2   tablespoons cold butter
   2   packages (3 ounces *each*) cream cheese, softened
 1/4   cup confectioners' sugar
   2   teaspoons *each* orange, lemon and lime juice
   1   teaspoon *each* grated orange, lemon and lime peel

1 In a blender or food processor, combine the nuts, sugar and flour; cover and process until blended. Add butter; blend until mixture forms coarse crumbs.

2 Press onto the bottom and up the sides of two greased 4-in. tartlet pans with removable bottoms. Bake at 350° for 13-15 minutes or until golden brown. Cool completely.

3 In a mixing bowl, beat cream cheese until fluffy. Add the confectioners' sugar, citrus juices and peels; beat until blended. Spoon into crusts. Refrigerate for at least 1 hour.

DESSERTS

Desserts

Cream Puffs & Eclairs

Almond Puffs

PREP: 25 min. **BAKE:** 50 min. + cooling
YIELD: 24 servings

Mary Ims, Yankton, South Dakota

This old-fashioned Danish has a tender crust, a cream puff layer and an almond glaze.

- 1/2 **cup cold butter**
- 1 **cup all-purpose flour**
- 1 **to 2 tablespoons water**

PUFF LAYER:
- 1 **cup water**
- 1/2 **cup butter**
- 1 **cup all-purpose flour**
- 1 **teaspoon almond extract**
- 3 **eggs**

GLAZE:
- 1-1/2 **cups confectioners' sugar**
- 2 **tablespoons butter, softened**
- 1/2 **teaspoon almond extract**
- 1 **to 2 tablespoons warm water**
- 2 **tablespoons sliced almonds, toasted and chopped**

1 In a bowl, cut butter into flour until mixture resembles coarse crumbs. Add water and toss with a fork. Shape into a ball. Divide in half. Pat into two 12-in. x 3-in. strips, 2 in. apart on an ungreased baking sheet. Set aside.

2 In a large saucepan, bring the water and butter to a boil over medium heat. Add flour all at once; stir until a smooth ball forms. Remove from the heat; stir in extract. Let stand for 5 minutes. Add eggs, one at a time, beating well after each addition. Continue beating until mixture is smooth and shiny. Spread over crusts, covering completely.

3 Bake at 325° for 50-55 minutes or until puffed and lightly browned. Cool on a wire rack for 5 minutes. In a bowl, combine the confectioners' sugar, butter, extract and enough water to achieve spreading consistency. Spread over warm puffs. Sprinkle with almonds. Cut into 1-in. strips. Refrigerate leftovers.

secrets for *successful cream puffs and eclairs*

- When baking the dough, it's important not to crowd the baking pan. Leave about 3 inches of space around each puff or eclair. The dough needs room to expand during baking and needs air to circulate so the steam it gives off can evaporate.

- Cream puffs and eclairs are done when they are golden brown and have a dry, crisp exterior.

- For the best flavor, serve cream puffs and eclairs the same day they're made. If necessary, they can be prepared a day in advance. Store the unfilled pastries in a plastic bag in the refrigerator and fill just before serving.

- For longer storage, arrange unfilled pastries in a single layer on a baking sheet and freeze. Once they're frozen, transfer to heavy-duty resealable plastic bags and freeze for up to 2 months. Thaw at room temperature for 15-20 minutes before using. If the thawed pastries are a little soggy, reheat them in the oven for a few minutes.

State Fair Cream Puffs

PREP: 25 min. **BAKE:** 35 min. + cooling
YIELD: 10 servings

Ruth Jungbluth, Dodgeville, Wisconsin

The Wisconsin Bakers Association has been serving these treats at the Wisconsin State Fair since 1924. In recent years, more than 300,000 are sold annually!

1	cup water
1/2	cup butter
1/4	teaspoon salt
1	cup all-purpose flour
4	eggs
2	tablespoons milk
1	egg yolk, lightly beaten
2	cups heavy whipping cream
1/4	cup confectioners' sugar
1/2	teaspoon vanilla extract

Additional confectioners' sugar

1 In a large saucepan, bring the water, butter and salt to a boil over medium heat. Add flour all at once and stir until a smooth ball forms. Remove from the heat; let stand for 5 minutes. Add eggs, one at a time, beating well after each addition. Continue beating until mixture is smooth and shiny.

2 Drop by 1/4 cupfuls 3 in. apart onto greased baking sheets. Combine milk and egg yolk; brush over puffs. Bake at 400° for 30-35 minutes or until golden brown. Remove to wire racks. Immediately cut a slit in each for steam to escape; cool.

3 In a chilled large mixing bowl, beat cream until it begins to thicken. Add sugar and vanilla; beat until almost stiff. Split cream puffs open; discard soft dough from inside. Fill the cream puffs just before serving. Dust with confectioners' sugar. Refrigerate leftovers.

STATE FAIR CREAM PUFFS

making *cream puffs*

1. Bring water, butter and salt to a boil in a saucepan. Add the flour all at once; stir briskly until the mixture leaves the sides of the pan and forms a ball.

2. Remove from the heat and let stand for 5 minutes to allow mixture to cool before adding the eggs. Beat well after adding each egg. Continue beating until mixture is smooth and shiny.

3. Drop dough 3 in. apart onto a greased baking sheet. Bake as directed.

4. Remove puffs from pan to a wire rack. Immediately cut a slit in each puff to allow steam to escape; cool. Split puffs and set tops aside; remove soft dough from inside with a fork and discard. Fill as directed.

Cream Puff Dessert

PREP: 20 min. + chilling **BAKE:** 30 min. + cooling
YIELD: 12 servings

Lisa Nash, Blaine, Minnesota

Instead of making individual cream puffs, try this rich dessert with a cream puff base and sweet toppings.

CREAM PUFF DESSERT

1 cup water
1/2 cup butter
1 cup all-purpose flour
4 eggs
FILLING:
1 package (8 ounces) cream cheese, softened
3-1/2 cups cold milk
2 packages (3.9 ounces *each*) instant chocolate pudding mix
TOPPING:
1 carton (8 ounces) frozen whipped topping, thawed
1/4 cup chocolate ice cream topping
1/4 cup caramel ice cream topping
1/3 cup chopped almonds

1 In a large saucepan, bring the water and butter to a boil over medium heat. Add flour all at once; stir until a smooth ball forms. Remove from the heat; let stand for 5 minutes. Add the eggs, one at a time, beating well after each addition. Continue beating until mixture is smooth and shiny.

2 Spread into a greased 13-in. x 9-in. x 2-in. baking dish. Bake at 400° for 30-35 minutes or until puffed and golden brown. Remove to a wire rack to cool completely.

3 For filling, beat the cream cheese, milk and pudding mix in a large mixing bowl until smooth. Spread over puff; refrigerate for 20 minutes.

4 Spread with whipped topping; refrigerate until serving. Drizzle with the chocolate and caramel toppings; sprinkle with almonds. Refrigerate leftovers.

Cream Puff Heart

PREP: 35 min. **BAKE:** 40 min. + cooling
YIELD: 14-16 servings

Edna Hoffman, Hebron, Indiana

This scrumptious treat looks great on a buffet table or makes a tasty finale for a special-occasion meal. The strawberries provide color and refreshing flavor.

1 cup water
1/2 cup butter
1/4 teaspoon salt
1 cup all-purpose flour
4 eggs
1-1/2 cups milk
1 package (3 ounces) cook-and-serve vanilla pudding mix
1 cup heavy whipping cream, whipped
1 teaspoon vanilla extract
2 packages (10 ounces *each*) frozen strawberries, thawed and drained *or* 2 cups sliced fresh strawberries
Confectioners' sugar

1 Cover a baking sheet with foil; grease foil. Trace a 12-in. heart onto foil and set aside. In a large saucepan, bring the water, butter and salt to a boil over medium heat. Add flour all at once and stir until a smooth ball forms. Remove from the heat; let stand for 5 minutes. Add eggs, one at a time, beating well after each addition. Continue beating until mixture is smooth and shiny.

2 Drop batter by rounded tablespoonfuls along the outside of the heart (mounds should be almost touching). Bake at 400° for 40-45 minutes or until golden. Lift foil and transfer to a wire rack. Immediately cut a slit in each puff to allow steam to escape; cool.

3 In a saucepan, cook milk and pudding mix according to package directions. Cool. Fold in whipped cream and vanilla.

4 Place cream puffs on a serving plate. Split puffs open; discard soft dough from inside. Fill cream puffs just before serving; top with strawberries and replace tops. Dust with confectioners' sugar. Refrigerate leftovers.

Banana Split Cream Puffs

PREP: 30 min. **BAKE:** 30 min. + cooling
YIELD: 12 servings

Sandra McKenzie, Braham, Minnesota

Banana split ingredients are cleverly sandwiched inside these cream puffs. You can use whatever ice cream and toppings your family prefers.

1	**cup water**
1/2	**cup butter**
1/4	**teaspoon salt**
1	**cup all-purpose flour**
4	**eggs**
12	**scoops vanilla ice cream**
1	**cup sliced fresh strawberries**
1	**large *or* 2 medium bananas, thinly sliced**
3/4	**cup pineapple tidbits, drained**
1/2	**cup hot fudge ice cream topping**

1 In a large saucepan, bring the water, butter and salt to a boil over medium heat. Add flour all at once and stir until a smooth ball forms. Remove from the heat; let stand for 5 minutes. Add eggs, one at a time, beating well after each addition. Continue beating until mixture is smooth and shiny.

2 Drop by rounded tablespoonfuls 3 in. apart onto a greased baking sheet. Bake at 400° for 30-35 minutes or until golden brown. Remove to a wire rack. Immediately cut a slit in each to allow steam to escape; cool. Split puffs open; remove tops and set aside. Discard soft dough from inside.

3 Fill each puff with a scoop of ice cream and top with fruit. Drizzle with hot fudge topping; replace tops. Serve immediately.

Graham Cream Puffs

PREP: 35 min. **BAKE:** 30 min. **YIELD:** 10 servings

Iola Egle, Bella Vista, Arkansas

These "berry" special cream puffs are made with graham cracker crumbs, filled with raspberries and cream and topped with a tangy raspberry sauce.

1	**cup water**
1/2	**cup butter**
1/4	**teaspoon salt**
1/2	**cup all-purpose flour**
1/2	**cup graham cracker crumbs**
4	**eggs**

GLAZE:

1/2	**cup raspberries**
2	**tablespoons sugar**
1	**teaspoon cornstarch**
1/2	**cup orange juice**

FILLING:
- 1 cup heavy whipping cream
- 1 to 3 tablespoons sugar
- 1 teaspoon vanilla extract
- 2 cups raspberries, drained

1 Cover baking sheets with foil; grease foil and set aside. In a large saucepan, bring water, butter and salt to a boil over medium heat. Add flour and cracker crumbs all at once and stir until a smooth ball forms. Remove from the heat; let stand for 5 minutes. Add eggs, one at a time, beating well after each addition. Continue beating until mixture is smooth and shiny.

2 Drop batter by 1/4 cupfuls 3 in. apart onto prepared baking sheets. Bake at 400° for 30-35 minutes or until golden brown. Remove to wire racks. Immediately cut a slit in each for steam to escape; cool.

3 For glaze, place berries in a blender; cover and process until pureed. Strain berries and discard seeds. Set the puree aside. In a saucepan, combine sugar and cornstarch. Stir in orange juice and the reserved puree until blended. Bring to a boil over medium heat; cook and stir for 1 minute or until thickened. Remove from the heat; set aside.

4 For filling, beat cream in a chilled large mixing bowl until it begins to thicken. Add sugar and vanilla; beat until stiff peaks form. Fold in raspberries. Split cream puffs open; discard soft dough from inside. Fill the cream puffs just before serving. Drizzle with glaze. Refrigerate leftovers.

- 2 cups milk
- 2 eggs, lightly beaten
- 1 teaspoon vanilla extract
- 2 cups whipped cream, *divided*

Chocolate sauce *and/or* fresh raspberries, optional

1 In a large saucepan, bring the water, butter and salt to a boil over medium heat. Add flour all at once and stir until a smooth ball forms. Remove from the heat; let stand for 5 minutes. Add eggs, one at a time, beating well after each addition. Continue beating until mixture is smooth and shiny.

2 Spread onto the bottom and halfway up the sides of a well-greased 9-in. pie plate. Bake at 400° for 35-40 minutes. Cool completely on a wire rack.

3 For filling, combine the sugar, flour and salt in a large heavy saucepan. Stir in milk until smooth. Cook and stir over medium-high heat until thickened and bubbly. Reduce heat; cook and stir 2 minutes more. Remove from the heat. Stir a small amount of hot filling into eggs; return all to pan, stirring constantly. Bring to a gentle boil. Cook and stir for 2 minutes longer. Remove from the heat. Gently stir in vanilla. Cool to room temperature without stirring.

4 Fold in 1 cup of whipped cream. Pour into the crust. Top with remaining whipped cream. Refrigerate for 2 hours. Garnish with chocolate sauce and/or raspberries if desired. Refrigerate leftovers.

CREAM PUFF PIE

Cream Puff Pie

PREP: 20 min. **BAKE:** 30 min. + chilling
YIELD: 6-8 servings

Holly Camozzi, Rohnert Park, California

A rich homemade vanilla pudding fills this cream puff pie. Whipped cream, chocolate sauce and raspberries are flavorful finishing touches.

- 1/2 cup water
- 1/4 cup butter
- 1/2 teaspoon salt
- 1/2 cup all-purpose flour
- 2 eggs

FILLING:
- 3/4 cup sugar
- 1/3 cup all-purpose flour
- 1/8 teaspoon salt

3 For filling, combine the sugar and cornstarch in a small saucepan; gradually stir in milk until smooth. Bring to a boil over medium heat until thickened and bubbly, stirring constantly. Reduce heat; cook and stir 2 minutes longer. Remove from the heat. Stir 1 cup hot filling into egg yolks; return all to pan, stirring constantly. Bring to a gentle boil; cook and stir 2 minutes longer. Remove from the heat; stir in butter and vanilla. Cool.

4 Split eclairs open; discard soft dough from inside. Fill eclairs just before serving. Replace tops; dust with confectioners' sugar or spread with frosting. Refrigerate leftovers.

Traditional Eclairs

PREP: 40 min. **BAKE:** 30 min. + cooling
YIELD: 1 dozen

Taste of Home Test Kitchen

Do you recall the old-fashioned sweet eclairs like Grandma used to make? She baked the puffed pastries to a beautiful golden brown, filled them with creamy vanilla pudding and frosted them with chocolaty icing. Now you can make them in your own home!

1	**cup water**
1/2	**cup butter**
1	**teaspoon sugar**
1/4	**teaspoon salt**
1	**cup all-purpose flour**
4	**eggs**

FILLING:

1/3	**cup sugar**
3	**tablespoons cornstarch**
2-1/2	**cups milk**
2	**egg yolks**
1	**tablespoon butter**
1-1/2	**teaspoons vanilla extract**

Confectioners' sugar *or* **chocolate frosting**

1 In a large saucepan, bring water, butter, sugar and salt to a boil over medium heat. Add flour all at once; stir until a smooth ball forms. Remove from the heat; let stand for 5 minutes. Add eggs, one at a time, beating well after each addition. Continue beating until mixture is smooth and shiny.

2 Insert a 3/4-in. round tip into a pastry bag or heavy-duty resealable plastic bag; add batter. Pipe into 12 strips (about 3 in. long) 3 in. apart on a greased baking sheet. Bake at 400° for 30-35 minutes or until golden brown. Remove to a wire rack. Immediately cut a slit in each for steam to escape; cool.

piping *eclairs*

Cut a small hole in the corner of a disposable pastry bag or heavy-duty resealable plastic bag. Place a large round tip (about 3/4 in. in diameter) in bag. Fill bag with dough. Pipe 3-in.-long strips on a greased baking sheet, leaving 3 in. of space between each strip.

problem-solving
pointers *for Cream Puffs & Eclairs*

DOUGH IS DRY

• The water was boiled too long, causing too much liquid to be evaporated.

BOTTOMS ARE SOGGY

• Puffs or eclairs were filled too soon. Fill just before serving or no sooner than 2 hours beforehand.

PUFFS ARE NOT CRISP

• Puffs are underbaked. They should be golden brown, crisp and dry.

Puff Pastry

Palmiers

PREP: 20 min. **BAKE:** 20 min. **YIELD:** about 2 dozen

Taste of Home Test Kitchen

It takes just two ingredients to whip up these impressive but easy-to-make French pastries, which are often called palm leaves.

1 **cup sugar,** *divided*
1 **sheet frozen puff pastry, thawed**

1 Sprinkle a surface with 1/4 cup sugar; open the puff pastry sheet on surface. Sprinkle with 2 tablespoons sugar. Roll into a 14-in. x 10-in. rectangle. Sprinkle with 1/2 cup sugar to within 1/2 in. of edges. Lightly press into pastry.

2 With a knife, very lightly score a line widthwise across the middle of the pastry. Starting at one short side, roll up jelly-roll style, stopping at the score mark in the middle. Starting at the other side, roll up pastry jelly-roll style to score mark. Cut into 3/8-in. slices.

3 Place cut side up 2 in. apart on parchment paper-lined baking sheets. Sprinkle lightly with 1 tablespoon sugar. Bake at 425° for 12 minutes. Turn pastries over and sprinkle with remaining sugar. Bake 5 minutes longer or until golden brown and glazed. Remove to wire racks to cool completely. Store in airtight containers.

PALMIERS

making *palmiers*

Roll out dough into a 14-in. x 10-in. rectangle. Sprinkle sugar over dough to within 1/2 in. of edges. Lightly press into pastry. With a knife, very lightly score a line widthwise across the middle of the pastry. Starting at one short side, roll up pastry jelly-roll style, stopping at the score mark in the middle. Starting at the other short side, roll up pastry jelly-roll style to the score mark. Cut into 3/8-in. slices.

Cherry Cheesecake Tarts

PREP: 15 min. **BAKE:** 20 min. + cooling
YIELD: 6 servings

Mary Lindell, Sanford, Michigan

Frozen puff pastry shells, cream cheese and cherry pie filling make these attractive tarts simple to prepare. The recipe can easily be doubled if you will be entertaining a larger group.

1 **package (10 ounces) frozen puff pastry shells**
2 **packages (3 ounces** *each*) **cream cheese, softened**
1/4 **cup confectioners' sugar**
1/2 **teaspoon almond extract**
1 **can (21 ounces) cherry pie filling**
Additional confectioners' sugar

1 Bake the pastry shells according to package directions. In a small mixing bowl, beat the cream cheese, sugar and extract. With a fork, carefully remove the circular top of each baked shell and set aside. Discard any soft pastry from inside shells.

2 Spoon the cream cheese filling into shells; place on a baking sheet. Bake at 400° for 5 minutes. Remove to a wire rack; cool for 1 hour. Refrigerate until serving.

3 Just before serving, spoon pie filling into shells. Top with reserved pastry circles. Dust with confectioners' sugar. Refrigerate leftovers.

Elegant Raspberry Dessert

PREP: 50 min. + chilling **BAKE:** 15 min.
YIELD: 8 servings

Taste of Home Test Kitchen

If the eye-catching appearance of this dessert doesn't impress guests, the wonderful flavor will! The homemade pastry cream is rich and smooth.

PASTRY CREAM:
- 1/4 cup sugar
- 4 teaspoons cornstarch

Dash salt

- 3/4 cup milk
- 1 egg yolk, beaten
- 1/2 teaspoon vanilla extract

CRUST:
- 1 sheet frozen puff pastry, thawed
- 1 egg
- 1 tablespoon water

TOPPING:
- 1-1/2 cups fresh raspberries *or* other berries
- 2 tablespoons seedless raspberry jam, warmed

ELEGANT RASPBERRY DESSERT

1 In a saucepan, combine the sugar, cornstarch and salt. Stir in milk until smooth. Cook and stir over medium-high heat until thickened and bubbly. Reduce heat; cook and stir 2 minutes longer. Remove from the heat. Stir a small amount of hot filling into yolk; return all to the pan, stirring constantly. Bring to a gentle boil; cook and stir 2 minutes longer. Remove from the heat; stir in vanilla. Pour into a small bowl; cover surface with plastic wrap. Refrigerate, without stirring, until chilled.

2 On a large parchment paper-lined baking sheet, unfold puff pastry sheet and form a 10-in. square (lightly use a rolling pin if necessary). With a large sharp knife or pastry wheel, cut a strip of dough 2-in. wide, leaving a 10-in. x 8-in. rectangle. From the 2-in. strip, cut two 10-in. x 1/2-in. strips and two 7-in. x 1/2-in. strips. Discard trimmings.

3 Prick the 10-in. x 8-in. rectangle (pastry base) with a fork. Brush water 1/2 in. around edges. Place the 10-in. x 1/2-in. and 7-in. x 1/2-in. strips along edge of base to form the sides; press lightly.

4 In a small bowl, beat egg and water; brush over top of pastry, avoiding the edges. Bake at 400° for 15-20 minutes or until golden brown and puffed. Cool on a wire rack. To serve, place tart on a serving plate. Spread with pastry cream. Top with raspberries; brush with jam.

tips for working with & storing *puff pastry*

Frozen puff pastry dough is available in sheets or individual shells. It has dozens of paper-thin layers of dough separated by butter. As the pastry bakes, steam created from water in the dough makes the layers rise up and pull apart, resulting in a crisp, flaky pastry. Here are some tips for working with and storing frozen puff pastry:

- Thaw pastry at room temperature for about 20 minutes before handling. Handle as little as possible to avoid stretching and tearing.
- Preheat the oven as directed.
- Cut pastry with a sharp knife or cutter to get a clean edge.
- Only brush an egg wash on the top of the dough, not the edges. If the edges are brushed, they will stick together and the pastry won't rise during baking.
- Unbaked puff pastry dough may be wrapped tightly in plastic wrap and stored in the refrigerator for 2 or 3 days or frozen for up to 1 month.
- Baked filled pastries are best enjoyed the day they are made and don't refrigerate well.
- Baked unfilled pastry may be frozen in airtight containers for up to 6 weeks.

forming a
puff pastry *crust*

1. On a parchment paper-lined baking sheet, unfold puff pastry sheet and form a 10-in. square, using a rolling pin if necessary. With a ruler, measure 2 in. from one edge in several places and mark with toothpicks. Using the toothpicks as guides, cut a 10-in. x 2-in. rectangle with a long sharp knife or pastry wheel.

2. From the 10-in. x 2-in. strip, cut two 10-in. x 1/2-in. strips and two 7-in. x 1/2-in. strips. Remove and discard trimmings.

3. Prick the 10-in. x 8-in. pastry base all over with a fork.

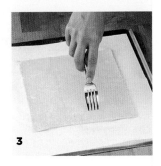

4. Brush water 1/2 in. around edges of pastry base. Place the 10-in. x 1/2-in. and 7-in. x 1/2-in. strips along edges to form sides. Press lightly.

Strawberry Napoleon

PREP: 15 min. + chilling **BAKE:** 30 min.
YIELD: 12 servings

Dean Barns, Farmington, New Mexico

Starting with frozen puff pastry makes the first step in this delightful dessert a snap to do.

>   1 **package (17-1/4 ounces) frozen puff pastry sheets, thawed**
>   3/4 **cup sugar**
>   2 **tablespoons cornstarch**
>   1/4 **teaspoon salt**
> 1-1/2 **cups milk**
>   3 **egg yolks, beaten**
>   1 **tablespoon butter**
>   3 **teaspoons vanilla extract**
> **TOPPING:**
>   2 **cups heavy whipping cream**
>   1/2 **cup confectioners' sugar**
>   1 **teaspoon vanilla extract**
>   3 **pints fresh strawberries, sliced**
> **Additional confectioners' sugar**

1 On a lightly floured surface, roll out each pastry sheet to a 9-in. square. Place on ungreased baking sheets. Bake at 350° for 30 minutes or until golden brown.

2 Meanwhile, in a saucepan, combine the sugar, cornstarch and salt. Gradually add milk until smooth. Cook and stir over medium-high heat until thickened and bubbly. Reduce heat; cook and stir 2 minutes longer. Remove from the heat. Stir a small amount of hot filling into egg yolks; return all to pan, stirring constantly. Bring to a gentle boil; cook and stir 2 minutes longer. Remove from the heat. Gently stir in butter and vanilla. Pour into a bowl; cover surface with plastic wrap. Refrigerate, without stirring, until chilled.

3 For topping, beat cream in a chilled large mixing bowl until it begins to thicken. Add sugar and vanilla; beat until soft peaks form.

4 Place one pastry square on a serving platter. Top with the custard, strawberries, sweetened whipped cream and second pastry. Dust with confectioners' sugar. Refrigerate leftovers.

Blueberry Turnovers

PREP: 45 min. **BAKE:** 15 min. **YIELD:** 8 servings

Taste of Home Test Kitchen

Bursting with juicy blueberries, these pastries are best served the day they're made.

    2   cups fresh *or* frozen blueberries, *divided*
    2   tablespoons sugar
    1   tablespoon cornstarch
    2   teaspoons grated lemon peel
    2   tablespoons butter
    1   package (17.3 ounces) frozen puff
        pastry, thawed
    1   egg
    1   tablespoon water
    1/2 cup confectioners' sugar
    1   tablespoon milk

1 In a saucepan, combine 1/2 cup blueberries, sugar, cornstarch and lemon peel. Mash well with a fork. Bring to a boil over low heat; cook and stir for 2 minutes or until thickened. Remove from the heat. Stir in butter and remaining blueberries.

2 On a lightly floured surface, roll out each pastry sheet into a 12-in. square. Cut each into four squares. Spoon 3 tablespoons of filling into the center of each square; fold diagonally in half and press edges to seal. Place on an ungreased baking sheet.

3 Beat egg and water; brush over pastry. Bake at 450° for 15 minutes or until golden brown. Combine the confectioners' sugar and milk; drizzle over turnovers. Serve warm or at room temperature.

Banana Bundles with Caramel Sauce

PREP: 25 min. **BAKE:** 15 min. **YIELD:** 4 servings

Taste of Home Test Kitchen

These attractive bundles have the fantastic flavor of Bananas Foster. It's best to use firm bananas...look for ones with a bright yellow peel.

CARAMEL SAUCE:
    1   cup packed brown sugar
    1   tablespoon water
    3   tablespoons cold butter, *divided*
    3/4 cup heavy whipping cream
    1/2 teaspoon vanilla extract
Dash salt

BANANA BUNDLES:
    1   cup sliced firm bananas
    1   tablespoon butter, melted
    1   tablespoon brown sugar
    1/4 teaspoon ground ginger
Dash ground cinnamon
    1   sheet frozen puff pastry, thawed
Confectioners' sugar

1 In a heavy saucepan, combine the brown sugar, water and 1 tablespoon butter. Bring to a boil over medium heat without stirring. Cover and cook for 3 minutes. Stir in cream. Cook and stir over medium-high heat just until mixture comes to a boil, about 1 minute. Remove from the heat. Whisk in vanilla and salt. Cut remaining butter into small pieces; whisk into sauce, a few pieces at a time, until smooth. Set aside and keep warm.

2 In a bowl, combine the bananas, butter, brown sugar, ginger and cinnamon. On a lightly floured surface, roll out pastry to a 12-in. square. Cut into four squares; lightly brush edges with water. Place 1/4 cup banana mixture in the center of each square. Bring corners of pastry over filling and twist to form a bundle; pinch edges closed.

3 Place on an ungreased baking sheet. Bake at 400° for 15-18 minutes or until golden brown. Sprinkle with confectioners' sugar; serve warm with caramel sauce.

Heart's Delight Dessert

PREP: 30 min. + chilling **BAKE:** 15 min.
YIELD: 10-12 servings

Lorene Milligan
Chemainus, British Columbia

This lovely and luscious treat will win the hearts of everyone you make it for. If you prefer, skip the step of cutting a heart shape in each pastry sheet and bake them as 12-inch squares.

    1   package (17.3 ounces) frozen puff
        pastry, thawed
    3   cups cold milk
    1   package (5.1 ounces) instant vanilla
        pudding mix
    2   cups heavy whipping cream
    1   teaspoon vanilla extract, *divided*
    1   cup confectioners' sugar
    1   tablespoon water
    1/4 teaspoon almond extract
    1/2 cup semisweet chocolate chips
    1   teaspoon shortening

HEART'S DELIGHT DESSERT

1 On a lightly floured surface, roll each puff pastry sheet into a 12-in. square. Using an 11-in. heart pattern, cut each square into a heart shape. Place on greased baking sheets. Discard trimmings. Bake at 400° for 12-15 minutes or until golden brown. Remove to wire racks to cool.

2 In a bowl, whisk milk and pudding mix for 2 minutes. Let stand for 2 minutes or until soft-set. In a chilled large mixing bowl, beat cream and 1/2 teaspoon vanilla until stiff peaks form. Carefully fold into pudding.

3 Split puff pastry hearts in half. Place one layer on a serving plate. Top with a third of the pudding mixture. Repeat twice. Top with remaining pastry.

4 In a bowl, combine the confectioners' sugar, water, almond extract and remaining vanilla until smooth. Spread over top pastry. In a heavy saucepan or microwave, melt chocolate chips and shortening; stir until smooth. Pipe in diagonal lines in one direction over frosting. Beginning

1 in. from side of heart, use a sharp knife to draw right angles across the piped lines. Refrigerate until set. Refrigerate leftovers.

problem-solving pointers *for Puff Pastry*

DOUGH DID NOT BAKE UP PUFFY

- The cut edges were brushed with an egg wash, preventing the dough from rising.

SIDES DID NOT RISE EVENLY

- Edges were not trimmed with a sharp knife.

DOUGH BAKED UNEVENLY

- Pastry was overhandled before baking.

Phyllo Dough

Cranberry Phyllo Triangles

PREP: 30 min. **BAKE:** 15 min. **YIELD:** 30 triangles

Taste of Home Test Kitchen

It's hard to eat just one of these crispy cranberry-filled triangles. If you prefer, make the chocolate version instead.

- 1/2 **cup chopped fresh *or* frozen cranberries**
- 3 **tablespoons sugar**
- 2 **tablespoons raisins**
- 2 **tablespoons chopped pecans**
- 1 **tablespoon honey**
- 1/4 **teaspoon shredded orange peel**
- 20 **sheets phyllo dough (14 inches x 9 inches)**
- 1/2 **cup butter, melted**

Confectioners' sugar

1 In a saucepan, combine the cranberries, sugar, raisins, pecans, honey and orange peel; bring to a boil. Reduce heat; simmer, uncovered, for 5 minutes, stirring occasionally. Drain and discard any juice. Cool to room temperature.

2 Lightly brush one sheet of phyllo with butter; place another sheet of phyllo on top and brush with butter. Keep remaining phyllo covered with plastic wrap and a damp towel to prevent drying. Cut the two layered sheets into three 14-in. x 3-in. strips. Place a teaspoon of cranberry filling in lower corner on each strip. Fold dough over filling, forming a triangle. Fold triangle up, then fold triangle over, forming another triangle. Continue folding, like a flag, until you come to the end of the strip. Brush end of dough with butter and press onto triangle to seal. Turn triangle and brush top with melted butter. Repeat with remaining strips of dough and remaining sheets of phyllo.

3 Place triangles on a greased baking sheet. Bake at 375° for 15-17 minutes or until golden brown. Cool on a wire rack. Sprinkle with confectioners' sugar.

For Chocolate Phyllo Triangles: In a microwave or heavy saucepan, melt 8 oz. of chopped semisweet chocolate. Stir in 3/4 cup toasted chopped pecans. Place a heaping teaspoonful on phyllo strip. Fold up as directed above.

CRANBERRY PHYLLO TRIANGLES

tips for
working with
& storing *phyllo dough*

Phyllo (pronounced FEE-lo) is a tissue-thin dough, generally sold in the freezer section of grocery stores. Phyllo dough is liberally basted with melted butter between each sheet so that it bakes up crisp and flaky. Phyllo dough is used for desserts, appetizers and savory main dishes. Follow these pointers for perfect phyllo:

- Thaw phyllo according to package directions. Always have all the other ingredients assembled and ready to go before unwrapping the dough.

- Because phyllo is thin, fragile and tears easily, work on a smooth dry surface.

- Phyllo dries out quickly. So once the dough is unwrapped and unrolled, cover it with plastic wrap, then a damp kitchen towel. Work with one sheet at a time and keep the other sheets covered.

- Preheat the oven as directed.

- Refrigerate unopened phyllo dough for up to 3 weeks or freeze for up to 3 months. Opened dough can be refrigerated for up to 3 days. Baked phyllo should be stored in an airtight container for up to 3 days or frozen for up to 3 months.

making *phyllo triangles*

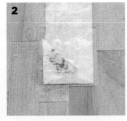

1. Place 1 teaspoon of filling in lower corner on each strip. Fold dough over filling, forming a triangle.

2. Fold triangle up.

3. Fold triangle over, forming another triangle.

4. Continue folding like a flag, until you come to the end of the strip. Brush end of dough with melted butter and press onto triangle to seal. Turn triangle and brush top with melted butter.

Chocolate Almond Mousse Napoleons

PREP/TOTAL TIME: 30 min. + chilling **YIELD:** 8 servings

Taste of Home Test Kitchen

The chocolate almond mousse is creamy and delicious. You can also serve it in parfait glasses with a crisp cookie.

- 6 **sheets phyllo dough (14 inches x 9 inches)**
- 1/4 **cup butter, melted**
- 2 **tablespoons sugar**

MOUSSE:
- 2 **cups heavy whipping cream**
- 1 **cup (6 ounces) semisweet chocolate chips**
- 1/4 **teaspoon almond extract**

GLAZE:
- 1 **cup confectioners' sugar**
- 1/4 **teaspoon vanilla extract**

Dash salt
- 4 **to 5 teaspoons half-and-half cream**
- 3 **tablespoons semisweet chocolate chips, melted**

1 Place one phyllo sheet on a work surface; keep remaining phyllo sheets covered with plastic wrap and a damp towel. Brush phyllo with melted butter; sprinkle with 1 teaspoon sugar.

Top with second phyllo sheet. Brush with butter; sprinkle with 1 teaspoon sugar. Repeat with third phyllo sheet, butter and sugar. Cut stack into twelve 3-in. squares. Transfer stacks to a greased baking sheet; place about 1 in. apart. Repeat with remaining three phyllo sheets, butter and sugar. Bake at 350° for 8-9 minutes or until golden brown, watching carefully. Cool on wire racks.

2 For mousse, heat heavy cream in a small saucepan over medium heat until cream begins to simmer, about 180°. Remove from the heat. Whisk in chocolate and extract until smooth. Transfer to a mixing bowl and refrigerate until chilled. Beat cream mixture until soft peaks form. Refrigerate until serving.

3 For glaze, combine the confectioners' sugar, vanilla and salt. Add enough half-and-half to achieve a spreading consistency. Spread over eight squares of phyllo. Drizzle with melted chocolate.

4 To serve, spread about 1/4 cup mousse over a square of phyllo. Add a second phyllo square and more mousse. Top with one of the glazed phyllo squares. Repeat with remaining phyllo, mousse and glazed phyllo. Serve immediately.

HAZELNUT APRICOT STRUDEL

Hazelnut Apricot Strudel

PREP: 30 min. + cooling **BAKE:** 15 min. + cooling
YIELD: 8 servings

Taste of Home Test Kitchen

Did you know that strudel is the German word for whirlpool? The swirling layers of this filled and rolled dessert likely led to its unusual name.

- 1 package (6 ounces) dried apricots, chopped
- 1/4 cup sugar
- 1 teaspoon orange peel
- 1/2 cup orange juice
- 1/4 cup water
- 1/3 cup chopped hazelnuts
- 6 sheets phyllo dough (14 inches x 9 inches)
- 2 tablespoons butter, melted
- 1/3 cup graham cracker crumbs (about 5 squares)

1 In a saucepan, combine the apricots, sugar and orange peel. Stir in orange juice and water. Bring to a boil. Reduce heat; simmer, uncovered, for 15 minutes or until liquid is absorbed, stirring occasionally. Remove from the heat; cool to room temperature. Set aside 1 tablespoon nuts; toast the remaining nuts. Stir toasted nuts into apricot mixture.

making *strudel*

1. Cover a smooth dry work surface with a piece of plastic wrap that is larger than the phyllo sheets. Place first sheet of phyllo on the plastic wrap. Working quickly, layer the phyllo sheets over each other, brushing with butter between each sheet and sprinkling with cracker crumbs.

2. Carefully spread filling to within 1 in. of edges.

3. Fold one long side over the filling, then the two short sides. Using the plastic wrap to help lift the remaining long side, roll up jelly-roll style.

4. Use the plastic wrap to help transfer strudel to greased baking sheet. Roll strudel off of plastic wrap and center on baking sheet. Discard plastic wrap.

2 Cover a work surface with a piece of plastic wrap larger than the phyllo sheet. Place one sheet of phyllo on the plastic wrap. Keep remaining phyllo sheets covered with plastic wrap and a damp towel. Working quickly, layer the phyllo sheets over each other, brushing each sheet with butter and sprinkling with a tablespoon of crumbs. Carefully spread apricot filling along one long edge to within 1 in. of short sides. Fold the two short sides over filling. Using the plastic wrap to help lift one long side, roll up jelly-roll style.

3 Use the plastic wrap to help transfer strudel to a greased baking sheet; discard plastic wrap. Brush top with butter; score top lightly at 1-1/2-in. intervals. Sprinkle with reserved nuts. Bake at 375° for 15-18 minutes or until golden brown. Cool on a wire rack. Slice at scored marks.

Baklava

PREP: 30 min. **BAKE:** 40 min. **YIELD:** 4 dozen

Judy Losecco, Buffalo, New York

Baklava is a traditional Middle Eastern pastry made with phyllo dough, nuts and honey. This dessert is very rich, so one pan goes a long way.

1-1/2	pounds finely chopped walnuts
1/2	cup sugar
1/2	teaspoon ground cinnamon
1/8	teaspoon ground cloves
1	pound butter, melted, *divided*
2	packages (16 ounces *each*, 18-inch x 14-inch sheet size) phyllo dough

SYRUP:

2	cups sugar
2	cups water
1	cup honey
1	tablespoon grated lemon *or* orange peel

1 In a small bowl, combine the walnuts, sugar, cinnamon and cloves; set aside. Brush a 15-in. x 10-in. x 1-in. baking pan with some of the butter. Unroll each package of phyllo sheets; trim each stack to fit into pan. Cover dough with plastic wrap and a damp cloth while assembling. Place one sheet of phyllo in pan; brush with butter. Repeat 14 times.

2 Spread with 2 cups walnut mixture. Layer with five sheets of phyllo, brushing with butter between each. Spread with remaining walnut mixture. Top with one sheet of phyllo; brush with butter. Repeat 14 times. Cut into 2-1/2-in. squares; cut each square in half diagonally. Brush remaining butter over top. Bake at 350° for 40-45 minutes or until golden brown.

3 In a large saucepan, bring the syrup ingredients to a boil. Reduce heat; simmer for 10 minutes. Strain and discard peel; cool to lukewarm. Pour over warm baklava.

Lime Mousse in Phyllo Cups

PREP: 25 min. **BAKE:** 10 min. **YIELD:** 6 servings

Taste of Home Test Kitchen

Lime gives a tart refreshing flavor to sweetened whipped cream. You can also use the lime mousse to fill individual purchased tart cups.

12	sheets phyllo dough (14 inches x 9 inches)
3	tablespoons butter, melted
1	cup heavy whipping cream
2	tablespoons sugar
2	tablespoons lime juice
1-1/2	teaspoons grated lime peel
1	drop green food coloring, optional

Fresh lime slices, optional

1 Place two sheets of phyllo dough on top of each other. Keep remaining phyllo covered with plastic wrap and a damp towel to prevent drying. Cut layered sheets in half widthwise. Brush top sheet of each with butter. Lightly press one stack into a 6-oz. custard cup coated with nonstick cooking spray. Lightly press second stack on top. Repeat with five more cups.

2 Bake at 375° for 8-10 minutes or until golden brown. Cool for 5 minutes before carefully removing pastry to a wire rack to cool completely.

3 For mousse, beat cream in a chilled small mixing bowl until thickened. Add the sugar, lime juice, lime peel and food coloring if desired; beat until soft peaks form. Just before serving, fill phyllo cups with mousse. Garnish with lime slices if desired.

problem-solving **pointers** *for Phyllo Dough*

DOUGH IS CRUMBLY

- The dough was not thawed completely at room temperature before using.
- The dough was kept in the freezer too long.

DOUGH IS BRITTLE

- The dough became dry. Be sure to properly keep it covered. (See Tips for Working with & Storing Phyllo Dough on page 250.)

Pastries

Raspberry Custard Kuchen

PREP: 15 min. **BAKE:** 40 min. **YIELD:** 10-12 servings

Virginia Arndt, Sequim, Washington

Kuchen is German for cake and usually refers to a sweet yeast dough coffee cake, often containing fruit and nuts. It can be served for breakfast or as a special dessert.

- 1-1/2 cups all-purpose flour, *divided*
- 1/2 teaspoon salt
- 1/2 cup cold butter
- 2 tablespoons heavy whipping cream
- 1/2 cup sugar

FILLING:
- 3 cups fresh raspberries
- 1 cup sugar
- 1 tablespoon all-purpose flour
- 2 eggs, beaten
- 1 cup heavy whipping cream
- 1 teaspoon vanilla extract

1 In a bowl, combine 1 cup flour and salt; cut in butter until mixture resembles coarse crumbs. Stir in cream. Pat into a greased 13-in. x 9-in. x 2-in. baking pan. Combine the sugar and remaining flour; sprinkle over crust.

2 Arrange raspberries over crust. In a large bowl, combine sugar and flour. Stir in the eggs, cream and vanilla; pour over berries. Bake at 375° for 40-45 minutes or until lightly browned. Serve warm or chilled. Store in the refrigerator.

RASPBERRY CUSTARD KUCHEN

Summer Dessert Pizza

PREP: 35 min. + chilling **BAKE:** 15 min. + cooling
YIELD: 12-16 servings

Ida Ruth Wenger, Harrisonburg, Virginia

This colorful dessert is especially refreshing during the hot summer months.

- 1/4 cup butter, softened
- 1/2 cup sugar
- 1 egg
- 1/4 teaspoon lemon extract
- 1/4 teaspoon vanilla extract
- 1-1/4 cups all-purpose flour
- 1/4 teaspoon baking powder
- 1/4 teaspoon baking soda
- 1/4 teaspoon salt

GLAZE:
- 1/4 cup sugar
- 2 teaspoons cornstarch
- 1/4 cup water
- 1/4 cup orange juice

TOPPING:
- 4 ounces cream cheese, softened
- 1/4 cup confectioners' sugar
- 1 cup whipped topping
- 1 firm banana, sliced
- 1 cup sliced fresh strawberries
- 1 can (8 ounces) mandarin oranges, drained
- 2 kiwifruit, peeled and thinly sliced
- 1/3 cup fresh blueberries

1 In a small mixing bowl, cream butter and sugar until light and fluffy. Beat in egg and extracts. Combine the flour, baking powder, baking soda and salt; add to creamed mixture and beat well. Cover and refrigerate for 30 minutes.

2 Press dough into a greased 12-in. or 14-in. pizza pan. Bake at 350° for 12-14 minutes or until light golden brown. Cool completely on a wire rack.

3 For glaze, combine sugar and cornstarch in a small saucepan. Stir in the water and orange juice until smooth. Bring to a boil; cook and stir for 1-2 minutes or until thickened. Cool to room temperature, about 30 minutes.

4 For topping, in a small mixing bowl, beat cream cheese and confectioners' sugar until smooth. Add whipped topping; mix well. Spread over crust. Arrange fruit on top. Brush glaze over fruit. Store in the refrigerator.

Super Strawberry Shortcake

PREP: 20 min. **BAKE:** 15 min. + cooling
YIELD: 8 servings

Renee Bisch, Wellesley, Ontario

Yum! is what people will say when you set this dessert on the table. It's fun to serve since it's attractive, not overly sweet and bursting with flavor.

- 1 **quart fresh strawberries, sliced**
- 1 **to 2 tablespoons sugar**

SHORTCAKE:
- 1-3/4 **cups all-purpose flour**
- 2 **tablespoons sugar**
- 1 **teaspoon baking powder**
- 1/2 **teaspoon baking soda**
- 1/2 **teaspoon salt**
- 1/4 **cup cold butter**
- 1 **egg**
- 3/4 **cup sour cream**

TOPPING:
- 1 **cup heavy whipping cream**
- 1 **to 2 tablespoons sugar**
- 1 **teaspoon vanilla extract**

1 In a large bowl, combine the strawberries and sugar; set aside. For shortcake, in another bowl, combine the flour, sugar, baking powder, baking soda and salt; cut in the butter until mixture resembles coarse crumbs.

2 In a small bowl, beat egg; add sour cream. Stir into the crumb mixture just until moistened. Knead dough on a floured surface 25 times or until smooth.

3 Roll out into a 7-1/2-in. circle on a lightly greased baking sheet. Cut a 2-in. hole in center to form a ring. Bake at 425° for 12-14 minutes or until golden brown. Remove from baking sheet to a wire rack to cool completely.

4 For topping, beat cream in a chilled small mixing bowl until it begins to thicken. Add sugar and vanilla; beat until stiff peaks form.

5 Just before serving, split shortcake into two horizontal layers. Spoon juice from berries over bottom layer. Spoon half of berries over juice. Spread with half of the topping. Cover with the top cake layer, then spread with remaining topping and berries. Cut into wedges.

CHEESE DANISH

Cookie Sheet Apple Pie

PREP: 20 min. + chilling BAKE: 40 min.
YIELD: 16-20 servings

Bertha Jeffries, Great Falls, Montana

When there's a large crowd to be fed, this dessert is a real time-saver. It serves more than a traditional pie with about the same amount of effort.

3-3/4   cups all-purpose flour
1-1/2   teaspoons salt
  3/4   cup shortening
    3   eggs, lightly beaten
  1/3   cup milk
    8   cups sliced peeled tart apples (7 to 8 large)
1-1/2   cups sugar
    1   cup crushed cornflakes
    1   teaspoon ground cinnamon
  1/2   teaspoon ground nutmeg
    1   egg white, beaten

1 In a bowl, combine the flour and salt. Cut in shortening until mixture resembles coarse crumbs. Combine eggs and milk; add to crumb mixture, tossing with a fork until dough forms a ball. Cover and refrigerate for 20 minutes.

2 Divide dough in half so that one piece is slightly larger than the other. On a lightly floured surface, roll out large half to fit the bottom and sides of a greased 15-in. x 10-in. x 1-in. baking pan. Arrange apples over crust. Combine the sugar, cornflakes, cinnamon and nutmeg; sprinkle over apples.

3 Roll out remaining dough to fit top of pan; place over apples. Seal edges; cut slits in top. Brush with egg white. Bake at 400° for 15 minutes. Reduce heat to 350°; bake 25-30 minutes longer or until golden.

Cheese Danish

PREP/TOTAL TIME: 30 min. YIELD: 2 servings

**Mary Margaret Merritt
Washington Court House, Ohio**

This sweet treat is delicious and prep time is minimal. The recipe can easily be doubled.

  1   tube (4 ounces) refrigerated crescent rolls
  1   package (3 ounces) cream cheese, softened
1/4   cup sugar
1/4   teaspoon vanilla extract
  1   teaspoon butter, melted
Cinnamon-sugar

1 Unroll crescent roll dough and separate into two rectangles; place on an ungreased baking sheet. Press perforations together.

2 In a small mixing bowl, beat cream cheese, sugar and vanilla until smooth. Spread over half of each rectangle; fold dough over filling and pinch to seal. Brush with butter; sprinkle with cinnamon-sugar. Bake at 350° for 15-20 minutes or until golden brown.

Quick Cherry Turnovers

PREP/TOTAL TIME: 20 min. YIELD: 4 servings

Elleen Oberrueter, Danbury, Iowa

Refrigerated crescent rolls help you make these fruit-filled pastries in a hurry. Feel free to experiment with other pie fillings besides cherry.

  1   tube (8 ounces) refrigerated crescent rolls
  1   cup cherry pie filling
1/2   cup confectioners' sugar
  1   to 2 tablespoons milk

1 Unroll crescent roll dough and separate into four squares; place on an ungreased baking sheet. Press seams and perforations together. Spoon 1/4 cup pie filling in one corner of each square. Fold to make triangles; pinch to seal.

2 Bake at 375° for 10-12 minutes or until golden. Combine sugar and enough milk to achieve drizzling consistency. Drizzle over turnovers; serve warm.

Ladyfingers

PREP: 25 min. **BAKE:** 15 min. per batch
YIELD: about 2 dozen

Mary Beth de Ribeaux
Gaithersburg, Maryland

These light sponge cakes can be served with ice cream or can be used to make tiramisu.

    3   **eggs,** *separated*
  1/3   **cup sugar**
    1   **teaspoon almond extract**
  1/3   **cup all-purpose flour**
Dash salt
  1/2   **cup confectioners' sugar**

1 Let eggs stand at room temperature for 30 minutes. Grease and lightly flour two baking sheets; set aside. In a large mixing bowl, beat egg yolks on high speed for 3 minutes. Gradually add sugar, beating until thick and pale yellow. Beat in extract. Gradually add flour and salt, beating until well blended. In a small mixing bowl and with clean beaters, beat egg whites on high speed until soft peaks form. Fold into yolk mixture.

2 Cut a 1/2-in. hole in a corner of a heavy-duty plastic bag, or use a pastry bag with round tip #808. Fill bag with batter. Form 4-in.-long finger shapes 1 in. apart on prepared baking sheets. Dust with confectioners' sugar. Bake at 350° for 12-15 minutes or until golden. Remove to wire racks to cool.

Fresh Plum Kuchen

PREP: 20 min. **BAKE:** 40 min. + chilling
YIELD: 10-12 servings

Anna Daley
Montague, Prince Edward Island

In late summer when plums are in season, this tender fruit-topped cake is delectable! For variety, you can substitute fresh pears or apples instead.

  1/4   **cup butter, softened**
  3/4   **cup sugar**
    2   **eggs**
    1   **cup all-purpose flour**
    1   **teaspoon baking powder**
  1/4   **cup milk**
    1   **teaspoon grated lemon peel**
    2   **cups sliced fresh plums (about 4 medium)**
  1/2   **cup packed brown sugar**
    1   **teaspoon ground cinnamon**

1 In a small mixing bowl, cream butter and sugar until light and fluffy. Beat in eggs. Combine flour and baking powder; add to the creamed mixture alternately with milk, beating well after each addition. Add lemon peel. Pour into a greased 10-in. springform pan. Arrange plums on top, overlapping slices. Gently press into batter. Sprinkle with brown sugar and cinnamon.

2 Place pan on a baking sheet. Bake at 350° for 40-50 minutes or until top is golden and a toothpick inserted near the center comes out clean. Cool for 10 minutes. Run a knife around edge of pan; remove sides. Cool on a wire rack.

FRESH PLUM KUCHEN

Almond Rhubarb Pastry

PREP: 40 min. **BAKE:** 50 min. **YIELD:** 16-20 servings

Lois Dyck, Coaldale, Alberta

Classic desserts like this stand the test of time. The rosy rhubarb filling contrasts beautifully with the flakey, golden brown crust.

1-1/2	cups sugar
1/4	cup quick-cooking tapioca
6	cups chopped fresh *or* frozen rhubarb

PASTRY:

4	cups all-purpose flour
4	teaspoons baking powder
1-1/4	teaspoons salt
1-1/4	cups shortening
3	eggs, beaten
1/3	to 1/2 cup milk, *divided*

TOPPING:

1/2	cup butter
3/4	cup sugar
2	tablespoons milk
1/2	teaspoon vanilla extract
1	cup slivered almonds

1 In a large bowl, combine the sugar, tapioca and rhubarb; let stand for 15 minutes. In a large bowl, combine the flour, baking powder and salt; cut in shortening until mixture resembles coarse crumbs. Combine the eggs and 1/3 cup milk; add to crumb mixture, tossing with a fork until dough forms a ball. Add some or all of remaining milk if necessary.

2 Divide dough in half so that one piece is slightly larger than the other. On a lightly floured surface, roll out large half into a 17-in. x 12-in. rectangle. Transfer to a greased 15-in. x 10-in. x 1-in. baking pan.

3 Spoon rhubarb filling into crust. Roll out remaining dough into a 15-in. x 10-in. rectangle. Place over filling. Fold bottom edge of dough over top layer of dough; press edges together to seal.

4 For topping, melt butter in a small saucepan; add sugar and milk. Bring to a gentle boil; cook and stir 2-3 minutes longer or until thickened. Remove from the heat; stir in vanilla. Spread over pastry. Sprinkle almonds on top. Bake at 400° for 20 minutes. Reduce heat to 325°; bake 20-25 minutes longer or until golden brown. Serve warm or cold.

Editor's Note: If using frozen rhubarb, measure rhubarb while still frozen, then thaw completely. Drain in a colander, but do not press liquid out.

Peach Kuchen

PREP: 20 min. **BAKE:** 45 min. **YIELD:** 8-10 servings

Barbara White, Cross Plains, Wisconsin

For this not-too-sweet dessert, you can customize it by using virtually any of your favorite fruits. It's great served warm with a dollop of whipped cream.

CRUST:

1	cup all-purpose flour
1/4	cup confectioners' sugar
1/4	teaspoon salt
1/2	cup cold butter

FILLING:

2	cans (one 29 ounces, one 15-1/4 ounces) sliced peaches, drained
2	eggs
1	cup sugar
1/4	teaspoon salt
3	tablespoons all-purpose flour
1	cup (8 ounces) sour cream

1 In a small bowl, combine the flour, confectioners' sugar and salt. Cut in butter until mixture resembles coarse crumbs. Pat lightly into an ungreased 11-in. x 7-in. x 2-in. baking dish.

2 Arrange peaches over the crust; set aside. In another bowl, beat eggs. Whisk in the sugar, salt, flour and sour cream until mixture is smooth. Pour over the peaches.

3 Bake at 450° for 10 minutes. Reduce heat to 325°; bake 35 minutes longer or until center is set. Serve warm or chilled. Store in the refrigerator.

Meringue Desserts

Holiday Meringue Dessert

PREP: 15 min. + standing **BAKE:** 35 min. + cooling
YIELD: 2 servings

Catherine Morrison, Newport, Pennsylvania

This recipe is perfect for two. For variety, use fresh fruit or lemon pudding for the filling.

- 1 **egg white**
- 1/8 **teaspoon cream of tartar**
- 1/8 **teaspoon almond extract**
- **Dash salt**
- 1/3 **cup sugar**
- 2 **scoops chocolate ice cream**
- **Chocolate sauce**
- 2 **tablespoons flaked coconut, toasted**
- **Maraschino cherries**

1 Place egg white in a mixing bowl and let stand at room temperature for 30 minutes. Add the cream of tartar, extract and salt. Beat on medium speed until soft peaks form. Gradually beat in sugar, 1 tablespoon at a time, on high until stiff glossy peaks form and sugar is dissolved.

2 Cover a baking sheet with parchment paper. Spoon the egg mixture into two mounds on paper. Using the back of a spoon, build up the edges slightly. Bake at 250° for 35 minutes. Turn off oven and do not open door; let shells dry in the oven for at least 1 hour.

3 To serve, fill shells with ice cream; top with chocolate sauce, coconut and cherries.

types of *meringue*

Meringue is a sweetened egg white foam that can be shaped into cups to hold fruit or mousse or made into a golden crown on Baked Alaska.

Depending on the amount of sugar beaten into the egg whites, meringue is classified as a soft meringue (as used for Baked Alaska or meringue-topped pies) or hard meringue (as used for meringue shells or cookies). For more information on making meringues, see Tips for Making Meringue on page 221.

HOLIDAY MERINGUE DESSERT

LEMON SCHAUM TORTE

Lemon Schaum Torte

PREP: 50 min. + chilling **BAKE:** 1 hour + standing
YIELD: 12-15 servings

Cindy Steffen, Cedarburg, Wisconsin

Lemon pairs well with the fluffy meringue and sweetened whipped cream. This version of a classic Austrian dessert conveniently bakes in a 13-inch x 9-inch pan.

- 6 **egg whites**
- 1 **teaspoon vanilla extract**
- 1/8 **teaspoon cream of tartar**
- 2 **cups sugar,** *divided*
- 9 **egg yolks**
- 1/2 **cup lemon juice**
- 1 **tablespoon grated lemon peel**
- 4 **cups heavy whipping cream**
- 2/3 **cup confectioners' sugar**

Ground cinnamon

1 Place egg whites in a large mixing bowl and let stand at room temperature for 30 minutes. Add vanilla and cream of tartar. Beat on medium speed until soft peaks form. Gradually beat in 1 cup sugar, 2 tablespoons at a time, on high until stiff glossy peaks form and sugar is dissolved.

2 Spread meringue over the bottom and up the sides of a greased 13-in. x 9-in. x 2-in. baking dish. Bake at 275° for 1 hour. Turn off oven and do not open door; let meringue dry in oven for at least 1 hour. Remove from the oven; cool on a wire rack.

3 In the top of a double boiler, beat egg yolks and remaining sugar. Stir in lemon juice and peel. Cook and stir over simmering water for 15 minutes or until mixture thickens and reaches 160°. Cover and refrigerate until cool.

4 In a chilled mixing bowl, beat cream until it begins to thicken. Add confectioners' sugar; beat until stiff peaks form. Spread half over meringue; cover with lemon mixture. Top with remaining cream mixture. Sprinkle with cinnamon. Chill overnight.

makeshift *double boiler*

If you don't have a double boiler, you can create your own using a metal mixing bowl and a saucepan. The water in the saucepan should not touch the bottom of the bowl.

Brownie Baked Alaska

PREP: 40 min. + freezing **BAKE:** 25 min. + cooling
YIELD: 12 servings

Carol Twardzik, Spy Hill, Saskatchewan

No one can resist the combination of brownies and two kinds of ice cream with a light meringue topping in this impressive dessert.

2 squares (1 ounce *each*) unsweetened chocolate
1/2 cup shortening
1 cup sugar
1 teaspoon vanilla extract
2 eggs
3/4 cup all-purpose flour
1/2 teaspoon baking powder
1/2 teaspoon salt
1 cup chopped walnuts, optional
1 quart strawberry ice cream, slightly softened
1 quart vanilla ice cream, slightly softened

MERINGUE:
5 egg whites
2/3 cup sugar
1/2 teaspoon cream of tartar

1 In a large saucepan, melt the chocolate and shortening; remove from the heat. Stir in sugar and vanilla. Add eggs, one at a time, beating well after each addition. Combine the flour, baking powder and salt; stir into chocolate mixture. Add nuts if desired. Spread into a greased 9-in. round baking pan.

2 Bake at 350° for 25-30 minutes or until a toothpick inserted near the center comes out with moist crumbs (do not overbake). Cool for 10 minutes before removing from pan to a wire rack to cool completely.

BROWNIE BAKED ALASKA

3 Line an 8-in. or 9-in. round bowl (1-1/2 qts.) with foil. Quickly spread strawberry ice cream over bottom and up sides of bowl, leaving center hollow; cover and freeze for 30 minutes. Pack vanilla ice cream into center; cover and freeze.

4 To assemble, place the brownie base on a 10-in. ovenproof serving plate. Unmold ice cream onto brownie. Return to freezer while preparing meringue.

5 In a heavy saucepan or double boiler over simmering water, combine the eggs whites, sugar and cream of tartar. Heat over low heat while beating egg white mixture with a portable mixer on low speed for 1 minute, scraping down sides of bowl. Continue beating until egg mixture reaches 160°. Remove from the heat. Beat on high speed until stiff peaks form.

6 Quickly spread over ice cream and brownie. Bake at 500° for 2-5 minutes or until meringue is lightly browned. (Or return to freezer until ready to bake.) Transfer to a plate; serve immediately.

making *a meringue for baked alaska*

1. In a double boiler over simmering water, beat egg whites and cream of tartar with a portable mixer on low speed for 1 minute.

2. Continue beating on low speed until meringue reaches 160°, about 12 minutes. Remove from the heat; add vanilla. Beat on high speed until stiff peaks form.

3. Quickly spread over ice cream, sealing meringue to cake layer.

Chocolate-Filled Meringue Cups

PREP: 20 min. + standing **BAKE:** 35 min. + cooling
YIELD: 6 servings

Mary Lou Wayman, Salt Lake City, Utah

These lovely delicate meringue shells are easy to make, and their crisp texture is a perfect complement to the creamy chocolate filling. Trace circles onto the parchment paper to use as a guide when making meringue cups.

> 2　**egg whites**
> 1/4　**teaspoon cream of tartar**
> 1/4　**teaspoon vanilla extract**
> **Dash salt**
> 1/2　**cup sugar**
> **FILLING:**
> 1　**package (8 ounces) cream cheese,**
> 　**softened**
> 1　**cup confectioners' sugar**
> 1/4　**cup baking cocoa**
> 1　**cup whipped topping**
> 1　**package (10 ounces) frozen sweetened**
> 　**sliced strawberries, thawed**

1 Place egg whites in a small mixing bowl; let stand at room temperature for 30 minutes. Add the cream of tartar, vanilla and salt; beat on medium speed until soft peaks form. Gradually beat in sugar, 1 tablespoon at a time, on high until stiff glossy peaks form and sugar is dissolved.

2 Line a baking sheet with parchment paper. Spoon meringue into six mounds on paper. Using the back of a spoon, shape into 3-in. cups. Bake at 250° for 35 minutes. Turn off oven and do not open door; let meringues dry in oven for 1 hour. Cool on baking sheet on a wire rack.

3 For filling, in a mixing bowl, beat cream cheese, confectioners' sugar and cocoa until smooth and fluffy. Fold in whipped topping. Place strawberries in a blender or food processor; cover and process until pureed. To serve, spoon filling into meringue shells. Top with strawberry sauce.

Strawberry Schaum Torte

PREP: 25 min. **BAKE:** 45 min. + cooling
YIELD: 12 servings

Geraldine Sauke, Alberta Lea, Minnesota

This schaum torte features a quick-to-fix strawberry gelatin filling.

> 6　**egg whites**
> 2　**teaspoons water**
> 2　**teaspoons white vinegar**
> 2　**teaspoons vanilla extract**
> 1　**teaspoon baking powder**

CHOCOLATE-FILLED MERINGUE CUPS

1/4   teaspoon salt
2   cups sugar

FILLING:
1   package (3 ounces) strawberry gelatin
1/2   cup boiling water
1   cup fresh *or* frozen sliced strawberries
1   teaspoon lemon juice

Dash salt
1-1/2   cups whipped cream

1 Place egg whites in a large mixing bowl and let stand at room temperature for 30 minutes. Add the water, vinegar, vanilla, baking powder and salt. Beat on medium speed until soft peaks form. Gradually beat in sugar, 2 tablespoons at a time, on high until stiff glossy peaks form and sugar is dissolved.

2 Spread evenly into a greased 13-in. x 9-in. x 2-in. baking pan. Bake at 300° for 45 minutes. Turn off oven and do not open door; let crust dry in oven overnight.

3 For filling, dissolve gelatin in boiling water in a bowl. Stir in the strawberries, lemon juice and salt (mixture will thicken quickly). Fold in cream. Spread over crust. Store in the refrigerator.

problem-solving **pointers** *for Meringue*

MERINGUE DID NOT REACH FULL VOLUME

- The egg whites were beaten when cold. They should stand at room temperature for 30 minutes before beating.
- Next time, make sure there are no egg yolks in with the whites and beat in a grease-free bowl.

BEADS FORMED ON THE TOP OF THE MERINGUE AND/OR THE MERINGUE IS STICKY

- Meringue was made on a humid or rainy day.
- Meringue was underbaked or overbaked.
- Meringue was baked at too high a temperature.

MERINGUE HAS SHRUNK DURING BAKING

- Seal meringue to edges of the cake or pie before baking.

MERINGUE HAS A SOFT TEXTURE

- Meringue was made on a humid or rainy day.
- Not enough sugar was used. Be sure to use 2 to 4 tablespoons of sugar for each egg white.

making *meringue cups*

1. In a mixing bowl, beat egg whites, cream of tartar, vanilla and salt on medium speed until the egg whites begin to increase in volume and soft peaks form.
   To test for soft peaks, lift the beaters from the whites, and the peaks of egg white should curl down.

2. Add sugar, 1 tablespoon at a time, beating on high speed until stiff peaks form and sugar is dissolved.
   To test for stiff peaks, lift the beaters from the whites, and the peaks of egg white should stand straight up; if you tilt the bowl, the whites should not slide around. Sugar is dissolved when mixture feels silky-smooth between your fingers.

3. Line a baking sheet with parchment paper. Drop meringue into mounds on the paper. Using the back of a spoon, make an indentation in the center of each mound to form a 3-in. cup.

4. Bake as recipe directs. After drying in the oven for 1 hour, remove meringues and cool completely on baking sheet. Carefully remove meringues from paper and store in an airtight container at room temperature for up to 2 days.

Special Souffles

Chocolate Souffle

PREP: 25 min. **BAKE:** 1 hour **YIELD:** 6 servings

Carol Ice, Burlingham, New York

Every bite of this creamy souffle will melt in your mouth. The sweetened cream sauce balances the richness of the chocolate.

- 2 **squares (1 ounce *each*) unsweetened chocolate**
- 1/4 **cup butter**
- 5 **tablespoons all-purpose flour**
- 1/3 **cup plus 1 teaspoon sugar, *divided***
- 1/4 **teaspoon salt**
- 1 **cup milk**
- 3 **eggs, *separated***
- 1 **teaspoon vanilla extract**
- 1/4 **teaspoon almond extract**

TOPPING:
- 1 **cup heavy whipping cream**
- 1/4 **cup confectioners' sugar**
- 1/4 **teaspoon vanilla extract**

Baking cocoa *or* ground cinnamon, optional

1 In a heavy saucepan, melt chocolate and butter over low heat, stirring until smooth. In a small bowl, combine the flour, 1/3 cup sugar and salt. Add milk; stir into the melted chocolate. Cook and stir over medium heat until thickened and bubbly. Reduce heat; cook and stir 2 minutes longer. Remove from the heat.

2 In a small bowl, beat egg yolks. Stir a small amount of hot filling into yolks; return all to the pan, stirring constantly. Add extracts.

3 In a small mixing bowl and with clean beaters, beat egg whites on medium speed until soft peaks form. Gradually beat in remaining sugar on high until

stiff peaks form. With a spatula, stir a fourth of the egg whites into chocolate batter until no white streaks remain, then fold in remaining egg whites.

4 Grease the bottom of a 1-1/2-qt. baking dish; add souffle batter. Place dish in a larger pan. Fill large pan with hot water to a depth of 1 in. Bake at 325° for 1 hour or until a knife inserted near the center comes out clean.

5 For topping, beat the cream in a chilled small mixing bowl until it begins to thicken. Add confectioners' sugar and vanilla; beat until soft peaks form. Serve souffle warm with a dollop of topping. Sprinkle with cocoa or cinnamon if desired.

secrets for successful *souffles*

Souffles are made from an egg yolk-based custard that is lightened with beaten egg whites. This mixture bakes up into a light airy creation that makes an impressive dessert.

The following guidelines help ensure success when baking a souffle:

- Separate eggs (see page 14) when they are cold. Let the separated eggs or egg whites stand at room temperature for 30 minutes before beating.

- Make sure there are no specks of egg yolk in the white.

- Before beating egg whites, remove all fat residue from your mixing bowl and beaters by washing them thoroughly in hot soapy water and drying with a clean kitchen towel. Use metal or glass mixing bowls. Plastic bowls, even freshly washed and dried ones, may have an oily film on them.

- To lighten the batter, fold about a third of the beaten egg whites into the custard base. Then fold in the remaining egg whites.

- Spoon or pour custard into baking dish. Souffles rise two to three times the volume of the batter. A four-egg souffle should be baked in a 1-1/2- to 2-qt. dish.

- Bake on the middle rack of a preheated oven according to recipe directions.

- A souffle is done when the top feels firm and a knife inserted near the center comes out clean.

- A souffle will fall slightly once it's removed from the oven. For best results, serve the souffle immediately.

- An unbaked souffle may be refrigerated up to 2 hours before baking or frozen for 3 weeks. Thaw a frozen souffle in the refrigerator before baking. A frozen souffle will not bake up as high as a freshly prepared souffle.

CHOCOLATE SOUFFLE

Baked Orange Souffle

PREP: 50 min. **BAKE:** 25 min. **YIELD:** 6-8 servings

Taste of Home Test Kitchen

This souffle with a distinctive orange flavor makes a light ending to any meal.

- 1 **teaspoon plus 2 tablespoons butter,** *divided*
- 2 **tablespoons plus 1/2 cup sugar,** *divided*
- 5 **tablespoons all-purpose flour**
- 1/4 **teaspoon salt**
- 1 **cup milk**
- 4 **eggs,** *separated*
- 2 **tablespoons grated orange peel**
- 1 **to 1-1/4 teaspoons orange extract**
- 1/8 **teaspoon cream of tartar**

1 Use 1 teaspoon butter to grease bottom and sides of a 6-cup souffle dish. Thoroughly coat inside of dish with 2 tablespoons sugar; tap out excess sugar and discard.

2 In a saucepan, combine flour, salt and 1/4 cup sugar; gradually whisk in milk until smooth. Bring to a boil over medium heat; cook and stir for 2 minutes or until thickened. Transfer to a bowl; whisk in egg yolks, orange peel, extract and remaining butter.

3 In a mixing bowl, beat egg whites and cream of tartar on medium speed until foamy. Gradually add remaining sugar, 1 tablespoon at a time, beating until soft peaks form. With a spatula, stir 1 cup of the whites into the orange batter until no white streaks remain. Fold in remaining egg whites until combined. Gently pour into the prepared dish.

4 Bake at 400° for 25-30 minutes or until a knife inserted near the center comes out clean. Serve immediately.

making *a souffle*

1. Temper the egg yolks by stirring a small amount of hot filling into egg yolks; return all to the pan, stirring constantly.

2. After adding the sugar, beat egg white mixture on high speed just until stiff peaks form; do not overbeat.

3. Stir about a fourth of the egg whites into the egg yolk mixture to lighten.

4. Fold in remaining egg whites.

5. Transfer to prepared baking dish.

problem-solving pointers *for Souffles*

SOUFFLE DID NOT RISE

- Egg whites were overbeaten. Beat just until they reach a stiff peak.
- Ingredients weren't gently folded together.
- The batter wasn't gently spooned into the dish.
- The oven wasn't preheated properly.

SOUFFLE OVERFLOWED THE DISH

- Next time, make a foil collar for the dish or use a larger dish.

SOUFFLE FELL

- A souffle will begin to fall shortly after it is removed from the oven. Plan the serving time well and have the guests waiting for the souffle.

Custards & Puddings

Pumpkin Custard

PREP: 10 min. **BAKE:** 50 min. **YIELD:** 4 servings

Andrea Holcomb, Torrington, Connecticut

This dessert is a refreshing departure from pumpkin pie, but it has the same good old-fashioned flavor.

  1 **can (15 ounces) solid-pack pumpkin**
  2 **eggs**
  1 **cup half-and-half cream**
2/3 **cup packed brown sugar**
1-1/2 **teaspoons pumpkin pie spice**
1/2 **teaspoon salt**
TOPPING:
1/4 **cup packed brown sugar**
1/4 **cup chopped pecans**
  1 **tablespoon butter, melted**
Whipped cream and ground cinnamon, optional

1 In a large mixing bowl, combine the first six ingredients; beat until smooth. Pour into four greased 10-oz. custard cups.

2 Place cups in a 13-in. x 9-in. x 2-in. baking pan. Fill pan with hot water to a depth of 1 in. Bake, uncovered, at 350° for 20 minutes.

3 For topping, combine the brown sugar, pecans and butter in a small bowl. Sprinkle over custard. Bake 30-35 minutes longer or until a knife inserted near the center comes out clean. Serve warm or chilled; top with whipped cream and cinnamon if desired. Store in the refrigerator.

PUMPKIN CUSTARD

Baked Custard

PREP: 10 min. **BAKE:** 50 min. + cooling
YIELD: 4 servings

Mary Kay Morris, Cokato, Minnesota

Adults and kids alike get a kick out of having their own individual custard set before them. Serving the custards warm or chilled is a matter of preference.

  2 **eggs**
  2 **cups milk**
1/3 **cup sugar**
1/4 **teaspoon salt**
Dash ground cinnamon
Dash ground nutmeg

the basics about *custards & puddings*

- Baked custards are a sweetened mixture of milk, eggs and flavoring. They can be baked individually in custard cups or in one large baking dish. They are usually baked in a water bath to help ensure gentle and even baking. (For directions, see Making a Water Bath on page 267.)

- Custards are done when a knife inserted about halfway to the center comes out clean and the top looks set.

- To unmold a cooled custard, carefully run a knife around the edge of dish to loosen. If possible, lift the bottom edge of the custard with the tip of the knife blade to loosen. Place a serving dish over the top of the baking dish. Invert and remove custard dish.

- Bread puddings are made with cubes or slices of bread baked in a custard mixture. They can be enriched with fruits, nuts, chocolate and spices. Bread puddings are served warm or cold and may be accompanied by a sauce. Bread puddings are done when a knife inserted near the center comes out clean.

- Rice puddings are made with cooked rice, a custard mixture, flavoring and spices. They can be served warm or cold. Rice puddings are done when a knife inserted near the center comes out clean.

- Store baked custards and puddings in the refrigerator for 1 to 2 days.

BAKED CUSTARD

1 In a small bowl, whisk the eggs, milk, sugar and salt. Pour into four ungreased 8-oz. custard cups; sprinkle with cinnamon and nutmeg.

2 Place cups in a 13-in. x 9-in. x 2-in. baking pan. Fill pan with hot water to a depth of 3/4 in. Bake, uncovered, at 350° for 50-55 minutes or until a knife inserted near the center comes out clean. Remove cups to a wire rack to cool. Serve warm or chilled. Store in the refrigerator.

Baked Barley Pudding

PREP: 35 min. **BAKE:** 30 min. **YIELD:** 8 servings

Judy Berarducci, Port St. Lucie, Florida

Smooth and custardy, this pudding bakes up firm and golden. Barley is an interesting twist to the usual rice.

1-1/4	cups water
1/2	cup uncooked medium pearl barley
1/4	teaspoon salt
2	cups milk
1	cup heavy whipping cream
1/2	cup sugar
2	eggs
1	teaspoon vanilla extract
1/2	cup golden raisins
1/4	teaspoon ground cinnamon

1 In a saucepan, bring water to a boil. Stir in barley and salt. Reduce heat; simmer, uncovered, for 15 minutes, stirring occasionally. Add milk; cook over medium-low heat for 10 minutes or until barley is almost tender, stirring frequently. In a bowl, whisk the cream, sugar, eggs and vanilla; gradually stir into the barley mixture.

2 Spoon into eight greased 6-oz. custard cups. Sprinkle with raisins and cinnamon. Place custard cups in two 9-in. baking pans. Fill both pans with boiling water to a depth of 1 in. Bake, uncovered, at 350° for 30-35 minutes or until a knife inserted near the center comes out clean. Store in the refrigerator.

Editor's Note: Pudding will appear layered when baked.

BAKED BARLEY PUDDING

making a
water bath for
custards & puddings

Place baking dish in a larger baking pan or dish, then place on rack in oven. Using a kettle or large measuring cup, carefully pour hot or boiling water into larger pan or dish. Fill according to recipe directions, generally to a depth of 1 in. or halfway up the sides of the larger pan or dish.

Traditional Caramel Flan

PREP: 20 min. **BAKE:** 55 min. + chilling
YIELD: 6 servings

Mary Ann Kosmas, Minneapolis, Minnesota

This delectable dessert is baked over a layer of caramelized sugar. When inverted, a delicious golden sauce runs down the edges of the flan and forms a tantalizing pool on the serving platter.

1-1/4	cups sugar, *divided*
2-3/4	cups milk
5	eggs
1/8	teaspoon salt
1	teaspoon vanilla extract

1 In a heavy saucepan or skillet over medium-low heat, melt 3/4 cup sugar. Do not stir. When sugar is melted, reduce heat to low; cook until syrup is golden brown, stirring constantly. Quickly pour into an ungreased souffle dish or 2-qt. round baking dish, tilting to coat the bottom of the dish. Let stand for 10 minutes.

2 In a saucepan, heat milk over medium heat until bubbles form around sides of saucepan. Remove from the heat. In a bowl, whisk eggs, salt and remaining sugar. Stir 1 cup of warm milk into egg mixture; return all to the pan, stirring constantly. Add vanilla. Pour into prepared dish.

3 Place dish in a large baking pan. Fill larger pan with boiling water to a depth of 1 in. Bake at 325° for 55-60 minutes or until center is just set (mixture will jiggle). Remove flan dish to a wire rack; cool for 1 hour. Refrigerate for 3-4 hours or until thoroughly chilled. Run a knife around edge

and invert onto a rimmed serving platter. Refrigerate leftovers.

Coconut Cream Pudding

PREP: 25 min. + cooling **BAKE:** 10 min.
YIELD: 9 servings

Verona Koehlmoos, Pilger, Nebraska

A golden baked meringue is the crowning touch to this mouth-watering dessert.

1-1/4	cups sugar, *divided*
1/4	cup cornstarch
3	cups milk
4	eggs, *separated*
1	cup flaked coconut
1	teaspoon vanilla extract

1 In a large heavy saucepan, combine 3/4 cup sugar and cornstarch; stir in milk until smooth. Cook and stir over medium heat until thickened and bubbly. Reduce heat; cook and stir 2 minutes longer. Remove from the heat.

2 In a bowl, beat egg yolks. Stir 1 cup hot milk mixture into egg yolks; return to pan, stirring constantly. Bring to a gentle boil over medium heat; cook and stir 2 minutes longer. Remove from the heat. Stir in coconut and vanilla. Cool to lukewarm without stirring.

3 Pour into an ungreased 8-in. square baking dish. In a large mixing bowl and with clean beaters, beat egg whites on medium speed until soft peaks form. Gradually beat in remaining sugar, 1 tablespoon at a time, on high until stiff peaks form. Spread over pudding, sealing to edges. Bake, uncovered, at 350° for 10-15 minutes. Serve warm.

caramelizing *sugar*

In a heavy saucepan or skillet, melt sugar over medium-low heat, about 10 minutes. Do not stir. When sugar is melted, reduce heat to low. Cook for about 5 minutes or until syrup is golden, stirring constantly with a metal spoon.

problem-solving pointers
for Custard

CUSTARD IS CURDLED

- It's overbaked. Bake only until a knife inserted about halfway to the center comes out clean, not until the center is completely set.
- Next time, bake the custard in a water bath.
- After baking, immediately remove custard from water bath; otherwise, it will continue to cook in the hot water.

CUSTARD HAS BUBBLES ON THE TOP

- Next time, beat eggs only until they are blended, not foamy.

Butterscotch Rice Pudding

PREP: 1-1/4 hours **BAKE:** 20 min. **YIELD:** 6-8 servings

Faye Hintz, Springfield, Missouri

Brown sugar in this rice pudding's unique meringue topping gives a pretty golden color.

      3 **cups milk,** *divided*
    1/2 **cup uncooked long grain rice**
    1/2 **teaspoon salt**
    3/4 **cup packed brown sugar,** *divided*
      2 **tablespoons butter**
      2 **eggs,** *separated*
      1 **teaspoon vanilla extract**

1 In a large heavy saucepan, bring 2 cups milk to a gentle boil. Stir in rice and salt. Cover and cook over medium-low heat for 45 minutes, stirring occasionally. Remove from the heat; set aside.

2 In a small saucepan, heat 1/2 cup brown sugar, butter and remaining milk until simmering. Remove from the heat. In a small bowl, beat egg yolks. Add a small amount of hot milk mixture to yolks; return to the pan, stirring constantly. Stir into rice mixture; cook and stir over medium heat for 5 minutes. Remove from the heat. Stir in vanilla.

3 Pour into a greased 1-1/2-qt. baking dish; set aside. In a small mixing bowl and with clean beaters, beat egg whites on medium speed until soft peaks form. Gradually beat in remaining brown sugar, 1 tablespoon at a time, on high until stiff peaks form. Spread over rice mixture, sealing to edges. Bake, uncovered, at 300° for 20-25 minutes.

Grandma's Rice Pudding

PREP: 10 min. **BAKE:** 45 min. **YIELD:** 4-6 servings

Margaret DeChant, Newberry, Michigan

You can whip up this classic dessert on short notice if you keep cooked rice on hand. Cooked rice can be frozen in an airtight container for up to 3 months. Thaw in the refrigerator before using.

    1-1/2 **cups cooked rice**
      1/4 **cup raisins**
        2 **eggs**
    1-1/2 **cups milk**
      1/2 **cup sugar**
      1/2 **teaspoon ground nutmeg**
Additional milk, optional

1 Place the rice and raisins in a greased 1-qt. baking dish. In a small mixing bowl, beat the eggs, milk, sugar and nutmeg; pour over rice.

2 Bake, uncovered, at 375° for 45-50 minutes or until a knife inserted near the center comes out clean. Cool. Pour additional milk over each serving if desired. Refrigerate leftovers.

GRANDMA'S RICE PUDDING

SAUCY MOCHA PUDDING CAKE

Saucy Mocha Pudding Cake

PREP: 20 min. **BAKE:** 45 min. **YIELD:** 9 servings

Kathy Koch, Smoky Lake, Alberta

This pudding cake goes great with ice cream and whipped cream, but it's just as scrumptious served alone. It's very easy to prepare. Don't wait for a special occasion to try it!

  1/2 **cup sugar**
  1/2 **cup packed brown sugar**
  1/4 **cup baking cocoa**
1-1/2 **cups strong brewed coffee**
CAKE:
  1/3 **cup butter, softened**
  2/3 **cup sugar**
    1 **egg**
  1/2 **teaspoon vanilla extract**
    1 **cup all-purpose flour**
1-1/2 **teaspoons baking powder**
  1/4 **teaspoon salt**
  1/3 **cup milk**
Fresh raspberries and mint, optional

1 In a saucepan, combine the sugars and cocoa. Stir in coffee; keep warm over low heat. For cake, in a mixing bowl, cream butter and sugar until light and fluffy. Beat in egg and vanilla. Combine the flour, baking powder and salt; add to creamed mixture alternately with milk, beating well after each addition. Spread into a greased 8-in. square baking dish. Pour mocha sauce slowly over batter. Do not stir.

2 Bake, uncovered, at 350° for 45-50 minutes or until a toothpick inserted near the center of the cake comes out clean. When finished, the cake will float in the hot mocha sauce. Garnish with raspberries and mint if desired.

Lemon Pudding Cake

PREP: 15 min. **BAKE:** 45 min. **YIELD:** 4 servings

Ann Berg, Chesapeake, Virginia

The tart taste of lemon brings the perfect finish to any meal. The fluffy, light cake texture is appealing.

   2 **eggs,** *separated*
   1 **cup sugar**
   3 **tablespoons all-purpose flour**
3/4 **cup milk**
1/4 **cup lemon juice**
   1 **tablespoon butter, melted**
   2 **teaspoons grated lemon peel**

1 Let eggs stand at room temperature for 30 minutes. In a large bowl, combine sugar and flour. Stir in the milk, lemon juice, butter and lemon peel. Beat egg yolks; add to lemon mixture. In a small mixing bowl and with clean beaters, beat egg whites on high speed until stiff peaks form. Fold into lemon mixture.

2 Pour into a greased 1-qt. baking dish. Place in a larger baking pan. Fill larger pan with hot water to a depth of 1 in. Bake, uncovered, at 350° for 45-50 minutes or until a knife inserted near the center comes out clean. Serve warm. Refrigerate leftovers.

what is a *pudding cake?*

Pudding cakes offer two treats in one. While baking, the cake portion rises to the top and a creamy pudding-like sauce forms on the bottom.

Blueberry Pudding Cake

PREP: 15 min. BAKE: 45 min. YIELD: 9 servings

Jan Bamford, Sedgwick, Maine

A tasty and different way to use blueberries...this dessert is sure to delight your family.

     2 cups fresh *or* frozen blueberries
     1 teaspoon ground cinnamon
     1 teaspoon lemon juice
     1 cup all-purpose flour
   3/4 cup sugar
     1 teaspoon baking powder
   1/2 cup milk
     3 tablespoons butter, melted
TOPPING:
   3/4 cup sugar
     1 tablespoons cornstarch
     1 cup boiling water

1 Toss the blueberries with cinnamon and lemon juice; place in a greased 8-in. square baking dish. In a small bowl, combine the flour, sugar and baking powder; stir in milk and butter. Spoon over berries.

2 Combine sugar and cornstarch; sprinkle over batter. Slowly pour boiling water over all. Bake at 350° for 45-50 minutes or until a toothpick inserted into the cake portion comes out clean.

Editor's Note: If using frozen blueberries, do not thaw before using.

Cherry Pudding Cake

PREP: 10 min. BAKE: 40 min. YIELD: 10-12 servings

Brenda Parker, Kalamazoo, Michigan

A cross between a cake and a cobbler, this cherry dessert is awesome. Add it to your potluck recipe collection, because this one is sure to go fast.

     2 cups all-purpose flour
 2-1/2 cups sugar, *divided*
     4 teaspoons baking powder
     1 cup milk
     2 tablespoons vegetable oil
     2 cans (14-1/2 ounces *each*) water-packed
        pitted tart red cherries, well drained
     2 to 3 drops red food coloring, optional
   1/8 teaspoon almond extract
Whipped cream *or* ice cream, optional

1 In a mixing bowl, combine flour, 1 cup sugar, baking powder, milk and oil; pour into a greased shallow 3-qt. baking dish. In a bowl, combine cherries, food coloring if desired, extract and remaining sugar; spoon over batter.

2 Bake at 375° for 40-45 minutes or until a toothpick inserted in the cake portion comes out clean. Serve dessert warm with whipped cream or ice cream if desired.

BLUEBERRY PUDDING CAKE

Bread Pudding

PREP: 10 min. **BAKE:** 50 min. **YIELD:** 12-16 servings

Evette Rios, Westfield, Massachusetts

Comforting desserts like this are always welcome at potlucks. It serves 12, which makes it ideal for a crowd.

    3   eggs
    3   cans (12 ounces *each*) evaporated milk
1-1/4   cups sugar
  1/4   cup butter, melted
  1/2   to 1 cup raisins
    2   teaspoons vanilla extract
    1   teaspoon ground cinnamon
  1/2   teaspoon salt
    1   loaf (1 pound) bread, cut into cubes

1 In a large bowl, beat eggs. Add the milk, sugar, butter, raisins, vanilla, cinnamon and salt; mix well. Add bread cubes; stir gently.

2 Pour into a greased 13-in. x 9-in. x 2-in. baking dish. Bake, uncovered, at 325° for 50-60 minutes or until a knife inserted near the center comes out clean. Serve warm or cold. Refrigerate leftovers.

Cajun Bread Pudding

PREP: 20 min. + soaking **BAKE:** 45 min.
YIELD: 12 servings

Linda Walter, Jetmore, Kansas

A pleasing praline sauce puts a spin on traditional bread pudding.

4-3/4   cups milk, *divided*
    4   eggs
  2/3   cup sugar
    1   teaspoon vanilla extract
  1/4   teaspoon salt
  1/3   cup butter, softened
   11   cups cubed French bread (1-inch cubes)
  1/2   teaspoon ground cinnamon
  2/3   cup raisins, optional
  2/3   cup chopped pecans, optional

PRALINE SAUCE:

  1/4   cup water
  1/3   cup packed brown sugar
  1/3   cup corn syrup
  1/2   cup coarsely chopped pecans
  1/2   teaspoon vanilla extract
    2   tablespoons butter

Dash salt

BREAD PUDDING

1 In a large saucepan, heat 4 cups of milk until warm; set aside. In a large mixing bowl, combine the eggs, sugar, vanilla, salt and remaining milk. Gradually add warmed milk, stirring constantly. Stir in butter. Add the bread cubes; let soak 10 minutes. Add the cinnamon, and raisins and/or pecans if desired.

2 Pour into a 13-in. x 9-in. x 2-in. baking dish. Bake, uncovered, at 400° for 45-60 minutes or until a knife inserted in center comes out clean.

3 For sauce, bring water to a boil in a small saucepan. Add brown sugar; stir to dissolve. Add corn syrup. Bring to boil; cook 15-20 seconds. Remove from the heat. Stir in the pecans, vanilla, butter and salt. Cut pudding into squares and serve with sauce.

LEMON BREAD PUDDING

Lemon Bread Pudding

PREP: 15 min. **BAKE:** 50 min. **YIELD:** 6 servings

Mildred Sherrer, Fort Worth, Texas

Sweet raisins and a smooth hot lemon sauce make this dessert extra special.

 3 **slices day-old bread, cubed**
3/4 **cup raisins**
 2 **cups milk**
1/2 **cup sugar**
 2 **tablespoons butter**
1/4 **teaspoon salt**
 2 **eggs**
 1 **teaspoon vanilla extract**
LEMON SAUCE:
3/4 **cup sugar**
 2 **tablespoons cornstarch**
 1 **cup water**
 3 **tablespoons lemon juice**
 2 **teaspoons grated lemon peel**
 1 **tablespoon butter**

1 Toss bread and raisins in an ungreased 1-1/2-qt. baking dish. In a small saucepan, combine the milk, sugar, butter and salt; cook and stir until butter is melted. Remove from the heat. Whisk eggs and vanilla in a small bowl. Stir a small amount of the hot milk mixture into the egg mixture; return all to the pan, stirring constantly. Pour over bread and raisins.

2 Place dish in a larger baking pan. Fill larger pan with hot water to a depth of 1 in. Bake, uncovered, at 350° for 50-60 minutes or until a knife inserted near the center comes out clean.

3 For sauce, combine the sugar and cornstarch in a saucepan. Stir in water until smooth. Bring to a boil over medium heat; cook and stir for 1-2 minutes or until thickened. Remove from the heat. Stir in lemon juice, peel and butter until butter melts. Serve over warm or cold pudding. Refrigerate leftovers.

testing
bread pudding for *doneness*

Insert a knife near the center of the bread pudding. It's done when the knife comes out clean.

Fruit Desserts

Rhubarb Granola Crisp

PREP: 15 min. **BAKE:** 30 min. **YIELD:** 9 servings

Arlene Beitz, Cambridge, Ontario

This will be a hit with your family—whether it's served warm with ice cream or chilled.

> 4 **cups chopped fresh *or* frozen rhubarb, thawed and drained**
> 1-1/4 **cups all-purpose flour, *divided***
> 1/4 **cup sugar**
> 1/2 **cup strawberry jam**
> 1-1/2 **cups granola cereal**
> 1/2 **cup packed brown sugar**
> 1/2 **cup chopped pecans**
> 1/2 **teaspoon ground cinnamon**
> 1/2 **teaspoon ground ginger**
> 1/2 **cup cold butter**
> **Ice cream, optional**

1 In a large bowl, combine the rhubarb, 1/4 cup flour and sugar; stir in jam and set aside. In another large bowl, combine the granola, brown sugar, pecans, cinnamon, ginger and remaining flour. Cut in butter until the mixture resembles coarse crumbs.

2 Press 2 cups of the granola mixture into a greased 8-in. square baking dish; spread rhubarb mixture over the crust. Sprinkle with remaining granola mixture.

3 Bake, uncovered, at 375° for 30-40 minutes or until filling is bubbly and topping is golden brown. Serve warm with ice cream if desired.

RHUBARB GRANOLA CRISP

Editor's Note: If using frozen rhubarb, measure rhubarb while still frozen, then thaw completely. Drain in a colander, but do not press liquid out.

Cranberry Apple Betty

PREP: 30 min. **BAKE:** 1 hour **YIELD:** 6-8 servings

Leona Cullen, Melrose, Massachusetts

For a tart autumn dessert, this one is hard to beat. You'll love the way the sweet apples and brown sugar complement the tangy cranberries. Topped off with lemon sauce, it's a winner!

> 4 **cups soft bread crumbs**
> 6 **tablespoons butter, *divided***
> 5 **cups sliced peeled tart apples (4 to 5 large)**
> 1 **cup packed brown sugar**
> 3/4 **teaspoon ground nutmeg**
> 2 **cups fresh *or* frozen cranberries, thawed**
> **LEMON SAUCE:**
> 1/2 **cup sugar**
> 1 **tablespoon cornstarch**
> **Dash salt**
> 1 **cup water**
> 1 **teaspoon grated lemon peel**
> 2 **tablespoons lemon juice**
> 2 **tablespoons butter**

1 In a skillet, brown the bread crumbs in 3 tablespoons butter. Place half of the apples in a greased 8-in. square baking dish. Combine brown sugar and nutmeg; sprinkle half over the apples. Top with half of the bread crumbs. Dot with half of the remaining butter. Place the cranberries on top. Layer with the remaining apples, brown sugar mixture, bread crumbs and butter.

2 Cover and bake at 350° for 45 minutes. Uncover; bake 15-20 minutes longer or until fruit is tender.

3 For lemon sauce, combine the sugar, cornstarch and salt in a small saucepan. Stir in water and lemon peel until smooth. Bring to a boil; cook and stir for 2 minutes or until thickened. Remove from the heat; stir in lemon juice and butter until butter is melted. Serve over warm betty.

Old-Fashioned Apple Crisp

PREP: 15 min. **BAKE:** 30 min. **YIELD:** 4-6 servings

Grace Yaskovic, Branchville, New Jersey

Nostalgic, comforting, luscious—call it what you will, this is one of those simple, old-time treats that never goes out of style.

OLD-FASHIONED APPLE CRISP

4 cups sliced peeled tart apples (about 3 medium)
3/4 cup packed brown sugar
1/2 cup all-purpose flour
1/2 cup old-fashioned oats
1 teaspoon ground cinnamon
1/4 to 1/2 teaspoon ground allspice
1/3 cup cold butter
Vanilla ice cream, optional

1 Place the apples in a greased 8-in. square baking dish. In a small bowl, combine the brown sugar, flour, oats, cinnamon and allspice; cut in butter until mixture is crumbly. Sprinkle over apples.

2 Bake, uncovered, at 375° for 30-35 minutes or until apples are tender. Serve warm with ice cream if desired.

Quick Strawberry Cobbler

PREP: 10 min. **BAKE:** 30 min. **YIELD:** 12 servings

Sue Poe, Hayden, Alabama

Thanks to canned fruits and packaged cake mix, this extra easy recipe offers old-fashioned goodness.

2 cans (21 ounces *each*) strawberry pie filling *or* fruit filling of your choice
1/2 cup butter, softened
1 package (3 ounces) cream cheese, softened
2 teaspoons vanilla extract
2 packages (9 ounces *each*) yellow cake mix

1 Pour pie filling into a greased 13-in. x 9-in. x 2-in. baking dish. Bake at 350° for 5-7 minutes or until heated through.

2 Meanwhile, cream butter and cream cheese in a small mixing bowl until fluffy. Beat in vanilla. Place dry cake mixes in a large bowl; cut in cream cheese mixture until crumbly. Sprinkle over hot filling. Bake, uncovered, 25-30 minutes longer or until topping is golden brown.

Praline Peach Cobbler

PREP: 30 min. **BAKE:** 25 min. **YIELD:** 12 servings

Maithel Martin, Kansas City, Missouri

Cobbler is a delicious dessert for picnics and potluck dinners. It can be served cold or warm and is especially good topped with a generous scoop of vanilla ice cream.

1-1/2 cups plus 2 teaspoons sugar, *divided*
2 tablespoons cornstarch
1 teaspoon ground cinnamon
1 cup water
8 cups sliced peeled fresh peaches
2 cups self-rising flour
1/2 cup shortening
1/2 cup buttermilk
Additional buttermilk, optional
3 tablespoons butter, melted
1/4 cup packed brown sugar
1 cup chopped pecans

1 In a large saucepan, combine 1-1/2 cups sugar, cornstarch and cinnamon. Stir in water until smooth. Add peaches. Bring to a boil over medium heat; cook and stir for 2 minutes or until thickened. Pour into a lightly greased 13-in. x 9-in. x 2-in. baking dish; set aside.

2 In a bowl, combine the flour and remaining sugar; cut in shortening until mixture resembles coarse crumbs. Add buttermilk and stir just until moistened. If needed, add additional buttermilk, 1 tablespoon at a time, until the dough clings together. Turn onto a floured surface; knead gently for 6-8 times. Roll into a 12-in. x 8-in. rectangle.

3 Combine the butter, brown sugar and pecans; spread over dough to within 1/2 in. of edges. Roll up jelly-roll style, starting with a long side. Cut into twelve 1-in. pieces. Place over peach mixture. Bake, uncovered, at 400° for 25-30 minutes or until golden brown.

Editor's Note: As a substitute for the self-rising flour, place 3 teaspoons baking powder and 1 teaspoon salt in a measuring cup. Add all-purpose flour to measure 1 cup. Then add an additional cup of all-purpose flour.

LEMON WHIRLIGIGS WITH RASPBERRIES

Lemon Whirligigs With Raspberries

PREP: 35 min. **BAKE:** 25 min. **YIELD:** 10 servings

Vicky Ayres, Wappingers Falls, New York

Golden pastry swirls with a tart lemon flavor float on a raspberry sauce in this whimsically named treat.

- 2/3 **cup sugar**
- 2 **tablespoons cornstarch**
- 1/4 **teaspoon ground cinnamon**
- 1/8 **teaspoon ground nutmeg**
- 1/8 **teaspoon salt**
- 1 **cup water**
- 3 **cups fresh raspberries**

WHIRLIGIGS:
- 1 **cup all-purpose flour**
- 2 **teaspoons baking powder**
- 1/2 **teaspoon salt**
- 3 **tablespoons shortening**
- 1 **egg, lightly beaten**
- 2 **tablespoons half-and-half cream**
- 1/4 **cup sugar**
- 2 **tablespoons butter, melted**
- 1 **teaspoon grated lemon peel**

Heavy whipping cream and additional raspberries, optional

1 In a saucepan, combine the sugar, cornstarch, cinnamon, nutmeg and salt. Stir in water until smooth. Bring to a boil; cook and stir for 2 minutes or until thickened.

2 Place the raspberries in an ungreased 1-1/2-qt. shallow baking dish; pour hot sauce over top. Bake, uncovered, at 400° for 10 minutes; remove from the oven and set aside.

3 For whirligigs, combine the flour, baking powder and salt in a small bowl. Cut in shortening until crumbly. Combine egg and half-and-half; stir into crumb mixture to form a stiff dough.

4 Shape into a ball. On a lightly floured surface, roll out into a 12-in. x 6-in. rectangle. Combine the sugar, butter and lemon peel; spread over dough to within 1/2 in. of edges. Roll up jelly-roll style, starting with a long side. Cut into 10 slices; pat slightly to flatten. Place over berry mixture.

5 Bake, uncovered, at 400° for 15 minutes or until whirligigs are golden. Garnish servings with cream and raspberries if desired.

Blackberry Buckle

PREP: 20 min. **BAKE:** 45 min. **YIELD:** 9-12 servings

Taste of Home Test Kitchen

This homey dessert can be made with blueberries or raspberries instead.

- 1/2 **cup shortening**
- 1 **cup sugar,** *divided*
- 1 **egg, beaten**
- 2-1/2 **cups all-purpose flour,** *divided*
- 2-1/2 **teaspoons baking powder**
- 1/2 **teaspoon salt**
- 1/2 **cup milk**
- 2 **cups fresh** *or* **frozen blackberries**
- 2 **teaspoons lemon juice**
- 1/2 **teaspoon ground cinnamon**
- 1/4 **cup cold butter**

1 In a large mixing bowl, cream the shortening and 1/2 cup sugar until light and fluffy. Add the egg and mix well. Combine 2 cups flour, baking powder and salt; add to the creamed mixture alternately with the milk, beating well after each addition.

2 Spread into a greased 9-in. square baking dish. Toss the blackberries with lemon juice; sprinkle over batter. In a small bowl, combine cinnamon and remaining sugar and flour; cut in the butter until mixture resembles coarse crumbs. Sprinkle over berries.

3 Bake, uncovered, at 350° for 45-50 minutes or until a toothpick inserted near the center comes out clean. Refrigerate leftovers.

Editor's Note: If using frozen berries, do not thaw before adding to batter.

Nutty Peach Crisp

PREP: 10 min. **BAKE:** 55 min. + standing
YIELD: 12-15 servings

Nancy Carpenter, Sidney, Montana

A moist bottom layer made with canned peaches and a boxed cake mix is covered with a lovely golden topping of coconut and pecans.

> 1　can (29 ounces) sliced peaches, undrained
> 1　package (18-1/4 ounces) yellow *or* butter pecan cake mix
> 1/2　cup butter, melted
> 1　cup flaked coconut
> 1　cup chopped pecans

1 Arrange peaches in an ungreased 13-in. x 9-in. x 2-in. baking dish. Sprinkle dry cake mix over the top. Drizzle with butter; sprinkle with coconut and pecans.

2 Bake, uncovered, at 325° for 55-60 minutes or until golden brown. Let stand for 15 minutes before serving. Serve warm or cold.

Strawberry Pretzel Dessert

PREP: 20 min. **BAKE:** 10 min. + chilling
YIELD: 12-16 servings

Aldene Belch, Flint, Michigan

A salty pretzel crust nicely contrasts cream cheese and gelatin layers.

> 2　cups crushed pretzels (about 8 ounces)
> 3/4　cup butter, melted
> 3　tablespoons sugar
> **FILLING:**
> 2　cups whipped topping
> 1　package (8 ounces) cream cheese, softened
> 1　cup sugar
> **TOPPING:**
> 1　package (6 ounces) strawberry gelatin
> 2　cups boiling water
> 2　packages (16 ounces *each*) frozen sliced strawberries with syrup, thawed

Additional whipped topping, optional

1 In a bowl, combine the pretzels, butter and sugar. Press into the bottom of an ungreased 13-in. x 9-in. x 2-in. baking pan. Bake at 350° for 10 minutes. Cool on a wire rack.

STRAWBERRY PRETZEL DESSERT

2 For filling, in a mixing bowl, beat the whipped topping, cream cheese and sugar until smooth. Spread over crust. Refrigerate until chilled.

3 For topping, dissolve the gelatin in boiling water. Stir in the strawberries with syrup; refrigerate until partially set. Carefully spoon over filling. Refrigerate for 4-6 hours or until firm. Cut into squares; serve with whipped topping if desired.

facts about *fruit desserts*

Apple, pears, peaches and berries lend themselves to so many delicious desserts. Here is a description of the old-fashioned desserts featured in this section.

- Betty is made with alternate layers of sweetened fruit and cake, cookie or bread crumbs. The top layer of crumbs brown as it bakes.

- Buckle is a cake-like dessert made with berries and may or may not have a crumb topping. It got its name because the cake sometimes buckles under the weight of the topping.

- Cobbler has a biscuit topping over the fruit. The topping can be either in a single layer or dropped over the fruit to give a cobblestone effect.

- Crisps have a crumb topping over the fruit. The topping has flour, sugar and butter and may or may not have oats, nuts and spices. The topping gets crisp while baking.

- Dessert dumplings use a flaky pastry to enclose the fruit.

3 Divide pastry into six portions. On a lightly floured surface, roll each portion into a 6-in. square. Place an apple in the center of each. Sprinkle with cinnamon-sugar; dot with remaining butter. Bring corners of pastry to center. Brush edges with milk; pinch edges to seal.

4 Place in a greased 13-in. x 9-in. x 2-in. baking dish; drizzle with the reserved syrup. Bake, uncovered, at 375° for 35-40 minutes or until golden brown.

Pumpkin Pie Squares

PREP: 15 min. **BAKE:** 1 hour 20 min. + cooling
YIELD: 16-20 servings

Denise Goedeken, Platte Center, Nebraska

This dessert has all the spicy pumpkin goodness of the traditional pie without the fuss of a pastry crust.

       1 cup all-purpose flour
    1/2 cup quick-cooking oats
    1/2 cup packed brown sugar
    1/2 cup cold butter
FILLING:
       2 cans (15 ounces *each*) solid-pack pumpkin
       2 cans (12 ounces *each*) evaporated milk
       4 eggs
   1-1/2 cups sugar
       2 teaspoons ground cinnamon
       1 teaspoon ground ginger
    1/2 teaspoon ground cloves
       1 teaspoon salt
TOPPING:
    1/2 cup packed brown sugar
    1/2 cup chopped pecans
       2 tablespoons butter, softened

1 In a small bowl, combine the flour, oats and brown sugar. Cut in butter until mixture is crumbly. Press into a greased 13-in. x 9-in. x 2-in. baking pan. Bake at 350° for 20 minutes or until golden brown.

2 In a large mixing bowl, beat filling ingredients until smooth; pour over crust. Bake for 45 minutes.

3 Combine topping ingredients; sprinkle over filling. Bake 15-20 minutes longer or until a knife inserted near the center comes out clean. Cool on a wire rack. Store in the refrigerator.

APPLE DUMPLINGS

Apple Dumplings

PREP: 25 min. **BAKE:** 35 min. **YIELD:** 6 servings

Marilyn Strickland, Williamson, New York

Instead of an apple pie, why not make these individual pastry-wrapped apples?

   2-1/2 cups water
   1-1/4 cups sugar
    1/2 teaspoon ground cinnamon
    1/4 cup plus 6 teaspoons butter, *divided*
       2 cups all-purpose flour
       2 teaspoons baking powder
       1 teaspoon salt
    3/4 cup shortening
    1/2 cup milk
       6 small tart apples, peeled and cored
Cinnamon-sugar
Additional milk

1 In a small saucepan, combine the water, sugar and cinnamon. Cook and stir over medium until sugar is dissolved, about 5 minutes. Add 1/4 cup butter; stir until melted. Remove from the heat; set aside.

2 In a bowl, combine the flour, baking powder and salt. Cut in the shortening until the mixture resembles coarse crumbs. Stir in milk.

Quick Breads

The convenience of quick breads comes from the fact that they're leavened with baking powder and/or baking soda, not yeast. So you can mix, bake and enjoy these baked goods in less time than traditional yeast breads. Like yeast breads, quick breads can be sweet or savory.

secrets for *successful quick breads*

- Measure ingredients accurately, using the measuring tools and techniques suggested on pages 7 and 8.
- Before preheating the oven, arrange the oven racks so that the bread will bake in the center of the oven.
- Preheat the oven for 10-15 minutes before baking.
- Be sure your baking powder and baking soda are fresh. (See Testing Baking Powder & Soda for Freshness on page 287.) Always check the expiration date on the packages before using.
- Mix the liquid and dry ingredients only until moistened. A few lumps in the batter is fine. Overmixing causes the gluten in the flour to develop and the texture to be coarse and tough.
- Grease aluminum baking pans and sheets with a dull rather than shiny or dark finish. Fill pans two-thirds full.
- Most quick breads should be baked shortly after dry ingredients and liquid ingredients are combined because the leaveners will begin producing gas once they are moistened. If allowed to stand too long before baking, the bread may have a sunken center.

- To allow for good air circulation while baking, leave at least 1 inch of space between pans and between pans and sides of oven. Switch pan positions and rotate pans halfway through baking.
- Use a kitchen timer. Check for doneness 10-15 minutes before the end of the recommended baking time. The bread is done if a toothpick inserted near the center comes out clean. If it is not done, test again in a few more minutes. The bread may have a split in the center, which is typical of a quick bread.
- Cool in the pan for 10 minutes, unless recipe directs otherwise. Turn loaves out onto a wire rack to cool. Most quick breads should be cooled completely before slicing to prevent crumbling.
- Quick breads such as banana, zucchini and cranberry slice and taste best when served a day after baking. Wrap the cooled bread in foil or plastic wrap; leave at room temperature overnight. Others like corn bread and coffee cakes are best served warm.
- Using a sawing motion, cut loaves with a thin sharp knife. Use a serrated knife for quick breads that have fruits and/or nuts.
- Most quick breads can be stored at room temperature. Quick breads with a cream cheese filling should be stored in the refrigerator.

Sweet Quick Breads

Strawberry Ribbon Bread

PREP: 15 min. **BAKE:** 70 min. + cooling
YIELD: 2 loaves

Carol Wilson, Missoula, Montana

The cream cheese filling in this loaf pairs well with the strawberry flavor.

- 3 **cups all-purpose flour**
- 2 **cups sugar**
- 1 **teaspoon baking soda**
- 1 **teaspoon salt**
- 1 **teaspoon ground cinnamon**
- 4 **eggs, beaten**
- 1/4 **cup vegetable oil**
- 2 **packages (10 ounces *each*) frozen sliced strawberries, thawed**
- 1 **teaspoon red food coloring, optional**

FILLING:
- 2 **packages (3 ounces *each*) cream cheese, softened**
- 1 **egg**
- 1/3 **cup sugar**
- 1 **tablespoon all-purpose flour**
- 1/2 **teaspoon orange extract**

1 In a large bowl, combine the flour, sugar, baking soda, salt, cinnamon. In another bowl, beat the eggs, oil, strawberries and food coloring if desired. Stir into dry ingredients just until moistened.

2 For filling, beat cream cheese in a small mixing bowl. Add the egg, sugar, flour and extract; beat well.

3 Spoon a fourth of the batter into each of two greased 8-in. x 4-in. x 2-in. loaf pans. Spread half of the filling over each. Top with the remaining batter.

4 Bake at 350° for 70-80 minutes or until a toothpick comes out clean (cover loosely with foil if top browns too quickly). Cool for 10 minutes before removing from pans to wire racks to cool completely. Store in the refrigerator.

LEMON POPPY SEED BREAD

Lemon Poppy Seed Bread

PREP: 10 min. **BAKE:** 35 min. + cooling
YIELD: 2 loaves

Karen Dougherty, Freeport, Illinois

If the days that you have time for baking are few and far between, try this extra-quick bread. You'll love the delicious bread and the ease of preparation.

- 1 **package (18-1/4 ounces) white cake mix**
- 1 **package (3.4 ounces) instant lemon pudding mix**
- 4 **eggs**
- 1 **cup warm water**
- 1/2 **cup vegetable oil**
- 4 **teaspoons poppy seeds**

1 In a large mixing bowl, combine the dry cake and pudding mixes, eggs, water and oil; beat until well mixed. Fold in poppy seeds.

2 Pour into two greased 9-in. x 5-in. x 3-in. loaf pans. Bake at 350° for 35-40 minutes or until a toothpick inserted near the center comes out clean. Cool for 10 minutes before removing from pans to wire racks to cool completely.

Apple Nut Bread

PREP: 15 min. **BAKE:** 1 hour + cooling **YIELD:** 1 loaf

June Mullins, Livonia, Missouri

Your family will love the nutty texture and fresh apple taste of this standby.

- 1/2 **cup butter, softened**
- 1 **cup plus 2 tablespoons sugar,** *divided*
- 2 **eggs**
- 1/2 **teaspoon vanilla extract**
- 2 **cups all-purpose flour**
- 1 **teaspoon baking soda**
- 1/2 **teaspoon salt**
- 2 **tablespoons buttermilk**
- 1 **cup grated peeled apple**
- 1 **cup chopped nuts**
- 3/4 **teaspoon ground cinnamon**

1 In a large mixing bowl, cream butter and 1 cup sugar until light and fluffy. Add eggs, one at a time, beating well after each addition. Stir in vanilla. Combine the flour, baking soda and salt; add to the creamed mixture alternately with buttermilk, beating well after each addition. Fold in apple and nuts.

2 Pour into a greased 9-in. x 5-in. x 3-in. loaf pan. Combine the cinnamon and remaining sugar; sprinkle over batter. Bake at 350° for 60-65 minutes or until a toothpick inserted near the center comes out clean. Cool for 10 minutes before removing from pan to a wire rack to cool completely.

APPLE NUT BREAD

making quick bread with a *creamed batter*

When a quick bread is made with solid fat, like softened butter or shortening, the fat and sugar are first creamed together. Then the eggs, dry ingredients and any liquids are added. This method incorporates air bubbles into the fat, resulting in a cake-like texture. For best results, make sure the butter is softened, not melted. (A knife should be able to glide through the butter.)

1. In a mixing bowl, cream butter and sugar. Add eggs, one at a time, beating well after each addition.

2. Combine the dry ingredients to evenly distribute the baking powder or soda.

3. Add the flour mixture alternately with milk or other liquid to the creamed mixture, beating well after each addition.

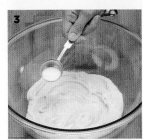

4. Fold in any other ingredients. Bake as directed.

Mango Nut Bread

PREP: 10 min. **BAKE:** 50 min. + cooling
YIELD: 2 loaves

Jo Sherley, Kahului, Hawaii

It can be difficult to remove the large flat oval pit inside a mango. Try cutting along each side of the mango next to the pit, resulting in two large sections. Then remove the fruit from the peel and chop.

2	cups all-purpose flour
1-1/2	cups sugar
1	teaspoon baking soda
1/2	teaspoon salt
1/2	teaspoon ground cinnamon
3	eggs
1/2	cup vegetable oil
1	teaspoon vanilla extract
2	cups chopped mangoes
1/2	cup chopped dates
1/2	cup chopped walnuts *or* macadamia nuts

1 In a large bowl, combine the flour, sugar, baking soda, salt and cinnamon. In another bowl, beat the eggs, oil and vanilla; stir into dry ingredients just until moistened. Fold in mangoes, dates and nuts (batter will be stiff).

2 Spoon into two greased 8-in. x 4-in. x 2-in. loaf pans. Bake at 350° for 50-55 minutes or until a toothpick inserted near the center comes out clean. Cool for 10 minutes before removing from pans to wire racks to cool completely.

MANGO NUT BREAD

making quick bread with a *stirred batter*

When a quick bread is made with liquid fat (melted butter or oil), the fat, eggs and any liquid are first combined, then stirred into the dry ingredients.

1. In a large bowl, combine dry ingredients to evenly distribute the baking powder or soda. Make a well in the center.

2. Beat eggs and combine with any liquid ingredients.

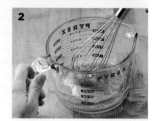

3. Pour egg mixture into the well all at one time.

4. Stir the ingredients together just until moistened, leaving a few lumps. Overmixing will result in a tough baked product.

5. Fold in any other ingredients. Bake as directed.

CINNAMON SWIRL QUICK BREAD

Cinnamon Swirl Quick Bread

PREP: 15 min. **BAKE:** 45 min. + cooling
YIELD: 1 loaf

Helen Richardson, Shelbyville, Michigan

While cinnamon bread is a natural for breakfast, it's great served around the clock! This is a nice twist on traditional cinnamon swirl yeast breads.

2	cups all-purpose flour
1-1/2	cups sugar, *divided*
1	teaspoon baking soda
1/2	teaspoon salt
1	cup buttermilk
1	egg
1/4	cup vegetable oil
1	tablespoon ground cinnamon

GLAZE:

1/4	cup confectioners' sugar
1-1/2	to 2 teaspoons milk

1 In a large bowl, combine the flour, 1 cup sugar, baking soda and salt. Combine the buttermilk, egg and oil; stir into dry ingredients just until moistened. In a small bowl, combine the cinnamon and remaining sugar.

2 Grease the bottom only of a 9-in. x 5-in. x 3-in. loaf pan. Pour half of the batter into pan; sprinkle with half of the cinnamon-sugar. Carefully spread with remaining batter and sprinkle with remaining cinnamon-sugar; swirl a knife through batter. Bake at 350° for 45-50 minutes or until a toothpick inserted near the center comes out clean. Cool for 10 minutes before removing from pan to a wire rack to cool completely.

3 For glaze, combine confectioners' sugar and enough milk to achieve drizzling consistency. Drizzle over bread.

Autumn Pear Mini Loaves

PREP: 15 min. **BAKE:** 35 min. + cooling
YIELD: 2 loaves

Mary Lynn Wilson, Linden, Texas

Pears give these little loaves delicious flavor and help keep them nice and moist. They're great to wrap up in plastic wrap and give as gifts.

2	cups all-purpose flour
1	cup sugar
1	teaspoon baking powder
1/2	teaspoon baking soda
1/2	teaspoon salt
1/8	teaspoon ground nutmeg
1/2	cup cold butter
2	eggs
1/4	cup buttermilk
1	teaspoon vanilla extract
1	cup finely chopped peeled ripe pears

1 In a large bowl, combine the flour, sugar, baking powder, baking soda, salt and nutmeg. Cut in butter until mixture is crumbly. In a small bowl, beat the eggs, buttermilk and vanilla; stir into crumb mixture just until moistened. Fold in the pears.

2 Spoon into two greased 5-3/4-in. x 3-in. x 2-in. loaf pans. Bake at 350° for 35-40 minutes or until a toothpick inserted near the center comes out clean. Cool for 10 minutes before removing from pans to a wire rack to cool completely.

checking quick breads *for doneness*

Insert a toothpick near the center of the bread. If the toothpick comes out clean—without any crumbs—the bread is done.

Pineapple Carrot Bread

PREP: 10 min. **BAKE:** 65 min. + cooling
YIELD: 2 loaves

Paula Spink, Elkins Park, Pennsylvania

This bread has the wonderful flavor of carrot cake but is jazzed up with crushed pineapple.

- 3 cups all-purpose flour
- 2 cups sugar
- 1 teaspoon baking soda
- 1 teaspoon ground cinnamon
- 3/4 teaspoon salt
- 3 eggs
- 2 cups shredded carrots
- 1 cup vegetable oil
- 1 can (8 ounces) crushed pineapple, drained
- 2 teaspoons vanilla extract
- 1 cup chopped pecans *or* walnuts
- 3/4 cup confectioners' sugar, optional
- 1 to 1-1/2 teaspoons milk, optional

1 In a large bowl, combine the flour, sugar, baking soda, cinnamon and salt. In another bowl, beat the eggs; add carrots, oil, pineapple and vanilla. Stir into dry ingredients just until moistened. Fold in nuts.

2 Spoon into two greased 8-in. x 4-in. x 2-in. loaf pans. Bake at 350° for 65-75 minutes or until a toothpick inserted near the center comes out clean. Cool for 10 minutes before removing from pans to wire racks to cool completely. If glaze is desired, combine confectioners' sugar and milk; drizzle over loaves.

Southern Banana Nut Bread

PREP: 15 min. **BAKE:** 45 min. + cooling
YIELD: 2 loaves

Viva Forman, Tallahassee, Florida

With bananas and pecans in both the bread and topping, this bread really is one of a kind. Use ripe bananas for the most intense flavor.

- 1/2 cup butter-flavored shortening
- 1-1/2 cups sugar
- 2 eggs
- 1 cup mashed ripe bananas (2 to 3 medium)
- 1 teaspoon vanilla extract
- 2 cups self-rising flour
- 1/2 cup buttermilk
- 3/4 cup chopped pecans

TOPPING:
- 1/4 to 1/3 cup mashed ripe banana
- 1-1/4 cups confectioners' sugar
- 1 teaspoon lemon juice
- Additional chopped pecans

1 In a large mixing bowl, cream shortening and sugar until light and fluffy. Beat in eggs. Blend in bananas and vanilla. Add flour alternately with buttermilk, beating well after each addition. Fold in pecans.

2 Pour into two greased 8-in. x 4-in. x 2-in. loaf pans. Bake at 350° for 45-55 minutes or until a toothpick inserted near the center comes out clean. Cool for 10 minutes before removing from pans to wire racks to cool completely.

3 For topping, combine the banana, confectioners' sugar and lemon juice in a small bowl. Spread over loaves. Sprinkle with pecans.

Editor's Note: As a substitute for the self-rising flour, place 3 teaspoons baking powder and 1 teaspoon salt in a measuring cup. Add all-purpose flour to equal 1 cup. Then add another cup of all-purpose flour.

SOUTHERN BANANA NUT BREAD

Pumpkin Spice Bread

PREP: 10 min. **BAKE:** 1 hour + cooling
YIELD: 2 loaves

Delora Lucas, Belle, West Virginia

One bite and you'll agree this moist bread tastes just like pumpkin pie without the crust. It's perfect for dinner on a cool crisp fall night.

- 3 cups sugar
- 1 cup vegetable oil
- 4 eggs, lightly beaten
- 1 can (15 ounces) solid-pack pumpkin
- 3-1/2 cups all-purpose flour
- 1 teaspoon baking soda
- 1 teaspoon salt
- 1 teaspoon ground cinnamon
- 1 teaspoon ground nutmeg
- 1/2 teaspoon baking powder
- 1/2 teaspoon ground cloves
- 1/2 teaspoon ground allspice
- 1/2 cup water

1 In a large bowl, combine the sugar, oil and eggs. Add pumpkin and mix well. Combine the flour, baking soda, salt, cinnamon, nutmeg, baking powder, cloves and allspice; add to the pumpkin mixture alternately with water, beating well after each addition.

2 Pour into two greased 9-in. x 5-in. x 3-in. loaf pans. Bake at 350° for 60-65 minutes or until a toothpick inserted near the center comes out clean. Cool for 10 minutes before removing from pans to wire racks to cool completely.

testing
baking powder & soda
for freshness

Much of a quick bread's success depends upon baking powder and baking soda. So test them for freshness before using.

- For baking powder, mix 1 teaspoon baking powder and 1/3 cup hot water.
- For baking soda, mix 1/4 teaspoon baking soda and 2 teaspoons vinegar.

If bubbling occurs, the products are still fresh. If not, they should be replaced.

TRIPLE-CHOCOLATE QUICK BREAD

Triple-Chocolate Quick Bread

PREP: 20 min. **BAKE:** 35 min. + cooling
YIELD: 4 mini loaves

Karen Grimes, Stephens City, Virginia

Chocolate lovers will beg you to bake this bread! Chocolate chips dot the chocolate batter, while melted chips form the delectable glaze.

1-1/2 cups miniature semisweet chocolate chips, *divided*
1/2 cup butter, softened
2/3 cup packed brown sugar
2 eggs
1-1/2 cups applesauce
2 teaspoons vanilla extract
2-1/2 cups all-purpose flour
1 teaspoon baking powder
1 teaspoon baking soda
1 teaspoon salt
GLAZE:
1/2 cup miniature semisweet chocolate chips
1 tablespoon butter
2 to 3 tablespoons half-and-half cream
1/2 cup confectioners' sugar
1/4 teaspoon vanilla extract
Pinch salt

1 In a microwave-safe bowl, melt 1 cup chocolate chips; set aside. In a large mixing bowl, cream butter and brown sugar until light and fluffy. Add eggs and melted chocolate; mix well. Add the applesauce and vanilla. Combine the flour, baking powder, baking soda and salt; add to creamed mixture and mix well. Stir in the remaining chocolate chips.

2 Spoon into four greased 5-3/4-in. x 3-in. x 2-in. loaf pans. Bake at 350° for 35-40 minutes or until a toothpick inserted near the center comes out clean. Cool for 10 minutes before removing from pans to wire racks.

3 For glaze, melt chocolate chips and butter in a small heavy saucepan; stir in cream. Remove from the heat. Stir in the confectioners' sugar, vanilla and salt. Drizzle over warm bread. Cool completely.

Orange Yogurt Bread

PREP: 15 min. **BAKE:** 55 min. + cooling **YIELD:** 1 loaf

Nancy Juntunen, Prattville, Alabama

This moist bread is complemented by a slightly tangy glaze. It makes a nice addition to a breakfast buffet.

2/3 cup butter, softened
1-1/4 cups sugar
2 eggs
1/2 cup plain yogurt
1/2 cup orange juice
1 tablespoon grated orange peel
2-1/2 cups all-purpose flour
1/2 teaspoon baking powder
1/2 teaspoon baking soda
1/2 teaspoon salt
GLAZE:
1/2 cup confectioners' sugar
2 to 3 teaspoons orange juice

1 In a large mixing bowl, cream butter and sugar until light and fluffy. Add eggs, one at a time, beating well after each addition. Add the yogurt, orange juice and peel. Combine the flour, baking powder, baking soda and salt; add to the creamed mixture and mix well.

2 Pour into a greased 9-in. x 5-in. x 3-in. loaf pan. Bake at 350° for 55-65 minutes or until a toothpick inserted near the center comes out clean (cover loosely with foil if top browns too quickly). Cool for 10 minutes before removing from pan to a wire rack to cool completely.

3 For glaze, combine confectioners' sugar and enough orange juice to achieve desired consistency. Drizzle over cooled bread.

Coconut Bread

PREP: 10 min. **BAKE:** 1 hour + cooling
YIELD: 2 loaves

Virginia Doyle, Pinedale, Wyoming

Fans of coconut will really enjoy this moist bread studded with walnuts. Get ready for recipe requests!

- 2 **cups sugar**
- 3/4 **cup vegetable oil**
- 4 **eggs**
- 2 **teaspoons coconut extract**
- 3 **cups all-purpose flour**
- 1 **teaspoon baking powder**
- 1/2 **teaspoon baking soda**
- 1/2 **teaspoon salt**
- 1 **cup buttermilk**
- 1 **cup flaked coconut**
- 1 **cup chopped walnuts**

1 In a large mixing bowl, combine the sugar, oil, eggs and extract. Combine the flour, baking powder, baking soda and salt; add to sugar mixture alternately with buttermilk, stirring just until moistened. Fold in coconut and walnuts.

2 Pour into two greased 8-in. x 4-in. x 2-in. loaf pans. Bake at 325° for 60-65 minutes or until a toothpick inserted near the center comes out clean. Cool for 10 minutes before removing from pans to wire racks to cool completely.

COCONUT BREAD

Lemon Blueberry Bread

PREP: 15 min. **BAKE:** 1 hour + cooling **YIELD:** 1 loaf

Julianne Johnson, Grove City, Minnesota

The lemon glaze adds a lustrous finish and locks in moisture. To have more of the glaze soak into the bread, first prick the top with the tines of a fork.

- 1/3 **cup butter, softened**
- 1 **cup sugar**
- 2 **eggs**
- 3 **tablespoons lemon juice**
- 1-1/2 **cups all-purpose flour**
- 1 **teaspoon baking powder**
- 1/2 **teaspoon salt**
- 1/2 **cup milk**
- 2 **tablespoons grated lemon peel**
- 1/2 **cup chopped nuts**
- 1 **cup fresh *or* frozen blueberries**

GLAZE:

- 2 **tablespoons lemon juice**
- 1/4 **cup sugar**

1 In a large mixing bowl, cream butter and sugar until light and fluffy. Beat in eggs and lemon juice. Combine the flour, baking powder and salt; add to the creamed mixture alternately with milk, beating well after each addition. Fold in the lemon peel, nuts and blueberries.

2 Pour into a greased 8-in. x 4-in. x 2-in. loaf pan. Bake at 350° for 60-70 minutes or until a toothpick inserted near the center comes out clean. Cool for 10 minutes before removing from pan to a wire rack. Combine glaze ingredients; drizzle over warm bread. Cool completely.

Editor's Note: If using frozen blueberries, do not thaw before adding to batter.

Peachy Peach Bread

PREP: 15 min. **BAKE:** 40 min. + cooling
YIELD: 2 mini loaves

Leanne Fried, Bismarck, North Dakota

Since this recipe calls for canned peaches, you can enjoy a taste of summer even when the weather turns cool.

- 2 **cups all-purpose flour**
- 3/4 **cup packed brown sugar**
- 2 **teaspoons baking powder**
- 1/2 **teaspoon salt**
- 1 **can (15-1/4 ounces) sliced peaches**
- 2 **eggs**
- 6 **tablespoons butter, melted**
- 3/4 **cup chopped pecans**

Peach preserves

1 In a large bowl, combine the flour, brown sugar, baking powder and salt. Drain peaches, reserving 1/4 cup syrup. Finely chop 1 cup of the peaches; set aside. Place remaining peaches and reserved syrup in a blender or food processor; add eggs and butter. Cover and process until smooth. Stir into dry ingredients just until moistened. Fold in the pecans and chopped peaches.

2 Spoon into two greased 5-3/4-in. x 3-in. x 2-in. loaf pans. Bake at 350° for 40-45 minutes or until a toothpick inserted near the center comes out clean. Cool for 10 minutes before removing from pans to a wire rack to cool completely. Serve with peach preserves.

Mocha Nut Bread

PREP: 10 min. **BAKE:** 55 min. + cooling **YIELD:** 1 loaf

Winnie Higgins, Salisbury, Maryland

The unbeatable combination of coffee and chocolate is featured in this rich, dark-colored loaf.

- 2 **cups all-purpose flour**
- 1 **cup sugar**
- 1/3 **cup baking cocoa**
- 2 **tablespoons instant coffee granules**
- 1 **teaspoon baking soda**
- 1/4 **teaspoon salt**
- 2 **eggs**
- 1-1/4 **cups sour cream**
- 1/3 **cup butter, melted**
- 1-1/2 **cups semisweet chocolate chips**
- 1/2 **cup chopped pecans**

1 In a large bowl, combine the flour, sugar, cocoa, coffee granules, baking soda and salt. In another bowl, beat the eggs, sour cream and butter until smooth. Stir into dry ingredients just until moistened. Fold in chocolate chips and pecans.

2 Pour into a greased 9-in. x 5-in. x 3-in. loaf pan. Bake at 350° for 55-60 minutes or until a toothpick inserted near the center comes out clean. Cool for 10 minutes before removing from pan to a wire rack to cool completely.

Zucchini Chip Bread

PREP: 15 min. **BAKE:** 55 min. + cooling
YIELD: 2 loaves

Edie DeSpain, Logan, Utah

These mild orange-flavored loaves are chock-full of nuts, chocolate chips and spices.

- 3 **cups all-purpose flour**
- 2 **cups sugar**
- 1 **teaspoon baking soda**
- 1 **teaspoon salt**
- 1 **teaspoon ground nutmeg**
- 1/2 **teaspoon ground cinnamon**
- 1/4 **teaspoon baking powder**
- 3 **eggs**
- 1/2 **cup unsweetened applesauce**
- 1/2 **cup vegetable oil**
- 1 **tablespoon grated orange peel**
- 2 **teaspoons vanilla extract**
- 2 **cups shredded zucchini**
- 1 **cup chopped walnuts**
- 1 **cup (6 ounces) semisweet chocolate chips**

ZUCCHINI CHIP BREAD

1 In a large bowl, combine the flour, sugar, baking soda, salt, nutmeg, cinnamon and baking powder. In another bowl, beat the eggs, applesauce, oil, orange peel and vanilla. Stir into dry ingredients just until moistened. Fold in the zucchini, nuts and chocolate chips.

2 Transfer to two greased 8-in. x 4-in. x 2-in. loaf pans. Bake at 350° for 55-60 minutes or until a toothpick inserted near the center comes out clean. Cool for 10 minutes before removing from pans to wire racks to cool completely.

Date Pecan Tea Bread

PREP: 20 min. **BAKE:** 65 min.
YIELD: 1 loaf (1/2 cup spread)

Carole Resnick, Cleveland, Ohio

Packed with dates and pecans, this moist sweet bread is excellent on its own and even better topped with the chunky cream cheese spread.

2-1/2   cups chopped dates
1-1/2   cups boiling water
1-1/2   teaspoons baking soda
    2   tablespoons butter, softened
1-1/4   cups sugar
    1   egg
    2   teaspoons vanilla extract
1-3/4   cups all-purpose flour
  1/4   teaspoon *each* ground ginger,
        cinnamon, nutmeg and cloves
1-1/2   cups coarsely chopped pecans
SPREAD:
    1   package (3 ounces) cream cheese,
        softened
    2   tablespoons chopped dates
    2   tablespoons coarsely chopped pecans
    1   tablespoon milk

1 Place dates in a bowl. Combine boiling water and baking soda; pour over dates. In a large mixing bowl, cream butter and sugar until light and fluffy. Beat in egg and vanilla. Combine flour and spices; add to the creamed mixture alternately with date mixture, beating well after each addition. Fold in pecans.

2 Pour into a greased 9-in. x 5-in. x 3-in. loaf pan. Bake at 350° for 65-75 minutes or until a toothpick inserted near the center comes out clean. Cool for 10 minutes before removing from pan to a wire rack to cool completely.

3 Combine spread ingredients in a bowl. Cover and refrigerate for 1 hour. Serve with the bread.

DATE PECAN TEA BREAD

problem-solving **pointers** *for Quick Breads*

BREAD IS TOUGH AND DENSE OR HAS TUNNELS

• Batter was overmixed.

BREAD IS SOGGY

• Batter had too much liquid or fat.

CENTER OF BREAD HAS SUNK

• There was too little or too much leavening.
• Bread was underbaked.
• Batter stood too long before baking.

BREAD HAS A THICK BROWN CRUST

• Batter had too much sugar.

BREAD HAS A BITTER AFTERTASTE

• Batter had too much leavener.

BREAD CRUMBLED WHILE BEING CUT

• Bread was still warm. Cool completely before slicing.

NUTS, FRUIT OR CHOCOLATE CHIPS SINK TO BOTTOM OF BREAD

• Batter was too thin to hold the fruit, nuts or chips. Next time, chop them smaller or use miniature chocolate chips.

Savory Quick Breads

Round Cheese Bread

PREP: 10 min. **BAKE:** 20 min. + cooling
YIELD: 6-8 servings

Deborah Bitz, Medicine Hat, Alberta

This savory loaf has an Italian flair. Warm buttery wedges are tasty with a pasta dinner or tossed salad.

- 1-1/2 **cups biscuit/baking mix**
- 1 **cup (4 ounces) shredded part-skim mozzarella cheese**
- 1/4 **cup grated Parmesan cheese**
- 1/2 **teaspoon dried oregano**
- 1/2 **cup milk**
- 1 **egg, beaten**
- 2 **tablespoons butter, melted**

Additional Parmesan cheese

1 In a bowl, combine the biscuit mix, mozzarella cheese, Parmesan cheese, oregano, milk and egg (batter will be thick). Spoon into a greased 9-in. round baking pan. Drizzle with butter; sprinkle with additional Parmesan cheese.

2 Bake at 400° for 20-25 minutes or until a toothpick inserted near the center comes out clean. Cool for 10 minutes. Cut into wedges; serve warm.

storing *quick breads*

- Quick breads may be wrapped in foil or plastic wrap and stored at room temperature for up to 3 days. If made with cheese, cream cheese or other perishable foods, they should be refrigerated.

- For longer storage, place quick breads in heavy-duty resealable plastic bags and freeze for 3 months.

Hearty Oat Loaf

PREP: 15 min. **BAKE:** 40 min. **YIELD:** 1 loaf

Judi Havens, Denton, Texas

Offer wedges of this bread when making stew or bean soup. Or top a warm slice with jam and serve alongside your favorite breakfast.

- 2 **cups all-purpose flour**
- 1 **cup whole wheat flour**
- 1/2 **cup plus 2 tablespoons quick-cooking oats, *divided***
- 1/4 **cup sugar**
- 3 **teaspoons baking powder**
- 3/4 **teaspoon salt**
- 1 **egg**

ROUND CHEESE BREAD

1-1/2 cups milk
3 tablespoons vegetable oil

1 In a large bowl, combine the flours, 1/2 cup oats, sugar, baking powder and salt. In another bowl, combine the egg, milk and oil; stir into dry ingredients just until moistened. Spread into a greased 9-in. round baking pan. Sprinkle with remaining oats.

2 Bake at 350° for 40-50 minutes or until a toothpick inserted near the center comes out clean. Cool for 5 minutes before removing from pan to a wire rack. Serve warm.

Jalapeno Corn Bread

PREP: 10 min. **BAKE:** 50 min. **YIELD:** 9 servings
Anita LaRose, Benavides, Texas

With cream-style corn, cheddar cheese and buttermilk, this golden corn bread is more moist than others.

1 cup cornmeal
1/2 cup shredded cheddar cheese
2 teaspoons baking powder
3/4 teaspoon salt
2 eggs
1 can (8-3/4 ounces) cream-style corn
1 cup buttermilk
1/4 cup vegetable oil
1 to 2 tablespoons minced seeded jalapeno peppers

1 In a large bowl, combine the cornmeal, cheese, baking powder and salt. In another bowl, beat the eggs; add corn, buttermilk, oil and jalapenos. Stir into dry ingredients just until moistened.

2 Transfer to a greased 9-in. square baking pan. Bake at 350° for 50-55 minutes or until a toothpick inserted near the center comes out clean. Cut into squares; serve warm.

Editor's Note: When cutting or seeding hot peppers, use rubber or plastic gloves to protect your hands. Avoid touching your face.

Savory Onion Corn Bread

PREP: 25 min. **BAKE:** 30 min. **YIELD:** 9 servings
Ruth Chastain, Bellflower, California

Thanks to hot pepper sauce, this corn bread is sweet and spicy. Serve it with chili to warm everyone up on a cold winter evening.

1 medium sweet onion, chopped
1/4 cup butter
1 egg
1 cup cream-style corn
1/3 cup milk
2 drops hot pepper sauce
1 package (8-1/2 ounces) corn bread/muffin mix
1 cup (8 ounces) sour cream
1 cup (4 ounces) shredded cheddar cheese, *divided*
1/4 teaspoon salt
1/4 teaspoon dill weed

1 In a small skillet, saute onion in butter until tender; set aside. In a bowl, combine the egg, corn, milk and hot pepper sauce; stir in muffin mix just until moistened. Pour into a greased 8-in. square baking dish.

2 Combine the sour cream, 1/2 cup cheese, salt, dill and sauteed onion; spoon over batter. Sprinkle with remaining cheese. Bake at 425° for 30-35 minutes or until a toothpick inserted near the center comes out clean. Cut into squares; serve warm.

Caraway Cheese Bread

PREP: 10 min. **BAKE:** 30 min. + cooling
YIELD: 1 loaf

Mrs. Homer Wooten, Ridgetown, Ontario

*In this savory bread, cheddar cheese blends beautifully
with just the right amount of caraway.*

2-1/2 **cups all-purpose flour**
   2 **cups (8 ounces) shredded cheddar
      cheese**
1-1/2 **to 2 teaspoons caraway seeds**
 3/4 **teaspoon salt**
 1/2 **teaspoon baking powder**
 1/2 **teaspoon baking soda**
   2 **eggs**
   1 **cup (8 ounces) plain yogurt**
 1/2 **cup butter, melted**
   1 **tablespoon Dijon mustard**

1 In a large bowl, combine the flour, cheese,
caraway seeds, salt, baking powder and baking
soda. In another bowl, beat the eggs, yogurt,
butter and mustard. Stir into dry ingredients just
until moistened.

2 Pour into a greased 9-in. x 5-in. x 3-in. loaf pan.
Bake at 375° for 30-35 minutes or until a toothpick inserted near the center comes out clean.
Cool for 10 minutes before removing from pan
to a wire rack. Serve warm. Refrigerate leftovers.

Herbed Monkey Bread

PREP: 10 min. **BAKE:** 20 min. + cooling **YIELD:** 1 loaf

Donna Gordon, Averill Park, New York

*Most folks are familiar with the sweet version of monkey
bread. Here a blend of herbs makes a savory bread perfect
for pairing with a variety of main courses.*

1/2 **cup butter, melted**
  1 **garlic clove, minced**
  2 **teaspoons dried parsley flakes**
  1 **teaspoon dried chives**
1/2 **teaspoon dried basil**
1/2 **teaspoon dried oregano**
  2 **packages (12 ounces *each*) refrigerated
     buttermilk biscuits**

1 In a small bowl, combine the butter, garlic and
seasonings. Dip biscuits in butter mixture; place
in a greased 10-in. fluted tube pan.

2 Bake at 400° for 18-20 minutes or until golden
brown. Cool for 10 minutes before removing
from pan to a wire rack. Serve warm.

Irish Soda Bread

PREP: 20 min. **BAKE:** 40 min. **YIELD:** 2 loaves

Anne Flanagan, Laguna Hills, California

*Legend has it that the cross cut on the top of traditional
Irish soda bread before baking will ward off evil spirits.*

   4 **cups all-purpose flour**
 1/4 **cup sugar**
   1 **teaspoon baking powder**
   1 **teaspoon baking soda**
 1/2 **teaspoon salt**
   6 **tablespoons shortening**
 1/2 **cup raisins**
   1 **tablespoon caraway seeds**
1-1/4 **cups buttermilk**
   1 **egg, lightly beaten**
   2 **tablespoons butter, melted**
Cinnamon-sugar

1 In a large bowl, combine the flour, sugar, baking
powder, baking soda and salt. Cut in shortening
until mixture is crumbly. Stir in raisins and
caraway seeds. Combine buttermilk and egg; stir
into the crumb mixture. Turn onto a lightly
floured surface; knead gently 5-6 times.

2 Divide dough in half; shape into two balls. Place
on a lightly greased baking sheet. Pat each ball
into a 6-in. round loaf. Using a sharp knife, cut a
4-in. cross about 1/4 in. deep on top of each loaf.
Brush with butter and sprinkle with cinnamon-
sugar. Bake at 375° for 40-45 minutes or until
golden brown. Remove from pans to wire racks.

IRISH SODA BREAD

Finnish Flat Bread

PREP: 20 min. **BAKE:** 30 min. + cooling
YIELD: 6-8 servings

Anne Heinonen, Howell, Michigan

It's so nice to have homemade bread with a stew, and it's even nicer when you don't have to fuss.

- 1-1/2 **cups all-purpose flour**
- 3/4 **cup whole wheat flour**
- 2 **tablespoons sugar**
- 1-1/2 **teaspoons baking powder**
- 1 **teaspoon salt**
- 1/2 **teaspoon baking soda**
- 1/4 **cup shortening**
- 1 **cup buttermilk**

1 In a large bowl, combine the flours, sugar, baking powder, salt and baking soda. Cut in shortening until mixture is crumbly. Stir in buttermilk just until moistened.

2 Turn dough onto a floured surface; knead for 3-5 minutes. Pat onto an ungreased 12-in. pizza pan. Bake at 350° for 30-35 minutes or until golden. Cool for 10 minutes before removing from pan to a wire rack.

FINNISH FLAT BREAD

Boston Brown Bread

PREP: 10 min. **BAKE:** 80 min. + cooling
YIELD: 2 loaves

Shellie Robb, Cleveland, Ohio

Whole wheat, brown sugar and molasses lend to the rich brown color of this hearty bread.

- 2 **eggs**
- 2 **cups packed brown sugar**
- 1 **cup molasses**
- 4 **cups buttermilk**
- 4 **cups whole wheat flour**
- 2 **cups all-purpose flour**
- 2 **teaspoons salt**
- 2 **teaspoons baking soda**
- 1 **cup raisins**
- 1 **cup chopped walnuts**

Butter *or* cream cheese, optional

1 In a large mixing bowl, beat the eggs and brown sugar. Add molasses and buttermilk; mix well. Combine the flours, salt and baking soda; stir into egg mixture just until moistened. Fold in raisins and walnuts.

2 Transfer to two greased 9-in. x 5-in. x 3-in. loaf pans. Bake at 325° for 80-85 minutes or until a

toothpick inserted near the center comes out clean. Cool for 10 minutes before removing from pans to wire racks to cool completely. Serve with butter or cream cheese if desired.

Pizza Bread

PREP: 10 min. **BAKE:** 15 min. **YIELD:** 8-10 servings

Carla Hodenfield, Mandan, North Dakota

Use this moist cheesy bread as a fun appetizer, or to complement Italian meals and main-dish salads.

- 2 **teaspoons cornmeal**
- 1 **tube (12 ounces) refrigerated biscuits**
- 1/2 **cup pizza sauce**
- 3/4 **cup shredded part-skim mozzarella cheese**

1 Sprinkle cornmeal on the bottom of a greased 8-in. square baking dish. Cut each biscuit into quarters; toss with pizza sauce.

2 Place in dish; sprinkle with cheese. Bake at 400° for 14 minutes or until golden brown.

Quick Coffee Cakes

Cinnamon Coffee Cake

PREP: 20 min. **BAKE:** 1 hour + cooling
YIELD: 16-20 servings

Eleanor Harris, Cape Coral, Florida

You'll love the texture of this old-fashioned, streusel-topped coffee cake. Always a crowd-pleaser, its sweet vanilla flavor is enhanced by sour cream.

> 1 cup butter, softened
> 2-3/4 cups sugar, *divided*
> 4 eggs
> 2 teaspoons vanilla extract
> 3 cups all-purpose flour
> 1 teaspoon baking soda
> 1 teaspoon salt
> 2 cups (16 ounces) sour cream
> 2 tablespoons ground cinnamon
> 1/2 cup chopped walnuts

1 In a large mixing bowl, cream butter and 2 cups sugar until light and fluffy. Add eggs, one at a time, beating well after each addition. Beat in vanilla. Combine the flour, baking soda and salt; add to the creamed mixture alternately with sour cream, beating just enough after each addition to keep batter smooth.

2 Spoon a third of the batter into a greased 10-in. tube pan. Combine the cinnamon, nuts and remaining sugar; sprinkle a third over batter.

CINNAMON COFFEE CAKE

making a streusel-filled *coffee cake*

Spoon about a third of the batter into greased pan. Sprinkle with a third of the streusel mixture. Repeat layers twice. Bake as directed.

Repeat layers twice. Bake at 350° for 60-65 minutes or until a toothpick inserted near the center comes out clean. Cool for 15 minutes before removing from pan to a wire rack to cool completely.

Monkey Bread

PREP: 15 min. **BAKE:** 30 min. + cooling
YIELD: 10-12 servings

Carol Allen, McLeansboro, Illinois

Let your children help by having them shake the biscuits in the sugar mixture and arrange the biscuits in the pan. It will be fun for them to make as well as to eat this treat.

> 1 package (3-1/2 ounces) cook-and-serve butterscotch pudding mix
> 3/4 cup sugar
> 1 tablespoon ground cinnamon
> 1/2 cup finely chopped pecans, optional
> 1/2 cup butter, melted
> 3 tubes (10 ounces *each*) refrigerated biscuits

1 In a large resealable plastic bag, combine the pudding mix, sugar, cinnamon and pecans if desired. Pour the butter into a shallow bowl. Cut the biscuits into quarters. Dip several pieces into the butter, then place in bag and shake to coat.

2 Arrange in a greased 10-in. fluted tube pan. Repeat until all the biscuit pieces are coated. Bake at 350° for 30-35 minutes or until browned. Cool for 30 minutes before inverting onto a plate.

Cherry Swirl Coffee Cake

PREP: 15 min. **BAKE:** 40 min. **YIELD:** 18-20 servings

Charlene Griffin, Minocqua, Wisconsin

A pretty cherry pie filling peeks out from the golden brown sweet dough in this classic recipe that has mass appeal.

1-1/2 **cups sugar**
  1/2 **cup butter, softened**
  1/2 **cup shortening**
    1 **teaspoon almond extract**
    1 **teaspoon vanilla extract**
  1/2 **teaspoon baking powder**
    4 **eggs**
    3 **cups all-purpose flour**
    1 **can (21 ounces) cherry pie filling**
    1 **cup confectioners' sugar**
    1 **to 2 tablespoons milk**

1 In a large mixing bowl, combine the sugar, butter, shortening, extracts, baking powder and eggs. Beat on low speed until blended; beat on high for 3 minutes. Stir in flour.

2 Spread two-thirds of the batter into a greased 15-in. x 10-in. x 1-in. baking pan. Spread pie filling over batter. Drop remaining batter by tablespoonfuls over filling. Bake at 350° for 40-45 minutes or until a toothpick inserted near the center comes out clean and top is golden. Combine the confectioners' sugar and milk; drizzle over coffee cake. Serve warm.

Strawberry Rhubarb Coffee Cake

PREP: 20 min. + cooling **BAKE:** 45 min. + cooling
YIELD: 12-16 servings

Benita Thomas, Falcon, Colorado

Even people who don't care for rhubarb will find this coffee cake hard to resist.

  2/3 **cup sugar**
  1/3 **cup cornstarch**
    2 **cups chopped fresh *or* frozen rhubarb**
    1 **package (10 ounces) frozen sweetened sliced strawberries, thawed**
    2 **tablespoons lemon juice**
CAKE:
    3 **cups all-purpose flour**
    1 **cup sugar**
    1 **teaspoon baking powder**
  1/2 **teaspoon baking soda**
    1 **cup cold butter**
    2 **eggs**
    1 **cup buttermilk**

STRAWBERRY RHUBARB COFFEE CAKE

    1 **teaspoon vanilla extract**
TOPPING:
  3/4 **cup sugar**
  1/2 **cup all-purpose flour**
  1/4 **cup cold butter**

1 In a saucepan, combine sugar and cornstarch; stir in rhubarb and strawberries. Bring to a boil over medium heat; cook for 2 minutes or until thickened. Remove from the heat; stir in lemon juice and cool.

2 In a large bowl, combine the flour, sugar, baking powder and baking soda; cut in butter until mixture is crumbly. In another bowl, beat the eggs, buttermilk and vanilla; stir into crumb mixture just until moistened. Spoon two-thirds of the batter into a greased 13-in. x 9-in. x 2-in. baking pan. Top with the fruit mixture and the remaining batter.

3 For topping, combine sugar and flour in a small bowl; cut in butter until mixture is crumbly. Sprinkle over batter. Bake at 350° for 45-50 minutes or until a toothpick inserted near the center comes out clean and cake is golden brown. Cool on a wire rack.

Editor's Note: If using frozen rhubarb, measure rhubarb while still frozen, then thaw completely. Drain in a colander, but do not press liquid out.

BLUEBERRY ALMOND COFFEE CAKE

Blueberry Almond Coffee Cake

PREP: 15 min. **BAKE:** 25 min. + cooling
YIELD: 9 servings

Brenda Carr, Houston, Texas

Since this chock-full of blueberries coffee cake is not overly sweet, it's just the thing for breakfast or a light dessert.

  1 **cup all-purpose flour**
1/2 **cup sugar**
3/4 **teaspoon baking powder**
1/2 **teaspoon salt**
1/4 **teaspoon baking soda**
  1 **egg**
2/3 **cup buttermilk**
  2 **tablespoons butter, melted**
  1 **teaspoon vanilla extract**
1/4 **teaspoon almond extract**
  1 **cup fresh *or* frozen blueberries, *divided***
1/2 **cup sliced almonds**
  1 **tablespoon brown sugar**
1/4 **teaspoon ground cinnamon**

1 In a large bowl, combine the flour, sugar, baking powder, salt and baking soda. In another bowl, whisk the egg, buttermilk, butter and extracts until blended. Stir into dry ingredients just until moistened. Stir in 2/3 cup blueberries.

2 Pour into a greased 8-in. square baking dish. Top with remaining blueberries. Combine the almonds, brown sugar and cinnamon; sprinkle over the top. Bake at 350° for 25-30 minutes or until a toothpick inserted near the center comes out clean. Cool on a wire rack.

Editor's Note: If using frozen blueberries, do not thaw before adding to batter.

Hazelnut Crumb Coffee Cake

PREP: 15 min. **BAKE:** 35 min. **YIELD:** 4 servings

Donna Cattanach, Redding, California

This recipe started as a plain brunch cake with some modifications. It now tastes like a hot fudge sundae cake.

  2 **tablespoons all-purpose flour**
1/4 **cup packed brown sugar**
  2 **tablespoons cold butter**
1/4 **cup finely chopped hazelnuts**
BATTER:
  1 **square (1 ounce) semisweet chocolate**
  1 **cup all-purpose flour**
1/2 **cup sugar**
1/2 **teaspoon baking soda**
1/4 **teaspoon salt**
1/2 **cup sour cream**
1/4 **cup butter, softened**
  1 **egg, beaten**

1 In a small bowl, combine the flour and sugar; cut in butter until crumbly. Stir in nuts; set aside.

2 In a small saucepan, melt chocolate over low heat. Stir until smooth; cool. In a small mixing bowl, combine the flour, sugar, baking soda and salt. Add the sour cream, butter and egg; beat until blended. Remove 1 cup of batter; stir in chocolate.

3 Spread the remaining batter into a greased 8-in. square baking dish; spoon chocolate batter over the top. Cut through batters with a knife to swirl. Sprinkle with reserved nut topping. Bake at 350° for 35-40 minutes or until a toothpick inserted near center comes out clean. Cool on a wire rack.

choosing a *nut*

Most coffee cake recipes that use nuts will list a specific kind of nut. If you don't have that type in your pantry, feel free to substitute one that you have on hand.

Raspberry Crumb Cake

PREP: 20 min. + cooling **BAKE:** 50 min.
YIELD: 12-16 servings

Pat Habiger, Spearville, Kansas

A cake spiced with cinnamon and mace, a yummy rasp-berry filling and a crunchy almond topping assures this tempting treat will brighten any buffet.

2/3	cup sugar
1/4	cup cornstarch
3/4	cup water
2	cups fresh *or* frozen unsweetened raspberries
1	tablespoon lemon juice

CAKE:

3	cups all-purpose flour
1	cup sugar
3	teaspoons baking powder
1	teaspoon salt
1	teaspoon ground cinnamon
1/4	teaspoon ground mace
1	cup cold butter
2	eggs
1	cup milk
1	teaspoon vanilla extract

TOPPING:

1/2	cup all-purpose flour
1/2	cup sugar
1/4	cup cold butter
1/4	cup sliced almonds

1 In a saucepan, combine sugar, cornstarch, water and raspberries. Bring to a boil over medium heat; boil for 5 minutes or until thickened, stirring constantly. Remove from the heat; stir in lemon juice. Cool.

2 In a large bowl, combine the flour, sugar, baking powder, salt, cinnamon and mace. Cut in butter until mixture is crumbly. In another bowl, beat the eggs, milk and vanilla; add to crumb mixture and mix well. Spread two-thirds of the batter into a greased 13-in. x 9-in. x 2-in. baking dish. Spoon raspberry filling over the top to within 1 in. of edges. Top with remaining batter.

3 For topping, combine flour and sugar in a bowl; cut in butter until mixture is crumbly. Stir in almonds. Sprinkle over batter. Bake at 350° for 50-55 minutes or until a toothpick inserted near center comes out clean and top is lightly browned.

RASPBERRY CRUMB CAKE

Cranberry Coffee Cake

PREP: 15 min. **BAKE:** 50 min. + cooling
YIELD: 12-16 servings

Judith Casserly, York Beach, Maine

This recipe uses cranberry sauce, making it great for when cranberries aren't in season.

- 1/2 **cup butter, softened**
- 1 **cup sugar**
- 2 **eggs**
- 1 **teaspoon almond extract**
- 2 **cups all-purpose flour**
- 1 **teaspoon baking powder**
- 1/2 **teaspoon baking soda**
- 1/2 **teaspoon salt**
- 1 **cup (8 ounces) sour cream**
- 1/3 **cup chopped walnuts**
- 1 **can (16 ounces) whole-berry cranberry sauce**

GLAZE:
- 3/4 **cup confectioners' sugar**
- 2 **tablespoons milk**
- 1/2 **teaspoon vanilla extract**

1 In a large mixing bowl, cream butter and sugar until light and fluffy. Add eggs, one at a time, beating well after each addition. Stir in almond extract. Combine the flour, baking powder, baking soda and salt; add to the creamed mixture alternately with sour cream, beating well after each addition.

CRANBERRY COFFEE CAKE

2 Sprinkle the walnuts into a greased 10-in. fluted tube pan. Spread half of the batter over nuts; top with half of the cranberry sauce. Repeat layers.

3 Bake at 350° for 50-55 minutes or until a toothpick inserted near the center comes out clean. Cool for 10 minutes before removing from pan to a wire rack to cool completely. Combine glaze ingredients; drizzle over coffee cake.

Peachy Sour Cream Coffee Cake

PREP: 25 min. **BAKE:** 70 min. + cooling
YIELD: 12 servings

Alice Brandt, Marengo, Illinois

The top of this coffee cake is adorned with fresh peaches.

- 2 **cups chopped pecans**
- 1/3 **cup packed brown sugar**
- 3 **tablespoons sugar**
- 1 **teaspoon ground cinnamon**

CAKE:
- 1/2 **cup butter-flavored shortening**
- 1 **cup sugar**
- 2 **eggs**
- 1 **teaspoon vanilla extract**
- 2 **cups all-purpose flour**
- 1/2 **teaspoon baking powder**
- 1/2 **teaspoon baking soda**
- 1/2 **teaspoon salt**
- 1 **cup (8 ounces) sour cream**
- 2 **cups sliced peeled fresh peaches (about 3 medium)**

1 In a small bowl, combine the pecans, sugars and cinnamon; set aside. In a large mixing bowl, cream shortening and sugar until light and fluffy. Add eggs, one at a time, beating well after each addition. Beat in vanilla. Combine the flour, baking powder, baking soda and salt; add to the creamed mixture alternately with sour cream, beating well after each addition.

2 Pour half of batter into a greased 10-in. tube pan with removable bottom. Sprinkle with 1 cup pecan mixture. Top with remaining batter and 1/2 cup pecan mixture. Bake at 350° for 40 minutes.

3 Arrange peaches over cake; sprinkle with remaining pecan mixture. Bake 30-35 minutes longer or until a toothpick inserted near the center comes out clean. Cool for 10 minutes. Run a knife around edge of pan to loosen. Lift cake with removable bottom from pan. Cool. Just before serving, carefully remove cake from pan bottom. Store in the refrigerator.

Banana Coffee Cake

PREP: 15 min. **BAKE:** 25 min. + cooling
YIELD: 12-15 servings

Georgia Courtney, Las Cruces, New Mexico

You'll go bananas over this yummy coffee cake topped with cinnamon, sugar and pecans! It's easy to transport to potlucks and parties.

- 1 package (8 ounces) cream cheese, softened
- 1/2 cup butter, softened
- 1-1/4 cups sugar
- 2 eggs
- 1 cup mashed ripe bananas (2 to 3 medium)
- 1 teaspoon vanilla extract
- 2-1/4 cups all-purpose flour
- 1-1/2 teaspoons baking powder
- 1/2 teaspoon baking soda

TOPPING:
- 1 cup chopped pecans
- 2 tablespoons sugar
- 1 teaspoon ground cinnamon

1 In a large mixing bowl, beat the cream cheese, butter and sugar until blended. Add eggs, one at a time, beating well after each addition. Add the bananas and vanilla. Combine the flour, baking powder and baking soda; gradually add to the creamed mixture. Combine topping ingredients; stir half into the batter.

2 Transfer to a greased 13-in. x 9-in. x 2-in. baking pan. Sprinkle with the remaining topping. Bake at 350° for 25-30 minutes or until a toothpick inserted near the center comes out clean. Cool on a wire rack.

CARAMEL APPLE COFFEE CAKE

Caramel Apple Coffee Cake

PREP: 25 min. **BAKE:** 1-1/4 hours + cooling
YIELD: 12-16 servings

Ruth Turner, Marinette, Wisconsin

A rich caramel topping is the crowning touch on this delicious apple coffee cake.

- 3 eggs
- 2 cups sugar
- 1-1/2 cups vegetable oil
- 2 teaspoons vanilla extract
- 3 cups all-purpose flour
- 1 teaspoon baking soda
- 1 teaspoon salt
- 3 cups chopped peeled apples
- 1 cup coarsely chopped pecans

TOPPING:
- 1/2 cup butter
- 1/4 cup milk
- 1 cup packed brown sugar

Pinch salt

1 In a large mixing bowl, beat the eggs until foamy; gradually add sugar. Blend in oil and vanilla. Combine the flour, baking soda and salt; add to egg mixture. Stir in apples and pecans. Pour into a greased 10-in. tube pan. Bake at 350° for 1-1/4 hours or until a toothpick inserted near the center comes out clean. Cool for 10 minutes before inverting onto a serving plate.

2 In a small saucepan, combine topping ingredients. Bring to a boil; boil for 3 minutes, stirring constantly. Slowly pour over warm cake (some topping will run down onto the plate).

reheating *coffee cakes*

If you make a coffee cake in advance but want fresh-from-the-oven flavor when you serve it to guests, try this trick.

Wrap an unfrosted coffee cake in foil. Reheat at 350° for a few minutes or until warm.

ALMOND APRICOT COFFEE CAKE

Almond Apricot Coffee Cake

PREP: 20 min. **BAKE:** 55 min. + cooling
YIELD: 12-16 servings

Sharon Mensing, Greenfield, Iowa

The nutty aroma and delicate fruit flavor make this cake special enough to serve to company. Strawberry or raspberry preserves can be used as a tasty variation.

- 1 **cup butter, softened**
- 2 **cups sugar**
- 3 **eggs**
- 1 **cup (8 ounces) sour cream**
- 1 **teaspoon almond extract**
- 2 **cups all-purpose flour**
- 1/2 **teaspoon baking powder**
- 1/2 **teaspoon baking soda**
- 1/4 **teaspoon salt**
- 3/4 **cup slivered almonds**, *divided*
- 1 **jar (10 to 12 ounces) apricot preserves,** *divided*

1 In a large mixing bowl, cream butter and sugar until light and fluffy. Add the eggs, sour cream and extract; mix well. Combine the flour, baking powder, baking soda and salt; add to the creamed mixture and mix well.

2 Spread half of the batter into a greased and floured 10-in. fluted tube pan. Sprinkle with half of the almonds. Spread half of the preserves to within 1/2 in. of the edges. Cover with remaining batter. Spoon remaining preserves over batter to within 1/2 in. of edges. Sprinkle with remaining almonds.

3 Bake at 350° for 55-60 minutes or until a toothpick inserted near the center comes out clean. Cool for 15 minutes before inverting onto a serving plate.

Chocolate Chip Coffee Cake

PREP: 10 min. **BAKE:** 25 min. + cooling
YIELD: 12-16 servings

Trish Quinn, Middletown, Pennsylvania

With chocolate chips and cinnamon in the middle and on top, this special breakfast treat never fails to please all ages.

- 1/2 **cup butter, softened**
- 1-1/2 **cups sugar,** *divided*
- 2 **eggs**
- 1 **cup (8 ounces) sour cream**
- 1 **teaspoon vanilla extract**
- 2-1/2 **cups all-purpose flour**
- 1-1/2 **teaspoons baking powder**

- 1 teaspoon baking soda
- 1 cup (6 ounces) semisweet chocolate chips
- 1 teaspoon ground cinnamon

1 In a large mixing bowl, cream butter and 1 cup sugar until light and fluffy. Add the eggs, sour cream and vanilla; mix well. Combine the flour, baking powder and baking soda; add to the creamed mixture (batter will be thick).

2 Spread half of the batter into a greased 13-in. x 9-in. x 2-in. baking pan. Combine chocolate chips, cinnamon and remaining sugar; sprinkle half over batter. Drop remaining batter by spoonfuls over the top. Sprinkle with remaining chip mixture. Bake at 350° for 25-30 minutes or until a toothpick inserted near the center comes out clean. Cool on a wire rack.

Graham Streusel Coffee Cake

PREP: 20 min. **BAKE:** 40 min. + cooling
YIELD: 12-16 servings

Blanche Whytsell, Arnoldsburg, Wyoming

This coffee cake is also delicious with just a dusting of confectioners' sugar instead of the drizzle.

- 1-1/2 cups graham cracker crumbs
- 3/4 cup packed brown sugar
- 3/4 cup chopped pecans

GRAHAM STREUSEL COFFEE CAKE

- 1-1/2 teaspoons ground cinnamon
- 2/3 cup butter, melted
- 1 package (18-1/4 ounces) yellow cake mix
- 1/2 cup confectioners' sugar
- 1 tablespoon milk

1 In a small bowl, combine the cracker crumbs, brown sugar, pecans and cinnamon. Stir in butter; set aside. Prepare cake mix according to package directions.

2 Pour half of the batter into a greased 13-in. x 9-in. x 2-in. baking pan. Sprinkle with half of the graham cracker mixture. Carefully spoon the remaining batter on top. Sprinkle with the remaining graham cracker mixture.

3 Bake at 350° for 40-45 minutes or until a toothpick inserted near the center comes out clean. Cool on a wire rack. Combine confectioners' sugar and milk; drizzle over coffee cake.

Berry Cream Coffee Cake

PREP/TOTAL TIME: 30 min. **YIELD:** 8-10 servings

Marjorie Miller, Haven, Kansas

For easy instructions on assembling this heavenly coffee cake, see Braiding a Filled Bread on page 391.

- 1 package (3 ounces) cream cheese
- 1/4 cup cold butter
- 2 cups biscuit/baking mix
- 1/3 cup milk
- 1/2 cup raspberry preserves

GLAZE:
- 1 cup confectioners' sugar
- 1 to 2 tablespoons milk
- 1/2 teaspoon vanilla extract

1 In a bowl, cut cream cheese and butter into biscuit mix until crumbly. Stir in milk just until moistened. Turn onto a floured surface; knead 8-10 times or until dough is smooth. On waxed paper, roll dough into a 12-in. x 8-in. rectangle. Turn onto a greased 15-in. x 10-in. x 1-in. baking pan. Remove waxed paper.

2 Spread preserves down center third of rectangle. On each long side, cut 1-in.-wide strips about 2-1/2 in. into center. Starting at one end, fold alternating strips at an angle across preserves; seal end. Bake at 425° for 12-15 minutes. Combine the glaze ingredients; drizzle over warm coffee cake. Cool on a wire rack.

Raspberry Cheese Coffee Cake

PREP: 20 min. **BAKE:** 55 min. + cooling
YIELD: 9-12 servings

Susan Litwiller, Medford, Oregon

Since this recipe calls for raspberry jam and not fresh raspberries, you can make this coffee cake any time of year and bring a touch of spring to your table.

- 2-1/4 **cups all-purpose flour**
- 3/4 **cup sugar**
- 3/4 **cup cold butter**
- 1/2 **teaspoon baking powder**
- 1/2 **teaspoon baking soda**
- 1/2 **teaspoon salt**
- 3/4 **cup sour cream**
- 1 **egg, beaten**
- 1-1/2 **teaspoons almond extract**

FILLING:
- 1 **package (8 ounces) cream cheese, softened**
- 1/2 **cup sugar**
- 1 **egg**
- 1/2 **cup raspberry jam**
- 1/2 **cup slivered almonds**

1 In a large mixing bowl, combine flour and sugar; cut in butter until mixture is crumbly. Remove 1 cup and set aside. To the remaining crumb mixture, add baking powder, baking soda, salt, sour cream, egg and almond extract; mix well. Spread onto the bottom and 2 in. up the sides of a greased 9-in. springform pan.

RASPBERRY CHEESE COFFEE CAKE

2 For filling, combine cream cheese, sugar and egg in a small mixing bowl; beat well. Spoon over batter. Top with raspberry jam. Sprinkle with almonds and reserved crumb mixture. Bake at 350° for 55-60 minutes or until a toothpick inserted near the center comes out clean. Cool on a wire rack for 15 minutes. Carefully run a knife around edge of pan to loosen. Remove sides of pan. Cool completely. Store in the refrigerator.

Apple Coffee Cake

PREP: 20 min. **BAKE:** 40 min. + cooling
YIELD: 12-16 servings

Oriana Churchill
Londonderry, New Hampshire

This tried-and-true recipe tastes wonderful. The apple filling makes it moist, while the crispy nut mixture adds a bit of crunch.

- 1/2 **cup butter, softened**
- 1-1/2 **cups sugar, *divided***
- 2 **eggs**
- 1 **teaspoon vanilla extract**
- 2 **cups all-purpose flour**
- 1 **teaspoon baking powder**
- 1/2 **teaspoon baking soda**
- 1/2 **teaspoon salt**
- 1 **cup (8 ounces) sour cream**
- 1/2 **cup chopped walnuts**
- 2 **teaspoons ground cinnamon**
- 1 **medium apple, peeled and thinly sliced**

1 In a large mixing bowl, cream the butter and 1 cup sugar until light and fluffy. Add eggs, one at a time, beating well after each addition. Beat in vanilla. Combine the flour, baking powder, baking soda and salt; add to the creamed mixture alternately with sour cream, beating well after each addition. In a small bowl, combine the nuts, cinnamon and remaining sugar.

2 Spread half of the batter into a well-greased 10-in. tube pan with removable bottom. Top with apple slices; sprinkle with half of the nut mixture. Top with remaining batter and nut mixture. Bake at 375° for 40-45 minutes or until a toothpick inserted near the center comes out clean. Cool in pan for 30 minutes.

3 Carefully run a knife around edge of pan to loosen. Lift cake with removable bottom from pan. Cool completely. Before serving, carefully remove cake from pan bottom.

Muffins, Biscuits & Scones

Muffins, biscuits and scones fall under the quick bread category because they're leavened with baking powder or baking soda instead of yeast. Plus, they require very little mixing…little or no kneading and shaping… and bake in minutes. No wonder these hand-held goodies are favored by both beginning and well-seasoned bakers!

Whether sweet or savory, the aroma of muffins, biscuits and scones baking in the oven will beckon your brood to the table.

secrets for *successful muffins*

- Use butter, stick margarine (with at least 80% oil) or shortening. For best results, do not use whipped, tub, soft, liquid or reduced-fat products. The fat should be softened (at room temperature), meaning it is pliable when touched.
- Measure ingredients accurately, using the measuring tools and techniques suggested on pages 7 and 8.
- Before preheating the oven, arrange the oven racks so that the muffins will bake in the center of the oven.
- Preheat the oven for 10-15 minutes before baking.
- Standard muffin pans come in different sizes, which affect baking time. The muffin pans we used in this book measure 2-1/2 inches across.
- Most muffin batters can be baked in jumbo-, standard- or mini-muffin pans. Just be sure to adjust the baking time in the recipe (more time for jumbo and standard muffins, less time for mini-muffins). A larger muffin pan will yield fewer muffins than a smaller muffin cup.
- Fill muffin cups from two-thirds to three-fourths full, wiping off any spills. If your muffin recipe does not fill all the cups in your pan, fill the empty cups with water. The muffins will bake more evenly.
- Unless directed otherwise, muffins should go directly into the oven as soon as the batter is mixed.
- Use a kitchen timer. Check for doneness 5-7 minutes before the end of the recommended baking time to avoid overbaking. Muffins are done when a toothpick inserted near the center comes out clean. For muffins with a filling, make sure the toothpick is inserted into the muffin and not the filling.
- Cool in the pan for 5 minutes, unless the recipe directs otherwise. Muffins are best served warm, fresh from the oven.

Muffins

Berry Cream Muffins

PREP: 10 min. **BAKE:** 20 min. per batch
YIELD: about 2-1/2 dozen

Linda Gilmore, Hampstead, Maryland

If you can't decide which berries to use in these delightful muffins, use half raspberries and half blueberries for a berry good treat.

- 4 **cups all-purpose flour**
- 2 **cups sugar**
- 1 **teaspoon baking powder**
- 1 **teaspoon baking soda**
- 1 **teaspoon salt**
- 3 **cups fresh *or* frozen raspberries *or* blueberries**
- 4 **eggs, lightly beaten**
- 2 **cups (16 ounces) sour cream**
- 1 **cup vegetable oil**
- 1 **teaspoon vanilla extract**

1 In a large bowl, combine the flour, sugar, baking powder, baking soda and salt. Add berries and toss gently. In another bowl, combine the eggs, sour cream, oil and vanilla; mix well. Stir into dry ingredients just until moistened.

2 Fill greased or paper-lined muffin cups two-thirds full. Bake at 400° for 20-25 minutes or until a toothpick comes out clean. Cool for 5 minutes before removing from pans to wire racks.

Editor's Note: If using frozen berries, do not thaw before adding to batter.

BERRY CREAM MUFFINS

- 1 **teaspoon baking soda**
- 1/2 **teaspoon baking powder**
- 1/2 **to 1 teaspoon pumpkin pie spice**
- 1/4 **teaspoon salt**

STREUSEL TOPPING:
- 1/3 **cup all-purpose flour**
- 3 **tablespoons brown sugar**
- 2 **tablespoons cold butter**

1 In a large mixing bowl, cream butter and sugars until light and fluffy. Add the pumpkin, buttermilk, eggs, molasses and orange peel; mix well. Combine the flour, baking soda, baking powder, pumpkin pie spice and salt; gradually add to pumpkin mixture just until blended. Fill greased or paper-lined muffin cups two-thirds full.

2 For topping, combine flour and brown sugar in a bowl; cut in butter until mixture is crumbly. Sprinkle over batter. Bake at 375° for 20-25 minutes or until a toothpick comes out clean. Cool for 5 minutes before removing from pan to a wire rack.

Pumpkin Streusel Muffins

PREP: 15 min. **BAKE:** 20 min. **YIELD:** 1 dozen

Connie Pietila, Atlantic Mine, Michigan

The pumpkin flavor of these nicely spiced muffins is complemented by a sweet brown-sugar topping. One batch disappears quickly.

- 1/4 **cup butter, softened**
- 1/2 **cup sugar**
- 1/4 **cup packed brown sugar**
- 2/3 **cup canned pumpkin**
- 1/2 **cup buttermilk**
- 2 **eggs, lightly beaten**
- 2 **tablespoons molasses**
- 1 **teaspoon grated orange peel**
- 2 **cups all-purpose flour**

Cinnamon Doughnut Muffins

PREP: 15 min. **BAKE:** 20 min. **YIELD:** 10 muffins

Sharon Pullen, Alvinston, Ontario

With a jam-filled center, these cinnamon-topped muffins are similar to a jelly doughnut, but they are much easier to prepare.

1-3/4 cups all-purpose flour
1-1/2 teaspoons baking powder
1/2 teaspoon salt
1/2 teaspoon ground nutmeg
1/4 teaspoon ground cinnamon
3/4 cup sugar
1/3 cup vegetable oil
1 egg, lightly beaten
3/4 cup milk
Jam
TOPPING:
1/4 cup butter, melted
1/3 cup sugar
1 teaspoon ground cinnamon

1 In a large bowl, combine flour, baking powder, salt, nutmeg and cinnamon. In a small bowl, combine the sugar, oil, egg and milk. Stir into dry ingredients just until moistened.

2 Fill greased or paper-lined muffin cups half full; place 1 teaspoon of jam on top. Cover jam with enough batter to fill cups three-fourths full. Bake at 350° for 20-25 minutes or until a toothpick inserted 1 in. from the edge comes out clean.

3 Place melted butter in a small bowl; combine the sugar and cinnamon in another bowl. Immediately after removing muffins from the oven, dip tops in butter, then in cinnamon-sugar. Serve warm.

CINNAMON DOUGHNUT MUFFINS

making *muffins*

1. In a large bowl, combine dry ingredients with a fork.

2. Beat eggs and combine with liquid ingredients.

3. Make a well in the dry ingredients and pour egg mixture into the well all at one time.

4. With a spoon or spatula, stir the ingredients together just until moistened. Fill greased or paper-lined muffin cups about two-thirds to three-fourths full, wiping off any spills.

5. Bake until golden or test for doneness by inserting a tooth-pick into the center of the muffin. If the toothpick comes out clean, the muffins are done. Cool for 5 minutes before removing from pan to a wire rack.

Apple Streusel Muffins

PREP: 15 min. **BAKE:** 20 min. **YIELD:** 1 dozen

Cynthia Kolberg, Syracuse, Indiana

You'll find yourself making these fruity muffins often. Their wonderful aroma smacks of fall!

1-1/2 cups all-purpose flour
 1/4 cup sugar
   2 teaspoons baking powder
 1/2 teaspoon ground cinnamon
 1/4 teaspoon salt
 1/8 teaspoon ground nutmeg
   1 egg
 1/2 cup milk
 1/4 cup vegetable oil
   1 cup shredded peeled tart apple
STREUSEL TOPPING:
 1/3 cup packed brown sugar
   2 tablespoons all-purpose flour
 1/2 teaspoon ground cinnamon
   2 tablespoons butter, softened
 1/3 cup chopped pecans

1 In a large bowl, combine the flour, sugar, baking powder, cinnamon, salt and nutmeg. In a small bowl, whisk the egg, milk and oil. Stir into dry ingredients just until moistened. Fold in apple. In another small bowl, combine topping ingredients. Set aside 3 tablespoons topping.

2 Spoon half of the batter into 12 greased muffin cups. Sprinkle with the remaining topping. Cover with enough batter to fill muffin cups two-thirds full. Sprinkle with reserved topping. Bake at 400° for 20-25 minutes or until a toothpick comes out clean. Cool for 5 minutes before removing from pan to a wire rack.

Rhubarb Nut Muffins

PREP: 15 min. **BAKE:** 20 min. **YIELD:** about 10 muffins

Mary Kay Morris, Cokato, Minnesota

A brown sugar topping adds to the richness of these tasty, nutty morsels.

1-1/2 cups all-purpose flour
 3/4 cup packed brown sugar
 1/2 teaspoon baking soda
 1/2 teaspoon salt
   1 egg
 1/3 cup vegetable oil
 1/2 cup buttermilk
   1 teaspoon vanilla extract
   1 cup diced fresh *or* frozen rhubarb

RHUBARB NUT MUFFINS

 1/2 cup chopped walnuts
TOPPING:
 1/4 cup packed brown sugar
 1/4 cup chopped walnuts
 1/2 teaspoon ground cinnamon

1 In a large bowl, combine the flour, brown sugar, baking soda and salt. In a small bowl, whisk the egg, oil, buttermilk and vanilla. Stir into dry ingredients just until moistened. Fold in rhubarb and walnuts.

2 Fill greased or paper-lined muffin cups two-thirds full. Combine the topping ingredients; sprinkle over batter. Bake at 375° for 20-25 minutes or until a toothpick comes out clean. Cool for 5 minutes before removing from pan to a wire rack.

Editor's Note: If using frozen rhubarb, measure rhubarb while still frozen, then thaw completely. Drain in a colander, but do not press liquid out.

filling
muffin cups
with *ease*

Using a spoon to fill muffin cups with batter can get messy. To quickly put batter into muffin cups with little mess, use an ice cream scoop with a quick release. Or pour the batter from a measuring cup.

Morning Glory Muffins

PREP: 20 min. **BAKE:** 25 min. **YIELD:** about 1-1/2 dozen

Richard Case, Johnstown, Pennsylvania

For a hearty morning treat, try these muffins full of carrots, raisins, walnuts, coconut and apple.

1	cup whole wheat flour
3/4	cup sugar
1/2	cup all-purpose flour
1/2	cup oat bran
2	teaspoons baking soda
1/2	teaspoon salt
3	eggs
3/4	cup applesauce
1/4	cup vegetable oil
1/4	cup molasses
2	teaspoons vanilla extract
1/4	teaspoon orange extract
2	cups grated carrots
1/2	cup raisins
1/2	cup walnuts
1/2	cup flaked coconut
1	medium tart apple, peeled and finely chopped

1 In a large bowl, combine the first six ingredients. In a small bowl, combine the eggs, applesauce, oil, molasses and extracts; mix well. Stir into dry ingredients just until moistened. Fold in the carrots, raisins, walnuts, coconut and apple.

LEMON TEA MINI MUFFINS

2 Fill greased or paper-lined muffin cups three-fourths full. Bake at 350° for 25-30 minutes or until toothpick comes out clean. Cool 5 minutes; remove from pans to wire racks.

Lemon Tea Mini Muffins

PREP: 20 min. **BAKE:** 20 min. **YIELD:** about 2 dozen

Terrie Cox, Honeyville, Utah

These light lemon muffins pair well with hot cocoa in winter and cool lemonade in summer.

2	eggs, *separated*
1/2	cup butter, softened
1/2	cup sugar
1	cup all-purpose flour
1	teaspoon baking powder
1/4	teaspoon salt
3	tablespoons lemon juice
1	teaspoon grated lemon peel

TOPPING:

1	tablespoon sugar
1/8	teaspoon ground cinnamon

Dash ground nutmeg

1 In a small mixing bowl, beat egg yolks until light and lemon-colored, about 5 minutes. In a large mixing bowl, cream butter and sugar until light and fluffy. Fold in yolks. Combine the flour, baking powder and salt; add to the creamed mixture alternately with lemon juice and peel, stirring just until combined.

2 In another small mixing bowl and with clean beaters, beat egg whites on high speed until stiff peaks form. Fold into batter.

3 Fill greased or paper-lined miniature muffin cups two-thirds full. Combine the topping ingredients; sprinkle over the batter. Bake at 350° for 16-18 minutes or until a toothpick comes out clean. Cool for 5 minutes before removing from pan to a wire rack.

Editor's Note: Batter may be baked in 8 regular-size muffin cups for 20-25 minutes.

Cranberry Almond Muffins

PREP: 20 min. BAKE: 20 min. YIELD: 8 muffins

Janice Pletscher
Basking Ridge, New Jersey

You can enjoy these wonderful muffins as a special breakfast treat or afternoon snack.

1-1/2 cups all-purpose flour
  1/2 cup sugar
    1 teaspoon baking powder
  1/4 teaspoon baking soda
  1/4 teaspoon salt
    2 eggs
  1/2 cup sour cream
  1/4 cup butter, melted
  1/4 teaspoon almond extract
  3/4 cup sliced almonds, *divided*
  1/2 cup whole-berry cranberry sauce

1 In a large bowl, combine the flour, sugar, baking powder, baking soda and salt. In another bowl, whisk the eggs, sour cream, butter and extract; stir into dry ingredients just until moistened. Fold in 1/2 cup almonds.

2 Fill greased or paper-lined muffin cups half full; drop 1 tablespoon cranberry sauce into the center of each muffin. Cover with enough batter to fill cups three-fourths full; sprinkle with remaining almonds.

3 Bake at 375° for 20-25 minutes or until a toothpick inserted 1 in. from the edge comes out clean. Cool for 5 minutes before removing from pan to a wire rack. Serve warm.

Banana Chip Muffins

PREP: 15 min. BAKE: 20 min. YIELD: 1 dozen

Joanne Shields, Olds, Alberta

Mini chocolate chips are just the right size for these muffins. They don't overpower the terrific banana flavor.

    1 egg
  1/3 cup vegetable oil
  3/4 cup sugar
    3 medium ripe bananas, mashed
       (about 1-1/3 cups)
    2 cups all-purpose flour
  1/2 cup old-fashioned oats
  3/4 teaspoon baking soda
  1/2 teaspoon baking powder
  1/2 teaspoon salt
  3/4 cup miniature semisweet chocolate
       chips

1 In a large mixing bowl, beat egg, oil and sugar until smooth. Stir in bananas. Combine the flour, oats, baking soda, baking powder and salt; stir into the banana mixture just until moistened. Stir in chocolate chips.

2 Fill greased muffin cups three-fourths full. Bake at 375° for 18-20 minutes or until a toothpick comes out clean. Cool for 5 minutes before removing from pan to a wire rack.

Poppy Seed Orange Muffins

PREP/TOTAL TIME: 30 min. YIELD: 16 muffins

Cindy Kroon, Hartford, South Dakota

With their burst of orange flavor, these muffins make a delicious way to start the day.

  2/3 cup butter, softened
    1 cup sugar
    2 eggs
    1 cup (8 ounces) plain yogurt
  1/4 cup orange juice concentrate
    1 tablespoon grated orange peel
    1 teaspoon orange extract
2-2/3 cups all-purpose flour

CRANBERRY ALMOND MUFFINS

2 tablespoons poppy seeds
1 teaspoon baking soda
1 teaspoon salt

1 In a large mixing bowl, cream butter and sugar until light and fluffy. Add eggs, one at a time, beating well after each addition. Stir in the yogurt, orange juice concentrate, orange peel and extract. Combine the flour, poppy seeds, baking soda and salt; add to creamed mixture just until moistened.

2 Fill paper-lined muffin cups two-thirds full. Bake at 400° for 15-18 minutes or until a toothpick comes out clean. Cool for 5 minutes before removing from pans to wire racks.

Cappuccino Muffins

PREP: 15 min. **BAKE:** 20 min.
YIELD: about 14 muffins (1 cup spread)

Janice Bassing, Racine, Wisconsin

Not only are these chocolate and coffee muffins great for breakfast, they make a tasty dessert or midnight snack. Serve them with a cup of coffee or tall glass of cold milk.

ESPRESSO SPREAD:
4 ounces cream cheese, cubed and softened
1 tablespoon sugar
1/2 teaspoon instant coffee granules
1/2 teaspoon vanilla extract
1/4 cup miniature semisweet chocolate chips

MUFFINS:
2 cups all-purpose flour
3/4 cup sugar
2-1/2 teaspoons baking powder
1 teaspoon ground cinnamon
1/2 teaspoon salt
1 cup milk
2 tablespoons instant coffee granules
1/2 cup butter, melted
1 egg
1 teaspoon vanilla extract
3/4 cup miniature semisweet chocolate chips

1 In a food processor or blender, combine the spread ingredients; cover and process until well blended. Transfer to a small bowl; cover and refrigerate until serving.

2 In a large bowl, combine the flour, sugar, baking powder, cinnamon and salt. In a small bowl, stir

CAPPUCCINO MUFFINS

milk and coffee granules until granules are dissolved. Add butter, egg and vanilla; mix well. Stir into dry ingredients just until moistened. Fold in chocolate chips.

3 Fill greased or paper-lined muffin cups two-thirds full. Bake at 375° for 17-20 minutes or until a toothpick comes out clean. Cool for 5 minutes before removing from pans to wire racks. Serve with espresso spread.

storing
muffins, biscuits
& scones

• Store muffins, biscuits and scones in an airtight container at room temperature. (If made with cheese, cream cheese or other perishable foods, they should be stored in the refrigerator.)

• Muffins stay fresh for up to 3 days. Biscuits and scones should be eaten within 1 to 2 days.

• You can freeze muffins for up to 1 month and biscuits and scones for up to 3 months.

GREEN CHILI CORN MUFFINS

Moist Bran Muffins

PREP/TOTAL TIME: 30 min. **YIELD:** 4 muffins

Mildred Ross, Badin, North Carolina

Tender muffins are a tasty way to complete any meal. This recipe makes a small quantity perfect for a couple or single person.

1/2	cup All-Bran
1/2	cup milk
2	tablespoons vegetable oil
1/2	cup all-purpose flour
2	tablespoons sugar
1	teaspoon baking powder
1/4	teaspoon salt

1 In a large bowl, combine the bran and milk; let stand for 5 minutes. Stir in the oil. Combine the flour, sugar, baking powder and salt; stir into bran mixture just until moistened.

2 Fill greased or paper-lined muffin cups half full. Bake at 400° for 18-22 minutes or until a toothpick comes out clean. Cool for 5 minutes before removing from pan to a wire rack.

Green Chili Corn Muffins

PREP: 15 min. **BAKE:** 20 min. **YIELD:** 16 muffins

Melissa Cook, Chico, California

The addition of cake mix makes these corn muffins a little more moist than most. With zesty green chilies, they really round out a Mexican dinner.

1	package (8-1/2 ounces) corn bread/muffin mix
1	package (9 ounces) yellow cake mix
2	eggs
1/2	cup milk
1/3	cup water
2	tablespoons vegetable oil
1	can (4 ounces) chopped green chilies, drained
1	cup (4 ounces) shredded cheddar cheese, *divided*

1 In a large bowl, combine the dry corn bread and cake mixes. In another bowl, combine the eggs, milk, water and oil. Stir into dry ingredients just until moistened. Add the chilies and 3/4 cup cheese.

2 Fill greased or paper-lined muffin cups two-thirds full. Bake at 350° for 20-22 minutes or until a toothpick comes out clean. Immediately sprinkle with the remaining cheese. Cool for 5 minutes before removing from pans to wire racks. Serve warm.

Yankee Corn Muffins

PREP/TOTAL TIME: 25 min. **YIELD:** 8 muffins

Barb Marshall, Pickerington, Ohio

These tried-and-true corn muffins have a delightful aroma as they bake. They're so good we rarely have leftovers.

  1 **cup all-purpose flour**
3/4 **cup yellow cornmeal**
  3 **tablespoons sugar**
  2 **teaspoons baking powder**
  1 **teaspoon salt**
  1 **egg**
  1 **cup milk**
1/4 **cup vegetable oil**

1 In a large bowl, combine the flour, cornmeal, sugar, baking powder and salt. In a small bowl, beat the egg, milk and oil. Stir into the dry ingredients just until moistened.

2 Fill greased muffin cups two-thirds full. Bake at 400° for 16-18 minutes or until a toothpick comes out clean. Cool for 5 minutes before removing from pan to a wire rack.

SWEET ONION MINI MUFFINS

Maple Bacon Muffins

PREP: 15 min. **BAKE:** 20 min. **YIELD:** about 1-1/2 dozen

Louise Biela, Hamburg, New York

Great for breakfast on the run, these hearty muffins combine the fabulous flavors of pancakes and bacon.

  1 **cup quick-cooking oats**
3/4 **cup all-purpose flour**
3/4 **cup whole wheat flour**
1/2 **cup packed dark brown sugar**
  2 **teaspoons baking powder**
  1 **teaspoon baking soda**
1/2 **teaspoon salt**
  2 **eggs**
  1 **cup buttermilk**
  1 **cup maple syrup**
 10 **bacon strips, cooked and crumbled**

1 In a large mixing bowl, combine the oats, flours, brown sugar, baking powder, baking soda and salt. In a small bowl, beat the eggs, buttermilk and syrup. Stir into dry ingredients just until moistened. Fold in bacon.

2 Fill greased or paper-lined muffin cups two-thirds full. Bake at 350° for 20-25 minutes or until a toothpick comes out clean. Cool for 5 minutes before removing from pans to wire racks. Serve warm. Refrigerate leftovers.

Sweet Onion Mini Muffins

PREP/TOTAL TIME: 10 min. per batch **YIELD:** 3 dozen

Mildred Spinn, Cameron, Texas

These savory morsels are wonderful alongside any main dish and also make a tasty snack warm or cold. It's hard to stop eating them!

1-1/2 **cups all-purpose flour**
 1/2 **cup sugar**
1-1/2 **teaspoons baking powder**
 1/2 **teaspoon salt**
   2 **eggs**
   1 **cup finely chopped onion**
 1/2 **cup butter, melted**
1-1/2 **cups chopped walnuts**

1 In a large bowl, combine the flour, sugar, baking powder and salt. In another bowl, beat the eggs, onion and butter until blended. Stir into dry ingredients just until moistened. Fold in walnuts.

2 Fill greased or paper-lined miniature muffin cups three-fourths full. Bake at 400° for 10-12 minutes or until a toothpick comes out clean. Cool for 5 minutes before removing from pans to wire racks.

Editor's Note: Batter may be baked in 1 dozen regular-size muffin cups for 20-25 minutes.

Three-Grain Muffins

PREP/TOTAL TIME: 20 min. per batch
YIELD: 3-1/2 dozen

Dorothy Collins, Winnsboro, Texas

This batter can be stored in the refrigerator for up to 1 week, so you can whip up a batch of oven-fresh muffins even on busy mornings.

        2   cups quick-cooking oats
        2   cups crushed Shredded Wheat
            (about 5 large)
        2   cups All-Bran
        4   cups buttermilk
        1   cup boiling water
        1   cup vegetable oil
        4   eggs, beaten
    2-1/4   cups packed brown sugar
        5   cups all-purpose flour
        5   teaspoons baking soda
        1   teaspoon salt

1 In a large bowl, combine the oats, Shredded Wheat and bran. Add the buttermilk, water, oil and eggs; stir for 1 minute. Stir in the brown sugar. Combine the flour, baking soda and salt; add to the oat mixture and stir well.

2 Fill greased or paper-lined muffin cups two-thirds full. Bake at 400° for 18-20 minutes or until a toothpick comes out clean. Cool for 5 minutes before removing from pans to wire racks.

Zucchini Oat Muffins

PREP: 10 min. **BAKE:** 20 min. **YIELD:** 1 dozen

Janet Bonarski, Perry, New York

Oats and pecans add heartiness to these slightly sweet muffins. Your family will never know you're sneaking a vegetable into these treats!

    2-1/2   cups all-purpose flour
    1-1/2   cups sugar
        1   cup chopped pecans
      1/2   cup quick-cooking oats
        3   teaspoons baking powder
        1   teaspoon salt
        1   teaspoon ground cinnamon
        4   eggs
        1   medium zucchini, shredded
            (about 3/4 cup)
      3/4   cup vegetable oil

THREE-GRAIN MUFFINS

1 In a large mixing bowl, combine the flour, sugar, pecans, oats, baking powder, salt and cinnamon. In a small bowl, beat the eggs; add zucchini and oil. Stir into dry ingredients just until moistened (batter will be lumpy).

2 Fill greased muffin cups three-fourths full. Bake at 400° for 20-25 minutes or until a toothpick comes out clean. Cool for 5 minutes before removing from pan to a wire rack.

CHEDDAR CHIVE MUFFINS

Dijon Ham Muffins

PREP/TOTAL TIME: 30 min. **YIELD:** 14 muffins

Karen Davis, Springfield, Missouri

Easy to fix, these muffins are great for breakfast with scrambled eggs or on a brunch buffet. They're also super with soup for lunch.

- 1-2/3   **cups all-purpose flour**
- 1/3   **cup cornmeal**
- 1/4   **cup sugar**
-    1   **teaspoon baking powder**
-    1   **to 2 teaspoons ground mustard**
- 1/2   **teaspoon baking soda**
- 1/2   **teaspoon salt**
- 1/8   **teaspoon ground cloves**
-    2   **eggs**
-    1   **cup buttermilk**
- 1/3   **cup vegetable oil**
-    3   **tablespoons Dijon mustard**
-    1   **cup finely chopped fully cooked ham**

1 In a large bowl, combine first eight ingredients. In a small bowl, combine the eggs, buttermilk, oil and mustard. Stir into dry ingredients just until moistened. Fold in the ham.

2 Fill greased muffin cups three-fourths full. Bake at 375° for 20-25 minutes or until a toothpick comes out clean. Cool for 5 minutes before removing from pans to wire racks.

Cheddar Chive Muffins

PREP: 15 min. **BAKE:** 20 min. **YIELD:** 1 dozen

Donna Royer, Largo, Florida

These savory muffins go so well with many entrees. And, they are made with pantry staples for added convenience.

- 1-1/4   **cups milk**
- 3/4   **cup mashed potato flakes**
-    1   **egg**
- 1/3   **cup vegetable oil**
-    1   **cup (4 ounces) shredded cheddar cheese**
- 1-2/3   **cups all-purpose flour**
-    3   **tablespoons sugar**
-    2   **tablespoons minced chives**
-    1   **tablespoon dried parsley flakes**
-    2   **teaspoons baking powder**
-    1   **teaspoon salt**

1 In a small saucepan, bring milk to a boil. Remove from the heat; stir in potato flakes. Let stand for 2 minutes. Whip with a fork until smooth; cool slightly. Transfer to a large bowl. Beat in the egg, oil and cheese. Combine the flour, sugar, chives, parsley, baking powder and salt; stir into potato mixture just until moistened (batter will be thick).

2 Fill greased muffin cups three-fourths full. Bake at 400° for 20-25 minutes or until a toothpick comes out clean. Cool for 5 minutes before removing from pan to a wire rack. Serve warm.

Biscuits & Scones

Buttermilk Biscuits

PREP: 25 min. **BAKE:** 15 min. **YIELD:** 1 dozen

Jean Parsons, Sarver, Pennsylvania

You can't go wrong with a basic biscuit like this. Your family will gobble them up when served warm with butter.

- 2 **cups all-purpose flour**
- 1 **tablespoon sugar**
- 1 **teaspoon baking powder**
- 1/2 **teaspoon salt**
- 1/2 **teaspoon baking soda**
- 1/4 **cup shortening**
- 3/4 **cup buttermilk**

1 In a large bowl, combine the flour, sugar, baking powder, salt and baking soda. Cut in shortening until mixture is crumbly. Add buttermilk; stir just until the dough clings together.

2 Turn dough onto a lightly floured surface; knead gently 10-12 times. Roll out to 1/2-in. thickness. Cut with a floured 2-1/2-in. biscuit cutter. Place 1 in. apart on a greased baking sheet. Bake at 450° for 11-12 minutes or until lightly browned. Serve warm.

Garlic Potato Biscuits

PREP: 25 min. **BAKE:** 10 min. **YIELD:** 12-15 biscuits

Diane Hixon, Niceville, Florida

The beauty of biscuits is you can enjoy the aroma of oven-fresh bread with less work than yeast breads.

- 1 **large potato (1/2 pound), peeled and diced**
- 3 **to 4 garlic cloves, peeled**
- 1/3 **cup butter, softened**
- 1 **teaspoon salt**
- 1/4 **teaspoon pepper**
- 2 **cups all-purpose flour**
- 3 **teaspoons baking powder**
- 1/3 **cup milk**

1 Place potato and garlic in a saucepan; cover with water. Bring to a boil. Reduce heat; cover and simmer until potato is tender. Drain. Add butter, salt and pepper to potato and garlic; mash. In a large bowl, combine flour and baking powder; stir in potato mixture until mixture is crumbly. Add milk and stir well.

2 Turn dough onto a lightly floured surface. Roll out to 1/2-in. thickness. Cut with a floured 2-1/2-in. biscuit cutter. Place 1 in. apart on an ungreased baking sheet. Bake at 450° for 10-12 minutes or until golden brown. Serve warm.

BUTTERMILK BISCUITS

making & shaping *biscuits*

1. Combine all dry ingredients with a fork. With a pastry blender or two knives, cut shortening into flour until mixture resembles coarse crumbs.

4. Roll dough evenly to 1/2-in. to 3/4-in. thickness. Cut with a floured biscuit cutter, using a straight downward motion; do not twist cutter.

2. Make a well in the center of the crumb mixture. Pour in the liquid all at once and mix with a fork just until dry ingredients are moistened and the mixture begins to cling together.

5. Place biscuits on a baking sheet. Place 1 to 1-1/2 in. apart for biscuits with crusty sides or almost touching for softer-sided biscuits.

3. Turn onto a lightly floured surface and knead gently for as many times as recipe directs.

6. Gently gather trimmings into a ball. Do not knead. Roll and cut out as in Step 4.

Caraway Wheat Biscuits

PREP/TOTAL TIME: 30 min. **YIELD:** about 1 dozen

Nancy Messmore, Silver Lake Village, Ohio

Whole wheat flour and caraway make these hearty biscuits terrific for wintertime meals.

2-1/2 **cups whole wheat flour**
2 **tablespoons caraway seeds**
1 **tablespoon baking powder**
1/8 **teaspoon salt**
1-1/3 **cups grated onions (about 3 medium)**
2 **eggs, beaten**
1/2 **cup vegetable oil**

1 In a large bowl, combine the flour, caraway seeds, baking powder and salt. In a small bowl, combine the onions, eggs and oil; stir into dry ingredients just until moistened.

2 Turn dough onto a floured surface. Roll out to 3/4-in. thickness. Cut with a floured 2-1/2-in. biscuit cutter. Place 1 in. apart on a greased baking sheet. Bake at 425° for 10-15 minutes or until golden brown. Serve warm.

Garlic Cheese Biscuits

PREP/TOTAL TIME: 30 min. **YIELD:** about 1-1/2 dozen

Gayle Becker, Mt. Clemens, Michigan

Shredded cheddar cheese adds nice color to these biscuits, while a tasty butter mixture brushed on top provides a burst of garlic flavor.

- 2 cups all-purpose flour
- 3 teaspoons garlic powder, *divided*
- 2-1/2 teaspoons baking powder
- 1/2 teaspoon baking soda
- 1/2 teaspoon chicken bouillon granules
- 1/2 cup butter-flavored shortening
- 3/4 cup shredded cheddar cheese
- 1 cup buttermilk
- 3 tablespoons butter, melted

1 In a small bowl, combine the flour, 2 teaspoons garlic powder, baking powder, baking soda and bouillon; cut in shortening until mixture is crumbly. Add cheese. Stir in buttermilk just until moistened.

2 Drop by heaping tablespoonfuls 1 in. apart onto a greased baking sheet. Bake at 450° for 10 minutes. Combine the butter and remaining garlic powder; brush over biscuits. Bake 4 minutes longer or until golden brown. Serve warm.

Nutty Cream Cheese Biscuits

PREP: 25 min. **BAKE:** 20 min. **YIELD:** about 1-1/2 dozen

Claudia Beene, Bossier, Louisiana

Folks are surprised to hear this recipe starts with refrigerated biscuits.

- 2 tubes (10 ounces *each*) refrigerated biscuits
- 2 packages (3 ounces *each*) cream cheese
- 1/2 cup sugar
- 1 teaspoon ground cinnamon
- 1/4 teaspoon *each* ground cloves, nutmeg and allspice
- 6 tablespoons butter, melted, *divided*
- 1 cup chopped pecans

1 Roll each biscuit into a 3-1/2-in. to 4-in. circle. Cut cream cheese into 20 equal cubes; place one cube in the center of each biscuit. Combine the sugar, cinnamon, cloves, nutmeg and allspice; sprinkle 1/2 teaspoon over each biscuit. Set remaining sugar mixture aside. Moisten edges of dough with water; fold over cheese and press edges with a fork to seal.

GARLIC CHEESE BISCUITS

BAKING POWDER BISCUITS

biscuit cutter. Place 1 in. apart on an ungreased baking sheet. Bake at 450° for 10-12 minutes or until golden brown. Serve warm.

Rye Drop Biscuits

PREP/TOTAL TIME: 20 min. **YIELD:** 4 biscuits

Nancy Zimmerman

Cape May Court House, New Jersey

These rich, rugged, melt-in-your-mouth biscuits are so easy to make since you don't have to knead them or cut them out. They go with any meal.

1/3	cup all-purpose flour
1/4	cup rye flour
1	tablespoon brown sugar
1	teaspoon baking powder
1/4	teaspoon dried parsley flakes
1/8	teaspoon salt
1/4	cup cold butter
1	egg
1	tablespoon milk

1 In a bowl, combine the flours, sugar, baking powder, parsley and salt. Cut in butter until crumbly. Stir in the egg and milk just until combined.

2 Drop by 1/4 cupfuls 2 in. apart onto a greased baking sheet. Bake at 400° for 7-10 minutes or until golden brown. Remove from pan to a wire rack. Serve warm.

2 Pour 2 tablespoons butter into each of two 9-in. round baking pans; sprinkle 1 tablespoon of reserved sugar mixture into each pan. Dip one side of each biscuit in remaining butter. Arrange in pans, forming a pinwheel pattern, with butter side up. Sprinkle pecans and remaining sugar mixture on top. Bake at 375° for 20-25 minutes or until golden brown. Serve warm. Refrigerate leftovers.

Baking Powder Biscuits

PREP/TOTAL TIME: 25 min. **YIELD:** 10 biscuits

Catherine Yoder, Bertha, Minnesota

These flaky biscuits have great flavor and bake to a beautiful golden brown.

2	cups all-purpose flour
2	tablespoons sugar
3	teaspoons baking powder
1/2	teaspoon salt
1/2	cup shortening
1	egg
2/3	cup milk

1 In a large bowl, combine the flour, sugar, baking powder and salt. Cut in shortening until mixture is crumbly. Beat egg and milk; stir into dry ingredients just until moistened.

2 Turn dough onto a lightly floured surface; roll out to 1/2-in. thickness. Cut with a floured 2-1/2-in.

shaping *drop biscuits*

Drop dough from a tablespoon or 1/4 cup measure onto a greased baking sheet. Use a rubber spatula, knife or another spoon to push the dough off of the spoon.

Lemon-Berry Biscuits

PREP/TOTAL TIME: 25 min. **YIELD:** 1 dozen

Kristin Dallum, Vancouver, Washington

Lemon and blueberries pair well in a variety of breads, and these biscuits are no exception.

  2 **cups all-purpose flour**
1/3 **cup sugar**
  2 **teaspoons baking powder**
1/2 **teaspoon baking soda**
1/4 **teaspoon salt**
  1 **cup (8 ounces) lemon yogurt**
  1 **egg, lightly beaten**
1/4 **cup butter, melted**
  1 **teaspoon grated lemon peel**
  1 **cup fresh *or* frozen blueberries**
GLAZE:
1/2 **cup confectioners' sugar**
  1 **tablespoon lemon juice**
1/2 **teaspoon grated lemon peel**

1 In a large bowl, combine the flour, sugar, baking powder, baking soda and salt. In a small bowl, combine the yogurt, egg, butter and lemon peel. Stir into dry ingredients just until moistened. Fold in blueberries.

2 Drop by tablespoonfuls 1 in. apart onto a greased baking sheet. Bake at 400° for 15-18 minutes or until lightly browned. Combine glaze ingredients; drizzle over warm biscuits.

Editor's Note: If using frozen blueberries, do not thaw before adding to batter.

LEMON-BERRY BISCUITS

Cheddar-Salsa Biscuit Strips

PREP/TOTAL TIME: 30 min. **YIELD:** about 3 dozen

Peggy Key, Grant, Alabama

A few ingredients are all you'll need for these tender breadsticks that get their kick from salsa. They're an excellent finger food for parties and equally good alongside a hot bowl of soup or chili.

1-2/3 **cups self-rising flour**
    1 **cup (4 ounces) shredded cheddar cheese**
  1/2 **cup salsa**
  1/4 **cup butter, melted**
  1/4 **cup water**
Additional melted butter, optional

1 In a bowl, combine the flour and cheese. Stir in the salsa, butter and water just until combined.

2 Turn dough onto a floured surface; knead gently 6-8 times or until smooth. Roll out into a 12-in. x 6-in. rectangle. Cut into 2-in. x 1-in. strips. Place 1 in. apart on a greased baking sheet. Bake at 425° for 6-8 minutes or until golden brown. Brush with butter if desired. Remove from pan to wire racks. Serve warm.

Editor's Note: As a substitute for the self-rising flour, place 2-1/2 teaspoons baking powder and 3/4 teaspoon salt in a measuring cup. Add all-purpose flour to measure 1 cup. Add additional 2/3 cup all-purpose flour.

Onion Dill Biscuits

PREP/TOTAL TIME: 15 min. **YIELD:** 6 servings

Marcille Meyer, Battle Creek, Nebraska

A quick coating in a mixture of melted butter, chopped onion and dill weed dresses up refrigerated biscuits in a hurry. Keep the ingredients on hand for biscuits in a snap.

1/4 **cup butter, melted**
  1 **tablespoon finely chopped onion**
  1 **teaspoon dill weed**
  1 **tube (10 ounces) refrigerated buttermilk biscuits**

1 In a bowl, combine the butter, onion and dill. Cut biscuits in half lengthwise; toss in the butter mixture.

2 Arrange in a single layer in an ungreased 9-in. square baking pan. Bake at 450° for 8-10 minutes or until lightly browned. Serve warm.

Rosemary Buttermilk Biscuits

PREP/TOTAL TIME: 30 min. **YIELD:** about 1 dozen

Debbie Smith, Crossett, Arkansas

The delicate herb flavor of these biscuits is special alongside any entree. Use fresh rosemary for the best flavor.

2-1/4 **cups all-purpose flour**
  2 **tablespoons sugar**
  2 **teaspoons minced fresh rosemary** *or* 3/4 **teaspoon dried rosemary, crushed**
1-1/2 **teaspoons baking powder**
 3/4 **teaspoon salt**
 1/2 **teaspoon baking soda**
 1/2 **cup plus 1 tablespoon shortening**
 3/4 **cup buttermilk**
 1/4 **cup butter, melted**

1 In a large bowl, combine the flour, sugar, rosemary, baking powder, salt and baking soda. Cut in shortening until mixture is crumbly. Stir in buttermilk just until moistened (dough will be dry).

2 Turn dough onto a lightly floured surface. Roll out to 1/2-in. thickness. Cut with a floured 2-1/2-in. biscuit cutter. Place 1 in. apart on a greased baking sheet. Brush with butter. Bake at 400° for 10-12 minutes or until golden brown. Serve warm.

CORNMEAL CHEDDAR BISCUITS

on a greased baking sheet. Bake at 425° for 12-15 minutes or until golden brown. Remove from pan to a wire rack. Serve warm.

Editor's Note: As a substitute for the self-rising flour, place 3 teaspoons baking powder and 1 teaspoon salt in a measuring cup. Add all-purpose flour to measure 1 cup. Then add another cup of all-purpose flour.

Bacon Cheese Biscuits

PREP/TOTAL TIME: 30 min. **YIELD:** 9 biscuits

Kimberly Harrell, Douglas, Georgia

It takes no time to stir up a batch of these golden, savory biscuits. With bacon and cheese throughout, they make a great breakfast on the go.

  2 **cups self-rising flour**
  1 **tablespoon sugar**
 1/2 **teaspoon baking soda**
 1/2 **cup shortening**
  1 **cup buttermilk**
 3/4 **pound sliced bacon, cooked and crumbled**
  1 **cup (4 ounces) shredded cheddar cheese**

1 In a large bowl, combine the flour, sugar and baking soda. Cut in shortening until crumbly. Stir in buttermilk just until combined. Fold in the bacon and cheese.

2 Turn onto a lightly floured surface; knead 4-5 times. Roll out to 1/2-in. thickness. Cut with a floured 2-1/2-in. biscuit cutter. Place 1 in. apart

Cornmeal Cheddar Biscuits

PREP/TOTAL TIME: 25 min. **YIELD:** 1 dozen

Taste of Home Test Kitchen

These cheesy cornmeal biscuits are a wonderful addition to a chili dinner.

1-1/2 **cups all-purpose flour**
 1/2 **cup cornmeal**
  3 **teaspoons baking powder**
  2 **teaspoons sugar**
 1/4 **to 1/2 teaspoon salt**
 1/2 **cup cold butter**
 1/2 **cup shredded cheddar cheese**
  1 **cup milk**

1 In a large bowl, combine the flour, cornmeal, baking powder, sugar and salt. Cut in butter until mixture is crumbly. Stir in cheese and milk just until moistened.

2 Drop by 1/4 cupfuls 2 in. apart onto an ungreased baking sheet. Bake at 450° for 12-15 minutes or until golden brown. Serve warm.

2 For scones, combine the flour, sugar, baking powder and salt in a bowl. Cut in butter until mixture resembles fine crumbs. Add the apricots, pecans and orange peel. With a fork, rapidly stir in 1 cup cream just until moistened.

3 Turn dough onto a floured surface; knead gently 5-6 times. Divide in half; shape each portion into a ball. Flatten each ball into a 6-in. circle; cut each circle into eight wedges. Separate wedges and place 1 in. apart on an ungreased baking sheet. Brush with remaining cream.

4 Bake at 375° for 13-15 minutes or until a toothpick comes out clean. Remove to a wire rack. Serve warm with Devonshire cream and jam.

Buttermilk Scones

PREP: 15 min. **BAKE:** 25 min. **YIELD:** 6 scones

Ruth LeBlanc, Nashua, New Hampshire

Scones are best served fresh—so this recipe is ideal for a small household.

> 1 cup all-purpose flour
> 2 tablespoons plus 1/2 teaspoon sugar, *divided*
> 1 teaspoon baking powder
> 1/8 teaspoon baking soda
> 1/4 cup cold butter
> 1/3 cup buttermilk
> 3 tablespoons dried currants *or* raisins
> 1/4 teaspoon grated lemon *or* orange peel
> 1/8 teaspoon ground cinnamon

1 In a small bowl, combine the flour, 2 tablespoons sugar, baking powder and baking soda. Cut in butter until mixture is crumbly. Stir in the buttermilk, currants or raisins and lemon peel until a soft dough forms.

2 Turn dough onto a lightly floured surface; knead gently 5-6 times or until no longer sticky. On a lightly greased baking sheet, pat dough into a 5-in. circle, about 3/4 in. thick. Score the top, making six wedges.

3 Combine the cinnamon and remaining sugar; sprinkle over dough. Bake at 375° for 23-25 minutes or until golden brown. Remove from pan to a wire rack. Break into wedges. Serve warm.

Apricot Scones

PREP: 20 min. **BAKE:** 15 min.
YIELD: 16 scones (1 cup cream)

Robin Fuhrman, Fond du Lac, Wisconsin

The dried apricots and Devanshire cream make these scones so special that they are perfect for brunch.

DEVONSHIRE CREAM:
> 1 package (3 ounces) cream cheese, softened
> 1 tablespoon confectioners' sugar
> 1/2 teaspoon vanilla extract
> 1/4 to 1/3 cup heavy whipping cream

SCONES:
> 2 cups all-purpose flour
> 1/4 cup sugar
> 3 teaspoons baking powder
> 1/4 teaspoon salt
> 1/3 cup cold butter
> 1/2 cup chopped dried apricots
> 1/2 cup chopped pecans
> 1 teaspoon grated orange peel
> 1 cup plus 2 tablespoons heavy whipping cream, *divided*

Jam of your choice

1 For Devonshire cream, beat cream cheese, confectioners' sugar and vanilla in a mixing bowl until fluffy. Gradually beat in enough cream to achieve a spreading consistency. Cover and refrigerate for at least 2 hours.

Chocolate Chip Scones

PREP: 15 min. **BAKE:** 20 min. **YIELD:** 6 scones

Diane LaFurno, College Point, New York

These scones are delicious warm, served with butter, when the chips are melted and gooey.

>   1   cup all-purpose flour
>   3   tablespoons sugar
> 1-1/2 teaspoons baking powder
> Pinch salt
>   2   tablespoons cold butter
>   1   egg
>   3   tablespoons heavy whipping cream
>   1/2   cup miniature semisweet chocolate chips

1 In a bowl, combine the flour, sugar, baking powder and salt. Cut in butter until crumbly. In a small bowl, combine egg and cream; stir into dry ingredients just until moistened. Fold in chocolate chips.

2 Turn onto a floured surface; knead gently 6-8 times. Pat into a 6-in. circle. Cut dough into six wedges. Separate wedges and place 1-in. apart on an ungreased baking sheet. Bake at 350° for 18-20 minutes or until golden brown. Remove from pan to a wire rack. Serve warm.

COUNTRY SCONES

Country Scones

PREP: 20 min. **BAKE:** 15 min. **YIELD:** 16 scones

Martha Plassmeyer, St. Elizabeth, Missouri

These tempting triangles perfectly balance a light and airy texture with a rich and moist flavor.

>   3/4   cup dried currants *or* raisins
>   2   cups all-purpose flour
>   3   tablespoons sugar
>   2   teaspoons baking powder
>   3/4   teaspoon salt
>   1/2   teaspoon baking soda
>   5   tablespoons cold butter
>   1   cup (8 ounces) sour cream
>   2   egg yolks
> **TOPPING:**
>   1   egg white
>   1   teaspoon sugar
>   1/8   teaspoon ground cinnamon

1 Place currants in a bowl; cover with hot water and let stand for 5 minutes. Drain well and set aside. In a bowl, combine the flour, sugar, baking powder, salt and baking soda. Cut in butter until mixture is crumbly. In a small bowl, combine sour cream and egg yolks; add to crumb mixture. Stir in currants just until blended.

2 Turn dough onto a floured surface; knead gently 8-10 times. Pat into a 9-in. circle. Cut into 4-in. circles; place on ungreased baking sheets. Cut each circle into four wedges but do not separate.

3 Beat egg white; brush over dough. Combine sugar and cinnamon; sprinkle over tops. Bake at 425° for 15-18 minutes or until golden brown. Remove from pans to wire racks. Serve warm.

shaping *scones*

Divide dough if directed by recipe. Shape dough into a circle about 1/2-in. thick. Cut into wedges with a sharp knife.

Double Orange Scones

PREP/TOTAL TIME: 30 min. **YIELD:** 8 scones

Margaret Frayser, Linton, Indiana

Orange butter adds the perfect finishing touch to each hearty bite of these scones.

    1   cup all-purpose flour
    1   cup whole wheat flour
    3   tablespoons sugar
2-1/2   teaspoons baking powder
    2   teaspoons grated orange peel
  1/4   teaspoon salt
  1/3   cup cold butter
    1   egg
  1/3   cup milk
  1/2   cup chopped mandarin oranges, well
        drained
Additional sugar
ORANGE BUTTER:
  1/2   cup butter, softened
    2   tablespoons orange marmalade

1 In a small bowl, combine the flours, sugar, baking powder, orange peel and salt. Cut in butter until mixture is crumbly. Combine the egg and milk; add to crumb mixture. Stir in oranges just until moistened.

2 Turn onto a floured surface; knead gently 10 times. Pat into a 6-in. circle; sprinkle with additional sugar. Cut into eight wedges; separate wedges and place 1 in. apart on a greased baking

DOUBLE ORANGE SCONES

sheet. Bake at 400° for 15-20 minutes or until golden brown. Remove from pan to a wire rack.

3 For orange butter, beat butter and marmalade in a small mixing bowl until fluffy. Serve with warm scones.

Gingerbread Scones

PREP: 20 min. **BAKE:** 15 min. **YIELD:** 1 dozen

Reverend David Bostedt
Zephyrhills, Florida

These moist gingerbread-flavored scones are a delight to share at Christmastime.

    2   cups all-purpose flour
    3   tablespoons brown sugar
    2   teaspoons baking powder
    1   teaspoon ground ginger
  1/2   teaspoon baking soda
  1/2   teaspoon salt
  1/2   teaspoon ground cinnamon
  1/4   cup cold butter
  1/3   cup molasses
  1/4   cup milk
    1   egg, *separated*
Sugar

1 In a large bowl, combine the flour, brown sugar, baking powder, ginger, baking soda, salt and cinnamon. Cut in the butter until mixture is crumbly. In a small bowl, combine the molasses, milk and egg yolk until smooth; stir into the crumb mixture just until moistened.

2 Turn dough onto a floured surface; knead gently 6-8 times. Pat into an 8-in. circle; cut into 12 wedges. Separate wedges and place 1 in. apart on a greased baking sheet. Beat egg white until frothy; brush over scones. Sprinkle with sugar. Bake at 400° for 12-15 minutes or until golden brown. Remove from pan to a wire rack. Serve warm.

Apple 'n' Honey Scones

PREP/TOTAL TIME: 30 min. **YIELD:** 8 scones

Bernadette Colvin, Houston, Texas

Round out a flavorful fall meal with these fruity scones. Wheat germ adds a little extra nutrition.

    2   cups all-purpose flour
  2/3   cup wheat germ
    2   teaspoons baking powder

    1 teaspoon ground cinnamon
 1/4 teaspoon baking soda
 1/4 teaspoon salt
 1/4 teaspoon ground nutmeg
 1/3 cup cold butter
    1 large tart apple, peeled and chopped
 1/2 cup milk
 1/4 cup honey
TOPPING:
    2 teaspoons wheat germ
    2 teaspoons sugar
 1/4 teaspoon ground cinnamon

1 In a large bowl, combine the flour, wheat germ, baking powder, cinnamon, baking soda, salt and nutmeg. Cut in butter until mixture is crumbly. Combine the apple, milk and honey; stir into crumb mixture just until moistened.

2 Turn dough onto a floured surface; knead gently 5-6 times. Gently pat into a 9-in. circle, about 1/2 in. thick. Combine topping ingredients; sprinkle over dough. Cut into eight wedges. Separate wedges and place 1 in. apart on a greased baking sheet. Bake at 400° for 15-18 minutes or until lightly browned. Remove from pan to a wire rack. Serve warm.

POPPY SEED LEMON SCONES

Poppy Seed Lemon Scones

PREP: 30 min. **BAKE:** 15 min.
YIELD: 8 scones (1-1/2 cups lemon curd)

Linda Murray, Allenstown, New Hampshire

You'll love the appealing look and delicate texture of these lightly sweet scones. They're wonderful served warm with homemade lemon curd for breakfast or with a salad for lunch.

LEMON CURD:
    2 eggs
    1 cup sugar
    6 tablespoons butter, melted
 1/4 cup lemon juice
    2 tablespoons grated lemon peel
SCONES:
    2 cups all-purpose flour
 1/4 cup sugar
    1 tablespoon poppy seeds
    2 teaspoons baking powder
 1/2 teaspoon baking soda
 1/4 teaspoon salt
 1/3 cup cold butter
 3/4 cup milk
    2 tablespoons lemon juice
Additional sugar

1 In a heavy saucepan or top of a double boiler, beat eggs and sugar. Stir in the butter, lemon juice and peel. Cook and stir over low heat or simmering water for 15 minutes or until mixture reaches 160° and is thickened. Cover and refrigerate until chilled (may be stored in the refrigerator for up to 1 week).

2 For scones, combine the flour, sugar, poppy seeds, baking powder, baking soda and salt in a bowl. Cut in butter until the mixture resembles fine crumbs. Combine milk and lemon juice; stir into crumb mixture just until blended (dough will be soft).

3 Turn dough onto a floured surface; knead gently 6 times. Shape into a ball. Pat dough into an 8-in. circle; cut into eight wedges. Separate wedges and place 1 in. apart on a greased baking sheet. Sprinkle with additional sugar. Bake at 425° for 12-15 minutes or until lightly browned. Remove from pan to a wire rack. Serve warm with lemon curd.

the
history
of *scones*

It's believed this Scottish quick bread originated between 1505 and 1515. Scones are named after the Stone of Destiny (or Scone), the place where Scottish kings were once crowned.

Heart-Shaped Cheese Scones

PREP/TOTAL TIME: 30 min. **YIELD:** about 1 dozen

Edna Hoffman, Hebron, Indiana

When you set out a plate of these golden scones flecked with bits of cheddar cheese, everyone will know you've put your heart into your baking! If you don't have a heart-shaped cutter, use a round one instead.

- 2 cups all-purpose flour
- 2 tablespoons sugar
- 3 teaspoons baking powder
- 1 teaspoon salt
- 1/4 teaspoon baking soda
- 1-1/2 cups (6 ounces) shredded cheddar cheese
- 1 egg
- 1/2 cup sour cream
- 1/4 cup vegetable oil
- 3 tablespoons milk

1 In a large bowl, combine the flour, sugar, baking powder, salt and baking soda. Stir in cheese. In a small bowl, combine the egg, sour cream, oil and milk. Make a well in the center of dry ingredients; stir in egg mixture just until moistened.

2 Turn dough onto a floured surface; knead gently 10-12 times. Pat out to 1/3-in. thickness. Cut with a floured 3-in. heart-shaped cutter. Place 2 in. apart on a greased baking sheet. Bake at 425° for 15-20 minutes or until golden brown. Remove from pan to a wire rack. Serve warm.

HEART-SHAPED CHEESE SCONES

problem-solving pointers
for Muffins, Biscuits & Scones

MUFFINS, BISCUITS OR SCONES ARE TOUGH

- Batter/dough was overmixed or overhandled. Next time, mix just until combined.

MUFFINS HAVE TUNNELS AND/OR PEAKS

- Batter was overmixed.

MUFFINS HAVE A BITTER AFTERTASTE

- Too much leavener was used.

BISCUITS BAKED UNEVENLY

- Batter was not patted or rolled out evenly. Next time, use a ruler to measure thickness.

Oat Scones

PREP/TOTAL TIME: 30 min. **YIELD:** about 15 scones

Barbara Chornoboy, Thunder Bay, Ontario

Unlike other scones, this recipe instructs you to use a round biscuit cutter.

- 2 cups all-purpose flour
- 1/2 cup packed brown sugar
- 2 teaspoons baking powder
- 1 teaspoon baking soda
- 1 teaspoon salt
- 1/2 cup shortening
- 1-1/4 cups quick-cooking oats
- 3/4 cup milk

1 In a large bowl, combine the flour, brown sugar, baking powder, baking soda and salt. Cut in shortening until mixture is crumbly. Stir in oats and milk just until moistened.

2 Turn dough onto a lightly floured surface. Roll out to 3/4-in. thickness. Cut with a floured 2-1/2-in. biscuit cutter. Place 1 in. apart on an ungreased baking sheet. Bake at 375° for 15-20 minutes or until lightly browned. Serve warm.

329

Savory Yeast Breads

Yeast breads, rolls, pretzels, biscuits and more can be made completely from scratch, can start with convenience products such as frozen bread dough or hot roll mix and can even be made in a bread machine.

They can be savory (like the recipes in this chapter) or sweet (like the recipes featured in the Sweet Yeast Breads chapter beginning on page 387).

All yeast breads are divided into the two following basic categories: kneaded yeast breads and batter yeast breads.

- Kneaded yeast breads are usually mixed, kneaded, allowed to rise, then shaped, allowed to rise again and finally baked. The rise times may be shortened or one may be eliminated if quick-rise yeast is used. Bread machine breads are also kneaded breads.

- For batter breads, the ingredients are beaten, allowed to rise once or twice, then baked. They have a coarse texture and rugged crust.

The ingredients you use in bread making will affect the texture, density and crust. Lean breads (like French bread) are made with yeast, flour, water, salt and a minimal amount of sugar to produce a dense, chewy bread with a crisp crust.

Rich or short breads (like Brioche) are made with fat such as butter or shortening, eggs and/or milk to produce a tender bread with a soft crust. For more information on ingredients and how they affect bread, see the Common Baking Ingredients on pages 12 through 17.

secrets for *successful savory yeast breads*

- Use butter, stick margarine (with at least 80% oil) or shortening. Do not use light or whipped butter, diet spread or tub margarine.

- Measure ingredients accurately, using the measuring tools and techniques suggested on pages 7 and 8.

- Arrange the oven racks so that the bread will bake in the center of the oven.

- Preheat oven for 10 to 15 minutes before baking.

- When mixing dough, always start with a minimum amount of flour until dough reaches desired consistency (soft, sticky, stiff or firm).

- Knead dough only until it does not tear easily when stretched.

- Let dough rise in a warm (80° to 85°) draft-free area. Proper rising helps in the development of the bread texture.

- Use aluminum pans with a dull rather than shiny or dark finish. Glass baking dishes and dark finishes will produce darker crusts.

- To allow for good air circulation while baking, leave at least 1 in. of space between pans and between pans and sides of oven.

- Use a kitchen timer and test for doneness at the minimum recommended baking time. Bread is done when it is golden brown and sounds hollow when tapped on the bottom. Or, insert an instant-read thermometer in the thickest part of the loaf. The bread is done when the thermometer reads 200°.

- Remove breads from pans and cool on wire racks. Let breads cool for at least 20 minutes before slicing. Use a serrated knife and a sawing motion when cutting.

kneading, shaping and baking *yeast bread*

1. Turn dough onto a lightly floured surface; shape into a ball. Fold top of dough toward you. With palms, push with a rolling motion away from you. Turn dough a quarter turn; repeat until dough is smooth and elastic. Add flour to surface only as needed.

2. Place the dough in a bowl greased with butter, oil or nonstick cooking spray. Turn dough over to grease the top. This prevents the dough from drying out while rising. Cover with a clean towel or plastic wrap.

3. Place covered dough in a warm draft-free area (80° to 85°) until dough has doubled. (Place covered bowl on the top rack in a cold oven with a pan of steaming hot water under-neath. Or turn your oven to its lowest setting for no longer than 40 to 50 seconds. Turn off and let dough rise in the oven.)

4. Press two fingers 1/2 in. into the dough. If the dents remain, the dough is doubled in size and ready to punch down.

5. To punch dough down, make a fist and push it into the center. Gather the dough to the center and shape into a ball. Place on a floured surface.

6. Divide the dough if the recipe directs; shape into balls. Roll each ball into a 12-in. x 8-in. rectangle. You will hear air bubbles "popping" as you roll the dough.

7. Dust off any loose flour that might cling to the dough. Beginning at the short end, roll up each rectangle firmly. If it's too loose, you'll see air pockets when the bread is cut. If it's too tight, the bread will crack while baking.

8. Pinch seam and each end to seal. Place seam side down in a greased pan; cover with a towel and allow to double in size in a warm draft-free area.

9. When dough has doubled, remove towel; place pans several inches apart in the center of the preheated oven.

10. When bread is golden brown, test for doneness by carefully removing loaves from pans and tapping the bottom crusts. If it sounds hollow, the bread is done. If the bread is browning too fast and it's not done, tent with foil and continue baking. Unless recipe directs otherwise, immediately remove breads from pans. Cool completely on a wire rack.

Loaves

Home-Style Yeast Bread

PREP: 25 min. + rising **BAKE:** 25 min. + cooling
YIELD: 3 loaves

Launa Shoemaker, Midland City, Alabama

Everyone will like the tender texture and slightly sweet taste of this homemade bread.

- 3 packages (1/4 ounce *each*) active dry yeast
- 2 cups warm water (110° to 115°)
- 1 cup sugar
- 1/2 cup butter, melted
- 1-1/2 teaspoons salt
- 2 eggs, beaten
- 7-3/4 to 8-1/4 cups bread flour

1 In a large mixing bowl, dissolve yeast in warm water. Add the sugar, butter, salt, eggs and 4 cups flour; beat until smooth. Stir in enough remaining flour to form a soft dough.

2 Turn onto a floured surface; knead until smooth and elastic, about 6-8 minutes. Place in a greased bowl, turning once to grease top. Cover and let rise in a warm place until doubled, about 45 minutes.

3 Punch dough down. Turn onto a heavily floured surface; divide into thirds. Shape each portion into a loaf. Place in three greased 9-in. x 5-in. x 3-in. loaf pans. Cover and let rise until doubled, about 45 minutes.

4 Bake at 350° for 25-30 minutes or until golden brown. Remove from pans to wire racks to cool.

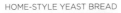
HOME-STYLE YEAST BREAD

CRUSTY FRENCH BREAD

Crusty French Bread

PREP: 30 min. + rising **BAKE:** 20 min. + cooling
YIELD: 2 loaves

Christy Freeman, Central Point, Oregon

Don't hesitate to try this recipe even if you're not an accomplished baker…there's no kneading required.

- 1 package (1/4 ounce) active dry yeast
- 1-1/2 cups warm water (110° to 115°), *divided*
- 1 tablespoon sugar
- 2 teaspoons salt
- 1 tablespoon shortening, melted
- 4 cups all-purpose flour
Cornmeal

1 In a large mixing bowl, dissolve yeast in 1/2 cup warm water. Add the sugar, salt, shortening and remaining water; stir until blended. Stir in flour until smooth. Do not knead. Cover and let rise in a warm place until doubled, about 1 hour.

2 Punch dough down. Turn onto a floured surface; divide in half. Cover and let rest for 10 minutes. Roll each portion into a 10-in. x 8-in. rectangle. Roll up jelly-roll style, starting with a long side; pinch seam to seal. Sprinkle greased baking sheets with cornmeal. Place loaves seam side down on prepared pans. Sprinkle tops with cornmeal. Cover and let rise until doubled, about 45 minutes.

3 With a sharp knife, make five diagonal cuts across the top of each loaf. Bake at 400° for 20-30 minutes or until lightly browned. Remove from pans to wire racks to cool.

Italian Bread

PREP: 20 min. + rising **BAKE:** 45 min. + cooling
YIELD: 2 loaves

Virginia Slater, West Sunbury, Pennsylvania

Years ago in Italian villages, bread was baked only once a week. They made the loaves just a little bigger so they'd last for 7 days.

- 2 **packages (1/4 ounce** *each***) active dry yeast**
- 3 **cups warm water (110° to 115°),** *divided*
- 3 **tablespoons sugar**
- 3 **tablespoons shortening**
- 1 **tablespoon salt**
- 1 **egg**
- 8 **to 9 cups all-purpose flour**

Melted butter

1 In a large mixing bowl, dissolve yeast in 1/2 cup warm water. Add the sugar, shortening, salt, egg, remaining water and 4 cups flour; beat until smooth. Stir in enough remaining flour to form a soft dough. Turn onto a floured surface; knead until smooth and elastic, about 6-8 minutes. Place in a greased bowl, turning once to grease top. Cover and let rise in a warm place until doubled, about 1 hour.

2 Punch dough down. Turn onto a lightly floured surface; divide in half. Shape each portion into a loaf. Place seam side down on greased baking sheets. With a sharp knife, make four shallow diagonal slashes across the top of each loaf. Cover and let rise until doubled, about 1 hour.

3 Bake at 350° for 37-42 minutes or until golden brown. Remove from pans to wire racks. Brush with melted butter. Cool.

Easter Bread

PREP: 45 min. + rising **BAKE:** 45 min. + cooling
YIELD: 3 loaves

Rose Kostynuik, Calgary, Alberta

This traditional Ukranian bread can be served for breakfast or afternoon tea.

- 2 **packages (1/4 ounce** *each***) active dry yeast**
- 1/2 **cup warm water (110° to 115°)**
- 4 **eggs**
- 6 **egg yolks**
- 1 **cup sugar**
- 3/4 **cup butter, melted**
- 2 **teaspoons salt**

EASTER BREAD

- 1 **teaspoon vanilla extract**
- 1 **teaspoon lemon juice**
- 2 **tablespoons grated lemon peel**
- 2 **cups warm milk (110° to 115°)**
- 9-3/4 **to 10-1/4 cups all-purpose flour**
- 1 **cup golden raisins**

1 In a small bowl, dissolve yeast in warm water; set aside. In a large mixing bowl, beat the eggs and yolks until lemon-colored; gradually add sugar. Add the butter, salt, vanilla, lemon juice and peel; beat well. Blend in milk and yeast mixture. Add 6 cups flour; beat until smooth. By hand, stir in enough remaining flour to form a soft dough.

2 Turn onto a lightly floured surface; knead until smooth and elastic, about 10 minutes. Sprinkle with raisins; knead for 5 minutes longer. Place in a greased bowl, turning once to grease top. Cover and let rise in a warm place until doubled, about 1 hour.

3 Punch dough down. Turn onto a lightly floured surface; divide into thirds. Cover and let rest 10 minutes. Shape each portion into a loaf and place in greased 8-in. x 4-in. x 2-in. loaf pans. Cover and let rise in a warm place until almost doubled, about 30 minutes.

4 Bake at 325° for 45 minutes or until golden brown. Remove from pans to cool on wire racks.

Milk-and-Honey White Bread

PREP: 15 min. + rising **BAKE:** 30 min. + cooling
YIELD: 2 loaves

Kathy McCreary, Goddard, Kansas

Honey gives a special flavor to this traditional white bread.

> 2 **packages (1/4 ounce *each*) active dry
> yeast**
> 2-1/2 **cups warm milk (110° to 115°)**
> 1/3 **cup honey**
> 1/4 **cup butter, melted**
> 2 **teaspoons salt**
> 8 **to 8-1/2 cups all-purpose flour**

1 In a large mixing bowl, dissolve yeast in warm milk. Add the honey, butter, salt and 5 cups flour; beat until smooth. Stir in enough remaining flour to form a soft dough.

2 Turn onto a floured surface; knead until smooth and elastic, about 6-8 minutes. Place in a greased bowl, turning once to grease top. Cover and let rise in a warm place until doubled, about 1 hour.

3 Punch dough down. Divide in half; shape each portion into a loaf. Place in two greased 9-in. x 5-in. x 3-in. loaf pans. Cover and let rise until doubled, about 30 minutes.

4 Bake at 375° for 30-35 minutes or until golden brown (cover loosely with foil if top browns too quickly). Remove from pans to wire racks to cool.

MILK-AND-HONEY WHITE BREAD

CHEESY ITALIAN BREAD

Cheesy Italian Bread

PREP: 20 min. + rising **BAKE:** 20 min. + cooling
YIELD: 2 loaves

Cookie Curci-Wright, San Jose, California

Romano cheese adds a little more flavor to plain Italian bread. This goes so well with an Italian meal or alongside a big bowl of soup.

> 1 **package (1/4 ounce) active dry yeast**
> 1-1/4 **cups warm water (110° to 115°)**
> 2 **tablespoons sugar**
> 1 **teaspoon garlic salt**
> 1/2 **teaspoon salt**
> 1/2 **cup grated Romano cheese**
> 3 **to 3-1/2 cups all-purpose flour**
> **Cornmeal**

1 In a large mixing bowl, dissolve yeast in warm water. Add the sugar, garlic salt, salt, cheese and 2 cups flour; beat until smooth. Stir in enough remaining flour to form a soft dough. Turn onto a floured surface; knead until smooth and elastic, about 6-8 minutes. Place in a greased bowl, turning once to grease top. Cover and let rise in a warm place until doubled, about 1 hour.

2 Punch dough down. Turn onto a lightly floured surface; divide in half. Shape each portion into a 14-in. loaf. Place on a greased baking sheet that has been sprinkled with cornmeal. Cover and let rise until doubled, about 45 minutes.

3 Brush loaves with water. With a sharp knife, make three diagonal slashes about 1/2 in. deep in each loaf. Fill a 13-in. x 9-in. x 2-in. baking dish with 1 in. of hot water; place on the bottom rack of oven. Place pan with loaves on middle rack. Bake at 400° for 20-25 minutes. Remove from pan to a wire rack to cool.

Irish Bread

PREP: 15 min. + rising **BAKE:** 30 min. + cooling
YIELD: 1 loaf

Martha Glenn, Enid, Oklahoma

Unlike traditional Irish Soda Bread, this version calls for yeast, giving it a slightly different texture.

2-1/2 to 2-3/4 cups all-purpose flour
   3 tablespoons sugar
   1 package (1/4 ounce) active dry yeast
1/2 teaspoon salt
1/2 teaspoon baking soda
   1 cup warm buttermilk (120° to 130°)
   2 tablespoons butter, melted
3/4 cup raisins
Additional all-purpose flour

1 In a large mixing bowl, combine 2 cups flour, sugar, yeast, salt and baking soda. Combine buttermilk and butter; gradually add to dry ingredients, beating well. Stir in enough remaining flour to form a soft dough.

2 Turn onto a lightly floured surface; knead in raisins until dough is smooth and elastic, about 6-8 minutes. Place in a greased bowl, turning once to grease top. Cover and let rise in a warm place until doubled, about 1-1/2 hours.

3 Punch dough down. Turn onto a lightly floured surface; knead about 15 times, forming a smooth round ball. Place on a greased baking sheet. Press dough down to form an 8-in. circle. Cover and let rise until doubled, about 45 minutes.

4 Sprinkle dough lightly with additional flour. With a sharp knife, make a 4-in. cross about 1/4 in. deep on top of loaf. Bake at 350° for 30 minutes or until browned. Remove from pan to a wire rack to cool.

Editor's Note: Warmed buttermilk will appear curdled.

HONEY MUSTARD LOAF

Honey Mustard Loaf

PREP: 20 min. + rising **BAKE:** 45 min. + cooling
YIELD: 1 loaf

Dorine Arvidson, Eudora, Kansas

For a flavorful variation to this golden bread, add a 1/2 teaspoon dried oregano and thyme to the dough.

   1 package (1/4 ounce) active dry yeast
3/4 cup warm water (110° to 115°)
   2 eggs
   3 tablespoons honey
   3 tablespoons Dijon mustard
   2 tablespoons butter, softened
   1 teaspoon salt
1/8 teaspoon ground turmeric, optional
   3 to 3-3/4 cups all-purpose flour

1 In a large mixing bowl, dissolve yeast in warm water. Add 1 egg, honey, mustard, butter, salt, turmeric if desired and 2 cups flour. Beat until smooth. Stir in enough remaining flour to form a soft dough.

2 Turn onto a floured surface; knead until smooth and elastic, about 6-8 minutes. Place in a greased bowl, turning once to grease top. Cover and let rise in a warm place until doubled, about 1 hour.

3 Punch dough down. Turn onto a lightly floured surface; shape into a loaf. Place in a greased 9-in. x 5-in. x 3-in. loaf pan. Cover and let rise until doubled, about 1 hour.

4 Beat remaining egg; brush over top. Bake at 400° for 20 minutes. Cover loosely with foil. Bake 15-17 minutes longer or until golden brown. Remove from pan to a wire rack to cool.

storing *yeast breads*

- Cool unsliced yeast bread completely before placing in an airtight container or resealable plastic bag. Yeast bread will stay fresh at room temperature for 2 to 3 days. Bread with cream cheese or other perishable ingredients should be stored in the refrigerator.

- For longer storage, freeze bread in an airtight container or resealable plastic bag for up to 3 months.

Garlic Bubble Loaves

PREP: 35 min. + rising **BAKE:** 35 min. **YIELD:** 2 loaves

Lynn Nichols, Bartlett, Nebraska

Complete your next spaghetti dinner with this eye-catching loaf. Family and friends will have fun pulling off each rich and buttery piece.

> 2 **packages (1/4 ounce *each*) active dry yeast**
> 1/4 **cup warm water (110° to 115°)**
> 2 **cups warm milk (110° to 115°)**
> 2 **tablespoons sugar**
> 1 **tablespoon shortening**
> 2 **teaspoons salt**
> 6-1/4 **to 6-1/2 cups all-purpose flour**
> 1/2 **cup butter, melted**
> 1 **tablespoon dried parsley flakes**
> 2 **teaspoons garlic powder**

1 In a large mixing bowl, dissolve yeast in warm water. Add the milk, sugar, shortening, salt and 2 cups flour; beat until smooth. Stir in enough remaining flour to form a soft dough.

2 Turn onto a floured surface; knead until smooth and elastic, about 6-8 minutes. Place in a greased bowl, turning once to grease top. Cover and let rise in a warm place until doubled, about 1 hour.

3 Punch dough down. Turn onto a lightly floured surface; divide into fourths. Divide each portion into 12 pieces. In a shallow bowl, combine the butter, parsley and garlic powder. Shape each piece of dough into a ball; dip into butter mixture. Place in two greased 9-in. x 5-in. x 3-in. loaf pans. Pour any remaining butter mixture over dough. Cover and let rise until doubled, about 30 minutes.

4 Bake at 375° for 35-40 minutes or until golden brown. Cool for 10 minutes. Remove from pans to wire racks. Serve warm.

GARLIC BUBBLE LOAVES

traditional
mixing method
for *yeast bread*

1. In a saucepan or microwave, heat liquid to 110° to 115°. Use a thermometer to check the temperature. Measure liquid and place in a large mixing bowl. Add active dry yeast; stir until dissolved.

2. Add sugar, salt, fat, eggs (if using) and about half of the flour. Beat with an electric mixer or by hand until smooth.

3. Gradually stir in enough of the remaining flour by hand to form a dough of the consistency stated in the recipe. The amount of flour depends on the humidity in the air.

Butternut Squash Bread

PREP: 25 min. + rising **BAKE:** 25 min. + cooling
YIELD: 3 loaves

Agnes Miller, Marshall, Illinois

Squash gives the loaves a pretty golden color. One pound of squash yields about 1 cup mashed.

- 2 **packages (1/4 ounce *each*) active dry yeast**
- 1/2 **cup warm water (110° to 115°)**
- 1-1/4 **cups mashed cooked butternut squash**
- 1 **cup warm milk (110° to 115°)**
- 2 **eggs**
- 1/3 **cup sugar**
- 1/3 **cup butter, melted**
- 1 **teaspoon salt**
- 7 **to 7-1/2 cups all-purpose flour**

1 In a large mixing bowl, dissolve yeast in warm water. Add the squash, milk, eggs, sugar, butter and salt; beat well. Gradually add 3-1/2 cups flour, beating until smooth. Stir in enough remaining flour to form a soft dough.

2 Turn onto a floured surface; knead until smooth and elastic, about 6-8 minutes. Place in a greased bowl, turning once to grease top. Cover and let rise in a warm place until doubled, about 1 hour.

3 Punch dough down. Turn onto a lightly floured surface; divide into thirds. Shape each portion into a loaf. Place in three greased 8-in. x 4-in. x 2-in. loaf pans. Cover and let rise until doubled, about 30 minutes.

4 Bake at 375° for 25-30 minutes or until golden. Remove from pans to wire racks to cool.

SWISS-ONION BREAD RING

oven temperatures for *baking bread*

The oven temperature for bread baking varies according to the ingredients used to make the bread.

- Generally, leaner breads (made with flour, water and yeast) are baked at 400° to 425°. Richer breads (made with more fat and eggs) are baked at lower temperatures.
- Breads made with less than 1/2 cup sugar are generally baked at 375° and breads with more are baked at 350°.
- A loaf of bread can bake from 25 to 45 minutes. The baking time depends on the size and shape of the loaf and the temperature of the oven.

Swiss-Onion Bread Ring

PREP: 10 min. **BAKE:** 25 min. **YIELD:** 1 loaf

Judi Messina, Coeur d'Alene, Idaho

With the ease of refrigerated bread dough, this tempting cheesy bread offers delicious, down-home goodness. It is crisp and golden on the outside, and rich and buttery on the inside.

- 2-1/2 **teaspoons poppy seeds, *divided***
- 2 **tubes (11 ounces *each*) refrigerated white bread dough**
- 1 **cup (4 ounces) shredded Swiss cheese**
- 3/4 **cup sliced green onions**
- 6 **tablespoons butter, melted**

1 Sprinkle 1/2 teaspoon poppy seeds into a greased 10-in. fluted tube pan. Cut the bread dough into 40 1-in. pieces; place half in prepared pan. Sprinkle with half of the cheese and onions. Top with 1 teaspoon poppy seeds; drizzle with half of the butter. Repeat layers.

2 Bake at 375° for 30-35 minutes or until golden brown. Immediately invert onto a wire rack. Serve warm.

Rosemary Orange Bread

PREP: 20 min. + rising **BAKE:** 45 min. + cooling
YIELD: 1 loaf

Deidre Fallavollita, Vienna, Virginia

Rosemary is the perfect herb to pair with homemade bread.

- 1 **package (1/4 ounce) active dry yeast**
- 3/4 **cup warm water (110° to 115°)**
- 3/4 **cup orange juice**
- 2 **tablespoons honey**
- 1 **tablespoon vegetable oil**
- 1 **tablespoon minced fresh rosemary**
  or 1 **teaspoon dried rosemary, crushed**
- 2 **teaspoons salt**
- 1 **teaspoon grated orange peel**
- 3-3/4 **to 4-1/2 cups all-purpose flour**
- 1 **egg white, lightly beaten**

Whole peppercorns and small rosemary sprigs, optional

1 In a large mixing bowl, dissolve yeast in warm water. Add the orange juice, honey, oil, rosemary, salt, orange peel and 2 cups flour; beat until smooth. Stir in enough remaining flour to form a soft dough.

2 Turn onto a floured surface; knead until smooth and elastic, about 6-8 minutes. Place in a greased bowl, turning once to grease top. Cover and let rise in a warm place until doubled, about 1 hour.

3 Punch dough down. Turn onto a lightly floured surface; roll into a 15-in. x 10-in. rectangle. Roll up jelly-roll style, starting with a short side; pinch edges to seal. Shape into an oval. Place seam side down on a greased baking sheet. Cover and let rise until nearly doubled, about 30 minutes.

4 Bake at 375° for 20 minutes. Brush egg white over loaf. Place peppercorns and rosemary sprigs on top if desired. Bake 25 minutes longer or until browned. Remove from pan to a wire rack to cool.

Rosemary Focaccia

PREP: 30 min. + rising **BAKE:** 25 min. + cooling
YIELD: 2 loaves

Debrah Peoples, Calgary, Alberta

This classic Italian flat bread rivals any store-bought focaccia. Serve slices as a side dish or snack.

- 2 **medium onions, chopped**
- 1/4 **cup plus 3 tablespoons olive oil,** *divided*
- 1-1/2 **teaspoons active dry yeast**
- 1/2 **teaspoon sugar**
- 1-1/2 **cups warm water (110° to 115°),** *divided*
- 1/2 **teaspoon salt**
- 3 **to 4 cups all-purpose flour**
- 2 **tablespoons snipped fresh rosemary**
  ***or* 2 teaspoons dried rosemary,**
  crushed, *divided*
- **Cornmeal**
- **Coarse salt**

1 In a skillet, saute onions in 1/4 cup oil until tender; cool. In a large mixing bowl, dissolve yeast and 1/2 teaspoon sugar in 1/4 cup warm water; let stand for 5 minutes. Add 2 tablespoons oil, salt and remaining water. Add 2 cups flour. Beat until smooth. Stir in enough remaining flour to form a soft dough.

2 Turn onto a floured surface; knead until smooth and elastic, about 6-8 minutes. Add onions and half of the rosemary; knead 1 minute longer. Place in a greased bowl, turning once to grease top. Cover and let rise in a warm place until doubled, about 40 minutes.

3 Punch dough down. Turn onto a lightly floured surface; divide in half. Pat each portion flat. Cover and let rest for 5 minutes. Grease two baking sheets and sprinkle with cornmeal. Stretch each portion of dough into a 10-in. circle on prepared pans. Cover and let rise until doubled, about 40 minutes.

4 Brush with remaining oil. Sprinkle with coarse salt and remaining rosemary. Bake at 375° for 25-30 minutes or until golden brown. Remove from pans to wire racks to cool.

Anadama Bread

PREP: 40 min. + rising **BAKE:** 25 min. + cooling
YIELD: 1 loaf

Taste of Home Test Kitchen

This Early American recipe from New England features an interesting combination of cornmeal and molasses.

- 1/2 **cup water**
- 1/4 **cup cornmeal**
- 1/2 **cup molasses**
- 2 **tablespoons butter**
- 1 **package (1/4 ounce) active dry yeast**
- 1/2 **cup warm water (110° to 115°)**
- 1 **teaspoon salt**
- 3 **to 3-1/2 cups all-purpose flour**

1 In a small saucepan, bring water and cornmeal to a boil. Reduce heat; cook for 2 minutes or until mixture thickens, stirring constantly. Remove from the heat; stir in molasses and butter. Cool to 110°-115°.

2 In a large mixing bowl, dissolve yeast in warm water. Add the cornmeal mixture, salt and 2 cups flour; beat until smooth. Stir in enough remaining flour to form a soft dough.

3 Turn onto a floured surface; knead until smooth and elastic, about 6-8 minutes. Place in a greased bowl, turning once to grease top. Cover and let rise in a warm place until doubled, about 1 hour.

4 Punch dough down. Turn onto a lightly floured surface; shape into a loaf. Place in a greased 9-in. x 5-in. x 3-in. loaf pan. Cover and let rise until doubled, about 1 hour.

5 Bake at 375° for 25-30 minutes or until browned (cover loosely with foil if top browns too quickly). Remove from pan to a wire rack to cool.

Golden Sesame Braids

PREP: 25 min. + rising **BAKE:** 30 min. + cooling
YIELD: 2 loaves

Barbara Sunberg, Camden, Ohio

With a crisp crust and tender inside, these loaves will be gobbled up in a hurry. Slices also make great sandwiches.

- **2** **packages (1/4 ounce *each*) active dry yeast**
- **1/2** **cup warm water (110° to 115°)**
- **1-1/2** **cups warm milk (110° to 115°)**
- **1/4** **cup shortening**
- **1/4** **cup sugar**
- **1** **tablespoon salt**
- **3** **eggs**
- **7-1/2** **to 8 cups all-purpose flour**

TOPPING:
- **1** **egg**
- **1** **tablespoon cold water**
- **2** **tablespoons sesame seeds**

GOLDEN SESAME BRAIDS

1 In a large mixing bowl, dissolve yeast in warm water. Add the milk, shortening, sugar, salt, eggs and 4 cups flour; beat until smooth. Stir in enough remaining flour to form a soft dough.

2 Turn onto a floured surface; knead until smooth and elastic, about 6-8 minutes. Place in a greased bowl, turning once to grease top. Cover and let rise in a warm place until doubled, about 1 hour.

3 Punch dough down. Turn onto a lightly floured surface; divide in half. Divide each portion into thirds. Shape each piece into a 12-in. rope. Place three ropes on a greased baking pan and braid; pinch ends to seal and tuck under. Repeat with remaining dough. Cover and let rise until doubled, about 45 minutes.

4 Beat egg and cold water; brush over braids. Sprinkle with sesame seeds. Bake at 350° for 30-35 minutes or until golden brown. Remove from pans to wire racks to cool.

braiding *breads*

1. Arrange three ropes of dough lengthwise on a greased baking sheet, so they are almost touching. Starting in the middle, loosely bring the left rope under the center rope. Bring the right rope under the new center rope and repeat until you reach the end.

2. Turn the pan and repeat braiding.

3. Press each end to seal and tuck ends under.

proofing *yeast*

To make sure active dry yeast (not quick-rise yeast) is alive and active, you may first want to proof it. Here's how:

Dissolve one package of yeast and 1 teaspoon sugar in 1/4 cup warm water (110° to 115°). Let stand for 5 to 10 minutes. If the mixture foams up, the yeast mixture can be used because the yeast is active. If it does not foam, the yeast should be discarded.

Challah

PREP: 30 min. + rising **BAKE:** 30 min. + cooling
YIELD: 2 loaves

Taste of Home Test Kitchen

Eggs lend to the richness of this traditional braided bread. The attractive golden color and delicious flavor make it hard to resist.

- 2 **packages (1/4 ounce *each*) active dry yeast**
- 1 **cup warm water (110° to 115°)**
- 1/2 **cup vegetable oil**
- 1/3 **cup sugar**
- 1 **tablespoon salt**
- 4 **eggs**
- 6 **to 6-1/2 cups all-purpose flour**

TOPPING:
- 1 **egg**
- 1 **teaspoon cold water**
- 1 **tablespoon sesame *or* poppy seeds, optional**

1 In a large mixing bowl, dissolve yeast in warm water. Add the oil, sugar, salt, eggs and 4 cups flour; beat until smooth. Stir in enough remaining flour to form a firm dough.

2 Turn onto a floured surface; knead until smooth and elastic, about 6-8 minutes. Place in a greased bowl, turning once to grease top. Cover and let rise in a warm place until doubled, about 1 hour.

3 Punch dough down. Turn onto a lightly floured surface; divide in half. Divide each portion into thirds. Shape each piece into a 15-in. rope. Place three ropes on a greased baking sheet and braid; pinch ends to seal and tuck under. Repeat with remaining dough. Cover and let rise until doubled, about 1 hour.

4 Beat egg and cold water; brush over braids. Sprinkle with sesame or poppy seeds if desired. Bake at 350° for 30-35 minutes or until golden brown. Remove from pans to wire racks to cool.

Cheddar Chili Braid

PREP: 20 min. + rising **BAKE:** 30 min. + cooling
YIELD: 1 loaf

Katie Dreibelbis
State College, Pennsylvania

Hot roll mix gives you a head start when preparing this savory bread. Make it with a big pot of chili and serve thick warm slices for "dunking."

- 1 **package (16 ounces) hot roll mix**
- 1 **cup warm water (120° to 130°)**
- 2 **eggs**
- 2 **cups (8 ounces) shredded cheddar cheese**
- 2 **tablespoons canned chopped green chilies, drained**
- 2 **tablespoons grated Parmesan cheese**

1 In a large bowl, combine contents of roll mix and yeast packet; stir in water, one egg, cheddar cheese and chilies. Turn onto a floured surface; knead until smooth and elastic, about 5 minutes. Cover and let rest for 5 minutes.

2 Divide dough into thirds. Shape each portion into a 14-in. rope. Place ropes on a greased baking sheet and braid; pinch ends to seal and tuck under. Cover and let rise in a warm place until doubled, about 30 minutes.

3 Beat remaining egg; brush over dough. Sprinkle with Parmesan cheese. Bake at 375° for 30 minutes or until golden brown. Remove from pan to a wire rack to cool.

Onion Poppy Seed Twist

PREP: 25 min. + rising **BAKE:** 40 min. + cooling
YIELD: 1 loaf

Florence Leitgeb, Medford, New York

Savory slices of this bread are great served with stews, soups and salads.

- 2 **packages (1/4 ounce** *each***) active dry yeast**
- 1/4 **cup warm water (110° to 115°)**
- 1 **cup warm milk (110° to 115°)**
- 1/2 **cup butter, softened**
- 1/4 **cup sugar**
- 1 **egg**
- 1-3/4 **teaspoons salt**
- 4-1/2 to 5 **cups all-purpose flour**
FILLING:
- 1 **cup chopped onion**
- 1/4 **cup butter, melted**
- 3 **tablespoons poppy seeds**
- 1/4 **teaspoon salt**
- 1 **egg, lightly beaten**
Additional poppy seeds

1 In a large mixing bowl, dissolve yeast in warm water. Add the milk, butter, sugar, egg, salt and 2 cups flour. Beat on medium speed for 2 minutes. Stir in enough remaining flour to form a soft dough.

2 Turn onto a floured surface; knead until smooth and elastic, about 6-8 minutes. Place in a greased bowl, turning once to grease top. Cover and let rise in a warm place until doubled, about 1 hour.

3 Punch dough down. Turn onto a floured surface; roll into a 20-in. x 8-in. rectangle. Cut in half lengthwise, forming two 20-in. x 4-in. rectangles.

4 In a small bowl, combine the onion, butter, poppy seeds and salt. Spread over dough to within 1/2 in. of edges. Fold rectangles in half lengthwise; pinch seams to seal, forming two ropes. Place ropes side by side on a greased baking sheet; twist together and shape into a ring. Pinch ends together. Cover and let rise in a warm place until doubled, about 30 minutes.

5 Brush with egg. Sprinkle with additional poppy seeds. Bake at 350° for 40-45 minutes or until golden brown. Remove from pan to a wire rack to cool.

problem-solving pointers *for Yeast Breads*

BREAD DID NOT RISE WELL OR DID NOT RISE AT ALL

- Yeast was not fresh. Next time, proof the yeast (see page 341).
- Liquid was too hot and killed the yeast.
- Dough was kneaded too much or not enough.
- Oven temperature was too low.

BREAD IS HEAVY AND COARSE

- There's too much liquid or not enough flour in dough.
- Next time, use a lower-gluten flour such as whole wheat, rye or oat.
- Dough was allowed to rise too long.
- Oven temperature was too low.

BREAD IS DRY AND CRUMBLY

- Too much flour was used.
- Dough was allowed to rise too long.

BREAD IS DOUGHY ON THE BOTTOM OR HAS A SLIGHTLY GUMMY TEXTURE

- Bread was underbaked.
- Bread stayed in the pan too long after baking.

LOAF SINKS IN THE CENTER

- Dough rose too long during the second rise time in the pan.

BREAD HAS LARGE HOLES

- Dough was not kneaded enough.
- Air was not compressed out of the dough during shaping.

BREAD CRUMBLES WHEN CUT

- Too much flour was used.
- Dough was kneaded too much or not enough.
- Dough was allowed to rise too long or not long enough.
- Oven temperature was too high.

BREAD HAS A YEASTY TASTE

- Dough had too much yeast or rose too long.

Maple Oat Batter Bread

PREP: 15 min. + rising **BAKE:** 40 min. **YIELD:** 1 loaf

Denise Frink, Henderson, Iowa

Maple flavor make this moist hearty bread very appealing.

1-1/4	cups warm milk (120° to 130°)
1	cup quick-cooking oats
1/4	cup butter, softened
1	package (1/4 ounce) active dry yeast
1/4	cup warm water (110° to 115°)
1/3	cup maple syrup
1-1/2	teaspoons salt
1	egg, lightly beaten
3/4	cup whole wheat flour
2	cups all-purpose flour

Additional oats

1 In a large mixing bowl, combine the milk, oats and butter; cool to 110°-115°. In a small bowl, dissolve yeast in warm water; add to the oat mixture. Add the syrup, salt, egg, whole wheat flour and 1 cup all-purpose flour. Beat on low speed for 30 seconds; beat on high for 3 minutes. Stir in remaining all-purpose flour (batter will be thick). Do not knead.

2 Sprinkle additional oats into a greased 1-1/2-qt. baking dish. Spoon batter into dish. Cover; let rise in a warm place until doubled, about 50 minutes.

3 Bake at 350° for 40-45 minutes or until golden brown. Cool for 10 minutes before removing from pan to a wire rack. Serve warm.

Cheese Batter Bread

PREP: 20 min. + rising **BAKE:** 25 min. **YIELD:** 1 loaf

Shirley Ramsey, Wymore, Nebraska

This bread has a unique flavor and will become a family favorite. Slices pair well with soup and chili.

1	package (1/4 ounce) active dry yeast
1	cup warm chicken broth (110° to 115°)
1	tablespoon butter
2	tablespoons sugar
1/2	teaspoon salt
1/2	teaspoon poultry seasoning
1	egg
3	cups all-purpose flour
1-1/4	cups finely shredded cheddar cheese, *divided*

Onion salt, optional

1 In a large mixing bowl, dissolve yeast in warm broth. Add the butter, sugar, salt, poultry seasoning, egg and 1 cup flour; beat until smooth, about 1 minute. Add 1 cup cheese and the remaining flour; stir for 1 minute. Do not knead. Cover and let rise in a warm place until doubled, about 30 minutes.

2 Stir batter down, about 25 strokes. Spread evenly into a greased 9-in. x 5-in. x 3-in. loaf pan. Cover and let rise until doubled, about 20 minutes. Top with the remaining cheese. Sprinkle with onion salt if desired. Bake at 375° for 25-30 minutes or until golden brown. Remove from pan to a wire rack. Serve warm.

English Muffin Bread

PREP: 15 min. + rising **BAKE:** 20 min. + cooling
YIELD: 3 loaves

Donna Meyer, Dayton, Ohio

Slices of this traditional batter bread are terrific when toasted and slathered with butter.

6	cups all-purpose flour
2	packages (1/4 ounce *each*) active dry yeast
1	tablespoon sugar
2	teaspoons salt
1/4	teaspoon baking soda
2	cups warm milk (120° to 130°)
1/2	cup warm water (120° to 130°)

Cornmeal

1 In a large mixing bowl, combine 3 cups flour, yeast, sugar, salt and baking soda. Add milk and water; mix well. Stir in remaining flour (batter will be soft). Do not knead.

2 Sprinkle three greased 8-in. x 4-in. x 2-in. loaf pans with cornmeal. Spoon batter into prepared pans; sprinkle cornmeal on top. Cover and let rise in a warm place until doubled, about 45 minutes.

3 Bake at 400° for 20-25 minutes or until golden brown. Remove from pans to cool on wire racks.

Dilly Bread Ring

PREP: 15 min. + rising **BAKE:** 30 min. + cooling
YIELD: 1 loaf

Natercia Yailaian, Somerville, Massachusetts

Parsley, dill and chives plus cream give this tender bread a delicious flavor.

2	**packages (1/4 ounce *each*) active dry yeast**
1/3	**cup warm water (110° to 115°)**
1/3	**cup warm milk (110° to 115°)**
6	**tablespoons butter, softened**
1/3	**cup sugar**
2	**eggs**
1	**cup (8 ounces) sour cream**
2	**tablespoons minced fresh parsley**
1	**to 2 tablespoons dill weed**
2	**teaspoons salt**
1-1/2	**teaspoons minced chives**
4-1/2	**cups all-purpose flour**

1 In a large mixing bowl, dissolve yeast in warm water. Add the milk, butter, sugar, eggs, sour cream, seasonings and 3 cups flour. Beat on low speed for 30 seconds; beat on high for 3 minutes. Stir in remaining flour (batter will be sticky). Do not knead. Cover and let rise in a warm place until doubled, about 1 hour.

2 Stir dough down. Spoon into a greased 10-in. tube or fluted tube pan. Cover and let rise until nearly doubled, about 45 minutes.

3 Bake at 375° for 30-35 minutes or until golden brown (cover loosely with foil if top browns too quickly). Cool for 10 minutes before removing from pan to a wire rack.

the basics of
batter breads

- Batter bread is beaten with an electric mixer to help develop the gluten faster and give the bread a better texture. Because these breads are not kneaded, it is important to beat them until the batter comes away from the bowl and appears to be stringy.

- Stir in the remaining flour with a sturdy wooden spoon until you have a stiff batter. Since less flour is used for batter breads, it forms a batter rather than a dough and is stickier than a kneaded dough.

- If a recipe directs you to stir the batter after the first rising, stir it enough to bring it down to the original volume.

- Most batter breads are spooned or spread into a baking pan or dish. Push batter evenly to the edge of pan or into corners with a rubber spatula. Some batter breads can be shaped.

- Follow the directions given for rising in each recipe. Batter breads rise until doubled or almost doubled—they don't rise to the top of the pan. If left to rise too long, they may fall during baking.

- Batter breads are best served the day they are made.

DILLY BREAD RING

THREE-FLOUR BRAID

Three-Flour Braid

PREP: 40 min. + rising **BAKE:** 25 min. **YIELD:** 2 loaves

Audrey Benson, Flagler, Colorado

Beautiful sliced or whole, this pretty multicolored bread freezes well, so you can enjoy it anytime of year.

> 2 packages (1/4 ounce *each*) active dry yeast
> 2-1/4 cups warm water (110° to 115°)
> 1/4 cup vegetable oil
> 2 tablespoons sugar
> 1 teaspoon salt
> 3-1/4 cups all-purpose flour
> **RYE DOUGH:**
> 2 tablespoons molasses
> 1 tablespoon baking cocoa
> 1 teaspoon caraway seed
> 1-1/4 cups rye flour
> **WHEAT DOUGH:**
> 2 tablespoons molasses
> 1 cup whole wheat flour
> **WHITE DOUGH:**
> 1-1/4 cups all-purpose flour
> 1 tablespoon butter, melted

1 In a large mixing bowl, dissolve yeast in warm water. Add oil, sugar, salt and 2-1/4 cups flour; beat for 2 minutes. Add remaining flour; beat 2 minutes longer. Divide evenly into three mixing bowls.

2 To the first bowl, add the molasses, cocoa and caraway seed; mix well. Gradually add rye flour. Turn onto a floured surface; knead until smooth and elastic, about 6-8 minutes. Place in a greased bowl, turning once to grease top. Cover and set aside.

3 To the second bowl, add molasses; mix well. Gradually add whole wheat flour. Turn onto a floured surface; knead until smooth and elastic, about 6-8 minutes. Place in a greased bowl, turning once to grease top. Cover and set aside.

4 To the third bowl, gradually add all-purpose flour. Turn onto a floured surface; knead until smooth and elastic, about 6-8 minutes. Place in a greased bowl, turning once to grease top. Cover all three bowls and let rise in a warm place until doubled, about 1 hour.

5 Punch doughs down. Turn onto a lightly floured surface; divide each in half. Shape each half into a 15-in. rope. Place a rope of each dough on a greased baking sheet and braid; pinch ends to seal and tuck under. Repeat with remaining ropes. Cover and let rise until nearly doubled, about 30 minutes.

baking yeast breads at *high altitudes*

High altitude (over 3,000 feet) affects bread baking because the lower air pressure allows the yeast to rise 25 to 50 percent faster, and the drier air makes the flour drier. If the dough over-rises, the results might be a heavy, dry loaf or misshapen or collapsed loaf. Make these adjustments when baking bread at high altitudes:

• Start checking the dough halfway through the recommended rise time to see if it has doubled. If the dough has over-risen, punch it down and allow it to rise again.

• Use about a third less yeast. If a recipe calls for one package of active dry yeast (2-1/4 teaspoons), you would need to use about 1-1/2 teaspoons.

• Add flour slowly when mixing the dough and use only enough to make the dough easy to handle. If the dough is sticky, use greased rather than floured hands for kneading.

• Oil the dough and cover with greased plastic wrap to prevent it from drying out while waiting to be shaped.

• Check doneness a few minutes before the minimum recommended baking time. Tent with foil if it's browning too quickly.

6 Bake at 350° for 25-30 minutes or until golden brown. Brush with butter.

Editor's Note: Use all purpose flour on kneading surface for all three doughs.

Herbed Whole Wheat Bread

PREP: 20 min. + rising BAKE: 45 min. + cooling
YIELD: 2 loaves

Barbara Glover, Port St. Lucie, Florida

A blend of dill, parsley and sage dresses up ordinary wheat bread. The flavor pairs well with a poultry dinner.

  1 **medium onion, chopped**
  3 **tablespoons vegetable oil**
  2 **packages (1/4 ounce *each*) active dry yeast**
1/2 **cup warm water (110° to 115°)**
  1 **can (12 ounces) evaporated milk**
1/2 **cup minced fresh parsley**
  3 **tablespoons sugar**
  1 **teaspoon salt**
1/2 **teaspoon dill weed**
1/4 **teaspoon rubbed sage**
3/4 **cup cornmeal**
  2 **cups whole wheat flour**
1-3/4 **to 2-1/4 cups all-purpose flour**

1 In a skillet, saute onion in oil until tender; cool. In a large mixing bowl, dissolve yeast in warm water. Add the milk, parsley, sugar, salt, dill, sage and onion mixture; mix well. Add cornmeal; mix well. Stir in whole wheat flour and enough all-purpose flour to form a soft dough.

2 Turn onto a floured surface; knead until smooth and elastic, about 3-5 minutes. Place in a greased bowl, turning once to grease top. Cover and let rise in a warm place until doubled, about 1 hour.

3 Punch dough down. Turn onto a lightly floured surface; divide in half. Shape each portion into a loaf. Place in two greased 9-in. x 5-in. x 3-in. loaf pans. Cover and let rise until doubled, about 30-45 minutes.

4 Bake at 350° for 30 minutes. Cover loosely with foil. Bake 15-20 minutes longer or until golden brown. Remove from pans to wire racks to cool.

Whole Wheat Braids

PREP: 20 min. + rising BAKE: 40 min. + cooling
YIELD: 3 loaves

Suella Miller, LaGrange, Indiana

A hearty loaf of bread completes any meal. Braiding the dough makes an appealing presentation.

  3 **packages (1/4 ounce *each*) active dry yeast**
  3 **cups warm water (110° to 115°)**
1/2 **cup sugar**
  3 **eggs**
1/3 **cup vegetable oil**
  1 **tablespoon salt**
  5 **cups whole wheat flour**
  4 **to 4-1/2 cups all-purpose flour**

1 In a large mixing bowl, dissolve yeast in warm water. Add the sugar, eggs, oil, salt and whole wheat flour; beat until smooth. Stir in enough all-purpose flour to form a soft dough.

2 Turn onto a floured surface; knead until smooth and elastic, about 6-8 minutes. Place in a greased bowl, turning once to grease top. Cover and let rise in a warm place until doubled, about 1 hour.

3 Punch dough down. Turn onto a lightly floured surface; divide into nine pieces. Shape each piece into a 14-in. rope. Braid three ropes together; pinch ends to seal and tuck under. Place in three greased 8-in. x 4-in. x 2-in. loaf pans. Cover and let rise until doubled, about 30 minutes.

4 Bake at 350° for 40-45 minutes. Remove from pans to wire racks to cool.

WHOLE WHEAT BRAIDS

Light Rye Sandwich Loaves

PREP: 20 min. + rising **BAKE:** 30 min. + cooling
YIELD: 2 loaves

Katie Koziolek, Hartland, Minnesota

This bread may also be shaped into two round loaves.

- 4 to 4-1/2 cups all-purpose flour
- 2-1/2 cups rye flour
- 1/3 cup packed brown sugar
- 2 packages (1/4 ounce *each*) active dry yeast
- 1 tablespoon grated orange peel
- 2 teaspoons salt
- 1/2 teaspoon fennel seed *or* aniseed, crushed
- 2-1/4 cups water
- 1/4 cup shortening
- 1-1/2 teaspoons molasses
- Cornmeal
- Melted butter

1 In a large mixing bowl, combine 2 cups all-purpose flour, rye flour, brown sugar, yeast, orange peel, salt and fennel seed. In a saucepan, heat the water, shortening and molasses to 120°-130°. Add to dry ingredients; beat until smooth. Stir in enough remaining all-purpose flour to form a soft dough.

2 Turn onto a floured surface; knead until smooth and elastic, about 6-8 minutes. Place in a greased bowl, turning once to grease top. Cover and let rise in a warm place until doubled, about 1-1/4 hours.

3 Punch dough down. Turn onto a lightly floured surface; divide in half. Shape each portion into a loaf. Greased two 8-in. x 4-in. x 2-in. loaf pans; sprinkle with cornmeal. Place loaves in prepared pans. Cover and let rise until doubled, about 45 minutes.

4 With a sharp knife, make three shallow slashes across the top of each loaf. Bake at 375° for 30-35 minutes or until golden brown. Remove from pans to wire racks. Brush with melted butter. Cool.

Old-World Rye Bread

PREP: 25 min. + rising **BAKE:** 35 min. + cooling
YIELD: 2 loaves

Perlene Hoekema, Lynden, Washington

Rye and caraway lend to this bread's wonderful flavor, while the surprise ingredient of baking cocoa gives it a rich, dark color. For variation, stir in a cup each of raisins and walnuts.

- 2 packages (1/4 ounce *each*) active dry yeast
- 1-1/2 cups warm water (110° to 115°)
- 1/2 cup molasses
- 6 tablespoons butter, softened
- 2 cups rye flour
- 1/4 cup baking cocoa
- 2 tablespoons caraway seeds
- 2 teaspoons salt
- 3-1/2 to 4 cups all-purpose flour
- Cornmeal

1 In a large mixing bowl, dissolve yeast in warm water. Beat in the molasses, butter, rye flour, cocoa, caraway seeds, salt and 2 cups all-purpose flour until smooth. Stir in enough remaining all-purpose flour to form a stiff dough.

2 Turn onto a floured surface; knead until smooth and elastic, about 6-8 minutes. Place in a greased bowl, turning once to grease top. Cover and let rise in a warm place until doubled, about 1-1/2 hours.

3 Punch dough down. Turn onto a lightly floured surface; divide in half. Shape each piece into a loaf, about 10 in. long. Grease two baking sheets and sprinkle with cornmeal. Place loaves on prepared pans. Cover and let rise until doubled, about 1 hour.

4 Bake at 350° for 35-40 minutes or until bread sounds hollow when tapped. Remove from pans to wire racks to cool.

OLD-WORLD RYE BREAD

Cornmeal Mini Loaves

PREP: 20 min. + rising **BAKE:** 15 min. + cooling
YIELD: 6 loaves

Ellen Govertsen, Wheaton, Illinois

This recipe makes six miniature loaves that can be baked, cooled and tucked into your freezer.

- 2 packages (1/4 ounce *each*) active dry yeast
- 1 cup warm water (110° to 115°)
- 1 cup warm milk (110° to 115°)
- 1/2 cup shortening
- 1/2 cup sugar
- 2 eggs
- 2 teaspoons salt
- 1 cup cornmeal
- 6 to 6-1/2 cups all-purpose flour
- Additional cornmeal

1 In a mixing bowl, dissolve yeast in warm water. Add milk, shortening, sugar, eggs, salt, cornmeal and 4 cups flour; beat until smooth. Stir in enough remaining flour to form a soft dough.

2 Turn onto a floured surface; knead until smooth and elastic, about 6-8 minutes. Place in a greased bowl, turning once to grease top. Cover and let rise in a warm place until doubled, about 1 hour.

3 Punch dough down. Turn onto a lightly floured surface; divide into six pieces. Shape each piece into a 6-in. oval loaf. Sprinkle two greased baking sheets with cornmeal. Place three loaves 3 in. apart on each prepared pan. Cover and let rise until doubled, about 30 minutes.

4 With a sharp knife, make three shallow diagonal slashes across the top of each loaf. Bake at 400° for 15-20 minutes or until golden brown. Remove from pans to wire racks to cool.

Dill Rye Rounds

PREP: 20 min. + rising **BAKE:** 30 min. + cooling
YIELD: 2 loaves

Betty Pittman, Letts, Iowa

The rye flour adds a delicious, mild flavor to this bread.

- 3-1/2 to 4 cups all-purpose flour
- 1-1/2 cups rye flour
- 1/2 cup nonfat dry milk powder
- 2 packages (1/4 ounce *each*) active dry yeast
- 2 teaspoons sugar
- 1 teaspoon salt
- 1 teaspoon caraway seeds
- 1 teaspoon dill seed
- 1 teaspoon dill weed
- 1-3/4 cups water
- 2 teaspoons shortening

1 In a mixing bowl, combine 2 cups all-purpose flour and next eight ingredients. Heat water and shortening to 120°-130°. Add to dry ingredients; beat until smooth. Stir in enough remaining all-purpose flour to form a soft dough.

2 Turn onto a floured surface; knead until smooth and elastic, about 6-8 minutes. Place in a greased bowl, turning once to grease top. Cover and let rise in a warm place until doubled, about 45 minutes.

3 Punch dough down. Turn onto a floured surface; divide in half. Shape each piece into a ball. Place on two greased baking sheets. Cover and let rise in a warm place until doubled, about 35 minutes.

4 With a sharp knife, make several shallow slashes across the top of each loaf. Bake at 375° for 30-35 minutes or until golden brown. Remove from pans to wire racks to cool.

making slashes on
top of a *loaf*

Slashing or scoring the top of a bread loaf allows steam to vent and helps prevent cracking. With a sharp knife, make shallow slashes across top of loaf.

Herbed Oatmeal Pan Bread

PREP: 25 min. + rising **BAKE:** 20 min.
YIELD: 8-10 servings

Karen Bourne, Magrath, Alberta

This beautiful golden pan bread is especially good with a steaming bowl of homemade soup. The oats in the dough and Parmesan topping give it a distinctive flavor.

- 1-1/2 cups boiling water
- 1 cup old-fashioned oats
- 2 packages (1/4 ounce *each*) active dry yeast
- 1/2 cup warm water (110° to 115°)
- 1/4 cup sugar
- 3 tablespoons butter, softened
- 2 teaspoons salt
- 1 egg
- 4 to 4-3/4 cups all-purpose flour

TOPPING:
- 1/4 cup butter, melted, *divided*
- 2 tablespoons grated Parmesan cheese
- 1 teaspoon dried basil
- 1/2 teaspoon dried oregano
- 1/2 teaspoon garlic powder

1 In a small bowl, combine boiling water and oats; cool to 110°-115°. In a large mixing bowl, dissolve yeast in warm water. Add the sugar, butter, salt, egg, oat mixture and 2 cups flour; beat until smooth. Stir in enough remaining flour to form a soft dough.

2 Turn onto a floured surface; knead until smooth and elastic, about 6-8 minutes. Place in a greased bowl, turning once to grease top. Cover and let rise in a warm place until doubled, about 45 minutes.

3 Punch dough down. Press evenly into a greased 13-in. x 9-in. x 2-in. baking pan. With a very sharp knife, cut diagonal lines 1-1/2 in. apart completely through dough. Repeat in opposite direction, creating a diamond pattern. Cover and let rise until doubled, about 1 hour.

4 Redefine pattern by gently poking along cut lines with knife tip. Brush with 2 tablespoons melted butter. Bake at 375° for 15 minutes. Meanwhile, combine Parmesan cheese, basil, oregano and garlic powder. Brush bread with remaining butter; sprinkle with cheese mixture. Bake for 5 minutes. Cover loosely with foil; bake 5 minutes longer. Serve warm.

HERBED OATMEAL PAN BREAD

mixing method
for yeast breads

1. In a mixing bowl, combine flour (about 2 cups), the sugar, active dry or quick-rise yeast, salt and any seasonings.

2. In a saucepan, heat the liquid ingredients (water, milk, honey, molasses and butter or oil) to 120°-130°. Add to dry ingredients and beat just until moistened.

3. Add any eggs; beat until smooth. Gradually stir in enough of the remaining flour to form a dough of the desired consistency. The amount of flour will vary with the humidity in the air.

3 tablespoons cornmeal
4 ounces string cheese
1 can (15 ounces) pizza sauce
1/2 cup sliced fresh mushrooms
1 cup (4 ounces) shredded part-skim mozzarella cheese
1/4 cup shredded cheddar cheese

1 In a skillet, cook beef and onion over medium heat until meat is no longer pink; drain and set aside. In a mixing bowl, combine 2-1/2 cups flour, 1 tablespoon Italian seasoning, yeast, sugar and salt.

2 In a saucepan, heat water and oil to 120°-130°. Add to the dry ingredients; beat just until moistened. Stir in enough remaining flour to form a soft dough. Let rest for 5 minutes. Sprinkle cornmeal over a greased 14-in. pizza pan.

3 On a lightly floured surface, roll dough into a 15-in. circle. Transfer to prepared pan, letting dough drape 1 in. over the edge. Cut string cheese in half lengthwise; place around edge of pan. Fold dough over string cheese; pinch to seal. Prick dough thoroughly with a fork. Bake at 375° for 5 minutes.

4 Combine pizza sauce and 2 teaspoons Italian seasoning; spread half over crust. Sprinkle with beef mixture and mushrooms; cover with remaining pizza sauce mixture. Sprinkle with shredded cheeses and remaining Italian seasoning. Bake 18-20 minutes longer or until cheese is melted and crust is golden brown.

STUFFED-CRUST PIZZA

Stuffed-Crust Pizza

PREP: 30 min. **BAKE:** 25 min. **YIELD:** 8 slices

Renae Jacobson, Elm Creek, Nebraska

The edges of the no-fail homemade crust are filled with string cheese, and the hearty toppings can be varied to suit your preference. Also try the dough for making breadsticks or bread bowls.

1 pound ground beef
1 small onion, chopped
2-1/2 to 3 cups all-purpose flour
2 tablespoons Italian seasoning, *divided*
1 package (1/4 ounce) quick-rise yeast
1 tablespoon sugar
1/2 teaspoon salt
1 cup water
3 tablespoons olive oil

Sausage Calzones

PREP: 35 min. + rising **BAKE:** 20 min. **YIELD:** 6 calzones

Janine Colasurdo, Chesapeake, Virginia

In these pizza turnovers, Italian sausage combines with ricotta, Parmesan and spinach.

- 1 package (1/4 ounce) active dry yeast
- 1/2 cup warm water (110° to 115°)
- 3/4 cup warm milk (110° to 115°)
- 2 tablespoons olive oil
- 1-1/2 teaspoons salt
- 1 teaspoon sugar
- 3 to 3-1/4 cups all-purpose flour
- 1 pound bulk Italian sausage
- 1 package (10 ounces) frozen chopped spinach, thawed and squeezed dry
- 1 carton (15 ounces) ricotta cheese
- 1/2 cup grated Parmesan cheese
- 1 tablespoon minced fresh parsley
- 1/8 teaspoon pepper
- 2 tablespoons cornmeal

Additional oil

- 1/2 teaspoon garlic salt
- 1-1/2 cups pizza sauce, warmed

1 In a large mixing bowl, dissolve yeast in warm water. Add the milk, oil, salt, sugar and 2 cups flour; beat until smooth. Stir in enough remaining flour to form a soft dough.

2 Turn onto a floured surface; knead until smooth and elastic, about 6-8 minutes. Place in a greased bowl, turning once to grease top. Cover and let rise in a warm place until doubled, about 1 hour. Meanwhile, in a large skillet, cook sausage over medium heat until no longer pink; drain. Stir in the spinach, cheeses, parsley and pepper; set aside.

3 Punch dough down. Turn onto a lightly floured surface; divide into six pieces. Roll each piece into an 8-in. circle. Top each with 2/3 cup filling. Fold dough over filling; pinch edges to seal. Sprinkle greased baking sheets with cornmeal. Place calzones on prepared pans. Brush tops lightly with oil; sprinkle with garlic salt. Bake at 400° for 20-25 minutes or until golden brown. Serve with pizza sauce. Refrigerate leftovers.

Basic Pizza Crust

PREP: 10 min. + resting **BAKE:** 25 min. **YIELD:** 1 pizza

Beverly Anderson, Sinclairville, New York

Store-bought pizza crusts and boxed mixes just can't compare to this homemade version.

- 1 package (1/4 ounce) active dry yeast
- 1 cup warm water (110° to 115°)
- 2 tablespoons vegetable oil
- 1 teaspoon sugar
- 1/4 teaspoon salt
- 2-1/2 to 2-3/4 cups all-purpose flour

Cornmeal

Pizza toppings of your choice

1 In a large mixing bowl, dissolve yeast in warm water. Add the oil, sugar, salt and 1-1/2 cups flour; beat until smooth. Stir in enough remaining flour to form a firm dough. Turn onto a floured surface; cover and let rest for 10 minutes.

2 Roll into a 13-in. circle. Grease a 12-in. pizza pan; sprinkle with cornmeal. Transfer dough to prepared pan, building up edges slightly. Do not let rise. Bake at 425° for 12-15 minutes or until browned. Add toppings; bake 10-15 minutes longer.

Special Savory Loaves

PREP: 35 min. + rising **BAKE:** 40 min. **YIELD:** 2 loaves

Alanna Petrone, Terryville, Connecticut

Tomato soup beautifully colors the dough, while herbs, tomatoes and cheese provide lots of flavor.

    2 packages (1/4 ounce *each*) active dry
       yeast
1-1/3 cups warm water (110° to 115°)
    1 can (10-3/4 ounces) condensed tomato
       soup, undiluted
  1/4 cup olive oil
  1/2 teaspoon salt
6-1/4 to 6-3/4 cups all-purpose flour
FILLING:
    1 cup minced fresh basil
  1/2 cup minced fresh parsley
  1/4 cup minced garlic
  1/2 cup olive oil
    2 large tomatoes, thinly sliced
  1/2 cup grated Romano cheese

TOPPING:
    1 egg white, lightly beaten
    2 tablespoons sesame seeds
    1 tablespoon cracked black pepper
  1/2 teaspoon garlic salt
  1/2 teaspoon crushed red pepper flakes

1 In a large mixing bowl, dissolve yeast in warm water. Add the soup, oil, salt and 3 cups flour; beat until smooth. Stir in enough remaining flour to form a soft dough.

2 Turn onto a floured surface; knead until smooth and elastic, about 10 minutes. Place in a greased bowl, turning once to grease top. Cover and let rise in a warm place until doubled, about 1 hour. For filling, combine the basil, parsley, garlic and oil in a bowl; let stand for 30 minutes.

3 Punch dough down. Turn onto a lightly floured surface; divide in half. Roll each portion into a 16-in. x 12-in. rectangle. Spread filling over dough to within 1 in. of edges. Cover with tomatoes; sprinkle with cheese. Roll up jelly-roll style, starting with a long side; pinch seams to seal and tuck ends under.

4 Place loaves on greased baking sheets; brush tops with egg white. Combine the sesame seeds, pepper, garlic salt and red pepper flakes; sprinkle over loaves. With a sharp knife, cut four 1/2-in. slits on top of each loaf. Cover and let rise until doubled, about 30-45 minutes.

5 Bake at 350° for 40-45 minutes or until golden brown. Cool on a wire rack. Serve warm.

SPECIAL SAVORY LOAVES

Stromboli

PREP: 30 min. + rising **BAKE:** 25 min.
YIELD: 2 loaves (about 8 servings each)

Erma Yoder, Millersburg, Indiana

This specialty sandwich, which originated in Philadelphia, features pizza dough wrapped around savory ingredients like cheese, herbs, meat and sausage.

1	package (1/4 ounce) active dry yeast
1-1/3	cups warm water (110° to 115°)
1/4	cup vegetable oil
1/2	teaspoon salt
4	to 5 cups all-purpose flour

FILLING:

1-1/2	pounds ground beef
3	tablespoons prepared mustard
12	slices American cheese
12	slices hard salami
1/2	pound thinly sliced deli ham
4	cups (16 ounces) shredded part-skim mozzarella cheese

Vegetable oil
Oregano to taste

1 In a large mixing bowl, dissolve yeast in warm water. Add the oil, salt and 2 cups flour; beat until smooth. Stir in enough flour to form a soft dough.

2 Turn onto a lightly floured surface; knead until smooth and elastic, about 10 minutes. Place in a greased bowl, turning once to grease top. Cover and let rise in a warm place until doubled, about 45 minutes. Meanwhile, in a large skillet, cook beef over medium heat until no longer pink; drain and set aside.

3 Punch dough down. Turn onto a lightly floured surface; divide in half. Roll each portion into a 15-in. x 12-in. rectangle. Spread mustard lengthwise down half of each rectangle; layer with American cheese, salami, beef, ham and mozzarella. Fold plain half of dough over filling and seal ends well. Brush with oil; sprinkle with oregano. Bake at 400° for 25-30 minutes or until lightly browned. Cool slightly; cut into 1-in. slices.

Country Ham Bread

PREP: 25 min. + rising **BAKE:** 25 min.
YIELD: 2 loaves (2/3 cup butter)

Sue Stamper, Grayson, Kentucky

This hearty bread is delicious served warm from the oven with the herb butter.

- 1 package (1/4 ounce) active dry yeast
- 1/2 cup warm water (110° to 115°)
- 2 cups warm buttermilk (110° to 115°)
- 1 egg
- 3 tablespoons sugar
- 3 tablespoons butter, melted
- 1 to 2 teaspoons coarsely ground pepper
- 1 teaspoon salt
- 1/2 teaspoon cayenne pepper
- 1 cup plus 2 tablespoons cornmeal, *divided*
- 5 to 5-1/2 cups all-purpose flour
- 2-1/2 cups ground fully cooked ham

HERB BUTTER:
- 1 cup butter, softened
- 1 cup chopped chives
- 1/2 cup minced fresh parsley
- 2 tablespoons lemon juice

Dash pepper

1 In a large mixing bowl, dissolve yeast in warm water. Add the buttermilk, egg, sugar, butter, pepper, salt, cayenne, 1 cup cornmeal and 3 cups flour; beat until smooth. Beat in ham. Stir in enough remaining flour to form a soft dough.

2 Turn onto a floured surface; knead until smooth and elastic, about 6-8 minutes. Place in a greased bowl, turning once to grease top. Cover and let rise in a warm place until doubled, about 1-1/4 hours.

3 Punch dough down. Turn onto a lightly floured surface; divide in half. Shape each portion into a round loaf. Sprinkle two greased 9-in. round baking pans with remaining cornmeal. Place loaves in prepared pans. Cover and let rise until doubled, about 45 minutes. Bake at 375° for 25-30 minutes or until golden brown. Remove from pans to wire racks.

4 In a small mixing bowl, beat the butter, chives, parsley, lemon juice and pepper. Serve with bread. Store ham bread and herb butter in the refrigerator.

Editor's Note: Warmed buttermilk will appear curdled.

Ham and Swiss Braid

PREP: 25 min. + rising **BAKE:** 30 min. **YIELD:** 8 servings

Rose Randall, Derry, Pennsylvania

The ham and cheese makes this substantial bread suitable for a brunch buffet or lunch. It also makes a tasty addition to a potluck.

- 4 cups all-purpose flour
- 2 tablespoons sugar
- 2 packages (1/4 ounce *each*) quick-rise yeast
- 1/2 teaspoon salt
- 1 cup water
- 1/4 cup Dijon mustard
- 2 tablespoons butter
- 1 pound thinly sliced deli ham
- 1 cup (4 ounces) shredded Swiss cheese
- 1/2 cup chopped dill pickles
- 1 egg, lightly beaten

1 In a large mixing bowl, combine 3 cups flour, sugar, yeast and salt. In a small saucepan, heat water, mustard and butter to 120°-130°. Add to flour mixture. Stir in enough remaining flour to form a soft dough (dough will be stiff).

2 Turn onto a lightly floured surface; knead until smooth and elastic, about 6-8 minutes. Roll dough into a 14-in. x 12-in. rectangle on a greased baking sheet. Arrange half of the ham over dough. Top with cheese, pickles and remaining ham. On each long side, cut 3/4-in.-wide strips about 2-1/2 in. into center. Starting at one end, fold alternating strips at an angle across filling. Pinch ends to seal. Cover and let rise for 15 minutes.

3 Brush with egg. Bake at 375° for 30-35 minutes or until golden brown. Serve warm.

HAM AND SWISS BRAID

Rolls, Buns & Beyond

Dinner Rolls

PREP: 30 min. + rising **BAKE:** 20 min. **YIELD:** 2 dozen

Anna Baker, Blaine, Washington

A basic roll like this can be served with dinner or used for small appetizer sandwiches. Either way, it's a recipe you'll come to rely on.

> 2   packages (1/4 ounce *each*) active dry yeast
> 1   teaspoon plus 1/3 cup sugar, *divided*
> 1/2 cup warm water (110° to 115°)
> 1-1/4 cups warm milk (110° to 115°)
> 1/2 cup butter, melted and cooled
> 1-1/2 teaspoons salt
> 2   eggs, beaten
> 6   to 6-1/2 cups all-purpose flour
> Additional melted butter, optional

1 In a large mixing bowl, dissolve yeast and 1 teaspoon sugar in warm water. Add the milk, butter, salt, remaining sugar, eggs and 3 cups flour; beat until smooth. Stir in enough remaining flour to form a soft dough.

2 Turn onto a floured surface; knead until smooth and elastic, about 6-8 minutes. Place in a greased bowl, turning once to grease top. Cover and let rise in a warm place until doubled, about 1 hour.

DINNER ROLLS

3 Punch dough down. Turn onto a lightly floured surface; divide in half. Divide each portion into 12 pieces. Shape each piece into a ball. Place in two greased 13-in. x 9-in. x 2-in. baking pans. Cover and let rise until doubled, about 30 minutes.

4 Bake at 375° for 20-25 minutes or until golden brown. Lightly brush with melted butter if desired. Remove from pans to wire racks. Serve warm.

Green Onion Potato Rolls

PREP: 25 min. + rising **BAKE:** 25 min. **YIELD:** 2 dozen

Louise Beaulieu, Monticello, Maine

The mild green onion flavor of these tender rolls appeals to all. Keep the ingredients on hand to bake up a batch on a moment's notice.

> 4-1/2 to 5-1/2 cups bread flour
> 1-1/4 cups mashed potato flakes, *divided*
> 3   tablespoons sugar
> 2   packages (1/4 ounce *each*) active dry yeast
> 2   teaspoons salt
> 2   cups milk
> 1/2 cup butter
> 4   to 6 green onions, sliced
> 2   eggs
> All-purpose flour

1 In a mixing bowl, combine 1-1/2 cups bread flour, 1 cup potato flakes, sugar, yeast and salt. In a saucepan, heat the milk, butter and onions to 120°-130°. Add to dry ingredients; beat until moistened. Add eggs; beat on medium speed for 3 minutes. Stir in enough remaining bread flour to form a soft dough.

2 Turn onto a surface floured with all-purpose flour; knead until smooth and elastic, about 8-10 minutes. Place in a greased bowl, turning once to grease top. Cover and let rise in a warm place until doubled, about 45 minutes.

3 Punch dough down. Cover and let rest for 15 minutes. Turn onto a lightly floured surface; divide into 24 pieces. Shape each piece into a ball. Dip each ball into remaining potato flakes. Place in a greased 13-in. x 9-in. x 2-in. baking pan. Cover and let rise in a warm place until doubled, about 30 minutes.

4 Bake at 375° for 25-35 minutes or until golden brown. Remove from pan to wire racks.

Golden Carrot Buns

PREP: 35 min. + rising **BAKE:** 20 min. **YIELD:** 4 dozen

Katharine Groine, Altona, Manitoba

These rolls have a one-of-a-kind flavor…folks usually don't guess that carrots are one of the ingredients!

- 4 **cups sliced carrots**
- 2 **eggs, beaten**
- 1 **cup warm water (110° to 115°),** *divided*
- 2 **packages (1/4 ounce** *each***) active dry yeast**
- 3/4 **cup vegetable oil**
- 1/2 **cup sugar**
- 1 **tablespoon molasses**
- 2 **teaspoons salt**
- 8-1/2 **to 9 cups all-purpose flour**

1 Place carrots in a saucepan and cover with water; cook until tender. Drain and cool slightly. Place carrots in a blender or food processor. Add eggs and 1/2 cup warm water; cover and process until smooth.

2 In a large mixing bowl, dissolve yeast in remaining water. Add the carrot mixture. Stir in the oil, sugar, molasses, salt and 5 cups flour; beat until smooth. Stir in enough remaining flour to form a soft dough.

3 Turn onto a floured surface; knead until smooth and elastic, about 6-8 minutes. Place in a greased bowl, turning once to grease top. Cover and let rise in a warm place until doubled, about 1 hour.

4 Punch dough down. Turn onto a floured surface; shape into 48 balls. Place 2 in. apart on greased

GOLDEN CARROT BUNS

baking sheets. Cover and let rise until almost doubled, about 1 hour.

5 Bake at 350° for 18-20 minutes or until browned. Remove from pans to wire racks.

Garlic Parmesan Rolls

PREP: 15 min. + rising **BAKE:** 10 min. **YIELD:** 16 rolls

Loretta Ruda, Kennesaw, Georgia

Just four ingredients are all you need to make fresh-from-the-oven dinner rolls that are dripping with butter and cheese!

- 1 **loaf (1 pound) frozen bread dough, thawed**
- 6 **tablespoons grated Parmesan cheese**
- 1 **teaspoon garlic powder**
- 1/2 **cup butter, melted**

1 Cut bread dough into 16 pieces; shape each piece into a ball. Place on a floured surface; cover and let rise in a warm place for 10 minutes. In a bowl, stir Parmesan cheese and garlic powder into butter. Using a spoon, roll balls in butter mixture. Arrange loosely in a 9-in. round baking pan. Cover and let rise in a warm place until doubled, about 30 minutes.

2 Bake at 375° for 10-15 minutes or until golden brown. Warm leftover butter mixture; when rolls are baked, pull them apart and dip again. Serve warm.

shaping *plain rolls*

Divide dough into equal pieces as recipe directs. Shape each piece into a ball, pulling edges under to smooth top. Place 2 in. apart on greased baking sheets. For pan rolls, place eight balls in a greased 9-in. round baking pan or 12 balls in a greased 13-in. x 9-in. x 2-in. baking pan.

BRIOCHE

Brioche

PREP: 30 min. + rising **BAKE:** 15 min. **YIELD:** 1 dozen

Wanda Kristoffersen, Owatonna, Minnesota

These classic French rolls (pronounced BREE-osh) are rich in butter and eggs. The unique shape resembles a muffin.

3-1/2 **cups all-purpose flour**
  1/2 **cup sugar**
    2 **packages (1/4 ounce *each*) active dry yeast**
    1 **teaspoon grated lemon peel**
  1/2 **teaspoon salt**
  2/3 **cup butter**
  1/2 **cup milk**
    5 **eggs**

1 In a large mixing bowl, combine 1-1/2 cups flour, sugar, yeast, lemon peel and salt. In a saucepan, heat butter and milk to 120°-130°. Add to dry ingredients; beat until moistened. Add four eggs; beat on medium speed for 2 minutes. Add 1 cup flour; beat until smooth. Stir in the remaining flour. Do not knead. Spoon into a greased bowl. Cover and let rise in a warm place until doubled, about 1 hour. Stir dough down. Cover and refrigerate overnight.

2 Punch dough down. Turn onto a lightly floured surface. Cover with a bowl; let rest for 15 minutes. Cut one-sixth from the dough; set aside. Shape remaining dough into 12 balls (about 2-1/2 in.); place in well-greased muffin cups. Divide reserved dough into 12 small balls (about 1 in.). Make an indentation in the top of each large ball; place a small ball in each indentation. Cover and let rise in a warm place until doubled, about 1 hour.

3 Beat remaining egg; brush over rolls. Bake at 375° for 15-20 minutes or until golden brown. Remove from pan to a wire rack.

making *brioche*

1. Shape dough into equal numbers of large and small balls (about 2-1/2 in. and 1 in.)

2. Place large balls in greased muffin cups. Using the end of a wooden spoon handle, make a deep indentation in the center of each large ball.

3. Place a small ball in each indentation.

Basil Tomato Rolls

PREP: 30 min. + rising **BAKE:** 25 min. **YIELD:** 1 dozen

Betty Jane Custer
Fishertown, Pennsylvania

The tomato herb filling rises and spills over the top of the crusty roll tops.

1 **package (1/4 ounce) active dry yeast**
1-1/3 **cups warm water (110° to 115°)**
1 **tablespoon sugar**
1 **tablespoon olive oil**
1 **teaspoon salt**
3-1/2 **to 4 cups all-purpose flour**
FILLING:
1 **small onion, finely chopped**
1 **tablespoon olive oil**
1 **medium tomato, peeled and chopped**
1 **can (8 ounces) tomato sauce**
1 **garlic clove, minced**
1-1/4 **teaspoons salt**
1 **teaspoon dried basil**
Dash pepper
1/4 **cup grated Parmesan cheese**

1 In a large mixing bowl, dissolve yeast in warm water. Add the sugar, oil, salt and 2-1/2 cups flour; beat until smooth. Stir in enough remaining flour to form a stiff dough.

2 Turn onto a floured surface; knead until smooth and elastic, about 6-8 minutes. Place in a greased bowl, turning once to grease top. Cover and let rise in a warm place until doubled, about 1 hour.

3 Meanwhile, in a skillet, saute onion in oil until tender. Add the tomato, tomato sauce, garlic, salt, basil and pepper. Bring to a boil; cook and stir until thickened. Cool to 110°-115°.

4 Punch dough down. Turn onto a lightly floured surface; divide into 12 pieces. Shape each into a ball. Place 3 in. apart on a greased baking sheet. Make an indention in center of each ball; add 1 tablespoon of filling. Sprinkle with Parmesan cheese. Cover and let rise in a warm place until doubled, about 20 minutes.

5 Bake at 375° for 25-30 minutes or until golden brown. Remove from pan to wire rack. Serve warm.

Poppy Seed Rolls

PREP: 25 min. + rising **BAKE:** 15 min. **YIELD:** 1-1/2 dozen

Dottie Miller, Jonesborough, Tennessee

Homemade rolls like these make a delicious addition to any meal.

1 **package (1/4 ounce) active dry yeast**
1 **teaspoon plus 1/4 cup sugar, divided**
1/4 **cup warm water (110° to 115°)**
1 **cup warm milk (110° to 115°)**
1/2 **cup shortening**
1-1/2 **teaspoons salt**
1 **egg, beaten**
3-3/4 **to 4 cups all-purpose flour**
Melted butter
Poppy seeds

1 In a large mixing bowl, dissolve yeast and 1 teaspoon sugar in warm water; let stand for 5 minutes. Beat in the milk, shortening, salt, egg and remaining sugar. Stir in enough flour to form a soft dough.

2 Turn onto a floured surface; knead until smooth and elastic, about 6-8 minutes. Place in a greased bowl, turning once to grease top. Cover and let rise in a warm place until doubled, about 1 hour.

3 Punch the dough down. Turn onto a lightly floured surface; divide into 18 pieces. Shape into balls. Place in greased muffin cups. Cover and let rise until doubled, about 30 minutes.

4 Brush tops with butter; sprinkle with poppy seeds. Bake at 375° for 11-13 minutes or until golden brown. Remove from pans to wire racks.

POPPY SEED ROLLS

MULTIGRAIN BUNS

2 Turn onto a floured surface; knead until smooth and elastic, about 6-8 minutes. Place in a greased bowl, turning once to grease top. Cover and let rise in a warm place until doubled, about 1 hour.

3 Punch dough down. Turn onto a lightly floured surface; shape into 18 round balls. Roll each ball into a 4-1/2-in. circle. Place on greased baking sheets. Cover and let rise until doubled, about 45 minutes.

4 Beat egg yolk and cold water; brush over buns. Sprinkle with additional oats. Bake at 350° for 20 minutes or until golden brown. Remove from pans to wire racks.

Caraway Cloverleaf Rolls

PREP: 30 min. + rising **BAKE:** 15 min. **YIELD:** 2 dozen

Ruth Reid, Jackson, Minnesota

It takes a little more time to shape these cloverleaf rolls, but the pretty presentation is worth it.

2	packages (1/4 ounce *each*) active dry yeast
1-1/2	cups warm water (110° to 115°)
1	cup whole wheat flour
1/2	cup sugar
1/2	cup vegetable oil
2	teaspoons caraway seeds
1-1/2	teaspoons salt
3-1/2	to 4 cups all-purpose flour

1 In a large mixing bowl, dissolve yeast in warm water. Add the whole wheat flour, sugar, oil, caraway seeds, salt and 2 cups all-purpose flour; beat until smooth. Stir in enough remaining all-purpose flour to form a soft dough.

Multigrain Buns

PREP: 20 min. + rising **BAKE:** 20 min.
YIELD: 1-1/2 dozen

Josie Drzewicki, Spirit River, Alberta

Delicious with a meal or to make a sandwich, these light and tasty rolls have a super nutty flavor.

2	packages (1/4 ounce *each*) active dry yeast
3	cups warm water (110° to 115°)
1-1/2	cups whole wheat flour
1	cup old-fashioned oats
1	egg
1/4	cup sesame seeds
1/4	cup salted sunflower kernels
1/4	cup vegetable oil
3	tablespoons butter, softened
2	tablespoons sugar
1-1/2	teaspoons salt
1	teaspoon caraway seeds
1/2	teaspoon white vinegar
5-1/2	to 6 cups all-purpose flour
1	egg yolk
2	tablespoons cold water

Additional oats

1 In a bowl, dissolve yeast in warm water. Add the whole wheat flour, oats, egg, sesame seeds, sunflower kernels, oil, butter, sugar, salt, caraway seeds, vinegar and 2 cups all-purpose flour; beat until smooth. Stir in enough remaining flour to form a soft dough.

shaping *cloverleaf rolls*

Divide dough into 1-1/2-in. balls. Make each ball smooth by pulling the edges under. Place three balls smooth side up in each greased muffin cup.

2 Turn onto a floured surface; knead until smooth and elastic, about 6-8 minutes. Place in a greased bowl, turning once to grease top. Cover and let rise in a warm place until doubled, about 1 hour.

3 Punch dough down. Turn onto a lightly floured surface; divide in half. Divide each portion into 36 pieces. Shape each piece into a ball; place three balls in each greased muffin cup. Cover and let rise until doubled, about 30 minutes.

4 Bake at 375° for 15-18 minutes or until golden brown. Remove from pans to wire racks.

CARAWAY CLOVERLEAF ROLLS

Grammy's Oat Rolls

PREP: 20 min. + rising **BAKE:** 25 min. **YIELD:** 16 rolls

Kathy Bungard, Ione, Washington

Hearty and flavorful, these old-fashioned multigrain rolls are sure to be a hit when you serve them.

- 1/2 **cup quick-cooking oats**
- 1/2 **cup whole wheat flour**
- 1/4 **cup butter**
- 2 **tablespoons plus 1 teaspoon honey, *divided***
- 2 **tablespoons molasses**
- 2 **teaspoons salt**
- 1 **cup boiling water**
- 2 **packages (1/4 ounce *each*) active dry yeast**
- 1/2 **cup warm water (110° to 115°)**
- 1 **egg**
- 3 **to 3-1/2 cups all-purpose flour**

1 In a large mixing bowl, combine the oats, whole wheat flour, butter, 2 tablespoons honey, molasses and salt. Stir in boiling water; cool to 110°-115°. Dissolve yeast in warm water; add remaining honey and let stand for 5 minutes. Stir yeast mixture into oat mixture with egg and enough all-purpose flour to form a soft dough.

2 Turn onto a floured surface; knead until smooth and elastic, about 6-8 minutes. Place in a greased bowl, turning once to grease top. Cover and let rise in a warm place until doubled, about 1 hour.

3 Punch dough down. Turn onto a lightly floured surface; divide into 16 pieces. Shape each piece into a ball. Place in two greased 9-in. round baking pans. Cover and let rise until doubled, about 45 minutes.

4 Bake at 350° for 25-30 minutes or until golden brown. Remove from pans to wire racks.

Bran Buns

PREP: 25 min. + rising **BAKE:** 15 min. **YIELD:** 2 dozen

Julie Eblen, Belgrade, Montana

These are wonderful served warm and also make small sandwich buns for cold cuts when you're having a party.

- 1 **cup All-Bran**
- 2 **cups water, *divided***
- 2 **tablespoons active dry yeast**
- 8 **tablespoons sugar, *divided***
- 2 **eggs**
- 3/4 **cup vegetable oil**
- 2 **teaspoons salt**
- 5-1/2 **to 6 cups all-purpose flour**

1 Place bran in a bowl. Heat 1 cup water to 120°-130°; pour over cereal to soften. Set aside. Place yeast in a mixing bowl. Heat remaining water to 110°-115°; pour over yeast and 2 tablespoons sugar and let stand for 5 minutes. Add the eggs, oil, salt, bran mixture and remaining sugar; mix well. Stir in enough flour to form a soft dough.

2 Turn onto a floured surface; knead until smooth and elastic, about 6-8 minutes. Place in a greased bowl, turning once to grease top. Cover and let rise in a warm place until doubled, about 1-1/2 hours.

3 Punch dough down. Turn onto a lightly floured surface; divide into 24 pieces. Shape each into a ball. Place 2 in. apart on greased baking sheets. Cover and let rise until doubled, about 30 minutes.

4 Bake at 350° for 15-20 minutes or until golden brown. Remove from pans to wire racks.

Spoon Rolls

PREP: 15 min. + rising **BAKE:** 25 min. **YIELD:** 16 rolls

Oma Rollison, El Cajon, California

The batter for these rolls may be refrigerated overnight. The next day, simply spoon the batter into muffin cups for homemade rolls in no time.

- 1 **package (1/4 ounce) active dry yeast**
- 2 **cups warm water (110° to 115°)**
- 1/2 **cup butter, melted**
- 1/4 **cup sugar**
- 1 **egg**
- 4 **cups self-rising flour**

1 In a large mixing bowl, dissolve yeast in warm water. Add the butter, sugar and egg; beat well. Stir in flour until thoroughly combined (batter will be soft). Cover and refrigerate overnight.

2 Spoon batter into greased or paper-lined muffin cups. Bake at 375° for 25-30 minutes or until golden brown. Remove from pans to wire racks.

Editor's Note: As a substitute for the self-rising flour, place 6 teaspoons baking powder and 2 teaspoons salt in a measuring cup. Add all-purpose flour to measure 1 cup. Then add an additional 3 cups all-purpose flour.

CARAWAY RYE ROLLS

SPOON ROLLS

Caraway Rye Rolls

PREP: 15 min. + rising **BAKE:** 20 min. **YIELD:** 2 dozen

Dot Christiansen, Bettendorf, Iowa

So easy—yet so good. Simply spoon the batter into muffin cups, bake and enjoy!

- 2 **packages (1/4 ounce *each*) active dry yeast**
- 1/2 **cup warm water (110° to 115°)**
- 2 **cups warm small-curd cottage cheese (110° to 115°)**
- 1/2 **cup sugar**
- 2 **eggs**
- 2 **tablespoons caraway seeds**
- 2 **teaspoons salt**
- 1/2 **teaspoon baking soda**
- 1 **cup rye flour**
- 3 **to 4 cups all-purpose flour**

1 In a large mixing bowl, dissolve yeast in warm water. Add the cottage cheese, sugar, eggs, caraway seeds, salt, baking soda, rye flour and 1 cup all-purpose flour; mix well. Stir in enough remaining all-purpose flour to form a sticky batter. Do not knead. Cover and let rise in a warm place until doubled, about 1 hour.

2 Stir batter down. Spoon into well-greased muffin cups. Cover and let rise until doubled, about 35 minutes. Bake at 350° for 18-20 minutes or until golden brown. Cool for 1 minute before removing from pans to wire racks.

shaping
crescent rolls

Roll a portion of the dough into a 12-in. circle. Cut into 12 wedges and roll up, beginning at the wide end. Place pointed side down 2 in. apart on greased baking sheets. Curve ends to form crescent shape.

No-Knead Tarragon Rolls

PREP: 15 min. + rising BAKE: 15 min. YIELD: 1 dozen

Polly Miller, Himrod, New York

Because no kneading is required, these golden brown rolls are quite simple to make.

2-3/4 **cups all-purpose flour, *divided***
   1 **package (1/4 ounce) active dry yeast**
   2 **tablespoons sugar**
   1 **tablespoon dried parsley flakes**
   1 **tablespoon minced fresh tarragon**
     ***or* 1 teaspoon dried tarragon**
 1/2 **teaspoon celery seed**
 1/2 **teaspoon salt**
   1 **cup warm water (120° to 130°)**
   1 **egg**
   2 **tablespoons vegetable oil**

1 In a large mixing bowl, combine 1-1/2 cups of flour, yeast, sugar, parsley, tarragon, celery seed and salt. Add the water, egg and oil; beat on low speed for 30 seconds, scraping bowl occasionally. Beat on high for 1 minute. Stir in remaining flour. Do not knead. Cover and let rise in a warm place until doubled, about 30 minutes.

2 Stir dough down. Spoon into greased muffin cups. Cover and let rise in a warm place until doubled, about 20-30 minutes.

3 Bake at 375° for 15-18 minutes or until golden brown. Remove from pans to wire racks.

Icebox Butterhorns

PREP: 15 min. + chilling BAKE: 15 min. + rising
YIELD: 2 dozen

Judy Clark, Elkhart, Indiana

These moist, golden rolls just melt in your mouth! People will be impressed when these appear on your table.

   2 **packages (1/4 ounce *each*) active dry yeast**
 1/4 **cup warm water (110° to 115°)**
   2 **cups warm milk (110° to 115°)**
 1/2 **cup sugar**
   1 **egg**
   1 **teaspoon salt**
6-1/2 **cups all-purpose flour**
 3/4 **cup butter, melted**
Additional melted butter

1 In a large mixing bowl, dissolve yeast in warm water. Add the milk, sugar, egg, salt and 3 cups flour; beat until smooth. Beat in butter and remaining flour (dough will be slightly sticky). Do not knead. Place in a greased bowl, turning once to grease top. Cover and refrigerate overnight.

2 Punch dough down. Turn onto a lightly floured surface; divide in half. Roll each portion into a 12-in. circle. Cut each circle into 12 wedges. Roll up wedges from the wide end and place pointed side down 2 in. apart on greased baking sheets. Cover and let rise in a warm place until doubled, about 1 hour.

3 Bake at 350° for 15-20 minutes or until golden brown. Immediately brush tops with melted butter. Remove from pans to wire racks.

ICEBOX BUTTERHORNS

CHILI CORNMEAL CRESCENTS

Flaky Croissants

PREP: 25 min. + chilling **BAKE:** 20 min.
YIELD: 8 croissants

Pam Butler, Branson, Missouri

It's worth the extra effort and calories to make these croissants—especially for holidays and special occasions.

2-1/2 to 3 cups all-purpose flour
   1 tablespoon sugar
   1 package (1/4 ounce) active dry yeast
 3/4 teaspoon salt
   1 cup warm water (120° to 130°)
   1 tablespoon shortening
   1 cup cold butter, cubed
   1 egg, beaten

1 In a large mixing bowl, combine 1 cup flour, sugar, yeast and salt. Add water and shortening; beat on medium speed for 2 minutes. Add 1/2 cup flour; beat 2 minutes longer. Stir in enough remaining flour to form a soft dough.

2 Turn onto a floured surface; knead until smooth and elastic, about 6-8 minutes. Place in a greased bowl, turning once to grease top. Cover and let rise in a warm place until doubled, about 45 minutes. Punch dough down. Cover and refrigerate for 2 hours.

3 Turn dough onto a lightly floured surface; roll into a 15-in. x 10-in. rectangle. In a small mixing bowl, beat cold butter until softened but still cold. Spread a fourth of the butter over dough. Fold dough into thirds, starting with a short side. Turn dough a quarter turn. Repeat rolling, buttering and folding three times. Wrap in plastic wrap. Refrigerate overnight.

4 On a floured surface, roll the dough into a 14-in. square. With a sharp knife, cut into quarters. Cut each quarter diagonally in half, forming two triangles. Roll up triangles from the wide end; place point side down 2 in. apart on a greased baking sheet. Curve ends to form a crescent. Cover and refrigerate for 20 minutes.

5 Brush with egg. Bake at 425° for 13-18 minutes or until golden brown. Remove from pan to a wire rack.

Chili Cornmeal Crescents

PREP: 20 min. + rising **BAKE:** 20 min. **YIELD:** 2 dozen

Marion Lowery, Medford, Oregon

These unique rolls are tender, light and delicious, with a bit of chili tang. They always spark recipe requests.

     1 package (1/4 ounce) active dry yeast
1-3/4 cups warm water (110° to 115°)
1-1/2 cups cornmeal
  1/3 cup sugar
     1 egg
     2 tablespoons olive oil
     1 tablespoon chili powder
     1 teaspoon salt
     4 to 4-1/2 cups all-purpose flour

1 In a large mixing bowl, dissolve yeast in warm water. Add the cornmeal, sugar, egg, oil, chili powder, salt and 2 cups flour; beat until smooth. Stir in enough remaining flour to form a soft dough.

2 Turn onto a floured surface; knead until smooth and elastic, about 6-8 minutes. Place in a greased bowl, turning once to grease top. Cover and let rise in a warm place until doubled, about 1 hour.

3 Punch dough down. Turn onto a lightly floured surface; divide in half. Roll each portion into a 12-in. circle. Cut each circle into 12 wedges. Roll up wedges from the wide end and place point side down 2 in. apart on greased baking sheets. Curve ends to form a crescent. Cover and let rise until doubled, about 30 minutes.

4 Bake at 375° for 20 minutes or until browned. Remove from pans to wire racks.

Golden Crescents

PREP: 25 min. + rising **BAKE:** 10 min. **YIELD:** 2 dozen

Bertha Johnson, Indianapolis, Indiana

Warm from the oven, these slightly sweet, tender rolls make any meal special.

> 2 **packages (1/4 ounce *each*) active dry yeast**
> 3/4 **cup warm water (110° to 115°)**
> 1/2 **cup sugar**
> 1/4 **cup plus 2 tablespoons butter, softened, *divided***
> 2 **tablespoons shortening**
> 2 **eggs**
> 1 **teaspoon salt**
> 4 **to 4-1/2 cups all-purpose flour**

1 In a mixing bowl, dissolve yeast in water. Add sugar, 1/4 cup butter, shortening, eggs, salt and 2 cups flour; beat until smooth. Stir in enough remaining flour to form a soft dough.

2 Turn onto a floured surface; knead until smooth and elastic, about 6-8 minutes. Place in a greased bowl, turning once to grease top. Cover and let rise in a warm place until doubled, about 1-1/4 hours.

3 Punch the dough down; divide in half. Roll each portion into a 12-in. circle. Melt remaining butter; brush over dough. Cut each circle into 12 wedges. Roll up wedges from the wide end and place point side down 2 in. apart on greased baking sheets. Curve ends to form a crescent. Cover and let rise until doubled, about 45 minutes.

4 Bake at 375° for 8-10 minutes or until golden. Remove from pans to wire racks.

FREEZE-AND-BAKE KNOTS

forming *knot-shaped rolls*

Divide dough into 3-in. balls. Roll each ball into a 10-in. rope; tie into a knot. Tuck and pinch ends under.

Freeze-and-Bake Knots

PREP: 30 min. + rising **BAKE:** 15 min. + freezing
YIELD: 4 dozen

Jayne Duce, Raymond, Alberta

Almost any occasion's right for these handy rolls. You can keep them in the freezer for Sunday meals and for company…they never fail to taste fresh.

> 2 **packages (1/4 ounce *each*) active dry yeast**
> 1-1/2 **cups warm water (110° to 115°)**
> 2 **teaspoons plus 1/2 cup sugar, *divided***
> 1-1/2 **cups warm milk (110° to 115°)**
> 1/4 **cup vegetable oil**
> 4 **teaspoons salt**
> 7-1/2 **to 8-1/2 cups all-purpose flour**
> **Melted butter**

1 In a large mixing bowl, dissolve yeast in warm water. Add 2 teaspoons sugar; let stand for 5 minutes. Add the milk, oil, salt, remaining sugar and 2 cups flour; beat until smooth. Stir in enough remaining flour to form a stiff dough.

2 Turn onto a floured surface; knead until smooth and elastic, about 6-8 minutes. Place in a greased bowl, turning once to grease top. Cover and let rise in a warm place until doubled, about 1-1/2 hours.

3 Punch dough down. Turn onto a lightly floured surface; divide into four pieces. Cover three pieces with plastic wrap. Divide remaining piece into 12 balls. To form knots, roll each ball into a 10-in. rope; tie into a knot and pinch ends together. Repeat with remaining dough. Place rolls on greased baking sheets; brush with butter. Cover and let rise until doubled, about 20-30 minutes.

4 To serve immediately, bake at 375° for 15-18 minutes. To freeze for later use, partially bake at 300° for 15 minutes. Remove from pans to wire racks to cool; freeze. Reheat frozen rolls at 375° for 12-15 minutes or until browned.

PIZZA POPPERS

3 Punch dough down. Turn onto a lightly floured surface; divide into four pieces. Divide each piece into eight balls. Roll each ball into a 12-in. rope. Tie into a loose knot, leaving two long ends. Fold top end under roll; bring bottom end up and press into center of roll. Place on greased baking sheets. Cover and let rise until doubled, about 30 minutes.

4 Bake at 375° for 10-12 minutes or until golden brown. Serve warm with pizza sauce.

Whole Wheat English Muffins

PREP: 20 min. + rising **BAKE:** 20 min. + cooling
YIELD: about 10 muffins

Mildred Decker, Sandy, Oregon

Whole wheat flour gives these muffins a hearty taste, but they still have a light texture. Plus, they keep well in the refrigerator or freezer.

- 1 package (1/4 ounce) active dry yeast
- 3 tablespoons sugar, *divided*
- 1/4 cup warm water (110° to 115°)
- 1 cup warm milk (110° to 115°)
- 3 tablespoons butter
- 3/4 teaspoon salt
- 1 egg, beaten
- 1 cup whole wheat flour
- 3 cups all-purpose flour, *divided*

1 In a large mixing bowl, dissolve yeast and 1 tablespoon sugar in warm water; let stand for 5 minutes. Add the milk, butter, salt, egg, whole wheat flour, 1 cup all-purpose flour and remaining sugar; beat until smooth. Stir in enough remaining all-purpose flour to form a soft dough.

2 Turn onto a lightly floured surface; knead until smooth and elastic, about 6-8 minutes. Place in a greased bowl, turning once to grease top. Cover and let rise in a warm place until doubled, about 1 hour.

3 Punch dough down. Turn onto a lightly floured surface; roll out to 1/2-in. thickness. Cover and let rest for 5 minutes. Cut into 4-in. circles. Place 2 in. apart on greased baking sheets.

4 Bake at 375° for 8 minutes or until bottom is browned. Turn muffins over; bake 7 minutes longer or until second side is browned. Remove from pans to wire racks to cool. Store in the refrigerator. To serve, split with a fork and toast.

Pizza Poppers

PREP: 35 min. + rising **BAKE:** 10 min.
YIELD: 32 appetizers

Denise Sargent, Pittsfield, New Hampshire

These pizza rolls are a welcomed addition to potlucks.

- 4 to 4-1/2 cups all-purpose flour
- 1/3 cup sugar
- 1 package (1/4 ounce) active dry yeast
- 1 teaspoon dried oregano
- 1/2 teaspoon salt
- 1 cup water
- 1 tablespoon shortening
- 1 egg
- 3 cups (12 ounces) shredded part-skim mozzarella cheese
- 1-1/3 cups minced pepperoni (about 5 ounces)
- 2 cups pizza sauce, warmed

1 In a large mixing bowl, combine 2 cups of flour, sugar, yeast, oregano and salt. In a saucepan, heat water and shortening to 120°-130°. Add to dry ingredients; beat until moistened. Add egg; beat on medium speed for 1 minute. Stir in cheese and pepperoni; mix well. Stir in enough remaining flour to form a soft dough.

2 Turn onto a floured surface; knead until smooth and elastic, about 6-8 minutes. Place in a greased bowl, turning once to grease top. Cover and let rise in a warm place until doubled, about 1 hour.

Topknot Rolls

PREP: 25 min. + rising **BAKE:** 10 min.
YIELD: 2-1/2 dozen

Bernadine Stine, Roanoke, Indiana

These golden dinner rolls have a fine texture and a delightful buttery flavor. Even though they look special, they're not difficult to make.

> 2 packages (1/4 ounce *each*) active dry yeast
> 2 teaspoons plus 1/2 cup sugar, *divided*
> 1-1/4 cups warm water (110° to 115°)
> 3 eggs
> 3/4 cup butter, melted, cooled, *divided*
> 5-1/2 cups all-purpose flour
> 2 teaspoons salt
> Additional butter, softened

1 In a large mixing bowl, dissolve yeast and 2 teaspoons sugar in warm water. Let stand for 5 minutes. Add the eggs, 1/2 cup melted butter, 2 cups flour, salt and remaining sugar; beat until smooth. Stir in enough remaining flour to form a soft dough.

2 Turn onto a floured surface; knead until smooth and elastic, about 6-8 minutes. Place in a greased bowl, turning once to grease top. Cover and let rise in a warm place for 45 minutes or until doubled, about 45 minutes.

3 Punch dough down. Turn onto a heavily floured surface; divide in half. Roll each portion into a 15-in. x 8-in. rectangle. Spread generously with softened butter. Roll up jelly-roll style, starting

TOPKNOT ROLLS

with a long side. Using a sharp knife, cut into 1-in. slices. Place cut side up in greased muffin cups. Cover and let rise until doubled, about 45 minutes.

4 Bake at 375° for 12-15 minutes or until golden brown. Brush with remaining melted butter. Remove from pans to wire racks.

Handy Sausage Biscuits

PREP: 25 min. **BAKE:** 10 min. **YIELD:** 2-3 dozen

Nancy Parker, Seguin, Texas

The addition of tasty browned sausage makes these biscuits similar to, but better than, old-fashioned biscuits.

> 3/4 pound bulk pork sausage
> 2-2/3 cups all-purpose flour
> 2 tablespoons sugar
> 1-1/2 teaspoons baking powder
> 1/2 teaspoon baking soda
> 1/2 teaspoon salt
> 1/2 cup shortening
> 1 package (1/4 ounce) active dry yeast
> 1/4 cup warm water (110° to 115°)
> 1 cup warm buttermilk (110° to 115°)
> Melted butter

1 In a skillet, cook sausage over medium heat until no longer pink; drain well and set aside. In a bowl, combine the flour, sugar, baking powder, baking soda and salt; cut in shortening until mixture is crumbly. Stir in sausage. In another bowl, dissolve yeast in warm water; add buttermilk. Stir into sausage mixture just until moistened.

2 Turn onto a lightly floured surface; knead gently 6-8 times. Roll out to 1/2-in. thickness; cut with a floured 2-1/2-in. biscuit cutter. Place on lightly greased baking sheets. Brush tops with butter. Bake at 450° for 10-12 minutes or until golden brown. Serve warm.

Editor's Note: No rising time is necessary before baking these biscuits. The dough can be rerolled. Warmed buttermilk will appear curdled.

Accordion Rye Rolls

PREP: 30 min. + standing **BAKE:** 20 min. + chilling
YIELD: 2 dozen

Alyson Armstrong
Parkersburg, West Virginia

These rolls will make anyone like rye bread. Although you conveniently make the dough ahead, bake them right before serving so they're hot and fresh.

- 2 packages (1/4 ounce *each*) active dry yeast
- 1/2 cup warm water (110° to 115°)
- 1-1/2 cups warm milk (110° to 115°)
- 1/4 cup molasses
- 4 tablespoons butter, softened, *divided*
- 1 tablespoon sugar
- 1 tablespoon plus 1/2 teaspoon salt, *divided*
- 3 to 3-1/2 cups all-purpose flour
- 2-1/2 cups rye flour
- Vegetable oil
- 1 egg white
- 2 teaspoons caraway seeds

1 In a large mixing bowl, dissolve yeast in warm water. Add the milk, molasses, 2 tablespoons butter, sugar and 1 tablespoon salt. Add 2 cups all-purpose flour; beat until smooth. Stir in rye flour and enough remaining all-purpose flour to form a soft dough.

2 Turn onto a floured surface; knead until smooth and elastic, about 6-8 minutes. Place in a greased bowl, turning once to grease top. Cover and let rest for 20 minutes.

3 Punch dough down. Turn onto a lightly floured surface; divide into four portions. Roll out each portion into a 14-in. x 6-in. rectangle. Brush with the remaining butter.

4 With dull edge of a table knife, score dough widthwise at 2-in. intervals. Using those marks as a guideline, make score marks widthwise across the dough. Fold dough accordion-style back and forth along creased lines. Cut folded dough into 1-in. pieces. Place each piece cut side down in a greased muffin cup. Brush with oil. Cover loosely with plastic wrap. Refrigerate for 4 to 24 hours.

5 When ready to bake, uncover dough and let stand at room temperature for 10 minutes. In a small mixing bowl, beat egg white until stiff peaks form; brush over dough. Sprinkle with caraway seeds and remaining salt. Bake at 375° for 20-25 minutes or until lightly browned. Remove from pans to wire racks.

ACCORDION RYE ROLLS

making *accordion rolls*

1. Roll dough into a 14-in. x 6-in. rectangle. Brush with butter. With the dull edge of a table knife, score dough widthwise at 2-in. intervals.

2. Fold dough accordion-style back and forth along crease lines.

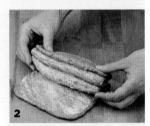

3. Cut dough into 1-in. pieces. Place each piece cut side down in a greased muffin cup.

Parker House Rolls

PREP: 30 min. + rising **BAKE:** 10 min.
YIELD: about 2-1/2 dozen

Sandra Melnychenko, Grandview, Manitoba

When a basket of these rolls is passed around the table, people will want to take two.

- 2 **packages (1/4 ounce** *each***) active dry yeast**
- 1 **teaspoon plus 6 tablespoons sugar,** *divided*
- 1 **cup warm water (110° to 115°),** *divided*
- 1 **cup warm milk (110° to 115°)**
- 2 **teaspoons salt**
- 1 **egg**
- 2 **tablespoons plus 2 teaspoons vegetable oil**
- 5-1/2 **to 6 cups all-purpose flour**
- 3 **tablespoons butter, melted, optional**

1 In a large mixing bowl, dissolve yeast and 1 teaspoon sugar in 1/2 cup warm water; let stand for 5 minutes. Add the milk, salt, egg, oil and remaining sugar and water.

2 Gradually add 2 cups flour; beat until smooth. Stir in enough remaining flour to form a soft dough.

3 Turn onto a floured surface; knead until smooth and elastic, about 6-8 minutes. Place in a greased bowl, turning once to grease top. Cover and let rise in a warm place until doubled, about 45 minutes.

forming *parker house rolls*

Roll out to 1/2-in. thickness. Cut with a floured 2-1/2-in. biscuit cutter. Brush with melted butter. Using the dull edge of a table knife, make an off-center crease in each roll. Fold along crease.

4 Punch dough down. Turn onto a lightly floured surface; divide in half. Roll out each portion to 1/3-in. or 1/2-in. thickness. Cut with a floured 2-1/2-in. round cutter. Brush with butter if desired.

5 Using the dull edge of a table knife, make an off-center crease in each roll. Fold along crease so the large half is on top; press along folded edge. Place 2 in. apart on greased baking sheets. Cover and let rise until doubled, about 30 minutes.

6 Bake at 375° for 10-15 minutes or until golden brown. Remove from pans to wire racks.

PARKER HOUSE ROLLS

YOGURT YEAST ROLLS

Yogurt Yeast Rolls

PREP: 30 min. + rising **BAKE:** 15 min. **YIELD:** 2 dozen

Carol Forcum, Marion, Illinois

People will snap up these fluffy golden rolls in a hurry whenever you take them to a potluck. It's a nice contribution since rolls are easy to transport and one batch goes a long way.

1-1/2   **cups whole wheat flour**
3-1/4   **cups all-purpose flour**
    2   **packages (1/4 ounce *each*) active dry yeast**
    2   **teaspoons salt**
  1/2   **teaspoon baking soda**
1-1/2   **cups (12 ounces) plain yogurt**
  1/2   **cup water**
    3   **tablespoons butter**
    2   **tablespoons honey**
Additional butter, melted

1 In a large mixing bowl, combine whole wheat flour, 1/2 cup all-purpose flour, yeast, salt and baking soda. In a saucepan over low heat, heat yogurt, water, butter and honey to 120°-130°. Add to dry ingredients; beat well. Beat on medium speed for 3 minutes. Stir in enough remaining all-purpose flour to form a soft dough.

2 Turn onto a floured surface; knead until smooth and elastic, about 6-8 minutes. Place in a greased bowl, turning once to grease top. Cover and let rise in a warm place until doubled, about 1 hour.

3 Punch dough down. Turn onto a lightly floured surface; divide into 2-in. balls. Roll each piece into a 10-in. rope. To form S-shaped rolls, coil each end of rope toward center in opposite directions. Place 3 in. apart on greased baking sheets. Cover and let rise until doubled, about 30 minutes.

4 Bake at 400° for 15 minutes or until golden brown. Brush tops with melted butter while warm. Remove from pans to wire racks.

forming *s-shaped rolls*

Divide dough into 2-in. balls. Shape each ball into a 10-in. rope. On a greased baking sheet, coil each end in opposite directions until it touches the center and forms an S-shape.

Pretzels with Cheese Dip

PREP: 35 min. + rising **BAKE:** 10 min.
YIELD: 1 dozen pretzels and 1-1/4 cups dip

Shannon Cooper
South Gibson, Pennsylvania

Chewy and golden brown, these soft pretzels are the best by far. Pair them with this warm cheese dip for a snack.

- 1 **package (1/4 ounce) active dry yeast**
- 1 **cup warm water (110° to 115°)**
- 2 **tablespoons butter, softened**
- 1 **tablespoon sugar**
- 1/2 **teaspoon salt**
- 2-3/4 **cups all-purpose flour**
- 4 **cups water**
- 2 **tablespoons baking soda**
- **Coarse salt**
- 8 **ounces process cheese (Velveeta), cubed**
- 1 **package (3 ounces) cream cheese, cubed**
- 1 **to 2 tablespoons milk**
- **Prepared mustard**

1 In a large mixing bowl, dissolve yeast in warm water. Add the butter, sugar, salt and 2 cups flour; beat until smooth. Stir in enough remaining flour to form a soft dough. Cover and let rise in a warm place for 20 minutes.

PRETZELS WITH CHEESE DIP

PRETZELS WITH CHEESE DIP

forming *pretzels*

1. Roll each piece of dough into a 15-in. rope and taper the ends. Shape rope into a circle with about 3 in. of each end overlapping.

2. Twist ends where they overlap.

3. Flip the twisted ends over the circle; place ends around edge and pinch under.

2 Punch dough down. Divide into 12 equal pieces. On a lightly floured surface, roll each piece into a 15-in.-long strip; twist into a pretzel shape.

3 In a large nonaluminum saucepan, bring water to a boil; add baking soda. Drop two pretzels into water; boil for 1 minute. Remove with a slotted spoon; drain. Place on a greased baking sheet; sprinkle with coarse salt. Repeat with remaining pretzels. Bake at 475° for 10-12 minutes. Remove from pan to wire rack.

4 For dip, combine cheeses in a microwave-safe bowl. Microwave on high for 2-3 minutes or until melted, stirring occasionally. Stir in milk. Serve pretzels with the cheese dip and mustard.

making *herbed bread twists*

1. Roll dough into a 12-in. square. Spread butter mixture to within 1/2 in. of edges. Top with cheese. Fold dough into thirds.

2. Cut dough widthwise into 24 strips.

3. Twist each strip twice; pinch ends to seal.

2 Fold dough into thirds. Cut widthwise into 24 strips. Twist each strip twice; pinch ends to seal. Place 2 in. apart on greased baking sheets. Cover and let rise in a warm place until doubled, about 40 minutes.

3 Beat egg and water; brush over dough. Sprinkle with sesame seeds. Bake at 375° for 10-12 minutes or until light golden brown. Remove from pans to wire racks.

Best-Ever Breadsticks

PREP: 20 min. + rising **BAKE:** 10 min.
YIELD: about 1-1/2 dozen

Carol Wolfer, Lebanon, Oregon

Present these long and thin breadsticks in a tall clear glass alongside an Italian favorite like lasagna or spaghetti.

>   3 to 3-1/4 cups all-purpose flour, *divided*
>   1 tablespoon sugar
>   1 package (1/4 ounce) quick-rise yeast
>   1 teaspoon salt
>   3/4 cup milk
>   1/4 cup water
>   1 tablespoon butter
>   1 egg white
>   1 tablespoon cold water
> Coarse salt

1 In a large mixing bowl, combine 1-1/2 cups flour, sugar, yeast and salt. In a saucepan, heat the milk,

Herbed Bread Twists

PREP: 30 min. + rising **BAKE:** 10 min. **YIELD:** 2 dozen

Deb Stapert, Comstock Park, Michigan

A blend of herbs and a special shape dress up ordinary frozen bread dough in this unbelievably easy recipe.

>   1/4 cup butter, softened
>   1/4 teaspoon *each* garlic powder, dried basil, marjoram and oregano
>   1 loaf (1 pound) frozen bread dough, thawed
>   3/4 cup shredded part-skim mozzarella cheese
>   1 egg
>   1 tablespoon water
>   4 teaspoons sesame seeds

1 In a small bowl, combine butter and seasonings. On a lightly floured surface, roll dough into a 12-in. square. Spread with butter mixture to within 1/2 in. of edges; sprinkle with mozzarella cheese.

HERBED BREAD TWISTS

shaping *breadsticks*

Divide dough into 2-1/2-in. balls. Roll each ball back and forth with both hands until they are shaped into 10-in. x 1/2-in. ropes.

water and butter to 120°-130°. Add to dry ingredients; beat just until moistened. Stir in enough remaining flour to form a stiff dough.

2 Turn onto a lightly floured surface; knead until smooth and elastic, about 6-8 minutes. Place in a greased bowl, turning once to grease top. Cover and let rise in a warm place until doubled, about 30 minutes.

3 Punch dough down. Pinch off golf ball-size pieces. On a lightly floured surface, roll into pencil-size strips. Place on greased baking sheets 1 in. apart. Cover and let rise for 15 minutes.

4 Beat the egg white and cold water; brush over breadsticks. Sprinkle with coarse salt. Bake at 400° for 10 minutes or until golden. Remove from pans to wire racks.

Homemade Bagels

PREP: 30 min. + rising **BAKE:** 20 min. + cooling
YIELD: 1 dozen

Rebecca Phillips, Burlington, Connecticut

Instead of going to a bakery, head to the kitchen and surprise your family with homemade bagels. For variation and flavor, sprinkle the tops with cinnamon-sugar instead of sesame and poppy seeds.

      1   teaspoon active dry yeast
1-1/4   cups warm milk (110° to 115°)
   1/4   cup butter, softened
      2   tablespoons sugar
      1   teaspoon salt
      1   egg yolk
3-3/4   to 4-1/4 cups all-purpose flour
      2   quarts water
Sesame *or* poppy seeds, optional

1 In a large mixing bowl, dissolve yeast in warm milk. Add the butter, sugar, salt, egg yolk and 1 cup flour; beat until smooth. Stir in enough remaining flour to form a soft dough.

2 Turn onto a floured surface; knead until smooth and elastic, about 6-8 minutes. Place in a greased bowl, turning once to grease top. Cover and let rise in a warm place until doubled, about 1 hour.

3 Punch dough down. Turn onto a lightly floured surface; divide into 12 pieces. Shape each piece into a ball. Push thumb through the center to form a 1-in. hole. Stretch and shape dough to form an even ring. Place on a floured surface. Cover and let rest for 10 minutes; flatten rings slightly.

4 In a large nonaluminum saucepan, bring water to a boil. Drop bagels, one at a time, into boiling water. Cook for 45 seconds; turn and cook 45 seconds longer. Remove with a slotted spoon; drain well on paper towels.

5 Sprinkle with sesame or poppy seeds if desired. Place 2 in. apart on greased baking sheets. Bake at 400° for 20-25 minutes or until golden brown. Remove from pans to wire racks to cool.

shaping *bagels*

1. Shape dough into balls. Push your thumb through the center of the dough, forming a 1-in. hole.

2. Stretch and shape dough to form an even ring.

Sourdough Breads

Sourdough Starter

PREP: 10 min. + standing **YIELD:** about 3 cups

Delila George, Junction City, Oregon

Sourdough breads have a unique tangy flavor, which is achieved from the use of a yeast starter. A portion of the starter is used to make bread, and the remaining starter is replenished to use another day.

- 1   **package (1/4 ounce) active dry yeast**
- 2   **cups warm water (110° to 115°)**
- 2   **cups all-purpose flour**

1 In a 4-qt. nonmetallic bowl, dissolve yeast in warm water; let stand for 5 minutes. Add flour; stir until smooth. Cover loosely with a clean towel. Let stand in a warm place (80°-90°) to ferment for 48 hours; stir several times daily (the mixture will become bubbly and rise, have a "yeasty" sour aroma and a transparent yellow liquid will form on the top).

2 Use starter for your favorite sourdough recipes. The starter will keep in the refrigerator for up to 2 weeks. Use and replenish or nourish at least once every 2 weeks. Refer to the Secrets for Successful Sourdough Starters at left.

Sourdough French Bread

PREP: 15 min. + rising **BAKE:** 20 min. + cooling
YIELD: 2 loaves

Delila George, Junction City, Oregon

These loaves rival any found in stores and can be made with relative ease.

- 1   **package (1/4 ounce) active dry yeast**
- 1-3/4   **cups warm water (110° to 115°)**
- 4-1/4   **cups all-purpose flour**
- 1/4   **cup Sourdough Starter (recipe above)**
- 2   **tablespoons vegetable oil**
- 2   **tablespoons sugar**
- 2   **teaspoons salt**

CORNSTARCH WASH:
- 1-1/2   **teaspoons cornstarch**
- 1/2   **cup water**

1 In a large mixing bowl, dissolve yeast in warm water. Add the flour, Sourdough Starter, oil, sugar and salt; mix well. Turn onto a floured surface; knead gently 20-30 times (dough will be slightly sticky). Place in a greased bowl, turning once to grease top. Cover and let rise in a warm place until doubled, about 1 to 1-1/2 hours.

2 Punch dough down. Turn onto a lightly floured surface; divide in half. Roll each portion into a 12-in. x 8-in. rectangle. Roll up jelly-roll style, starting with a long side; pinch ends to seal. Place seam side down on two greased baking sheets; tuck ends under. Cover and let rise until doubled, about 30 minutes.

3 With a sharp knife, make four shallow diagonal slashes across the top of each loaf. In a small saucepan, combine cornstarch and water until smooth. Cook and stir over medium heat until thickened. Brush some over loaves. Bake at 400° for 15 minutes. Brush loaves with the remaining cornstarch wash. Bake 5-10 minutes longer or until lightly browned. Remove from pans to wire racks to cool.

Honey Wheat Sourdough Bread

PREP: 20 min. + rising **BAKE:** 25 min. + cooling
YIELD: 2 loaves

Evelyn Newlands, Sun Lakes, Arizona

Honey adds a slightly sweet taste to this bread, which nicely complements the tangy sourdough.

1   **tablespoon active dry yeast**
1   **cup warm milk (110° to 115°)**
3   **tablespoons butter, softened**
2   **tablespoons honey**
2   **tablespoons molasses**
2   **cups Sourdough Starter (recipe on opposite page)**
3   **tablespoons wheat germ**
1   **tablespoon sugar**
1   **teaspoon baking soda**
1   **teaspoon salt**
1   **cup whole wheat flour**
3-1/4   **to 3-3/4 cups all-purpose flour**
Vegetable oil

1 In a large mixing bowl, dissolve yeast in warm milk. Add the butter, honey, molasses, Sourdough Starter, wheat germ, sugar, baking soda, salt, whole wheat flour and 2 cups all-purpose flour; beat until smooth. Stir in enough remaining all-purpose flour to form a soft dough.

2 Turn onto a floured surface; knead until smooth and elastic, about 6-8 minutes. Place in a greased bowl, turning once to grease top. Cover and let rise in a warm place until doubled, about 1 hour.

3 Punch dough down. Turn onto a lightly floured surface; divide in half. Shape each portion into a loaf. Place in two greased 8-in. x 4-in. x 2-in. loaf pans. Cover and let rise until doubled, about 1 hour.

4 Brush loaves with oil. Bake at 375° for 25-30 minutes or until browned. Remove from pans to wire racks to cool.

SOURDOUGH FRENCH BREAD, HONEY WHEAT SOURDOUGH BREAD

SOURDOUGH HAM CRESCENT ROLLS

Sourdough Ham Crescent Rolls

PREP: 30 min. + rising **BAKE:** 15 min. **YIELD:** 32 rolls

Jean Graf-Joyce, Albany, Oregon

These eye-appealing crescent rolls are loaded with ham and hard-cooked eggs. They're a terrific main course for a ladies' luncheon.

- 2 **packages (1/4 ounce *each*) active dry yeast**
- 1/2 **cup warm water (110° to 115°)**
- 1 **cup warm milk (110° to 115°)**
- 1 **cup Sourdough Starter (recipe on page 374)**
- 1/2 **cup vegetable oil**
- 1/4 **cup sugar**
- 2 **teaspoons salt**
- 5 **to 5-1/2 cups all-purpose flour**

FILLING:
- 2 **cups finely chopped fully cooked ham**
- 2 **hard-cooked eggs, chopped**
- 1 **small onion, chopped**
- 1/2 **cup condensed cream of mushroom soup, undiluted**

1 In a large mixing bowl, dissolve yeast in warm water. Add the milk, Sourdough Starter, oil, sugar, salt and 2 cups flour; beat until smooth. Stir in enough remaining flour to form a medium-stiff dough.

2 Turn onto a floured surface; knead until smooth and elastic, about 6-8 minutes. Place in a greased bowl, turning once to grease top. Cover and let rise in a warm place until doubled, about 1 hour.

3 Punch dough down. Turn onto a lightly floured surface; divide into four pieces. Roll each piece into a 12-in. circle; cut each into eight wedges. Combine the filling ingredients; spread over wedges. Roll up from the wide end and place point side down 2 in. apart on greased baking sheets. Curve ends to form a crescent shape. Cover and let rise until doubled, about 45 minutes.

4 Bake at 375° for 12-15 minutes or until golden brown. Remove from pans to wire racks. Serve warm. Refrigerate leftovers.

Golden Sourdough Biscuits

PREP/TOTAL TIME: 30 min. + cooling
YIELD: 1 dozen

Stephanie Church, Delaware, Ohio

These soft biscuits are best enjoyed straight from the oven.

- 2 **cups all-purpose flour**
- 1 **teaspoon baking powder**
- 1 **teaspoon salt**
- 1/2 **teaspoon baking soda**
- 1/2 **cup cold butter**
- 1 **cup Sourdough Starter (recipe on page 374)**
- 1/2 **cup buttermilk**

Additional butter, melted

1 In a bowl, combine the flour, baking powder, salt and baking soda; cut in butter until mixture resembles coarse crumbs. Combine Sourdough Starter and buttermilk; stir into crumb mixture with a fork.

2 Turn onto a well-floured surface; knead 10-12 times. Roll to 1/2-in. thickness. Cut with a floured 2-1/2-in. biscuit cutter. Place 2 in. apart on a greased baking sheet.

3 Bake at 425° for 12-15 minutes or until golden brown. Brush with melted butter. Remove from pan to a wire rack to cool.

Country Crust Sourdough Bread

PREP: 20 min. + rising **BAKE:** 30 min. + cooling
YIELD: 2 loaves

Beverley Whaley
Camano Island, Washington

Brushing the top of these baked loaves with melted butter gives them a beautiful golden color.

2	**packages (1/4 ounce *each*) active dry yeast**
1-1/4	**cups warm water (110° to 115°)**
1	**cup Sourdough Starter (recipe on page 374)**
2	**eggs**
1/4	**cup sugar**
1/4	**cup vegetable oil**
1	**teaspoon salt**
6	**to 6-1/2 cups all-purpose flour**

Melted butter

1 In a large mixing bowl, dissolve yeast in warm water. Add the Sourdough Starter, eggs, sugar, oil, salt and 3 cups flour; beat until smooth. Stir in enough remaining flour to form a soft dough.

2 Turn onto a floured surface; knead until smooth and elastic, about 6-8 minutes. Place in a greased bowl, turning once to grease top. Cover and let rise in a warm place until doubled, about 1 hour.

3 Punch dough down. Turn onto a lightly floured surface; divide in half. Shape each portion into a loaf. Place in two greased 8-in. x 4-in. x 2-in. loaf pans. Cover and let rise until doubled, about 45 minutes.

4 Bake at 375° for 30-35 minutes or until golden brown. Remove from pans to wire racks. Brush with butter. Cool.

Sourdough Bread

PREP: 20 min. + rising **BAKE:** 45 min. + cooling
YIELD: 2 loaves

Evelyn Gebhardt, Kasilof, Alaska

This no-knead bread is no fuss to make and delicious, too! It has a crisp crust and distinctive sourdough flavor from the starter yeast mixture, which is stirred up in advance.

1	**recipe Sourdough Starter (recipe on page 374)**
1/4	**cup nonfat dry milk powder**
2	**tablespoons butter, melted**
2	**tablespoons sugar**
2	**teaspoons salt**
1-1/2	**cups warm water (100° to 115°)**
5	**cups all-purpose flour**

Cornmeal

1 In a large mixing bowl, combine the Sourdough Starter, milk powder, butter, sugar, salt, water and 2 cups flour. Stir in enough remaining flour to form a soft dough. Do not knead. Place in a greased bowl, turning once to grease the top. Cover and let rise in a warm place until doubled, about 1-1/2 hours.

2 Punch dough down. Turn onto a floured surface; divide in half. Shape each into a round loaf. Sprinkle cornmeal on two heavily greased baking sheets. Place loaves on prepared pans. Cover and let rise until doubled, about 30 minutes.

3 With a sharp knife, make three diagonal slashes across tops of loaves. Bake at 350° for 10 minutes. Brush loaves with cold water. Bake 35-40 minutes longer or until golden brown. Remove from pans to wire racks to cool.

SOURDOUGH BREAD

Bread Machine Recipes

secrets for *success with bread machines*

- Before beginning, carefully read your bread machine owner's manual.
- All liquid ingredients should be at room temperature (70° to 80°). This includes water, milk, yogurt, juice, cottage cheese, eggs and applesauce.
- Measure ingredients accurately, using the measuring tools and techniques suggested on pages 7 and 8 before adding to your machine. Then add in the order suggested by your bread machine manufacturer.
- For best results, use bread flour.
- If a recipe calls for softened butter, cut it into pieces, then let it stand at room temperature until softened. This way the butter will mix into the dough more uniformly.
- While either active dry yeast or bread machine yeast can be used in bread machines, bread machine yeast is a little finer, which allows for better dispersion during mixing and kneading. For 1 cup of flour, it is generally recommended to use 3/4 teaspoon of active dry yeast or 1/2 teaspoon of bread machine yeast.
- Check dough after 5 minutes of mixing. The dough should feel smooth, soft and slightly tacky. If it's moist or sticky, add 1 tablespoon of flour and check again after a few more minutes of mixing. If it's dry and crumbly, add 1 tablespoon of liquid, then check again.
- Recipes containing eggs, milk, sour cream, cottage cheese and other dairy or perishable products should be baked immediately and not placed on a "timed-bake" cycle.

Grandma's Molasses Bread

PREP: 5 min. **BAKE:** 3-4 hours
YIELD: 1 loaf (about 1-1/2 pounds)

Jeannie Thomas, Kokomo, Indiana

This dark, slightly sweet bread is great toasted.

- 1 cup warm milk (70° to 80°)
- 2 tablespoons butter, softened
- 2 tablespoons molasses
- 1 egg
- 1-1/2 teaspoons salt
- 2-1/2 cups bread flour
- 4-1/2 teaspoons sugar
- 1/2 cup rye flour
- 1/4 cup whole wheat flour
- 2-1/4 teaspoons active dry yeast

In bread machine pan, place all ingredients in order suggested by manufacturer. Select basic bread setting. Choose crust color and loaf size if available. Bake according to bread machine directions (check dough after 5 minutes of mixing; add 1 to 2 tablespoons of water or flour if needed).

Editor's Note: If your bread machine has a time-delay feature, we recommend you do not use it for this recipe.

Home-Style White Bread

PREP: 5 min. **BAKE:** 3-4 hours
YIELD: 1 loaf (about 1-1/2 pounds)

Yvonna Nave, Lyons, Kansas

Serve this basic white bread with butter and jam. Or use slices to assemble your favorite sandwiches.

- 1 cup water (70° to 80°)
- 2 tablespoons butter, softened
- 1 teaspoon salt
- 2 tablespoons sugar
- 2 tablespoons nonfat dry milk powder
- 3 cups bread flour
- 2 teaspoons active dry yeast

In bread machine pan, place all ingredients in order suggested by manufacturer. Select basic bread setting. Choose crust color and loaf size if available. Bake according to bread machine directions (check dough after 5 minutes of mixing; add 1 to 2 tablespoons of water or flour if needed).

HOME-STYLE WHITE BREAD

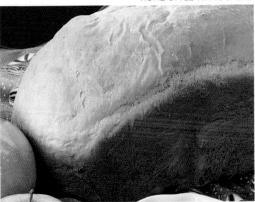

MULTIGRAIN BREAD

Multigrain Bread

PREP: 10 min. **BAKE:** 3-4 hours
YIELD: 1 loaf (2 pounds)

Michele MacKinlay, Madoc, Ontario

Cornmeal and wheat germ give this bread a wonderful texture and nutty flavor.

1	cup water (70° to 80°)
2	tablespoons vegetable oil
2	egg yolks
1/4	cup molasses
1	teaspoon salt
1-1/2	cups bread flour
1	cup whole wheat flour
1/2	cup rye flour
1/2	cup nonfat dry milk powder
1/4	cup quick-cooking oats
1/4	cup wheat germ
1/4	cup cornmeal
2-1/4	teaspoons active dry yeast

In bread machine pan, place all ingredients in order suggested by manufacturer. Select basic bread setting. Choose crust color and loaf size if available. Bake according to bread machine directions (check dough after 5 minutes of mixing; add 1 to 2 tablespoons water or flour if needed).

Editor's Note: If your bread machine has a time-delay feature, we recommend you do not use it for this recipe.

Greek Loaf

PREP: 10 min. **BAKE:** 3 hours
YIELD: 1 loaf (about 1-1/2 pounds)

Melanie Parker, Gloucester, Ontario

Feta cheese and olives star in this zesty bread. Leftovers make great salad croutons.

1	cup milk (70° to 80°)
1	tablespoon olive oil
1/2	to 1-1/2 teaspoons salt
3/4	cup crumbled feta cheese
3	cups bread flour
1	tablespoon sugar
2-1/4	teaspoons active dry yeast
1/4	cup sliced ripe olives

1 In bread machine pan, place the first seven ingredients in order suggested by manufacturer. Select basic bread setting. Choose crust color and loaf size if available. Bake according to bread machine directions (check dough after 5 minutes of mixing; add 1 to 2 tablespoons of water or flour if needed).

2 Just before the final kneading (your machine may audibly signal this), add the olives.

Editor's Note: If your bread machine has a time-delay feature, we recommend you do not use it for this recipe.

Cracked Pepper Bread

PREP: 10 min. **BAKE:** 3 hours **YIELD:** 1 loaf (2 pounds)

Joy McMillan, The Woodlands, Texas

Herbs and Parmesan cheese lend big flavor to this bread.

1-1/2	cups water (70° to 80°)
3	tablespoons olive oil
3	tablespoons sugar
2	teaspoons salt
3	tablespoons minced chives
2	garlic cloves, minced
1	teaspoon garlic powder
1	teaspoon dried basil
1	teaspoon cracked black pepper
1/4	cup grated Parmesan cheese
4	cups bread flour
2-1/2	teaspoons active dry yeast

In bread machine pan, place all ingredients in order suggested by manufacturer. Select basic bread setting. Choose crust color and loaf size if available. Bake according to bread machine directions (check the dough after 5 minutes of mixing; add 1 to 2 tablespoons of water or flour if needed).

PUMPERNICKEL CARAWAY BREAD

Garlic Herb Bubble Loaf

PREP: 25 min. + rising **BAKE:** 35 min.
YIELD: 1 loaf (1-1/2 pounds)

Katie Crill, Priest River, Idaho

This pull-apart loaf smells heavenly while baking. It has a light crust, tender interior and is packed with herb flavor.

1/2	cup water (70° to 80°)
1/2	cup sour cream
2	tablespoons butter, softened
3	tablespoons sugar
1-1/2	teaspoons salt
3	cups bread flour
2-1/4	teaspoons active dry yeast

GARLIC HERB BUTTER:

1/4	cup butter, melted
4	garlic cloves, minced
1/4	teaspoon *each* dried oregano, thyme and rosemary, crushed

1 In bread machine pan, place the first seven ingredients in order suggested by manufacturer. Select dough setting (check dough after 5 minutes of mixing; add 1 to 2 tablespoons of water or flour if needed).

2 When cycle is completed, turn dough onto a lightly floured surface. Cover and let rest for 15 minutes. Divide dough into 36 pieces. Shape each piece into a ball. In a shallow bowl, combine the butter, garlic and herbs. Dip each ball in mixture; place in an ungreased 9-in. x 5-in. x 3-in. loaf pan. Cover and let rise in a warm place until doubled, about 45 minutes. Bake at 375° for 35-40 minutes or until golden brown. Remove from pan to a wire rack. Serve warm.

Editor's Note: If your bread machine has a time-delay feature, we recommend you do not use it for this recipe.

Pumpernickel Caraway Bread

PREP: 10 min. **BAKE:** 3-4 hours **YIELD:** 1 loaf (1 pound)

Lorraine Darocha, Berkshire, Massachusetts

This rich dark bread has an old-fashioned homemade taste that's oh-so-satisfying. Made with molasses and caraway seeds, it's moist and flavorful.

3/4	cup water (70° to 80°)
2	tablespoons molasses
4-1/2	teaspoons butter
1	teaspoon salt
1	cup bread flour
2/3	cup rye flour
1/3	cup whole wheat flour
2	tablespoons cornmeal
5	teaspoons baking cocoa
4-1/2	teaspoons sugar
3	teaspoons nonfat dry milk powder
1	teaspoon caraway seeds
1/4	teaspoon instant coffee granules
1-1/2	teaspoons active dry yeast

In bread machine pan, place all ingredients in order suggested by manufacturer. Select basic bread setting. Choose crust color and loaf size if available. Bake according to bread machine directions (check dough after 5 minutes of mixing; add 1 to 2 tablespoons of water or flour if needed).

GARLIC HERB BUBBLE LOAF

Herbed Tomato Bread

PREP: 15 min. **BAKE:** 3-4 hours
YIELD: 1 loaf (1-1/2 pounds) and 1/2 cup spread

Sherry Letson, Trinity, Alabama

Slices of this moist bread are terrific when eaten alone, with Garlic Chive Spread or when used to make grilled cheese sandwiches.

- 1/2 cup plus 2 tablespoons warm milk (70° to 80°)
- 1 can (6 ounces) tomato paste
- 1 egg
- 2 tablespoons olive oil
- 1/2 teaspoon salt
- 2 tablespoons minced fresh parsley
- 1 tablespoon sugar
- 2 teaspoons dried minced onion
- 1/2 teaspoon garlic powder
- 1/2 teaspoon dried tarragon
- 3 cups bread flour
- 2-1/4 teaspoons active dry yeast

GARLIC CHIVE SPREAD:
- 1/2 cup butter, softened
- 1 tablespoon minced chives
- 1 garlic clove, minced

1 In bread machine pan, place the first 12 ingredients in order suggested by manufacturer. Select basic bread setting. Choose crust color and loaf size if available. Bake according to bread machine directions (check dough after 5 minutes of mixing; add 1 to 2 tablespoons of water or flour if needed).

2 In a small bowl, combine the spread ingredients. Serve with bread.

Editor's Note: If your bread machine has a time-delay feature, we recommend you do not use it for this recipe.

converting recipes for use in *bread machines*

Converting a traditional yeast bread recipe for the bread machine will require some experimentation on your part. We've included some pointers to help get you started.

First, determine the size of your bread machine. Look at the recipes that came with your bread machine and note the amount of flour and liquid called for in most of those recipes. The chart below gives a general guideline for the ratio of ingredients for bread machines yielding 1 pound, 1-1/2 pound and 2 pound loaves.

- Flour includes dry ingredients such as any type of flour, oats, cereal and cornmeal. Liquid includes milk, water, yogurt, sour cream, applesauce, eggs (1/4 cup liquid per egg), cottage cheese, etc. Sugar includes other sweeteners such as honey, molasses or brown sugar. Fat includes shortening, butter, margarine and oil.
- It's best to start with a bread recipe you are familiar with and have successfully made. Once you've mastered those familiar recipes, look for other bread recipes that use the amount of flour needed for your bread machine. Or, look for a recipe that makes two loaves and can be easily divided in half. Divide all the ingredients in half. When recipes give a range of flour, always start with the lower amount.

- Avoid sourdough recipes, recipes that require refrigerating the dough or recipes with a high ratio of fat. These types of recipes won't be successful in the bread machine.
- For breads with topping or fillings as well as ones that require special shapes or rolls—just mix, knead and proof the dough in the bread machine. Punch the dough down, fill and/or shape. Then follow the original recipe to finish the bread.
- Add ingredients to the bread pan in the order your manufacturer recommends. Check the dough after 5 minutes of mixing. Add 1 to 2 tablespoons of flour or liquid if necessary.
- Make notes on your recipe for reference. If it wasn't quite right, make an adjustment in one ingredient and try again.

BREAD MACHINE SIZE	FLOUR BY CUPS	LIQUID BY CUP	ACTIVE DRY YEAST BY TEASPOONS	SUGAR BY TABLESPOONS	SALT BY TEASPOONS	FAT BY TEASPOONS
1 pound	2 to 2-1/2	2/3	1-1/2	2	1	4
1-1/2 pounds	3 to 3-1/2	1	2-1/2	3	1-1/2	6
2 pounds	4 to 4-1/2	1-1/3	3	4	2	8

Sour Cream Lemon Bread

PREP: 15 min. **BAKE:** 3-4 hours
YIELD: 1 loaf (1 pound) and about 1/2 cup spread

Barbara Strickler, Syracuse, Indiana

Serve slices of this light and tender bread with a creamy lemon spread for an early-morning treat or late-night snack that's simply dreamy.

- 1/4 **cup sour cream**
- 2 **tablespoons lemon juice**
- 2 **to 3 tablespoons warm milk (70° to 80°)**
- 2 **tablespoons butter, softened**
- 1 **egg**
- 2 **teaspoons grated lemon peel**
- 2 **tablespoons sugar**
- 1 **teaspoon salt**
- 1/4 **teaspoon baking soda**
- 2 **cups bread flour**
- 1-1/2 **teaspoons active dry yeast**

LEMON SPREAD:

- 1 **package (3 ounces) cream cheese, softened**
- 1/4 **cup confectioners' sugar**
- 1 **tablespoon lemon juice**
- 1 **teaspoon grated lemon peel**

1 In a measuring cup, combine sour cream and lemon juice. Add enough warm milk to measure 1/2 cup. In bread machine pan, place the sour cream mixture, butter, egg, lemon peel, sugar, salt, baking soda, flour and yeast in order suggested by manufacturer. Select sweet bread setting. Choose crust color and loaf size if available. Bake according to bread machine directions (check dough after 5 minutes of mixing; add 1 to 2 tablespoons of water or flour if needed).

2 In a small mixing bowl, combine the spread ingredients; beat until smooth. Serve with bread. Store in the refrigerator.

Editor's Note: If your bread machine has a time-delay feature, we recommend you do not use it for this recipe. If your bread machine does not have a sweet bread setting, follow the manufacturer's directions using the basic setting.

Jalapeno Bread

PREP: 10 min. **BAKE:** 3-4 hours **YIELD:** 1 loaf (1 pound)

Lola Gangwer, Burgoon, Ohio

Ordinary sandwiches become extraordinary when made with slices of this pretty corn-flecked loaf. For a milder chili taste, use green chilies in place of the jalapenos.

- 1/2 **cup water (70° to 80°)**
- 1 **tablespoon butter, softened**
- 1 **tablespoon sugar**

SOUR CREAM LEMON BREAD

1 teaspoon salt
1/2 cup whole kernel corn
2 tablespoons chopped jalapenos *or* green chilies
1 teaspoon chopped fresh cilantro
2 cups bread flour
1/3 cup cornmeal
1-1/2 teaspoons active dry yeast

In bread machine pan, place all ingredients in order suggested by manufacturer. Select basic bread setting. Choose crust color and loaf size if available. Bake according to bread machine directions (check dough after 5 minutes of mixing; add 1 to 2 table-spoons of water or flour if needed).

Editor's Note: If your bread machine has a time-delay feature, we recommend you do not use it for this recipe.

Three-Seed Bread

PREP: 5 min. **BAKE:** 3-4 hours
YIELD: 1 loaf (about 1 pound)

Melissa Vannoy, Childress, Texas

Here's a hearty whole wheat bread that's chock-full of sunflower kernels and poppy and sesame seeds. It rivals any gourmet bakery bread.

2/3 cup plus 2 teaspoons water (70° to 80°)
1 tablespoon butter, softened
1 tablespoon honey
2 tablespoons sesame seeds
2 tablespoons sunflower kernels
2 tablespoons poppy seeds
3/4 teaspoon salt
1 cup bread flour
1 cup whole wheat flour
3 tablespoons nonfat dry milk powder
2 teaspoons active dry yeast

In bread machine pan, place all ingredients in order suggested by manufacturer. Select basic bread setting. Choose crust color and loaf size if available. Bake according to bread machine directions (check dough after 5 minutes of mixing; add 1 to 2 table-spoons of water or flour if needed).

Apricot Nutmeg Bread

PREP: 10 min. **BAKE:** 3-4 hours
YIELD: 1 loaf (1-1/2 pounds)

Anna Kinney, Farmington, New Mexico

This fruity bread is good for breakfast when toasted and spread with strawberry jam. Nutmeg complements the apricot flavor in this golden, soft-textured loaf.

APRICOT NUTMEG BREAD

1 cup water (70° to 80°)
3 tablespoons vegetable oil
1 teaspoon lemon juice
2 tablespoons plus 1-1/2 teaspoons brown sugar
1 teaspoon salt
2-1/4 teaspoons active dry yeast
3 cups bread flour
1 tablespoon plus 1-1/2 teaspoons nonfat dry milk powder
1 cup chopped dried apricots
3/4 teaspoon ground nutmeg

1 In bread machine pan, place the first eight ingre-dients in order suggested by manufacturer. Select sweet bread cycle. Choose medium crust color and loaf size if available. Bake according to bread machine directions (after 5 minutes of mixing, check dough; add 1 to 2 tablespoons of water or flour if needed).

2 Just before the final kneading (your machine may audibly signal this), add apricots and nutmeg.

Editor's Note: If your bread machine does not have a sweet bread setting, follow the manufacturer's directions using the basic setting.

Golden Honey Pan Rolls

PREP: 35 min. + rising **BAKE:** 20 min. **YIELD:** 2 dozen

Sara Wing, Philadelphia, Pennsylvania

Using your bread machine to make the dough saves about 2 hours compared to the traditional method. The rich buttery taste of these honey-glazed rolls will be popular with your family and friends.

    1   cup warm milk (70° to 80°)
    1   egg
    1   egg yolk
  1/2   cup vegetable oil
    2   tablespoons honey
1-1/2   teaspoons salt
3-1/2   cups bread flour
2-1/4   teaspoons active dry yeast
GLAZE:
  1/3   cup sugar
    2   tablespoons butter, melted
    1   tablespoon honey
    1   egg white
Additional honey, optional

1 In bread machine pan, place the first eight ingredients in order suggested by manufacturer. Select dough setting (check dough after 5 minutes of mixing; add 1 to 2 tablespoons of water or flour if needed).

2 When cycle is completed, turn dough onto a lightly floured surface. Cover and let rest for 15 minutes. Divide into 24 pieces; shape each piece into a ball. Place 12 balls each in two greased 9-in. square baking pans. Cover and let rise in a warm place until doubled, about 30 minutes.

3 For glaze, combine sugar, butter, honey and egg white; drizzle over dough. Bake at 350° for 20-25 minutes or until golden brown. Brush with additional honey if desired.

Editor's Note: If your bread machine has a time-delay feature, we recommend you do not use it for this recipe.

Cranberry Nut Bagels

PREP: 30 min. + rising **BAKE:** 20 min. **YIELD:** 8 bagels

John Russell, Greentown, Indiana

Do you love homemade bagels but not the time commitment? This convenient recipe lets you prepare those delicious baked goods in a lot less time.

    1   cup plus 2 tablespoons water (70° to 80°)
    2   tablespoons sugar
    1   teaspoon salt
1-1/4   teaspoons ground cinnamon
  1/4   cup quick-cooking oats
    3   cups bread flour
2-1/2   teaspoons active dry yeast
  3/4   cup dried cranberries
  1/4   cup chopped pecans
    2   quarts water
TOPPING:
    2   tablespoons brown sugar
    1   teaspoon ground cinnamon

1 In bread machine pan, place the first seven ingredients in order suggested by manufacturer. Select dough setting (check dough after 5 minutes of mixing; add 1 to 2 tablespoons of water or flour if needed). Just before the final kneading (your machine may audibly signal this), add the cranberries and pecans.

2 When cycle is completed, turn dough onto a lightly floured surface. Cover and let rest for 15 minutes. Divide into eight balls. Push thumb through the center of each ball to form a 1-in. hole. Stretch and shape dough to form an even ring. Place on a floured surface. Cover and let rest for 10 minutes; flatten rings slightly.

3 In a large nonaluminum saucepan, bring water to a boil. Drop rings, one at a time, into boiling water. Cook for 45 seconds; turn and cook 45 seconds longer. Remove with a slotted spoon; drain well on paper towels.

GOLDEN HONEY PAN ROLLS

SOFT ITALIAN BREADSTICKS

dough setting (check dough after 5 minutes of mixing; add 1 to 2 tablespoons of water or flour if needed).

2 When cycle is completed, turn dough onto a lightly floured surface; divide in half. Cut each portion into 12 pieces; roll each into a 4-in. to 6-in. rope. Place 2 in. apart on greased baking sheets. Cover and let rise in a warm place until doubled, about 20 minutes.

3 Bake at 350° for 15-18 minutes or until golden brown. Immediately brush with butter; sprinkle with Parmesan cheese. Serve warm.

4 Combine brown sugar and cinnamon; sprinkle over bagels. Place 2 in. apart on greased baking sheets. Bake at 375° for 20-25 minutes or until golden brown. Remove from pan to a wire rack to cool.

Soft Italian Breadsticks

PREP: 25 min. + rising **BAKE:** 15 min. **YIELD:** 2 dozen

Christy Eichelberger, Jesup, Iowa

Use the dough-only cycle on your bread machine to prepare these melt-in-your-mouth breadsticks. The soft, chewy breadsticks are irresistible when brushed with butter and sprinkled with Parmesan cheese. They're the perfect accompaniment to soups or Italian entrees.

        1   cup water (70° to 80°)
        3   tablespoons butter, softened
    1-1/2   teaspoons salt
        3   cups bread flour
        2   tablespoons sugar
        1   teaspoon Italian seasoning
        1   teaspoon garlic powder
    2-1/4   teaspoons active dry yeast
TOPPING:
        1   tablespoon butter, melted
        1   tablespoon grated Parmesan cheese

1 In bread machine pan, place the water, butter, salt, flour, sugar, Italian seasoning, garlic powder and yeast in order suggested by manufacturer. Select

problem-solving pointers *for Bread Machines*

BREAD IS LUMPY OR DOUGH APPEARS DRY

• Dough is too dry. Add a little more water during the kneading cycle.

DOUGH IS STICKY AND WON'T FORM A BALL

• Dough is too moist. Add a little more flour during the kneading cycle.

BREAD HAS A MUSHROOM TOP

• Water was too warm.

BREAD HAS AN UNDERBAKED, GUMMY CENTER

• Dough was too moist.

TOP IS SUNKEN

• Too much yeast or liquid and/or not enough flour was used.

BREAD ROSE TOO HIGH OR OVERFLOWED PAN

• Next time, reduce the amount of yeast slightly and remember to add the salt.

Hawaiian Dinner Rolls

PREP: 35 min. + rising **BAKE:** 15 min. **YIELD:** 15 rolls

Kathy Kurtz, Glendora, California

Pineapple and coconut give a subtle sweetness to these golden rolls. Leftovers are great for sandwiches.

- 1 can (8 ounces) crushed pineapple, undrained
- 1/4 cup warm pineapple juice (70° to 80°)
- 1/4 cup water (70° to 80°)
- 1 egg
- 1/4 cup butter, cubed and softened
- 1/4 cup nonfat dry milk powder
- 1 tablespoon sugar
- 1-1/2 teaspoons salt
- 3-1/4 cups bread flour
- 2-1/4 teaspoons active dry yeast
- 3/4 cup flaked coconut

1 In bread machine pan, place the first 10 ingredients in order suggested by manufacturer. Select dough setting (check dough after 5 minutes of mixing; add 1 to 2 tablespoons of water or flour if needed). Just before final kneading (your machine may audibly signal this), add coconut.

2 When cycle is complete, turn dough onto a lightly floured surface. Cover with plastic wrap; let rest for 10 minutes. Divide into 15 portions; roll each into a ball. Place in a greased 13-in. x 9-in. x 2-in. baking pan. Cover and let rise in a warm place for 45 minutes or until doubled.

3 Bake at 375° for 15-20 minutes or until golden brown. Remove from pan to a wire rack. Serve warm.

Editor's Note: If your bread machine has a time-delay feature, we recommend you do not use it for this recipe.

Stuffed-to-the-Gills Pizza

PREP: 1 hour **BAKE:** 35 min. **YIELD:** 8 slices

Dyann Schieltz, Parker, Colorado

While the bread machine makes the dough, you can cook the sausage and chop up the other ingredients.

- 1-1/2 cups water (70° to 80°)
- 2 teaspoons salt
- 2 teaspoons sugar
- 2 teaspoons olive oil
- 5 cups all-purpose flour
- 4 teaspoons active dry yeast

- 1 can (8 ounces) tomato sauce
- 3 tablespoons tomato paste
- 1 garlic clove, minced
- 1 teaspoon Italian seasoning
- Dash crushed red pepper flakes
- 1/2 pound Italian sausage, cooked and crumbled
- 1/4 pound hard salami, diced
- 30 slices pepperoni
- 1/2 cup chopped red onion
- 1 cup (4 ounces) shredded cheddar cheese, *divided*
- 1 cup (4 ounces) shredded part-skim mozzarella cheese, *divided*
- 1 plum tomato, diced

1 In bread machine pan, place the first six ingredients in order suggested by manufacturer. Select dough setting (check dough after 5 minutes or mixing; add 1 to 2 tablespoons of water or flour if needed). When cycle is completed, turn dough onto a lightly floured surface and punch down; divide in half. Roll one portion into a 13-in. circle. Place on a greased 14-in. pizza pan.

2 In a bowl, combine the tomato sauce, tomato paste, garlic, Italian seasoning and pepper flakes. Spread 3/4 cup over dough to within 1 in. of edge. Sprinkle with the sausage, salami, pepperoni, onion, 1/2 cup cheddar cheese and 1/2 cup mozzarella cheese.

3 Roll the remaining dough into a 12-1/2-in. circle. Place over the pizza; seal edges. Cut four slits in top. Spread with the remaining sauce. Bake at 375° for 35 minutes. Sprinkle with diced tomato and remaining cheese. Bake 5-10 minutes longer or until golden brown.

STUFFED-TO-THE-GILLS PIZZA

Sweet Yeast Breads

The Basics of Sweet Yeast Breads

Sweet yeast breads fall into two basic categories sweet loaves and sweet rolls. The dough can be made by hand or in a bread machine.

- Sweet loaves include fruit-filled breads and a variety of coffee cakes.
- Sweet rolls refer to fruit-filled rolls, sticky buns, cinnamon rolls, doughnuts, kolachkes and individual Danishes.
- Sweet and savory yeast breads are prepared in the same manner. For information and techniques on mixing and kneading, see Traditional Mixing Method for Yeast Bread, page 337; Rapid Mixing Method for Yeast Bread, page 351; Kneading, Shaping and Baking Yeast Bread, page 332; and Secrets for Success with Bread Machines, page 378.

secrets for *successful* *sweet yeast breads*

- Use butter, stick margarine (with at least 80% oil) or shortening. Do not use light or whipped butter, diet spread or tub margarine.
- Measure ingredients accurately, using the measuring tools and techniques suggested on pages 7 and 8.
- Arrange the oven racks so that the bread will be baked in the center of the oven.
- Preheat oven for 10 to 15 minutes before baking.
- When mixing dough, always start with a minimum amount of flour until dough reaches desired consistency (soft, sticky, stiff or firm).
- Knead dough only until it does not tear easily when stretched.

- Let dough rise in a warm (80° to 85°) draft-free area. Proper rising helps in the development of the bread texture.
- Use aluminum pans with a dull rather than a shiny or dark finish. Glass baking dishes and dark finishes will produce darker crusts.
- To allow for good air circulation while baking, leave at least 1 in. of space between pans and between pans and sides of oven.
- Use a kitchen timer and test for doneness at the minimum recommended baking time. Bread is done when it is golden brown and sounds hollow when tapped on the bottom. Or, insert an instant-read thermometer in the thickest part of the loaf. The bread is done when the thermometer reads 200°.
- Remove breads from pans and cool on wire racks. Let breads cool for at least 20 minutes before slicing. Use a serrated knife and sawing motion when cutting.

Sweet Breads & Coffee Cakes

Pineapple Cheese Braids

PREP: 45 min. + rising **BAKE:** 25 min. + cooling
YIELD: 2 loaves

Shirley Kensinger
Roaring Spring, Pennsylvania

*Folks will be pleasantly surprised by this bread's pineapple
filling. If you're in a hurry, you can use canned pie filling.*

- 2 packages (1/4 ounce *each*) active dry yeast
- 1 cup warm water (110° to 115°)
- 1/2 cup butter, softened
- 5 tablespoons sugar
- 2 eggs
- 1/4 teaspoon salt
- 4-1/4 to 4-1/2 cups all-purpose flour
- **PINEAPPLE FILLING:**
  - 1 can (8 ounces) crushed pineapple, undrained
  - 1/2 cup sugar
  - 3 tablespoons cornstarch
- **CREAM CHEESE FILLING:**
  - 2 packages (8 ounces *each*) cream cheese, softened
  - 1/3 cup sugar
- 1 tablespoon lemon juice
- 1/2 teaspoon vanilla extract
- **ICING (optional):**
  - 1 cup confectioners' sugar
  - 2 to 3 tablespoons milk

1 In a large mixing bowl, dissolve yeast in warm water. Add the butter, sugar, eggs, salt and 2 cups flour; beat on low speed for 3 minutes. Stir in enough remaining flour to form a soft dough.

2 Turn onto a floured surface; knead until smooth and elastic, about 6-8 minutes. Place in a greased bowl, turning once to grease top. Cover and let rise in a warm place until doubled, about 45 minutes.

3 For pineapple filling, combine the pineapple, sugar and cornstarch in a small saucepan. Bring to a boil. Reduce heat; cook and stir until thickened. Cool. In a mixing bowl, combine the cream cheese filling ingredients; mix well.

4 Punch dough down. Turn onto a lightly floured surface; divide in half. Roll each portion into a 15-in. x 9-in. rectangle. Place on greased baking sheets. Spread the cream cheese filling lengthwise down the center third of each rectangle. Spread the pineapple filling on top.

5 On each long side, cut 1-in.-wide strips about 3 in. into the center. Starting at one end, fold alternating strips at an angle across filling; seal ends. Cover and let rise for 20 minutes.

PINEAPPLE CHEESE BRAIDS

braiding *a filled bread*

1. Roll dough into a rectangle; place on a greased baking sheet. Spread filling down center of rectangle. On each long side, cut 1 in. wide strips, about 1/2 in. from the filling.

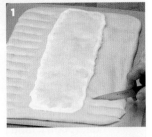

2. Starting at one end, fold alternating strips at an angle across filling. Seal ends.

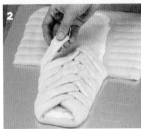

6 Bake at 350° for 25-30 minutes or until golden brown. Remove from pans to wire racks to cool. If desired, combine icing ingredients and drizzle over braids. Store in the refrigerator.

Fruit 'n' Nut Bread

PREP: 15 min. BAKE: 20 min. + cooling YIELD: 1 loaf

Mary Hansen, St. Louis, Missouri

Keep frozen bread dough on hand during the holidays so you can bake this favorite in brisk fashion!

- 1/2 cup chopped pecans
- 1/2 cup raisins
- 1/2 cup chopped dates
- 1/2 cup halved candied cherries
- 2 teaspoons orange juice
- 1 loaf (1 pound) frozen bread dough, thawed
- 1 tablespoon butter, melted

GLAZE:
- 1/2 cup confectioners' sugar
- 1 tablespoon orange juice
- 1 tablespoon butter, melted
- 1/8 teaspoon grated orange peel

Pecan halves

1 In a small bowl, combine the pecans, raisins, dates, cherries and orange juice; set aside. Shape bread dough into a ball. Turn onto a floured surface; roll out to about 1 in. thick.

2 Spread pecan mixture over dough; fold over and knead well until the fruit and nuts are evenly mixed into dough. Shape into a flattened ball; place on a greased baking sheet. Brush with butter. Cover and let rise until doubled, about 1 hour.

3 Bake at 375° for 20-25 minutes or until golden brown. Remove from pan to a wire rack to cool. For glaze, combine the confectioners' sugar, orange juice, butter and orange peel. Spread over bread. Top with pecan halves.

Cheery Cherry Christmas Bread

PREP: 25 min. + rising BAKE: 30 min. + cooling
YIELD: 16-20 servings

Robyn Wegelin, Bridgeport, Nebraska

The convenience of the hot roll mix makes this recipe a time-saver and perfect for the busy holiday season.

- 1 package (16 ounces) hot roll mix
- 1 can (21 ounces) cherry pie filling

FILLING:
- 1/2 cup sour cream
- 1 egg
- 2 tablespoons sugar
- 1/2 teaspoon almond extract

TOPPING:
- 1 cup all-purpose flour
- 1/4 cup sugar
- 1/2 cup cold butter

1 Prepare hot roll mix and knead dough according to package directions. Cover and let rest for 5 minutes.

2 Turn onto a lightly floured surface; roll into a 15-in. x 10-in. rectangle. Press dough onto the bottom and up the sides of a greased 15-in. x 10-in. x 1-in. baking pan. Cover and let rise in a warm place until doubled, about 30 minutes.

3 Spread pie filling over dough. Combine the sour cream, egg, sugar and almond extract; drizzle over filling. In small bowl, combine flour and sugar; cut in butter until mixture is crumbly. Sprinkle over filling.

4 Bake at 375° for 30-35 minutes or until golden brown. Cool on a wire rack. Store in the refrigerator.

Fruited Swedish Tea Ring

PREP: 45 min. + rising **BAKE:** 20 min. + cooling
YIELD: 2 tea rings

Betty Murray, Hamiota, Manitoba

These tasty "wreaths" are wonderful gifts from the kitchen at Christmastime.

1	cup chopped candied fruit
1/2	cup raisins
2/3	cup packed brown sugar
1/4	cup butter, melted
1	teaspoon grated orange peel

1/2	teaspoon ground cardamom

DOUGH:

2	packages (1/4 ounce *each*) active dry yeast
1/3	cup sugar, *divided*
1-1/4	cups warm water (110° to 115°), *divided*
2	eggs
1/4	cup shortening
1-1/2	teaspoons salt
4-1/4	to 4-3/4 cups all-purpose flour

ICING:

1	cup confectioners' sugar
1	tablespoon lemon juice
1	tablespoon milk

Candied cherries, optional

1 In a bowl, combine the first six ingredients. Cover and refrigerate. In a small bowl, dissolve yeast and 1 teaspoon sugar in 1/4 cup warm water; let stand for 5 minutes. In a large mixing bowl, stir remaining water and sugar until dissolved. Add the yeast mixture, eggs, shortening, salt and 3 cups flour; beat until smooth. Stir in enough remaining flour to form a soft dough.

2 Turn onto a floured surface; knead until smooth and elastic, about 6-8 minutes. Place in a greased bowl, turning once to grease top. Cover and let rise in a warm place until doubled, about 1 hour.

3 Punch dough down. Turn onto a lightly floured surface; divide in half. Roll each portion into a 16-in. x 9-in. rectangle. Sprinkle fruit mixture over each rectangle to within 1/2 in. of edges.

shaping *a coffee cake ring*

1. Roll into a rectangle. Spread filling evenly over dough to within 1/2 in. of edges. Roll up jelly-roll style, starting with a long side; pinch seam to seal.

2. Place seam side down on greased baking sheets; pinch ends together to form a ring.

3. With scissors, cut from outside edge to two-thirds of the way toward center of ring at 1-in. intervals.

4. Separate the cut pieces slightly, twisting each individually to allow filling to show.

4 Roll up jelly-roll style, starting with a long side; pinch seam to seal. Place seam side down on greased baking sheets; pinch ends together to form a ring. With scissors, cut from outside edge two-thirds of the way toward center of ring at 1-in. intervals. Separate strips slightly; twist to allow filling to show. Cover and let rise until doubled, about 1 hour.

5 Bake at 350° for 20-25 minutes or until golden brown. Cool on wire racks for 20 minutes. For icing, combine the confectioners' sugar, lemon juice and milk; drizzle over warm rings. Decorate with cherries if desired.

Apple Ladder Loaf

PREP: 70 min. + chilling **BAKE:** 30 min. **YIELD:** 2 loaves

Norma Foster, Compton, Illinois

This pretty filled bread makes a nice breakfast pastry or— with a scoop of ice cream—a lovely dessert.

APPLE LADDER LOAF

   2   **packages (1/4 ounce *each*) active dry yeast**
1/4   **cup warm water (110° to 115°)**
1/2   **cup warm milk (110° to 115°)**
1/2   **cup butter, softened**
1/3   **cup sugar**
   1   **teaspoon salt**
   4   **eggs**
4-1/2 **to 4-3/4 cups all-purpose flour**
FILLING:
1/4   **cup butter, softened**
1/3   **cup packed brown sugar**
   2   **tablespoons all-purpose flour**
1-1/4 **teaspoons ground cinnamon**
1/2   **teaspoon ground nutmeg**
1/8   **teaspoon ground allspice**
   4   **cups thinly sliced peeled tart apples**
ICING:
   1   **cup confectioners' sugar**
1/4   **teaspoon vanilla extract**
   1   **to 2 tablespoons orange juice**

1 In a large mixing bowl, dissolve yeast in warm water. Add the milk, butter, sugar, salt, eggs and 2 cups flour. Beat on low speed for 3 minutes. Stir in enough remaining flour to form a soft dough.

2 Turn onto a lightly floured surface; knead until smooth and elastic, about 6-8 minutes. Place in a greased bowl, turning once to grease top. Cover and refrigerate for 1-2 hours; punch down. Cover and refrigerate overnight.

3 Punch dough down. Turn onto a lightly floured surface; divide in half. Roll each portion into a 12-in. x 9-in. rectangle. Place on greased baking sheets. Spread with 1/4 cup butter.

4 For filling, combine the brown sugar, flour, cinnamon, nutmeg and allspice in a large bowl; add apples and toss to coat. Spoon down the center third of each rectangle.

5 On each long side, cut 1-in.-wide strips about 3 in. into the center. Starting at one end, fold alternating strips at an angle across filling; seal ends. Cover and let rise until nearly doubled, about 45-50 minutes.

6 Bake at 350° for 30-40 minutes or until golden brown. Remove from pans to wire racks. Combine confectioners' sugar, vanilla and enough orange juice to achieve a drizzling consistency; drizzle over warm loaves. Serve warm or at room temperature.

vanilla glaze *recipe*

Add a sweet finishing touch to coffee cakes, sweet rolls and many other breads with a flavorful Vanilla Glaze. Follow this easy recipe:

For 1/2 cup glaze, combine 1 cup onfectioners' sugar and 1/4 teaspoon vanilla extract in a bowl. Add 1 to 2 tablespoons milk to achieve desired consistency.

Danish Kringle

PREP: 30 min. + rising **BAKE:** 20 min. + cooling
YIELD: 1 kringle

Lorna Jacobsen, Arrowwood, Alberta

This traditional Scandinavian yeast bread has flaky layers of tender dough flavored with almond paste. The unique sugar cookie crumb coating adds the perfect amount of sweetness.

        8 **tablespoons butter, softened, *divided***
  1-1/2 **to 2 cups all-purpose flour, *divided***
        1 **package (1/4 ounce) active dry yeast**
        2 **tablespoons warm water (110° to 115°)**
      1/4 **cup warm half-and-half cream (110° to 115°)**
        2 **tablespoons sugar**
      1/4 **teaspoon salt**
        1 **egg, beaten**
      1/2 **cup almond paste**
        1 **egg white, beaten**
      1/4 **cup sugar cookie crumbs**
        2 **tablespoons sliced almonds**

1 In a small mixing bowl, cream 6 tablespoons butter and 2 tablespoons flour. Spread into an 8-in. x 4-in. rectangle on a piece of waxed paper. Cover with another piece of waxed paper; refrigerate.

2 In a large mixing bowl, dissolve yeast in warm water. Add the cream, sugar, salt and egg; beat until smooth. Stir in enough remaining flour to form a soft dough.

3 Turn onto a floured surface; knead until smooth and elastic, about 6-8 minutes. Do not let rise. Roll into an 8-in. square. Remove top sheet of waxed paper from butter mixture; invert onto center of dough. Peel off waxed paper. Fold plain dough over butter layer; fold widthwise into thirds. Roll into a 12-in. x 6-in. rectangle. Fold into thirds. Repeat rolling and folding twice. Wrap in waxed paper; refrigerate for 30 minutes.

4 On a lightly floured surface, roll dough into a 24-in. x 5-in. rectangle. In a small mixing bowl, beat almond paste and remaining butter until smooth. Spread lengthwise down the center of dough. Fold dough over filling to cover; pinch seam to seal. Place on a greased baking sheet. Shape into a pretzel. Flatten lightly with a rolling pin. Cover and let rise in a warm place until doubled, about 1 hour.

5 Brush egg white over dough. Sprinkle with cookie crumbs and almonds. Bake at 350° for 20-25 minutes or until golden brown. Carefully remove from pan to a wire rack to cool.

DANISH KRINGLE

Cinnamon Raisin Bread

PREP: 40 min. + rising **BAKE:** 30 min. + cooling
YIELD: 2 loaves

Joan Hutter, Warnick, Rhode Island

Two kinds of raisins are swirled into each slice of this heavenly bread. Use leftovers to make French toast.

        2 **packages (1/4 ounce *each*) active dry yeast**
      1/3 **cup warm water (110° to 115°)**
        1 **cup warm milk (110° to 115°)**
      1/2 **cup sugar**
        6 **tablespoons butter, softened**
        2 **eggs, lightly beaten**
  1-1/4 **teaspoons salt**
  5-1/2 **to 6 cups all-purpose flour**
FILLING:
  1-1/3 **cups raisins**
  1-1/3 **cups golden raisins**
        1 **cup water**

6 Bake at 350° for 35-40 minutes or until bread sounds hollow when tapped. Cover loosely with foil if top browns too quickly. Remove from pans to cool on a wire rack.

Apricot Cheese Danish

PREP: 25 min. **BAKE:** 20 min. + cooling
YIELD: 2 loaves

Florence Schafer, Jackson, Minnesota

It's easy to offer your family a fresh-from-the-oven morning treat with this recipe. You mix it up at night, then just roll it out and bake the next morning.

1	package (1/4 ounce) active dry yeast
1/4	cup warm water (110° to 115°)
3	tablespoons sugar
1/2	cup butter, softened
2	eggs
1/2	cup sour cream
1/4	teaspoon salt
3	cups all-purpose flour

FILLING:

2	packages (8 ounces *each*) cream cheese, softened
1/2	cup sugar
2	egg yolks
2	teaspoons vanilla extract
1/4	cup apricot preserves

Confectioners' sugar

1 In a large mixing bowl, dissolve yeast in warm water. Add the sugar, butter, eggs and sour cream. Gradually add salt and 2 cups flour; beat until smooth. Stir in all of the remaining flour (dough will be soft and sticky). Place in a greased bowl. Cover and refrigerate overnight.

2 Punch dough down. Turn onto a lightly floured surface; knead 2-3 times. Divide in half. Roll each portion into a 16-in. x 10-in. oval; place on greased baking sheets.

3 For filling, combine the cream cheese, sugar, egg yolks and vanilla in a large mixing bowl; beat until smooth. Spread 1-1/4 cups filling over each oval to within 1 in. of edges. Fold longest side over filling; pinch edges to seal. Cover and let rise in a warm place until doubled, about 1 hour.

4 Bake at 375° for 20-22 minutes or until golden brown. Remove from pans to wire racks to cool. Spread preserves on top. Dust with confectioners' sugar. Store in the refrigerator.

CINNAMON RAISIN BREAD

1/3	cup apple juice *or* cider
1	tablespoon ground cinnamon
1	egg, beaten

1 In a large mixing bowl, dissolve yeast in warm water. Add the milk, sugar, butter, eggs, salt and 2 cups flour; beat on medium speed for 2 minutes. Stir in enough remaining flour to form a soft dough.

2 Turn onto a floured surface; knead until smooth and elastic, about 6-8 minutes. Place in a greased bowl, turning once to grease top. Cover and let rise in a warm place until doubled, about 1 hour.

3 In a large saucepan, bring the first five filling ingredients to a boil. Reduce heat to medium; cook for 15-20 minutes until almost all of the liquid is absorbed, stirring occasionally. Remove from the heat; set aside.

4 Punch dough down. Turn onto a lightly floured surface; knead for 1 minute. Divide in half. Roll each portion into a 12-in. x 8-in. rectangle; brush with egg. Spread half of the filling over each rectangle to within 1/2 in. of edges.

5 Roll up jelly-roll style, starting with a short side; pinch to seal. Place each loaf seam side down in a greased 9-in. x 5-in. x 3-in. loaf pan. Cover and let rise until doubled, about 1 hour.

Maple Nut Coffee Cake

PREP: 35 min. + rising **BAKE:** 20 min. + cooling
YIELD: 1 coffee cake

Rosadene Herold, Lakeville, Indiana

This flower-shaped coffee cake is actually quite easy to make. The impressive presentation makes it great to serve guests.

    1   **package (16 ounces) hot roll mix**
    3   **tablespoons sugar**
  3/4   **cup warm water (120° to 130°)**
    1   **egg**
    1   **teaspoon maple flavoring**
  1/2   **cup butter, melted, *divided***
FILLING:
  1/2   **cup sugar**
    1   **teaspoon ground cinnamon**
  1/2   **teaspoon maple flavoring**
  1/3   **cup chopped walnuts**
GLAZE:
 1-1/2 **cups confectioners' sugar**
  1/4   **teaspoon maple flavoring**
    1   **to 2 tablespoons milk**

1 In a large bowl, combine contents of hot roll mix and sugar. Stir in the water, egg, maple flavoring and 6 tablespoons butter; mix well.

2 Turn onto a floured surface; knead until smooth and elastic, about 2-3 minutes. Place in a greased bowl, turning once to grease top. Cover and let rise in a warm place until doubled, about 45-60 minutes.

3 Punch dough down. Turn onto a lightly floured surface; divide into thirds. Roll one portion into a 12-in. circle; transfer to a greased 12-in. pizza pan. Brush with some of the remaining butter. Combine sugar, cinnamon and maple flavoring; add nuts. Sprinkle a third of the filling over butter. Roll out second portion of dough into a 12-in. circle; place over filling. Brush with butter; sprinkle with a third of the remaining filling. Repeat with remaining dough, butter and filling.

4 Pinch dough around outer edge to seal. Place a small glass in center. Cut from outside edge just to the glass, forming 16 wedges. Remove the glass. Twist each wedge five to six times. Tuck edge under. Cover and let rise until doubled, about 30-45 minutes.

5 Bake at 375° for 20-25 minutes or until golden brown. Remove from pan to a wire rack to cool. Combine glaze ingredients; drizzle over warm coffee cake.

making a
flower-shaped
coffee cake

1. Divide dough into thirds and roll each piece into a 12-in. circle. Place one on prepared pan. Brush with a third of the butter. Sprinkle with a third of the filling. Repeat layers.

2. Pinch around edges to seal. Carefully place a glass in center of circle. With scissors, cut from outside edge just to the glass, forming 16 wedges.

3. Remove glass; twist each wedge five to six times. Tuck edges under.

1-1/2 teaspoons salt
   1 egg
6-1/2 to 7 cups all-purpose flour
Additional water
   2 teaspoons ground cinnamon
GLAZE:
   1 cup confectioners' sugar
   2 tablespoons orange juice

1 In a large mixing bowl, dissolve yeast in warm water. In a saucepan, heat milk and orange juice to 110°; add to yeast mixture. Stir in 1/2 cup sugar, orange peel, salt, egg and 3 cups flour; beat until smooth. Stir in enough remaining flour to form a soft dough.

2 Turn onto a floured surface; knead until smooth and elastic, about 6-8 minutes. Place in a greased bowl, turning once to grease top. Cover and let rise in a warm place until doubled, about 1 hour.

3 Punch dough down. Turn onto a lightly floured surface; divide in half. Roll each portion into a 15-in. x 7-in. rectangle. Brush with water. Combine cinnamon and remaining sugar; sprinkle over dough to within 1 in. of edges.

4 Tightly roll up jelly-roll style, starting with a short side; pinch seams to seal. Place seam side down in two greased 9-in. x 5-in. x 3-in. loaf pans. Cover and let rise until doubled, about 1 hour.

5 Bake at 350° for 35-40 minutes or until golden brown. Remove from pans to wire racks to cool. Combine glaze ingredients; drizzle over bread.

ORANGE CINNAMON BREAD

Orange Cinnamon Bread

PREP: 35 min. + rising **BAKE:** 35 min. + cooling
YIELD: 2 loaves

Cindy Anderson, Delhi, New York

This citrusy cinnamon bread is a hit with anyone who has a sweet tooth. You can also make a loaf that's terrific for toasting by eliminating the glaze.

   2 packages (1/4 ounce *each*) active dry yeast
1/4 cup warm water (110° to 115°)
   1 cup milk
3/4 cup orange juice
   1 cup sugar, *divided*
   1 tablespoon grated orange peel

Chocolate Marble Bread

PREP: 45 min. + rising **BAKE:** 40 min. + cooling
YIELD: 1 loaf

Rosina Sacks, Copley, Pennsylvania

This is just the recipe for folks who think chocolate should be served at every meal! It will be the highlight of your breakfasts and brunches.

    7   to 7-1/2 cups all-purpose flour
    1/2 cup sugar
    1   package (1/4 ounce) active dry yeast
    1   teaspoon salt
    2   cups milk
    1/4 cup butter
    2   eggs
    1/4 cup baking cocoa
GLAZE:
    1   cup confectioners' sugar
    1   tablespoon milk
    1/4 cup chopped walnuts

1 In a large mixing bowl, combine 3 cups flour, sugar, yeast and salt. In a saucepan, heat milk and butter to 120°-130°. Add to dry ingredients; beat until moistened. Add eggs; beat on low speed for 30 seconds. Beat on high for 3 minutes. Stir in enough remaining flour to form a soft dough.

2 Turn onto a floured surface; knead until smooth and elastic, about 6-8 minutes. Divide dough into thirds. Knead cocoa into one portion of dough (this may take 5-6 minutes). Shape into a ball. Shape remaining portions of dough into one ball. Place each ball in a lightly greased bowl, turning once to grease top. Cover and let rise in a warm place until doubled, about 1-1/4 hours.

CHOCOLATE MARBLE BREAD

3 Punch dough down. Turn onto a lightly floured surface; cover and let rest for 10 minutes. Roll chocolate dough into a 20-in. x 10-in. rectangle; repeat with plain dough. Place chocolate layer on top of plain layer.

4 Roll up jelly-roll style, starting with a long side; pinch seam to seal. Cut into 20 slices; place in a greased 10-in. tube pan in about three layers. Cover and let rise until nearly doubled, about 30-40 minutes.

5 Bake at 350° for 40-45 minutes or until lightly browned. Immediately remove from pan to a wire rack to cool. For the glaze, combine confectioners' sugar and milk; drizzle over bread. Sprinkle with walnuts.

Plum Coffee Loaf

PREP: 30 min. + rising **BAKE:** 20 min. + cooling
YIELD: 1 loaf

Janet Snider, Kalamazoo, Michigan

A simple-to-make filling and hot roll mix make it easy to whip up this delicious bread on a moment's notice. People are pleasantly surprised to see plum in the filling instead of the more traditional apple or cherry.

    1   package (16 ounces) hot roll mix
    2   tablespoons butter, melted
    1   can (30 ounces) purple plums, drained, halved and pitted
    1/4 cup sugar
    1/4 teaspoon ground cinnamon
    1/8 teaspoon ground cloves
GLAZE:
    1   cup confectioners' sugar
    1/4 teaspoon almond extract
    1   to 2 tablespoons milk
    1/3 cup slivered almonds

1 Prepare hot roll mix and knead dough according to package directions. Place in a greased bowl, turning once to grease top. Cover and let rise in a warm place until doubled, about 30 minutes.

2 Punch dough down. Turn onto a lightly floured surface; roll into a 15-in. x 10-in. rectangle. Brush with butter. Place plums cut side down lengthwise down the center third of rectangle. Combine the sugar, cinnamon and cloves; sprinkle over plums.

3 Fold both long sides of dough over filling; pinch seam to seal and tuck ends under. Place a baking sheet on work surface next to the loaf. Carefully slide loaf onto baking sheet. With a sharp knife, make slashes 1 in. apart across top of loaf. Cover and let rise until doubled, about 30 minutes.

4 Bake at 350° for 20-25 minutes or until golden brown. Remove from pan to a wire rack. For glaze, combine confectioners' sugar, almond extract and milk; drizzle over warm loaf. Sprinkle with almonds. Cool. Store in the refrigerator.

RASPBERRY COFFEE CAKE

Apple Pull-Apart Bread

PREP: 40 min. + rising **BAKE:** 35 min. + cooling
YIELD: 1 loaf

Carolyn Gregory, Hendersonville, Tennessee

Drizzled with icing, each finger-licking "piece" of this bread has a yummy filling of apples and pecans. It's well worth the bit of extra effort.

- 1 **package (1/4 ounce) active dry yeast**
- 1 **cup warm milk (110° to 115°)**
- 1/2 **cup butter, melted, *divided***
- 1 **egg**
- 2/3 **cup plus 2 tablespoons sugar, *divided***
- 1 **teaspoon salt**
- 3 **to 3-1/2 cups all-purpose flour**
- 1 **medium tart apple, peeled and chopped**
- 1/2 **cup finely chopped pecans**
- 1/2 **teaspoon ground cinnamon**

ICING:
- 1 **cup confectioners' sugar**
- 1/2 **teaspoon vanilla extract**
- 3 **to 4-1/2 teaspoons hot water**

1 In a large mixing bowl, dissolve the yeast in warm milk. Add 2 tablespoons butter, egg, 2 tablespoons sugar, salt and 3 cups flour; beat until smooth. Stir in enough remaining flour to form a stiff dough.

2 Turn onto a floured surface; knead until smooth and elastic, about 6-8 minutes. Place in a greased bowl, turning once to grease top. Cover and let rise in a warm place until doubled, about 1 hour.

3 Punch dough down. Turn onto a lightly floured surface; divide in half. Cut each portion into 16 pieces. Pat or roll each piece into a 2-1/2-in. circle. Combine the apple, pecans, cinnamon and remaining sugar; place 1 teaspoonful in the center of each circle. Pinch edges together and seal, forming a ball. Dip in remaining butter.

4 In a greased 10-in. tube pan, place 16 balls seam side down; sprinkle with 1/4 cup apple mixture. Layer with remaining balls; sprinkle evenly with

remaining apple mixture. Cover and let rise until nearly doubled, about 45 minutes.

5 Bake at 350° for 35-40 minutes or until golden brown. Cool for 10 minutes before removing from pan to a wire rack to cool completely. Combine icing ingredients; drizzle over bread.

Raspberry Coffee Cake

PREP: 20 min. **BAKE:** 25 min. + cooling
YIELD: 1 coffee cake

Lisa Schulz, Madison, Wisconsin

This fresh and fruity coffee cake looks elegant but is so simple to make, thanks to frozen bread dough.

- 1 **loaf (1 pound) frozen bread *or* sweet bread dough, thawed**
- 1 **pint fresh raspberries**
- 1/2 **cup all-purpose flour**
- 1/4 **cup sugar**
- 1/4 **cup cold butter**
- 1/8 **teaspoon vanilla extract**

GLAZE:
- 1/2 **cup confectioners' sugar**
- 3 **to 4 teaspoons milk**

1 On a lightly floured surface, roll dough into a 14-in. circle. Transfer to a greased 14-in. pizza pan. Build up edges slightly. Bake at 350° for 5 minutes. Sprinkle with raspberries. In a small bowl, combine flour and sugar; cut in butter and vanilla until mixture is crumbly. Sprinkle over berries.

2 Bake at 350° for 25-30 minutes or until golden. Cool on a wire rack. Combine glaze ingredients; drizzle over coffee cake. Store in the refrigerator.

Sally Lunn Batter Bread

PREP: 15 min. + rising **BAKE:** 25 min. + cooling
YIELD: 12-16 servings

Jeanne Voss, Anaheim Hills, California

The tantalizing aroma of this golden loaf baking will draw people into your kitchen. Once they see it's pretty, circular shape, it won't last long.

- 1 package (1/4 ounce) active dry yeast
- 1/2 cup warm water (110° to 115°)
- 1 cup warm milk (110° to 115°)
- 1/2 cup butter, softened
- 1/4 cup sugar
- 2 teaspoons salt
- 3 eggs
- 5-1/2 to 6 cups all-purpose flour

HONEY BUTTER:
- 1/2 cup butter, softened
- 1/2 cup honey

1 In a large mixing bowl, dissolve yeast in warm water. Add the milk, butter, sugar, salt, eggs and 3 cups flour; beat until smooth. Stir in enough remaining flour to form a soft dough. Do not knead. Place in a greased bowl, turning once to grease the top. Cover and let rise in a warm place until doubled, about 1 hour.

2 Stir the dough down. Spoon into a greased and floured 10-in. tube pan. Cover and let rise until doubled, about 1 hour.

3 Bake at 400° for 25-30 minutes or until golden brown. Remove from pan to a wire rack to cool.

4 Combine the honey butter ingredients until smooth. Serve with bread.

Peach Flip

PREP: 30 min. + rising **BAKE:** 20 min. + cooling
YIELD: 2 loaves

Helen Millhouse, Piqua, Ohio

This recipe is a little less time-consuming than most because the dough only needs to rise once.

- 2 packages (1/4 ounce *each*) active dry yeast
- 1/2 cup warm water (110° to 115°)
- 1/2 cup plus 2/3 cup sugar, *divided*
- 3/4 cup butter, softened, *divided*
- 1/2 cup warm milk (110° to 115°)
- 2 teaspoons salt
- 3 eggs
- 5 to 5-1/2 cups all-purpose flour
- 1 cup peach preserves
- 1 cup chopped pecans
- 2 teaspoons ground cinnamon

1 In a large mixing bowl, dissolve yeast in warm water. Add 1/2 cup sugar, 1/2 cup butter, milk, salt, eggs and 2-1/2 cups flour; beat until smooth. Stir in enough remaining flour to form a stiff dough.

2 Turn onto a floured surface; knead until smooth and elastic, about 6-8 minutes. Place in a greased bowl, turning once to grease top. Cover and let rise in a warm place until doubled, about 1-1/4 hours.

3 Punch dough down. Turn onto a lightly floured surface; divide in half. Roll each portion into a 21-in. x 13-in. rectangle. Spread each with the remaining butter to within 1/2 in. of edges. Spread 1/4 cup preserves over butter. Combine the pecans, cinnamon and remaining sugar; sprinkle over preserves.

4 Roll up jelly-roll style, starting with a long side; pinch seam to seal. Place seam side down on greased baking sheets; curve to form a crescent shape. With a sharp knife, make a lengthwise slash a third of the way through the center to within 2 in. of each end. Spoon 1/4 cup preserves into each roll.

5 Bake at 350° for 25-30 minutes or until golden brown. Remove from pans to wire racks to cool. Store in the refrigerator.

Apricot Braids

PREP: 1 hour + rising **BAKE:** 20 min. + cooling
YIELD: 3 braids

Paula Wipf, Arlington, Virginia

These lovely yeast braids are light and tender and have a delightful apricot filling.

2-1/4 **cups chopped dried apricots**
1-1/2 **cups water, *divided***
1-1/2 **cups packed brown sugar**
5-1/2 **to 6 cups all-purpose flour**
3/4 **cup sugar**
3 **packages (1/4 ounce *each*) active dry yeast**
1 **teaspoon salt**
1/2 **cup butter, softened**
3 **eggs, beaten**
Vanilla Glaze (page 393)

1 In a saucepan, bring apricots and 1/2 cup water to a boil. Reduce heat; cover and simmer until water is absorbed and fruit is tender, about 20 minutes. Cool slightly. Transfer to a food processor; add brown sugar. Cover and process until smooth.

2 In a mixing bowl, combine 2 cups of flour, sugar, yeast and salt. In a saucepan, heat butter and remaining water to 120°-130°. Add to the dry ingredients; beat just until moistened. Add eggs; beat until smooth. Stir in enough remaining flour to form a soft dough.

3 Turn onto a floured surface; knead until smooth and elastic, about 6-8 minutes. Place in a greased bowl, turning once to grease top. Cover and let rise in a warm place until doubled, about 40-45 minutes.

4 Punch dough down; divide into thirds. On greased baking sheets, roll out each portion into a 12-in. x 8-in. rectangle. Spread filling down the center of each rectangle. On each long side, cut 1-in.-wide strips about 2 in. into center. Starting at one end, fold alternating strips at an angle across filling. Pinch ends to seal. Cover and let rise for 30 minutes.

5 Bake at 375° for 20-25 minutes or until golden brown. Remove from pans to wire racks to cool. Drizzle with Vanilla Glaze.

Cherry Kringle

PREP: 30 min. + chilling **BAKE:** 25 min. + cooling
YIELD: 4 loaves

Mary Christianson, Carmel, Indiana

The soft dough in this recipe is so easy to work with. It bakes into a golden tender pastry that surrounds a luscious cherry center. The loaves freeze well, too.

1 **package (1/4 ounce) active dry yeast**
1 **cup warm milk (110° to 115°)**
4 **cups bread flour**
2 **tablespoons sugar**
1 **teaspoon salt**
1/2 **cup cold butter**
1/2 **cup shortening**
2 **eggs, lightly beaten**
4 **cups cherry pie filling**
ICING:
2 **cups confectioners' sugar**
2 **to 3 tablespoons milk**

1 In a large mixing bowl, dissolve yeast in warm milk. In another bowl, combine the flour, sugar and salt; cut in butter and shortening until crumbly. Add to yeast mixture. Add eggs; beat to form a very soft dough (do not knead). Cover and refrigerate for at least 8 hours.

2 Turn onto a lightly floured surface; divide into fourths. Roll each portion into a 14-in. x 11-in. rectangle; spread cherry pie filling down the center third of each rectangle. Starting at a long side, fold a third of the dough over filling. Fold other third over top; pinch to seal. Pinch ends and tuck under. Place 2 in. apart on greased baking sheets.

3 Bake at 350° for 25 minutes or until golden brown. Remove from pans to wire racks to cool completely. Combine icing ingredients; drizzle over kringles.

CHERRY KRINGLE

Cherry Almond Wreath

PREP: 30 min. + rising **BAKE:** 35 min. + cooling
YIELD: 20 servings

Gwen Roffler, Grassy Butte, North Dakota

For gift-giving at the holidays, try this recipe. It's flavorful and gorgeous.

       1 **package (1/4 ounce) active dry yeast**
    1/2 **cup warm milk (110° to 115°)**
    1/4 **cup warm water (110° to 115°)**
    1/4 **cup butter, softened**
       3 **tablespoons sugar**
  1-1/2 **teaspoons salt**
       1 **teaspoon grated lemon peel**
    1/2 **teaspoon ground cardamom**
       2 **eggs**
       3 **to 4-1/2 cups all-purpose flour**
FILLING:
    1/4 **cup butter, softened**
    1/4 **cup all-purpose flour**
       2 **tablespoons sugar**
       1 **teaspoon almond extract**
    1/2 **teaspoon grated lemon peel**
    2/3 **cup finely chopped blanched almonds**
    1/2 **cup chopped red and green candied cherries**
GLAZE:
    2/3 **cup confectioners' sugar**
       2 **teaspoons lemon juice**
       1 **teaspoon water**

1 In a large mixing bowl, dissolve yeast in warm milk and water. Add the butter, sugar, salt, lemon peel, cardamom, eggs and 2 cups flour; beat until smooth. Stir in enough remaining flour to form a soft dough.

2 Turn onto a floured surface; knead until smooth and elastic, about 6 to 8 minutes. Place in a greased bowl, turning once to grease top. Cover and let rise in a warm place until doubled, about 1-1/2 hours.

3 In a small mixing bowl, beat butter, flour, sugar, almond extract and lemon peel. Stir in almonds and cherries. Refrigerate.

4 Punch dough down. Turn on a lightly floured surface. Roll into a 30-in. x 9-in. rectangle. Crumble filling over rectangle to within 1/2 in. of edges.

5 Roll up jelly-roll style, starting with a long side; pinch seam to seal. Place seam side down on a greased baking sheet. With a scissors, cut lengthwise down the middle of the roll; carefully turn cut sides up. Loosely twist strips around each other, keeping cut sides up. Shape into a ring and pinch ends together. Cover and let rise for 1 hour.

6 Bake at 350° for 35-40 minutes or until browned. cool for 15 minutes on a wire rack. Combine glaze ingredients; drizzle over warm coffee cake. Cool completely.

CHERRY ALMOND WREATH

Hawaiian Sweet Bread

PREP: 20 min. + rising **BAKE:** 20 min. + cooling
YIELD: 3 loaves

Ruthie Banks, Pryor, Oklahoma

Pineapple juice lends to the slightly sweet flavor of this delicious bread. The recipe makes three loaves, so you can keep one and give two away.

- 7 to 7-1/2 cups all-purpose flour
- 3/4 cup mashed potato flakes
- 2/3 cup sugar
- 2 packages (1/4 ounce *each*) active dry yeast
- 1 teaspoon salt
- 1/2 teaspoon ground ginger
- 1 cup milk
- 1/2 cup water
- 1/2 cup butter, softened
- 1 cup pineapple juice
- 3 eggs
- 2 teaspoons vanilla extract

1 In a large mixing bowl, combine 3 cups flour, potato flakes, sugar, yeast, salt and ginger. In a saucepan, heat the milk, water, butter and pineapple juice to 120°-130°. Add to dry ingredients; beat just until moistened. Beat in eggs until smooth. Beat in vanilla. Stir in enough remaining flour to form a soft dough.

2 Turn onto a floured surface; knead until smooth and elastic, about 6-8 minutes. Place in a greased bowl, turning once to grease top. Cover and let rise in a warm place until doubled, about 1-1/4 hours.

3 Punch dough down. Turn onto a lightly floured surface; divide into thirds. Shape each into a ball. Place in three greased 9-in. round baking pans. Cover; let rise until doubled, about 45 minutes.

4 Bake at 375° for 20-25 minutes or until golden brown. Cover loosely with foil if top browns too quickly. Remove from pans to wire racks to cool.

Walnut Cream Braids

PREP: 30 min. + rising **BAKE:** 15 min. + cooling
YIELD: 2 loaves

Jean Erickson, North Pole, Alaska

A nutty cheese filling is tucked inside each bite of these pretty braided breads.

- 1 package (1/4 ounce) active dry yeast
- 1/4 cup warm water (110° to 115°)
- 1/2 cup butter, softened

shaping *a pan bread*

To easily shape a round loaf of bread, place ball of dough in a greased 9-in. round baking pan. Flatten into a 6- or 7-in. circle.

- 2 tablespoons sugar
- 1/2 teaspoon salt
- 1 egg
- 2 to 2-1/2 cups all-purpose flour

FILLING:
- 2 packages (3 ounces *each*) cream cheese, softened
- 3/4 cup sugar
- 1/2 cup finely chopped walnuts

Confectioners' sugar, optional

1 In a large mixing bowl, dissolve yeast in warm water. Add the butter, sugar, salt, egg and 1-1/2 cups flour; beat on low speed for 3 minutes. Stir in enough remaining flour to form a soft dough.

2 Turn onto a floured surface; knead until smooth and elastic, about 6-8 minutes. Place in a greased bowl, turning once to grease top. Cover and let rise in a warm place until doubled, about 1 hour. Meanwhile, in a small mixing bowl, beat the cream cheese and sugar; set aside.

3 Punch dough down. Turn onto a lightly floured surface; divide in half. Roll each portion into a 12-in. x 8-in. rectangle; place on greased baking sheets. Spread half of the cream cheese mixture down the center third of each rectangle. Sprinkle with walnuts.

4 On each long side, cut 1-in. wide strips about 2-1/2 in. into center. Starting at one end, fold alternating strips at an angle across filling; seal ends. Cover and let rise for 30 minutes.

5 Bake at 375° for 15-20 minutes or until browned. Cool on wire racks. Dust with confectioners' sugar if desired. Store in the refrigerator.

POTECA NUT ROLL

Poteca Nut Roll

PREP: 30 min. + rising **BAKE:** 35 min. + cooling
YIELD: 1 coffee cake

Mrs. Anthony Setta
Saegertown, Pennsylvania

You'll need a large surface to roll out the dough for this traditional Yugoslavian treat.

- 1 package (1/4 ounce) active dry yeast
- 1/4 cup warm water (110° to 115°)
- 3/4 cup warm milk (110° to 115°)
- 1/4 cup sugar
- 1 teaspoon salt
- 1 egg, lightly beaten
- 1/4 cup shortening
- 3 to 3-1/2 cups all-purpose flour

FILLING:
- 1/2 cup butter, softened
- 1 cup packed brown sugar
- 2 eggs, lightly beaten
- 1 teaspoon vanilla extract
- 1 teaspoon lemon extract, optional
- 4 cups ground *or* finely chopped walnuts

Confectioners' sugar icing, optional

1 In a large mixing bowl, dissolve yeast in warm water. Add the milk, sugar, salt, egg, shortening, and 1-1/2 cups flour; beat until smooth. Stir in enough remaining flour to form a soft dough.

2 Turn onto a floured surface; knead until smooth and elastic, about 6-8 minutes. Place in a greased bowl, turning once to grease top. Cover and let rise in a warm place until doubled, about 1 hour.

3 Punch down. Turn onto a lightly floured surface; roll into a 30-in. x 20-in. rectangle. In a bowl, combine the butter, brown sugar, eggs, vanilla, lemon extract if desired and nuts. Add milk until mixture reaches spreading consistency, about 1/2 cup. Spread over rectangle to within 1 in. of edges.

4 Roll up jelly-roll style, starting with a long side; pinch seams and ends to seal. Place on a greased baking sheet; shape into a tight spiral. Cover and let rise until nearly doubled, about 1 hour.

5 Bake at 350° for 35 minutes or until golden brown. Remove from pan to a wire rack to cool. If desired, combine confectioners' sugar and enough milk to make a thin glaze; brush over roll.

Cinnamon-Apricot Daisy Ring

PREP: 30 min. + rising **BAKE:** 15 min. + cooling
YIELD: 1 ring loaf

Sherri Rush, Converse, Indiana

"Just stunning" is how people describe the look of this apricot-filled coffee cake.

- 3-1/2 cups all-purpose flour
- 2 tablespoons sugar
- 1 package (1/4 ounce) active dry yeast
- 1 teaspoon salt
- 3/4 cup milk
- 1/4 cup butter
- 2 eggs

FILLING:
- 2 tablespoons butter, melted
- 1/4 cup sugar
- 2 teaspoons ground cinnamon
- 1 egg yolk
- 2 tablespoons water
- 1/2 cup apricot preserves

Vanilla Glaze (page 393)
Slivered almonds, toasted

1 In a large mixing bowl, combine 1-1/2 cups flour, sugar, yeast and salt. In a saucepan, heat milk and butter to 120°-130°. Add to dry ingredients; beat until moistened. Add eggs; beat on low speed for 30 seconds. Beat on high for 3 minutes. Stir in remaining flour; beat well.

2 Turn onto a floured surface; knead until smooth and elastic, about 6-8 minutes. Place in a greased bowl, turning once to grease top. Cover and let rise in a warm place until doubled, about 1 hour.

3 Punch dough down. On a lightly floured surface, roll into a 16-in. circle; place on a greased baking sheet (circle will be larger than the baking sheet). Place a glass in the center of dough. Brush dough with melted butter. Combine the sugar and cinnamon; sprinkle over butter. Cut from the glass to the outside edge, forming 16 wedges. Remove glass.

4 Place one slice over the top of the next slice, cinnamon-sugar sides together; pinch edges to seal. Continue around circle until there are eight strips. Twist each strip four to five times. Loop to the center to make daisy petals. Cut off one roll to place in the center. Cover and let rise until doubled, about 1 hour.

5 Beat egg yolk and water; brush over ring. Bake at 375° for 15-20 minutes. Remove from pan to a wire rack to cool. Top with preserves. Drizzle with Vanilla Glaze. Sprinkle with almonds.

Cream Cheese Coffee Cake

PREP: 35 min. + rising **BAKE:** 20 min. + cooling
YIELD: 20-24 servings

Mary Anne McWhirter, Pearland, Texas

These impressive loaves really sparkle on the buffet. You can't just eat one slice of this treat.

 1 cup (8 ounces) sour cream
1/2 cup sugar
1/2 cup butter
 1 teaspoon salt
 2 packages (1/4 ounce *each*) active dry yeast
1/2 cup warm water (110° to 115°)
 2 eggs, beaten
 4 cups all-purpose flour
FILLING:
 2 packages (8 ounces *each*) cream cheese, softened
3/4 cup sugar
 1 egg, beaten
 2 teaspoons vanilla extract
1/8 teaspoon salt
GLAZE:
2-1/2 cups confectioners' sugar
1/4 cup milk
 1 teaspoon vanilla extract
Toasted sliced almonds, optional

1 In a saucepan, combine the sour cream, sugar, butter and salt. Cook over medium-low heat, stirring constantly, for 5-10 minutes or until well blended. Cool to room temperature.

2 In a large mixing bowl, dissolve yeast in warm water. Add sour cream mixture and eggs; mix well. Gradually stir in flour (dough will be very soft). Cover and refrigerate overnight.

3 Punch dough down. Turn onto a floured surface; knead 5-6 times. Divide into fourths. Roll each piece into a 12-in. x 8-in. rectangle. In a large mixing bowl, combine the filling ingredients until well blended. Spread over each rectangle to within 1 in. of edges.

4 Roll up jelly-roll style, starting with a long side; pinch seams and ends to seal. Place seam side down on greased baking sheets. Cut six X's on top of loaves. Cover and let rise until nearly doubled, about 1 hour.

5 Bake at 375° for 20-25 minutes or until golden brown. Remove from pans to wire racks to cool. In a small bowl, combine the confectioners' sugar, milk and vanilla; drizzle over loaves. Sprinkle with almonds if desired. Store in the refrigerator.

CREAM CHEESE COFFEE CAKE

ALMOND RING COFFEE CAKE

until moistened. Add egg; beat for 3 minutes. Stir in enough remaining flour to form a soft dough.

2 Turn onto floured surface; knead until smooth and elastic, about 4-6 minutes. Place in a greased bowl, turning once to grease top. Cover and let rise in a warm place until doubled, about 1 hour.

3 Punch dough down. Turn on a lightly floured surface; roll into an 18-in. x 12-in. rectangle. In a small mixing bowl, beat filling ingredients until smooth. Spread over dough to within 1 in. of edges.

4 Roll up jelly-roll style, starting with a long side; pinch seam to seal. Place on a greased baking sheet, sealing ends to form a ring. Cover and let rise until doubled, about 30 minutes.

5 Bake at 375° for 20-25 minutes or until golden. Remove from pan to a wire rack to cool. In a small mixing bowl, combine milk and almond extract; whisk in confectioners' sugar until smooth. Drizzle over coffee cake. Sprinkle with almonds if desired.

Almond Ring Coffee Cake

PREP: 35 min. + rising **BAKE:** 20 min. + cooling
YIELD: 8-10 servings

Vie Spence, Woburn, Massachusetts

The coffee cake gets a delicate almond flavor from the extract in the filling and the glaze.

3-1/2 to 3-3/4 cups all-purpose flour, *divided*
  1 package (1/4 ounce) active dry yeast
  1 cup milk
1/3 cup butter
1/3 cup sugar
1/2 teaspoon salt
  1 egg
FILLING:
1/4 cup butter, softened
1/2 cup sugar
1/2 teaspoon almond extract
GLAZE:
  2 to 3 tablespoons milk
  1 teaspoon almond extract
1-3/4 cups confectioners' sugar
Sliced almonds, toasted, optional

1 In a large mixing bowl, combine 2 cups flour and yeast. In a saucepan, heat the milk, butter, sugar and salt to 120°-130°. Add to dry ingredients; beat

Chocolate Coffee Cake

PREP: 35 min. + rising **BAKE:** 45 min. + standing
YIELD: 1 coffee cake

Deborah Keller
Goose Creek, South Carolina

Chocolate and cinnamon combine for a scrumptious filling in this tender coffee cake. For added sweetness, drizzle with Vanilla Glaze (page 393).

  1 package (1/4 ounce) active dry yeast
  1 cup warm water (110° to 115°)
  3 tablespoons butter, softened
  3 tablespoons sugar
  1 egg, beaten
  1 teaspoon salt
  2 tablespoons nonfat dry milk powder
  3 to 3-1/2 cups all-purpose flour
FILLING:
  1 cup (6 ounces) semisweet chocolate chips
1/3 cup evaporated milk
  2 tablespoons sugar
1/2 teaspoon ground cinnamon
TOPPING:
1/4 cup all-purpose flour
1/4 cup sugar
  1 teaspoon ground cinnamon
1/4 cup cold butter

1 In a mixing bowl, dissolve yeast in warm water. Add butter, sugar, egg, salt and milk powder. Add 2 cups flour; beat until smooth. Stir in enough remaining flour to form a soft dough.

2 Turn onto a floured surface; knead until smooth and elastic, about 6-8 minutes. Place in a greased bowl, turning once to grease top. Cover and let rise in a warm place until doubled, about 1 hour.

3 For filling, combine the chocolate chips, milk and sugar in a small saucepan; cook and stir over low heat until smooth. Stir in cinnamon; set aside. For topping, combine the flour, sugar and cinnamon in a small bowl; cut in butter until mixture is crumbly. Set aside.

4 Punch dough down. Turn onto a floured surface; roll into a 20-in. x 10-in. rectangle. Spread with filling. Roll up jelly-roll style, starting with a long side; pinch seam to seal. Place in a well-greased 10-in. fluted tube pan, with seam facing the inside of pan. Sprinkle with topping. Cover and let rise until doubled, about 30 minutes.

5 Bake at 350° for 45-50 minutes or until golden brown. Let stand for 10 minutes before inverting onto a wire rack to cool.

1 In a large mixing bowl, dissolve yeast in warm water. Add the milk, butter, eggs, sugar, salt and 2 cups flour; beat until smooth. Stir in enough remaining flour to form a soft dough.

2 Turn onto a floured surface and knead until smooth and elastic, about 6-8 minutes. Place in a greased bowl, turning once to grease top. Cover and let rise in a warm place until doubled, about 1 hour.

3 Punch dough down. Turn onto a lightly floured surface; divide in half. Roll each portion into a 14-in. x 8-in. rectangle. Combine filling ingredients; spread over each rectangle to within 1/2 in. of edges.

4 Roll up jelly-roll style, starting with a long side; pinch seam to seal. Place seam side down on greased baking sheets. With a sharp knife, cut each roll in half lengthwise; carefully turn cut sides up. Loosely twist strips around each other, keeping cut sides up. Shape into a ring and pinch ends together. Cover and let rise for 30 minutes.

5 Bake at 350° for 25-30 minutes or until browned. Remove from pans to wire racks to cool.

MAPLE BUTTER TWISTS

Maple Butter Twists

PREP: 25 min. + rising **BAKE:** 25 min. + cooling
YIELD: 2 coffee cakes

Marna Krause, Las Vegas, Nevada

If you like the flavor of maple, you'll really enjoy this appealing coffee cake. Brush a Vanilla Glaze (page 393) over warm twists for a little shine.

1	package (1/4 ounce) active dry yeast
1/4	cup warm water (110° to 115°)
1/2	cup warm milk (110° to 115°)
1/4	cup butter, melted
2	eggs, beaten
3	tablespoons sugar
1-1/2	teaspoons salt
3-1/4	to 3-1/2 cups all-purpose flour

FILLING:

1/2	cup packed brown sugar
1/2	cup chopped walnuts
1/3	cup sugar
1/4	cup maple syrup
1/4	cup butter, softened
2	tablespoons all-purpose flour
1/2	teaspoon ground cinnamon
1/2	teaspoon maple flavoring

GERMAN CHOCOLATE RING

3 Punch dough down; turn onto lightly floured surface. Roll dough into 18-in. x 10-in. rectangle. Melt remaining 1 tablespoon butter and brush over dough; spread with reserved chocolate mixture.

4 Roll up dough jelly-roll style, starting with a long side; pinch seam to seal. Place seam side down on greased baking sheet. Pinch ends together to form a ring. With scissors, cut from outside edge to two-thirds of the way toward center of ring at 1-in. intervals. Separate strips slightly; twist to allow filling to show. Cover and let rise until doubled, about 1 hour.

5 Bake at 350° for 20-25 minutes or until golden brown. Sprinkle with remaining chocolate chips; let stand for 5 minutes. Spread melted chips; sprinkle with remaining coconut. Carefully remove from pan to a wire rack to cool.

German Chocolate Ring

PREP: 30 min. + rising **BAKE:** 20 min. + cooling
YIELD: 20-24 servings

Anne Frederick, New Hartford, New York

This sweet-tasting bread is modeled after German sweet chocolate cake. It can be made ahead and stored in the freezer for convenience.

1	cup semisweet chocolate chips, *divided*
1-1/4	cups flaked coconut, *divided*
3/4	cup chopped pecans
3	eggs
4-1/2	to 5 cups all-purpose flour
1/2	cup sugar
1	teaspoon salt
1	package (1/4 ounce) active dry yeast
1	cup milk
5	tablespoons butter, *divided*

1 In bowl, mix 3/4 cup chocolate chips, 1 cup coconut, pecans and 1 egg; set aside. In large mixing bowl, combine 1 cup flour, sugar, salt and yeast. In saucepan, heat milk and 4 tablespoons butter to 120°-130°; add to flour mixture, beating until smooth. Add remaining eggs and enough remaining flour to form a soft dough.

2 Turn onto a lightly floured surface. Knead until smooth and elastic, about 6-8 minutes. Place in greased bowl, turning once to grease top. Cover; let rise in warm place until doubled, about 1 hour.

Braided Date Coffee Cake

PREP: 45 min. + rising **BAKE:** 15 min. + cooling
YIELD: 3 loaves

Muriel Lerdal, Humboldt, Iowa

For a Christmas look, decorate these braids with candied cherries and pecans.

2	packages (1/4 ounce *each*) active dry yeast
1/2	cup warm water (110° to 115°)
1/2	cup sugar
1/2	cup warm milk (110° to 115°)
1/4	cup vegetable oil
1-1/2	teaspoons salt
2	eggs
4	to 4-1/2 cups all-purpose flour

FILLING:

1	cup chopped dates
2/3	cup water
1/2	cup chopped pecans
1/4	cup sugar
1	teaspoon lemon juice
1/2	cup apricot preserves

ICING:

1-1/2	cups confectioners' sugar
3	tablespoons butter, softened
2	tablespoons boiling water
1/2	teaspoon vanilla extract

1 In a large mixing bowl, dissolve yeast in warm water. Add the sugar, milk, oil, salt, eggs and 2 cups flour; beat on low speed 3 minutes. Stir in enough remaining flour to form a soft dough.

2 Turn onto a floured surface; knead until smooth and elastic, 6-8 minutes. Place in a greased bowl, turning once to grease top. Cover and let rise in a warm place until doubled, about 1 hour.

3 Meanwhile, combine the dates, water, pecans, sugar and lemon juice in a saucepan. Cook and stir over medium heat until thickened, 7-8 minutes. Stir in preserves; let cool.

4 Punch dough down. Turn on a lightly floured surface; divide into thirds. Roll each portion into a 15-in. x 6-in. rectangle. Place on greased baking sheets. Spread a third of filling down the center third of each rectangle.

5 On each long side, cut 1-1/2-in. wide strips 1-3/4 in. into center. Starting at one end, fold alternating strips at an angle across filling; seal ends. Cover; let rise until doubled, about 30 minutes.

6 Bake at 375° for 15-20 minutes or until browned. Remove from pans to wire racks to cool. Combine icing ingredients; drizzle over braids.

Martha Washington's Fans

PREP: 40 min. + rising **BAKE:** 20 min. + cooling
YIELD: 3 loaves

Susan Peck, Springfield, Missouri

Guests will be quite impressed with the look of this coffee cake. It's actually easy to make into the fan shape.

> 6 **to 7 cups all-purpose flour,** *divided*
> 1/2 **cup sugar**
> 2 **tablespoons nonfat dry milk powder**
> 2 **packages (1/4 ounce** *each***) active dry yeast**
> 1-1/4 **teaspoons salt**
> 2/3 **cup butter, softened**
> 1-1/4 **cups warm water (120° to 130°)**
> 3 **eggs**
> **FILLING:**
> 6 **tablespoons butter, melted,** *divided*
> 1-1/2 **cups flaked coconut**
> 1 **cup chopped pecans**
> 1/2 **cup packed brown sugar**
> **ICING:**
> 1 **cup confectioners' sugar**
> 2 **to 3 tablespoons milk**

1 In a large mixing bowl, combine 2 cups flour, sugar, dry milk, yeast and salt. Add butter and water; beat on low for 2 minutes. Add eggs; beat on high for 2 minutes. Stir in enough remaining flour to form a soft dough.

2 Turn onto a floured surface; knead until smooth and elastic, 6-8 minutes. Place in a greased bowl, turning once to grease top. Cover and let rise in a warm place until doubled, about 1 hour.

3 Turn onto a lightly floured surface; divide into thirds. Roll one portion into a 20-in. x 6-in. rectangle, with a short side facing you. Brush top two-thirds of dough with 1 tablespoon melted butter. In a bowl, combine the coconut, pecans and brown sugar; blend in 3 tablespoons butter. Sprinkle a third of the mixture over buttered portion of dough. Starting at the plain short side, fold dough over half of filling; fold over again. Pinch edges and end to seal.

4 Place on a greased baking sheet with folded edge facing away from you. With scissors, cut into eight strips to within 1 in. from folded edge. Separate strips slightly; twist to allow filling to show. Pinch ends into points. Repeat with remaining dough and filling to make two more fans. Cover and let rise until doubled, about 45 minutes.

5 Bake at 350° for 20-25 minutes. Remove from pans to wire racks to cool. Combine icing ingredients; drizzle over fans.

MARTHA WASHINGTON'S FANS

Sweet Rolls

Sticky Buns

PREP: 30 min. + rising **BAKE:** 20 min. + cooling
YIELD: 1 dozen

Dorothy Showalter, Broadway, Virginia

It's impossible to eat just one of these soft, yummy sticky buns—they have wonderful old-fashioned goodness.

STICKY BUNS

  2 teaspoons active dry yeast
1-1/4 cups warm water (110° to 115°)
  3 tablespoons butter, softened
  3 tablespoons sugar
  2 tablespoons nonfat dry milk powder
  1 teaspoon salt
  3 to 3-1/4 cups bread flour

FILLING:
1/3 cup butter, softened
  1 tablespoon sugar
  1 teaspoon ground cinnamon

SAUCE:
1/2 cup packed brown sugar
1/4 cup butter
1/4 cup corn syrup
1/2 cup chopped pecans

1 In a large mixing bowl, dissolve yeast in warm water. Add the butter, sugar, milk powder, salt and 2 cups flour; beat on low speed for 3 minutes. Stir in enough remaining flour to form a soft dough.

2 Turn onto a floured surface; knead until smooth and elastic, about 6-8 minutes. Place in a greased bowl, turning once to grease top. Cover and let rise in a warm place until doubled, about 1 hour.

3 Punch dough down. Turn onto a lightly floured surface; roll into a 16-in. x 10-in. rectangle. Spread with butter; sprinkle with sugar and cinnamon. Roll up jelly-roll style, starting from a long side; pinch seam to seal. Cut into 12 slices; set aside.

4 In a saucepan, combine the brown sugar, butter and corn syrup; cook over medium heat until the sugar is dissolved. Stir in pecans. Pour into a greased 13-in. x 9-in. x 2-in. baking pan. Place rolls cut side down over sauce. Cover and let rise until doubled, about 1 hour.

5 Bake at 375° for 20-25 minutes or until golden brown. Cool for 3 minutes. Invert onto a serving platter.

shaping *cinnamon rolls & sticky buns*

1. Roll dough into a rectangle. Spread or brush with butter; sprinkle with filling. Roll up, starting from a long end, and pinch seam to seal.

2. Slice into rolls. Place cut side down in a greased baking pan.

3. Cover and let rise until doubled. Rolls will begin to touch each other.

4. After baking, combine glaze ingredients if desired; spoon in a thin stream over warm rolls.

Chocolate Sticky Buns

PREP: 35 min. + rising **BAKE:** 20 min.
YIELD: 1-1/2 dozen

Jean Seidel, Wadena, Iowa

The fudge-like topping pairs well with the chocolate-cinnamon filling.

- 1 package (1/4 ounce) active dry yeast
- 1/3 cup warm water (110° to 115°)
- 3/4 cup warm milk (110° to 115°)
- 1/2 cup butter, softened
- 1/3 cup sugar
- 1 teaspoon salt
- 1 egg
- 4-1/2 to 5 cups all-purpose flour

SYRUP:
- 1 cup packed brown sugar
- 1/2 cup butter
- 1/4 cup corn syrup
- 3 tablespoons baking cocoa
- 1-1/2 cups chopped pecans

FILLING:
- 1/4 cup butter, melted
- 1 cup sugar
- 2 tablespoons baking cocoa
- 2 teaspoons ground cinnamon

1 In a large mixing bowl, dissolve yeast in warm water. Add the milk, butter, sugar, salt, egg and 1-1/2 cups flour. Beat on medium speed for 2-3 minutes or until smooth. Stir in enough remaining flour to form a soft dough.

2 Turn onto a floured surface; knead until smooth and elastic, about 6-8 minutes. Place in a greased bowl, turning once to grease top. Cover and let rise in a warm place until doubled, about 1 hour.

3 Combine the first four syrup ingredients in a saucepan. Bring to a boil; cook and stir for 1 minute. Pour into two greased 9-in. round baking pans; sprinkle with pecans. Set aside.

4 Punch dough down. Turn onto a lightly floured surface; divide in half. Roll each portion into a 12-in. x 10-in. rectangle; brush with melted butter. Combine the sugar, cocoa and cinnamon; sprinkle over rectangles to within 1/2 in. of edges.

5 Roll up jelly-roll style, starting with a short side; pinch seam to seal. Cut each roll into nine slices; place cut side down over syrup and pecans. Cover and let rise until doubled, about 40 minutes.

6 Bake at 375° for 20-25 minutes or until well browned. Cool for 1 minute before inverting onto serving platters.

Quick 'n' Easy Cinnamon Rolls

PREP: 15 min. + rising **BAKE:** 25 min. + cooling
YIELD: 1 dozen

Gayle Grigg, Phoenix, Arizona

The delectable homemade taste of these cinnamon rolls will bring raves. With raisins and a light lemon glaze, these rolls are perfect for a special brunch.

- 1 loaf (1 pound) frozen bread dough, thawed
- 3 tablespoons butter, melted
- 1/3 cup sugar
- 2 teaspoons ground cinnamon
- 1 teaspoon grated lemon peel
- 1/2 cup raisins

GLAZE:
- 1/2 cup confectioners' sugar
- 2 tablespoons lemon juice

1 On a lightly floured surface, roll the dough into a 14-in. x 10-in. rectangle. Brush with butter. Combine the sugar, cinnamon and lemon peel; sprinkle evenly over butter. Sprinkle with raisins.

2 Roll up jelly-roll style, starting with a long side; pinch seam to seal. Cut into 12 rolls. Place cut side down in a greased 11-in. x 7-in. x 2-in. baking pan. Cover and let rise until doubled, about 45 minutes.

3 Bake at 350° for 25-30 minutes or until golden brown. Cool for 10 minutes. Combine glaze ingredients; brush over rolls.

secrets for *successful sweet rolls*

- After punching down the dough, let it rest for 10 minutes. This allows the dough to relax, which makes it easier to roll out.

- Roll up dough firmly. If it's too loose, you'll see air pockets or large gaps when cut. If it's too tight, the bread will crack.

- A simple way to slice cinnamon rolls or sticky buns is to place a piece of unflavored dental floss or heavy-duty thread under the rolled dough, 1 in. from the end. Bring the floss up around the dough and cross it over the top, cutting through the dough and filling. Repeat at 1-in. intervals.

- Evenly space the cut rolls in the pan, leaving room around each to allow for the final rising.

CRANBERRY SWEET ROLLS

1/4   **cup butter, softened**
1/2   **teaspoon vanilla extract**
1/2   **teaspoon milk**

1 In a saucepan, bring sugar and water to a boil. Add cranberries; return to a boil. Boil, uncovered, for 20 minutes, stirring occasionally. Remove from the heat. Stir in orange peel; cover and refrigerate.

2 In a large mixing bowl, dissolve yeast in warm water. Add 1/2 cup butter, milk, eggs, sugar, salt, cinnamon, nutmeg and 3 cups flour; beat until smooth. Stir in enough remaining flour to form a soft dough.

3 Turn onto a floured surface; knead until smooth and elastic, about 6-8 minutes. Place in a greased bowl, turning once to grease top. Cover and let rise in a warm place until doubled, about 1 hour.

4 Punch dough down. Turn onto a lightly floured surface; roll into a 20-in. x 10-in. rectangle. Melt the remaining butter; brush over dough. Spread with cranberry filling to within 1 in. of edges. Roll up jelly-roll style, starting with a long side; pinch seam to seal. Cut into 15 slices. Place cut side down in a greased 13-in. x 9-in. x 2-in. baking pan. Cover and let rise until doubled, about 30 minutes.

5 Bake at 375° for 25-30 minutes. Cool for 5 minutes before removing from pans to a wire rack. In a small mixing bowl, combine frosting ingredients; beat until smooth. Spread over warm rolls. Store in the refrigerator.

Cranberry Sweet Rolls

PREP: 55 min. + rising   **BAKE:** 25 min.   **YIELD:** 15 rolls

Germaine Stank, Pound, Wisconsin

Christmas morning will be sweeter than ever when you serve these festive rolls topped with a rich and creamy frosting. They rise high and hold their shape. Plus, the tart cranberry filling is a nice change of pace from traditional cinnamon rolls.

  3/4   **cup sugar**
  1/2   **cup water**
    2   **cups fresh *or* frozen cranberries**
    1   **teaspoon grated orange peel**
DOUGH:
    2   **packages (1/4 ounce *each*) active dry yeast**
  1/2   **cup warm water (110° to 115°)**
  1/2   **cup plus 2 tablespoons butter, softened, *divided***
  1/2   **cup milk**
    2   **eggs**
  1/2   **cup sugar**
    1   **teaspoon salt**
    1   **teaspoon ground cinnamon**
  1/2   **teaspoon ground nutmeg**
4-1/2   **to 5 cups all-purpose flour**
CREAM CHEESE FROSTING:
    1   **cup confectioners' sugar**
  1/2   **of a 3-ounce package cream cheese, softened**

Blueberry Pinwheels

PREP: 30 min. + rising   **BAKE:** 20 min. + cooling
YIELD: 2 dozen

Betsy Stoner, Elmira, New York

Juicy blueberries peek out from the swirls of these tender, flaky sweet rolls. A succulent sauce settles on the bottom of the pan.

    2   **cans (5 ounces *each*) evaporated milk**
    6   **tablespoons butter, softened**
    1   **package (1/4 ounce) active dry yeast**
  1/4   **cup sugar**
    1   **teaspoon salt**
    1   **egg**
3-1/2   **to 4 cups all-purpose flour**
FILLING:
    3   **tablespoons butter, melted**
  1/2   **cup sugar**

1-1/2 to 2 teaspoons ground cinnamon
1 teaspoon grated lemon peel
2 cups fresh *or* frozen blueberries

GLAZE:
1 cup confectioners' sugar
1/2 teaspoon vanilla extract
1 to 2 tablespoons water

1 In a saucepan, heat milk and butter to 110°-115°. In a large mixing bowl, dissolve yeast in warm milk mixture. Add the sugar, salt, egg and 2 cups flour; beat until smooth. Stir in enough remaining flour to form a soft dough.

2 Turn onto a floured surface; knead until smooth and elastic, about 6-8 minutes. Place in a greased bowl, turning once to grease top. Cover and let rise in a warm place until doubled, about 1-1/4 hours.

3 Punch dough down. Turn onto a floured surface; divide in half. Roll each portion into a 14-in. x 8-in. rectangle; brush with melted butter. Combine the sugar, cinnamon and lemon peel; sprinkle over each rectangle to within 1/2 in. of edges. Top with blueberries; press into dough.

4 Roll up jelly-roll style, starting with a long side; pinch seam to seal. Cut each roll into 12 slices. Place cut side down in two greased 13-in. x 9-in. x 2-in. baking pans. Cover and let rise until doubled, about 1-1/4 hours.

5 Bake at 375° for 20-25 minutes or until golden brown. Cool for 5 minutes. Combine glaze ingredients; drizzle over warm rolls. Cool in pans on wire racks.

Editor's Note: If using frozen blueberries, do not thaw.

Orange Knots

PREP: 25 min. + rising **BAKE:** 10 min. + cooling
YIELD: 20 rolls

Bernice Morris, Marshfield, Missouri

These orange rolls are a little time-consuming to prepare, but they're worth the extra effort. They bake up feather-light with a sweet and tangy flavor.

2 packages (1/4 ounce *each*) active dry yeast
1/4 cup warm water (110° to 115°)
1 cup warm milk (110° to 115°)
1/3 cup sugar
1/2 cup butter, softened
1 teaspoon salt

2 eggs
1/4 cup orange juice
2 tablespoons grated orange peel
5-1/4 to 5-3/4 cups all-purpose flour

ORANGE ICING:
1 cup confectioners' sugar
2 tablespoons orange juice
1 teaspoon grated orange peel

1 In a large mixing bowl, dissolve yeast in warm water. Add the milk, sugar, butter, salt, eggs, orange juice, orange peel and 3 cups flour; beat until smooth. Stir in enough remaining flour to form a soft dough.

2 Turn onto a floured surface; knead until smooth and elastic, about 6-8 minutes. Place in a greased bowl, turning once to grease top. Cover and let rise in a warm place until doubled, about 1 hour.

3 Punch dough down. Turn onto a lightly floured surface; roll into a 16-in. x 10-in. rectangle, about 1/2 in. thick. Cut into 10-in. x 3/4-in. strips; roll lightly and tie into knots. Place on greased baking sheets; tuck ends under. Cover and let rise until doubled, about 45 minutes.

4 Bake at 400° for 10-12 minutes or until golden brown. Remove from pans to wire racks to cool. Combine icing ingredients; drizzle over rolls.

ORANGE KNOTS

CHERRY DANISH

beat until smooth. Stir in enough remaining flour to form a soft dough.

2 Turn onto a floured surface; knead until smooth and elastic, about 6-8 minutes. Place in a greased bowl, turning once to grease top. Cover and let rise in a warm place until doubled, about 1 hour.

3 Punch dough down. Turn onto a lightly floured surface; roll into a 24-in. x 16-in. rectangle. Dot half of the dough with 1/4 cup shortening; fold dough in half lengthwise. Dot with shortening and fold lengthwise into thirds. Dot with remaining shortening and fold widthwise into thirds.

4 Roll dough into a 16-in. x 15-in. rectangle. Cut into 8-in. x 3/4-in. strips; coil into spiral shapes, tucking end underneath the coil. Place on greased baking sheets. Cover and let rise until doubled, about 1 hour. Beat remaining egg. Make a depression in the center of each roll; brush with egg. Fill each with pie filling.

5 Bake at 375° for 15-18 minutes or until golden brown. Remove from pans to wire racks to cool. For glaze, combine the confectioners' sugar, milk and vanilla; drizzle over rolls. Sprinkle with almonds.

Cherry Danish

PREP: 30 min. + rising **BAKE:** 15 min. + cooling
YIELD: 40 rolls

Christie Cochran, Canyon, Texas

These ruby-colored pastries will be the first to disappear from your brunch table. You can use apple pie filling with equally good results.

- 1 **package (1/4 ounce) active dry yeast**
- 1/4 **cup warm water (110° to 115°)**
- 1 **cup warm milk (110° to 115°)**
- 3/4 **cup shortening,** *divided*
- 1/3 **cup sugar**
- 3 **eggs**
- 1 **teaspoon salt**
- 1/4 **teaspoon ground mace**
- 1/4 **teaspoon lemon extract**
- 1/4 **teaspoon vanilla extract**
- 4 **to 4-1/2 cups all-purpose flour**
- 1 **can (21 ounces) cherry pie filling**

GLAZE:
- 1-1/2 **cups confectioners' sugar**
- 2 **to 3 tablespoons milk**
- 1/2 **teaspoon vanilla extract**
- 1/4 **cup chopped almonds**

1 In a large mixing bowl, dissolve yeast in warm water. Add the milk, 1/4 cup shortening, sugar, two eggs, salt, mace, extracts and 2 cups flour;

Cranberry Almond Sweet Rolls

PREP: 35 min. + rising **BAKE:** 20 min. **YIELD:** 1 dozen

Marian Platt, Sequim, Washington

These sweet rolls feature tangy cranberries, crunchy almonds and vanilla chips.

- 1 **package (16 ounces) hot roll mix**
- 2 **tablespoons sugar**
- 1/2 **teaspoon ground cinnamon**
- 1/2 **teaspoon ground ginger**
- 1/4 **teaspoon ground nutmeg**
- 1 **cup warm water (110° to 115°)**
- 2 **tablespoons butter, softened**
- 1 **egg, beaten**
- 1 **cup finely chopped fresh** *or* **frozen cranberries**
- 1 **package (10 to 12 ounces) vanilla** *or* **white chips**
- 1 **cup slivered almonds**
- 1/4 **cup confectioners' sugar**
- 1/2 **teaspoon lemon juice**
- 3 **to 4 teaspoons milk**

1 In a large bowl, combine the contents of hot roll mix, sugar, cinnamon, ginger and nutmeg; mix well. Stir in the water, butter and egg to form a soft dough. Turn onto a floured surface; knead until smooth and elastic, about 6-8 minutes. Cover and let rest for 5 minutes.

2 Roll into a 15-in. x 10-in. rectangle; sprinkle with cranberries. Set aside 1/2 cup vanilla chips for glaze. Sprinkle almonds and remaining chips over cranberries.

3 Roll up jelly-roll style, starting with a long side; pinch seam to seal. Cut into 12 slices; place in a greased 13-in. x 9-in. x 2-in. baking pan. Cover and let rise in a warm place until doubled, about 30 minutes.

4 Bake at 375° for 18-20 minutes or until lightly browned. In a saucepan over low heat, melt reserved vanilla chips. Stir in the confectioners' sugar, lemon juice and milk. Drizzle over warm rolls.

NO-KNEAD CITRUS ROLLS

No-Knead Citrus Rolls

PREP: 20 min. + chilling **BAKE:** 20 min.
YIELD: 2-1/2 dozen

Margaret Otley, Waverly, Nebraska

These flavorful homemade rolls can come fresh from the oven any morning. Besides the fact that they don't require kneading, the goodies are ideal to start preparing the night before, then bake for breakfast.

>   2   **packages (1/4 ounce *each*) active dry yeast**
>   7   **tablespoons sugar, *divided***
> 1/4   **cup warm water (110° to 115°)**
>   1   **cup warm heavy whipping cream (110° to 115°)**
>   3   **egg yolks, beaten**
> 3-1/2   **to 4 cups all-purpose flour**
>   1   **teaspoon salt**
> 3/4   **cup cold butter, *divided***
> **FILLING:**
> 1/2   **cup sugar**
>   2   **tablespoons grated lemon peel**
>   2   **tablespoons grated orange peel**
> **GLAZE:**
> 1-1/3   **cups confectioners' sugar**
>   2   **tablespoons milk**
>   1   **tablespoon lemon juice**
>   1   **tablespoon orange juice**

1 In a bowl, dissolve yeast and 1 tablespoon sugar in warm water. Let stand for 5 minutes. Stir in cream and egg yolks; mix well. In another bowl, combine 3-1/2 cups flour, salt and remaining sugar; cut in 1/2 cup butter until crumbly. Add yeast mixture; stir just until moistened. Add enough remaining flour to form a soft dough. Place in a greased bowl, turning once to grease top. Refrigerate for 6-8 hours or overnight.

2 Punch dough down. Turn onto a lightly floured surface. Divide in half; roll each into a 15-in. x 12-in. rectangle. Melt the remaining butter; brush over dough. Combine filling ingredients; sprinkle over the dough.

3 Roll up jelly-roll style, beginning with a long side; pinch seam to seal. Cut each roll into 15 slices; place cut side down in two greased 9-in. pie plates. Cover and let rise until doubled, about 45 minutes.

4 Bake at 375° for 20-25 minutes or until golden brown. Combine glaze ingredients until smooth; drizzle over warm rolls. Cool in pans on wire racks.

storing *coffee cakes & sweet rolls*

- Cool coffee cakes and sweet rolls completely. Place in an airtight container or plastic bag; keep at room temperature for 2 to 3 days. Breads containing perishable items should be refrigerated.

- For longer storage, unfrosted sweet breads can be frozen for up to 3 months. Thaw at room temperature, then frost or glaze as desired.

BEAR CLAWS

Bear Claws

PREP: 1 hr. + rising **BAKE:** 10 min. + cooling
YIELD: 9 rolls

Taste of Home Test Kitchen

You don't have to head to gourmet bakeries to indulge in this sweet pastry. This recipe lets you master rich, flaky pastries at home.

> 1 package (1/4 ounce) active dry yeast
> 1/2 cup warm milk (110° to 115°)
> 2 tablespoons sugar
> 1 teaspoon salt
> 1 egg, lightly beaten
> 1-1/2 cups plus 2 tablespoons all-purpose flour

BUTTER MIXTURE:
> 2 tablespoons all-purpose flour, *divided*
> 3/4 cup cold butter, cut into tablespoon-size pieces

FILLING:
> 6 tablespoons prepared almond filling *or* filling of your choice
> 1 egg, beaten

GLAZE:
> 3/4 cup confectioners' sugar
> 2 to 3 teaspoons water

1 In a large mixing bowl, dissolve yeast in warm milk. Stir in the sugar, salt and egg; mix well. Add the flour all at once, stirring until mixed. Set aside.

2 For butter mixture, sprinkle 1 tablespoon flour on a work surface; place butter on surface and sprinkle with 1 teaspoon flour. Press and roll out with a rolling pin. Scrape butter from rolling pin and continue to work the butter until it forms a smooth mass without any hard lumps. Knead in remaining flour, working quickly to keep butter cold. Place butter mixture on a sheet of plastic wrap and shape into a small rectangle. Cover with another sheet of plastic wrap; roll into a 9-in. x 6-in. rectangle. Set aside.

3 Turn dough onto a floured work surface; roll into a 14-in. x 10-in. rectangle, with a 10-in. side toward the bottom. Unwrap butter mixture; place on dough 1 in. above bottom edge and 1/2 in. from each side edge. Fold top half of dough over butter and pinch edges to seal.

shaping *bear claws*

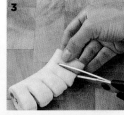

1. Roll dough into a 12-in. square, then cut each square into three 12-in. x 4-in. strips.

2. Spread 2 tablespoons of filling down the center of each strip to within 1 in. of long edge. Fold lengthwise over filling; pinch seam to seal. Cut into three pieces.

3. With scissors, cut each strip four times, starting from pinched seam to about 1/2 in. from the folded side.

4. Place 2 in. apart on greased baking sheets. Curve folded side slightly to separate strips and show the filling.

4 Turn dough a quarter turn to the right; sprinkle lightly with additional flour. Lightly roll into a 16-in. x 8-in. rectangle. Fold bottom third of rectangle up and top third down, as when folding a business letter, making a 5-1/2-in. x 8-in. rectangle (this is called one turn). Rotate dough a quarter turn to the right. Lightly roll into a 16-in. x 8-in. rectangle and again fold into thirds, finishing the second turn. Repeat rotating, rolling and folding two more times for a total of four turns. Wrap loosely in plastic wrap; refrigerate for 30 minutes.

5 Roll dough into a 12-in. square; cut square into three 12-in. x 4-in. strips. Spread 2 tablespoons filling down the center of each strip to within 1 in. of long edge. Fold lengthwise over filling and pinch seam to seal. Cut each strip into three pieces. With scissors, cut each piece four times from pinched seam to about 1/2 in. from folded side. Place 2 in. apart on greased baking sheets. Curve folded side slightly to separate strips and allow filling to show. Cover and let rise in a warm place until almost doubled, about 1 hour.

6 Brush with egg. Bake at 400° for 10-14 minutes or until puffy and golden brown. Remove from pans to wire racks. Combine glaze ingredients; brush over warm rolls. Cool.

2 Turn onto a floured surface; knead until smooth and elastic, about 6-8 minutes. Place in a greased bowl, turning once to grease top. Cover and let rise in a warm place until doubled, about 1 hour.

3 Punch dough down. Turn onto a lightly floured surface; roll into a large rectangle, 1/4 in. thick. Spread with 2 tablespoons butter; sprinkle with 1/3 cup of the remaining sugar. Fold dough in half lengthwise; roll out to 1/4-in. thickness. Spread with 2 tablespoons butter; sprinkle with 1/3 cup sugar. Fold in half widthwise; roll out to 1/4-in. thickness. Spread with remaining butter; sprinkle with 1/3 cup sugar. Fold in half lengthwise; roll into an 18-in. x 10-in. rectangle. Combine the cinnamon and remaining sugar; sprinkle half over the dough to within 1/4 in. of edges.

4 Roll up jelly-roll style, starting with a short side; pinch seams to seal. Cut into 1/2-in. slices; place on greased baking sheets (four to six slices per sheet). Cover with waxed paper and flatten with palm of hand. Sprinkle with remaining cinnamon-sugar. Let stand for 30 minutes.

5 Bake at 400° for 12-15 minutes. Immediately remove from pans to wire racks to cool.

MORNING CRISPIES

Morning Crispies

PREP: 30 min. + rising **BAKE:** 15 min. + cooling
YIELD: about 1-1/2 dozen

Emily Goad, Franklin, Indiana

These large, cinnamon-sugar pastries make quite an impression on the table. Every bite melts in your mouth.

- 1 **package (1/4 ounce) active dry yeast**
- 1/2 **cup warm water (110° to 115°)**
- 1 **cup warm milk (110° to 115°)**
- 2 **cups sugar,** *divided*
- 1/2 **cup vegetable oil**
- 1-1/4 **teaspoons salt**
- 2 **eggs**
- 1-1/2 **teaspoons lemon extract**
- 5-1/2 **to 6 cups all-purpose flour**
- 6 **tablespoons butter, softened,** *divided*
- 1 **tablespoon ground cinnamon**

1 In a large mixing bowl, dissolve yeast in warm water. Add the milk, 1/2 cup sugar, oil, salt, eggs, extract and 2 cups flour; beat well. Stir in enough remaining flour to form a soft dough.

No-Fry Doughnuts

PREP: 30 min. + rising **BAKE:** 20 min. **YIELD:** 2 dozen

Susie Baldwin, Columbia, Tennessee

These glazed doughnuts are finger-licking good! They bake in the oven, so there's no greasy mess to clean up.

2	**packages (1/4 ounce** *each***) active dry yeast**
1/4	**cup warm water (110° to 115°)**
1-1/2	**cups warm milk (110° to 115°)**
1/3	**cup shortening**
1/2	**cup sugar**
2	**eggs**
1	**teaspoon salt**
1	**teaspoon ground nutmeg**
1/4	**teaspoon ground cinnamon**
4-1/2	**to 5 cups all-purpose flour**
1/4	**cup butter, melted**

GLAZE:

1/2	**cup butter**
2	**cups confectioners' sugar**
5	**teaspoons water**
2	**teaspoons vanilla extract**

1 In a large mixing bowl, dissolve yeast in warm water. Add milk and shortening; stir for 1 minute. Add the sugar, eggs, salt, nutmeg, cinnamon and 2 cups flour; beat on low speed until smooth. Stir in enough remaining flour to form a soft dough (do not knead). Cover and let rise in a warm place until doubled, about 1 hour.

2 Punch dough down. Turn onto a floured surface; roll out to 1/2-in. thickness. Cut with a floured 2-3/4-in. doughnut cutter; place 2 in. apart on greased baking sheets. Brush with butter. Cover and let rise in a warm place until doubled, about 30 minutes.

3 Bake at 350° for 20 minutes or until lightly browned. Meanwhile, for glaze, melt butter in a saucepan. Add the confectioners' sugar, water and vanilla; cook and stir over low heat until smooth (do not boil). Keep warm. Dip warm doughnuts in glaze, one at a time, and turn to coat. Drain on a wire rack. Serve immediately.

Potato Doughnuts

PREP: 50 min. + rising **BAKE:** 15 min.
YIELD: about 2-1/2 dozen

Jill Shramek, Smith, Nevada

For ease of preparation, the dough for these baked favorites is made in a bread machine. The cinnamon-sugar topping is irresistible.

3	**medium potatoes, peeled and quartered**
1	**cup warm milk (70° to 80°)**
2	**eggs, well beaten**

3/4 cup shortening
1/2 cup sugar
1 teaspoon salt
4-1/2 cups bread flour
2-1/4 teaspoons active dry yeast
TOPPING:
3/4 cup sugar
1-1/4 teaspoons ground cinnamon
1/4 cup butter, melted

1 Place potatoes in a saucepan and cover with water. Bring to a boil; cook until tender. Drain, reserving 1/4 cup cooking liquid; set liquid aside to cool to 70°-80°. Mash potatoes; set aside 1 cup to cool to room temperature. (Refrigerate any remaining mashed potatoes for another use.)

2 In bread machine pan, place milk, eggs, shortening, sugar, salt, bread flour and yeast in order suggested by manufacturer, adding reserved cooking liquid and mashed potatoes. Select dough setting (check dough after 5 minutes of mixing; some flour may remain on top; add 1 to 2 tablespoons water or flour if needed).

3 When cycle is completed, turn dough onto a lightly floured surface. Knead in an additional 1/4 to 1/2 cup flour if necessary. Roll out to 1/2-in. thickness. Cut with a floured 2-1/2-in. doughnut cutter. Place on greased baking sheets; cover and let rise until almost doubled, about 25 minutes.

4 Bake at 350° for 15-20 minutes or until lightly browned. Combine sugar and cinnamon. Brush warm doughnuts with butter; dip in cinnamon-sugar.

Editor's Note: If your bread machine has a time-delay feature, we recommend you do not use it for this recipe.

Almond Apricot Logs

PREP: 30 min. + rising **BAKE:** 15 min. + cooling
YIELD: 5 dozen

L. Kniffin, Hockessin, Delaware

This recipe makes 5 dozen delicious rolls, so bake and take them to your next potluck.

2 packages (1/4 ounce *each*) active dry yeast
1/3 cup warm water (110° to 115°)
1-1/2 cups warm milk (110° to 115°)
1/3 cup vegetable oil
1/2 cup sugar
2 eggs

2 teaspoons salt
2 teaspoons ground nutmeg
5 to 5-1/2 cups all-purpose flour
1-1/2 cups coarsely chopped dried apricots
1 cup chopped almonds
GLAZE:
1-1/2 cups confectioners' sugar
1/2 teaspoon vanilla extract
2 to 3 tablespoons milk

1 In a large mixing bowl, dissolve yeast in warm water. Add milk, oil, sugar, eggs, salt, nutmeg and 2 cups flour; beat until smooth. Add apricots and almonds. Stir in enough remaining flour to form a soft dough.

2 Turn onto a floured surface; knead until smooth and elastic, about 6-8 minutes. Place in a greased bowl, turning once to grease top. Cover and let rise in a warm place until doubled, about 1-1/2 hours.

3 Punch dough down. Turn onto a lightly floured surface; cover and let rest for 10 minutes. Roll into a 15-in. x 12-in. rectangle. Cut into 3-in. x 1-in. strips. Place 1 in. apart on greased baking sheets. Cover and let rise until doubled, about 30 minutes.

4 Bake at 375° for 15 minutes or until light golden brown. Remove from pans to wire racks. Combine glaze ingredients; brush over warm logs. Cool.

ALMOND APRICOT LOGS

FRUIT-FILLED KOLACHKES

Fruit-Filled Kolachkes

PREP: 30 min. + rising **BAKE:** 10 min. + cooling
YIELD: 2 dozen

Mary Pecinovsky, Calmar, Iowa

Kolachkes are a small, flaky Polish pastry made with sweet yeast dough and filled with fruit, jam, poppy seeds or nuts.

1-1/4 cups water (70° to 80°)
1/2 cup butter, softened
1 egg
1 egg yolk
1 teaspoon lemon juice
1/3 cup nonfat dry milk powder
1/4 cup mashed potato flakes
1/4 cup sugar
1 teaspoon salt
3-3/4 cups plus 3 tablespoons bread flour
2 teaspoons active dry yeast
1 can (12 ounces) apricot *or* raspberry filling
Additional butter, melted

1 In bread machine pan, place first 11 ingredients in order suggested by manufacturer. Select dough setting (check dough after 5 minutes of mixing; add 1 to 2 tablespoons of water or flour if needed).

2 When cycle is completed, turn dough onto a lightly floured surface. Pat or roll into a 15-in. x 10-in. rectangle. Cover with plastic wrap; let rest for 10 minutes. Cut dough into 24 squares. Place a heaping teaspoon of filling in the center of each square. Overlap two opposite corners of dough over filling; pinch tightly to seal. Place 2 in. apart on greased baking sheets. Cover and let rise in a warm place until doubled, about 1 hour.

3 Bake at 425° for 8-10 minutes or until lightly browned. Brush with melted butter. Remove from pans to paper towels to cool.

Editor's Note: This recipe was tested with Solo fruit filling. If your bread machine has a time-delay feature, we recommend you do not use it for this recipe.

shaping fruit-filled *kolachkes*

1. Roll dough into a 15-in. x 10-in. rectangle. Cover with plastic wrap; let rest for 10 minutes. Cut dough into 24 squares.

2. Place a heaping teaspoonful of filling in the center of each square. Overlap two opposite corners of dough over filling; pinch tightly to seal.

Bohemian Kolachkes

PREP: 30 min. + rising **BAKE:** 15 min.
YIELD: about 2-1/2 dozen

Maxine Hron, Quincy, Illinois

In Eastern Europe, a kolachke is typically shaped into a circle, which is a symbol of good luck, prosperity and eternity.

- 2 packages (1/4 ounce *each*) active dry yeast
- 1/2 cup sugar, *divided*
- 2 cups warm milk (110° to 115°)
- 5-3/4 to 6-1/2 cups all-purpose flour
- 4 egg yolks
- 1 teaspoon salt
- 1/4 cup butter, softened
- 2 cups canned prune, poppy seed, cherry *or* lemon pie filling
- 1 egg white, beaten

1 In a small bowl, dissolve yeast and 1 tablespoon sugar in warm milk; let stand for 5 minutes. In a large mixing bowl, combine 2 cups flour, egg yolks, salt, butter, yeast mixture and remaining sugar; beat until smooth. Stir in enough of the remaining flour to form a stiff dough.

2 Turn onto a floured surface; knead until smooth and elastic, about 6-8 minutes. Add additional flour if necessary. Place dough in a greased bowl, turning once to grease top. Cover and let rise in a warm place until doubled, about 1 hour.

3 Punch dough down. Turn onto a lightly floured surface; roll out to 1/2-in. thickness. Cut with a large glass or a 2-1/2-in. cutter. Place on greased baking sheets. Let rise until doubled, about 45 minutes.

4 Firmly press an indentation in the center of each roll; fill each with a heaping tablespoon of filling. Brush dough with egg white. Bake at 350° for 15-20 minutes or until rolls are light golden brown.

Butter Nut Twists

PREP: 30 min. + chilling **BAKE:** 15 min.
YIELD: 5-6 dozen

Joyce Hallisey, Mt. Gilead, North Carolina

Not only are these rolls filled with a crunchy coconut-nut filling, they are also rolled in the extra filling after they are twisted into shape.

- 2 packages (1/4 ounce *each*) active dry yeast
- 1/4 cup warm water (110° to 115°)
- 1 cup cold butter
- 4 cups all-purpose flour
- 2 eggs, beaten
- 3/4 cup buttermilk
- 1/3 cup sugar
- 1/2 teaspoon salt

FILLING:
- 1/2 pound ground walnuts
- 1 cup flaked coconut
- 1/3 cup sugar
- 4-1/2 teaspoons butter, melted

1 In a small bowl, dissolve yeast in warm water; set aside. In a large bowl, cut butter into flour until crumbly. Add the yeast mixture, eggs, buttermilk, sugar and salt; mix lightly. Divide dough into thirds. Cover and refrigerate overnight.

2 On a sugared surface, roll out one portion of dough into a 12-in. x 9-in. rectangle. Combine filling ingredients; sprinkle 1/3 cupful on half of the 12-in. edge of dough. Fold over lengthwise and seal, forming a 12-in. x 4-1/2-in. rectangle. Pat out to press filling into dough. Sprinkle another 1/3 cup filling on half of the 12-in. edge of dough. Fold over lengthwise, forming a 12-in. x 2-in. rectangle. Pat down to 12 in. x 4 in. Cut into 4-in. x 1/2-in. pieces. Repeat with remaining dough. Twist each slice and roll in remaining filling. Place on greased baking sheets.

3 Bake at 350° for 15-18 minutes or until golden brown. Remove from pans to wire racks. Serve warm or at room temperature.

BUTTER NUT TWISTS

Butterscotch Crescents

PREP: 50 min. + rising **BAKE:** 15 min. + cooling
YIELD: 3 dozen

Phyllis Hofer, De Witt, Iowa

With a coconut and pecan filling and a brown sugar frosting, these flaky rolls are loaded with flavor. Butterscotch pudding mix in the dough makes them nice and moist.

- 1 **can (12 ounces) evaporated milk**
- 1 **package (3-1/2 ounces) cook-and-serve butterscotch pudding mix**
- 1/2 **cup butter, cubed**
- 2 **packages (1/4 ounce *each*) active dry yeast**
- 1/4 **cup warm water (110° to 115°)**
- 2 **eggs**
- 2 **teaspoons salt**
- 5 **to 5-1/2 cups all-purpose flour**

FILLING:
- 2/3 **cup packed brown sugar**
- 2/3 **cup flaked coconut**
- 1/3 **cup chopped pecans**
- 1/4 **cup butter, melted**
- 2 **tablespoons all-purpose flour**

FROSTING:
- 1/4 **cup packed brown sugar**
- 2 **tablespoons butter**
- 1 **cup confectioners' sugar**
- 2 **to 3 tablespoons hot water, optional**

1 Set aside 2 tablespoons evaporated milk for frosting. In a saucepan, combine pudding mix and remaining milk until smooth. Bring to a boil over medium heat, stirring constantly. Remove from the heat; stir in butter until melted. Let stand until mixture cools to 110°-115°.

2 In a large mixing bowl, dissolve yeast in warm water. Beat in eggs, salt, 2 cups flour and pudding mixture until smooth. Stir in enough remaining flour to form a soft dough.

3 Turn onto a floured surface; knead until smooth and elastic, about 6-8 minutes. Place in a greased bowl, turning once to grease top. Cover and let rise in a warm place until doubled, about 1 hour.

4 Punch dough down. Turn onto a lightly floured surface; divide into thirds. Roll each portion into a 15-in. circle. Combine filling ingredients; spread 1/2 cup over each circle. Cut each circle into 12 wedges. Roll up wedges from the wide end. Place pointed side down 2 in. apart on greased baking sheets. Curve ends to form a crescent shape. Cover and let rise until doubled, about 45 minutes.

5 Bake at 375° for 15-18 minutes or until golden brown. Remove from pans to wire racks to cool.

6 For frosting, combine the brown sugar, butter and reserved evaporated milk in a saucepan. Cook and stir over low heat until smooth. Remove from the heat; stir in confectioners' sugar until smooth. Add water if needed to achieve desired consistency. Frost rolls.

BUTTERSCOTCH CRESCENTS

Almond Croissants

PREP: 30 min. + chilling **BAKE:** 15 min. + cooling
YIELD: 16 rolls

Patricia Glass, East Wenatchee, Washington

These tender croissants are a little lighter than others. The subtle flavor of almond pairs well with a cup of hot coffee or a glass of cold milk.

- 1 **package (1/4 ounce) active dry yeast**
- 1/4 **cup warm water (110° to 115°)**
- 4 **cups all-purpose flour**
- 1/4 **cup sugar**
- 1 **teaspoon salt**
- 1 **cup cold butter**
- 3/4 **cup warm milk (110° to 115°)**
- 3 **egg yolks**

FILLING:
- 1/2 **cup almond paste**
- 1 **egg white**
- 1/4 **cup confectioners' sugar**

EGG WASH:
- 1 **egg white**
- 1 **tablespoon water**
- 1/4 **cup sliced almonds**

1 In a bowl, dissolve yeast in warm water. In a large bowl, combine the flour, sugar and salt. Cut in butter until mixture is crumbly. Add milk and egg yolks to yeast mixture; mix well. Stir into flour mixture; mix well. Do not knead. Cover and refrigerate overnight.

2 In a mixing bowl, beat filling ingredients until smooth. Punch dough down. Turn onto a lightly floured surface; divide in half. Roll each portion into a 12-in. circle; cut each circle into eight wedges. Spread filling over wedges; roll up from wide end.

3 Place pointed side down 3 in. apart on ungreased baking sheets. Curve ends to form a crescent shape. Cover and let rise in a warm place for 1 hour (dough will not double).

4 Beat egg white and water; brush over croissants. Sprinkle with almonds. Bake at 350° for 15-20 minutes. Remove from pans to wire racks to cool.

Austrian Apple Twists

PREP: 30 min. + chilling **BAKE:** 20 min. + cooling
YIELD: 64 rolls

Kathy Bless, Fayetteville, Pennsylvania

The addition of apple makes these butterhorns stand out from all the rest. No rising time is needed to make this.

- 1 package (1/4 ounce) active dry yeast
- 3 cups all-purpose flour
- 1 cup butter, softened

- 3 egg yolks, beaten
- 1 cup (8 ounces) sour cream
- 1/2 cup sugar
- 1/2 cup finely chopped pecans
- 3/4 teaspoon ground cinnamon
- 1 medium tart apple, peeled, cored and finely chopped

ICING:
- 1 cup confectioners' sugar
- 4 teaspoons milk
- 1/4 teaspoon vanilla extract

Finely chopped pecans

1 In a large mixing bowl, combine the yeast and flour. Add butter and mix well. Add egg yolks and sour cream; mix well. Shape into four balls. Place in separate resealable plastic bags or wrap in plastic wrap; refrigerate overnight.

2 On a floured surface, roll each ball of dough into a 9-in. circle. Combine sugar, pecans and cinnamon; sprinkle over each circle. Top with apple. Cut each circle into 16 wedges. Roll up wedges from the wide end and place pointed side down 2 in. apart on greased baking sheets.

3 Bake at 350° for 16-20 minutes or until lightly browned. Immediately remove from pans to wire racks to cool. For the icing, combine the confectioners' sugar, milk and vanilla until smooth; drizzle over rolls. Sprinkle with pecans.

Editor's Note: The yeast does not need to be dissolved in liquid, and no rising time is necessary before baking.

SOUR CREAM TWISTS

4 Bake at 375° for 12-14 minutes or until lightly browned. Immediately remove from pans to wire racks to cool.

Fan Rolls

PREP: 35 min. + rising **BAKE:** 15 min. + cooling
YIELD: 8 rolls

Christine Wahlgren, Sandwich, Illinois

The dough for these rolls can be made and refrigerated for up to 24 hours.

3-1/4	cups all-purpose flour
1/4	cup sugar
1	package (1/4 ounce) active dry yeast
1	teaspoon grated lemon peel
1/2	teaspoon salt
1	cup milk
1/4	cup shortening
1	egg

FILLING:

2	tablespoons butter, softened
1/2	cup packed brown sugar
1/2	cup raisins
1	teaspoon ground cinnamon

Vanilla Glaze (recipe on page 393)

1 In a large mixing bowl, combine 1-1/4 cups flour, sugar, yeast, lemon peel and salt. In a saucepan, heat milk and shortening to 120°-130°. Add to dry ingredients; beat until moistened. Add egg; beat on high speed for 3 minutes. Stir in enough remaining flour to form a soft dough. Do not knead. Cover and refrigerate for 2-24 hours.

2 Let dough stand at room temperature for 10 minutes. On a lightly floured surface, roll dough into a 16-in. x 12-in. rectangle. Cut in half lengthwise; spread with butter. Combine the brown sugar, raisins and cinnamon; sprinkle down the center third of each rectangle. Fold one long side of dough over filling, then fold the other long side of dough over, forming a 16-in. x 2-in. rectangle. Pat lightly to flatten.

3 Cut each rectangle into four 4-in. rolls. Line a baking sheet with foil and grease the foil. Place rolls seam side down 3 in. apart on foil. With scissors, cut five strips two-thirds of the way through each roll. Separate each strip slightly, curving to form a fan shape. Cover and let rise in a warm place until doubled, about 45 minutes.

4 Bake at 350° for 15-20 minutes or until lightly browned. Remove from pan to a wire rack to cool. Drizzle with glaze.

Sour Cream Twists

PREP: 40 min. + chilling **BAKE:** 15 min. + cooling
YIELD: 4 dozen

Linda Welch, North Platte, Nebraska

Keep some of these terrific flaky twists in your freezer to serve in a pinch at breakfast, lunch or dinner.

1	package (1/4 ounce) active dry yeast
1/4	cup warm water (110° to 115°)
3	cups all-purpose flour
1-1/2	teaspoons salt
1/2	cup cold butter
1/2	cup shortening
2	eggs
1/2	cup sour cream
3	teaspoons vanilla extract, *divided*
1-1/2	cups sugar

1 In a small bowl, dissolve yeast in warm water. In a mixing bowl, combine flour and salt. Cut in butter and shortening until mixture is crumbly. Stir in the eggs, sour cream, 1 teaspoon vanilla and the yeast mixture; mix well. Cover and refrigerate overnight.

2 Combine sugar and remaining vanilla; lightly sprinkle 1/2 cup over a pastry cloth or work surface. Divide dough in half; put one portion back in the refrigerator. On the sugared surface, roll the other portion into a 12-in. x 8-in. rectangle. Sprinkle with about 1 tablespoon sugar mixture. Fold rectangle into thirds.

3 Give dough a quarter turn; repeat rolling, sugaring and folding two more times. Roll into a 12-in. x 8-in. rectangle. Cut into 4-in. x 1-in. strips; twist each strip two or three times. Place on chilled ungreased baking sheets. Repeat with the remaining dough and sugar mixture.

Fanciful Creations

Maple Tree Cake

PREP: 25 min. **BAKE:** 30 min. + cooling
YIELD: 12 servings
Taste of Home Test Kitchen

Here's a colorful dessert that's perfect for fall. A chocolate tree with pretty dried-fruit leaves tops off the scrumptious maple-flavored cake.

    4 **eggs**
    2 **cups sugar**
    2 **cups (16 ounces) sour cream**
    2 **teaspoons maple flavoring**
2-1/2 **cups all-purpose flour**
    2 **teaspoons baking soda**
Dash salt
  1/2 **cup chopped pecans**
FROSTING:
  1/4 **cup butter, softened**
    3 **cups confectioners' sugar**
  1/2 **cup plus 1 tablespoon maple syrup**
  1/4 **cup semisweet chocolate chips**
  1/4 **cup peanut butter chips**
    2 **tablespoons dried cranberries**
    2 **tablespoons golden raisins**
    2 **tablespoons chopped dried apricots**
    2 **tablespoons chopped dried apples**

1 In a large mixing bowl, beat the eggs and sugar. Add sour cream and maple flavoring. Combine the flour, baking soda and salt; add to sour cream mixture and mix well. Fold in pecans.

2 Pour into two greased and floured 9-in. round baking pans. Bake at 350° for 30 minutes or until a toothpick inserted near the center comes out clean. Cool for 10 minutes before removing from pans to wire racks to cool completely.

3 For frosting, in a mixing bowl, cream butter and confectioners' sugar until blended. Add syrup; mix well. Spread between layers and over top and sides of cake.

4 In a microwave-safe bowl, melt chocolate and peanut butter chips; stir until smooth. Transfer to a pastry bag or a heavy-duty resealable plastic bag; cut a small hole in the corner of bag. Pipe a tree and branches on top of the cake. Combine dried fruit; sprinkle around tree base and at ends of branches to resemble leaves.

MAPLE TREE CAKE

Gift Box Wedding Cake

PREP: 1 hour 35 min. + soaking **BAKE:** 1 hour + cooling
YIELD: 50 servings

Taste of Home Test Kitchen

With the lovely cake "presented" here, you'll never need to special-order one for a wedding (or an anniversary) again! The recipe calls for pink icing, but feel free to use the food coloring of your choice.

1-1/3   cups poppy seeds, *divided*
    4   packages (18-1/4 ounces *each*) white cake mix
    1   package (3.4 ounces) instant lemon pudding mix

FROSTING:

1-1/2   cups butter, softened
  15   cups confectioners' sugar
  3/4   cup half-and-half cream
1-1/2   teaspoons vanilla extract
  1/2   teaspoon salt
Pink liquid *or* paste food coloring

1 Place 1/3 cup poppy seeds in each of four small bowls; add the water called for in cake mix directions to each bowl. Soak for 1 hour.

2 Prepare cake batters according to package directions, using the poppy seed water. Bake in three greased and floured 13-in. x 9-in. x 2-in. baking pans and two 8-in. square baking dishes. Cool for 10 minutes before removing from pans to wire racks to cool completely. Prepare pudding mix according to package directions; refrigerate.

3 For frosting, in a large mixing bowl, cream butter and confectioners' sugar. Add the cream, vanilla and salt; beat on medium speed until light and fluffy, about 3 minutes. (Frosting may need to be made in batches.) Add food coloring to 4-1/2 cups frosting.

4 Cut a small hole in the corner of two pastry bags or heavy-duty resealable plastic bags; insert round pastry tip #3 in one bag and round pastry tip #5 in the other. Place 1/2 cup white frosting in the bag with tip #3 and 1/2 cup pink frosting in the bag with tip #5. Cover remaining frosting with a damp clean cloth until ready to use.

5 Trim two 13-in. x 9-in. cakes into 12-in. x 8-in. rectangles (see Fig. 1a); level tops (see Leveling Cake Layers on page 119). Cut an 8-in. x 2-in. strip off each, leaving two pieces (A). Cut each strip in half, forming four 4-in. x 2-in. pieces. Attach two 4-in. x 2-in. pieces together lengthwise with white frosting to form a 4-in. x 4-in. piece (see Fig. 1b); repeat with two remaining pieces and set aside.

6 Trim remaining 13-in. x 9-in. cake into a 12-in. x 7-in. rectangle (see Fig. 2); level top. Cut cake in half to form two 7-in. x 6-in. pieces (C); set aside. Level tops of 8-in. square cakes.

7 Each frosted layer of the cake consists of two cake pieces with lemon pudding filling in between. Place one piece A on a covered board; spread with pudding to within 1/2 in. of edges. Place second piece A on top; set aside. Repeat filling procedure for remaining layers (pieces B, C and 8-in. square cakes) and place on covered boards.

8 For bottom layer, frost piece A with 3-1/2 cups white frosting. If desired, attach a ribbon across the corners of piece A (as shown in photo on opposite page).

9 For second layer, frost 8-in. cake with 2-1/2 cups pink frosting. With prepared bag of white frosting, pipe a continuous string, curving up, down and around so strings never touch or cross on cake.

10 For third layer, frost piece C with 2 cups white frosting. With prepared bag of pink frosting, pipe dots 1/2 in. apart over entire cake. Frost piece B with remaining pink frosting. Add bow on top.

11 For bottom three layers, cut a 1/4-in.-diameter dowel rod into five pieces the height of each layer. Insert dowels 1-2 in. apart in center of each cake to support the next layer. Carefully stack layers on a large serving platter, working from largest cake to smallest. Decorate with ribbon and silk flowers as desired. Remove dowels before cutting each layer.

Editor's Note: Unfrosted cakes can be frozen for up to 6 months wrapped in foil. Frosting can be prepared 2 weeks ahead; store in refrigerator. Rewhip before spreading. Cake can be assembled 8 hours before serving.

GIFT BOX WEDDING CAKE

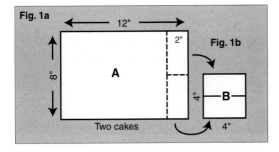

Fig. 1a

12"

2"

8"

A

Fig. 1b

4"

B

4"

Two cakes

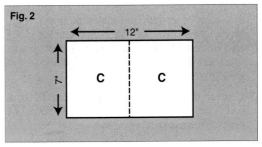

Fig. 2

12"

7"

C   C

the circles to form ears. Place M&M's in the center of each circle for eyes. Place a cashew in the center of the face for the beak.

4 Bake at 350° for 9-11 minutes or until edges are lightly browned. Cool for 2 minutes before removing to a wire rack.

OWL COOKIES

Owl Cookies

PREP: 25 min. + chilling **BAKE:** 10 min.
YIELD: about 1-1/2 dozen

Liz Clemons, Sumter, South Carolina

These cookies are a real hoot. They taste as good as they look, and make a great treat for Halloween.

- 3/4 cup butter, softened
- 1 cup packed brown sugar
- 1 egg
- 1 teaspoon vanilla extract
- 2-1/2 cups all-purpose flour
- 2 teaspoons baking powder
- 1/4 teaspoon salt
- 1 square (1 ounce) unsweetened chocolate, melted
- 1/4 teaspoon baking soda

Orange and yellow M&M's
Whole cashews

1 In a large mixing bowl, cream butter and brown sugar until light and fluffy. Beat in egg and vanilla. Combine the flour, baking powder and salt; add to creamed mixture. Remove two-thirds of the dough; roll into an 8-in. square on plastic wrap and set aside.

2 Combine melted chocolate and baking soda until thoroughly blended; beat into remaining dough. Shape into an 8-in. log. Place chocolate log at one end of the square and roll up; pinch seams together. Wrap in plastic wrap; refrigerate for at least 2 hours.

3 Unwrap dough; cut into 1/4-in. slices. To form owl's face, place two slices side by side on a lightly greased baking sheet. Pinch dough at the top of

Christmas Cookie Bowl

PREP: 30 min. + chilling **BAKE:** 30 min. + cooling
YIELD: 1 bowl and 1 dozen cookies

Jennifer Faus, Wichita, Kansas and
Taste of Home Test Kitchen

Spicy gingerbread cookie dough not only makes tasty cookies but a tasteful container to hold those cookies.

- 1/2 cup butter, softened
- 1/2 cup sugar
- 1/2 cup molasses
- 1/4 cup water
- 2-1/2 cups all-purpose flour
- 1 teaspoon ground allspice
- 1 teaspoon ground ginger
- 1 teaspoon ground nutmeg
- 1/2 teaspoon baking soda

ICING:
- 6 tablespoons butter, softened
- 2-2/3 cups confectioners' sugar
- 1 teaspoon vanilla extract
- 1 to 2 tablespoons milk

Food coloring
Assorted candy, optional

CHRISTMAS COOKIE BOWL

1. In a large mixing bowl, cream butter and sugar until light and fluffy. Add molasses and water; mix well. Combine the flour, allspice, ginger, nutmeg and baking soda. Add to creamed mixture; mix well. Cover and refirgerate for at least 3 hours.

2. Spray the outside of 1-1/2-quart ovenproof glass bowl with nonstick cooking spray. Invert bowl and place on ungreased baking sheet. On a floured surface, roll out chilled dough into a 1/4-in.-thick circle. Gently transfer dough circle to the outside of the bowl; press dough firmly around bowl. Trim edge of dough 1 in. above bowl rim with a pastry cutter or knife. Cover and refrigerate remaining dough to use for cookies.

3. If desired, use a 1-in. tree cookie cutter to cut out shapes around dough bowl. (Be sure to invert the cookie cutter so that when bowl is turned right side up, the shapes with be right side up also.) Chill for 20 minutes.

4. Bake at 350° for 20-25 minutes or until edges are lightly browned. Cool gingerbread on bowl. Gently twist bottom of gingerbread bowl until it releases; invert and carefully remove bowl. Place bowl on 9-in. plate or platter. Add candy around bottom of bowl, if desired.

5. On a floured surface, roll out reserved dough to 1/4-in. thickness. Cut with 2-1/2-in. cookie cutters. Place cutouts on a greased baking sheet. Bake at 350° for 10-12 minutes or until edges are lightly browned. Remove to a wire rack to cool completely.

6. In a large mixing bowl, beat the butter, confectioners' sugar, vanilla and enough milk to achieve spreading consistency. Tint as desired. Decorate cookies as desired and serve in bowl.

WEDDING PETITS FOURS

glazing *petits fours*

Place a wire rack over a sheet of waxed paper. Arrange petits fours on rack, leaving space between each. Spoon glaze over the top and sides, allowing excess to drip off. When glaze is dry, repeat with a second coat.

Wedding Petits Fours

PREP: 40 min. **BAKE:** 20 min. + cooling
YIELD: 1-1/2 dozen

Taste of Home Test Kitchen

Prepare these bite-size cakes for any occasion by changing the shape and food coloring.

- 1 **package (18-1/4 ounces) white cake mix**
- 3 **cups confectioners' sugar**
- 1/4 **cup water**
- 3 **tablespoons light corn syrup**
- 2 **tablespoons butter**
- 1/2 **teaspoon vanilla extract**
- 1/4 **teaspoon almond extract**

Food coloring, optional

1. Line a greased 15-in. x 10-in. x 1-in. baking pan with parchment paper. Prepare cake batter according to package directions; pour into prepared pan. Bake at 350° for 18-24 minutes or until a toothpick inserted near the center comes out clean. Cool completely in pan on a wire rack.

2. Invert cake onto a large cutting board or work surface. Gently peel off parchment paper. Cut cake into hearts (or other desired shapes) with a 2-1/2-in. to 3-in. cookie cutter.

3. For glaze, combine the confectioners' sugar, water, corn syrup, butter and extracts in a mixing bowl; beat on low speed until sugar is moistened. Beat on high until smooth. Tint with food coloring if desired. Add 2-3 teaspoons of additional water if needed for desired consistency.

4. Place petits fours on a wire rack with a piece of waxed paper beneath. Spoon glaze evenly over top and sides, letting excess drip off. When glaze is dry, repeat with a second coat.

Booties 'n' Rattles Cake

PREP: 1 hour **BAKE:** 25 min. + cooling
YIELD: 20 servings

Mary Cicio, Youngwood, Pennsylvania

Follow the easy instructions here for an adorably adorned baby shower dessert.

    6 **eggs,** *separated*
1-1/2 **cups butter, softened**
1-1/2 **cups sugar**
    3 **tablespoons grated orange peel**
    2 **cups all-purpose flour**
    2 **teaspoons baking powder**
  1/4 **teaspoon salt**
    6 **cups Easy Vanilla Buttercream Frosting**
       (page 164)

Pink and blue liquid food coloring

1 Let separated eggs stand at room temperature for 30 minutes. In a large mixing bowl, cream butter and sugar until light and fluffy. Add egg yolks and orange peel; beat well. Combine the flour, baking powder and salt; add to creamed mixture and mix well (batter will be thick). In a small mixing bowl and with clean beaters, beat the egg whites on high speed until stiff peaks form. Fold into batter.

2 Pour into a greased and floured 13-in. x 9-in. x 2-in. baking pan. Bake at 375° for 25-30 minutes or until a toothpick inserted near the center comes out clean. Cool for 10 minutes before inverting onto a wire rack to cool completely. Transfer cake to a large platter or covered board (about 15 in. x 12 in.).

3 Place 3/4 cup frosting each in two small bowls; tint one pastel pink and one pastel blue. Set aside 2-1/2 cups white frosting for trim and border. Cover and set bowls aside. Frost cake with the remaining white frosting.

4 Using dental floss or a sharp knife, mark a straight line lengthwise down the center of cake. Mark an additional lengthwise line on each side of the center line, dividing cake into four equal sections. Mark four lines widthwise, dividing cake into a total of 20 squares.

5 For booties, cut a small hole in the corner of a pastry bag or heavy-duty resealable plastic bag. Insert round pastry tip #8; fill bag with pink frosting. In alternating squares, pipe an elongated dot, raising up at one end to form the heel.

6 For rattles, use another pastry bag, round tip #8 and blue frosting. In each empty square, pipe one

large dot and one small dot, leaving 3/4 in. between. Use round pastry tip #2 and blue frosting to pipe a line connecting the dots.

7 For trim, use a third pastry bag, round tip #2 and reserved white frosting. Pipe a bow and trim on each bootie and a bow on each rattle.

8 Use star pastry tip #20 and white frosting to pipe rows of shells (see Shell Border on page 170) on top of the straight lines. Pipe a row of shells around top and bottom edges of cake.

Editor's Note: Use of a coupler ring will allow you to change tips easily for different designs.

BUTTERFLY CUPCAKES

decorating the
booties 'n' rattles *cake*

1. For booties, use round tip #8 and pink frosting to pipe an elongated dot, raising up at one end to form the heel.

2. For rattles, use round tip #8 and blue frosting to pipe one large dot and one small dot, leaving 3/4 in. of space between. Use round tip #2 to pipe a line to connect dots.

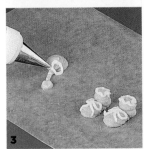

3. For trim, use round tip #2 and white frosting to pipe a bow and trim on each bootie and a bow on each rattle.

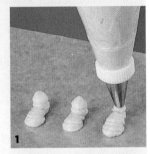

Butterfly Cupcakes

PREP: 35 min. **BAKE:** 15 min. + cooling
YIELD: 20 cupcakes

Adeline Piscitelle, Sayreville, New Jersey

Herald the arrival of spring with a platter of these eye-catching cupcakes bursting with lemon pie filling.

> 3/4 **cup butter, softened**
> 3/4 **cup sugar**
>   3 **eggs**
>   1 **teaspoon vanilla extract**
>   2 **cups self-rising flour**
> 1/2 **cup milk**
>   1 **can (15-3/4 ounces) lemon pie filling**
> 40 **pieces red *and/or* black shoestring licorice (2 inches)**

1 In a large mixing bowl, cream butter and sugar until light and fluffy. Beat in eggs and vanilla. Add flour to creamed mixture alternately with milk, beating well after each addition.

2 Fill greased muffin cups half full. Bake at 350° for 15-20 minutes or until a toothpick inserted near the center comes out clean. Cool for 10 minutes before removing from pans to wire racks to cool completely.

3 Cut off the top fourth of each cupcake; cut the slices in half. Spoon 1 tablespoon pie filling onto each cupcake. Place two halves upside down on top of filling for wings. Insert two pieces of licorice for antennae.

Editor's Note: As a substitute for the self-rising flour, place 3 teaspoons baking powder and 1 teaspoon salt in a measuring cup. Add all-purpose flour to measure 1 cup. Then add an additional 1 cup of all-purpose flour.

HAUNTED HOUSE CAKE

Haunted House Cake

PREP: 45 min. **BAKE:** 55 min. + cooling
YIELD: 12-15 servings

Taste of Home Test Kitchen

This eerie abode will be a haunting delight at Halloween parties! The ghostly home starts with handy cake mixes, plus common baking pans you likely already have.

- 1 package (18-1/4 ounces) chocolate cake mix
- 1 package (18-1/4 ounces) white cake mix
- 2 Nutter Butter cookies
- 3/4 cup shortening
- 3/4 cup butter, softened
- 6 cups confectioners' sugar
- 3 tablespoons plus 1-1/2 teaspoons milk
- 1-1/2 teaspoons vanilla extract
- 1 milk chocolate candy bar (1.55 ounces)
- 1 orange M&M miniature baking bit

Orange liquid *or* paste food coloring
- 1 cup Golden Grahams cereal

Stick of orange-striped fruit gum
Chocolate sprinkles
- 1/4 cup gold rock candy

1 Prepare chocolate cake batter according to package directions. Spoon 3 cups into a greased and floured 8-in. x 4-in. x 2-in. loaf pan. Set remaining batter aside. Bake loaf cake at 350° for 55-60 minutes or until a toothpick inserted near the center comes out clean. Cool for 10 minutes before removing from pan to a wire rack to cool completely.

2 Prepare white cake batter and pour into a greased and floured 13-in. x 9-in. x 2-in. baking pan. Drop reserved chocolate batter by 1/4 cupfuls onto white batter. Cut through batter with a knife to swirl. Bake at 350° for 35-40 minutes or until a toothpick inserted near the center comes out clean. Cool for 10 minutes before removing from pan to a wire rack to cool completely.

3 To assemble, place the marbled cake on a large platter or covered board (about 14 in. x 10 in.). Level top of chocolate cake (see Leveling Cake Layers on page 119). Cut chocolate cake in half widthwise. Referring to photo at left for position, place one half on the corner of the marbled cake for the house.

4 For the roof, cut remaining half of chocolate cake in half diagonally. Position the two halves together so they form a triangular shape on top of house. Cut each cookie in half widthwise and set aside.

5 In a mixing bowl, cream shortening and butter until light and fluffy. Gradually add the confectioners' sugar, milk and vanilla, mixing until smooth. Frost house, roof, sides of marble cake and cookie halves.

6 Break candy bar into rectangles. Place one on front of house for door (save remaining pieces for another use). Place a small dot of frosting on left side of door and attach M&M baking bits for doorknob. Tint remaining frosting orange; frost top of marble cake.

7 Place cereal on roof of house for shingles. Cut gum in half widthwise and then lengthwise. Place two pieces above the door for shutters. Use sprinkles to outline the window.

8 For tombstones, attach sprinkles to the cookies to read "RIP" and "BOO." Place cookies on the cake, lightly pushing them into frosting. Place rock candy in front of door for a walkway.

Sweet Stars Cake

PREP: 20 min. **BAKE:** 20 min. + cooling
YIELD: 12 servings

Flo Burtnett, Gage, Oklahoma

Three ingredients are all you need for this dazzling dessert perfect for a Fourth of July celebration.

- 1 package (18-1/4 ounces) chocolate cake mix
- 1 can (16 ounces) vanilla frosting
- 1 package (5 ounces) Fruit Roll-Ups

SWEET STARS CAKE

2 Place 1/2 cup coconut in a plastic bag; sprinkle 5-6 drops of yellow food coloring into bag and shake until color is evenly distributed. Repeat with 1/4 cup coconut and blue coloring, then with remaining coconut and green coloring. Reserve one licorice piece for mouth; cut remaining pieces into 2-in. to 3-in. pieces for hair.

3 Frost round cake with vanilla frosting; place on a large platter or covered board (about 22 in. x 15 in.). Press peanut butter cups upside down in place for eyes. Form long licorice piece into mouth and press into frosting (insert a small piece for smile if desired).

4 Remove liner from one cupcake and cut the top off. Cut the top in half again and press into sides of frosted cake for ears. Tint 2 tablespoons of frosting with red food coloring; frost bottom half of cupcake and press in place for nose.

5 Frost all remaining cupcakes. Remove liners from two cupcakes and cut in half; sprinkle with green coconut. Press flat sides against top of cake to form hat brim. Sprinkle five cupcakes with yellow coconut and one with blue coconut; stack in a pyramid on top of brim to make the hat.

6 Push ends of small licorice pieces into frosting for hair. Place remaining cupcakes at bottom of cake to make a bow tie; decorate those cupcakes with Skittles.

1 Prepare and bake cake according to package directions, using two greased and floured 9-in. round baking pans. Cool for 10 minutes; remove from pans to wire racks to cool completely.

2 Place bottom cake layer on a serving plate; spread with some of the frosting. Top with second layer; spread frosting over top and sides of cake.

3 Unroll Fruit Roll-Ups. Cut one blue, one green and one red star with a 2-3/4-in. star-shaped cookie cutter. Place on top of cake. Cut remaining Roll-Ups with a 2-in. star-shaped cookie cutter. Place a yellow star in the center of each large star. Arrange remaining stars on top and sides of cake.

Happy Clown Cake

PREP: 1 hour **BAKE:** 30 min. + cooling
YIELD: 16-20 servings

Taste of Home Test Kitchen

Children of all ages will find this fun-filled cake irresistible! To serve, first pass out the cupcakes, then cut up what's left.

> 1 **package (18-1/4 ounces) yellow cake mix**
> 1 **cup flaked coconut,** *divided*
> **Yellow, blue, green and red liquid food coloring**
> 1 **package (5 ounces) red shoestring licorice**
> 1 **can (16 ounces) vanilla frosting**
> 2 **miniature peanut butter cups**
> 1 **package (2.17 ounces) Skittles bite-size candies**

1 Prepare cake batter according to package directions. Fill 12 paper-lined muffin cups two-thirds full. Pour remaining batter into a greased 9-in. round baking pan. Bake cake and cupcakes according to package directions. Cool for 10 minutes before removing from pans to wire racks to cool completely.

HAPPY CLOWN CAKE

Snowman Cake

PREP: 40 min. **BAKE:** 1 hour + cooling
YIELD: 8-10 servings

Taste of Home Test Kitchen

The cute-as-can-be character is completely edible. And, you'll be able to build the confection without using a specially shaped pan.

- 2 **packages (16 ounces *each*) pound cake mix**
- 1 **cup shortening**
- 1 **cup butter, softened**
- 8 **cups confectioners' sugar**
- 2 **teaspoons vanilla extract**
- 4 to 6 **tablespoons milk**
- 1 **package (10 ounces) flaked coconut**
- 2 **brown M&M's**
- 3 **green M&M's**
- 1 **large orange gumdrops**
- 4-1/2 **teaspoons miniature chocolate chips**
- 1 **chocolate wafer**
- 6 **pieces red shoestring licorice, *divided***
- 1 **large green gumdrop**
- 2 **red M&M'S**

1 Prepare cake mixes according to package directions. Pour batter into two greased 1-quart ovenproof bowls, two greased 10-oz. custard cups and one greased muffin cup.

SNOWMAN CAKE

2 In a 350° oven, bake muffin cup for 18-20 minutes, custard cups for 45-50 minutes and bowls for 60-65 minutes or until a toothpick inserted near the center comes out clean. Cool for 5 minutes before removing cakes from pans to wire racks to cool completely.

3 For frosting, cream the shortening and butter in a mixing bowl until light and fluffy. Beat in the confectioners' sugar, vanilla and enough milk to achieve spreading consistency.

4 For body and head, use serrated knife to level the cakes.

5 For the body, place one large round cake flat side up on the 8-inch serving plate. Frost the top of the cake. Place the remaining large cake on top with the flat side down and edges even. Frost the top and sides.

6 For the head, place one custard cup cake with flat side up on top of body. Frost the top of the cake. Place the remaining custard cup cake on top with the flat side down and edges even. Set aside 1/4 cup of frosting for hat. Frost the top and sides with remaining frosting.

7 Press coconut over the top and sides of snowman, reserving some to sprinkle on plate later. Press two brown M&M's onto face for the eyes and three green M&M's onto body for the buttons. Use your fingers to shape the orange gumdrop into a carrot shape. Press wide end onto face for the nose.

8 For hat, place reserved frosting in a bowl. Melt chocolate chips. Stir melted chips into frosting until blended. Frost top of wafer. Center cupcake top side down on top of frosted wafer. Frost cupcake with remaining frosting. Place hat on snowman's head. Wrap two licorice pieces around hat just above brim and trim as needed. Flatten green gumdrop between waxed paper. Using sharp knife, cut a holly leaf shape from gumdrop and place on hat brim. Place two red M&M'S on brim next to holly leaf for the berries.

9 Press the ends of two licorice pieces together to create one long piece. Repeat with remaining two pieces of licorice. Tie long licorice pieces around neck for scarf. Sprinkle plate with reserved coconut.

RUDOLPH CUPCAKES

Rudolph Cupcakes

PREP: 20 min. **BAKE:** 25 min. per batch + cooling
YIELD: 2 dozen

Karen Gardiner, Eutaw, Alabama

Have your children help decorate these easy-to-make reindeer treats. They're great for class holiday parties.

- 1 **package (18-1/4 ounces) cake mix of your choice**
- 1 **can (16 ounces) chocolate frosting**
- 48 **animal crackers**
- 24 **miniature marshmallows, halved**
- 48 **miniature chocolate chips *or* raisins**
- 24 **red jelly beans**

1 Prepare and bake cake according to package directions for cupcakes, using foil or paper-lined muffin cups. Cool for 10 minutes before removing from pans to wire racks to cool completely.

2 Frost cupcake tops. Insert two animal crackers into each cupcake for antlers. For the eyes, place two marshmallow halves cut side up with a chocolate chip in the center of each. Add a jelly bean for nose.

ROLY-POLY
SANTA

Roly-Poly Santas

PREP: 1 hour **BAKE:** 15 min. + cooling **YIELD:** 1 dozen

Mrs. Andrew Seyer, Oak Ridge, Missouri

Tuck these fanciful Santas onto every gift cookie tray you make…they're guaranteed to be a hit.

- 1 **cup butter, softened**
- 1/2 **cup sugar**
- 1 **tablespoon milk**
- 1 **teaspoon vanilla extract**
- 2-1/4 **cups all-purpose flour**
- **Red paste food coloring**
- **Miniature chocolate chips**
- **FROSTING:**
- 1/2 **cup shortening**
- 1/2 **teaspoon vanilla extract**
- 2-1/3 **cups confectioners' sugar, *divided***
- 2 **tablespoons milk, *divided***

1 In a large mixing bowl, cream butter and sugar until light and fluffy. Add milk and vanilla; mix well. Add flour and mix well. Remove 1 cup dough; add red food coloring. Shape white dough into 12 balls, 3/4 in. each, and 48 balls, 1/4 in. each. Shape red dough into 12 balls, 1 in. each, and 60 balls, 1/2 in. each.

2 Place 1-in. red balls on two ungreased baking sheets for the body of 12 Santas; flatten to 1/2-in. thickness. Attach 3/4-in. white balls for heads; flatten to 1/2-in. thickness. Attach four 1/2-in. red balls to each Santa for arms and legs. Attach 1/4-in. white balls to ends of arms and legs for hands and feet. Shape remaining 1/2-in. red balls into hats (see photo at left). Add chocolate chip eyes and buttons.

3 Bake at 325° for 12-15 minutes or until set. Cool for 10 minutes; carefully remove from pans to wire racks (cookies will be fragile).

4 For frosting, in a small mixing bowl, beat shortening and vanilla. Gradually add 1-1/3 cups confectioners' sugar; add 1 tablespoon milk. Gradually add remaining sugar and milk.

5 Cut a small hole in the corner of a pastry bag or heavy-duty resealable plastic bag; insert round pastry tip #3. Fill bag with frosting. Pipe a band of icing on hat, cuffs at hands and feet, and down the front and at bottom of jacket. Use star pastry tip #16 to pipe beard and pom-pom on hat.

Editor's Note: Use of a coupler ring will allow you to easily change tips. Remaining dough may be shaped into balls and baked.

SPRING BONNET COOKIE TORTE

Spring Bonnet Cookie Torte

PREP: 1 hour + chilling
BAKE: 10 min. per batch + cooling   **YIELD:** 8-10 servings

Taste of Home Test Kitchen

Unlike other hat-shaped desserts, this one is fashioned from crisp cookies. A dreamy creamy filling holds the layers of cookies together and softens them, making it easy to slice. Add silk flowers to the brim as in the photo above.

3/4	cup butter, softened
1-1/2	cups sugar
2	eggs
3/4	teaspoon vanilla extract
3	cups all-purpose flour
1-1/2	teaspoons baking powder
3/4	teaspoon salt

Additional sugar
FILLING:

1	cup vanilla *or* white chips
1/4	cup half-and-half cream
1	cup heavy whipping cream, whipped
1	teaspoon vanilla extract

FROSTING:

1/2	cup butter, softened
1/2	cup shortening
4	cups confectioners' sugar
2	tablespoons heavy whipping cream
1	teaspoon almond extract

Pink *or* red liquid *or* paste food coloring

1 In a large mixing bowl, cream butter and sugar until light and fluffy. Beat in eggs and vanilla. Combine the flour, baking powder and salt; add to creamed mixture and mix well. Form seven balls, using 1/4 cup of dough for each. Form three balls, using about 1/2 cup of dough for each. Cover and refrigerate for 1 hour.

2 Sprinkle each ball with additional sugar, then place between two sheets of waxed paper. Roll smaller balls into 6-in. circles. Roll larger balls into 9-in. circles. Remove top sheet of waxed paper; invert circles onto ungreased baking sheets. Remove waxed paper; prick cookies with a fork.

3 Bake at 350° for 8-10 minutes or until edges are lightly browned. Carefully loosen cookies and place on paper towels to cool.

4 In a small heavy saucepan or microwave, melt chips with half-and-half; stir until smooth. Cool to room temperature. Combine whipped cream and vanilla; fold into melted mixture.

5 To form bonnet brim, layer 9-in. cookies on a large platter or covered board (about 15 in. square), spreading 1/2 cup filling between layers. For crown, spread 1/4 cup filling on the bottom of one 6-in. cookie and center cookie on top of the 9-in. layer. Layer remaining 6-in. cookies, spreading 1/4 cup filling between layers. Refrigerate overnight.

6 For frosting, in a large mixing bowl, beat butter, shortening and sugar on low speed until blended; beat on high for 5 minutes. Reduce speed to medium. Gradually add cream and extract, beating until smooth. Set aside 3/4 cup; tint remaining frosting pink.

7 Spread pink frosting over top and sides of cookies. Cut a small hole in the corner of a pastry bag or heavy-duty resealable plastic bag; insert star pastry tip #20. Fill bag with white frosting. Holding bag at a 45° angle, form shell border at base of bonnet (see Making a Shell Border on page 170). Using the same tip, form a reverse shell border on top of bonnet.

8 Using another pastry bag, basketweave pastry tip #48 and white frosting, hold bag at a 45° angle to form a ribbed border at base of crown. Decorate with silk flowers on one side of bonnet. Tie a piece of ribbon into a bow and place on opposite side of bonnet.

TEDDY BEAR ROLLS

Teddy Bear Rolls

PREP: 30 min. + rising **BAKE:** 20 min. + cooling
YIELD: about 10 rolls (1-1/4 cups butter)

Annette Ellyson, Carolina, West Virginia

These cute rolls would be a nice addition to a "Teddy Bear" party. Their oven-fresh goodness is so appealing.

2	**packages (1/4 ounce *each*) active dry yeast**
1	**cup warm water (110° to 115°)**
1	**cup warm milk (110° to 115°)**
2	**tablespoons sugar**
2	**tablespoons vegetable oil**
1	**egg**
1	**teaspoon salt**
5-1/2	**to 6-1/2 cups all-purpose flour**

About 20 raisins
White frosting
HONEY BUTTER:

1	**cup butter, softened**
1/4	**cup honey**
1/4	**cup confectioners' sugar**

1 In a large mixing bowl, dissolve yeast in water. Add the milk, sugar, oil, egg, salt and 4 cups flour; beat until smooth. Stir in enough remaining flour to form a soft dough.

2 Turn onto a floured surface; knead until smooth and elastic, about 6-8 minutes. Place in a greased bowl, turning once to grease top. Cover and let rise in a warm place until doubled, about 1 hour.

3 Punch dough down. For each bear, shape a 2-in. ball for the body. Add a 1-1/4-in. ball for the head and six 1/2-in. balls for ears, arms and legs. Place 2 in. apart on greased baking sheets. Cover and let rise until doubled, about 20 minutes.

4 Bake at 400° for 17-20 minutes or until golden brown. Cool on wire racks. Add raisins for eyes, anchoring with a dab of frosting. Add a frosting smile.

5 In a small mixing bowl, beat honey butter ingredients until fluffy. Chill. Serve with rolls.

SWAN CREAM PUFFS

of each for head. Bake at 400° for 5-8 minutes or until golden brown. Remove to wire racks to cool.

3 For swan bodies, drop remaining batter by 36 level tablespoonfuls 2 in. apart onto greased baking sheets. With a small icing knife or spatula, shape batter into 2-in. x 1-1/2-in. teardrops. Bake at 400° for 30-35 minutes or until golden brown. Cool on wire racks.

4 Meanwhile, prepare pudding according to package directions for pie filling; chill.

5 Just before serving, cut off top third of swan bodies; set tops aside. Remove any soft dough inside. Spoon filling into bottoms of puffs. Top each with a small amount of jam if desired. Cut the reserved tops in half lengthwise to form wings; set wings in filling. Place necks in filling. Dust with confectioners' sugar; serve immediately.

Swan Cream Puffs

PREP: 55 min. + chilling **BAKE:** 35 min. + cooling
YIELD: 3 dozen

Carole Davis, Keene, New Hampshire

These pretty pastries can be prepared a day in advance, then stored at room temperature in an airtight container. Fill just before serving.

1	cup water
1/2	cup butter
1/4	teaspoon salt
1	cup all-purpose flour
4	eggs
2	packages (3.4 ounces *each*) instant vanilla pudding mix
2	tablespoons seedless raspberry jam, optional

Confectioners' sugar

1 In a heavy saucepan over medium heat, bring water, butter and salt to a boil. Add flour all at once; stir until a smooth ball forms. Remove from the heat; let stand for 5 minutes. Add eggs, one at a time, beating well after each addition. Beat until smooth and shiny.

2 Cut a small hole in the corner of a pastry bag or heavy-duty resealable plastic bag; insert round pastry tip #7. Fill bag with batter. On a greased baking sheet, pipe 3 dozen 2-in.-long S shapes for the swan necks, making a small dollop at the end

making *swan cream puffs*

1. To make swan necks, pipe batter into 3 dozen 2-in. long S shapes onto greased baking sheets, making a small dollop at the end of each for the head. Bake as directed.

2. To assemble cream puffs, cut off the top third of swan bodies. Remove any soft dough inside. Cut tops in half lengthwise to form wings. Fill bottoms of puffs with pudding. Place necks and wings in filling.

Chocolate Garnishes

Chocolate garnishes add a special touch to desserts. These garnishes can be made from either chocolate or candy coating. (In this section, the terms are used interchangeably.)

Most of these garnishes call for melted chocolate. Here's how:

Break or chop large pieces of chocolate. This gives it more surface area and it will melt more evenly. Melt in a heavy saucepan over low heat and stir until smooth. (High heat will scorch and ruin the chocolate.) Small amounts of water will cause chocolate to seize. So make sure the pan and spoon are dry.

To melt in the microwave, heat semisweet chocolate at 50% power. Heat milk chocolate and vanilla or white chocolate at 30% power. Stir during melting and don't overheat.

CUTOUTS

Melt 1 cup chips—semisweet, milk, vanilla or white—and 1/4 teaspoon shortening (do not use butter, margarine or oil).

Line a baking sheet with aluminum foil (shiny side up) or waxed paper. Smooth the foil or paper so there are not any wrinkles or bumps, which would make the chocolate uneven.

Pour melted chocolate onto foil or paper; spread with a spatula so the chocolate is about 1/8 in. thick. Let stand at room temperature until firm.

Using sharp metal cookie cutters, cut out desired shapes. (See photo.) Carefully lift off shapes with a metal spatula.

The chocolate scraps may be remelted and used to coat fruit or whole nuts for additional garnishes.

CURLS

Using a vegetable peeler, peel off curls from a solid block of chocolate. (See photo above left.) Allow curls to fall gently onto a work surface or plate in a single layer. If you get only shavings, try warming the chocolate slightly.

HEARTS AND ARROWS

Trace the design several times on a piece of paper. Place the paper on a baking sheet and cover with waxed paper.

Melt semisweet, milk, vanilla or white chocolate. The amount of melted chocolate needed depends on the number of garnishes you are making. Fill pastry bag or resealable plastic bag with melted chocolate. Cut a small hole in the bottom corner of bag. The more detailed the design, the smaller the hole in the bag should be. But remember, when finished, thicker designs will be sturdier and easier to remove.

Following traced designs, pipe chocolate onto waxed paper. (See photo 1.) Refrigerate until the chocolate is firm, about 15 minutes.

Just before serving, carefully remove the hearts with a metal spatula. (See photo 2.) If designs are not to be used immediately, store in a cool dry place in a covered plastic container until needed.

EDIBLE CLAY

Melt 10 oz. chocolate or white candy coating. Stir in 1/3 cup light corn syrup. If using white candy coating, you can divide between different bowls and tint with various liquid or paste food coloring. Spread on a sheet of waxed paper to 1/3-in. thickness. Let stand, uncovered, at room temperature for 2-3 hours or until dry to the touch. Remove clay from waxed paper and gather into a ball. Wrap tightly in plastic wrap; let stand overnight. Use immediately or store for up to 2 weeks.

To use, unwrap clay and knead until pliable but not soft. Roll between sheets of waxed paper to 1/8-in. thickness. Cut into desired shapes with a sharp knife or cookie cutters. Carefully lift up shapes with a spatula.

BUTTERFLIES

Melt about 10 oz. white candy coating.

Trace pattern (at right) onto tracing paper. Place butterfly pattern on a flat surface. Arrange wooden spoons with handles 2 in. apart. Place a 4-in. square of waxed paper directly over the pattern.

Cut a small hole in the bottom corner of a pastry bag or heavy-duty resealable plastic bag. Insert round pastry tip #4 if desired or pipe candy coating directly from the bag. Fill bag with some melted candy coating.

Pipe chocolate over the pattern, carefully tracing the butterfly outline. (See photo 1.) Continue with the inside design, then pipe the body and antennae. If mistakes are made when tracing over the pattern with chocolate, or if chocolate begins to harden while tracing, simply start over. Remove chocolate from bag before remelting. To fix broken wings or antennae, "glue" them back on with melted chocolate.

Immediately pick up the edges of waxed paper and place the completed butterfly between the spoon handles with the wings resting against the handles. (See photo 2.) This will create the curve of the wings. Repeat, lining up the butterflies down the length of the handles. Remove butterflies from waxed paper by carefully peeling away the waxed paper.

If butterflies are not to be used immediately, store in a cool dry place in a covered plastic container. Place butterflies on cakes, cupcakes or petit fours while frosting is still moist. This will help secure them in place.

LEAVES

Wash 10 to 12 lemon, rose or mint leaves and set aside until completely dry. Melt 1/2 cup chips—semisweet, milk, vanilla or white—and 1/4 teaspoon shortening (do not use butter, margarine or oil).

With a new small paintbrush, brush melted chocolate in a thin layer on the underside of each leaf. (See photo 1.) Refrigerate until set, about 10 minutes. Apply a second layer of melted chocolate; chill for at least 15 minutes or overnight. Gently peel leaf from

chocolate. (See photo 2.)

If leaves are not to be used immediately, store in a cool dry place in a covered plastic container until needed.

CHOCOLATE ALMOND PINECONES

Divide one 7-oz. tube almond paste into six equal portions. Form each into a cone shape, about 1-1/2 in. tall and 1 in. in diameter. Beginning at the base, insert pointed end of sliced almonds (4 ounces total) into paste to resemble a pinecone. (See photo 1.)

Melt 1-1/4 cups chips—semisweet, milk, vanilla or white—and 1 tablespoon shortening (do not use

butter, margarine or oil). Stir until smooth. Insert a toothpick into the bottom of each pinecone. Holding over a bowl, spoon melted chocolate over pinecone. (See photo 2.)

Use another toothpick to spread the chocolate to completely cover. Place on a wire rack over waxed paper; let stand until firm. (See photo 3.)

Use immediately or store in an airtight container at room temperature for several weeks.

HOLIDAY BAKING

Holiday Baking

Butterscotch Eggnog Stars

PREP: 25 min. + chilling **BAKE:** 10 min. per batch
YIELD: about 3 dozen

Cheryl Hemmer, Swansea, Illinois

These yellow star-shaped cookies with a stained-glass center are almost too pretty to eat! But they have a rich eggnog flavor that is irresistible.

2/3　**cup butter, softened**
1　**cup sugar**
1　**egg**
1/4　**cup eggnog**
2　**cups all-purpose flour**
3/4　**teaspoon baking powder**
1/4　**teaspoon salt**
1/4　**teaspoon ground nutmeg**
1/2　**cup crushed hard butterscotch candies**
ICING (OPTIONAL):
1-1/2　**cups confectioners' sugar**
1/4　**teaspoon rum extract**
2　**to 3 tablespoons eggnog**
Yellow colored sugar

1 Grease foil-lined baking sheets; set aside. In a large mixing bowl, cream butter and sugar until light and fluffy. Beat in egg and eggnog. Combine the flour, baking powder, salt and nutmeg; gradually add to creamed mixture and mix well. Divide dough in half.

2 On a lightly floured surface, roll out one portion at a time to 1/4-in. thickness. Cut with a floured 3-1/2-in. star cutter. Cut out centers with a 1-1/2-in. star cutter.

3 Place large stars 2 in. apart on prepared baking sheets. Sprinkle 1 teaspoon candy in center of each. Repeat with remaining dough; reroll small cutouts if desired.

4 Bake at 375° for 6-8 minutes or until edges are golden. Cool on baking sheets for 5 minutes. Carefully slide foil and cookies from baking sheets onto wire racks to cool.

5 For icing if desired, beat the confectioners' sugar, rum extract and enough eggnog to achieve drizzling consistency. Drizzle over cooled cookies if desired. Sprinkle with colored sugar if desired. Let stand until set.

Editor's Note: This recipe was tested with commercially prepared eggnog.

BUTTERSCOTCH EGGNOG STARS

Cookies

Holiday Nuggets

PREP: 25 min. **BAKE:** 25 min. per batch + cooling
YIELD: 3-1/2 dozen

Beverly Launius, Sandwich, Illinois

Hazelnuts give these delicious cookies a little different flavor from the usual pecans.

- 1/2 **cup butter, softened**
- 1/2 **cup sifted confectioners' sugar**
- 1 **tablespoon vanilla extract**
- 1 **teaspoon almond extract**
- 2 **cups all-purpose flour**
- 1/2 **teaspoon salt**
- 1/2 **cup chopped hazelnuts**

Confectioners' sugar
Colored crystallized sugar

1 In a large mixing bowl, cream butter and sugar until light and fluffy. Blend in vanilla and almond extract. Gradually add flour and salt. Stir in nuts.

2 Shape into 1-1/4-in. balls. Place 2 in. apart on ungreased baking sheets. Flatten slightly with fingers. Bake at 325° for 25 minutes or until the bottoms are lightly browned. Cool on a wire rack. When cool, sprinkle with a mixture of confectioners' and colored sugar.

Butter Cookie Snowmen

PREP: 40 min. **BAKE:** 15 min. **YIELD:** 2 dozen

Kathleen Taugher, East Troy, Wisconsin

The dough of these tasty cookies is easy to shape, which makes it a good choice to make with young children.

- 1 **cup butter, softened**
- 1/2 **cup sugar**
- 1 **tablespoon milk**
- 1 **teaspoon vanilla extract**
- 2-1/4 **cups all-purpose flour**

Red and yellow paste food coloring
Miniature chocolate chips

1 In a mixing bowl, cream butter and sugar until light and fluffy. Add milk and vanilla; mix well. Gradually add flour. Remove 1/3 cup of dough to a small bowl; tint with red food coloring. Repeat with 1/3 cup of dough and yellow food coloring; set aside.

BUTTER COOKIE SNOWMEN

2 For snowmen, shape white dough into 24 balls, 1-1/4 in. each; 24 balls, about 1/2 in. each; and 24 balls, about 1/8 in. each. For bodies, place large balls on two ungreased baking sheets; flatten to 3/8-in. thickness. Place 1/2-in. balls above bodies for heads; flatten.

3 Shape red dough into 24 balls, 1/8 in. each, and 24 triangles. Place triangles above heads for hats; attach 1/8-in. white balls for tassels. Place red balls on heads for noses. Divide the yellow dough into 24 pieces; shape into scarves and position on snowmen. Add chocolate chip eyes and buttons. Bake at 325° for 13-16 minutes or until set. Cool for 2 minutes, then carefully remove to wire racks.

Candy Cane Snowballs

PREP: 25 min. + chilling **BAKE:** 20 min. per batch + cooling **YIELD:** 5 dozen

Debby Anderson, Stockbridge, Georgia

These snowballs are dipped in a white candy coating, then into crushed peppermint candy, and make a great treat.

- 2 **cups butter, softened**
- 1 **cup confectioners' sugar**
- 1 **teaspoon vanilla extract**
- 3-1/2 **cups all-purpose flour**
- 1 **cup chopped pecans**
- 8 **ounces white candy coating**
- 1/3 **to 1/2 cup crushed peppermint candy**

1 In a large mixing bowl, cream butter and confectioners' sugar until light and fluffy. Stir in vanilla. Gradually add flour. Stir in pecans. Refrigerate for 3-4 hours or until easy to handle.

2 Shape into 1-in. balls. Place 2 in. apart on ungreased baking sheets. Bake at 350° for 18-20 minutes or until lightly browned. Remove to wire racks to cool.

3 In a heavy saucepan or microwave, melt candy coating; stir until smooth. Dip the top of each cookie into the candy coating, then into the peppermint candy.

HOLLY BERRY COOKIES

Holly Berry Cookies

PREP: 30 min. + chilling **BAKE:** 10 min. + cooling
YIELD: 2 dozen

Audrey Thibodeau, Mesa, Arizona

What would Christmas be without overflowing tins of cookies? These festive cookies can be baked one or two months in advance. Keep them in the freezer until you need them. Then thaw and decorate.

- 2 **cups all-purpose flour**
- 1 **cup sugar**
- 1 **teaspoon ground cinnamon**
- 3/4 **teaspoon baking powder**
- 1/4 **teaspoon salt**
- 1/2 **cup cold butter**
- 1 **egg**
- 1/4 **cup milk**
- 2/3 **cup seedless raspberry jam**

GLAZE:
- 2 **cups confectioners' sugar**
- 2 **tablespoons milk**
- 1/2 **teaspoon vanilla extract**

Red-hot candies
Green food coloring

1 In a large bowl, combine the first five ingredients. Cut in butter until mixture resembles coarse crumbs. In a small bowl, beat egg and milk. Add to crumb mixture just until moistened. Cover and refrigerate for 1 hour or until dough is easy to handle.

2 On a lightly floured surface, roll out dough to 1/8-in. thickness. Cut with a 2-in. round cookie cutter. Place 2 in. apart on ungreased baking sheets. Bake at 375° for 8-10 minutes or until edges are lightly browned. Cool on wire racks. Spread jam on half of the cookies; top each with another cookie.

3 In a small mixing bowl, combine the sugar, milk and vanilla until smooth; spread over cookies. Decorate with red-hots before glaze is set. Let dry. Using a small new paintbrush and green food coloring, paint holly leaves on cookies.

CANDY CANE SNOWBALLS

CREAM CHEESE SPRITZ

Cream Cheese Spritz

PREP: 15 min. **BAKE:** 10 min. per batch + cooling
YIELD: about 9 dozen

Sarah Bedia, Lake Jackson, Texas

A hint of orange and cinnamon highlights these Christmastime classics. For an extra touch, add colorful sprinkles before baking them.

    1 cup shortening
    1 package (3 ounces) cream cheese,
       softened
    1 cup sugar
    1 egg yolk
    1 teaspoon vanilla extract
    1 teaspoon grated orange peel
2-1/2 cups all-purpose flour
  1/2 teaspoon salt
  1/4 teaspoon ground cinnamon
Green food coloring, decorator candies and
   colored sugar, optional

1 In a mixing bowl, beat shortening and cream cheese until blended. Add sugar; beat until creamy. Beat in the egg yolk, vanilla and orange peel. Combine the flour, salt and cinnamon; gradually add to creamed mixture. Add food coloring if desired.

2 Using a cookie press fitted with the disk of your choice, press dough 1 in. apart onto ungreased baking sheets. Decorate if desired. Bake at 350° for 9-12 minutes or until set (do not brown). Remove to wire racks to cool.

Deluxe Sugar Cookies

PREP: 20 min. + chilling **BAKE:** 10 min. per batch
YIELD: 5 dozen (2-inch cookies)

Dawn Fagerstrom, Warren, Minnesota

Christmas cutouts signal the holiday season. For variety, sprinkle half of the cookies with colored sugar before baking and frost the remaining ones after they're cooled.

    1 cup butter, softened
1-1/2 cups confectioners' sugar
    1 egg, beaten
    1 teaspoon vanilla extract
  1/2 teaspoon almond extract
2-1/2 cups all-purpose flour
    1 teaspoon baking soda
    1 teaspoon cream of tartar

1 In a mixing bowl, cream butter and sugar until light and fluffy. Add egg and extracts. Combine the flour, baking soda and cream of tartar; gradually add to the creamed mixture and mix well. Cover and refrigerate for at least 1 hour.

2 On a surface lightly sprinkled with confectioners' sugar, roll out the dough to 1/8-in. thickness. Cut into desired shapes. Place 2 in. apart on ungreased baking sheets. Repeat with the remaining dough.

3 Bake at 350° for 7-8 minutes, or until the edges begin to brown. Remove to wire racks to cool.

DELUXE SUGAR COOKIES

HOLIDAY GINGER CUTOUTS

3 For icing, sift confectioners' sugar and meringue powder into a large mixing bowl. Add water; beat on low speed until blended. Beat on high for 5-6 minutes or until soft peaks form. Place a damp paper towel over bowl and cover tightly until ready to use.

4 Cut a small hole in the corner of a pastry or plastic bag; insert round pastry tip #2, #3 or #4. Fill bag with 1 cup icing. Outline each cookie with icing.

5 Tint remaining icing with food coloring if desired. Add water, a few drops at a time, until mixture is thin enough to flow smoothly. Prepare additional pastry or plastic bags with thinned icing. Fill in cookies, letting icing flow up to the outline.

6 Let cookies dry at room temperature overnight. With food coloring and small new paintbrush, paint designs on dry icing. Store cookies in airtight containers.

Holiday Ginger Cutouts

PREP: 40 min. + chilling **BAKE:** 10 min. per batch + standing **YIELD:** about 6 dozen

Joanne MacVey, Blue Grass, Iowa

Looking to get a little creative with your cookie decorating? Paint your own masterpieces on a ginger cookie canvas.

1	cup shortening
1	cup sugar
1	egg
1	cup molasses
2	tablespoons white vinegar
4-1/2	cups all-purpose flour
2	teaspoons ground ginger
1-1/2	teaspoons baking soda
1	teaspoon ground cinnamon
3/4	teaspoon ground cloves
1/2	teaspoon salt

ICING:

4	cups confectioners' sugar
2	tablespoons meringue powder
1/2	cup warm water

Assorted colors of liquid food coloring

1 In a mixing bowl, cream shortening and sugar until light and fluffy. Add the egg, molasses and vinegar; mix well. Combine dry ingredients; add to creamed mixture and mix well. Cover and refrigerate for 3 hours or overnight.

2 On a lightly floured surface, roll out dough to 1/8-in. thickness and cut into desired shapes. Place 1 in. apart on lightly greased baking sheets. Bake at 350° for 7-9 minutes or until set. Remove to wire racks to cool.

decorating cookies with *royal icing*

1. Cut a small hole in the corner of a pastry or plastic bag. Insert a round tip; fill bag with icing. Hold bag at a 45° angle to the cookie, and pipe a bead of icing around the edge. Stop squeezing the bag before you lift the tip from the cookie.

2. Thin remaining icing so that it will flow smoothly. Fill another bag with thinned icing. Starting in the middle, fill in the cookie with the thinned icing, letting icing flow up to the outline. Let cookies dry overnight.

3. With a new small paintbrush, paint your own designs on the cookies with liquid food coloring.

Jeweled Thumbprints

PREP: 20 min. + chilling BAKE: 15 min. per batch + cooling YIELD: 6 dozen

Maria Debono, New York, New York

The almond flavor of these delicate cookies complements the preserves.

3/4 cup butter, softened
3/4 cup confectioners' sugar
1 egg yolk
1/2 teaspoon almond extract
1-3/4 cups all-purpose flour
1/2 cup raspberry *or* apricot preserves

1 In a large mixing bowl, cream butter and sugar until light and fluffy. Beat in egg yolk and extract. Gradually add flour. Cover and refrigerate for 2 hours or until easy to handle.

2 Shape into 3/4-in. balls. Place 1 in. apart on greased baking sheets. Using the end of a wooden spoon handle, make an indentation in the center of each ball.

3 Bake at 350° for 12-14 minutes or until edges are lightly browned. Remove to wire racks to cool. Fill with preserves.

JEWELED TUMBPRINTS

3/4 cup butter, softened
3/4 cup shortening
1-1/4 cups packed brown sugar
2 eggs
1 teaspoon vanilla extract
4 cups all-purpose flour
2 teaspoons baking powder
1/2 teaspoon salt
1 can (8 ounces) crushed pineapple, drained
1/2 cup chopped dates
1/2 cup chopped red maraschino cherries
1/2 cup chopped green maraschino cherries
1/2 cup flaked coconut
1/2 cup chopped pecans *or* walnuts

1 In a large mixing bowl, cream the butter, shortening and brown sugar until light and fluffy. Add eggs, one at a time, beating well after each addition. Beat in vanilla. Combine the flour, baking powder and salt; gradually add to the creamed mixture. Stir in remaining ingredients. Shape into three 10-in. rolls; wrap each in plastic wrap. Refrigerate for 2 hours or until firm.

2 Unwrap and cut into 1/4-in. slices. Place 2 in. apart on ungreased baking sheets. Bake at 375° for 8-10 minutes or until golden brown. Remove to wire racks to cool.

Fruit 'n' Nut Cookies

PREP: 15 min. + chilling BAKE: 10 min. per batch + cooling YIELD: 7 dozen

Jennie Loftus, Gasport, New York

Dotted with red and green maraschino cherries, these soft cookies are a nice addition to a Christmas dessert tray.

FRUIT 'N' NUT COOKIES

Chocolate Island Cookies

PREP: 15 min. BAKE: 15 min. per batch
YIELD: about 4 dozen

Christine Harsh, Kerens, West Virginia

You'll get a double-dose of chocolate from these cookies and their creamy frosting.

1/2 cup shortening
1 cup packed brown sugar
1 egg
3 squares (1 ounce *each*) unsweetened chocolate, melted and cooled
1/4 cup strong brewed coffee
2 cups all-purpose flour
1/2 teaspoon baking soda
1/2 teaspoon salt
2/3 cup buttermilk
1/3 cup flaked coconut

FROSTING:
1-1/2 squares (1-1/2 ounces) unsweetened chocolate, melted and cooled
1/4 cup sour cream
1 tablespoon butter, softened
1 to 1-1/2 cups confectioners' sugar
2/3 cup flaked coconut

1 In a mixing bowl, cream shortening and sugar until light and fluffy. Add the egg, chocolate and coffee; mix well. Combine the flour, baking soda and salt; add to creamed mixture alternately with buttermilk. Stir in coconut.

2 Drop by tablespoonfuls 2 in. apart onto greased baking sheets. Bake at 375° for 12-15 minutes or until edges are browned. Remove to wire racks to cool.

3 For frosting, combine the chocolate, sour cream and butter in a small mixing bowl. Add enough sugar to achieve spreading consistency. Frost cooled cookies. Sprinkle with coconut.

Italian Horn Cookies

PREP: 30 min. + chilling **BAKE:** 10 min. per batch + cooling **YIELD:** about 5 dozen

Gloria Siddiqui, Houston, Texas

These delicate fruit-filled Christmas cookies are light and flaky. They have the look of elegant pastry.

1 cup cold butter
4 cups all-purpose flour
2 cups vanilla ice cream, softened
1 can (12-1/2 ounces) cherry filling

Sugar

1 In a large bowl, cut butter into flour until mixture resembles coarse crumbs. Stir in ice cream. Divide into four portions. Cover and refrigerate for 2 hours.

2 On a lightly floured surface, roll each portion to 1/8-in. thickness. With a fluted pastry cutting, cut into 2-in. squares. Place about 1/2 teaspoon filling in the center of each squares. Overlap two opposite corners of dough over the filling and seal. Sprinkle lightly with sugar.

3 Place 2 in. apart on ungreased baking sheets. Bake at 350° for 10-12 minutes or until bottoms are light brown. Remove to wire racks to cool.

ITALIAN HORN COOKIES

WALNUT-FILLED PILLOWS

Walnut-Filled Pillows

PREP: 30 min. + chilling **BAKE:** 10 min.
YIELD: 28 cookies

Nancy Kostrej, Canonsburg, Pennsylvania

These tender cookie pillows, filled with a delicious walnut mixture, will soon be your favorite.

- 1/2 **cup cold butter**
- 1 **package (3 ounces) cold cream cheese**
- 1-1/4 **cups all-purpose flour**
- 3/4 **cup ground walnuts**
- 1/4 **cup sugar**
- 2 **tablespoons milk**
- 1/2 **teaspoon vanilla *or* almond extract**
- 1 **egg, lightly beaten**

Confectioners' sugar

1 In a large bowl, cut butter and cream cheese into flour until mixture resembles coarse crumbs. Using your hands, blend mixture together until smooth dough forms, about 3 minutes. Pat into a rectangle; wrap in plastic wrap. Refrigerate for 1 hour or until firm. For filling, combine the walnuts, sugar, milk and vanilla.

2 Unwrap dough and place on a lightly floured surface. Roll into a 17-1/2-in. x 10-in. rectangle; cut into 2-1/2-in. squares. Place a level teaspoonful of filling in the center of each square. Moisten edges with water; fold in half and seal with a fork. Place 1 in. apart on ungreased baking sheets. Brush with egg.

3 Bake at 375° for 10-12 minutes or until edges are golden brown. Remove to wire racks to cool. Dust with confectioners' sugar.

Holiday Brownies

PREP: 15 min. + cooling **BAKE:** 35 min. + cooling
YIELD: 2 dozen

Erna Madsen, Bothell, Washington

The candied cherries make a festive addition to this basic brownie recipe.

- 1/2 **cup butter**
- 4 **squares (1 ounce *each*) unsweetened chocolate, coarsely chopped**
- 2 **cups sugar**
- 1-1/4 **cups all-purpose flour**
- 2 **teaspoons ground cinnamon**
- 1/2 **teaspoon salt**
- 4 **eggs, beaten**
- 1 **teaspoon vanilla extract**
- 1-1/2 **cups halved red *and/or* green candied cherries, *divided***
- 1 **cup chopped walnuts**

1 In a heavy saucepan, melt butter and chocolate over low heat. Cool for 10 minutes. In a bowl, combine the sugar, flour, cinnamon and salt. Stir in the cooled chocolate mixture, eggs and vanilla until smooth. Fold in 1-1/4 cups cherries and the walnuts.

2 Transfer to a greased 13-in. x 9-in. x 2-in. baking pan. Arrange remaining cherries over top. Bake at 350° for 35 minutes or until a toothpick inserted near the center comes out clean. Cool on a wire rack. Cut into bars.

HOLIDAY BROWNIES

CRANBERRY DATE BARS

Marzipan Bars

PREP: 30 min. **BAKE:** 35 min. per batch + cooling
YIELD: about 6-1/2 dozen

Jeanne Koniuszy, Nome, Texas

Almond paste gives these special bars a rich, sweet taste. They look festive when set out on a serving tray and will go quickly.

- 1/2 cup butter, softened
- 1/2 cup packed brown sugar
- 1 egg yolk
- 1 teaspoon vanilla extract
- 2 cups all-purpose flour
- 1/2 teaspoon baking soda
- 1/4 teaspoon salt
- 1/4 cup milk
- 1 jar (10 ounces) raspberry jelly

FILLING:
- 1 can (8 ounces) almond paste, cubed
- 3 tablespoons butter, softened
- 1/2 cup sugar
- 1 egg white
- 1 teaspoon vanilla extract
- 3 eggs
- 6 drops green food coloring

ICING:
- 2 squares (1 ounce *each*) unsweetened chocolate
- 1 tablespoon butter
- 2 cups confectioners' sugar
- 4 to 5 tablespoons milk
- 1 teaspoon vanilla extract

1 In a mixing bowl, cream butter and brown sugar until light and fluffy. Add egg yolk and vanilla; mix well. Combine the flour, baking soda and salt; add to creamed mixture alternately with milk, beating well after each addition. Press into a greased 15-in. x 10-in. x 1-in. baking pan. Spread with jelly.

2 For filling, combine almond paste, butter, sugar, egg white and vanilla in a mixing bowl. Beat in eggs. Add food coloring; mix well. Pour over jelly layer. Bake at 350° for 35 minutes or until set. Cool on a wire rack.

3 For icing, in a heavy saucepan or microwave, melt chocolate and butter; stir until smooth. Add confectioners' sugar and enough milk to make a smooth icing. Stir in vanilla. Immediately spread over bars. Cover and store overnight at room temperature before cutting.

Cranberry Date Bars

PREP: 20 min. **BAKE:** 30 min. per batch + cooling
YIELD: 4 dozen

Mrs. Richard Grams, La Crosse, Wisconsin

Stock up on cranberries when they're in season—that way you'll always have them on hand for this easy-to-make bar.

- 1 package (12 ounces) fresh *or* frozen cranberries
- 1 package (8 ounces) chopped dates
- 1 teaspoon vanilla extract
- 2 cups all-purpose flour
- 2 cups quick-cooking oats
- 1-1/2 cups packed brown sugar
- 1/2 teaspoon baking soda
- 1/4 teaspoon salt
- 1 cup butter, melted

ORANGE GLAZE:
- 2 cups confectioners' sugar
- 2 to 3 tablespoons orange juice
- 1/2 teaspoon vanilla extract

1 In a saucepan, combine cranberries and dates. Cover and cook over low heat for 15 minutes or until berries pop, stirring often. Remove from the heat and stir in vanilla; set aside.

2 In a bowl, combine the flour, oats, sugar, baking soda and salt. Stir in butter until crumbly. Press half into an ungreased 13-in. x 9-in. x 2-in. baking pan. Bake at 350° for 8 minutes.

3 Spoon cranberry mixture over the crust; spread gently. Sprinkle with remaining crumb mixture; pat down gently. Bake at 350° for 20-25 minutes or until golden brown. Cool in pan on a wire rack. Combine glaze ingredients; drizzle over bars.

Cakes

Eggnog Cake

PREP: 30 min. + cooling   **BAKE:** 30 min. + cooling
YIELD: 12 servings

Debra Frappolli, Wayne, New Jersey

This wonderful cake is full of eggnog flavor. It will be a special favorite with your family around Christmastime.

    1/2 cup butter, softened
  1-1/4 cups sugar
      3 eggs
    1/2 teaspoon vanilla extract
    1/2 teaspoon rum extract
      2 cups all-purpose flour
      2 teaspoons baking powder
      1 teaspoon salt
      1 cup eggnog
FROSTING:
    1/4 cup all-purpose flour
    1/4 teaspoon salt
  1-1/2 cups eggnog
      1 cup butter, softened
  1-1/2 cups sugar
  1-1/2 teaspoons vanilla extract
Red and green gel food coloring, optional

1 In a large mixing bowl, cream butter and sugar until light and fluffy. Add eggs, one at a time, beating well after each addition. Add extracts; mix well. Combine the flour, baking powder and salt; add to creamed mixture alternately with eggnog. Pour into two 9-in. round baking pans coated with nonstick cooking spray.

EGGNOG CAKE

2 Bake at 350° for 30-35 minutes or until a toothpick inserted near the center comes out clean. Cool for 10 minutes before removing from pans to wire racks.

3 For frosting, combine flour and salt in a saucepan. Gradually stir in eggnog until smooth. Bring to a boil over medium heat; cook and stir for 2 minutes or until thickened. Remove from the heat; cool to room temperature.

4 In a large mixing bowl, cream butter and sugar until light and fluffy. Add eggnog mixture and vanilla; beat on high until fluffy. Remove 1/4 cup frosting for decorating if desired; tint 3 tablespoons green and 1 tablespoon red. Spread plain frosting between layers and over top and sides of cake. Use green and red frosting to pipe leaves and berries on cake. Store in the refrigerator.

Editor's Note: This recipe was tested with commercially prepared eggnog

Chocolate Chiffon Valentine Cake

PREP: 30 min.   **BAKE:** 20 min. + cooling
YIELD: 12 servings

Pat Eastman, Provo, Utah

While this heart-shaped cake is perfect for Valentine's Day, it can be baked in round pans and used for any special occasion. You can also decorate the top with chocolate kisses.

    1/2 cup baking cocoa
    1/2 cup hot water
  1-1/4 cups sugar, *divided*
    3/4 cup all-purpose flour
    3/4 teaspoon baking soda
    1/2 teaspoon salt
      4 eggs, *separated*
    1/4 cup vegetable oil
      1 teaspoon vanilla extract
    1/4 teaspoon cream of tartar
FROSTING:
  1-1/2 cups heavy whipping cream
    1/4 cup confectioners' sugar
     15 small fresh strawberries, halved
Fresh mint, optional

1 In a small bowl, combine cocoa and water until smooth; cool. In a large mixing bowl, combine 1 cup sugar, flour, baking soda and salt. Add the egg yolks, oil, vanilla and cocoa mixture; stir until smooth. In a small mixing bowl, beat egg whites and cream of tartar until very foamy. Gradually add the remaining sugar, beating until soft peaks form. Gradually fold into chocolate mixture.

2 teaspoons ground cinnamon
1 teaspoon ground allspice
1 teaspoon ground nutmeg
1/2 teaspoon baking powder
1/2 teaspoon baking soda
1/4 teaspoon salt
1 cup unsweetened applesauce
3/4 cup chopped pecans, toasted
2/3 cup finely chopped peeled tart apple

BROWN SUGAR GLAZE:

3 tablespoons butter
3 tablespoons brown sugar
3 tablespoons heavy whipping cream
3/4 cup confectioners' sugar
1/2 teaspoon vanilla extract
2 tablespoons chopped pecans, toasted

2 Pour into two greased and floured 9-in. heart-shaped pans or two 9-in. round cake pans. Bake at 350° for 18-20 minutes or until top springs back when lightly touched. Cool for 10 minutes before removing from pans to wire racks to cool completely. Carefully removing waxed paper from cake layer.

3 In a chilled mixing bowl, beat cream until it begins to thicken. Add confectioners' sugar; beat until stiff peaks form. Spread frosting between layers and over top and sides of cake. Spoon 1-1/2 cups of frosting into a pastry bag with a star tip. Pipe a decorative lattice design on cake top and sides. Garnish with strawberries and mint if desired. Refrigerate until serving.

1 In a large mixing bowl, cream the butter, shortening, sugars and lemon peel until light and fluffy. Add eggs, one at a time, beating well after each addition. Beat in vanilla. Combine the flour, spices, baking powder, baking soda and salt; add to creamed mixture alternately with applesauce. Stir in the pecans and apple.

2 Pour into a greased and floured 10-in. fluted tube pan. Bake at 350° for 55-60 minutes or until a toothpick inserted near the center comes out clean. Cool for 10 minutes before removing from pan to a wire rack to cool completely.

3 For glaze, in a heavy saucepan, melt butter and brown sugar over low heat. Stir in cream. Cook and stir until mixture comes to a boil; boil for 1 minute. Remove from the heat; whisk in sugar and vanilla until smooth, about 1 minute. Pour over cake; immediately sprinkle with pecans.

Apple Spice Bundt Cake

PREP: 20 min. **BAKE:** 55 min. + cooling
YIELD: 12 servings

Laurel Leslie, Sonora, California

This cake is perfect for Thanksgiving—it's not too sweet and not too heavy. It's a moist cake with a mild fruit flavor and a pleasant spice level.

1/3 cup butter, softened
1/3 cup shortening
3/4 cup sugar
2/3 cup packed brown sugar
1 teaspoon grated lemon peel
2 eggs
1-1/4 teaspoons vanilla extract
2-1/4 cups all-purpose flour

CHRISTMAS PETITS FOURS

3 In a large saucepan, combine the sugar, water and cream of tartar. Bring to a boil, without stirring, until a candy thermometer reads 226°. Cool to 100°; beat in confectioners' sugar until smooth. Keeping glaze warm, dip cake squares into glaze with a two-tine fork, allowing excess to drip off. Place on wire racks over waxed paper. Add hot water, 1 teaspoon at a time, if glaze becomes too thick. Let dry completely. Decorate with frosting and sprinkles.

Editor's Note: We recommend that you test your candy thermometer before each use by bringing water to a boil; the thermometer should read 212°. Adjust your recipe temperature up or down based on your test.

Christmas Petits Fours

PREP: 40 min. **BAKE:** 15 min. + cooling
YIELD: 35 servings

Linda Ault, Newberry, Indiana

The dainty petits fours are attractive and fun to make. If time is short, just frost and dust with candy sprinkles.

- 2 **eggs**
- 2 **egg yolks**
- 1 **cup sugar**
- 2 **cups all-purpose flour**
- 2 **teaspoons baking powder**
- 1/2 **cup milk**
- 5 **tablespoons butter, melted**

GLAZE:

- 4 **cups sugar**
- 2 **cups water**
- 1/4 **teaspoon cream of tartar**
- 3 **cups confectioners' sugar**
- 1 **tube** *each* **red and green decorating frosting**

Holiday sprinkles

1 In a large mixing bowl, beat eggs and egg yolks until slightly thickened. Gradually add sugar, beating until thick and lemon-colored. Combine flour and baking powder. Add to egg mixture gradually with milk and butter; mix well. (Batter will be thick.)

2 Spread evenly into a greased and floured 15-in. x 10-in. x 1-in. baking pan. Bake at 350° for 12-15 minutes or until a toothpick inserted near the center comes out clean. Cool for 10 minutes before inverting onto a wire rack to cool completely. Cut a thin slice off each side of cake. Cut cake into 1-1/4-in. squares. Freeze cakes.

Pumpkin Pound Cake

PREP: 10 min. **BAKE:** 1 hour 5 min. + cooling
YIELD: 16 servings

Jean Volk, Jacksonville, Florida

This recipe for nicely spiced pumpkin pound cake is fabulous anytime of year. It's impossible to resist a slice topped with the sweet walnut sauce.

- 1-1/2 **cups butter, softened**
- 2-3/4 **cups sugar**
- 6 **eggs**
- 1 **teaspoon vanilla extract**
- 3 **cups all-purpose flour**
- 3/4 **teaspoon ground cinnamon**
- 1/2 **teaspoon baking powder**
- 1/2 **teaspoon salt**
- 1/2 **teaspoon ground ginger**

PUMPKIN POUND CAKE

1/4 teaspoon ground cloves
1 cup canned pumpkin
WALNUT SAUCE:
1 cup packed brown sugar
1/2 cup heavy whipping cream
1/4 cup corn syrup
2 tablespoons butter
1/2 cup chopped walnuts
1/2 teaspoon vanilla extract

1 In a large mixing bowl, cream butter and sugar until light and fluffy. Add eggs, one at a time, beating well after each addition. Stir in vanilla. Combine the flour, cinnamon, baking powder, salt, ginger and cloves; add to creamed mixture alternately with pumpkin, beating just until combined.

2 Pour into two greased and floured 9-in. x 5-in. x 3-in. loaf pans. Bake at 350° for 65-70 minutes or until a toothpick inserted near the center comes out clean. Cool for 10 minutes before removing form pans to wire racks to cool completely.

3 For sauce, combine the brown sugar, cream, corn syrup and butter in a saucepan. Bring to a boil over medium heat, stirring constantly. Reduce heat; cook and stir 5 minutes longer. Remove from the heat; stir in walnuts and vanilla. Serve warm over the cake.

Walnut Raspberry Torte

PREP: 20 min. + standing **BAKE:** 30 min. + chilling
YIELD: 16 servings

Janet Zoz, Alvo, Nebraska

Moist, tender and light describes this lovely three-layered cake. It rivals any cake from the finest bakery. Use black walnuts to add a more distinctive flavor.

5 eggs, *separated*
1/2 cup shortening
1/2 cup butter, softened
2 cups sugar
1-1/2 teaspoons vanilla extract
2 cups all-purpose flour
1/2 teaspoon baking soda
1 cup buttermilk
1 cup finely chopped walnuts, toasted
1/2 cup flaked coconut
1/2 teaspoon cream of tartar
FILLING/FROSTING:
1 cup raspberry preserves, warmed
2 packages (one 8 ounces, one 3 ounces) cream cheese, softened

WALNUT RASPBERRY TORTE

3/4 cup butter, softened
6-1/2 cups confectioners' sugar
2 teaspoons vanilla extract
1/2 cup chopped walnuts

1 Let eggs stand at room temperature for 30 minutes. In a large mixing bowl, cream the shortening, butter and sugar until light and fluffy. Add egg yolks, one at a time, beating well after each addition. Beat in vanilla. Combine the flour and baking soda; add to creamed mixture alternately with buttermilk, beating well after each addition. Stir in walnuts and coconut.

2 In another mixing bowl and with clean beaters, beat egg whites and cream of tartar on high speed until stiff peaks form. Fold a fourth of egg whites into the batter, then fold in remaining whites.

3 Pour into three greased and floured 9-in. round baking pans. Bake at 350° for 24-28 minutes or top springs back lightly when touched. Cool for 10 minutes before removing from pans to wire racks to cool completely.

4 Spread raspberry preserves over the top of two cake layers. Refrigerate for 30 minutes. Meanwhile, in a large mixing bowl, beat the cream cheese, butter and confectioners' sugar until fluffy. Beat in vanilla. Place one raspberry topped cake layer on a serving plate. Spread with some of the frosting. Repeat with second raspberry topped cake layer. Top with plain cake layer. Spread remaining frosting over the top and sides of cake. Sprinkle with the nuts. Store in the refrigerator.

Halloween Layer Cake

PREP: 20 min. **BAKE:** 30 min. + cooling
YIELD: 12-16 servings

Karen Wirth, Tavistock, Ontario

There's nothing scary about making this cake, and it makes a hauntingly good dessert for Halloween.

- 1 **cup butter, softened**
- 2 **cups sugar**
- 4 **eggs**
- 3 **cups all-purpose flour**
- 1 **tablespoon baking powder**
- 1/2 **teaspoon salt**
- 1 **cup milk**
- 1/4 **cup baking cocoa**
- 1/4 **cup water**
- 1/2 **teaspoon vanilla extract**
- 1/2 **teaspoon orange extract**
- 1 **tablespoon grated orange peel**
- 10 **drops yellow food coloring**
- 6 **drops red food coloring**

FROSTING:
- 3 **packages (3 ounces *each*) cream cheese, softened**
- 5-3/4 **cups confectioners' sugar**
- 2 **tablespoons milk**
- 8 **drops yellow food coloring**
- 6 **drops red food coloring**

GLAZE:
- 3 **squares (1 ounce *each*) semisweet chocolate, coarsely chopped**
- 1/3 **cup heavy whipping cream**

Candy corn for garnish

1 In a large mixing bowl, cream butter and sugar until light and fluffy. Add eggs, one at a time, beating well after each. Combine the flour, baking powder and salt; add alternately with milk to creamed mixture, beating well after each addition. Combine the cocoa, water and vanilla; stir in 2 cups cake batter.

2 Pour into a greased and floured 9-in. round baking pan. Add the orange extract, peel and food coloring to remaining batter. Pour into two greased and floured 9-in. cake pans. Bake at 350° for 30 minutes or until a toothpick inserted near the center comes out clean. Cool for 10 minutes before removing from pans to wire racks.

3 In a mixing bowl, beat all frosting ingredients until smooth. Place one orange cake layer on a cake plate; spread with 1/2 cup frosting. Top with chocolate layer; spread with 1/2 cup frosting. Top with second orange layer. Frost the top and sides.

4 Microwave chocolate and cream on high 1-1/2 minutes or, stirring once. Stir until smooth; let cool 2 minutes. Slowly pour over cake, letting glaze drizzle down sides. Garnish with candy corn.

White Christmas Cake

PREP: 30 min. **BAKE:** 25 min. + cooling
YIELD: 10-12 servings

Nancy Reichert, Thomasville, Georgia

Wow! That's the reaction you'll get from family and guests when they see and taste this lovely three-layer cake.

- 4 **eggs, *separated***
- 1/2 **cup water**
- 4 **ounces white candy coating *or* vanilla *or* white chips**
- 1 **cup butter, softened**
- 2 **cups sugar**
- 1 **tablespoon vanilla extract**
- 2-1/2 **cups all-purpose flour**
- 1/2 **teaspoon baking powder**
- 1/2 **teaspoon baking soda**
- 1 **cup buttermilk**
- 1 **cup flaked coconut**
- 1 **cup chopped pecans**

FROSTING:
- 1 **package (8 ounces) cream cheese, softened**
- 1/2 **cup butter, softened**
- 3-3/4 **cups confectioners' sugar**
- 1 **tablespoon milk**
- 1 **teaspoon vanilla extract**

HALLOWEEN LAYER CAKE

WHITE CHRISTMAS CAKE

Cranberry Bundt Cake

PREP: 10 min. **BAKE:** 45 min. + standing
YIELD: 8-10 servings

Esther McCoy, Dillonvale, Ohio

Along with pumpkin pies, this cake will become a traditional annual holiday dessert for Thanksgiving.

2/3	cup butter, softened
1	cup sugar
3	eggs
1-1/2	teaspoons vanilla extract
2	cups all-purpose flour
1	teaspoon baking powder
3/4	teaspoon baking soda
1/2	teaspoon salt
1	cup (8 ounces) sour cream
3/4	cup chopped dried cranberries
1/3	cup chopped pecans

Confectioners' sugar

1 In a large mixing bowl, cream butter and sugar until light and fluffy. Add the eggs, one at a time, beating well after each addition. Stir in vanilla. Combine the flour, baking powder, baking soda and salt; add to creamed mixture alternately with sour cream. Fold in the cranberries and pecans.

2 Pour into a greased and floured 8-in. fluted tube pan. Bake at 350° for 45-50 minutes or until a toothpick inserted near the center comes out clean. Cool for 10 minutes before removing from pan to a wire rack to cool completely. Dust with confectioners' sugar.

1 Let the eggs stand at room temperature for 30 minutes. In a saucepan, bring the water to a boil. Remove from the heat; stir in candy coating until melted. Cool for 20 minutes. Line three greased 8-in. square baking dishes with waxed paper and grease the paper; set aside.

2 Meanwhile, in a mixing bowl, cream butter and sugar until light and fluffy. Add egg yolks; mix well. Beat in coating and vanilla. Combine flour, baking powder and baking soda; add to creamed mixture alternately with buttermilk. Mix well. Stir in the coconut and pecans. Beat egg whites with clean beaters until stiff peaks form; fold into the batter.

3 Pour into prepared dishes. Bake at 350° for 25-30 minutes or until a toothpick inserted near the center comes out clean. Cool for 10 minutes before removing from pans to wire racks to cool completely.

4 For frosting, in a large mixing bowl, beat cream cheese and butter until light. Add confectioners' sugar, milk and vanilla; beat until smooth. Spread frosting between layers and over top and sides of the cake.

CRANBERRY BUNDT CAKE

Yule Log

PREP: 30 min. **BAKE:** 15 min. + cooling
YIELD: 8 servings

Taste of Home Test Kitchen

During the Middle Ages, people would cut down a huge tree to burn throughout the holiday season. Later on, folks sweetened the idea by making cakes that resembled the logs.

- 4 eggs, *separated*
- 1/3 cup sugar
- 1 teaspoon vanilla extract
- 4 squares (1 ounce *each*) semisweet chocolate, melted and cooled
- 1/3 cup water
- 1/2 cup all-purpose flour
- 1/2 teaspoon baking soda
- 2 tablespoons confectioners' sugar
- 1 can (16 ounces) coconut-pecan frosting
- 1 can (16 ounces) milk chocolate frosting, *divided*

Large marshmallows
Baking cocoa

1 Let eggs stand at room temperature for 30 minutes. Line a greased 15-in. x 10-in. x 1-in. baking pan with waxed paper; grease and flour the paper. Set aside.

2 In a large mixing bowl, beat the egg yolks, sugar and vanilla on high until thick and lemon-colored, about 5 minutes. Beat in chocolate and water on low until blended. Add flour and baking soda; mix well. In another large mixing bowl and with clean beaters, beat egg whites on high until stiff peaks form. Fold in the chocolate mixture.

3 Spread evenly in a greased and floured 15-in. x 10-in. x 1-in. baking pan. Bake at 375° for 15 minutes or until a toothpick inserted near the center comes out clean. Cool in pan on a wire rack for 5 minutes. Turn cake onto a kitchen towel dusted with confectioners' sugar. Gently peel off waxed paper. Roll up cake in the towel jelly-roll style, starting from a short side. Cool completely on a wire rack.

4 Unroll cake; spread coconut-pecan frosting to within 1 in. of edges. Roll up again.

5 Cut a 3-in. piece from one end of cake roll. Cut the piece diagonally in half. Reserve 2 tablespoons chocolate frosting for mushrooms. Attach diagonal cake slices with a little of the frosting to opposite sides of cake to resemble stumps. Frost entire cake with remaining frosting. With the tines of a fork, make strokes in the frosting to resemble bark on a tree trunk.

YULE LOG

6 For the mushrooms, half marshmallows widthwise. Flatten half of each marshmallow for cap of mushroom; roll other half between palms of hands for stem. Attach caps to stems with the reserved frosting. Dust tops of mushrooms with cocoa; place around the log.

Candy Cane Cheesecake

PREP: 30 min. + chilling **BAKE:** 35 min. + cooling
YIELD: 12-16 servings

Gwen Koob-Roach
Saskatoon, Saskatchewan

This pepperminty cheesecake says Christmas at first sight and first bite. You'll win compliments whenever you serve it at seasonal parties.

- 1-1/2 cups chocolate wafer crumbs
- 1/3 cup butter, melted
- 2 tablespoons sugar

FILLING:
- 3 packages (8 ounces *each*) cream cheese, softened
- 3/4 cup sugar
- 3 tablespoons all-purpose flour
- 4 eggs, lightly beaten
- 1 cup (8 ounces) sour cream
- 2 tablespoons vanilla *or* white chips
- 1/2 to 3/4 teaspoon peppermint extract

Red liquid *or* paste food coloring
Crushed peppermint candy and whipped topping, optional

1 Combine the first three ingredients; press onto the bottom of a greased 9-in. springform pan. Chill. In a mixing bowl, beat cream cheese and sugar until smooth; add flour and mix well. Add the eggs; beat on low speed just until combined. Stir in sour cream. Set aside.

2 In a small saucepan or microwave, melt vanilla chips; stir until smooth. Remove from the heat. Add 1/4 cup cream cheese mixture, extract and a few drops of food coloring; mix well. Pour half of the remaining cream cheese mixture over crust. Top with half of the peppermint mixture; swirl with a knife. Repeat layers.

3 Bake at 325° for 35-40 minutes or until the center is almost set. Cool on a wire rack for 10 minutes. Carefully run a knife around the edge of pan to loosen; cool 1 hour longer.

4 Refrigerate overnight. Just before serving, remove sides of pan. Garnish with crushed candy and whipped topping if desired. Refrigerate leftovers.

MOCHA TRUFFLE CHEESECAKE

Mocha Truffle Cheesecake

PREP: 20 min. **BAKE:** 50 min. + chilling
YIELD: 12-16 servings

Shannon Dormady, Great Falls, Montana

The brownie-like crust and creamy mocha layer will really hit the spot. It's excellent for get-togethers because it can be made in advance.

1 package (18-1/4 ounces) devil's food cake mix
6 tablespoons butter, melted
1 egg
1 to 3 tablespoons instant coffee granules

CANDY CANE CHEESECAKE

FILLING/TOPPING:

2 packages (8 ounces *each*) cream cheese, softened
1 can (14 ounces) sweetened condensed milk
2 cups (12 ounces) semisweet chocolate chips, melted and cooled
3 to 6 tablespoons instant coffee granules
1/4 cup hot water
3 eggs, lightly beaten
1 cup heavy whipping cream
1/4 cup confectioners' sugar
1/2 teaspoon almond extract

1 In a large mixing bowl, combine the dry cake mix, butter, egg and coffee granules. Press onto the bottom and 2 in. up the sides of a greased 10-in. springform pan.

2 In another large mixing bowl, beat cream cheese until smooth. Beat in milk and chips. Dissolve coffee granules in water. Add coffee and eggs to cream cheese mixture; beat on low speed just until combined. Pour into crust. Place pan on a baking sheet.

3 Bake at 325° for 50-55 minutes or until center is almost set. Cool on a wire rack for 10 minutes. Carefully run a knife around edge of pan to loosen; cool 1 hour longer. Chill overnight.

4 Remove sides of pan. Just before serving, in a mixing bowl, beat cream until it begins to thicken. Beat in sugar and extract until stiff peaks form. Spread over top of cheesecake. Refrigerate leftovers.

Pies & Tarts

Traditional Pumpkin Pie

PREP: 20 min. **BAKE:** 50 min. + cooling
YIELD: 2 pies (6-8 servings each)

Gloria Warczak, Cedarburg, Wisconsin

Most families would agree that Thanksgiving dinner isn't complete until slices of pumpkin pie are passed. Here, brown sugar, cinnamon, cloves, nutmeg and ginger add spark to canned pumpkin.

    2   cups all-purpose flour
    3/4 teaspoon salt
    2/3 cup shortening
    4   to 6 tablespoons cold water
FILLING:
    6   eggs
    1   can (29 ounces) solid-pack pumpkin
    2   cups packed brown sugar
    2   teaspoons ground cinnamon
    1   teaspoon salt
    1/2 teaspoon *each* ground cloves, nutmeg
        and ginger
    2   cups evaporated milk

1 In a bowl, combine flour and salt; cut in shortening until crumbly. Sprinkle with water, 1 tablespoon at a time, tossing with a fork until dough forms a ball. Divide dough in half.

2 On a floured surface, roll out each portion to fit a 9-in. pie plate. Place pastry in plates; trim pastry (set scraps aside if leaf cutouts are desired) and flute edges. Set shells aside.

TRADITIONAL PUMPKIN PIE

3 For filling, beat eggs in a mixing bowl. Add the pumpkin, sugar, cinnamon, salt, cloves, nutmeg and ginger; beat just until smooth. Gradually stir in milk. Pour into pastry shells. Bake at 450° for 10 minutes. Reduce heat to 350°; bake 40-45 minutes longer or until a knife inserted near the center comes out clean. Cool pies on wire racks. Store in the refrigerator.

4 If desired, cut the pastry scraps with a 1-in. leaf-shaped cookie cutter; place on an ungreased baking sheet. Bake at 350° for 10-15 minutes or until lightly browned. Place on baked pies.

Partridge in a Pear Tree Pie

PREP: 30 min. + cooling **BAKE:** 45 min.
YIELD: 6-8 servings

Jill Rens, Champlin, Minnesota

Delight guests and have a partridge in a pear tree make an appearance on your holiday table.

    1   can (15 ounces) pear halves, drained
    1   package (12 ounces) fresh *or* frozen
          cranberries
    1   can (8 ounces) crushed pineapple
    1-1/2 cups sugar
    3   tablespoons all-purpose flour
    1/4   teaspoon salt
    1/4   teaspoon ground cinnamon
Pastry of double-crust pie (9 inches)
Additional sugar, optional

1 Set aside five pear halves; chop any remaining pears. In a large saucepan, combine the chopped pears, cranberries, pineapple and sugar. Bring to a boil; cook and stir for 4-5 minutes or until some cranberries have popped. Cool for 30 minutes, stirring several times. In a bowl, combine the flour, salt and cinnamon. Stir in cooled cranberry mixture.

2 Line a 9-in. pie plate with bottom pastry; trim and flute edges. Spoon cranberry mixture into pastry shell; arrange pear halves on top. Bake at 400° for 35-40 minutes or until bubbly and crust is golden brown (cover edges with foil for last 15 minutes of baking if necessary). Cool on wire rack.

3 Roll remaining pastry. Using cookie cutters, cut out small leaves, small pears and a partridge. Place on an ungreased baking sheet; sprinkle with sugar if desired. Bake at 400° for 6-8 minutes or until golden brown. Place partridge in center of pie with leaves and pears around it.

PARTRIDGE IN A PEAR TREE

Coconut Cream Pie

PREP: 55 min. + chilling **BAKE:** 15 min.
YIELD: 2 pies (6-8 servings each)

Nancy Jo Leffler, DePauw, Indiana

This classic cream pie will be a hit on any holiday or with any family meal.

2-1/2 cups all-purpose flour
   2 teaspoons sugar
 1/4 teaspoon salt
 1/4 teaspoon baking powder
 3/4 cup shortening
   1 egg, *separated*
 1/2 cup plus 1 tablespoon cold water, *divided*

FILLING:
   2 cups sugar
 2/3 cup all-purpose flour
Pinch salt
   6 cups milk
   8 egg yolks, lightly beaten
   2 cups flaked coconut
   2 teaspoons vanilla extract
   1 teaspoon coconut extract

MERINGUE:
   6 tablespoons sugar
   3 tablespoons cornstarch
1-1/2 cups water
   8 egg whites
Additional flaked coconut

1 In a bowl, combine the flour, sugar, salt and baking powder. Cut in shortening until mixture resembles coarse crumbs. Combine egg yolk and 1/2 cup cold water; gradually add to crumb mixture, tossing with a fork until a ball forms. Cover and refrigerate for 1 hour.

2 Divide dough in half. Roll out each portion to fit a 9-in. pie plate. Place in plates; trim pastry even with edge. With a small round fluted cutter, cut small circles out of dough scraps. Beat egg white with remaining water; brush over edges of pastry. Arrange dough cutouts around edge.

3 Line unpricked pastry shells with a double thickness of heavy-duty foil. Bake at 400° for 12-15 minutes or until lightly browned. Cool on wire racks.

4 For filling, combine the sugar, flour and salt in a large saucepan. Stir in milk until smooth. Cook and stir over medium-high heat until thickened and bubbly. Reduce heat; cook and stir 2 minutes longer. Remove from the heat. Stir a small amount of hot filling into egg yolks; return all to pan, stirring constantly. Bring to a gentle boil; cook and stir 2 minutes longer. Remove from the heat. Stir in coconut and extracts; keep warm.

5 For meringue, combine the sugar, cornstarch and water in a saucepan until smooth. Bring to a boil over medium heat, stirring constantly. Cook and stir for 2 minutes or until clear. In a large mixing bowl, beat egg whites until soft peaks form. Pour hot sugar mixture in a small stream into egg whites, beating constantly until stiff peaks form.

6 Pour warm filling into pastry shells; immediately spread with meringue, sealing edges to crusts. Sprinkle with additional coconut. Bake at 350° for 12-15 minutes or until meringue is golden. Cool on wire racks. Store in the refrigerator.

COCONUT CREAM PIE

2 Layer the cranberries, vanilla chips and pecans in pastry. In a small mixing bowl, beat the egg, brown sugar, corn syrup, flour and peel until smooth; pour over nuts. Place pans on a baking sheet.

3 Bake at 400° for 15 minutes. Cover with foil; bake 15-20 minutes longer or until crust is golden brown and filling near center is set. Cool on a wire rack. Serve with whipped cream if desired.

Editor's Note: This recipe can be easily doubled to serve 4.

Mincemeat Cherry Pie

PREP: 15 min. **BAKE:** 40 min. + cooling
YIELD: 6-8 servings

Kathleen Tucker, Huachuca City, Arizona

Cherries and orange marmalade give a nice twist to traditional mincemeat pie. It's sure to add some old-fashioned flavor to your Yuletide festivities.

Pastry for double-crust pie (9 inches)
- 1 **can (21 ounces) cherry pie filling**
- 1-3/4 **cups prepared mincemeat**
- 1/3 **cup orange marmalade**
- 1/4 **cup chopped walnuts**
- 1 **tablespoon all-purpose flour**

1 Line a 9-in. pie plate with bottom pastry. Trim evenly with edge of plate. In a bowl, combine the remaining ingredients. Pour into crust. Roll out remaining pastry to fit top of pie; place over filling. Trim, seal and flute edges. Cut slits in top. Cover edges loosely with foil.

2 Bake at 400° for 40-45 minutes or until crust is golden brown and filling is bubbly. Cool on a wire rack. Store in the refrigerator.

Cranberry Pecan Tarts

PREP: 15 min. **BAKE:** 30 min. + cooling
YIELD: 2 servings

Melanie Bredeson, Milwaukee, Wisconsin

This recipe is a colorful alternative to traditional pecan pie.

- 1 **sheet refrigerated pie pastry**
- 1/4 **cup fresh *or* frozen cranberries, thawed**
- 1/4 **cup vanilla *or* white chips**
- 1/4 **cup pecan halves**
- 1 **egg**
- 3 **tablespoons packed brown sugar**
- 3 **tablespoons light corn syrup**
- 1-1/2 **teaspoons all-purpose flour**
- 1/4 **teaspoon grated orange peel**

Whipped cream, optional

1 Cut pastry sheet in half and roll each half into a 7-in. circle. Transfer pastry to two ungreased 4-in. fluted tart pans with removable bottoms. Trim pastry even with edge.

Horn of Plenty Pie

PREP: 40 min. **BAKE:** 20 min. + cooling
YIELD: 6-8 servings

Liz Fernald, Mashpee, Massachusetts

Tart apples, cranberries and raisins make this a perfect pie for autumn.

- 1-1/2 **cups sugar**
- 1/3 **cup water**
- 3 **cups fresh *or* frozen cranberries**
- 1/2 **cup raisins**
- 1/2 **cup chopped walnuts**
- 1/2 **cup chopped peeled tart apple**
- 1 **tablespoon butter**

Pinch salt
1 unpricked pastry shell (9 inches), baked

MERINGUE:
3 egg whites
6 tablespoons brown sugar

1 In a large saucepan, bring sugar and water to a boil. Add the cranberries, raisins, walnuts and apple; cover and simmer for 15 minutes, stirring occasionally. Stir in butter and salt. Spoon into pie shell.

2 In a mixing bowl, beat egg whites until soft peaks form. Gradually beat in sugar, 1 tablespoon at a time, until stiff glossy peaks form. Spread meringue evenly over hot filling, sealing to edges of pastry. Bake at 325° for 20 minutes or until golden brown. Cool completely on a wire rack. Store in the refrigerator.

EASTER PIE

Easter Pie

PREP: 25 min. + chilling **BAKE:** 55 min. + cooling
YIELD: 6-8 servings

Barbara Tierney, Farmington, Connecticut

Easter Pie is a specialty in many Italian homes, so mothers make sure their daughters master the recipe to ensure that the holiday tradition continues.

1-2/3 cups all-purpose flour
2 tablespoons sugar
1/2 teaspoon salt
1/4 teaspoon baking powder
1/4 cup cold butter
1/4 cup shortening
2 eggs, lightly beaten

HORN OF PLENTY PIE

FILLING:
1 carton (15 ounces) ricotta cheese
1 cup sugar
1 tablespoon all-purpose flour
1/4 teaspoon grated lemon peel
1/4 teaspoon grated orange peel

Pinch salt
4 eggs
2 teaspoons vanilla extract
1/3 cup semisweet chocolate chips
1/3 cup diced citron, optional
1/8 teaspoon ground cinnamon

Dash ground nutmeg

1 In a bowl, combine the flour, sugar, salt and baking powder; cut in butter and shortening until mixture resembles small crumbs. Add eggs; stir until moistened and mixture forms a ball. Cover and refrigerate for 1 hour. On a lightly floured surface, roll out dough to a 10-in. circle. Place in a 9-in. pie plate; flute crust. Refrigerate.

2 For filling, beat the ricotta, sugar and flour in a mixing bowl. Add peels and salt; beat until smooth. In another bowl, beat eggs until thick and lemon-colored, about 5 minutes; slowly fold into ricotta mixture. Gently mix in remaining ingredients. Pour into the crust.

3 Bake at 350° for 55 minutes or until a knife inserted near the center comes out clean. Cool on a wire rack. Store in the refrigerator.

Desserts

Chocolate-Filled Meringue

PREP: 25 min. + chilling BAKE: 20 min. + cooling
YIELD: 6-8 servings

Joan Totton, Stanfield, Oregon

This meringue has a nutty, chewy crust and dark chocolate filling that's not too sweet. Your guests will love the taste.

- 3 egg whites
- 1/2 teaspoon vanilla extract
- 1/4 teaspoon cream of tartar
- 1/4 teaspoon salt
- 1/2 cup sugar
- 1/4 cup confectioners' sugar
- 3/4 cup finely chopped pecans
- 1 cup (6 ounces) semisweet chocolate chips, optional

FILLING:
- 2 milk chocolate candy bars (1.55 ounces *each*)
- 1 square (1 ounce) unsweetened chocolate
- 1/4 cup water
- 1 teaspoon vanilla extract
- 1 cup heavy whipping cream

Additional whipped cream, optional

1 Place egg whites in a mixing bowl and let stand at room temperature for 30 minutes. Add the vanilla, cream of tartar and salt; beat on medium speed until soft peaks form. Gradually add sugars, beating on high until stiff peaks form. Fold in pecans.

2 Grease the bottom and sides of a 9-in. pie plate, leaving top edge ungreased. Spread meringue onto the bottom and up the sides of pie plate. Build up top edge. Bake at 350° for 20-30 minutes or until lightly browned. Cool on a wire rack.

3 If chocolate stars are desired, melt chocolate chips. Transfer chocolate to a small heavy-duty resealable bag; cut a small hole in one corner of bag. On a waxed paper-lined baking sheet, pipe chocolate into star shapes. Refrigerate until firm, about 15 minutes. When ready to serve, carefully remove stars with a metal spatula.

4 For filling, in a heavy saucepan, combine the candy bars, unsweetened chocolate and water. Cook and stir over low heat until melted. Pour into a large bowl; cool to room temperature. Stir in vanilla. Fold in whipped cream; pour into the crust. Top with additional whipped cream and chocolate stars if desired.

Christmas Bread Pudding

PREP: 15 min. BAKE: 50 min. + cooling
YIELD: 6-8 servings

Jennifer Dignin, Westerville, Ohio

Bread pudding gets a fruity update with this apple-and-cranberry-studded version!

- 8 cups day-old bread cubes, crust removed
- 2 medium tart apples, peeled and chopped
- 1/2 cup dried cranberries *or* raisins
- 6 egg yolks
- 3 eggs
- 1 cup heavy whipping cream
- 1/2 cup milk
- 1 cup sugar

CREAM SAUCE:
- 1 cup heavy whipping cream
- 3 tablespoons sugar
- 1 to 2 teaspoons vanilla *or* rum extract

Dash ground cinnamon and nutmeg

1 In a bowl, combine the bread cubes, apples and cranberries. Transfer to a greased 11-in. x 7-in. x 2-in. baking dish. In a bowl, combine the egg yolks, eggs, cream, milk and sugar. Pour over bread mixture.

2 Place dish in a larger baking dish. Fill larger dish with boiling water halfway up the sides. Bake at 350° for 50-55 minutes or until a knife inserted near the center comes out clean. Remove from water bath. Cool for 15 minutes.

CHOCOLATE-FILLED MERINGUE

CHRISTMAS BREAD PUDDING

3 For the cream sauce, in a saucepan, combine cream and sugar. Cook and stir until sugar is dissolved. Remove from the heat. Stir in the vanilla, cinnamon and nutmeg. Serve warm with pudding.

Holiday Cranberry Cobbler

PREP: 15 min. **BAKE:** 35 min. **YIELD:** 12-15 servings

Helen Weissinger, Caribou, Maine

For a change of pace from pumpkin pie, prepare this merry berry cobbler.

> 1 **can (21 ounces) peach pie filling**
> 1 **can (16 ounces) whole-berry cranberry sauce**
> 1 **package (18-1/4 ounces) yellow cake mix**
> 1 **teaspoon ground cinnamon**
> 1/4 **teaspoon ground nutmeg**
> 1 **cup cold butter**
> 1 **cup chopped nuts**
> **Vanilla ice cream *or* whipped cream**

1 Combine pie filling and cranberry sauce. Spread in an ungreased 13-in. x 9-in. x 2-in. baking dish. In a bowl, combine the dry cake mix, cinnamon and nutmeg; cut in butter until crumbly. Stir in nuts; sprinkle over fruit.

2 Bake at 350° for 35-40 minutes or until a toothpick inserted near the center of cake comes out clean. Serve warm with ice cream or whipped cream.

Creme Brulee

PREP: 30 min. **BAKE:** 45 min. + cooling
YIELD: 8 servings

Joylyn Trickel, Greendale, Wisconsin

For extra-fun, have your guests finish off their own desserts by broiling the sugar on their portions with a small torch.

> 4 **cups heavy whipping cream**
> 9 **egg yolks**
> 3/4 **cup sugar**
> 1 **teaspoon vanilla extract**
> **Brown sugar**

1 In a heavy saucepan, heat cream to 180° over medium heat, stirring frequently. Meanwhile, in a large bowl, whisk the egg yolks, sugar and vanilla. When cream reaches 180°, slowly stir into the egg yolk mixture.

2 Pour into eight 6-oz. custard cups; place cups in a baking pan. Add 1 in. of boiling water to pan. Bake, uncovered, at 325° for 45-50 minutes or until a knife inserted near the center comes out clean. Remove from water bath. Cool for 10 minutes.

3 Before serving, sprinkle each cup with 1 to 1-1/2 teaspoons brown sugar. Place on a baking sheet. Broil 6 in. from the heat for 3-5 minutes or until sugar is caramelized. Serve custard immediately. Refrigerate leftovers.

HOLIDAY CRANBERRY COBBLER

Valentine Napoleons

PREP/TOTAL TIME: 30 min. YIELD: 12 servings

Kathleen Taugher, East Troy, Wisconsin

These pastries are quick to fix, thanks to convenient puff pastry! The hearts are filled with a pudding and cream mixture and strawberries.

- 1 package (17-1/4 ounces) frozen puff pastry, thawed
- 1 cup cold milk
- 1 package (3.4 ounces) instant vanilla pudding mix
- 1 cup heavy whipping cream
- 1/4 cup confectioners' sugar
- 1-1/4 cups sliced fresh strawberries
- Additional confectioners' sugar

1 On a lightly floured surface, roll out each pastry sheet to 1/8-in. thickness. Using a 3-1/2-in. heart-shaped cookie cutter, cut out 12 hearts. Place on ungreased baking sheets. Bake at 400° for 8-11 minutes or until golden brown. Remove to wire racks to cool.

2 In a bowl, whisk milk and pudding mix for 2 minutes. In a chilled mixing bowl, beat cream until it begins to thicken. Beat in confectioners' sugar until soft peaks form. Fold into pudding.

3 Split puff pastry hearts in half. Place bottom halves on serving plates. Spoon 1/4 cup pudding mixture over each; top with strawberries and pastry tops. Sprinkle with confectioners' sugar. Serve immediately.

SWEETHEART BROWNIE SUNDAE

Sweetheart Brownie Sundae

PREP: 45 min. + freezing BAKE: 15 min. + cooling
YIELD: 2 servings

Dottie Miller, Jonesborough, Tennessee

For a special ending to a special meal for two, choose this heart-shaped dessert.

- 1/4 cup butter
- 2 squares (1 ounce *each*) semisweet chocolate, coarsely chopped
- 1 egg
- 1/2 cup packed brown sugar
- 1 teaspoon vanilla extract
- 1/4 teaspoon salt
- 1/4 cup all-purpose flour
- 1 cup vanilla ice cream, softened

CHOCOLATE SAUCE:
- 1 cup water
- 1/2 cup baking cocoa
- 1/4 cup sugar
- 2 tablespoons butter
- Confectioners' sugar

1 In a heavy saucepan or microwave, melt butter and chocolate; stir until smooth. Remove from the heat; cool for 10 minutes. In a small mixing bowl, beat the egg, brown sugar, vanilla and salt. Stir in chocolate mixture. Add flour; mix well.

2 Line an 8-in. square baking pan with foil and grease the foil. Spread batter evenly into pan (batter will be thin). Bake at 350° for 15 minutes or until a toothpick inserted near the center comes out clean. Cool completely on a wire rack. Cover and refrigerate until firm.

3 Using a 3-1/2-in. x 3-1/2-in. heart pattern or cookie cutter, mark four hearts on surface of brownies; cut with a knife. Spread ice cream on two hearts; top each with a second heart. Wrap in plastic wrap; freeze in a single layer overnight.

4 For chocolate sauce, combine the water, cocoa and sugar in a saucepan; bring to a boil over medium heat, stirring constantly. Reduce heat; simmer for 2-3 minutes or until thickened. Remove from the heat; stir in butter until melted.

5 To serve, dust brownie hearts with confectioners' sugar and drizzle with warm chocolate sauce. Store any leftover sauce in the refrigerator.

1. In a mixing bowl, beat cream cheese, butter and sugar. Add eggs, one at a time, beating well after each addition. Combine the flour, baking powder and salt; add to creamed mixture and mix well. Transfer half of the batter to another bowl; stir in nuts and chocolate. Spread into a greased 9-in. square baking pan.

2. Stir peppermint extract and food coloring if desired into remaining batter. Spoon over chocolate layer; cut through batter with a knife to swirl. Bake at 350° for 15-20 minutes or until a toothpick inserted near the center comes out clean. Cool on a wire rack.

3. In a saucepan or microwave, melt chocolate and butter; stir until smooth. Remove from the heat; stir in the confectioners' sugar, vanilla and enough water to achieve glaze consistency. Pour over brownies and spread evenly. Cut into bars.

Cherry Date Fruitcake

PREP: 15 min. **BAKE:** 1-3/4 hours + cooling
YIELD: 2 fruitcakes

Judy Schultz, Jamestown, New York

Brushing the baked fruitcakes with corn syrup adds a little extra sweetness, making each slice scrumptious!

- 1-1/2 cups all-purpose flour
- 1-1/2 cups sugar
- 1 teaspoon baking powder
- 1 teaspoon salt
- 5-1/2 cups pecan halves
- 2 jars (16 ounces *each*) maraschino cherries, drained and halved
- 1 pound diced candied pineapple
- 2 packages (8 ounces *each*) chopped pitted dates
- 6 eggs
- 1/2 cup apple juice
- 1/4 cup light corn syrup

1. In a large bowl, combine the first four ingredients. Add the pecans, cherries, pineapple and dates; toss to coat. Beat eggs and apple juice; add to fruit mixture and mix well. Grease two foil-lined 9-in. x 5-in. x 3-in. loaf pans. Press half of the mixture into each pan.

2. Bake at 300° for 1-3/4 to 2 hours or until a toothpick inserted near the center comes out clean. Cool for 10 minutes before removing from pan to wire racks; remove foil. Brush each loaf with corn syrup. Cool completely.

Mint Swirl Bars

PREP: 20 min. **BAKE:** 15 min. + cooling **YIELD:** 2 dozen

Debbie Devore, Fremont, Nebraska

The chocolaty mint cake-like bars look simply scrumptious and taste even better.

- 1 package (3 ounces) cream cheese, softened
- 1/4 cup butter, softened
- 3/4 cup sugar
- 2 eggs
- 2/3 cup all-purpose flour
- 1/2 teaspoon baking powder
- 1/2 teaspoon salt
- 1/3 cup chopped walnuts
- 1 square (1 ounce) semisweet chocolate, melted
- 1/2 teaspoon peppermint extract
- 2 to 3 drops green *or* red food coloring, optional

GLAZE:
- 1 square (1 ounce) semisweet chocolate
- 1 tablespoon butter
- 1 cup confectioners' sugar
- 1/2 teaspoon vanilla extract
- 2 to 3 tablespoons boiling water

Breads & Rolls

Sweet Potato Loaves

PREP: 15 min. **BAKE:** 35 min. + cooling
YIELD: 2 mini loaves

Joyce Randolph, Canton, Maine

The sweet potatoes make this nicely spiced bread moist. It makes a tasty addition to a Thanksgiving menu.

- 1/4 **cup butter, softened**
- 1/2 **cup sugar**
- 1 **egg**
- 1 **cup all-purpose flour**
- 1-1/2 **teaspoons baking powder**
- 1/2 **teaspoon ground cinnamon**
- 1/4 **teaspoon ground ginger**
- 1/4 **teaspoon salt**
- 1/2 **cup cold mashed sweet potatoes**
- 2 **tablespoons milk**
- 1/4 **cup raisins**

1 In a small mixing bowl, cream butter and sugar until light and fluffy. Add egg; mix well. Combine the flour, baking powder, cinnamon, ginger and salt; add to creamed mixture just until blended (batter will be thick). Combine sweet potatoes and milk; stir into batter until blended. Fold in raisins.

2 Transfer to two greased 5-3/4-in. x 3-in. x 2-in. loaf pans. Bake at 350° for 35-40 minutes or until lightly browned and a toothpick inserted near the center comes out clean. Cool for 10 minutes before removing from pans to wire racks.

SWEET POTATO LOAVES

BRAIDED ONION LOAF

Braided Onion Loaf

PREP: 30 min. + rising **BAKE:** 30 min. + cooling
YIELD: 1 loaf

Linda Knoll, Jackson, Michigan

One bite of this tender, savory loaf and you'll know it was worthwhile making this bread.

- 1 **package (1/4 ounce) active dry yeast**
- 3/4 **cup warm water (110° to 115°)**
- 1/2 **cup warm milk (110° to 115°)**
- 1/4 **cup butter, softened**
- 1 **egg**
- 1/4 **cup sugar**
- 1-1/2 **teaspoons salt**
- 4 **to 4-1/2 cups all-purpose flour**

FILLING:

- 1/4 **cup butter, softened**
- 3/4 **cup dried minced onion**
- 1 **tablespoon grated Parmesan cheese**
- 1 **teaspoon paprika**
- 1 **teaspoon garlic salt, optional**

Melted butter

1 In a large mixing bowl, dissolve yeast in warm water. Add the milk, butter, egg, sugar, salt and 2 cups flour; beat until smooth. Stir in enough remaining flour to form a soft dough. Turn onto a floured surface; knead until smooth and elastic, about 6-8 minutes. Place in a greased bowl, turning once to grease top. Cover and let rise in a warm place until doubled, about 1 hour.

2 For filling, in a bowl, combine the butter, onion, Parmesan cheese, paprika and garlic salt if desired; set aside. Punch dough down; turn onto a lightly floured surface. Divide into thirds. Roll each portion into a 20-in. x 4-in. rectangle. Spread filling over rectangles. Roll up jelly-roll style, starting from a long side.

3 Place ropes on an ungreased baking sheet; braid. Pinch ends to seal and tuck under. Cover and let rise until doubled, about 45 minutes. Bake at 350° for 30-35 minutes or until golden brown. Brush with butter. Remove from pan to a wire rack.

Orange-Chip Cranberry Bread

PREP: 20 min. **BAKE:** 50 min. + cooling **YIELD:** 2 loaves

Donna Smith, Fairport, New York

Tart berries, crunchy nuts and sweet chocolate are simply scrumptious when mixed together in this easy quick bread.

2-1/2	cups all-purpose flour
1	cup sugar
1/2	teaspoon baking powder
1/2	teaspoon baking soda
1/4	teaspoon salt
2	eggs
3/4	cup vegetable oil
2	teaspoons grated orange peel
1	cup buttermilk
1-1/2	cups chopped fresh *or* frozen cranberries, thawed
1	cup miniature semisweet chocolate chips
1	cup chopped walnuts
3/4	cup confectioners' sugar, optional
2	tablespoons orange juice, optional

1 In a mixing bowl, combine the flour, sugar, baking powder, baking soda and salt. In another bowl, combine eggs, oil and orange peel; mix well. Add to dry ingredients alternately with buttermilk. Fold in cranberries, chocolate chips and walnuts.

2 Pour into two greased 8-in. x 4-in. x 2-in. loaf pans. Bake at 350° for 50-60 minutes or until a toothpick inserted near the center comes out clean. Cool for 10 minutes before removing from pans to wire racks. If glaze is desired, combine confectioners' sugar and orange juice until smooth; spread over cooled loaves.

Turkey Stuffing Bread

PREP: 10 min. **BAKE:** 3-4 hours
YIELD: 1 loaf (1-1/2 pounds)

Gayl Koster, Nunica, Michigan

This unique bread tastes just like real turkey stuffing. It's fabulous with a chicken or turkey dinner...and works well with all those Thanksgiving leftovers, too.

1	cup plus 1 tablespoon warm milk (70° to 80°)
1	egg, beaten
1	tablespoon butter, softened
2	tablespoons brown sugar
1-1/2	teaspoons salt
1/3	cup cornmeal
3	cups bread flour
4-1/2	teaspoons dried minced onion
1-1/2	teaspoons celery seed
3/4	teaspoon poultry seasoning
1/2	teaspoon rubbed sage
1/2	teaspoon pepper
2-1/4	teaspoons active dry yeast

1 In bread machine pan, place all ingredients in order suggested by manufacturer. Select basic bread setting. Choose crust color and loaf size if available.

2 Bake according to bread machine directions (check dough after 5 minutes of mixing; add 1 to 2 tablespoons of water or flour if needed).

Editor's Note: If your bread machine has a time-delay feature, we recommend you do not use it for this recipe.

ORANGE-CHIP CRANBERRY BREAD

Easter Bunny Rolls

PREP: 30 min. + rising **BAKE:** 10 min. + cooling
YIELD: 2 dozen

Bonnie Myers, Callaway, Nebraska

These delicious herb rolls can be made anytime of the year, just shape into balls. But they are extra festive when they are made into cute bunnies.

1	package (1/4 ounce) active dry yeast
1/4	cup warm water (110° to 115°)
3/4	cup warm milk (110° to 115°)
2	tablespoons sugar
2	tablespoons shortening
1	egg, beaten
2	teaspoons celery seed
1	teaspoon rubbed sage
1	teaspoon salt
1/2	teaspoon ground nutmeg
3	to 3-1/2 cups all-purpose flour

Melted butter

1 In a large mixing bowl, dissolve yeast in warm water. Add the milk, sugar, shortening, egg, celery seed, sage, salt, nutmeg and 3 cups flour; beat until smooth. Stir in enough remaining flour to form a soft dough.

2 Turn onto a floured surface and knead until smooth and elastic; about 6-8 minutes. Place in a greased bowl, turning once to grease top. Cover and let rise in a warm place until doubled, about 1-1/2 hours.

3 Punch dough down; let rest 10 minutes. Divide dough into 24 pieces. For each bunny, roll one piece of dough into an 18-in. rope. Cut rope into one 10-in. piece, one 5-in. piece and three 1-in. pieces. Coil 10-in. piece for body; place on a greased baking sheet. Coil 5-in. piece for head; place next to body. Form ears from two 2-in. pieces; place next to head. Form tail from third 1-in. piece; place next to body. Pinch and seal pieces together. Repeat, placing bunnies 2 in. apart on the baking sheet. Cover and let rise until doubled, about 45 minutes.

4 Bake at 375° for 10-12 minutes or until lightly browned. Brush with melted butter. Cool on wire racks.

Old-Fashioned Stollen

PREP: 30 min. + rising **BAKE:** 25 min. + cooling
YIELD: 3 breads

Linda Hinners, Brookfield, Wisconsin

Stollen is a traditional German Christmas yeast bread. The fruit-filled loaf topped with a confectioners' sugar icing and candied cherries has a shape resembling a giant Parker House roll.

2	packages (1/4 ounce *each*) active dry yeast
1/2	teaspoon plus 1/2 cup sugar, *divided*
1/2	cup warm water (110° to 115°)
1	cup warm milk (110° to 115°)
3/4	cup butter, softened
1-1/2	teaspoons salt
1/2	teaspoon ground cardamom
2	eggs plus 2 egg yolks
6-1/4	to 6-3/4 cups all-purpose flour, *divided*

1/2 **cup raisins**

1/2 **cup diced citron *or* mixed candied fruit**
   and peel

1/2 **cup sliced candied cherries**

Melted butter

ICING:

   1 **cup confectioners' sugar**

   5 **to 6 teaspoons milk**

Blanched whole almonds and additional
   candied fruit

1 In a large mixing bowl, dissolve yeast and 1/2 teaspoon sugar in warm water; let stand for 5 minutes. Add the milk, butter, salt, cardamom, eggs, egg yolks, remaining sugar and 2 cups flour; beat until smooth. Stir in the raisins, citron, cherries and enough remaining flour to form a soft dough.

2 Turn out onto a lightly floured surface; knead until smooth and elastic, about 6-8 minutes. Place in a greased bowl, turning once to grease top. Cover and let rise in a warm place until doubled, about 1-1/4 hours.

3 Punch dough down; divide into thirds. Roll each piece on a floured surface into a 10-in. x 6-in. oval. Brush with the melted butter. Fold one long side over to within 1 in. of the opposite side. Press edges to seal.

4 Place on greased baking sheets. Brush with melted butter. Cover and let rise until doubled, about 45 minutes.

5 Bake at 375° for 25 minutes or until lightly browned. Remove to wire racks to cool. For icing, combine confectioners' sugar and milk; spread over cooled bread. Decorate with almonds and fruit.

Candy Cane Coffee Cakes

PREP: 25 min. + rising **BAKE:** 25 min. + cooling
YIELD: 4 loaves

Eleanor Gross, Bowdle, South Dakota

These moist, jolly loaves are a joy to share at Christmas-time. The hazelnut filling is a wonderful surprise.

   1 **package (1/4 ounces) active dry yeast**

3/4 **cup warm water (110° to 115°)**

1/2 **cup warm milk (110° to 115°)**

   4 **eggs**

   1 **cup sugar**

1/2 **cup butter, melted**

   2 **teaspoons salt**

CANDY CANE COFFEE CAKES

   7 **to 7-1/2 cups all-purpose flour**

FILLING:

   1 **cup chopped hazelnuts**

   1 **cup packed brown sugar**

   1 **cup raisins**

   2 **teaspoons ground cinnamon**

   3 **tablespoons butter, melted**

GLAZE:

   2 **cups confectioners' sugar**

   3 **to 4 tablespoons warm milk**

   1 **tablespoon butter, softened**

   1 **teaspoon vanilla extract**

1/2 **teaspoon lemon extract**

1/4 **cup chopped hazelnuts**

1 In a mixing bowl, dissolve yeast in warm water and milk. Add the eggs, sugar, butter, salt and 3 cups flour; beat until smooth. Stir in enough remaining flour to form a soft dough.

2 Turn onto a floured surface; knead until smooth and elastic, 6-8 minutes. Place in a greased bowl, turning once to grease top. Cover and let rise in a warm place until doubled, about 1-1/2 hours.

3 For filling, combine the nuts, brown sugar, raisins and cinnamon; set aside. Punch dough down and divide into fourths. Roll one portion into a 12-in. x 7-in. rectangle. Brush with some butter; sprinkle with 2/3 cup filling. Roll up jelly roll-style, starting with a long side; pinch to seal. Place on a greased baking sheet; shape top to form a cane. Repeat with remaining dough, filling and butter. Cover and let rise until doubled, about 35 minutes.

4 Bake at 350° for 25-30 minutes or until golden brown. Cool on wire racks. Combine the first five glaze ingredients; drizzle stripes over loaves. Sprinkle with nuts.

Braided Cardamom Rings

PREP: 30 min. + rising **BAKE:** 30 min. + cooling
YIELD: 2 coffee cakes

Jo Learman, Caro, Michigan

Red and green candied cherries look so festive on top of these mouth-watering rings, which may be iced and served warm, if desired.

> 2 **packages (1/4 ounce** *each***) active dry yeast**
> 1/4 **cup warm water (110° to 115°)**
> 2-1/2 **cups warm milk (110° to 115°)**
> 3/4 **cup butter, softened**
> 1 **egg, beaten**
> 1 **cup sugar**
> 1-1/2 **teaspoons ground cardamom**
> 1/2 **teaspoon salt**
> 8-3/4 **to 9-1/4 cups all-purpose flour**
> **LEMON ICING:**
> 2 **cups confectioners' sugar**
> 3 **to 4 tablespoons milk**
> 1/4 **teaspoon lemon extract**
> **Red and green candied cherries, halved, optional**

1 In a mixing bowl, dissolve yeast in warm water. Add the milk, butter, egg, sugar, cardamom and salt; mix well. Add 6 cups of flour; beat until smooth. Stir in enough of the remaining flour to form a soft dough.

2 Turn onto a floured surface; knead until smooth and elastic, about 6-8 minutes. Place in a greased bowl, turning once to grease top. Cover and let rise in a warm place until doubled, about 1 hour.

EASTER EGG BREAD

3 Punch dough down and divide in half. Divide each half into three portions. Shape each portion into a 24-in. long rope. Place three ropes on a greased baking sheet; braid. Form into a ring; pinch edges tightly together. Repeat with remaining dough. Cover and let rise until doubled, about 30 minutes.

4 Bake at 350° for 30-35 minutes or until golden brown. Cool on a wire racks. For icing, combine the sugar, milk and extract; spoon over rings, allowing icing to drizzle down the sides. Decorate with cherries if desired.

BRAIDED CARDAMOM RINGS

Easter Egg Bread

PREP: 35 min. + rising **BAKE:** 30 min. + cooling
YIELD: 1 loaf

Heather Durante, Wellsburg, Virginia

Colored hard-cooked eggs baked in the dough give this sweet bread such a festive look. Leave them out and it can be enjoyed anytime of year.

> 6 **to 6-1/2 cups all-purpose flour**
> 1/2 **cup sugar**
> 2 **packages (1/4 ounce** *each***) active dry yeast**
> 1 **to 2 teaspoons ground cardamom**
> 1 **teaspoon salt**
> 1-1/2 **cups milk**
> 6 **tablespoons butter, cubed**
> 4 **eggs**
> 3 **to 6 hard-cooked eggs**
> **Easter egg dye**
> **Vegetable oil**
> 2 **tablespoons cold water**

1. In a large mixing bowl, combine 2 cups flour, sugar, yeast, cardamom and salt. In a saucepan, heat milk and butter to 120°-130°. Add to dry ingredients; beat just until moistened. Add 3 eggs; beat until smooth. Stir in enough remaining flour to form a soft dough.

2. Turn onto a floured surface; knead until smooth and elastic, about 6-8 minutes. Place in a greased bowl, turning once to grease top. Cover and let rise in a warm place until doubled, about 45 minutes.

3. Dye hard-cooked eggs; lightly rub with oil. Punch dough down. Turn onto a lightly floured surface; divide dough into thirds. Shape each portion into a 24-in. rope.

4. Place ropes on a greased baking sheet and braid; bring ends together to form a ring. Pinch ends to seal. Gently separate braided ropes and tuck dyed eggs into openings. Cover and let rise until doubled, about 20 minutes.

5. Beat water and remaining egg; gently brush over dough. Bake at 375° for 28-32 minutes or until golden brown. Remove from pan to a wire rack to cool. Refrigerate leftovers.

Poppy Seed Sweet Rolls

PREP: 30 min. + rising **BAKE:** 15 min. + cooling
YIELD: about 2-1/2 dozen

Ruth Stahl, Shepherd, Montana

These freeze well—so when you make a batch tuck some into the freezer. Then surprise your family with them when they least expect it!

- 2 **tablespoons active dry yeast**
- 3 **tablespoons sugar,** *divided*
- 1/4 **cup warm water (110° to 115°)**
- 1-1/2 **cups warm buttermilk (110° to 115°)**
- 1/2 **cup vegetable oil**
- 1 **teaspoon salt**
- 1/2 **teaspoon baking soda**
- 4 **to 4-1/2 cups all-purpose flour**

FILLING:
- 1 **package (8 ounces) cream cheese, softened**
- 1/4 **cup butter, softened**
- 1 **cup packed brown sugar**
- 2 **tablespoons all-purpose flour**
- 1 **teaspoon vanilla extract**
- 1 **cup chopped pecans**
- 2 **tablespoons poppy seeds**

ICING:
- 2 **cups confectioners' sugar**
- 4 **teaspoons milk**
- 1 **teaspoon vanilla extract**

1. In a large mixing bowl, dissolve yeast and 1 tablespoon sugar in warm water; let stand for 5 minutes. Add the buttermilk, oil, salt, baking soda, 3 cups flour and remaining sugar; beat until smooth. Stir in enough remaining flour to form a soft dough.

2. Turn onto a lightly floured surface; knead until smooth and elastic, about 6-8 minutes. Place in a greased bowl, turning once to grease top. Cover and let rise in a warm place for 30 minutes.

3. For filling, in a small bowl, beat cream cheese and butter. Add the brown sugar, flour and vanilla; beat well. Stir in nuts and poppy seeds; set aside.

4. Punch dough down. Turn onto a floured surface; divide in half. Roll each portion into a 15-in. x 9-in. rectangle. Spread filling over rectangles to within 1/2 in. of edges. Roll up jelly-roll style, starting with a long side; pinch seams to seal. Cut into 1-in. pieces. Place 2 in. apart on greased baking sheets. Cover and let rise for 30 minutes.

5. Bake at 375° for 12-15 minutes. Remove from pans to wire racks to cool. Combine icing ingredients; drizzle over rolls.

POPPY SEED SWEET ROLLS

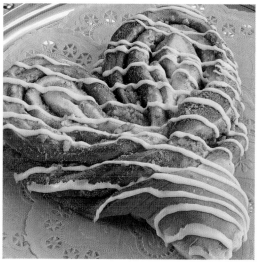

HEART-SHAPED COFFEE CAKE

3 Punch dough down; let rest for 10 minutes. Divide in half. On a floured surface, roll each portion into a 15-in. x 10-in. rectangle. Brush with remaining butter. Combine filling ingredients; sprinkle over dough to within 1/2 in. of edges. Roll up jelly-roll style, starting with a long side; pinch seams to seal.

4 Place seam side up on two greased baking sheets. Fold each roll in half lengthwise with seams touching, with one side 1-1/2 in. longer than the other. With scissors, make a lengthwise cut down the middle to within 1 in. of open ends. Open and lay flat; arrange into a heart shape. Cover and let rise until doubled, about 30 minutes.

5 Bake at 350° for 15-20 minutes or until golden brown. Cool on wire racks. In a mixing bowl, cream butter, sugar and vanilla. Add enough milk to achieve desired consistency; drizzle over hearts.

Heart-Shaped Coffee Cake

PREP: 40 min. + rising **BAKE:** 15 min. + cooling
YIELD: 2 coffee cakes

Norma Hammond, Leland, Iowa

You'll love to make this pretty coffee cake for Valentine's Day and anniversaries.

1	**package (1/4 ounce) active dry yeast**
1/4	**cup warm water (110° to 115°)**
1	**cup warm milk (110° to 115°)**
3/4	**cup butter, melted, *divided***
2	**eggs, beaten**
1/4	**cup sugar**
1	**teaspoon salt**
3-1/2	**to 4 cups all-purpose flour**

FILLING:

1/2	**cup sugar**
1/2	**cup finely chopped walnuts**
2	**teaspoons ground cinnamon**

ICING:

2	**tablespoons butter, softened**
2	**cups confectioners' sugar**
1	**teaspoon vanilla extract**
5	**to 6 tablespoons milk**

1 In a mixing bowl, combine yeast and warm water. Add milk, 1/2 cup butter, eggs, sugar, salt and 2 cups of flour; beat until smooth. Stir in enough remaining flour to form a soft dough.

2 Turn onto a floured surface; knead until smooth and elastic, about 6-8 minutes. Place in a greased bowl, turning once to grease top. Cover and let rise in a warm place until doubled, about 1 hour.

making *a heart-shaped coffee cake*

1. Roll dough into a 15-in. x 10-in. rectangle. Brush with melted butter. Spread filling to within 1/2 in. of edges. Roll up jelly-roll style, starting with a long side; pinch seams to seal. Fold roll in half with seams touching, making top half 1-1/2 in. longer than bottom half. Place on a greased baking sheet.

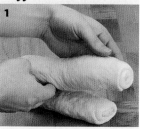

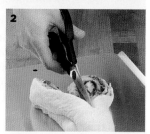

2. Starting at the folded end, cut lengthwise down the middle with scissors to within 1-1/2 in. of open ends.

3. Turn each side so that the cut side is up and shape into a heart. Tuck pointed end of heart under.

Holiday Breakfast Braid

PREP: 30 min. + rising **BAKE:** 30 min. + cooling
YIELD: 1 coffee cake (1/2 cup orange butter)

Sarah Miller, Wauconda, Washington

This fruity braid will round out your Christmas morning menu. Slathered with orange butter, the bread is just delicious.

- 1 package (1/4 ounce) active dry yeast
- 1/4 cup warm water (110° to 115°)
- 1/2 cup warm milk (110° to 115°)
- 1/3 cup sugar
- 1/3 cup butter, softened
- 2 eggs, beaten
- 1 teaspoon salt
- 1 teaspoon grated orange peel
- 1/2 teaspoon ground cardamom
- 1/8 teaspoon ground mace
- 3-1/2 cups all-purpose flour

FILLING:
- 1/4 cup butter, softened
- 2 tablespoons sugar
- 3/4 teaspoon almond extract
- 1/2 teaspoon grated orange peel
- 1/2 cup chopped mixed candied fruit
- 1/2 cup chopped almonds
- 2 teaspoons all-purpose flour

ORANGE BUTTER:
- 1/2 cup butter, softened
- 2 tablespoons confectioners' sugar
- 1 teaspoon grated orange peel

1 In a large mixing bowl, dissolve yeast in warm water. Add the milk, sugar, butter, eggs, salt, orange peel, cardamom, mace and 2 cups flour; beat until smooth. Stir in enough remaining flour to form a soft dough.

2 Turn onto a floured surface; knead until smooth and elastic, about 6-8 minutes. Place in a greased bowl, turning once to grease top. Cover and let rise in a warm place until doubled, about 1 hour.

3 Meanwhile, for filling, in a small mixing bowl, combine the butter, sugar, extract and orange peel; set aside. Toss the fruit and almonds with flour; set aside.

4 Punch dough down. Turn onto a lightly floured surface. Roll into a 30-in. x 9-in. rectangle. Spread filling to within 1/2 in. of edges; sprinkle with fruit mixture. Roll up jelly-roll style, starting with a long side; pinch seam to seal. With a sharp knife, cut roll in half lengthwise. Place on a greased baking sheet; gently twist the ropes together cut side up. Coil into a circle; tuck ends under. Cover and let rise until doubled, about 1 hour.

5 Bake at 325° for 30-35 minutes or until golden brown. Remove from pan to a wire rack to cool. In a mixing bowl, combine the orange butter ingredients. Refrigerate until serving. Serve with coffee cake.

HOLIDAY BREAKFAST BRAID

Cinnamon Love Knots

PREP: 45 min. + rising **BAKE:** 15 min.+ cooling
YIELD: 3 dozen

Marlene Fetter, Alpena, Michigan

Try these flavorful yeast rolls for breakfast or even dessert.

       2 **packages (1/4 ounce *each*) active dry yeast**
    1/2 **cup warm water (110° to 115°)**
    1/2 **cup warm milk (110° to 115°)**
    1/2 **cup butter, softened**
    1/2 **cup sugar**
       2 **eggs, beaten**
       1 **teaspoon salt**
 4-1/2 **to 5 cups all-purpose flour**
TOPPING:
       2 **cups sugar**
       2 **tablespoons ground cinnamon**
    3/4 **cup butter, melted**

1 In a large mixing bowl, dissolve yeast in warm water. Add the milk, butter, sugar, eggs and salt. Stir in enough flour to form a stiff dough.

2 Turn onto a floured surface; knead until smooth and elastic, about 6-8 minutes. Place in a greased bowl; turn once to grease top. Cover and let rise in a warm place until doubled, about 1-1/2 hours.

3 Punch dough down; divide into three portions. Cover two with plastic wrap. Shape one portion into 12 balls. Roll each ball into an 8-in. rope. Combine sugar and cinnamon. Dip rope into melted butter, then coat with cinnamon-sugar. Tie into a knot. Tuck and pinch ends under and place on ungreased baking sheets. Repeat with remaining dough. Cover and let rise until doubled, about 30 minutes.

CINNAMON LOVE KNOTS

4 Bake at 375° for 12-14 minutes or until golden brown. Remove to wire racks.

Traditional Hot Cross Buns

PREP: 20 min. + rising **BAKE:** 15 min. + cooling
YIELD: 2-1/2 dozen

Barbara Jean Lull, Fullerton, California

These yeast rolls dotted with raisins and currants are traditionally topped with a white glaze in the shape of a cross and served at Easter.

       2 **packages (1/4 ounce *each*) active dry yeast**
       2 **cups warm milk (110° to 115°)**
    1/3 **cup butter, softened**
       2 **eggs, lightly beaten**
    1/4 **cup sugar**
 1-1/2 **teaspoons salt**
       6 **to 7 cups all-purpose flour**
    1/2 **cup raisins**
    1/2 **cup dried currants**
       1 **teaspoon ground cinnamon**
    1/4 **teaspoon ground allspice**
       2 **tablespoons water**
       1 **egg yolk**
ICING:
 1-1/4 **cups confectioners' sugar**
    1/2 **teaspoon vanilla extract**
       1 **to 2 tablespoons milk**

1 In a large mixing bowl, dissolve yeast in warm milk. Stir in the butter, eggs, sugar and salt. Combine 3 cups flour, raisins, currants, cinnamon and allspice; add to yeast mixture and mix well. Stir in enough remaining flour to form a soft dough.

2 Turn onto a floured surface and knead until smooth and elastic, about 6-8 minutes. Place in a greased bowl, turning once to grease top. Cover and let rise in a warm place until doubled, about 1 hour.

3 Punch dough down; shape into 1-1/2- to 2-in. balls. Place 2 in. apart on greased baking sheets. Using a sharp knife, cut a cross on top of each roll. Cover and let rise until doubled, about 30 minutes. Beat water and egg yolk; brush over rolls.

4 Bake at 375° for 15-20 minutes or until golden brown. Cool on wire racks. In a small bowl, combine confectioners' sugar, vanilla and enough milk to achieve piping consistency. Pipe over rolls.

CHAPTER 14

ALPHABETICAL INDEX

Alphabetical Index

Refer to this index for a complete listing of all the recipes in this book.

Subject & Reference Indexes

This index lists every recipe by food category and/or major ingredient.

CAKES

REFERENCE INDEX

Use this index as a guide to the many helpful hints and step-by-step instructions throughout this book.

FOOD EQUIVALENTS

FOOD	EQUIVALENT
Apples	1 pound (3 medium) = 2-3/4 cups sliced
Apricots	1 pound (8 to 12 medium) = 2-1/2 cups sliced
Bananas	1 pound (3 medium) = 1-1/3 cups mashed *or* 1-1/2 to 2 cups sliced
Berries	1 pint = 1-1/2 to 2 cups
Bread	1 loaf = 16 to 20 slices
Bread Crumbs	1 slice = 1/2 cup soft crumbs *or* 1/4 cup dry crumbs
Butter *or* Margarine	1 pound = 2 cups *or* 4 sticks 1 stick = 8 tablespoons
Cheese Cottage Shredded	1 pound = 2 cups 4 ounces = 1 cup
Cherries	1 pound = 3 cups whole *or* 3-1/2 cups halved
Chocolate Chips	6 ounces = 1 cup
Cocoa, Baking	1 pound = 4 cups
Coconut, Flaked	14 ounces = 5-1/2 cups
Cornmeal	1 pound = 3 cups uncooked
Corn Syrup	16 ounces = 2 cups
Cranberries	12 ounces = 3 cups whole *or* 2-1/2 cups finely chopped
Cream Cheese	8 ounces = 16 tablespoons
Cream, Whipping	1 cup = 2 cups whipped
Dates, Dried	1 pound = 2-3/4 cups pitted and chopped
Dates, Dried and Chopped	10 ounces = 1-3/4 cups
Egg Whites	1 cup = 8 to 10 whites
Flour All-Purpose Cake Whole Wheat	1 pound = about 3-1/2 cups 1 pound = about 4-1/2 cups 1 pound = about 3-3/4 cups
Frozen Whipped Topping	8 ounces = 3-1/2 cups
Gelatin, Unflavored	1 envelope = 1 tablespoon
Graham Crackers	16 crackers = 1 cup crumbs
Grapefruit	1 medium = 3/4 cup juice *or* 1-1/2 cups segments

FOOD	EQUIVALENT
Grapes	1 pound = 3 cups
Honey	1 pound = 1-1/3 cups
Lemons	1 medium = 3 tablespoons juice *or* 2 teaspoons grated peel
Limes	1 medium = 2 tablespoons juice *or* 1-1/2 teaspoons grated peel
Marshmallows Large Miniature	1 cup = 7 to 9 marshmallows 1 cup = about 100 marshmallows
Nectarines	1 pound (3 medium) = 3 cups sliced
Nuts Almonds	1 pound = 3 cups halves *or* 4 cups slivered
Ground Hazelnuts Pecans Walnuts	3-3/4 ounces = 1 cup 1 pound = 3-1/2 cups whole 1 pound = 4-1/2 cups chopped 1 pound = 3-3/4 cups chopped
Oats Old-Fashioned Quick-Cooking	1 pound = 5 cups 1 pound = 5-1/2 cups
Oranges	1 medium = 1/3 to 1/2 cup juice *or* 4 teaspoons grated peel
Peaches	1 pound (4 medium) = 2-3/4 cups sliced
Pears	1 pound (3 medium) = 3 cups sliced
Pineapples	1 medium = 3 cups chunks
Popcorn	1/3 to 1/2 cup unpopped = 8 cups popped
Raisins	15 ounces = 2-1/2 cups
Rhubarb	1 pound = 3 cups chopped (raw) *or* 2 cups (cooked)
Shortening	1 pound = 2 cups
Strawberries	1 pint = 2 cups hulled and sliced
Sugar Brown Sugar Confectioners' Sugar Granulated	1 pound = 2-1/4 cups 1 pound = 4 cups 1 pound = 2-1/4 to 2-1/2 cups
Yeast, Active Dry	1 envelope = 2-1/4 teaspoons

INGREDIENT SUBSTITUTIONS

WHEN YOU NEED:	IN THIS AMOUNT:	SUBSTITUTE:
Allspice	1 teaspoon	1/2 teaspoon ground cinnamon plus 1/2 teaspoon ground cloves
Apple Pie Spice	1 teaspoon	1/2 teaspoon ground cinnamon plus 1/4 teaspoon ground nutmeg, 1/8 teaspoon ground allspice and 1/8 teaspoon ground cardamom, ginger *or* cloves
Baking Powder	1 teaspoon	1/2 teaspoon cream of tartar plus 1/4 teaspoon baking soda
Broth	1 cup	1 cup hot water plus 1 teaspoon bouillon granules *or* 1 bouillon cube
Buttermilk	1 cup	1 tablespoon lemon juice *or* white vinegar plus enough milk to measure 1 cup; let stand for 5 minutes. *Or* 1 cup plain yogurt
Chocolate, Semisweet	1 square (1 ounce)	1 square (1 ounce) unsweetened chocolate plus 1 tablespoon sugar *or* 3 tablespoons semisweet chocolate chips
Chocolate	1 square (1 ounce)	3 tablespoons baking cocoa plus 1 tablespoon shortening *or* vegetable oil
Cornstarch (for thickening)	1 tablespoon	2 tablespoons all-purpose flour
Corn Syrup, Dark	1 cup	3/4 cup light corn syrup plus 1/4 cup molasses
Corn Syrup, Light	1 cup	1 cup sugar plus 1/4 cup water
Cracker Crumbs	1 cup	1 cup dry bread crumbs
Cream, Half-and-Half	1 cup	1 tablespoon melted butter plus enough whole milk to measure 1 cup
Egg	1 whole	2 egg whites *or* 2 egg yolks *or* 1/4 cup egg substitute
Flour, Cake	1 cup	1 cup minus 2 tablespoons (7/8 cup) all-purpose flour
Flour, Self-Rising	1 cup	1-1/2 teaspoons baking powder plus 1/2 teaspoon salt and enough all-purpose flour to measure 1 cup
Garlic, Fresh	1 clove	1/8 teaspoon garlic powder
Gingerroot, Fresh	1 teaspoon	1/4 teaspoon ground ginger
Honey	1 cup	1-1/4 cups sugar plus 1/4 cup water
Lemon Juice	1 teaspoon	1/4 teaspoon cider vinegar
Lemon Peel, grated	1 teaspoon	1/2 teaspoon lemon extract
Mace	1 teaspoon	1 teaspoon ground allspice *or* nutmeg
Milk, Whole	1 cup	1/2 cup evaporated milk plus 1/2 cup water *or* 1 cup water plus 1/3 cup nonfat dry milk powder
Molasses	1 cup	1 cup honey
Onion	1 small (1/3 cup chopped)	1 teaspoon onion powder *or* 1 tablespoon dried minced onion
Pumpkin Pie Spice	1 teaspoon	1/2 teaspoon ground cinnamon plus 1/4 teaspoon ground ginger, 1/8 teaspoon ground nutmeg and 1/8 teaspoon ground cloves
Sour Cream	1 cup	1 cup plain yogurt
Sugar	1 cup	1 cup packed brown sugar *or* 2 cups sifted confectioners' sugar
Sugar, Light Brown	1 cup	1/2 cup dark brown sugar plus 1/2 cup granulated sugar
Yeast	1 package (1/4 ounce) active dry	1 cake (5/8-ounce) compressed yeast

taste of home